D1222656

The Investor's Guide to Mutual Funds

JOHN A. HASLEM
University of Maryland

Prentice Hall, Englewood Cliffs, NJ 07632

Haslem, John A.
    The investor's guide to mutual funds/John A. Haslem.
      p.   cm.
    Includes index.
    ISBN 0-13-504739-0
    1. Mutual funds.   I. Title.
  HG4530.H386   1988
  332.63'27—dc19

Editorial/production supervision
and interior design: TKM Productions
Cover design: Photo Plus Art
Manufacturing buyer: Marianne Gloriande

 © 1988 by Prentice-Hall, Inc.
A Division of Simon & Schuster
Englewood Cliffs, New Jersey 07632

All rights reserved. No part of this book may be
reproduced, in any form or by any means,
without permission in writing from the publisher.

The publisher offers discounts on this book when ordered
in bulk quantities. For more information, write:
    Special Sales/College Marketing
    Prentice Hall
    College Technical and Reference Division
    Englewood Cliffs, NJ 07632

Printed in the United States of America
10 9 8 7 6 5 4 3 2 1

ISBN   0-13-504739-0

Prentice-Hall International (UK) Limited, *London*
Prentice-Hall of Australia Pty. Limited, *Sydney*
Prentice-Hall Canada Inc., *Toronto*
Prentice-Hall Hispanoamericana, S.A., *Mexico*
Prentice-Hall of India Private Limited, *New Delhi*
Prentice-Hall of Japan, Inc., *Tokyo*
Simon & Schuster Asia Pte. Ltd., *Singapore*
Editora Prentice-Hall do Brasil, Ltda., *Rio de Janeiro*

This book is dedicated with love to
Florence Beck Morris
on her 100th birthday

Contents

Preface

This book has a specific purpose—to explain the nature of mutual funds and the method of selecting the appropriate fund for the individual investor by using straightforward criteria and readily available data. The approach promises no panacea to the uncertainties of investing, but it does attempt to shorten the odds for the investor who is willing to take a relatively long-term view of investment performance by using mutual funds. This approach can provide outstanding performance on a relatively consistent basis.

ACKNOWLEDGMENTS

This attempt to make life a little better for the individual investor has benefitted from several helpful friends, colleagues, and family members. They have my sincere thanks. This book could not have taken the investor so directly into the data needed to select an appropriate mutual fund without the generosity of Robert A. Levy, President of CDA Investment Technologies, Inc. The content of the book was enriched greatly by the literature on mutual funds provided by Dennis McConnell, University of Maine. My greatest appreciation goes to John A. Haslem, Jr., University of Denver, for his thorough and able editing of the manuscript. Kathryn M. Bartol, University of Maryland, kindly volunteered to read the manuscript and provided useful suggestions for improvement. Charles B. Edelson, University of Maryland, also provided useful suggestions for the manuscript. The College of Business and Management, University of Maryland, provided research and typing support for the project. Ev Lyn Brennan typed the manuscript through its many preliminary versions with kindness and patience. Jeanne M. Fineran arranged to provide the typing of the later versions of the manuscript in a timely fashion. Lynda Griffiths of TKM Productions provided excellent production editorial services. And, finally, Marcese E. Oakley, of Prentice Hall, sparked my interest in writing the book, and Jeffrey A. Krames, editor at Prentice Hall, managed everything with great skill and enthusiasm. I thank them all!

1

The Nature
of Mutual Funds:
An Introduction

ARE MUTUAL FUNDS FOR YOU?

Before we begin this chapter, answer the following questions concerning your investment behavior preferences:

1. I am more of a speculator, who is seeking short-term price appreciation rather than an investor who is seeking long-term and relatively consistent returns.
   Yes _____   No _____

2. I truly enjoy security analysis and management of my own portfolio.
   Yes _____   No _____

3. I have ample time to do a thorough job of security analysis and portfolio management.
   Yes _____   No _____

4. I generally earn higher rates of return on my portfolio than is earned on the overall stock market (exclusive of risk differences).
   Yes _____   No _____

    If you answered "Yes" to question 1, then mutual funds are not for you. Mutual funds generally follow an "investment" rather than a "speculative" approach to security analysis and portfolio management. If you answered "Yes" to Question 2, then you should probably manage your own portfolio *if* you also answered "Yes" to Questions 3 and 4, especially the latter. If you answered "No" to Question 1, then mutual funds may be for you, depending on your responses to Questions 2 through 4. If you answered "No" to Question 2, then you would probably prefer the professional management offered by a mutual fund. If you don't really enjoy security analysis and portfolio management, then chances are you also don't spend the time necessary (Question 3) to be able to attain superior returns to your portfolio (Question 4).

Individually, each of the following answers is consistent with the idea that mutual funds are appropriate for you:

Question 1:   "No"

Question 2:   "No"

Question 3:   "No"

Question 4:   "No"

However, which "No" answers are appropriate for you to consider mutual funds as an appropriate investment vehicle? A "No" answer to Question 1 is a prerequisite. Futhermore, a "No" response to any *one* or more of Questions 2 through 4, especially Question 4, is probably sufficient grounds for you to consider mutual funds. These latter three questions are doubtlessly interdependent. If a lack of experience suggests an "I Don't Know" response to any of these questions, then you should consider it a "No" answer for these purposes.

Therefore, if your responses to these questions suggest that mutual funds are not for you, then call your broker. Otherwise, read on—you can benefit from this book.

Some other questions the investor should consider in deciding whether or not to buy mutual funds include the following:[1]

1. Do you have less than $50,000 to invest?
   Yes ____   No ____
2. Do you own fewer than 15 stocks?
   Yes ____   No ____
3. Are you buying "odd lots" (fewer than 100 share trades) or paying full-service commission rates?
   Yes ____   No ____
4. Do you have difficulty in knowing either when to sell stocks or in selling stocks that you earlier thought were undervalued?
   Yes ____   No ____
5. Do you wish you could receive better advice and/or service from your broker?
   Yes ____   No ____

If your answer is "Yes" to most of these questions, then mutual funds may be for you. If you have less than $50,000 to invest, then you probably cannot get the same degree of portfolio diversification as you can in most mutual funds. However, it only takes a portfolio of twelve to eighteen stocks to obtain approximately 90 percent of the benefits of complete diversification.[2] This supports the notion that mutual funds can provide investors with an adequate amount of risk reduction through diversification.

Compared to the costs of buying "odd lots" or full-service brokerage commissions, "true" no-load mutual funds (discussed in Chapter 6) impose no sales charges and little or no redemption costs. This cost difference can be relatively significant.

Furthermore, many people find it difficult to know when to sell stocks (as do many professional portfolio managers). Many investors also form an emotional attachment with their stocks and find it difficult to sell them, especially if it means taking a loss or admitting an error in judgment. The danger involved in not knowing when to sell stocks or being emotionally unable to sell them is magnified if the portfolio is not adequately diversified.

Finally, some investors complain that brokers provide poor advice and/ or service. They feel that brokers take an individual rather than an overall (portfolio) approach to the investor's securities needs, and that they emphasize investor purchases of securities more so than any needed sale of securities.

WHAT ARE MUTUAL FUNDS?

Mutual funds are the major type of investment companies. *Investment companies* are financial intermediaries (middlemen) that pool the funds of investors who are seeking the same general investment objective and invest them in a number of frequently different types of securities (e.g., common stock, bonds, money market securities). These pooled funds provide thousands of investors with proportional ownership of diversified portfolios which are operated by professional investment managers.

Mutual funds are *open-end investment companies* that continuously sell new shares upon demand and normally stand ready to redeem (buy back) outstanding shares upon demand. The number of fund shares outstanding fluctuates as investors buy and sell them, and the shares fluctuate in value according to how well the pool of securities in the portfolio have performed. Mutual fund shares are sold in two basic ways: through salespeople or the funds themselves.

Mutual fund shares are valued at the *net asset value* (NAV) per share, which is computed by dividing the fund's total assets, less liabilities, by the number of shares outstanding. Thus, what a share is worth in the market is what the investor gets upon redemption (less any fees).

The Glossaries of this book include many of the terms commonly used in mutual fund investing. Those terms not included can generally be obtained from standard investments textbooks found in public libraries.

WHAT DO MUTUAL FUNDS OFFER?

Mutual funds provide investors with a number of desirable *services*, including:

1. Professional investment management
2. Diversification (risk reduction) through managed portfolios
3. Availability of alternative portfolio objectives (e.g., income, growth)
4. Shareholder account administration and services (e.g., tax record information)
5. Reduction in transaction costs

These and other advantages as well as the disadvantages of mutual funds are discussed in Chapters 7 and 8.

The alternative investment objectives available from mutual funds are generally defined by the various types of mutual funds (as classified here by the mutual fund industry):[3]

1. Aggressive Growth Funds (maximum capital appreciation)
2. Growth Funds (long-term capital appreciation)
3. Growth and Income Funds (long-term capital appreciation and current income)
4. Precious Metals Funds (gold and precious metals stocks)
5. International Funds (securities of foreign companies)
6. Balanced Funds (conservation of principal, current income, and long-term growth of income and capital)
7. Income Funds (high level of current income)
8. Option/Income Funds (high current income from dividends and options)
9. U.S. Government Income Funds (variety of government securities)
10. GNMA (Ginnie Mae) Funds (government-backed mortgage securities)
11. Corporate Bond Funds (high level of income)
12. Municipal Bond Funds (local government bonds with tax-free income)
13. Single State Municipal Bond Funds (issues of one state to provide tax-free income for residents of that state)
14. Money Market Mutual Funds (short-term, money-market securities)
15. Short-term Municipal Bond Funds, also known as Tax-Exempt Money Market Funds (short-term local government securities)

ARE MUTUAL FUNDS POPULAR?

Yes. The increasing popularity of mutual funds can be demonstrated in several ways. As indicated in Fig. 1.1, there were 68 *mutual funds* in 1940 and 1,843 in 1986—an average annual growth rate of approximately 7 percent. As shown in Figure 1.2, the number of mutual fund *shareholder accounts* grew from 0.3 million in 1940 to 46.1 million in 1986—an average annual growth rate of approximately 11 percent. Finally, Figure 1.3 shows that mutual fund *assets* increased from $0.4 billion in 1940 to $716.3 billion in 1986—an average annual growth rate of approximately *17 percent!*

Traditionally, mutual funds were organized primarily to meet the needs of small investors for professional management and diversification (among the other advantages discussed in Chapter 7). Today, however, institutional investors are turning to mutual funds in ever-increasing numbers. They include bank trust departments and other fiduciary institutions, employee pension funds, employee profit-sharing plans, insurance companies, and

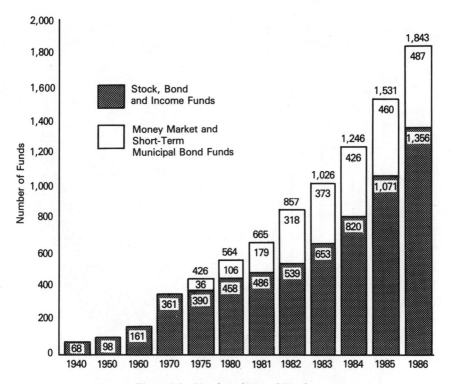

Figure 1.1 Number of Mutual Funds

Source: Investment Company Institute, *1987 Mutual Fund Fact Book*, p. 13. Reprinted with permission of Investment Company Institute.

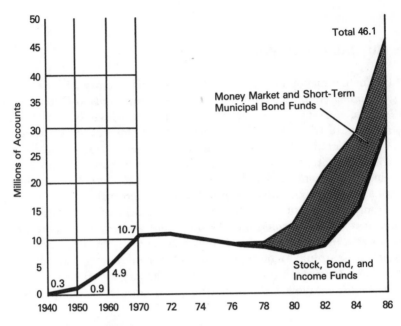

Figure 1.2 Mutual Fund Shareholder Accounts

Source: Investment Company Institute, *1987 Mutual Fund Fact Book*, p. 14. Reprinted with permission of Investment Company Institute.

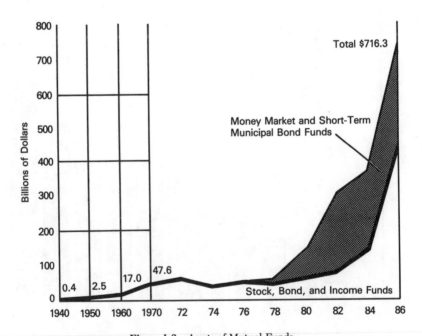

Figure 1.3 Assets of Mutual Funds

Source: Investment Company Institute, *1987 Mutual Fund Fact Book*, p. 14. Reprinted with permission of Investment Company Institute.

foundations. As a result, the value of institutional assets invested in mutual funds has increased from \$1.2 billion in 1960 to \$168.1 billion in 1985, the latter representing 33.9 percent of total mutual fund assets.[4] As indicated in Figure 1.4, fiduciary institutions represent the largest segment (over 50 percent) of total institutional investment in mutual funds.

The increasing use of mutual funds by institutional investors is easily explained. They like the (1) professional management; (2) diversified portfolios; (3) consistent performance of selected fund portfolio managers, especially relative to institutional portfolio managers; (4) reasonable fees; (5) liquidity, which is the ease of redemption and the ability to change the mix of fund holdings (and portfolio managers) easily; and (6) readily verifiable performance records that mutual funds provide.[5]

Contrasted to large pension funds, small pension funds are more likely to invest in mutual funds because they may provide greater diversification and, perhaps, better portfolio management. Some institutional investors tend to select mutual funds with portfolio managers who have been with their funds for several years and who have a relatively consistent record of high investment performance (discussed in Chapter 10). They also tend to avoid narrowly focused "sector" or specialty funds that invest in the securities of a specific industry or sector of the economy (e.g., health care), preferring broader-based funds in which the portfolio managers make diversification

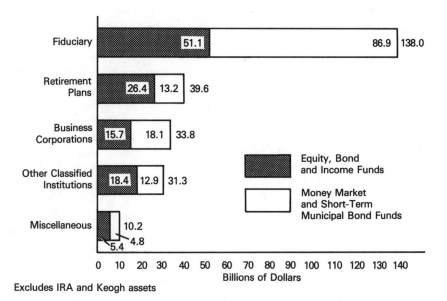

Figure 1.4   Institutional Assets by Type of Institution—1986

Source: Investment Company Institute, *1987 Mutual Fund Fact Book*, p. 46. Reprinted with permission of Investment Company Institute.

decisions. Sector funds are a hybrid product, somewhere between a diversified fund and a stock. Because they are not well diversified, they are very volatile in their price behavior. Individual as well as institutional investors in these funds should have a high tolerance for risk (Chapter 10). On the other hand, institutional investors may prefer to take a flexible, short-run view of investing by placing more money in those funds that are currently "hot."

DEVELOPMENTS FAVORING MUTUAL FUNDS

In addition to the personal reasons that investors might have for favoring mutual funds (discussed earlier), there are also several external reasons that favor their use. Since 1970, the securities markets have become increasingly volatile.[6] According to a study by Leuthold, there were 69 days during the period from 1973 through the third quarter of 1975 in which the Dow-Jones Industrial Average (DJIA) stock market index moved at least 2 percent.[7] This contrasts to 57 such high volatility days in the entire 24-year period from 1949 to 1972. Volatility continues in the 1980s. In 1971, the average daily price change in the DJIA was over 4 points, and by 1983, the average was over 8 points.

The market for debt securities has also become more volatile. During the 1970s, expansionary economic policies led to increased inflation. In its fight against inflation, the Federal Reserve began to focus more on the supply of money than on the level of interest rates. As a result, interest rates became higher and much more volatile. With more changeable interest rates, the prices of debt instruments not only necessarily become more volatile, but also, with fixed interest payments, they necessarily adjust to reflect current interest yields.

Another cause of increased volatility and, therefore, uncertainty in the securities markets is the growth in institutional trading. Institutional trading includes that done by financial institutions, trust companies, bank trust departments, private and public pension funds, insurance companies, investment advising firms, mutual funds, and so on. These firms deal with billions of dollars and their trades normally involve large blocks (e.g., 5,000 to 10,000 share trades). Large price concessions are frequently required to buy or sell these large blocks. And since these concessions, in themselves, cause increased volatility in stock price movements, consecutive stock prices are therefore less continuous (having larger gaps) than they were in the years before institutions represented over one-half of all trades. This increased volatility in the securities markets has generated several important problems for both professional and individual investors:

1. The response time of the committee decision process of institutional investors has frequently become too slow.

2. Securities prices have become less liquid (larger price concessions) as institutions program (predetermine) their trading responses.
3. The use of "fundamental" analysis to buy or sell stocks based on their "true" value relative to their market price has become less useful because the relationship changes too quickly.
4. The use of technical analysis to anticipate individual stock or stock market price trends has become more difficult to interpret and frequently too slow in anticipating trends.
5. Portfolios are more difficult to diversify in an effective and timely fashion because of the potentially large number of securities and their interactions to evaluate.
6. The *direct* participation of individual investors in the securities markets has become less with the increased domination of institutional investors.

In addition to a more volatile market environment, the market has also become more complex in terms of the number and type of investment vehicles available to investors.[8] Prior to the 1970s, investment in equity securities was concentrated in a small group of high quality ("blue chip") stocks. The bond market consisted primarily of U.S. government securities, U.S. Agency securities, and high-quality corporate bonds. There was little market volatility, therefore, there was little real need for the analysis of these high-quality securities.

Today, however, there is a great deal of volatility in the securities markets. As a result of rapid economic and financial growth in an increasingly complex and uncertain world, a wide spectrum of securities has developed. In some cases, these securities have facilitated risk-reduction strategies—the kind you can find discussed in the business section of your newspaper, where they make reference to such securities as financial futures contracts, option contracts, floating rate notes, clips, strips, collateralized mortgage obligation bonds, and "junk" bonds. (See an investments text or service at your public library for a discussion of these and other securities.)

As a result of the ever-increasing complexity of financial markets, the professional or individual investor is faced with several other problems:

1. A large and increasing number of investment alternatives
2. A complex and increasing number of investment strategies (e.g., buy stock and sell options, option arbitrage, hedging, put and call programs)
3. A decision to sell or buy a large number of securities (requiring broad expertise) or to specialize in a few securities (e.g., high-yielding bonds)
4. An overwhelming number of sources of information on each aspect of the market
5. The inability of any one information source of methodology to demonstrate consistent predictive ability

Thus, because of the difficulties involved in this volatile and complex investment environment, there is need for investment vehicles that provide investors, and some institutional investors as well, such benefits as professional management, appropriate investment objectives, compact portfolio diversification, liquidity, and numerous customer services, including timely and documented records of performance, and so on. As discussed in Chapter 7, mutual funds potentially offer benefits that make them desirable portfolio vehicles in today's investment environment.

STEPS TO MUTUAL FUND INVESTING

Because of the large number of funds, a structured approach is needed to assist the investor who seeks to select the "right" fund.[9] This approach might include the following questions:

1. *What are your objectives?*
   (Define your personal objectives and investment horizon. The appropriate fund investment objective will come into view.)
2. *How much should you diversify?*
   (Seek the degree of diversification that coincides with your investment objective and risk tolerance.)
3. *What are your performance goals?*
   (The historical performance figures you use should be weighed by the length of your investment horizon.)
4. *Do you want to manage your holdings?*
   (The more actively you manage your funds, the more important it is to select the "correct" family of funds to facilitate exchanges between funds and a satisfactory level of performance.)
5. *Will you pay for advice?*
   (Sales charges on funds become less important the more you need advice, the more the fund fits your needs, and the longer your investment horizon.)
6. *Which fund is for you?*
   (Steps 1–5 narrow your choices of funds, and the final selection is enhanced by studying the prospectus and analyses of the fund.)

This approach does not exactly follow that suggested in this book, but it does nonetheless ask basic questions that are relevant to all investors in mutual funds.

ENDNOTES

[1]Karen Slater, "Mutual Funds' Growth Requires Investors to Do More Studies, Make More Decisions," *Wall Street Journal*, May 21, 1984.

[2]This research is summarized in Frank K. Reilly, *Investment Analysis and Portfolio Management*, 2nd ed. (New York: Dryden Press, 1985), pp. 245–247.

[3]Investment Companies Institute, *1986 Mutual Fund Fact Book* (Washington, D.C.: 1986), pp. 8–9.

[4]Ibid., p. 45.

[5]For a discussion of this treatment of institutional investors in mutual funds, see Alice B. Knox, "The Feeling is Mutual," *Financial Planning* (November 1986), pp. 57–58.

[6]For a discussion of this treatment of market volatility, see Michael D. Hirsch, *Multifund Investing* (Homewood, Ill.: Dow Jones-Irwin, 1987), Chapters 1–2.

[7]Steven C. Leuthold, "The Causes (and Cures?) of Market Volatility," *Journal of Portfolio Management 2* (Winter 1976), pp. 21–25.

[8]For a discussion of this treatment of market complexity, see Hirsch, Chapters 3–4.

[9]For a discussion of this treatment of these steps, see Michael Silverstein, "The Mutual Fund Maze," *Sylvia Porter's Personal Finance* (October 1985), pp. 78–80.

2

Major Types of Investment Companies and Related Investments

BRIEF HISTORY

Historically, closed-end funds, not open-end funds, were the major type of investment company. As will be discussed, they differ from open-end funds primarily by *not* selling or redeeming shares upon demand. Closed-end funds were introduced in the United States during the late 1880s, followed by mutual funds in the 1920s. The 1920s was a period of financial growth accompanied by new types of investment products. With the increasingly speculative stock market in the 1920s, a number of closed-end funds engaged in complex financing schemes, speculative investments, and, unfortunately, even fraudulent sales and other practices. Even so, closed-end funds remained the dominant type of investment company until the stock market crash of 1929, which basically destroyed them. As a result, many investors turned to mutual funds, which propelled them toward becoming the dominant type of investment company.

Another major result of these fund practices was a legislative remedy for the perceived ills of the securities markets following the crash. A series of new federal laws were passed, which were designed to prevent fraud and manipulation of securities prices and to provide public disclosure of all relevant securities information. This remedy also included stricter securities laws and regulation at the state level.

Funds are subject to the laws of the state in which they are incorporated and, more importantly, they are regulated by the states in which they sell shares. If an investment company is not registered in a particular state, it is probably because that state has strict limits on the fees that can be paid to the investment adviser. In general, state securities ("blue sky") laws prohibit fraud in the sale of securities and require the registration under law of brokers, dealers, investment advisers, and certain securities.

Investment companies are regulated under several federal statutes: (1) Securities Act of 1933—established "truth-in-securities" legislation, which requires "full disclosure" in the registration statement and prospectus for *new* securities; (2) Securities Exchange Act of 1934—established the Securities and Exchange Commission (SEC), which extended the 1933 Act to existing (outstanding) securities and required registration with the SEC of the major participants in the securities markets (e.g., brokers); (3) Investment Company Act of 1940—provided for registration and regulation of investment companies and for the regulation of investment advisers; and (4) Federal Investment Company Amendments Act of 1970—established standards for mutual fund management fees and sales charges.

Some specifics of these federal statutes as they relate to the regulation of investment companies include the following:

1. The SEC must be given full information about securities offered to the public.
2. Potential investors must be given complete information about the fund's investment policies, management, and portfolio activities.
3. The sales practices of salespeople and investment advisers are regulated to prevent fraud; advertising activities are also limited.
4. The composition of the board of directors is restricted to avoid conflicts of interest.
5. Investment advisers must be approved by majority vote of the shareholders to whom they have a fiduciary responsibility.
6. Standards are provided to prevent excessive management fees and sales charges.
7. Mutual funds may sell only common stock and only at its net asset value.

The numerous federal and state laws offer a great deal of protection to the investor against fraud, inadequate disclosure, and improper management practices. Of all the legislation, the Investment Company Act of 1940 was instrumental in restoring public confidence in investment companies, expecially mutual funds. This restrictive law has been successful in protecting the fund-owning public against major incidences of fraud, malfeasance, and conflicts of interest. Nonetheless, there is *no* way to ensure through regulation that a particular investment company will provide adequate investment performance. It is the *investor's* responsibility to make the correct choice among the available investment companies. Furthermore, unlike most bank deposits, investor shares in investment companies are not federally insured. A more complete summary of the Investment Company Act of 1940 (as revised in 1970) is shown in Figure 2.1.

In more recent years, funds have passed through several growth phases. In the 1950s and early 1960s, mutual funds were not particularly popular. Individual investors seemed to feel, and/or they were told by their brokers, that they could do better by buying and selling their own securities. With the "bull market" of the 1960s, mutual funds were aggressively marketed to attract both old and new small investors who wanted a "piece of the action." Then, with the downturn in the market from 1968 to 1974, investors became disillusioned with the market and mutual funds and left in droves. The high

1. Provide for registration, "full" disclosure, and regulation of investment companies to prevent fraudulent abuses.
2. Not more than 60 percent of the board of directors may be affiliated with the fund, its bank or brokers. (No-load funds need only one outside director.)
3. May not purchase securities if one of its employees owns more than one-half of one percent of those outstanding (or five percent when all employee holdings are combined).
4. The company's investment policy must be contained in a prospectus which must be updated at least every 14 months. Policy cannot be changed without a majority vote.
5. Management (advisor) contracts cannot be for a term longer than two years and must be approved by shareholders.
6. The Company must redeem shares duly offered by shareholders within seven calendar days at per share net asset value.
7. Open-end companies (mutual funds) may borrow from a bank and use the proceeds for investment purposes (leverage). However, such debt must be collateralized three to one.
8. Shareholders must be sent complete financial reports at least semiannually and the SEC must be sent such reports quarterly.
9. To qualify as a registered investment company, the fund must have at least 75 percent of its total assets invested in securities such that: Not more than five percent of its assets are invested in the securities of any one issuer and not hold more than ten percent of the voting securities of any one corporation.
10. A prospectus must be given to a prospective fund investor before sales can be solicited.
11. The maximum load (commission) cannot exceed nine percent of the share's offering price.
12. Securities and cash must be kept by either a bank or a broker who is a member of a national securities exchange.

Figure 2.1 Summary of the Major Provisions and Rules of the Investment Company Act of 1940 (amended in 1970)

Source: Gerald W. Perritt and L. Kay Shannon, *The Individual Investor's Guide to No-Load Mutual Funds*, 3rd ed. (Chicago: Investment Information Services Press, 1984), p. 2.

inflation and interest rates that began in the early 1970s spurred a renewed interest in mutual funds via money market funds. Money market funds were introduced as a means of competing with banks by providing money market interest rates and check-writing capability to small investors.

The small investor's delight with competitive interest rates transferred interest to the entire mutual fund industry in the 1970s, especially with the introduction of IRA accounts for those not covered by corporate pension plans. This interest in mutual funds was increased in 1982 when IRA accounts became available to all wage earners. Many investors felt mutual funds were the ideal vehicle for these long-term retirement accounts. With the success of the money market funds, a variety of other types of money market and mutual funds was introduced to meet diverse investor needs. These included tax-exempt money market funds, municipal bond funds, option/income funds, government income funds, Ginnie Mae funds, and sector funds (defined in Chapter 3). All of these developments were greatly enhanced by the tremendous "bull market" that began in 1982.

LEGAL CLASSIFICATION

Legally, investment companies are corporations or trusts into which investors pool their capital and receive professional portfolio management in order to diversify (reduce) risk and improve returns. For the sake of completeness, it should be realized that there are actually three classes of investment companies: (1) *face-amount certificate companies*, which issue long-term "face-amount" certificates that guarantee a minimum rate of return (these companies are very rare); (2) *unit investment trusts*, which issue redeemable securities each of which represents a unit of interest in a fixed portfolio of securities deposited with a trustee; and (3) *management companies*, which are open-end (mutual fund) and closed-end investment companies.

OPEN-END (MUTUAL) FUNDS

As discussed in Chapter 1, open-end (mutual) funds are the major type of investment company—the other being closed-end investment companies (discussed next). The terms *open-end* and *closed-end* reflect a major difference between the two types of funds. Open-end means that the fund continuously has shares available for sale and that it normally stands ready to redeem outstanding shares upon request. As a result, the number of shares outstanding fluctuates as investors buy or redeem them. If new shares are sold, then the fund has additional cash for investment; if outstanding shares are redeemed, then the fund has fewer dollars invested. Thus, the dollar value of the portfolio changes with the number of shares sold or redeemed and with the changes in the prices of the securities in the portfolio. Shares are typically redeemed out of the fund's cash balance, which is primarily held for this purpose, but large redemptions could require the sale of securities to obtain cash.

To determine the value of an investor's investment in a mutual fund, the number of shares owned is multiplied by the net asset value (NAV) per share. The number of shares owned can increase without buying additional shares if the fund's dividend (including interest) and capital gains distributions are reinvested in shares rather than paid out to the investor (illustrated later in Figure 9.1). Also, the value of the shares increases as the securities in the portfolio increase in value (until they are sold). Mutual fund income is nontaxable as long as it follows IRS guidelines in paying out portfolio net income (or reinvesting the income in new shares at the investor's request) from interest, dividends, and capital gains. However, this income (distributed or reinvested) is taxable income to the investor.

The two basic types of mutual funds are *no-load funds* and *load funds*. This distinction is very important for investors. No-load funds sell their shares directly to investors at NAV. Load funds employ brokerage firms and other sales organizations to sell their shares. Load funds typically add a 7.5 to 8 percent sales or "load" charge to the NAV. This, of course, reduces the amount of investor's capital that is actually invested (e.g., $1,000 less 8 percent load charge) in the fund's portfolio, and this effectively increases the load charge as a percentage of the amount actually invested (e.g., 8 percent load charge is actually 8.7%). "True" no-load funds have no load charges, but some have small redemption fees, typically 1 percent. This fee, which discourages short-term trading of the fund, is generally eliminated after the fund has been held for a specified period of time. Whether the investor is better served by a load fund or a no-load fund depends on whether the assistance received (fund selection advice, etc.) from the broker or salesperson is perceived to be worth the load charge and whether the investment performance of load funds is superior to no-load funds with the same general investment objective. The specific varieties of load and no-load funds are discussed in Chapter 6.

Figure 2.2 indicates the sales prices of load and no-load funds. No-load funds sell at their NAVs, as indicated in the newspaper by "N.L." (no load) under "Offer Price." Specifically, N.L. means no "up-front" load charge, but it does not preclude other fees and charges, such as redemption fees. Thus, this abbreviation is often misleading. The sales prices of load funds are also listed in the newspaper under "Offer Price." These prices exceed the NAVs of the load funds by the amount of the load charges.

Figure 2.2 Mutual Fund Quotations

Source: Reprinted by permission of *The Wall Street Journal*, © Dow Jones & Company, Inc., November 13, 1987. All rights reserved.

CLOSED-END INVESTMENT COMPANIES

Contrasted to open-end funds, closed-end means that the number of shares outstanding are fixed by the number of shares that have been sold and subsequently traded. A closed-end fund does *not* stand ready to sell or redeem shares on a continuous basis, nor are the shares sold or purchased except through a broker. Thus, it has a type of "load" charge. The dollar value of its portfolio changes with changes in the prices of the securities in the portfolio and with the infrequent issuance of new shares through a stock offering.

Although closed-end funds do not buy and sell shares continuously, they do pay their investors the dividends, interest, and "realized" capital gains (net of losses) received (net of expenses). These realized capital gains arise from selling securities that have higher prices than when they were purchased.

Furthermore, whereas mutual fund shares are valued at NAV, closed-end fund shares are not. Closed-end fund shares are generally traded on a stock exchange where they are priced by the interplay of supply and demand. The shares either sell above (premium) or below (discount) their NAV, but generally they sell 5 to 20 percent below their NAV (Figure 2.3). These discounts make it possible to buy fund assets below their market value.[1] This increases the opportunity to earn above-average returns, especially if the discount gets smaller after purchase. On the other hand, the discount may get larger and reduce the return.

The explanation for this discount behavior is not definitely known, but

PUBLICLY TRADED FUNDS

Friday, November 13, 1987
Following is a weekly listing of unaudited net asset values of publicly traded investment fund shares, reported by the companies as of Friday's close. Also shown is the closing listed market price or a dealer-to-dealer asked price of each fund's shares, with the percentage of difference.

	N.A. Value	Stk Price	% Diff		N.A. Value	Stk Price	% Diff
Diversified Common Stock Funds				Claremont	a45.76	43½ −	4.9
				CounsTndC	6.37	4¾ −	25.4
AdmExp	18.64	19⅞ +	6.6	CypressFd	8.87	6¾ −	23.9
BakerFen	51.63	37½ −	27.4	DufPhUtils	7.77	8⅜ +	7.8
BlueChipVal	6.97	6 −	13.9	EllsworthCv	7.95	7¼ −	8.8
Clmnte-Gbl	b7.10	5 −	29.6	EmgMdTh	11.11	9½ −	14.5
EqGuard	b8.36	7⅛ −	14.81	Engex	11.22	7¾ −	30.9
GemIICap	14.47	11½ −	20.5	Fin NwCmp	16.32	14⅞ −	8.9
GemII Inc	9.74	11¾ +	20.6	1stAustralia	9.62	8 −	16.8
GenAmInv	16.85	15⅛ −	10.2	FstFnFd	7.09	5¾ −	18.9
GlobGrCap	7.90	9⅜ +	18.7	FranceFd	b10.87	8⅛ −	25.3
GlobGrInc	9.47	9⅛ −	3.6	GabelIIE	9.48	7½ −	20.9
GSO, Trust	9.56	9¼ −	3.2	GermanyFd	7.19	7 −	2.6
Lehman	14.94	13⅝ −	8.8	H&Q Health	7.10	5⅛ −	27.8
LbtyAll-Star	8.12	6½ −	20.0	Helvetia Fd	11.81	9¾ −	17.44
NiagaraSh	a13.87	13 −	6.3	HopperSol	17.34	9⅝ −	44.5
NchApGrEq	6.77	5 −	26.1	Italy Fd	b9.90	6⅞ −	30.56
QuestFVICp	9.28	6¾ −	27.37	Korea fd	30.43	48⅞ +	60.6
QuestFVIInc	11.89	9 −	24.3	Malaysia Fd	7.08	6½ −	13.5
RoyceValue	8.12	7 −	13.79	Mexico Fd	b8.01	5⅞ −	26.6
SchaferValu	f7.91	6⅜ −	19.4	MG SLCap	6.69	5⅛ −	23.0
Source	35.68	33 −	7.5	Pete&Res	26.62	24⅛ −	9.4

Figure 2.3   Publicly Traded Funds

Source: Reprinted by permission of *The Wall Street Journal*, © Dow Jones & Company, Inc., November 13, 1987. All rights reserved.

some reasons might include a built-in shareholder tax liability and the fund's past investment performance.[2] That is, investors tend to prefer those closed-end funds that do *not* have built-in capital gains tax liabilities from "unrealized" capital gains. These unrealized gains arise from a fund holding securities that have higher prices than when they were purchased. If a fund does have unrealized capital gains, a new shareholder could be faced with a built-in tax liability without any additional appreciation in the NAV of the shares when these gains are realized and distributed. Also, investors tend to prefer funds with superior performance in the preceding year on the assumption (unsupported) that this is a consistent predictor of future performance. Another explanation might point to the fact that closed-end fund shares are not redeemed at their NAV, but sold in the market with the payment of brokerage commissions. On the other hand, "true" no-load funds do not impose "up front" load charges and generally have no redemption fees.

There are several types of closed-end funds: (1) diversified closed-end funds, (2) dual-purpose funds, and (3) specialized closed-end funds. *Diversified companies* are invested in a wide range of securities with no special focus. They are primarily financed with common-stock capital. *Dual-purpose funds* have an equal number of income and capital shares. Investors who buy the income shares receive all the income generated by the portfolio, and those who buy the capital shares receive all of the net capital gains generated by the portfolio. These funds are also known as "leverage funds" because capital shareholders receive all of the portfolio's capital gains without having to own both classes of shares. Of course, they don't get the income generated by the entire portfolio. In recent years, most dual-purpose funds have been traded on the New York Stock Exchange. However, unlike corporations, dual-purpose funds do not have perpetual lives. At maturity, the income shares are redeemed at a fixed price or converted into mutual fund shares; the capital shares are converted into mutual fund shares. *Specialized closed-end funds* have portfolios that are limited either with respect to (1) type of security (e.g., common stock), (2) industry, (3) group of industries, or (4) geographic area.

UNIT INVESTMENT TRUSTS

A *unit investment trust* is a company with a *fixed portfolio* for the life of the trust. The sponsor (e.g., brokerage firm) of the trust purchases a portfolio of securities, typically fixed-income, which is then placed with a trustee (e.g., bank trust department) under an agreement for safekeeping and administrative services. In turn, the trustee issues *redeemable trust certificates* to the sponsor. Finally, these certificates of proportional interest (ownership) in the trust's assets are sold by the sponsor to investors, usually in minimums of

$1,000. The sponsor is rewarded for the risk of selling the trust certificates by adding a sales charge to the cost of the securities (analogous to a load charge).

Unit trust portfolios generally include either money-market securities (e.g., U.S. Treasury bills) or, more likely, corporate bonds, municipal (tax-exempt) bonds, or U.S. government bonds. Interest on the portfolio is passed through to the investors. The trust expires with the final maturity (or sale) of the securities in the portfolio (which could be, for example, 6 months for money market securities and 20 to 30 years for bonds).

If the investor desires to sell his or her certificates, the trustee generally redeems them for the seller at their NAV, using the market bid prices of the securities in the portfolio. These bid prices are the price quotations at which securities dealers are willing to *purchase* the securities. These prices are lower than the offer prices at which the securities dealers are willing to *sell* the securities. The cash for the redemption of investor shares is obtained from the sale of securities in the portfolio.

RELATED INVESTMENTS

A brief summary of a few of the other diversified investment pools follows as a means of familiarizing you with these alternatives.

Commingled funds. These funds are similar in concept to mutual funds. They provide an in-house alternative to the personal trust funds and individual retirement accounts managed by banks and insurance companies. Rather than being individually owned accounts, commingled funds are pooled investments of many investors, which are used to purchase a portfolio of securities (various issues and, perhaps, various types of securities). Each new "unit" in the portfolio is sold at NAV and each oustanding unit can be redeemed at NAV. Commingled funds have various general investment objectives, as reflected in the types of securities they may purchase: money market funds, common-stock funds, bond funds, and so forth.

Real Estate Investment Trusts (REITs). These funds are similar in concept to closed-end funds. REITs buy and manage portfolios of real estate and real estate mortgages. They obtain capital from the sale of common stock, bonds, warrants, and commercial paper (marketable short-term promissory notes) and from bank loans and mortgage loans. These corporations are not subject to federal income tax as long as they pay out at least 95 percent of their income in dividends. There are three basic types of REITs: *mortgage trusts*, which primarily invest in mortgages and construction and development loans; *equity trusts*, which primarily invest in real estate; and *hybrid* *trusts*, which are combinations of the other two types. REITs are not without substantial risk, and their use requires an informed investor and careful analysis.

Commingled Real Estate Funds (CREFs).   These funds are similar in concept to unit investment trusts. CREFs are real estate securities portfolios that expire upon maturity of the securities in the portfolio. CREFs are generally sponsored by life insurance companies and banks for their pension fund customers; banks also sponsor CREFs for their trust department customers. The sponsor receives a sales charge for initiating and managing the CREF. CREFs frequently have sizable liquidity risk because any subsequent buy or sell transactions occur in markets with only a limited volume of trading.

Tax shelters.   Tax shelters are partnerships or Subchapter S corporations designed to "shelter" income from income taxes. Limited partnerships are generally the preferred form of organization. In a limited partnership, the limited partners (investors) provide the capital by buying units in the partnership. Each investor's liability is limited to the amount of his or her contributed capital. The general partner sponsors the partnership, pools and invests the capital (e.g., in a commercial building), and provides partnership management, including financial responsibility. The general partner receives an ample percentage commission of the total investment, and at the scheduled expiration date of the partnership the property and the net proceeds are distributed to the limited partners. In the early years of their existence, tax shelters generally provided accounting and tax losses while generating positive cash flows. The tax losses arose from cash expenses and, especially, noncash partnership expenses such as depreciation and oil depletion allowances. These tax losses reduced the investors' taxable income. Tax shelters also allow the investors to transform ordinary income into capital gains through sale of partnership property. Investment in tax shelters requires very sophisticated legal and investor analysis which focuses on the investment worth of the tax shelter, with the tax benefits considered an addition to the return. Popular tax shelters include real estate, oil and gas drilling, equipment leasing, and some technology development.

The Tax Reform Act of 1986 severely limits the former (above) benefits of tax shelters by (1) imposing new limitations on the use of passive losses to shelter nonpassive income, (2) tightening further the limitations on the deductibility of investment interest expense, and (3) cutting back on the deductions and credits that produce tax shelters.[3] A "passive" investment usually refers to a trade or business in which the investor does not materially participate in the conduct of that activity. Salaries and income (loss) from the conduct of a trade or business in which the taxpayer materially participates are considered "active."

Some of the major provisions of this Act, as they apply to tax shelters, follow:

1. The ability of investors to offset losses or credits from passive business activity (i.e., tax shelters) against active (e.g., salary) or portfolio income is limited.

2. Losses and credits from passive activities are deductible *only* against income from other passive activities. Unused passive losses and credits can be carried forward to offset future passive income.

3. Interest expense and income attributable to a passive activity are generally subject to the passive loss limitation and are not treated as investment interest or income.

4. The passive loss limitation applies to individuals, estates, and trusts. It also applies to most personal service corporations and, in more generous form, to closely held corporations.

5. The rental of real (e.g., house) and personal property is generally treated as passive activity, regardless of whether the taxpayer materially participates in the activity. However, individuals who are active participants in rental real estate activities are permitted to offset up to $25,000 of nonpassive income with real estate losses.

6. The Act presumes that income and losses attributable to a limited partnership reflect a passive activity (except for oil and gas drilling interests).

7. Portfolio income is not passive income and, therefore, may not be sheltered by passive losses and credits. It includes dividends on stock, REIT dividends, interest, royalties, annuity income, and gains or losses on the sale of properties (portfolio income or loss). But it excludes income from business partnerships, Subchapter S corporations (treated like proprietorships for federal tax purposes), or property leases.

This tax law should increase the number of real estate syndicates created to produce passive income. These syndicates will purchase real estate with little or no use of debt because the interest payments will be considered passive and, therefore, deductible only against passive income.

Variable annuities. Variable and fixed annuities are retirement and savings plans offered by insurance companies and some nonprofit organizations representing particular occupations (e.g., professors).[4] They are discussed here as retirement vehicles. Variable annuities are tax-favored investments under the 1986 tax law, and they involve both accumulation and retirement (annuity) phases. During the accumulation phase, the investor makes contributions (premiums) that are used to pay the contract's various management fees and to purchase shares in the investment portfolio. At retirement, the investor chooses a lump-sum payment or annuity payments for life (or a related annuity option). The contracts also include a guaranteed death benefit equal to, or larger than, the market value of the investor's net contributions. The financial strength of the insurance company stands behind payment of a death benefit that exceeds the net market value of the contributions.

Under the newer variable plans, the net premiums are invested in a diversified portfolio of common stock or a mutual fund managed by the company. The retirement annuity payments are "variable," reflecting the investment performance of the portfolios. Under fixed-annuity plans, the net premiums are invested in a diversified portfolio of long-term debt securities. The minimum amounts of the retirement annuity payments are guaranteed, but under some contracts the early years pay a guaranteed "going rate" followed by payments reflecting actual portfolio performance, subject to the guaranteed minimum payments.

Variable annuities are tax-deferred retirement plans similar to the IRA accounts of those whose contributions are not tax deductible. However, there is no limit on the size of contributions and the beneficiary is guaranteed no less than the net amount invested. As with IRAs, the income earned by variable annuities accumulates without taxes. Thus, this tax benefit reduces the generally higher fees and lower investment performance of mutual funds owned by insurance companies relative to direct investment in mutual funds, especially no-load funds.

For annuity plans offering investment in mutual funds, the investor can select the allocation of his or her contributions among a limited number of available funds. Usually, these allocations can be changed only a limited number of times per year. However, the tax implications of early withdrawal and contract surrender charges make variable annuities especially useful as long-term investments, most suitable for older investors with immediate needs for retirement planning. Thus, these plans are less flexible and liquid than the direct investment in mutual funds. Also, the performance of the annuity contract is dependent upon the financial strength of the insurance company.

Variable life insurance.   This is one of several types of single-premium life insurance policies—the only one that gives the policyholders control over their investments and that invests in mutual funds offering "variable" rates of return.[5] They are also tax-favored investments under the 1986 tax law. Variable life policies combine some of the advantages of mutual-fund investing with the tax-deferral benefits of life insurance. The income earned is tax deferred until withdrawal or retirement. However, the tax implications and the surrender charges for early policy cancellation (which also apply to variable annuities) can be avoided. Policyholders have tax-free access to their investments through the use of policy loans, which are available at nominal rates of interest. Moreover, the interest is returned to the policyholder's account as long as the loan is taken only from the earnings on the investment.

As insurance, variable life policies require an initial lump-sum payment of $5,000 or more—thus, "single-premium" insurance. The policies guarantee a minimum rate of return on net premium payments, which provides the guaranteed cash value and death benefit of the policy. However, the sales administrative and "mortality" fees add up to more than the fees associated with variable annuities. As suggested earlier, the policies also have surrender charges if they are cancelled after only a few years. Thus, variable life insurance is especially useful for the investor who has an actual and long-term need for insurance coverage. At death the insurance proceeds pass tax-free to the beneficiaries. All in all, variable life insurance is a more flexible product than variable annuities. Again, the performance of the contract is backed by the financial strength of the insurance company.

The features of five retirement plans are summarized in Table 2.1, and one of them, tax-free municipal bond funds, is defined briefly in Chapter 3.

TABLE 2.1   Five Ways to Save for Retirement

Features	IRA	401(k)	Single-Premium Life Insurance	Annuity	Tax-free Municipal Bond Fund
Tax-deferred earnings	x	x	[1]	x	[2]
Automatic reinvestment	x	x	x	x	x
Safety of principal	3	3	x	x	
Guaranteed return			x	x	
Unlimited contributions			x	x	x
Direct loan provisions			x		
No mandatory withdrawal after age 70½			x		x
No early withdrawal penalty[4]			x		x

[1]All income from life insurance is *exempt* from federal taxes if you receive it by borrowing against your policy.

[2]Income from tax-free municipal bond funds is *exempt* from federal (and in many cases state) income taxes; capital gains earned from sale of municipal bond fund shares are not tax-exempt or tax-deferred, however.

[3]Only for IRAs or 401(k)s invested in money market funds or bank CDs.

[4]Under federal law, prior to age 59½; 10% penalty does not apply to annuity distributions made before age 59½ if payments are distributed over your lifetime, but insurance companies typically retain a percentage of your principal as a "surrender" charge if you take out more than 10% during the first five years of your contract—no matter what your age.

Source: Anita Saville, "A Different Shelter: Variable Annuities," *Independent Investor's Personal Investing Newsletter*, January 28, 1987, p. 9.

ENDNOTES

[1] For an informative discussion of closed-end funds, see Lindy Spellman, "A Close Look at Closed-end Funds," *Changing Times*, May 1987, pp. 87–92.

[2] Hans R. Stoll, "Discounts and Premiums on Shares of Diversified Closed-End Investment Funds" (Philadelphia: University of Pennsylvania, The Wharton School, Working Paper No. 11-7, 1978).

[3] For a more complete discussion of tax shelters and the 1986 tax law, see C. Clinton Stretch and Emil M. Sunley, *The Tax Revolution: A New Era Begins* (Washington, D.C.: Deloitte Haskins & Sells, 1986).

[4] For a discussion of this treatment of variable annuities, see Karen Slater, "Variable Annuities, Life Insurance: Tax-Favored Investing—At a Price," *The Wall Street Journal*, September 8, 1986; also, Anita Saville, "A Different Shelter: Variable Annuities," *Independent Investor's Personal Investing Newsletter*, January 28, 1987, pp. 9–12.

[5] For a discussion of this treatment of variable life insurance, see Anita Saville, "Single-Premium Life Insurance," *Independent Investor's Personal Investing Newsletter*, December 3, 1986, pp. 181–184.

3

Types of Mutual Funds
by Their Investment
Objectives

As discussed in Chapter 1, the types of mutual funds are classified by their general investment objectives. The mutual fund industry classifications and definitions are used here (Figure 3.1) to avoid the confusion of the variety of approaches used in the mutual fund literature. Of course, all of these funds seek to make money for their investors, but the investment objective suggests how the fund hopes to do this (types of securities) and/or the level and form of income (e.g., current income, high capital appreciation) it hopes to achieve. The degree of risk is implicit in these objectives. Figure 3.2 indicates the number of funds classified by their investment objective. The most common types of funds in 1986 are money market funds (360), growth funds (260), and growth and income funds (177).

Table 3.1 is helpful in providing some insight on the total return performance of *some* of the types of funds. It shows the five-year, ten-year, and fifteen-year performances of aggressive growth funds, growth funds, growth and income funds, precious metals funds, international funds, balanced funds, income funds, and option/income funds. When looking at their *total* reinvested cumulative total returns, it is important to remember that, on average, high return and high risk go hand in hand. For example, the ten-year and fifteen-year total returns on aggressive growth funds are the highest of the eight types of funds. However, in the five-year period, aggressive growth funds rank fifth of the eight funds. Aggressive growth funds are used in this example on the assumption that they have high risk relative to the

Aggressive Growth Funds seek maximum capital gains as their investment objective. Current income is not a significant factor. Some may invest in stocks that are somewhat out of the mainstream such as those in fledgling companies, new industries, companies fallen on hard times, or industries temporarily out of favor. They may also use specialized investment techniques such as option writing or engage in short-term trading.

Growth Funds invest in the common stock of more settled companies but, again, the primary aim is to produce an increase in the value of their investments rather than a steady flow of dividends.

Growth and Income Funds invest mainly in the common stock of companies with a longer track record that have the expectation of a higher share value but also have a solid record of paying dividends.

Precious Metals Funds invest in the stocks of gold mining companies and other companies in the precious metals business.

International Funds invest in the securities of foreign companies. Global funds, a segment of the international fund category, may also invest in U.S. securities.

Balanced Funds generally have a three-part investment objective: 1) to conserve the investors' initial principal, 2) to pay current income, and 3) long-term growth of both principal and income. They aim to achieve this by owning a mixture of bonds, preferred stocks and common stocks.

Income Funds seek a high level of current income for their shareholders. This may be achieved by investing in the common stock of companies which have good dividend-paying records. Often corporate and government bonds are also part of the portfolio.

Option/Income Funds seek a high current return by investing primarily in dividend-paying common stocks on which call options are traded on national securities exchanges. Current return generally consists of dividends, premiums from writing call options, net-short-term gains from sales of portfolio securities on exercises of options or otherwise, and any profits from closing purchase transactions.

U.S. Government Income Funds invest in a variety of government securities. These include U.S. Treasury bonds, federally guaranteed mortgage backed securities and other government notes.

GNMA or Ginnie Mae Funds (Government National Mortgage Association) invest in government backed mortgage securities. To qualify for this category, the majority of the portfolio must always be invested in mortgage backed securities.

Corporate Bond Funds, like income funds, seek a high level of income. They do so by buying bonds of corporations for the majority of the fund's portfolio. The rest of the portfolio may be in U.S. Treasury and other government entities' bonds.

Municipal Bond Funds invest in bonds issued by local governments—such as cities and states—which use the money to build schools, highways, libraries and the like. Income earned on these securities is not taxed by the federal government. The mutual fund buys the municipal bonds and then passes the tax-free income through to fund shareholders.

Single State Municipal Bond Funds work just like other municipal bond funds except their portfolios contain the issues of only one state. The advantage for a resident of that state is that income is free of both federal and state tax.

Money Market Mutual Funds invest in the short-term securities sold in the money market. (The money market is where large companies, banks and other institutions invest their surplus cash for short periods of time.) In the investment spectrum these are generally the safest, most stable securities available and include Treasury Bills, certificates of deposit of large banks, and commercial paper (the short-term IOUs of large U.S. corporations).

Short-Term Municipal Bond Funds invest in municipal securities with relatively short maturities. They are also known as tax-exempt money market funds.

Figure 3.1   Types of Mutual Funds

Source: Investment Company Institute, *1987 Mutual Fund Fact Book*, pp. 8–9. Reprinted with permission of Investment Company Institute.

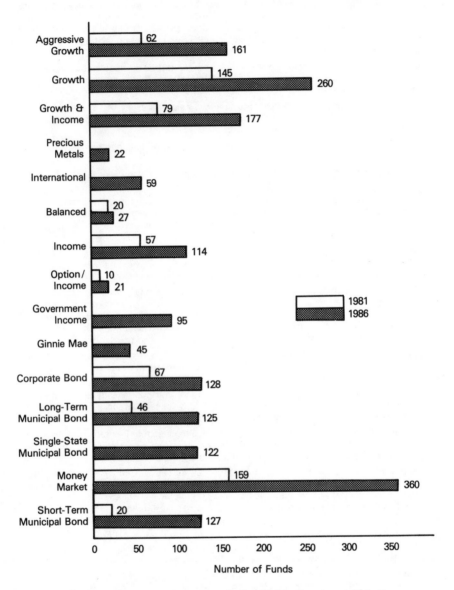

Figure 3.2   Number of Mutual Funds Classified by Investment Objective
Source: Investment Company Institute, *1987 Mutual Fund Fact Book,* p. 19.
Reprinted with permission of Investment Company Institute.

other types of funds. It would seem, on average, that their returns reflect their relative risk over the ten-year and fifteen-year periods, but not the shorter five-year period. The longer the period, the more likely the expected relationships will hold.

An additional bit of information in Table 3.1 is the relative performance of the various types of mutual funds compared to the Standard & Poor's 500 Composite Index (S&P 500). This index is used to approximate the performance of the overall stock market; it contains 400 industrial stocks, 40 utility stocks, 20 transportation stocks, and 40 financial stocks. By including the S&P 500 as a "fund," one can see that it performed fourth best of the nine funds for the fifteen-year period, sixth best of nine funds for the ten-year period, and third best of nine funds for the five-year period. Thus, it appears that some types of funds can outperform the stock market, especially over longer periods of time. But this is to be expected because some types of funds bear more risk than the overall market.

This conclusion is only barely substantiated in Figure 3.3. In the ten-year period ending 1986, equity funds (those investing only in equity securities) show an average annual return of 14.3 percent, whereas the S&P 500 Index shows a similar average annual return of 13.9 percent. Although the difference in returns is small, both the equity funds and the S&P 500 Index easily outperform the 6.6 percent average annual increase in inflation as measured by the Consumer Price Index. This provides support for the use of common-stock portfolios to outperform inflation.

MONEY MARKET FUNDS

Money market funds are discussed in Chapter 11 as the haven for monies transferred from mutual funds when the market declines sufficiently. They provide a safe refuge from the risk of capital loss due to such factors as

TABLE 3.1   Performance by Type of Mutual Fund

| | | Total Reinvested Cumulative Performance | | |
| | | 3/31/71–
3/31/86 | 3/31/76–
3/31/86 | 3/31/81–
3/31/86 |
Number	Type of Fund			
116	Aggressive growth	+484.82%	+417.50%	+ 97.13%
206	Growth	+366.74	+371.19	+ 98.97
123	Growth and income	+402.29	+316.33	+120.69
21	Precious metals	+295.26	+339.82	− 5.26
25	International	+317.30	+228.96	+ 96.34
24	Balanced	+358.81	+282.86	+134.50
24	Income	+332.15	+256.81	+123.49
19	Option/Income	+228.12	+204.12	+ 73.16
674	All equity funds	+406.10	+362.01	+103.45
973	All funds (median)	+335.07	+291.02	+111.22
	S&P 500 Index	+365.68	+279.45	+123.43

Source: Excerpted from "Mutual Fund Averages by Group" by Lipper Analytical Services, Inc., in Barrons, May 19, 1986, p. 73.

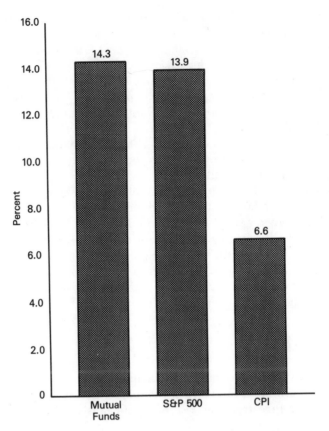

NOTE:

Mutual fund performance reflects a monthly weighted average for all equity funds.

Mutual fund and S&P 500 data prepared by Lipper Analytical Services. These indexes are not adjusted for sales charges.

Figure 3.3   Mutual Fund Investment Performance (10 Years through 12/31/85)

Source: Investment Company Institute, 1987 Mutual Fund Fact Book, p. 23. Reprinted with permission of Investment Company Institute.

increased interest rates, increased inflation, decreased security liquidity, and reduced security creditworthiness (see below). Thus, money market funds deserve some additional attention.

Money market funds are very advantageous because they provide investors with *competitive money market yields* (from money market instruments), *high liquidity, small minimum purchase requirements,* and *safety of principal.* These funds also have *professional management*, generally *low management fees*, and are generally "true" *no-load funds* with *no-redemption fees.*[1]

Money market funds have similarities to money market deposit accounts (MMDAs). MMDAs were authorized in 1982 to allow depository institutions to compete with money market funds. These accounts have no interest-rate ceilings, permit six transfers per month (including three checks), and have no regulatory minimum amount per check written on the account. Money market funds typically have higher minimum check denominations (e.g., $500). MMDAs are federally insured where the depository institution is so covered. They are also generously treated like savings deposits rather than demand deposits for purposes of federal legal reserve requirements.

The taxable funds are called *money market funds* because their portfolios include only the securities issued and traded in the so-called "money market." The money market is a wholesale market for low-risk, highly liquid, short-term debt securities.[2] *Low risk* means there is a high degree of safety of principal because the securities are of very high credit quality with low risk of default. It also means that, because of their short-term maturity (maximum one year), there is little risk of a significant price decline due to an increase in interest, including inflation rates. In any case, the securities can be held to maturity to avoid such losses and to maintain the stability of the fund's NAV, while earning current income on the securities. *Highly liquid* means that the volume of trading is active enough so that a security can be converted (sold) to cash quickly without substantial risk of loss in value due to an increase in the security's bid-ask spread in the market. This increase in the difference between the highest bid price and the lowest ask price requires a "price concession" to effect a sale at the market price.

Although referred to as a *money market*, it is, in fact, an interrelated collection of markets for distinct types of securities. The borrowers participating in the money market include foreign and domestic banks, U.S. Treasury, corporations, federal agencies, dealers in money market securities, and states and municipalities. The participating lenders include most of the above participants plus insurance companies, pension funds, and various other financial institutions. Dealers and brokers act to bridge the gap between borrowers and lenders. As a wholesale market, trades in the money market are large and generally made for the accounts of major institutions. Participants in the money market need skill in the narrow areas of expertise represented by each of the types of securities they trade. They also need the integrity to stand behind their trades.

Money market funds came into their own during the 1970s when interest rates on money market securities soared to unequaled heights. For example, the annualized yields on money market funds exceeded 20 percent for some time during this period—an historical high on these high-quality, low-risk, and short-maturity portfolios.

Although money market funds have low risk, there are differences in risk within and between categories of these funds. The lowest-risk category of money market funds is U.S. Treasury Money Funds. These funds seek *maximum* safety of capital, liquidity, and the highest yield consistent with these objectives. They also maintain stable NAV of $1.00 by seeking only dividend income. These funds invest in short-term U.S. Treasury securities, securities guaranteed by the U.S. government, and high-quality repurchase agreements involving the above securities. The securities they hold have maturities of one year or less and average no more than 120 days. The portfolio maturities are aggressively managed to reflect the outlook for short-term interest rates. During periods of rising interest rates, the maturities are below average; during periods of decreasing interest rates, they are above average.

The next category of money market funds is *Diversified Money Market Funds*. This is what is usually meant when one refers to "money market funds." These funds seek preservation of capital, liquidity, and the highest yield consistent with these objectives. They also maintain a stable net asset value of $1.00 by seeking only dividend income. In general, but not always, these funds invest from among eight types of short-term securities (defined on the next page). The major ones are *commercial paper*, followed by *U.S. Treasury securities* and *repurchase agreements*. These major types of securities are followed in importance by Eurodollar certificates of deposit, U.S. Government agency securities, certificates of deposit, bankers' acceptances, "Yankee" certificates of deposit, and all other such instruments. The funds may require that some percentage of their portfolios be invested only in the highest-quality securities, while the balance must be in high-quality securities. The securities have maturities of one year or less and average no more than 120 days. Again, the average maturities of the portfolios are aggressively managed to reflect the outlook for short-term interest rates.

The third category of money market funds is *Tax-Exempt Money Funds*. These funds seek safety of capital, liquidity, and the highest federal tax-exempt income compatible with these objectives. They also maintain a stable NAV of $1.00 by seeking only dividend income. Tax-exempt money funds invest in short-term, high-quality municipal securities, including municipal notes and municipal bonds. Municipal notes are used to finance short-term needs for capital, and they include project notes, tax anticipation notes, revenue anticipation notes, bond anticipation notes, construction loan notes, and tax-exempt commercial paper (defined in standard investments reference sources). Municipal bonds are used to finance long-term capital needs, and they include general obligation bonds, revenue bonds, and industrial development bonds. The securities in these money funds have maturities of one year or less and average no more than 120 days. Like the other fund types, these portfolio maturities are also aggressively managed to reflect the outlook for short-term interest rates.

On the basis of yield, the desirability of these funds depends on whether they or taxable funds provide the larger after-tax return. This can be determined by computing the taxable *equivalent* yield of a tax-exempt fund and comparing it to the yield on a taxable fund. The taxable-equivalent yield is computed by dividing the tax-exempt yield by the sum of one minus the investor's marginal tax rate (the rate applied to the last dollar of income). For example, assume the tax-exempt yield is 5 percent and the marginal tax rate is 28 percent. Dividing 5 percent by one minus 28 percent, the taxable-equivalent yield is 6.94 percent. If this is greater than the yield on the taxable fund, the tax-exempt fund is preferred on the basis of comparable yield (exclusive of risk).

Some of the major types of money market securities held by U.S. Treasury money funds and/or diversified money market funds include:

Bankers' acceptances—short-term obligations of large banks generally arising from financing foreign trade. More specifically, they are secured, short-term notes arising from foreign and domestic trade, which are accepted for payment at maturity value by large, high-quality banks that frequently sell them at a discount to maturity value. They are of excellent credit quality.

Commercial paper—short-term promissory notes of large corporations. More specifically, they are short-term (fixed maturity, maximum 270 days), unsecured promissory notes of large, high-quality corporations, which sell them at discount to maturity value. Generally, they are of high-credit quality.

Eurodollar CDs—dollar-denominated negotiable certificates of deposit issued by U.S. bank branches and foreign banks outside the United States. Generally, they are of high-credit quality.

Negotiable certificates of deposit (CDs)—large denomination deposit liabilities of major banks. More specifically, they are short-term (usually one to six months) time-deposit liabilities of large, high-quality foreign and domestic banks, usually sold in $1 million denominations. Generally, they are of high-credit quality.

Repurchase agreements (RPs)—sale of securities with an agreement to repurchase them at a fixed price and date. More specifically, RPs involve the sale ("loan") of U.S. Treasury or agency securities by dealers, financial institutions, and others with an agreement to repurchase them at a fixed yield and date, usually overnight. Reverse RPs are the same agreements from the standpoint of the purchasers of the securities (e.g., mutual funds). They are of excellent-credit quality.

Treasury bills—short-term debt obligations of the U.S. Treasury. More specifically, they are short-term (30, 90, 180, 360 days) noninterest securities sold at discount to maturity value by the U.S. Treasury. They are of the highest-credit quality.

U.S. Agency Securities—securities issued by agencies (e.g., housing and farm credit agencies) created by Congress, which are backed by their own assets, the full faith and credit of the United States, the guarantee of the Treasury, and the ability to borrow from the Treasury, or which have no direct or indirect Treasury backing. They are of excellent-credit quality, especially the "full faith and credit" securities.

Yankee CDs—negotiable certificates of deposit issued in the United States by branches of foreign banks. Generally, they are of high-credit quality.

Money market funds generally hold several types of money market securities. The risk of their portfolios also varies with respect to the credit quality and maturity of the individual issues held. For example, according to its February 28, 1986 Annual Report, the T. Rowe Price Prime Reserve Fund had the following characteristics:

PORTFOLIO COMPOSITION

Bankers' Acceptances (8 issues, foreign and domestic)	2.7%
Certificates of Deposit (41 issues, foreign and domestic)	50.6
Commercial Paper (49 issues, foreign and domestic)	46.0
Other Assets (net)	0.7
	100.0%

QUALITY DIVERSIFICATION

Fund Quality Rating 1	7.0%
2	40.0
3	53.0
	100.0%
Weighted-Average Rating	2.5

MATURITY DIVERSIFICATION

0–30 days	54.0%
31–60 days	36.0
61–90 days	10.0
	100.0%
Weighted-Average Maturity	31 days

Thus, this fund basically holds certificates of deposit and commercial paper. These issues appear to be of adequate (but not the highest) quality, and the resulting return (not shown here) is quite competitive. The weighted-average maturity of the portfolio (thirty-one days) reflects the fund's outlook for interest-rates. In this case, the fund's portfolio manager was anticipating a period of relative stability in short-term interest rates (within a two-year period of sharply declining interest rates).

ENDNOTES

[1]For a further discussion of the advantages and characteristics of money market funds, see Donald D. Rugg, *The Dow Jones Irwin Guide to Mutual Funds*, 3rd ed. (Homewood, Ill.: Dow Jones-Irwin, 1986), Chapter 6.

[2]For a complete discussion of this treatment of the money market and its securities, see Marcia Stigum, *Money Market*, rev. ed. (Homewood, Ill.: Dow Jones-Irwin, 1983).

4

Mutual Fund Management

A mutual fund is a corporation chartered to do business as an open-end investment company. Legally, it can issue only one class of securities—common stock—which provides shareholders with a mutuality of interest in the fund's assets and income. The fund invests the pool of funds provided by the shareholders in a securities portfolio, which is the fund's major asset. A mutual fund is required by federal law to be registered with the Securities and Exchange Commission (SEC), and it must also be registered with each state in which its shares are sold. As a corporation, a mutual fund is legally owned by the shareholders (investors) who elect the board of directors. The general duties of the board are described (italics added) in the prospectus of a major mutual fund:

> The Board of Directors of the Fund is elected annually by the shareholders. The Board has *responsibility* for the overall management of the Fund, including general supervision and review of its investment activities. The Directors elect the officers of the Fund, who are *responsible* for administering the day-to-day operations of the Fund.

As with most publicly held corporations, the fact that the fund is "owned" by the shareholders is somewhat misleading with respect to actual control of the fund. The fund is actually controlled and managed by a separate management company (fund sponsor) through its role as the fund's investment adviser. The investment adviser manages the fund's portfolio and most of its administrative responsibilities. The advisory contract between the fund and the management company as investment adviser specifies the duties to be performed and the fees to be paid. The major duties include securities research and analysis, portfolio management, and general fund administration. The fund's board of directors appoints the fund's officers and selects the investment adviser. The board normally selects the management company to be the investment adviser because the board is controlled by officers of the management company. After all, it is the principals of the management company who incorporate and organize the fund and select its initial board of directors. In addition to being a fund management company, some of these companies are, or are related to, investment advisory firms, insurance companies (for load funds), or brokerage firms (for load funds).

The fact that the fund's management company is almost always the investment adviser means that the investment adviser is seldom replaced. This is not necessarily bad from the shareholders' point of view if they selected the fund primarily on the basis of the adviser's ability to generate superior rates of return on the fund's portfolio (for the fund's investment objective).

Although the fund is controlled by its sponsoring management company (fund sponsor), fund shareholders do have the legal right to approve (affirm actually) certain of the major decisions made by the fund's board of directors. These decisions include (1) changes in the fund's investment objective, (2) selection of the investment adviser, (3) approval of the investment advisory fee schedule, (4) selection of the custodian, and (5) selection of the transfer agent.

INVESTMENT ADVISER

The investment adviser manages the fund's portfolio and its day-to-day operations. In this capacity, the adviser is responsible for providing and paying for several major items, including

1. Office space, personnel, and supplies
2. Security analysts and portfolio managers
3. Compliance with federal and state laws and regulations
4. Preparation and distribution of the fund's prospectus, annual and quarterly reports, and other shareholder communications
5. Provision of the methods of share sale or redemption, advertising, and other sales material
6. Provision for transfer of shares sold or redeemed
7. Provision for safekeeping of fund assets
8. Provision of accounting services and preparation of tax returns
9. Provision of insurance coverage.

These expenses are usually less than 1 percent of the net asset value of *large* funds. The fund's advisory contract with the investment adviser usually limits the total expenses the fund will pay. Also, these fees are limited by law in those states in which fund shares are sold. (A fund's advisory contract is described below.)

As mentioned above, the ability of the investment adviser to produce superior portfolio rates of return (for its investment objective) should be a primary criterion in selecting a mutual fund. Again, the fund's board of directors almost always names the management company as investment adviser because the fund was created by the management company as a vehicle for obtaining a pool of funds which, *for a fee*, the sponsor, as investment adviser, invests and manages. There is nothing sinister in this because the fund is a vehicle for creating a product—in this case, an investment product.

The investment adviser receives a fee for managing the fund. The annual fees tend to range from less than ¼ of 1 percent to over 1 percent of net assets. With the increased costs of business, new funds tend to have fees ranging from ¾ of 1 percent to 1 percent of net assets. Because the expenses of managing a mutual fund do not increase proportionately with the size of the fund, many advisory fee rate schedules decline as the fund increases in size (example below). Nonetheless, the total amount of the fees increases with the size of the fund. This provides a strong monetary incentive for fund managers to perform well and to attract more capital to invest. More recently, some funds pay their investment adviser a basic fee and, if earned, a performance "bonus" fee (see example that follows). Typically, the fund's investment performance is compared to a measure of the overall stock market, such as the S&P 500 Index. The difference in performance is used to compute the performance adjustment, which is either added to or subtracted from the basic fee, depending on the fund's performance relative to the S&P 500. For example, if the fund outperforms the S&P 500, the basic fee will be increased according to the performance adjustment formula approved by the fund's board of directors.

Today, it is common for management companies to offer families of mutual funds, each with a different basic investment objective. The management company's primary advantage in having a family of funds is the ability to offer a more diversified financial product line with which to obtain additional investor capital and revenue. Moreover, fund families provide shareholders with the ability to transfer their invested capital efficiently within the family to meet their changing investment needs.

The control of the investment adviser, the services it provides, and the fee it receives are described in the following prospectus of a leading mutual fund:

The Fund's Investment Adviser, _____ Management Corporation, is controlled by Mr. _____, who is an officer, sole director, and as of October 18, 1985, the holder of 59.12% of the voting securities of the Adviser. Mr. _____ is also the President, Treasurer and a Director of the Fund.

Under an Advisory Contract dated October 20, 1983, by vote of the shareholders on October 17, 1985, the Adviser provides the Fund with investment advisory services, office space, and personnel. Under the Advisory Contract, the Adviser pays the salaries and fees of the Fund's officers and directors who are interested persons of the Fund and all clerical services relating to the Fund's investments. The Adviser also pays all promotional expenses of the Fund. The Fund pays all other costs and expenses, including interest, taxes, fees of directors who are not interested persons of the Fund, other fees and commissions of every kind, administrative expenses directly related to the issuance and redemption of Shares including expenses of registering or qualifying Shares for sale, charges of custodians, transfer agents, and registrars, costs of printing and mailing reports and notices to shareholders, auditing services and legal services, and other expenses not expressly assumed by the Advisor.

The contract with the Investment Adviser, adopted by vote of the shareholders October 20, 1983, and extended October 17, 1985, provides for renewal annually by vote of the Fund's Board of Directors or by vote of a majority of the oustanding voting securities of the Fund. In addition, the terms of any continuance or modification of the contract must have been approved by the vote of a majority of those directors of the Fund who are not parties to such contract or interested persons of any such party, cast in person at a meeting called for the purpose of voting on such approval. The contract is terminable by either party on 60 days written notice and is terminated automatically in the event of its assignment.

The Adviser receives a basic fee of .7% per annum of the first $50 million average net assets of the Fund, plus .6% of the next $350 million and .5% of the excess over $400 million, subject to increase or decrease (performance bonus or penalty) depending on the Fund's investment performance compared with the investment record of the Standard & Poor's Stock Composite Index. Investment performance of the Fund means the sum of the change in its net asset value during the fiscal year and the value of dividends and capital gains distributions per share accumulated to the end of the fiscal year, expressed as a percentage of net asset value per share at the beginning of the fiscal year. In computing the investment performance of the Fund and the investment record of the Index, distributions of realized capital gains by the Fund, dividends paid by the Fund out of its investment income and all cash distributions of the Companies whose stocks comprise the Index, are treated as reinvested.

Fee Schedule	First $50 Million	Next $350 Million	Excess Over $400 Million
If the Fund's performance exceeds the Index by:			
more than 12 percentage points	0.9%	0.8%	0.7%
more than 6 but less than 12 percentage points	0.8%	0.7%	0.6%
less than 6 percentage points	0.7%	0.6%	0.5%
If the Fund's performance falls below the Index by:			
less than 6 percentage points	0.7%	0.6%	0.5%
more than 6 but less than 12 percentage points	0.6%	0.5%	0.4%
more than 12 percentage points	0.5%	0.4%	0.3%

The maximum fee possible, assuming maximum performance, is .9% of the first $50 million of average net assets, .8% of the next $350 million, and .7% of the excess over $400 million. The smallest fee possible, assuming poorest performance, is .5% of the first $50 million of average net assets, .4% for the next $350 million, and .3% of the excess over $400 million.

The basic fee may be increased or decreased, in accordance with the foregoing formula, during a particular year despite the fact (1) that there may be no change in the Index, if there is an increase or decrease in the net asset value per share of the Fund of at least 6%, or (2) that there may be no change in the net asset value per share of the Fund, if there is an increase or decrease in the Index of at least 6%.

If the ratio of annual operating expenses (excluding taxes and interest) exceeds 1½% of the first $30 million of average net assets of the Fund, plus 1% of average net assets in excess of $30 million, then the Contract requires the Adviser to reimburse the Fund for any such excess.

The net fee is accrued monthly. In partial payment of amounts so accrued, the Adviser is entitled to receive quarterly installments of ¹⁄₁₀ of 1% of average net assets toward the annual fee, subject to the foregoing expense limitation applied on a quarterly basis; the excess, if any, of the annual fee over the quarterly installments is payable annually, within thirty days after receipt of the Accountant's Report for the Fund's fiscal year.

BANK CUSTODIAN

To protect shareholder capital against the risk of theft by fund management, the Investment Company Act of 1940 requires SEC-registered mutual funds to have bank or trust company custodians hold their cash and securities in trust. To avoid any potential conflict of interest in this role, the custodian can have no other relationship with the fund. In holding the fund's assets in trust, the custodian typically

1. Makes payments for securities purchased
2. Receives and holds the certificates for the securities purchased
3. Receives payment for securities sold
4. Delivers the certificates for the securities sold
5. Receives the dividend and interest payments on the securities held
6. Releases cash for fund expenses

These rather specialized and bonded custodial duties are performed by a few large banks. The custodian is typically compensated based on the fund's average NAV.

The custodian's role and compensation is described in the prospectus of a leading mutual fund:

> The _____ Bank of _____ acts as custodian of all cash and securities of the Fund. The Bank is also responsible for the settlement of securities trades and collection of dividends and interest due the Fund. Its custody does not involve advice or decisions as to the purchase or sale of portfolio securities.
>
> The Custodian receives a monthly fee based on average net assets on an annualized basis of:
>
> $\frac{1}{10}$ of 1 % of the first $25,000,000,
> $\frac{1}{20}$ of 1 % of the next $50,000,000,
> $\frac{1}{30}$ of 1 % of the next $100,000,000,
> $\frac{1}{40}$ of 1 % of the next $200,000,000 and
> $\frac{1}{50}$ of 1 % of the next $125,000,000.

The description makes explicit that the custodian is not involved with portfolio selection and management.

TRANSFER AGENT

The transfer agent is a bank or organization that acts as the mutual fund's stock transfer and dividend disbursing agent. The transfer agent is frequently an affiliate of the fund's management company. The agent's duties include

1. Processing transfers in ownership of the fund's shares (sales and redemptions)
2. Maintaining shareholder records
3. Computing the fund's NAV
4. Maintaining the fund's portfolio and accounting records
5. Disbursing income payments to shareholders

The transfer agent typically receives payments from the fund and the investment adviser for its out-of-pocket expenses and fees.

The transfer agent's role and compensation is described in the prospectus of a large load fund:

> _____ Company, an affiliate of [the management company] is transfer and shareholders' servicing agent for the Fund, for which _____ Company received fees of $_____ for the year ended March 31, 1986. In addition, _____ Company was reimbursed $_____ for out-of-pocket expenses incurred in the performance of such services. The Fund and _____ Company also have an agreement under which _____ Company determines the net asset value per share and maintains the portfolio and general accounting records of the Fund, for which _____ Company received fees during the year ended March 31, 1986 of $_____ and out-of-pocket expenses of $_____ .

FUND DISTRIBUTOR/UNDERWRITER

Most mutual funds have underwriters that distribute their shares nationally on an exclusive basis. This section briefly describes the sales organizations of load and no-load mutual funds. As discussed earlier, _load funds_ add a sales charge to the NAV of their shares. The fund's distributor is typically an affiliate of the management company and is responsible for buying shares from the fund at NAV and selling them ("wholesalers") to securities dealers and others at NAV plus a commission. The securities dealers, their brokers, and the other "retailers" resell the shares to the public at NAV plus a commission. For example, assuming an 8 percent sales charge, the distributor might get a

1 percent commission and the securities dealer a 7 percent commission, with the dealer's commission being shared with the broker who made the sale. The relatively large commission available from the sale of load funds provides a great incentive for brokers, financial planners, insurance agents, and others to include load funds in their recommendations to clients.

The distributor is described briefly in the prospectus of a large load fund:

> Fund shares are sold with a sales commission, commonly referred to as "sales load." For the year ended March 31, 1986, _____ Distributors Corporation, a wholly-owned subsidiary of [the holding company of the management company and other fund-related companies] and the general distributor of the Fund, received $_____ as its portion of the sales charges on sales of shares of the Fund.

No-load funds also have fund underwriters, the functions of which are normally provided by the management company itself or an affiliated company. These distributors are responsible for buying shares from the fund at NAV and selling them *directly* to investors (also at NAV). To do this, they use periodical advertising, direct-mail advertising, and some use sales offices to reach potential investors. The investor's initial response to the fund is generally by letter or telephone. The methods of share purchase and redemption are discussed in Chapter 6.

An affiliated distributor is described briefly in the prospectus of a no-load fund:

> Each Fund is distributed by _____ Investment Services, Inc., a wholly-owned subsidiary of [the management company] . . . .

5

Mutual Fund Plans

ACCUMULATION PLANS

One of the advantages mutual funds offer is a number of flexible and convenient *accumulation plans* for the voluntary or systematic acquisition of fund
shares (these advantages are discussed in Chapter 7). The simplest accumulation plan is the *automatic reinvestment* of all income dividends (from
interest and dividends) and capital gains distributions (from realized net
capital gains). This plan allows shareholders to elect whether to have their
distributions paid in cash or reinvested in fund shares. Either choice is subject
to the same income tax liability. Automatic reinvestment is a convenient way
for shareholders to accumulate additional shares over time, and it is the plan
elected by most shareholders.

A less formal accumulation plan is the *voluntary plan*. This plan depends
on the shareholder's initiative to purchase additional fund shares. The only
limitation on the amount of an additional purchase is the minimum amount
imposed by the fund. These minimums range from zero to $1,000, with zero,
$50, or $100 frequently required. Voluntary plans may sometimes be formalized with the cooperation of a bank and the fund, whereby the shareholder
has the bank transfer monies electronically to the mutual fund to purchase
additional shares. The fixed-amount transfer (e.g., $100) takes place on a
predetermined schedule, for instance, the fifteenth of each month.

An obviously more formal accumulation plan is the *contractual
accumulation plan*. These plans are most commonly used in conjunction with
bond funds. Contractual accumulation plans call for the investor to purchase
a fixed dollar amount of the fund's shares on a predetermined schedule (e.g.,
monthly) for an extended period of years (e.g., five years). These plans generally "front load" the sales charge so that a large proportion of early payments

simply pay this charge. Thus, to the extent that investors do not complete their plan, they are paying a very high percentage of their payments in sales charges. Once involved in such a plan, the investor must complete it to minimize the average per share sales charge.

Because of abuses perceived in the nature and practice of these contracts and fund load charges, Congress passed the Investment Company Amendment Act of 1970. This Act (1) limits overall load charges on funds to 9 percent, (2) limits sales charges on contractual accumulation plans to no more than 50 percent of the first year's payments, and (3) provides that if the first year charges exceed this limit, the plan may be cancelled within eighteen months of its inception with an effective sales charge of 15 percent.

Voluntary withdrawal plans are the opposite of voluntary accumulation plans. These plans depend on the shareholder's initiative in redeeming fund shares. Voluntary withdrawal plans may also sometimes be formalized with the cooperation of a bank and the fund. Under these plans, the shareholder instructs the fund to redeem a fixed dollar amount of shares and transfer the proceeds electronically on a fixed schedule (e.g., monthly) to his or her account. These plans are most frequently used by retirees. One of the great advantages of voluntary withdrawal plans is that if the dollar amount of the yearly withdrawal is no more than the increased value of the remaining shares, then the market value of the retiree's investment remains the same or increases. The increased value of the shares can come from the increased NAV of the shares and/or any additional shares acquired from reinvestment of distributions, net of the value of any shares withdrawn in cash (redeemed).

RETIREMENT PLANS

Another advantage of mutual funds is that they offer investment vehicles for retirement plans. These plans, normally called *qualified* retirement plans, have several tax advantages: (1) tax-deferred income on plan contributions, (2) tax deductions for plan contributions, and (3) favorable tax treatment on lump-sum plan distributions.

To be able to provide these advantages, retirement plans must qualify by meeting IRS requirements. The qualified plans offered by mutual funds include individual retirement accounts (IRAs), Keogh plans, simplified employee pension plans (SEPs), Section 403(b) plans, Section 401(k) plans, and corporate-sponsored plans. The Tax Reform Act of 1986 made numerous changes in the rules governing these plans.[1] Thus, investors are advised to obtain needed assistance from experts on retirement plans.

Mutual funds are ideal investment vehicles for retirement plans.[2] In addition to the general advantages and disadvantages of mutual funds, funds have several particular advantages as vehicles for some retirement plans.

These advantages include (1) provision of new account forms that meet legal information requirements, (2) provision of any custodial/fiduciary relationship required by law, (3) provisions of assistance in meeting any periodic legal reporting requirements, (4) provision of reports to shareholders on legal changes, and (5) availability of mutual funds that emphasize long-term portfolio performance, consistent with the long investment horizon of most retirement accounts. This last advantage has been weakened by those funds that market their short-run performance as a means of attracting new investor capital.

Individual retirement accounts (IRAs) are designed to encourage individuals to save for their retirement. They allow each person under the age of 70½ to contribute a *maximum* amount equal to the first $2,000 of earned income (e.g., wages, personal services). If the investor's spouse has no earned income, a *maximum* of $2,250 may be contributed to two IRA accounts, with neither exceeding $2,000.

The IRA contribution is deductible from taxes if both the investor and spouse are not covered by a Keogh plan, company pension plan, or tax-deferred savings plan, and if income limits are not exceeded. The contribution is completely deductible for single persons with adjusted gross income under $25,000 and for married couples with adjusted gross incomes under $40,000. The deduction is gradually phased out above these income levels and is zero at $35,000 for single persons and at $50,000 for married couples.

Even if an investor does not qualify for a tax-deductible contribution, the compound income on the contributions is tax deferred until withdrawn. This is a worthwhile advantage of IRA accounts. Nonetheless, because of these newly imposed limitations on the deductibility of IRA contributions, many investors should consider other plans, such as 401(k), Keogh, and SEP, which may provide greater retirement benefits. IRAs must be maintained by trustees, which are usually banks. The fund's investment adviser selects the trustee and provides the contributor with the necessary legal paperwork to open the account and appoint the trustee.

Amounts withdrawn from the contributor's account after age 59½ are subject to ordinary income tax rates. Withdrawals may begin at age 59½ and they must begin by age 70½. Amounts withdrawn prior to age 59½, death, or disability are subject to a 10 percent penalty tax plus ordinary income taxes, unless received in the form of a life-time annuity. The limitations on withdrawals have the effect of reducing the liquidity of the account, and contributions to it should be made with this in mind. IRA contributions may be transferred from one mutual fund to another without payment of taxes. The recipient fund supplies the required form to be completed by the contributor and sends it to the current fund to effect the transfer.

Keogh ("HR-10") plans are designed for persons with full or part-time self-employment income (e.g., proprietors, partners). They provide the same essential features as corporate pension plans. Keogh plans must include accounts for all those full-time employees covered by law. The plans are maintained by approved custodians, which are usually banks. The mutual fund's investment adviser selects the custodian and provides the self-employed person (plan sponsor) with the required paperwork to establish the plan and appoint the custodian. The plan sponsor must also file an annual report with the IRS. The mutual fund usually provides information for this filing.

The self-employed person may make contributions under three types of *defined contribution* retirement plans: (1) profit sharing, (2) money purchase, and (3) paired. A *profit-sharing plan* permits a variable percentage contribution per year. Profit-sharing plans are flexible and involve low risk because the employer's contributions are optional and depend on the firm's ability to pay. A *money-purchase plan* is a fixed percentage plan that requires that the selected percentage contribution be made each year. Money-purchase plans are not flexible and involve sizable potential risk because the employer's contributions are mandatory, regardless of the ability to pay. The *paired plan* is a combination of the two plans. It permits higher contributions than a profit-sharing plan and also has more flexibility with less risk of not being able to make required payments than a money-purchase plan.

The allowable percentage contributions to the plan sponsor's own Keogh plan and those of the employees are defined with respect to the sponsor's *net earned income* (net income less the Keogh contribution) and each employee's company compensation, respectively. The maximum effective percentages of company *net profits* that equal the maximum percentages of net earned income are:

	Maximum Contribution for Plan Sponsor	*Maximum* Contribution for Employee
Profit-sharing plan	13.04%	15.00%
Money-purchase plan	20.00	25.00
Paired plan		
Profit sharing	13.04	15.00
Money purchase	6.96	10.00
Combined total	20.00	25.00

The maximum contribution paired plan with the most flexibility against having to meet large contributions under the fixed requirements of a money purchase plan is one with a 13.04 percent profit-sharing payment and only a 6.96 percent money purchase payment.

Thus, the maximum contribution to the plan sponsor's own Keogh plan is 20 percent of net income (up to a maximum of $30,000). The plan sponsor's maximum contribution to an employee's plan is 25 percent of the employee's compensation (also up to a maximum of $30,000). The qualified plan sponsor's contributions to employee plans are deductible expenses. The plan sponsor's qualified contributions to his or her Keogh plan are deductible expenses on the individual's personal federal income tax return, In addition, the compound income on contributions to participant plans is tax deferred until it is withdrawn. Plan contributions may also be transferred free of taxes from one mutual fund to another. The recipient fund provides the form to initiate the transfer.

In addition to defined contribution plans, there are also *defined benefit* plans. These plans permit employers to contribute the estimated amount needed to fund a predetermined annual retirement benefit. The *maximum* allowable contribution is that necessary to fund a retirement benefit of either 100 percent of compensation or $90,000, whichever is less. The size of the employer's contributions reflect the assumed rate of return on the invested money, employee's age and life expectancy, estimated future compensation, estimated cost-of-living adjustments, retirement age, and the definition of compensation for the plan. To the extent the actual return on the portfolio differs from that assumed, future contributions will have to be increased or decreased as needed to meet the plan's promised retirement benefits.

Participants may normally receive benefits from their plans upon termination of service or retirement after age 59½. Withdrawals must begin no later than age 70½. These withdrawals may be made under alternative distribution formulas, which are then subject to income taxes. The limitations on withdrawals reduce the liquidity of these plans and suggest that plan contributions should be made with this in mind.

Simplified employee pension plans (SEPs) are designed primarily for smaller corporations, partnerships, and proprietorships. They require no complex IRS approval procedures and are relatively simple to operate. They also provide flexibility with respect to employer contributions. However, they may be used only by employers that have never had a defined benefit pension plan and that have twenty-five or fewer employees. Under SEPs, the employers make tax-deductible contributions to individual IRA accounts they have established for their employees. These accounts are basically subject to the regulations that apply to regular IRAs. Although employer contributions are taxable income to employees, they may be deducted as expenses by both employers and employees. Under the Tax Reform Act of 1986, the deductibility of company contributions per employee are limited to $7,000 per year under rules similar to 401(k) plans (discussed below). Employees may also make their own contributions to these SEP IRAs or to their own IRAs. The deductibility of these employee contributions is limited by the law applying to IRAs (as discussed earlier).

Section 403(b) and 401(k) retirement plans are frequently offered to employees as optional and *supplemental* (to their regular retirement plans) tax-sheltered annuity plans. Section 403(b) refers to plans available only to employees of educational institutions and other nonprofit organizations. Section 401(k) refers to plans available to corporate employees. These plans are named after their sections in the Internal Revenue Code and related Treasury regulations. Under the tax-deferred provisions of these sections, employees may arrange with their employers to direct a portion of their gross (before-tax) salaries to purchase fully vested retirement annuity benefits. Employers may also make contributions to the plans. These "salary reduction" plans reduce employee salaries for tax purposes by the amounts of their contributions to the plans. Under the 1986 tax law, employees may defer limited amounts (see below) per year, less any payments to other tax-deferred plans. The compound income on these contributions is tax deferred until retirement or other eligible withdrawals are made. Withdrawals may be made after age $59\frac{1}{2}$, upon termination of service, for defined hardship cases, and upon plan termination. Withdrawals must begin no later than age $70\frac{1}{2}$. These plans may call for tax and investment assistance from retirement experts.

Under the 1986 tax reform act, employee tax-deferred salary contributions under 401(k) plans are limited to $7,000 per year. However, this amount is adjusted upwards with the cost of living. Employers may contribute up to the lesser of $30,000 or 25 percent of employee taxable compensation less the amount of any employee deferral. The act also limits the tax-deferred salary contributions made by defined "highly compensated" employees. There are also limits on employer matching contributions and employee *after-tax* contributions to 401(k) plans.

Under the 1986 tax reform act, employee tax-deferred salary contributions under 403(b) defined contribution (variable benefit) annuity plans are limited to the greater of $9,500 or the cost-of-living adjusted limit under 401(k) plans. Employer contributions are limited to the lesser of 25 percent of compensation or $30,000, the latter to be adjusted upwards with the cost of living beginning at a later date. Annual plan benefits are limited to the lesser of 100 percent of defined compensation or $90,000, the latter adjusted upwards with the cost of living. Employee *after-tax* contributions are treated as employer contributions for purposes of the maximum allowable employer contributions. The new act also reduces the maximum early retirement benefits under 403(b) plans.

Other retirement plans frequently offered by mutual funds include regular corporate retirement plans. These plans include defined contribution plans and defined benefit plans, the former including profit-sharing plans and money-purchase (pension) plans. These plans provide the same essential features as Keogh plans. The specific details of these plans are available from the employer, where offered.

As an example of the types of accumulation and retirement plans offered by mutual funds, one large fund provides the following:

Systematic investment plan

Systematic withdrawal plan

IRA plan

Keogh plan

403(b) tax-deferred annuity plan

401(k) retirement savings plan

Corporate pension and profit sharing plans

ENDNOTES

[1] These changes in the tax rules affecting retirement plans are described further in C. Clinton Stretch and Emil M. Sunley, *The Tax Revolution: A New Era Begins* (Washington, D.C.: Deloitte Haskins & Sells, 1986), pp. 61–71.

[2] For a discussion of this treatment of retirement plans, see Donald D. Rugg, *The Dow Jones-Irwin Guide to Mutual Funds*, 3rd ed. (Homewood, Ill.: Dow Jones-Irwin, 1986), Chapter 13.

6

Purchase and Redemption of Mutual Fund Shares

METHODS OF SHARE PURCHASE AND REDEMPTION

There are two major ways to purchase mutual fund shares, depending on whether the fund is a load fund or a no-load (or similar type) fund. The distribution of load fund shares through a sales distribution system is described in Chapter 4. On the other hand, no-load funds and related funds, such as low-load funds, sell their shares directly to the public. Low-load funds are funds with smaller load charges than load funds. They were originally no-load funds, but in recent years, as their market acceptance and investment performance made it feasible to do so, a sales charge was added. These load charges are normally explained as necessary (a debatable point) to cover the increased marketing costs of an increasingly competitive fund environment.

No-load funds use newspaper, periodical, and direct-mail advertising to stimulate the sale of shares. No salesforce is utilized. In most cases, the investor writes or calls the fund for a new account application. Under federal regulations, the fund (all types) must also provide all prospective shareholders with a *prospectus*. In completing the application form, the investor must certify that he or she has read the prospectus. The prospectus typically includes the fund's (1) financial history, (2) investment objective and policies, (3) income distributions and taxation, (4) management and service fees, (5) methods of share purchase, (6) income distribution options, (7) exchange privileges, (8) method of electronic money transfer system to purchase or redeem shares (if any), (9) tax-deferred retirement plans offered, (10) methods of share redemption, and (11) securities holdings.

In recent years, the SEC approved a shortened version of the prospectus for general distribution.[1] To obtain all of the information that used to be included in the prospectus, the investor should request it and a copy of the "Statement of Additional Information." The investor should also request the latest quarterly and annual reports. In reviewing this information, the investor could use the following preliminary checklist:

_____ Investment Objective
    _____ investment policies
    _____ risk level

_____ Past Performance
    _____ annual rates of return, latest and recent years
    _____ 10- to 15-year average annual rate of return
    _____ dividend yield, latest and recent years

_____ Officers and Directors
    _____ portfolio manager and time in job
    _____ backgrounds

_____ Portfolio
    _____ total assets
    _____ largest securities holdings
    _____ industry weighting in portfolio (%)
    _____ turnover rate (measure of purchase/sale activity)

_____ Fees
    _____ management fee
    _____ expense ratio (percentage of average net assets)
    _____ 12b-1* (advertising and sales expense) fees (if any)
    _____ load (sales) charges (if any)

_____ Services
    _____ telephone exchange ("switch")
    _____ automatic reinvestment of distributions
    _____ check-writing privilege
    _____ switching fees (if any)
    _____ other

Initial purchases of shares in no-load and low-load mutual funds may normally be made by mail or by wiring monies from the investor's bank account to his or her new fund account. Initial purchases by telephone are

---

*The 12b-1 fees and load charges are discussed later in this chapter.

sometimes available, but they normally require an identically registered account in one of the sponsor's other funds. To open an account by mail, the investor must complete the application form (available from the fund by mail or telephone) and attach a check for the initial required minimum amount of purchase, for instance, $1,000. The checks sent by mail are usually considered eligible for share purchase at NAV the day following the collection period of the check. These shares may typically be redeemed with fund payment by check upon receipt of a written request that arrives after collection of the monies used to purchase the shares. Share accounts opened by wiring monies through the banking system are typically eligible for share purchase at NAV on the day these monies are available as collected deposits. These shares may also be redeemed with fund payment by check immediately upon receipt of the shareholder's written request that arrives after collection of the monies used to purchase the shares.

Subsequent (additional) purchases of shares may normally be made by mail, telephone, or the wiring of funds through the banking system. These purchases must be for at least the subsequent required minimum amount (if any), for instance, $100. When additional shares are ordered by telephone, payment for them must usually be received within seven days. Other restrictions may also apply in this case.

SHARE REGISTRATION

In completing the new account application, the investor or fiduciary must register ownership of the shares. Mutual funds provide several registration options:

1. *Individual ownership*—sole ownership account
2. *Joint tenants with right of survivorship*—joint ownership account (e.g., man and wife) with ownership reverting to the surviving owner
3. *Joint tenant*—joint ownership account with the deceased owner's share reverting to his or her estate
4. *Corporation*—corporate ownership account registered by a duly constituted officer
5. *Custodian*—fiduciary account (e.g., child) registered and controlled by the beneficiary's custodian (e.g., father)
6. *Trust*—fiduciary account registered and owned by the beneficiary's trustee (e.g., bank)

Traditionally, a custodial account provided a simple way to accumulate wealth for a child's future use (e.g., college), while taxing the investment income from the account at the child's usually low tax bracket. Under the

1986 tax law, this advantage has been reduced. For a child under age fourteen, investment income over $1,000 is taxed at the parents' usually higher tax rate. Custodial accounts are usually registered under the Uniform Gifts to Minors Act of the child's state of residence. The parents' gifts to this account are subject to the relatively generous provisions of the federal gift tax laws. These accounts require a minimum of legal expertise and no additional cost.

INCOME DISTRIBUTION

Mutual fund payments of *realized net income* to shareholders are called *distributions*. They are of two basic types: (1) *dividend distributions*, which are payments from dividend and interest income net of fund expenses; and (2) *capital gains distributions*, which are payments from realized capital gains net of any capital losses.

Also in completing the new account application, the investor must choose a distribution option:

1. *Share option*—both dividend and capital gains distributions are automatically reinvested in additional shares, generally at NAV
2. *Income-earned option*—dividend distributions are paid in cash and capital gains distributions are reinvested in additional shares, generally at NAV
3. *Cash options*—both dividend and capital gains distributions are paid in cash

Most shareholders select the automatic reinvestment option. Some funds permit the distributions to be reinvested in selected other funds in the sponsor's "family" of funds.

ADDITIONAL PURCHASE OR REDEMPTION SERVICES

At the time the application form is completed, or at any later time, the investor may *apply* (prior to use) for *additional purchase or redemption services* provided by the fund. These services may include:

1. *Redemption by check*—the shareholder is permitted to write "special" checks (in at least a specified minimum dollar amount) drawn on his or her account in an agent bank which is paid by the redemption of shares in the shareholder's fund account
2. *Exchange by telephone (telephone "switch") or telegram*—the shareholder is permitted to transfer (generally for no more than a nominal

amount) at least a specified minimum dollar amount of his or her shares in one fund to another in the sponsor's family of funds

3. *Redemption by telephone or telegram*—the shareholder is permitted to call or send a telegram to redeem his or her shares in the fund (with payments as agreed either by check or by transfer to the shareholder's bank account)

4. *Electronic funds transfer* ("wiring federal funds" through the Federal Reserve System)—permits the shareholder to call routinely to authorize the purchase of shares by electronic funds transfer from his or her bank account to the fund's custodian bank account or to authorize the redemption of shares and the wire transfer of funds from the fund's custodian bank to the shareholder's bank account

5. *Automatic purchase or redemption*—permits the shareholder to authorize the systematic (e.g., monthly) purchase or redemption of shares by transferring money between his or her bank account and his or her fund account

This last service implements the formalized voluntary withdrawal and/or accumulation plans discussed in Chapter 5.

Shares purchased by treasurer's, certified, or cashier's checks may normally be redeemed immediately upon receipt of written request or through use of the fund's authorized check or telephone redemption services. However, shares purchased by corporate, government, or personal check, or through use of electronic funds transfer may not normally be redeemed until the fund is assured of having received collected monies (e.g., fifteen days for personal checks).

Use of these redemption services requires that the shareholder's shares be maintained electronically as book entry notations by the fund's transfer agent, rather than as actual share certificates in the investor's possession. Shareholders do not receive certificates unless they request them; if they do, the certificates should be kept in safekeeping. Also, funds may delay sending proceeds of redeemed shares for up to seven days if making immediate payment could adversely affect the fund. The Securities and Exchange Commission may also suspend fund share redemptions and payments under emergency financial market conditions.

COSTS OF INVESTING

Many mutual funds are charging new types of sales charges and fees to raise money for their sponsors and salespersons. Thus, investors need to search out any such costs by reading the fund prospectus, proxy statements, annual reports, and sales literature. To review the costs of purchasing mutual fund shares, the investor will find it useful to classify funds according to the size and nature of these sales charges and other fees: (1) "load" or "front-end load" funds, (2) "low-load" funds, (3) "back-end load" funds, (4) "12b-1" ("hidden") load funds, (5) miscellaneous load funds, and (6) "no-load" funds.[2]

Approximately 50 percent of mutual funds are *front-end load funds*. These are "full load" funds that charge an upfront sales charge, ranging from approximately 4.5 percent to a legal maximum of 9 percent. This load charge is allocated to the sales distribution system as described in Chapter 4. A few load funds also impose sales charges on dividend distributions which are reinvested in the fund.

The small number of *low-load funds* have significantly lower sales charges, normally 1 to 3 percent, than do "full-load" funds, reflecting their no-load background. Thus, the sales charges remain within the fund organization rather than going to commission salespersons. These charges permit the funds to offer the customer information services provided to shareholders in load funds. Large low-load funds were once generally successful no-load funds, which are now able to impose charges because of increased investor acceptance of their investment performance and shareholder services, such as telephone "switching." Because of the difficulty in reaching investors, some smaller no-load funds have become low-load funds in order to provide increased visibility through improved sales and advertising efforts. However, these developments do not represent a trend, especially for the larger no-load funds.

Back-end load funds represent less than 10 percent of mutual funds. They charge a fee upon share redemption (e.g., 4 percent) rather than at the time of purchase. Back-end load funds (and 12b-1 funds) were usually organized as front-end load funds. A major motivation for their becoming back-end load funds was to be categorized as "no-load" funds, which can be interpreted to mean no front-end load (and, unfortunately, probably interpreted by the public as actual no-load).

Back-end load funds impose *contingent deferred sales charges*. Former load funds, which have become 12b-1 funds, impose deferred sales charges on shares redeemed prior to a specified period since their purchase. These charges typically start at 4 to 6 percent and decline to zero over some four to six years. These deferred charges and the 12b-1 fees allow the fund to pay commissions to brokers and salespersons without imposing front-end load charges. It is important to research the prospectus to see whether these charges are applied to the amount of the investor's original investment, the current market value of the investment, or some related amount, such as the gain to date where it at least equals the amount of the original investment. The current market value method is the least preferred if the fund's NAV has increased.

Redemption fees have a long history. Today, less than 5 percent of funds are no-load funds that impose small *exit fees* (e.g., 1 percent) on the market value of redeemed shares to discourage frequent redemptions, such as telephone exchanges. Therefore, redemption fees could be considered "back-end loads" for no-load funds. Nonetheless, it seems reasonable that small fees for this purpose are consistent with a fund being considered a "true" no-load fund, if no other charges are imposed.

Since 1980, the Securities and Exchange Commission, under its Rule 12b-1, has permitted so-called *12b-1 load-funds* to take fund (investor) assets to pay for distribution (advertising and sales) expenses used to get new shareholders and also to pay for customer service expenses to keep shareholders. The initial idea behind 12b-1 funds was to help small no-load funds reach new shareholders and, thereby, reduce costs per dollar of assets. These unregulated fees must be approved (and so far they all have been) by the independent members of the fund's board of directors and by the shareholders.

In 1981, some no-load funds began to use 12b-1 fees to pay for promotional materials and advertising. Most of the approximately 100 no-load funds that have distribution fees charge ¼ of 1 percent or less per year. These funds do not impose back-end load charges (discussed earlier).

In 1982, some load funds began to replace their front-end load charges with 12b-1 distribution fees. These fees are currently *as high as 1.25 percent per year* and include sales commissions and retainers, annual ("trailing") royalty payments for servicing accounts, and the costs of advertising and sales materials. One reason for switching from front-load charges to 12b-1 fees is that the Securities and Exchange Commission has not (yet) required that 12b-1 load funds be called "load" funds, but it has warned them not to advertise as "no-load" funds. Nonetheless, 12b-1 fees make it possible for brokers to earn commissions on so-called "no-load" funds.

The 12b-1 load funds pay these sales commissions from the distribution fees charged to fund assets. The fund management company advances the 4 to 5 percent commission to the salesperson and then recoups it over the next few years from the fund's distribution fee. To ensure that the fund sponsor is reimbursed for its commission expenditures, even if investors redeem their shares too soon, a declining back-end load charge (see below) is imposed. To encourage follow-up services to shareholders, 12b-1 load funds also pay the salespersons annual royalties of some ¼ of 1 percent of the total value of each client's shareholdings.

For the short-term investor in a 12b-1 fund, these *annual* fees may be preferable to a one-time 8.5 percent load charge, but not for the long-term investor. For example, 9 years times a 1 percent annual fee exceeds 8.5 percent. Some 12b-1 funds deduct most of these fees from gross assets so that they are not included in the fund's "expense ratio" (discussed below). The fund's prospectus does not include any load charges in the performance data, and the 12b-1 fees may not be included in the expense ratio. Thus, the investor should read the prospectus carefully and compute the fund's performance net of all load charges, expenses, and 12b-1 distribution fees.

While the Securities and Exchange Commission is pressuring the approximately 900 12b-1 funds to keep these charges under control, their use is still growing, especially among funds that have the fastest asset growth. Another issue the SEC has not yet resolved is the question of responsibility for these expenses. If a fund management company spends money on marketing and sales commissions this year, it expects to be reimbursed for most of these expenditures from the fund's assets over the next few years. However, the legal issue is whether the management company or the fund is responsible for any questionable carryover charges. Given the hidden, continuous, and, perhaps, excessive nature of these fees and the legal issues surrounding them, *investors should normally avoid 12b-1 funds*, especially converted front-end load funds.

Miscellaneous load funds are those few that impose dollar amounts of sometimes unusual fees, including purchase fees, account maintenance fees, and exit fees.

There are nearly 400 *no-load funds*. These funds have no front-end load, no back-end load (except, perhaps, for small redemption fees for recently purchased shares), and no 12b-1 distribution fees. Assuming comparable investment performance among the various types of funds (based on their charges and fees), *the investor should invest in no-load funds to obtain the largest net return*. (See Table 6.1 for examples of how these various charges total as a percentage of investment.)

The above types of load and 12b-1 charges refer to those imposed on the investor's per share NAV at the time of purchase, time of redemption, or while the shares are held (12b-1). However, *all* funds pay *management advisory fees* and other *administrative expenses*. These expenses are, of course, deducted from the fund's investment income and, thus, reduce the distributions paid to shareholders. The management advisory fee (details in Chapter 4) is paid to the investment adviser for managing the day-to-day operations of the fund and its portfolio. The other administrative expenses are paid by the mutual fund.

It has been determined that common stock mutual funds have an average *expense ratio* (total expenses divided by average annual net assets) of 1.12, and load funds have an average ratio of 0.91.[3] Further, the average management advisory fee is ½ of 1 percent. Expense ratios tend to decrease as the size of the fund increases. Also, many advisory contracts call for advisory fee rate schedules to decline as the fund increases in size (Chapter 4). The investment adviser must reimburse the fund for total expenses that exceed the maximum expense ratio in the management advisory contract. State laws also impose maximum expense ratios, with the more restrictive states limiting total expenses to 1.5 percent of average net assets. Assuming

TABLE 6.1   The Real Costs of Investing in Four Typical Funds

When evaluating a fund's fees, you have to look at more than such highly visible charges as initial sales commissions or back-end loads (also called deferred sales charges) and exit fees that you must pay to get your money out. You should also examine the prospectus for the fund's internal charges—the fees that management deducts from your assets every year. The four funds in the table below levy fees that are typical in the industry. The top line after each fund's name shows how much you would pay in fees the first year. The second line tells how those charges add up over five years.

	Number of Years in Fund	% Maximum Initial Sales Charge	% Deferred Sales Charge	% Exit Fee	Expenses as Percentage of Assets*	Total Costs as a Percentage of Your Investment
Pennsylvania Mutual	1	None	None	1	1.03	2.02
	5	None	None	1	5.04	6.00
Hutton Special	1	None	5	None	2.20	7.09
Equities	5	None	1	None	10.53	11.42
Putnam Fund for	1	8½	None	None	.55	9.00
Growth & Income	5	8½	None	None	2.49	10.99
Fidelity Select-	1	2	None	1	1.50	4.44
Energy	5	2	None	1	7.13	10.04

*Five-year expense figure assumes that costs remain at current levels.

Source: Eric Schurenberg, "How Hidden Charges Snatch Away Profits," *Money* (November 1986), p. 232.

comparable overall performance among no-load funds, the investor should invest in those funds with the lowest expense ratios, all else being equal.

INVESTOR TAX FACTORS

As will be discussed in Chapter 7, mutual funds that perform as a legal conduit in making distributions to shareholders are not subject to federal income or excise taxes. The realized income that funds distribute is earned on a portfolio of securities. Its *dividend* payments are earned on equity securities, such as common stock and preferred stock. Its *interest* payments are earned on debt securities, such as government and corporate bonds and Treasury bills. Its payments from net *realized capital gains (losses)* arise from the sale of securities that have higher (or lower) prices than their cost at purchase.

These dividend and capital gains distributions are taxable income to the shareholders, whether they are received in cash or reinvested in fund shares (at NAV). Furthermore, fund distributions of dividend income (not interest) are generally partly eligible for the 80 percent dividend-received deduction for corporations. The portion of the dividends that qualifies for this deduction depends on the ratio of qualifying dividends to the fund's total taxable income, exclusive of capital gains. The fund informs its shareholders of the amount of the income distribution that qualifies for this treatment.

One unhappy aspect of the 1986 tax law is that fund shareholders are required to include their prorated share of the fund's investment expenses as additions to the distributions they receive in computing their federal taxable income. These additions are deductible only to the extent that the total of "miscellaneous deductions" exceeds 2 percent of adjusted gross income. In any case, the tax implications should not be significant for most investors.

A selected checklist of tax reminders for mutual fund investors includes the following:

_____ Capital gains and losses on the sales of fund shares are considered ordinary income and losses under the Tax Reform Act of 1986 (discussed above).

_____ Telephone and other exchanges ("switches") of mutual fund shares are considered a sale and purchase for tax purposes.

_____ Income (dividends and interest) distributions are treated as dividends for tax purposes.

_____ Reinvested dividend and capital gains distributions are taxable, and they should be included in the cost basis of the shares (for tax purposes) when sold.

_____ The cost basis of each fund's shares may be calculated on the basis of one of the following methods: (1) *average cost* per share, with the shares sold assumed to be those held the longest; (2) *first-in first out*, with the shares sold assumed to be those held longest; and (3) *specific share basis*, with the shares specified at their sale and confirmed by the fund.

_____ *Losses* on fund sales are disallowed for tax purposes if *identical* shares are repurchased within a sixty-one-day period beginning thirty days before and ending thirty days after the sale ("wash-sale" rule); however, *gains* are fully recognized even if they are repurchased immediately.

_____ Dividend distributions from tax-exempt money and bond funds are exempt from federal taxation; however, capital gains/losses from the sale of shares are considered ordinary income/losses.

_____ *State* taxation of the distributions from U.S. Treasury money or bond funds varies—check treatment in the investor's state.

_____ Most *states* tax the distributions from municipal money or bond funds—check treatment in the investor's state.

As suggested here, the method for determining the cost of fund shares redeemed can be an important tax matter. It is recommended that the specific-shares method be used, especially if the fund cooperates in the procedure.[4] It provides the greatest flexibility in controlling the tax consequences of each redemption. The records that should be kept, along with the transaction records provided by the fund, include the following ledger headings for each fund:

Date of transaction

Number of shares

Price per share

Cost-basis adjustment

Total amount invested

Total shares owned

Date redeemed

The investor should consult his or her tax advisor on issues concerning the tax implications of mutual fund investing.

Capital gains (losses) on securities that have *not* been sold are called *unrealized capital gains (losses)*. These gains (losses) do not have tax implications for shareholders. However, unrealized gains (losses) increase (decrease) NAV, and realized capital gains increase NAV until they are distributed and NAV is reduced by an equal amount.

Before the Tax Reform Act of 1986 was passed, net long-term capital gains (but not short-term gains) were taxed at 40 percent of the shareholder's marginal tax rate on ordinary income. Now all capital gains (losses) are taxed as ordinary income (losses). Capital gains (losses) on mutual funds are realized when fund shareholders sell shares at a price above (below) their purchase cost.

ENDNOTES

[1] For a discussion of the prospectus, see Janice Horowitz, "How to Pick a Mutual Fund," *Personal Investor* (May 1985), pp. 28–29.

[2] For a discussion of this treatment of load charges, see "New Ways Mutual Funds are Socking it to Investors," *Changing Times* (February 1984), pp. 37–38; Eric Schurenberg, "How Hidden Charges Snatch Away Profits," *Money* (November 1986), pp. 231–232; Laura R. Walbert, "Backdoor Loads," *Forbes* (April 8, 1985), p. 168; John Waggoner, "Loaded for Bull," *Financial Planning* (November 1986),

pp. 97–100; Pamela Sebastian, "Sales-Stimulus Plan May Have Side Effects," *Wall Street Journal*, July 21, 1986; and Jerry Edgerton, "When a Load Becomes a Burden," *Money* (July 1985), pp. 135–136, 138.

[3]For a discussion of the study of expenses and management fees, see Gerald W. Perritt and L. Kay Shannon, *The Individual Investor's Guide to No-Load Mutual Funds*, 3rd ed. (Chicago: Investment Information Services Press, 1984), p. 27.

[4]Linda Marsa, "Save on Mutual Fund Taxes," *Sylvia Porter's Personal Finances* (December 1986), pp. 27–29.

7

Potential Advantages
of Mutual Funds

Mutual funds offer several major and other potential advantages to investors.[1] These advantages are not equally important to all investors, but they do provide a wide opportunity for mutual funds to offer one or more advantages that are important to any given investor. These advantages are discussed in the remainder of this chapter.

PROFESSIONAL MANAGEMENT

This is the first major advantage stressed by mutual funds. By hiring its investment adviser (its own management company), funds assert that shareholders receive the expert management of professional securities analysts and portfolio managers. Also, because of the relatively large pool of investable funds, mutual funds have the resources to hire very qualified, full-time investment managers, obtain the needed research data and information, and use the most appropriate security analyses and portfolio management techniques. And investors only pay for this professional management on an as-needed basis. The large and growing number of mutual funds also includes, as defined by their investment objective and policies, portfolios with the increasing number of new types of securities. Thus, funds provide built-in expertise in both the traditional and newer areas of investment.

Fund portfolio managers are responsible for all aspects of the mutual fund's portfolio—type of securities, specific holdings, risk and return attributes, buying and selling decisions, investment performance, and so on. Because fund portfolio managers are not involved in the solicitation or retention of accounts, they are generally able to manage their portfolios without direct pressure from shareholders.

However, evidence suggests that many mutual funds do not provide the relative level of investment performance to justify the implicit assumption that mutual fund management provides, *by definition*, consistently superior portfolio management. Thus, mutual fund management may not be effective in managing fund expenses and/or in generating superior portfolio returns commensurate with the fund's risk. Superior professional fund mangement simply cannot be assumed—it must be found and then evaluated on a consistent, periodic basis.

PORTFOLIO DIVERSIFICATION

This is a second major advantage stressed by mutual funds. Mutual funds generally provide diversification in a manageable, compact way because each share represents a *pro rata* share of an entire portfolio. One of the important tasks performed by fund management is the reduction of portfolio risk by providing adequate diversification. In fact, both federal and state laws and regulations require that fund assets be diversified among issuers of securities. Under the Investment Company Act of 1940, a fund must meet specified asset, diversification, and other standards (discussed below) to qualify as a so-called "diversified investment company." The Internal Revenue Service also requires that a fund meet specified income and diversification criteria (discussed below) to qualify as a "regulated investment company." Furthermore, many states require funds to meet diversification requirements to be eligible to sell shares in their jurisdictions (discussed below).

Diversification may take several forms and/or combinations of forms. As discussed above, it may involve investing in securities offered by a variety of *issuers* (e.g., several different issues of common stock). It also involves spreading risk by investing in several *types of securities* (e.g., common stock, preferred stock, corporate bonds). Commonly, diversification involves investing in securities in a *variety of industries* (e.g., health care and steel) *and/or governments* (e.g., state and municipal bonds). In recent years, some newer mutual funds have foregone traditional industry diversification and, instead, focus on a *particular industry* (e.g., health care), *market segment* (e.g., high-tech firms), or *geographic area* (e.g., Sun Belt securities). However, even these sector funds normally have some *limited* diversification within their relatively narrow areas.

To the extent that mutual funds are reasonably well diversified, and most appear to be, this is an important advantage to the average shareholder. The investor with limited money to invest is likely to incur either excessive transactions costs due to small-quantity purchases of each security or an inadequate number and/or variety of securities to obtain adequate diversification. However, if the investor purchases shares in a mutual fund, the pooling of investor monies in a portfolio can provide a low-cost (especially in a "true" no-load fund) way of diversifying risk. Also, because the costs of managing the fund and its portfolio are spread over the pool of invested funds, total expenses relative to NAV are *generally modest*.

In the context of a portfolio, the risk that can be effectively eliminated through efficient diversification is the unique risk of each security and its industry. This *company-related risk* is called *unsystematic risk*. The other type of risk is *market-related risk* and it cannot normally be eliminated through diversification. This risk is called *systematic risk* and it is measured in terms of the variability of portfolio returns relative to market returns (as measured by the S&P 500 Index).

The relative importance of these basic types of risks were analyzed in a study of sixty-three stocks for the period from 1927–1960.[2] The purpose of this study was to find out how much the variability in stock prices was due to variability in stock market factors, industry factors, and the firm's own unique factors. Overall, market factors explained 52 percent of the variability in stock prices, industry factors explained 10 percent of the variability, and the unique firm factors explained the remaining 38 percent. Later studies confirmed these general findings, but found a decline to 30 to 35 percent in the relative importance of market factors.[3] The effectiveness of the *typical* (not all) mutual fund in significantly reducing its unsystematic risk through diversification *is* supported by research.

Another study found that the typical mutual fund was well diversified with respect to reducing significantly unsystematic risk.[4] Analysis of 100 mutual funds during the period from 1970 to 1974 found that 90 percent (ranging from 68 to 98 percent) of the quarterly variations in the typical fund's returns were attributable to systematic risk. Thus, unsystematic risk was not a significant factor in explaining these returns. This finding suggests that unless investors can obtain adequate diversification through their individual securities holdings, then *most* mutual funds provide a simple and inexpensive way to accomplish this important objective. Thus, while it cannot be assumed that a particular mutual fund is adequately diversified, the typical one is. This is especially true for funds with diversification as a stated objective.

INVESTMENT OBJECTIVES AND RISK MANAGEMENT

A third major advantage of mutual funds is the wide diversity in the available types of funds defined by their investment objective (Chapter 3). This large diversity permits the investor to find professional management of the ever-increasing and more complex types of investments (Chapter 1). Thus, the investor should have no trouble finding a fund with an objective consistent with his or her risk preference. If so, for example, an investor with a high tolerance for risk should first analyze "aggressive growth funds." As indicated in Table 3.1, this type of fund had the highest ten-year performance. It would also be expected to have had the largest risk—measured by variation in annual returns.

Although each fund's stated investment objective is necessarily somewhat general, there does appear to be a relationship between the stated objective and actual portfolio risk. A study of the risk of the various types of funds found that the level of actual risk was generally associated with the implied aggressiveness of the fund's objective.[5] This means that funds with conservative objectives normally have low risk, and vice versa. However, the dispersion around the average risk of a particular type of fund overlapped significantly with the risk dispersions of both more and less aggressive funds. This suggests that some funds with conservative objectives have more risk than other funds with more aggressive objectives, and vice versa. The implication of this is that investors may sometimes be able to obtain less risk, and higher return, by purchasing shares in a more aggressive type of fund. Thus, investors should not use fund investment objectives as the sole means of isolating funds for analysis and selection.

Another issue in selecting a mutual fund is whether it will continue to maintain the same general risk and return posture. For example, the fund's portfolio managers may decide to change the fund's risk posture if they anticipate a sharp decline in the market. This risk/return consistency is supported under the requirement in the Investment Company Act of 1940, which specifies that a fund must state its objective and follow the policy guidelines in its prospectus. This provides the investor with some assurance that the fund will follow an investment style consistent with its stated objective and policies.

Furthermore, a study of 90 mutual funds found a clear relationship between a fund's prior portfolio risk (systematic) and its present risk level.[6] This suggests that funds are reasonably consistent in maintaining their risk levels over time. This finding was supported by an earlier study of thirty-four mutual funds during the period from 1944 to 1963.[7] This latter study included an analysis of the consistency of fund returns over time and found that risk was reasonably consistent between the two halves of the time period studied. Another study found that fund unsystematic risk decreased over time due to increased effectiveness of diversification.[8] It was also found that fund systematic risk was fairly stationary over time. These studies suggest that a fund's current risk is normally a better indicator of its future risk than its investment objective.

The stated investment objective and policies of a large mutual fund follow:

_____ seeks capital appreciation by investing primarily in common stock and securities convertible into common stock. We may not always achieve our *objective*, but we will always follow the *investment style* described in the following paragraphs (italics added).

_____ , our Manager, seeks capital appreciation by primarily investing in common stock and securities convertible into common stock; up to 20% of our assets may also be invested in debt securities of all types and qualities issued by foreign and domestic issuers if our Manager believes that doing so will result in capital appreciation. We don't place any emphasis on dividend income except when our Manager believes this income will have a favorable influence on the market value of the security.

We look to the following areas for potential capital appreciation:

Domestic corporations operating primarily or entirely in the United States;

Domestic corporations which have significant activities and interests outside the United States; and

Foreign companies—principally large, well-known companies, but also smaller, less well-known companies which our Manager believes possess unusual values although they may involve greater risk.

Our emphasis on capital appreciation supersedes any attempt to balance our portfolio between investments in domestic and foreign issuers (which can be made without limitation).

Our Manager can also make substantial temporary investments in investment-grade debt securities for defensive purposes when it believes market conditions warrant.

As indicated, this stated fund objective also includes more specific policy guides to the fund's investment behavior.

The risk and return characteristics that accompany the investment objectives and policies of the various funds in a family of no-load funds are shown in Table 7.1. This type of information provides the investor with more specific guidance in matching his or her risk/return preferences to a fund with an appropriate investment objective.

Table 7.1 Mutual Fund Investment Characteristics Categorized by Investment Objectives

Investment Objective	Investment Policy	Potential Capital Appreciation	Stability of Income	Stability of Principal
Maximum capital growth	Aggressive growth stocks	Very high	Low	Very low
Capital appreciation	Growth stocks	High	Moderate	Low
Income and capital growth	Growth and income stocks	High	Tends to grow	Low to moderate
Current income and conservation of capital	Stocks and bonds	Moderate	Grows modestly	Moderate
Tax-free income	Municipal bonds	Moderate	Moderate to high	Low to moderate
Current income	Short-term corporate bonds	Low	High	Moderate
Current income	Long-term bonds	Moderate	High	Low to moderate
Current income plus capital protection	Money market instruments	None	Low	Very high

LIQUIDITY

A fourth major advantage of mutual funds is liquidity. As discussed here, liquidity refers to the speed with which fund shares may be converted into "cash" by investors for other purposes, such as emergency needs. It also refers to the risk of price concessions in redeeming fund shares. *There is no more liquid stock and bond investment medium than mutual funds.* Under the Investment Company Act of 1940, funds must honor purchases (of collected monies) and redemptions at NAV (less any fees) on the trading day received. An important convenience of mutual funds is the ease by which the share redemption process may be initiated and the normal expectation of prompt payment, depending upon the method of redemption requested (Chapter 6). Also, because the shares are redeemed at NAV (less any fees), the investor does not directly face the risk of price concessions in a falling market dominated by large, institutional orders.

Without a specific redemption agreement, shares are normally redeemed with payment by check upon receipt of a written request ("letter of instruction"). Where a fund is not a member of a fund "family" or does not offer telephone exchange, the use of letters of instruction can expedite share redemption. This letter and its bank signature guarantee may be prepared after a share purchase to be ready for immediate first class or express mailing once the redemption decision has been made.

By additional agreement, however, shares may also be redeemed by: (1) writing "special" checks indirectly drawn on the investor's fund account; (2) use of telephone or telegram, with payment by fund check or by transfer to the investor's bank account; (3) electronic funds transfer to the investor's account, or (4) automatic periodic redemption by transfer to the investor's bank account. The check-writing privilege is probably most convenient in most cases because "cash" is created by depositing the special check in the shareholder's regular bank account, and/or it may be used to make direct payments (minimum specified amount). It is generally safe to assume that mutual funds provide, through their regular and additional redemption services, a high degree of liquidity to meet shareholder needs for *cash*. However, fund liquidity may be temporarily reduced or stopped if the fund suffers financial difficulties or if the Securities and Exchange Commission declares an emergency in the securities markets.

SHAREHOLDER SERVICES

A fifth major advantage of mutual funds is the various useful customer services they provide. Because these services vary by fund, the investor should make sure the fund under consideration provides the services that are most important to him or her. These services include:

Accumulation plans—voluntary and contractual—Chapter 5

Withdrawal (redemption) plans—voluntary—Chapter 5

Various registration options (e.g., custodial)—Chapter 6

Shareholder information—funds are legally required to send periodic statements of shareholder accounts, information on fund investments and earnings, proxy statements, prospectus, and its semiannual and annual shareholder reports

Distribution options (e.g., reinvestment of income dividends and capital gains)—Chapter 6

Share purchase/redemption options (e.g., telephone exchange)—Chapter 6

Share ownership custodianship—Chapter 6

Retirement plans (e.g., IRA)—Chapter 5

Tax record information (Form 1099 DIV)—on income dividends and capital gains distributions

Share cost and redemption price information (for tax purposes)

Reduced investor stress—(perhaps) associated with individual investment management

Time savings in investment management (e.g., investment research, decision making, transaction making, record keeping for each transaction and each fund holding, tax records)—mutual funds collectivize investment activities

Daily publication of fund NAV in newspapers—provides timely, documented record of fund value for investors and other interested parties.

A more complete listing of shareholder services follows in Figure 7.1.

No-load mutual funds offer many special features and convenient shareholder services that are hard to match with any other type of investment. The following is a summary of the services and features now available from no-load funds. Please check individual listings to see the particular services each fund offers.

- Diversification. Mutual funds spread investment risk among a broad range of securities. Similar diversification is often difficult for individuals to achieve independently.
- Professional Management. Your money is managed by professionals working full time to achieve your investment goals.
- Convenience. You own just one security, rather than several, while still enjoying the benefits of a diversified portfolio and a wide range of shareholder services.
- No Sales Charge. 100% of your money goes to work for you the moment you invest.
- Privacy. Brokers, salespeople, and other middlemen are never needed. You deal directly with the no-load mutual fund of your choice, so your investments remain strictly your own business.
- Investor Information. Shareholders receive regular reports from the funds, including details of transactions on a year-to-date basis. Share values, usually available by phone from the fund, also appear in the daily newspapers.
- Liquidity. On any business day, no-load mutual fund shares can be redeemed at their current net asset value.
- Variety. This *Investor's Directory* shows the wide variety of no-load mutual funds available to you—serving virtually every investment goal.
- Ease of Investing. Accounts can be opened by mail, telephone, or bank wire. Investors can add to their holdings in the same easy manner, or by pre-authorized drafts against checking accounts.
- Exchange Privileges. Most fund families allow shares to be exchanged from one of their funds to another—at little or no cost. These switches can be executed quickly

Figure 7.1   The No-Load Fund Advantage: Convenient Services and Special Features

and easily, allowing you to adjust your investments to changing goals or changing market conditions.

- Dividend Options. You can receive dividend payments in cash. Or you can have them reinvested in the fund free of charge, in which case dividends are automatically compounded.

- Withdrawal Services. You can redeem shares by letter, telephone, bank wire, or check, depending on the fund.

- Systematic Withdrawal Plans. With most funds you can arrange to withdraw money at regular intervals to supplement your current income.

- Retirement Plans. No-load funds can be used for both individual and corporate tax-deferred retirement plans, and many funds provide master or prototype plans for interested investors—at very low costs. IRA, Keogh, and 401(k) plans are increasingly popular.

- Personal Service. The funds take care of record keeping, dividend and interest collection, and securities safekeeping, freeing the investor from these tasks. Fund personnel are always available to answer questions by telephone.

- ATMs. Some funds have Automatic Transaction Machines, which allow you to make fund transactions 24 hours a day—7 days a week—at convenient locations.

- Home Computer Access. With a growing number of funds, you can use your home computer to buy and redeem shares, check your account balance, and examine the fund's portfolio.

- Fund Centers. Some fund groups have conveniently located offices for walk-in transactions. And service representatives are always there to assist you.

- Sweep Accounts. With many funds, you can arrange to have excess assets in your equity account swept into your money market fund automatically. You get all the advantages of both accounts—with no extra effort.

- Asset Management Accounts. These master accounts, available from some of the larger fund groups, enable you to manage all your financial service needs under a single umbrella. From unlimited check writing and automatic bill paying to discount brokerage and credit card accounts.

- Automatic Direct Deposit. You can usually arrange to have regular, third-party payments—such as social security or pension checks—deposited directly in your fund account. This puts your money to work immediately, without even waiting to clear your checking account.

- Buying on Margin. No-load fund shares can be purchased using brokers' credit.

Source: Investor's Directory: Your Guide to Mutual Funds, 1985–1986 (New York: No-Load Mutual Fund Association, Inc., 1986), p. 3.

TRANSACTION COSTS

The lack of sales charges and redemption fees is a major advantage of investing in "true" *no-load funds*. Additionally, these no-loads impose no additional marketing expenses under SEC Section 12b-1. It should also be remembered that other types of funds have one or more of the following types of charges and expenses: low-load charges, back-load charges, redemption fees, and 12b-1 expenses (Chapter 6). Nonetheless, funds with only *small* redemption fees may be considered no-load funds (discussed in Chapter 10). Assuming that all other aspects of fund performance are comparable, investors should normally invest in no-load funds.

If the investor does purchase shares in a load fund, then the fund normally *accumulates* all of the previous purchases in the fund or fund family in calculating the load charge. The percentage of the load charge decreases as the size of the accumulated order increases. Furthermore, if shares in several funds in a fund family are purchased, then the *cumulative* total purchase determines the load charge. Again, the percentage of the load charge decreases as the size of the cumulative order increases.

FUND TAXATION

The nature of the taxation of mutual funds has implications for the fund's shareholders and their accounts. Under the Internal Revenue Code, a unit trust, closed-end fund, or open-end fund can avoid corporate income taxation by qualifying and electing to be a *regulated investment company*. This is a domestic corporation that is registered under the Investment Company Act of 1940 and satisfies the following prerequisites: (1) at least 90 percent of its gross income is from dividends, interest, and gains from the sale/disposition of securities; (2) less than 30 percent of its gross income is from the sale of securities held less than three months, and (3) its securities holdings are adequately diversified.

If the fund qualifies, then it will not be liable for federal income taxes if it distributes at least 90 percent of its net income and net realized capital gains. Also, it will not be subject to federal excise taxes if it distributes an amount equal to (1) 97 percent of its calendar year ordinary income, (2) 90 percent of its net capital gains income for the one-year period ending October 31, and (3) 100 percent of any undistributed ordinary or net capital gains income from the prior fiscal year. Dividends declared in December are considered paid by the fund and received by shareholders in the current year if they are paid before February 1 of the following year. Thus, a fund is not subject to federal income and excise taxes if it acts currently as a legal conduit in paying income dividends and capital gains distributions to shareholders.

To be qualified as a *diversified investment company* under the Investment Company Act of 1940, a fund must meet the following requirements: (1) at least 50 percent of its assets are in cash and securities at the end of each quarter, (2) no more than 5 percent of its assets are invested in the securities of any one issuer, and (3) it owns no more than 10 percent of the voting securities of any one issuer. Furthermore, later federal legislation allows municipal bond mutual funds to distribute their tax-exempt net income (exclusive of capital gains) to shareholders as income exempt from federal income taxation. To the extent the income is earned in the investor's state of residence, it would normally be tax exempt there as well.

The tax treatment of regulated investment companies (performing as "legal conduits") precludes adding to the "double taxation" burden of stockholders, which occurs when they directly own securities, such as common stock. A corporation's dividends are paid from after-tax income and are taxed again as income to shareholders. Thus, a regulated investment company pays no income or excise taxes if it meets legal requirements in making its distributions to shareholders.

ENDNOTES

[1] For discussions of the advantages of mutual funds, see Michael D. Hirsch, *Mutual Investing* (Homewood, Ill.: Dow Jones-Irwin, 1987), Chapters 6–7; Donald D. Rugg, *The Dow Jones-Irwin Guide to Mutual Funds*, 3rd ed. (Homewood, Ill.: Dow Jones-Irwin, 1986), Chapter 3; and Gerald W. Perritt and L. Kay Shannon, *The Individual Investor's Guide to No-Load Mutual Funds*, 3rd ed. (Chicago: Investment Information Services Press, 1984), pp. 30–31.

[2] Benjamin F. King, "Market and Industry Factors in Stock Price Behavior," *Journal of Finance 39*, Pt. 2 (January 1966), pp. 139–140.

[3] Stephen L. Myers, "A Re-Examination of Market and Industry Factors in Stock Price Behavior," *Journal of Finance 28* (June 1973), pp. 695–705; Marshall E. Blume, "On the Assessment of Risk," *Journal of Finance 26* (March 1971), pp. 1–10.

[4] *Investment Performance Analysis, Comparative Study, 1970–1974* (New York: Merrill Lynch, Pierce, Fenner and Smith, Inc., 1975).

[5] John G. McDonald, "Objectives and Performance of Mutual Funds, 1960–1969," *Journal of Financial and Quantitative Analysis 9* (June 1974), pp. 311–333.

[6] Gerald A. Pouge and Walter Conway, "On the Stability of Mutual Fund Beta Values" (Unpublished working paper, MIT, Sloan School of Management, June 1972).

[7] William F. Sharpe, "Mutual Fund Performance," *Journal of Business 39*, Pt. 2 (January 1966), pp. 119–138.

[8] Hany A. Shawkey, "An Update on Mutual Funds: Better Grades," *Journal of Portfolio Management 8* (Winter 1982), pp. 29–34.

8

Potential Disadvantages
of Mutual Funds

Whereas there are several potential advantages associated with mutual funds, there are also some important potential disadvantages. These potential disadvantages are described in the remainder of this chapter.

TYPES OF ASSETS

Mutual funds *generally* invest only in financial assets, such as common stock, corporate and U.S. government bonds, and money market instruments (e.g., negotiable certificates of deposits). Although, for example, there are also precious metals funds that invest in the stocks of gold-mining companies and other precious metals companies (e.g., silver, platinum), these types of funds are not among the mainstream of mutual funds. Interest in these funds derives primarily from the danger of inflation and the fact that there are times when investment in tangible assets (e.g., gold) and/or the firms producing them (e.g., oil-producing companies) is especially desirable.

Mutual funds do not provide opportunities for investment in tangible assets such as Chinese ceramics, diamonds, old master art works, coins, stamps, and so on. It must be assumed, therefore, that there is insufficient investor interest, asset liquidity, expected returns, sponsor knowledge, or legal authority to support funds investing in these more specialized types of assets. The same problems may also exist for much of the potential fund activity in tax-sheltered investments. Certainly, the Tax Reform Act of 1986 reduces the desirability of most traditional tax-sheltered investments (Chapter 2). Thus, mutual funds provide limited opportunities for investment in the diverse types of assets available to individually managed portfolios.

TRADING COSTS

The greatest cost assumed by mutual fund shareholders is that associated with the fund's buying and selling of securities. These costs include brokerage commissions and price concessions to dealers for the purchase or sale of large "blocks" of securities (e.g., 10,000 shares). It is usually assumed that these large transactions provide a reduction in the percentage of the transaction paid in brokerage commissions by mutual funds compared to the percentage paid by individual investors. One study found this to be true.[1] Its survey of fund prospectuses found average brokerage commissions to be only one-quarter to one-half of 1 percent. These commissions are not included in the fund's expense ratio because the "cost" of shares purchased includes the brokerage commission, and the "price" of shares sold is net of the brokerage commission.

But when the dealer's larger "bid-ask spread" is added to the fund's lower brokerage commissions, the total cost of fund transactions is often greater than it is for individual investors. This spread is the difference between the current highest bid to buy a security and the current lowest offer to sell the security. The bid-ask spread is generally larger for funds because they must make price concessions to buy or sell these large blocks of shares. These concessions are the amounts below (for a sale) or above (for a purchase) the current bid-ask quotations that the fund must accept to make the transaction ("trade"). Depending on the dollar size of the trade and the dollar equity value of the firm whose shares are traded, mutual fund total "round trip" (buy and sell) trading costs are estimated to range widely—from 3.1 percent to 30 percent! On the other hand, the maximum total round-trip trading costs for individual investors is estimated to be 7.6 percent with full-service brokers and 5.12 percent with discount brokers. Thus, overall trading costs are a potential disadvantage of mutual funds versus individual portfolios.

PORTFOLIO TURNOVER

Based on their trading costs, mutual fund shareholder costs are significantly affected by the "portfolio turnover" of the fund. The percentage turnover rate is a measure of the sales or purchase activity of the fund. It is measured by dividing the smaller figure by the monthly average value of securities with maturities exceeding one year. A 1982 study of 100 mutual funds found an average portfolio turnover of 86 percent, with 28 percent of the funds having turnover rates of over 100 percent.[2] For example, if a fund has a turnover rate of 172 percent, its trading cost as a percentage of asset value is twice that of the average fund. Thus, a fund's portfolio turnover rate magnifies any trading cost disadvantages it has relative to individual portfolios, given the likelihood that, on average, individual portfolios have smaller turnover rates.

CONTROL OVER TAXATION

As discussed in Chapter 7, mutual funds normally do not add significantly to the shareholder's tax burden, but they do have a disadvantage with respect to investor tax planning. Fund shareholders lack control over the *timing* and *nature* (the latter only relevant for taxes prior to implementation of the 1986 tax act) of the taxable distributions they receive from funds. Funds must make the legally or required distributions of income to shareholders if they are to maintain their roles as nontaxable conduits. Prior to the implementation of the 1986 tax act, this meant that if a fund took short-term (less than one year) capital gains, then shareholders paid ordinary income tax rates on this distribution (rather than the much lower long-term capital gains rates). Now, however, the 1986 tax law makes these two types of capital gains taxable as ordinary income.

Even so, there are several ways shareholders can reduce the tax implications resulting from their lack of control over the timing of fund distributions.[3] First, investors should normally purchase shares *after* the fund's ex-distribution date, the date after which the purchaser of shares will not receive the current distribution. Fund distributions result in a decrease in per share NAV equal to the per share distribution. Thus, the purchaser of fund shares just prior to the ex-distribution date receives a partial return of capital in the form of a *taxable* distribution equal to the amount of the reduction in NAV per share. If the investor waits until after the ex-distribution date, then the NAV paid per share will be reduced by the amount of the per share distribution and the individual would have no tax liability on the payment. Thus, the investor would get more shares for the amount of his or her investment due to the lower NAV, and there would be no immediate taxable income.

Second, assuming the fund's performance will become positive, investors should consider purchasing shares in a fund with a realized capital-loss carryforward (a loss that can be offset against future capital gains). Mutual funds are allowed to carry forward net-realized capital losses to future tax years. This is useful because funds can use these carryforward losses to offset current realized capital gains and thereby avoid having to distribute these current gains. The result is an increase in NAV, with *no* required taxable distribution to shareholders. Shareholders should prefer this nontaxable increase in the value of their shares.

Third, fund shareholders should consider selling those funds in which the NAV is less than it was at the time of purchase (capital loss) in order to provide a capital loss and a reduction in their taxable income. The redemption proceeds should normally be invested in another fund with the same investment objective and a superior investment performance. Remember— no transaction costs are involved in either the sale or purchase of "true" no-load funds.

Fourth, fund shareholders desiring to take *capital gains* in the current year (perhaps because they will be in a higher tax bracket next year) may be able to do so while effectively maintaining their investment in the same fund. If the fund is in a family of funds, then the shareholder can transfer ("switch") the investment in the fund to a money-market fund for at least one day. The switch establishes the sales price of the shares for tax purposes, and the next day the investor can switch the investment back to the fund. However, this approach cannot be used to establish a current-year capital loss for tax purposes.

Finally, the other strategies that were profitable prior to the implementation of the 1986 tax law, which removed the preferential treatment of long-term versus short-term capital gains, are no longer applicable.

REGULATORY SHORTCOMINGS

Currently, the Securities and Exchange Commission is reducing the time needed to respond to inquiries from mutual fund managers and to process applications for new funds. The SEC is also attempting to establish new fiduciary standards for fund advertising and fee disclosure.

A major regulatory concern is the increasing use and inadequate disclosure of 12b-1 fees (discussed in Chapter 6). These fees are used to pay advertising and marketing expenses, often without the knowledge of fund shareholders. The information is often "hidden" in the prospectus. These fees should be published with other relevant performance and expense information in a section at the front of the prospectus. Another shortcoming is the lack of a standard, uniform method for calculating and presenting fund rate-of-return performance. The rates of return should also be presented at the front of the prospectus on an annual basis for at least each of the last five years and on an average annual return basis over that five-year period. Another major problem is the confusion over what is meant by "no-load" and "load" funds with the development of low-load and 12b-1 funds. These terms should be officially defined and required to be included in the section at the front of the prospectus.

Although the SEC has made progress in these areas, the disclosure requirements are not yet sufficient to prevent some funds from attempting to hide or obfuscate their performance and expense figures.

ENDNOTES

[1]For a discussion of this treatment of trading costs, see Gerald W. Perritt and L. Kay Shannon, *The Individual Investor's Guide to No-Load Mutual Funds*, 3rd. ed. (Chicago: Investment Information Services Press, 1984), pp. 27–29.

[2]For a discussion of this treatment of portfolio turnover and trading costs, see Perritt and Shannon, pp. 29–30.

[3]For a discussion of this treatment of control over taxation, see Perritt and Shannon, pp. 33–35.

9

Mutual Fund Investment Performance

RETURN PERFORMANCE

Performance is most important when selecting a mutual fund. Investors need to know how well a fund has done as a basis to estimate how well the fund will perform in the future. They should seek superior levels of return for their desired investment objective (risk class). This issue is of particular importance because the so-called *efficient markets hypothesis* suggests that, on average, investors cannot earn superior returns for their desired level of risk. This hypothesis, in its general form, states that the market correctly prices securities based on known, relevant information. Thus, there are no opportunities for investors to buy securities for less than their true value. This does not necessarily mean that there are no exceptions to this hypothesis, as indicated by some of the studies reviewed in this chapter.[1]

The usual way to evaluate fund performance is to compare it with the performance of a *benchmark market portfolio* with comparable risk. Risk can be made comparable by assuming, first, that all monies are invested in the market portfolio (e.g., S&P 500 Index); second, that some of these monies are reinvested in Treasury bills; or third, that additional monies are borrowed to purchase more of the market portfolio so as to obtain the same risk level as the particular fund's portfolio. The fund's systematic risk—the so-called *beta coefficient*—is used to compare its risk relative to the market portfolio. Thus, the beta is a measure of the risk of the fund's portfolio relative to the risk of the market portfolio. A beta of 1.0 means the fund's portfolio is equally risky as the market; a beta greater than 1.0 means it is more risky than the market, and a beta less than 1.0 means it is less risky. Superior fund performance could then be indicated by a fund portfolio return that is greater than the benchmark market portfolio's return for the same level of risk. Other measures of relative importance are also used, including the Treynor measure, which is discussed in Chapter 10.

Some studies include fund management fees and other expenses in their analysis of fund performance; others do not. As discussed in Chapter 8, these expenses exclude total trading costs (broker commissions and bid-ask spreads). By adding back its operating expenses, the fund's portfolio performance can be compared to the performance of the market benchmark portfolio (which has no operating expenses).

Before discussing mutual fund performance, the investor needs to understand how total rates of return are computed for funds:

Market value of shares, end of period (NAV times number of shares, including reinvested distributions)	$1,800.00
Amount of capital gains distribution (if not reinvested in shares)	400.00
Amount of income distribution (if not reinvested in shares)	200.00
Market value of shares, beginning of period (NAV times number of shares)	1,400.00

The difference between the beginning and ending market values is the change in NAV, assuming that there is no reinvestment of distributions. If the distributions are reinvested, however, then the ending market value would reflect the change in NAV plus the increased total number of shares from the reinvestment. If it is assumed that the distributions are not reinvested in this case, then the total percentage return for the period would be:

Market value, end of period	$1,800.00
Capital gains distribution	400.00
Income distribution	200.00
Total value (shares plus distributions)	$2,400.00
Total cost (market value, beginning of period)	1,400.00
Total profit	$1,000.00

$$\text{Total return} = 71.4\% = \frac{\$1,000.00}{\$1,400.00}$$

Figure 9.1 provides a simple approach to the computation of a fund's annual return. It has been completed using the above assumptions and therefore also indicates a 71 percent annual return. The annual return can be computed by using either the assumption of no reinvestment of distributions or the assumption of reinvestment of all distributions.

An early and informative study by Sharpe investigated the performance of thirty-four mutual funds for the period from 1954 to 1963.[2] Performance was measured using a _reward-to-variability ratio_ (discussed in Chapter 11), which encompasses the fund's average return and its risk measured by the variability of its returns. When the returns were computed net of fund expenses (but excluding load charges), only eleven funds outperformed the Dow-Jones Industrial Average (DJIA). But when gross returns were computed, it was found that nineteen funds outperformed the DJIA. Thus, this study suggests that above-average fund performance is associated with a small expense ratio. The following were among this study's major findings:

1. Funds with large average returns normally had more variability than those with small average returns.

2. Past reward-to-variability performance appeared to provide a basis for predicting future performance, but did not necessarily imply that performance differences were due to differences in management skill in finding undervalued securities.

3. Differences in performance could only be imperfectly predicted, and past performance was not the best predictor of future performance.

4. Differences in fund performance were largely explained by differences in expense ratios, with high performance associated with low expense ratios (excluding broker commissions).

5. Fund size was not important in predicting fund performance.

6. Fund managers appeared to keep their portfolios within the risk classes defined by their investment objectives.

7. On average, fund managers selected portfolios at least equal to the DJIA, but shareholders did less well due to fund expenses.

Because the research suggests that fund performance can be largely explained by differences in expense ratios, good fund managers should focus on evaluating risk, providing diversification, and minimizing the expense of searching for undervalued securities.

Jensen studied 115 mutual funds during the period from 1945 to 1964 in order to develop an approach to the evaluation of the performance of portfolios relative to their level of systematic risk.[3] Superior rates of return were due to the superior ability of portfolio managers to select undervalued shares and/or superior ability to forecast market turns. On average, fund _net_ returns were smaller than they should have been for their risk class, and fund _gross_ returns were slightly smaller than they should have been. Thus, on average, it appears that the 115 funds did not have sufficient ability to select

Current mutual fund performance figures like those beginning on page 204 are useful for comparing overall track records, but they don't tell you how well these same funds would have served you during your own period of ownership. Everyone invests at different times and therefore at different share prices. Quite likely you also sent in more money since your first investment. Sure, your fund sends statements showing all your transactions—but that includes every number you need to know except the big one: your annualized gain or loss.

The worksheet at right, devised with the help of John Markese, director of research at the American Association of Individual Investors in Chicago, makes it possible to estimate your rate of return over the past two years or less. The bottom line should deviate no more than two or three percentage points from your actual return. To fill in the blanks, fish out your most recent statement and the last one from 1985. (For simplicity, the sample statement below combines both years' activity and the relevant entries.) If you're in a load fund, be sure to include your sales charges on line 2.

The worksheet takes account of shares you may have redeemed. *If redemptions exceed investments on line 5, show the net result as a minus number.*

— *Greg Anrig Jr.*

	Your Fund	Example
1. The number of months for which performance is being measured (not more than two years)	*12*	13
2. Your investment at the beginning of the period (from your statement if it shows your first investment in the fund; otherwise, multiply the number of shares you owned by their price per share)	*1400*	$5,407
3. The current value of your investment (multiply the number of shares you now own by the current net asset value per share)	*1800*	$9,221
4. Unreinvested income, if any (total dividends and capital-gains distributions you received in cash during the period)	*600*	$115
5. Net redemptions (−) or investments (+) during the period (do not include reinvested distributions)	*0*	$2,000
6. Computation of your gain or loss		
Step A: Add line 2 to half the total on line 5	*1400*	$6,407
Step B: Add line 3 and line 4, then subtract half the total on line 5 (add if negative)	*2400*	$8,336
Step C: Divide the Step B sum by the Step A sum	*1.71*	1.30
Step D: Subtract the numeral 1 from the result of Step C, then multiply by 100	*71%*	30.0%
7. Computation of your annualized return (divide the number of months on line 1 into 12; multiply the result by the Step D percentage)	*71%*	27.7%

YOUR MUTUAL FUND INC.
1000 MAIN ST.
NEW YORK, N.Y. 10020

JOHN A JOHNSON &
JOAN J JOHNSON
3 OAK RD
MAYFIELD MO 65010

ACCOUNT NO. 98765432101

YOUR DISTRIBUTION OPTION IS

STATEMENT DATE	TRANSACTION DATE	TRANSACTION DETAIL DESCRIPTION	DOLLAR AMOUNT OF TRANSACTION	SHARE PRICE	INCOME REINVEST SHARES THIS TRANSACTION	CAPITAL GAINS IN CASH	TOTAL SHARES OWNED
		BEGINNING BALANCE					82.435
1/4/85	1/4/85	INVESTMENT	1,000	53.46	18.706		101.141
2/18	2/8	INCOME REINVEST AT .250	25.29	52.25	.484		101.625
2/18	2/8	SHORT-TERM CAPITAL GAIN AT .450	45.52	—	—		101.625
4/1	4/1	INVESTMENT	2,000	55.37	36.121		137.746
6/17	6/4	INCOME REINVEST AT .250	34.44	57.04	.604		138.350
9/23	9/10	INCOME REINVEST AT .250	34.59	61.89	.559		138.909
12/26	12/17	INCOME REINVEST AT .200	27.78	66.13	.420		139.329
2/26/86	2/3	SHORT-TERM CAPITAL GAIN AT .500	69.66	—	—		139.329
2/26	2/3	INCOME REINVEST AT .300	41.80	65.88	.635		139.964

Figure 9.1 Figuring Your Own Fund's Performance

Source: Modified from Greg Anrig, Jr., "Figuring Your Own Fund's Performance," *Money* (May 1986), p. 113.

stocks and/or ability to time turns in the market to outperform a portfolio *buy-and-hold strategy* (no effort at stock selection and market timing) represented by the market. The major findings of Jensen's study follow:

1. Fund systematic risk was independent of the length of the investor's investment horizon and can thus be used for an investment horizon of any length.
2. Fund systematic risk was approximately stationary over time and thus the future risk of a portfolio can be estimated from its past risk.
3. Fund patterns of systematic risk and return were consistent with the notion that fund managers, on the average, are unable to forecast security prices.
4. Fund performance was inferior to market performance after deduction of all management expenses and broker commissions.
5. Fund performance was neutral with respect to the market when all management expenses and broker commissions were added back to fund returns and average fund cash balances were assumed to earn the riskless rate.
6. On average, the resources spent in attempting to forecast security prices did not yield higher portfolio returns than those that could have been earned by random portfolio selection or by combined investment in the market portfolio and government securities.
7. It appeared that the current prices of securities completely captured the effects of all currently available information; thus, attempts to analyze past information more thoroughly do not generate increased returns.
8. On average, mutual funds provided investors with inefficient portfolios relative to market returns because of excessive expenses.
9. Some funds had consistently superior performance relative to the market, and others had consistently inferior performance; the low-performing funds were most likely to perform consistently.

Because of the absence of superior forecasting ability, the results of the analysis suggested several investment policies that funds should follow:

1. Minimize management expenses and broker commissions by using a buy-and-hold investment policy.
2. Focus on maintaining a perfectly diversified portfolio.
3. Maintain a constant level of systematic risk—to attract and to keep an investor clientele for the fund's risk class.

Jensen also discussed this research in another article in which he evaluated the ability of fund managers to forecast security prices.[4] The evidence for funds in general and for individual funds (their returns adjusted for systematic risk) suggested that they were not able to predict security prices well enough to outperform a market buy-and-hold strategy. Furthermore, there was little evidence that any individual fund was able to earn significantly higher returns than might be expected by chance. These results held for both net returns and gross returns, the latter assuming no management expenses except for broker commissions. On average, then, the funds were not able to forecast security prices well enough to recover their management expenses or even their broker commissions.

Prompted by shortcomings he found in Jensen's research, Mains analyzed the monthly returns of seventy mutual funds during the period from 1955 to 1964.[5] He found that approximately 60 percent of the funds had larger *net* returns adjusted for systematic risk than the overall market returns. On the other hand, only 37 percent of Jensen's sample had larger net returns than they should have had for their risk class. However, Mains's *overall* sample only had a neutral risk-adjusted performance relative to market returns. On a *gross* returns basis, 80 percent of the funds had larger risk-adjusted returns than they should have had relative to market returns. On average, then, these funds earned 10.7 percent more than naive portfolios with the same level of systematic risk.

Mains's results *rejected* the idea that mutual fund managers should abandon their security selection and market-timing activities in favor of buy-and-hold strategies. Furthermore, if fund expenses are added back, the large majority of funds earned risk-adjusted gross returns that were in *excess* of market returns.

A study by the Securities and Exchange Commission examined the performance of 125 mutual funds for the period from 1960 to 1969, computing the differences in monthly returns for each fund and its benchmark portfolio.[6] It was found that the typical mutual fund outperformed its benchmark portfolio (with similar average risk) by only a little over one-half of 1 percent per year. Also, of the 125 funds studied, only 53 had larger average monthly rates of return than their benchmark portfolios.

A study by Merrill Lynch, Pierce, Fenner, and Smith examined the quarterly rates of 100 mutual funds during the period from 1970 to 1974.[7] It was found that the typical mutual fund's rate of return averaged 2 percent less than its benchmark portfolio. Over the five-year period, only 20 funds outperformed their benchmark portfolios.

In conclusion, the research in this area may be summarized as finding that mutual funds do not earn significantly larger or smaller rates of return than unmanaged market-based portfolios of similar risk. (Furthermore, although gross returns on fund portfolios are sometimes higher than on market portfolios of equal risk, it must be remembered that no one manages mutual funds for free and also pays the other fund expenses.) This finding may come as a shock to most investors, but the shock should be reduced if it is remembered that consistently superior performance requires consistently superior ability to select undervalued securities and/or consistently superior ability to time turns in the market and adjust portfolio risk accordingly. Because the market's overall performance includes the efforts of many market professionals to earn superior rates of return, a fund's average performance is never simply "average" in an absolute sense.

If the overall rates of return on mutual funds are necessarily "average," then particular fund segments have superior investment performance. Do *large funds* do better than small funds, perhaps because of superior management and/or the economies of large size? Do *load funds* do better than no-load funds, perhaps because of superior management which offsets the large load charge? Do funds that are in *families of funds* with substantial assets under common management do better than others, perhaps because of superior management and/or the economies of large size? Do funds that are *actively managed* (high portfolio turnover) do better than others that are less actively managed, perhaps because of superior security analysis and/or market-timing abilities?

The SEC study also tested the value of these possible performance factors, examining the performance of 132 mutual funds for the period from 1965 to 1969.[8] The differences in monthly returns for each fund and its benchmark portfolio were computed, and the sample was then segmented to test the performance factors. The results have important implications for mutual-fund investors:

1. Large funds performed no better than small funds (all else being equal).
2. Load funds performed no better than no-load funds, exclusive of load charges (all else being equal).
3. Funds in families of funds with substantial assets under common management performed no better than others (all else being equal).
4. Funds with high portfolio turnover performed *worse* than funds with low turnover (all else being equal).

The average investor in load funds was, therefore, worse off than the average no-load investor after deducting load charges from his or her return. Also, mutual funds with high portfolio turnover seemingly increased their trading costs with the additional trades, but without any measurable increase in portfolio performance.

Carlson applied a measure of investment performance to the portfolios of fifty-seven mutual funds for the period from 1948 to 1967.[9] The reward-to-variability ratios of groups of funds were analyzed by using various market indices (e.g., S&P 500 Index) as benchmark portfolios. The study criticized the effectiveness of market indices to evaluate the aggregate results of managed portfolios, tested the predictive value of past performance in forecasting future performance, and identified factors that are positively identified with fund performance.

The following fund-group performance rankings were found relative to the S&P 500 and DJIA market indices:

1. Balanced fund group (gross returns)
2. Common stock fund group (gross returns)
3. S&P 500 Index
4. Common stock fund group (net returns)
5. Balanced fund group (net returns)
6. DJIA
7. Income fund group (gross returns)
8. Income fund group (net returns)

Thus, none of the fund groups outperformed the S&P 500 on a net returns basis, and all but the income groups (net and gross returns) outperformed the DJIA. These findings suggested that the market index selected had a great deal to do with how well a fund performed relative to the benchmark. Specifically, 59 percent of the individual funds outperformed the S&P 500—a strong result compared to other studies of fund performance.

The major results and conclusions of the Carlson study follow:

1. Analysis of mutual funds supported a positive, linear relationship between expected returns and risk (e.g., high risk and high returns).
2. Fund performance relative to the market was greatly influenced by the type of fund, time period studied, and market index used.
3. Mutual funds should be grouped by their investment objectives before testing whether, on average, they outperformed the market.
4. The performance of portfolio managers should be compared with an index replicating the actual results of portfolio managers with similar investment objectives.
5. The past risk-adjusted performance of mutual funds was of little assistance in predicting future performance; however, *there was a slight tendency for funds to remain either in the top or bottom performance quartiles* (groups).
6. There was no significant relationship between fund risk-adjusted performance and portfolio size, age, or its expense ratio.
7. *There was a positive relationship between fund risk-adjusted performance and portfolio net cash inflow.*
8. No-load funds tended to have higher risk-adjusted performance than load funds.

IMPACT OF FUND OBJECTIVES

An important issue when selecting a mutual fund is to determine whether its performance is going to be consistent with its stated investment objective (e.g., aggressive growth fund). The risk aspects of fund performance and investment objectives are discussed in Chapter 7.

McDonald's study of 123 mutual funds for the period from 1960 to 1969 considered five issues: (1) the relationship between stated fund objectives and their risk and return attributes, (2) the relationship between the performance of funds with various objectives, (3) the relationship between fund risk and return, (4) the risk and return performance of the average mutual fund and the overall market, and (5) the risk and return performance of funds at either end of the risk spectrum.[10]

The funds in the study were categorized by the following objectives: (1) maximum capital gain, (2) growth, (3) income growth, (4) balanced, and (5) income. The results indicated that risk increased as fund objectives became more aggressive. Also, fund returns generally increased relative to the benchmark market portfolio as their objective became more aggressive. Using a reward-to-variability (return-to-risk) fund performance measure, the research showed that more aggressive funds outperformed the less aggressive ones.

This comprehensive study generated the following major results:

1. Stated fund objectives were significantly related to their systematic risk, total risk, and mean excess returns for their level of risk; more "aggressive" objectives generally produced larger mean returns both with respect to systematic risk and total risk.

2. Funds with more aggressive objectives generally produced larger mean excess returns with respect to both systematic risk and total risk.

3. Average fund returns increased with their risk levels.

4. On average, funds had smaller systematic risk but larger total risk than the market index, accordingly, fund excess returns were less than market returns.

5. Higher-risk funds generally appeared to produce larger returns for their risk levels than did lower-risk funds.

Excess returns are the fund's return *less* the risk-free interest rate. Overall, the data clearly showed that mutual funds did not have significantly superior or inferior performance relative to the market index.

To test the consistency of performance for mutual funds with different objectives, Ang and Chua analyzed sixty-two funds during the period from 1955 to 1979.[11] Using quarterly fund returns, they compared the performance of each fund against the S&P 500. They attempted to ascertain whether funds serve the function of providing different types of investors with portfolios that are preferable to the market portfolio and whether they perform this function consistently.

When the performance of the funds was tested against the market, taking into account differences in investor risk/return preferences, it was found that (1) all funds, at one time or another, provided superior or comparable risk-return performance relative to the market, but (2) only about one-half of the funds consistently achieved this degree of relative performance. Thus, it seemed that the majority of fund managers did not "deliver the goods." Although they did provide different investment objectives, fund managers did not generally perform their function well by providing consistently comparable or superior risk-return performance relative to the market.

Martin, Keown, and Farrell investigated the diversification policies of the December 31, 1977, portfolios of seventy-two mutual funds to see whether portfolios designed to achieve particular investment objectives were non-market sources of co-movement in their returns.[12] For example, did aggressive growth funds tend to concentrate their holdings in growth stocks that share a nonmarket source of co-movement in their returns?

Five types of fund investment objectives were tested to see if their portfolios hampered the diversification process by generating nonmarket co-movement in returns: (1) aggressive growth, (2) growth, (3) growth and income, (4) income, and (5) "other." The findings indicated that the investment objective was an important determinant of the level of nonmarket sources of co-movement in portfolio returns. Nonetheless, the investment objective explained only 15 percent of the variation in nonmarket sources of co-movement in returns. Thus, the research indicated that there were other important nonmarket sources of co-movement in fund portfolio returns.

Overall, their study found that a mutual fund's risk and return attributes were generally consistent with those implied by its type of investment objective. Thus, the types of investment objectives provided a useful aid in identifying funds with objectives consistent with investor risk and return preferences. However, each of these funds so identified should be investigated further to determine the relative level and the consistency of its risk-return performance.

MARKET TIMING

As discussed earlier, mutual funds may be able to achieve superior investment performance by superior ability to select securities that are *undervalued* (priced lower than their "true" value) and/or by superior market timing ability. If a fund successfully practices market timing, then it should earn a higher rate of return than its comparable benchmark portfolio. This section discusses the research findings on the ability of mutual funds to be successful "market timers."

Another early study by Treynor and Mazuy examined whether fifty-seven mutual funds were able to anticipate successfully the major turns in the stock market during the period from 1953 to 1962.[13] If funds believe the market is going to rise, then they shift the composition of their portfolios from less to more volatile securities, and vice versa. Thus, the tests of the ability of funds to anticipate market turns were based on the idea that fund volatility should be higher in years when the market did well than in years when it did badly. It was concluded that there was *no* evidence that funds are able to time market changes and adjust their portfolio risk accordingly.

The major results and conclusions of their study included the following:

1. There was no statistical evidence that the managers of the funds successfully "outguessed" the market (only one fund's behavior *suggested* this ability).

2. Mutual fund shareholders were completely dependent on fluctuations in the market. This does not mean that funds cannot earn higher rates of return than the market in both good and bad times, but that improvements in fund returns are due to the fund's ability to identify underpriced securities, rather than to any market-timing ability.

3. It should be assumed that fund managers cannot outguess the market, and they should not be held responsible for failing to do so.

Henriksson analyzed the monthly data of 116 mutual funds for the period from 1968 to 1980 to determine whether *active* fund management achieved a sufficient increase in returns to offset the information, transaction, and management expenses involved in security analysis and portfolio management.[14] To do this, he tested the ability of fund mangement to earn superior returns based on superior forecasting ability. The results showed little evidence of market-timing ability. One test indicated that 62 percent of the funds had negative market-timing ability, and only three funds showed any significantly positive market-timing ability. Thus, the research results *rejected* the idea that mutual fund managers were able to follow strategies that successfully timed turns in the market. Furthermore, there was no evidence that fund managers were more successful in forecasting large rather than small changes in the market.

Veit and Cheney investigated the effectiveness of mutual fund managers in making market-timing decisions to improve portfolio performance.[15] This investigation was based on an analysis of seventy-four randomly selected funds during the period from 1944 to 1978. They defined effective market-timing strategy as correctly forecasting "bull" and "bear" markets and making appropriate changes in the portfolio's risk relative to the market (systematic risk exposure). Superior portfolio performance requires the fund to earn a higher rate of return than would be expected for a given risk level. Superior portfolio performance can result from correct market-timing decisions and/ or identifying undervalued and overvalued securities. As discussed earlier, theory tells us that securities sell at their "true" values. If so, then repeated efforts to find undervalued securities will reduce fund performance as a result of the research expenses and transactions costs. Thus, if a fund has demonstrated some success in timing decisions, it may be better off by minimizing efforts to select undervalued securities; instead, it should concentrate on making correct market-timing decisions.

The Veit and Cheney study generated the following results and conclusions:

1. Mutual funds did not successfully employ market-timing strategies.

2. Of those few funds that had significantly different levels of systematic risk in bull and bear markets, 73 percent showed unsuccessful timing.

3. Under the four bull and bear market classification schemes tested, only three of the seventy-four funds indicated evidence of successful market timing by shifting their beta in anticipation of market movements.

4. The lack of successful market-timing strategies resulted either because fund managers did not attempt them or because they were unsuccessful at them.

5. Funds that did not attempt market timing were either not able to forecast market movements, unwilling to change the fund's risk class, or unwilling to pay the transaction costs of active portfolio management.

6. For funds that did not attempt market timing, their systematic risk was, nonetheless, unstable because of passive management—high-risk stocks changed price more than low-risk stocks as the market level changed, resulting in low beta portfolios prior to bull markets, and vice versa.

7. The efforts of funds that did attempt market timing may have failed because of the inability to forecast bull and bear markets (as reflected in changes in systematic risk).

8. Market-timing activities involved changing the proportion of fund portfolios invested in the various risk classes, as well as the proportion of funds invested in individual securities within the risk classes.

The study by Kon and Jen of forty-nine mutual funds from 1960 to 1971 included (1) an evaluation of the ability of portfolio managers to forecast security and market prices, (2) a test of the stability of portfolio risk and changes in portfolio diversification, and (3) an analysis of the ability of funds to select undervalued stocks.[16] The results indicated that many funds exhibited superior market timing, as reflected in significant changes in portfolio risk and diversification. However, *no* fund was able to earn *consistently superior returns.* In addition, many funds also exhibited superior ability to select undervalued stocks. However, average fund performance was less than that of an unmanaged portfolio of equal risk. Overall, and on average, the ability of funds to select superior portfolios was not high enough to recover fund expenses.

Shawky investigated the monthly performance of 255 mutual funds for the period from 1973 to 1977 to answer the following questions: (1) Has mutual fund performance improved? (2) Were there any differences in performance among funds with different investment objectives (e.g., growth)? (3) Have fund diversification policies improved? (4) Are there differences in the major measures of fund performance? (5) What do fund risk/return relationships look like relative to the market in bull and bear markets?[17] The results of the study follow:

1. The mutual fund industry made significant improvements in performance over time; they earned a return commensurate with systematic risk.

2. During the years studied, mutual funds performed *as well* as the overall market.

3. The diversification effectiveness of mutual funds increased considerably over the years—unsystematic risk was reduced, especially for balanced funds.

4. Fund returns conformed about exactly to equally weighted NYSE returns rather than to value-weighted NYSE returns.

5. The major reward-to-variability performance measures of mutual funds were highly correlated.

6. Mutual fund risk/return relationships were useful in describing the general risk/return relationship of the market; funds provided a better description than did individual securities or randomly selected portfolios.

7. General fund risk/return relationships were sensitive to the time intervals and market conditions (e.g., bull market) over which they were measured.

8. Fund systematic risk was fairly stationary over the period; thus, their risk/return relationships were sensitive to the pattern of historical market returns.

Chang and Lewellen examined sixty-seven mutual funds for the period from 1971 to 1979 to determine whether portfolio managers achieved differential return performance by engaging in market-timing strategies and

security-selection activities.[18] The funds represented a wide range of investment objectives, and the results indicated little evidence of successful market
timing by fund portfolio managers. The results of this study included the
following:

1. Overall, fund portfolio managers provided little evidence of any market-
   timing ability; indeed, if anything, the evidence suggested a reverse
   "skill."

2. Apparently, funds either did little in the way of market timing or, if
   they did, it was not implemented or it was overwhelmed by other
   portfolio considerations.

3. In the aggregate, funds gave little evidence of any stock selection ability.

4. The results indicated that neither skillful market timing nor clever
   security selection abilities was abundantly evident in fund return
   performance.

5. The general conclusion that mutual funds have been collectively unable
   to outperform a passive investment strategy remains valid.

CONSISTENCY OF PERFORMANCE

As discussed previously, average mutual fund investment performance net of
expenses is less than the market average (as measured by a market benchmark
portfolio). This being the case, then perhaps investors should avoid average
performance by focusing their attention on those funds with superior historical performance on the assumption that past performance is the best and
simplest guide to future performance.

The study by Sharpe (discussed earlier) evaluated whether past reward-
to-variability performance was a reliable prediction of future performance.[19]
Fund performance in each half of the period studied was investigated to see
if there was a degree of consistency between past and future fund performance. The results indicated that past performance provided a basis for
predicting future performance, but that it was not the best predictor. Expense
ratios were found to be the best predictors of fund performance.

A study by Klemkosky analyzed monthly rates of return for 158 mutual
funds during the period from 1968 to 1975 to see if past mutual fund performance was a good predictor of future performance.[20] The overall evidence
from adjacent three-year and four-year periods found little to support the
belief that a fund manager's past risk-adjusted performance is a good guide
to his or her future performance. This was particularly true with respect to
fund performance over adjacent two-year periods, but less so over four-year

periods. Nonetheless, there was not enough consistency in the results of the overall period to suggest that the future risk-adjusted return performance of funds can be predicted with any certainty.

In the study by Jensen (discussed earlier), part of the analysis was concerned with the consistency of mutual fund performance.[21] It was found that some funds may have had consistently superior risk-adjusted performance relative to the market, but others had consistently inferior risk-adjusted performance. The inferior-performing funds were found to be most likely to perform consistently in the next period because it does not take any action to continue holding a poorly performing portfolio. In another test, it was found that only about 50 percent of the funds had consistent performance from one period to the next. Thus, these results *do not* provide support for consistency of fund performance, especially for superior-performing funds.

IMPLICATIONS OF STUDIES

These studies have numerous implications for the investor, especially for the individual who wants to invest in mutual funds for the reasons discussed in Chapter 1. They also have implications for mutual fund advisory newsletters, for there are always those that sell their "proven" approach based on methods that research tells us generally cannot prove successful, *especially on a consistent basis*. In some cases, these approaches are "packaged" to appeal to the investor's fear of financial disaster (e.g., a forthcoming world banking crisis) or any underlying avarice (e.g., a "sure thing" opportunity for "smart money" people to "cash in" on).

Mutual fund advisory newsletters have grown with the bull market, reflecting the growing opportunities for profits from advising individual investors.[22] There are now approximately forty-five newsletters—about four times as many as there were in 1982. A few of these letters present original analysis and well-organized data and information. They assist investors in understanding current developments relevant to their securities holdings, in assessing risks, and in comparing investment performance. Of course, the ultimate test of a newsletter is the performance of its recommendations and the quality of its reasoning and research. (Some of the letters and services useful to the fund selection method advocated in this book are listed in the next chapter.)

The newsletters of uncertain quality tend to have one or more of the following characteristics:

1. Publishers with little investment experience
2. Dependent on subscribers who invest in the funds they write about

3. Tendency to make "promises, promises"

4. Inclusion of back-dated (misleading) performance on "model" portfolios

5. Coverage overly dependent on other newsletters

6. Excessive use of material from prospectuses

7. Too much rehash of old financial news

8. Use of nebulous advice based on confusing statistics and incoherent/invalid analysis

9. Use of "technical" approaches to fund timing and switching (lacking research validation)

10. Frequent use of "signals" to switch funds (with tax implications)

11. Use of too many "buy" recommendations (some must prove to be winners!)

12. Use of unreliable or confusing performance figures on past recommendations

Nonetheless, some fund advisory letters are helpful, if not infallible (see Chapter 11). They can help the investor (1) learn more about investments and mutual funds; (2) incorporate relevant present and likely future developments in the investor's training, and (3) make more informed decisions with some regard to timing. However, the research results discussed in this and other chapters must be considered when evaluating the worth of newsletters.

In conclusion, the *implications of these research studies (and those in Chapter 10) may be summarized as follows:*

1. Funds provide an adequate number of investment objectives to meet the diverse risk needs of investors.

2. Fund risks and returns are generally consistent with their investment objectives; risk and return generally increase with the aggressiveness of fund objectives.

3. Most funds are effectively diversified and have eliminated most risks except systematic risk (for those funds with the stated objective of providing diversification).

4. Funds are not generally consistent in maintaining their risk-adjusted performance relative to the market, but they are with respect to their risk class.

5. On average (but with individual exceptions), fund gross returns adjusted for risk approximate the market return; on the basis of the more realistic returns net of expenses, fund returns are smaller than the market return

(equivalent to the return on a diversified portfolio using a buy-and-hold strategy).

6. No-load funds perform as well as load funds; therefore, investors should not reduce their returns by paying load charges.[23]

ENDNOTES

[1]These research studies are reviewed in Frank K. Reilly, *Investments*, 2nd ed. (Hinesdale, Ill.: Dryden Press, 1986), Chapter 20; William F. Sharpe, *Investments*, 3rd ed. (Englewood Cliffs, N.J.: Prentice-Hall, 1985), Chapter 18.

[2]William F. Sharpe, "Mutual Fund Performance," *Journal of Business* 39, Pt. 2 (January 1966), pp. 119–138.

[3]Michael C. Jensen, "Risk, The Pricing of Capital Assets, and the Evolution of Investment Portfolios," *Journal of Business* 42 (April 1969), pp. 167–247.

[4]Michael C. Jensen, "The Performance of Mutual Funds in the Period 1945–1965," *Journal of Finance* 23 (May 1968), pp. 389–416.

[5]Norman E. Mains, "Risk, the Pricing of Capital Assets, and the Evolution of Investment Portfolios: Comment," *Journal of Business* 50 (July 1977), pp. 371–384.

[6]Securities and Exchange Commission, *Institutional Investor Study Report* (Washington, D.C.: U.S. Government Printing Office, March 10, 1971).

[7]*Investment Performance Analysis, Comparative Study 1970–1974* (New York: Merrill Lynch, Pierce, Fenner and Smith, Inc., 1975).

[8]Securities and Exchange Commission, *Institutional Investor Study Report*.

[9]Robert S. Carlson, "Aggregate Performance of Mutual Funds, 1948–1967," *Journal of Financial and Quantitative Analysis* 5 (March 1970), pp. 1–32.

[10]John G. McDonald, "Objectives and Performance of Mutual Funds, 1960–1967," *Journal of Financial and Quantitative Analysis* 9 (June 1974), pp. 311–333.

[11]James S. Ang and Jess H. Chua, "Mutual Funds: Different Strokes for Different Folks?" *Journal of Portfolio Management* 8 (Winter 1982), pp. 43–47.

[12]John D. Martin, Arthur J. Keown, Jr., and James L. Farrell, "Do Fund Objectives Affect Diversification Policies?" *Journal of Portfolio Management* 8 (Winter 1982), pp. 19–28.

[13]Jack L. Treynor and Kay K. Mazuy, "Can Mutual Funds Outguess the Market?" *Harvard Business Review* 44 (July–August 1966), pp. 131–136.

[14]Roy D. Henriksson, "Market Timing and Mutual Fund Performance: An Empirical Investigation," *Journal of Business* 57, Pt. 1 (January 1984), pp. 73–96.

[15]E. Theodore Veit and John M. Cheney, "Are Mutual Funds Market Timers?" *Journal of Portfolio Management* 8 (Winter 1982), pp. 35–42.

[16]Stanley J. Kon and Frank C. Jen, "The Investment Performance of Mutual Funds: An Empirical Investigation of Timing, Selectivity, and Market Efficiency," *Journal of Business* 52 (April 1979), pp. 263–289.

[17]Hany A. Shawky, "An Update on Mutual Funds: Better Grades," *Journal of Portfolio Management* 8 (Winter 1982), pp. 29–34.

[18]Eric C. Chang and Wilbur G. Lewellen, "Market Timing and Mutual Fund Investment Performance," *Journal of Business* 57, Pt. 1 (January 1984), pp. 57–72.

[19]Sharpe, "Mutual Fund Performance," pp. 114–138.

[20]Robert C. Klemkosky, "How Consistently Do Managers Manage?" *Journal of Portfolio Management* 3 (Winter 1977), pp. 11–15.

[21]Jensen, "Risk, the Pricing of Capital Assets, and the Evolution of Investment Portfolios."

[22]For a discussion of this treatment of fund newsletters, see Jan Wong, "Mutual Fund Newsletters Multiply, But What Do They Offer Readers?" *Wall Street Journal*, June 30, 1986; "Mutual Fund Advice in Your Mailbox," *Changing Times* (December 1985), pp. 71–73.

[23]For a discussion of the implications of these research studies, see Reilly, pp. 573–575.

10

Mutual Fund Selection

SPECIFICATION OF THE SELECTION CRITERIA

The selection of mutual funds can be simplified if the investor uses some specific criteria. In this way, most funds can be eliminated from consideration and attention can be focused on the high-performing fund(s). A discussion of the various selection criteria follows.[1]

Matching investor risk preferences and fund objectives. Because funds are categorized by their investment objectives (Chapter 3), the elimination of those funds with objectives that do not meet the investor's needs will remove most funds from further consideration. The investor should carefully review the fund's prospectus (obtained from the fund) to be sure that its objective is appropriate to his or her risk preference. The prospectus contains a statement of the fund's investment objective and policies, and includes information on its approach to security selection, fund investment performance, load charges, and expenses. This objective and its attendant investment policies should be consistent and understandable. For example, if the investor's needs call for aggressive growth funds, then only 141 (9.2%) of 1,531 mutual funds remain under consideration (Chapter 3). This topic will be discussed in greater detail later in this chapter.

Fund performance. Based on the research discussed in Chapter 9, there are exceptions to the general finding that net mutual fund performance is lower than a diversified market portfolio of the same risk class using a buy-and-hold strategy. This general finding suggests that funds are not, on average, effective market timers and/or security selectors. The exceptions to the general findings and other selected aspects of fund performance research provide the hope for being able to select funds that will have superior performance.

In this regard, there are several potential performance criteria for selecting mutual funds that are exceptions to the general research findings:

1. *Consistent long-run rate of return*—rate of return can be a predictor of future investment performance, especially when it is consistent over a long period of time. (The risk measures related to rate-of-return performance are also included in this criterion.)

2. *Low expense ratio*—the best predictor of future fund performance.

3. *Low portfolio turnover*—minimizes transactions costs (broker commissions and price concessions).

4. *Large net cash inflow* (net of redemption and distributions)—provides flexibility in portfolio management (as opposed to the constraint of net redemptions).

The selection of mutual funds that have consistently high long-term rates of return is not without its risks. One argument states that spectacular fund performance in any one period is no more likely to be followed by success than by failure.[2] For example, the 44 Wall Street Fund was the best performing fund from 1975 to 1979, but it was the worst performer from 1980 to 1986.

Results of this kind reflect the fact that investors may make one or more psychological errors in making decisions involving risk and chance. For example, "streak shooting" in basketball and a streak of high returns from a mutual fund are both due to chance. Thus, a mutual fund is no more likely to earn a high return after a string of good years than after a string of poor years. Investors tend to believe there is a pattern in these streaks because of the "representativeness" fallacy, which holds that patterns of investment performance revealed over a short period of time (say, five to ten years for purposes of statistical analysis) convey nothing about the pattern that will emerge over the next five to ten years. As a result, investors often act as if they can forecast fund performance over the next five to ten years based on its pattern over the previous five to ten years. Unfortunately, five to ten years may not be long enough to know whether consistent fund performance is due to randomness and luck or consistency and skill. Although some funds do perform better than average for some period of time, it is *unusual* for them to be consistently "lucky" on a long-term basis.

Investors have a difficult time learning the difference between skill and luck. One explanation is that they fail to learn that the return-performance process is random. They form an initial impression and search for confirming evidence, while ignoring the rest. Another explanation is that once investors have observed a performance pattern, they tend to see it as predictable. This gives investors exaggerated confidence in their ability to forecast.

Nevertheless, the *approach taken here is based on the premise that there are potentially rewarding exceptions to the general research findings.* It is also based on the premise that it may not matter significantly whether a fund's consistently high performance over five to ten years is due to luck or a superior portfolio manager. This is so because the fund's shares are sold once its long-term rate-of-return has been surpassed by another fund that also satisfies the other performance and selection criteria. (This approach is discussed in the next chapter.)

Furthermore, research in recent years has uncovered some "holes" (exceptions) in the efficient markets hypothesis.[3] These exceptions are in addition to those previously discussed. The so-called "semi-strong" version of this hypothesis states that investors cannot beat the market because the current price of a stock reflects all of what is publicly known about it. The computer-based research efforts of large institutional investors, portfolio managers, investment companies, and so on, to find undervalued stocks contributes to this efficiency by quickly pushing undervalued stocks to their "correct" price levels.

The exceptions to the efficient markets hypothesis include the following research findings:

1. Some stocks appear to offer higher returns than indicated by their risk levels.
2. Some analysts use "private" information (unique to the analyst or class of market participants) to earn above-average returns.
3. Not all market participants view "winning" in the stock market the same way; thus, there need not be a loser for every winner, and some can earn above-average returns over a long period of time.
4. Some research indicates that stocks with low price-earnings ratios have lower risk and higher returns than the overall market.
5. Some "contrarians" earn above-average returns by buying unpopular, undervalued stocks that reside in pockets of the market where stocks are not properly priced.
6. Research indicates that investments in the "one-ranked" stocks generated by the *Value Line Investment Survey* generally outperform the market.

Nonetheless, these exceptions do not change the general conclusion that *most* investors cannot outperform the market. For these investors, it is often recommended that they invest in a diversified portfolio or fund that attempts to mirror the market's performance as measured by an index, known as an *index fund.*

Load charges.   Based on the research discussed in Chapter 9, there is generally no reason to buy funds with significant load and other related charges, as they do not generate higher returns than no-load funds. No-load funds represent 109 (77.3%) of the 141 aggressive growth funds.[4] The 32 load funds are sold by sales organizations that represent each fund's distributor (underwriter) at the "wholesale" level, and by securities firms, insurance companies, and financial planners at the investor ("retail") level.

As discussed in Chapter 6, there are several types of funds that are classified according to their sales and other charges, if any: (1) load funds, (2) low-load funds, (3) back-end load funds, (4) 12b-1 funds, (5) miscellaneous load funds, and (6) no-load funds. The simplest way to deal with the increasingly complex combinations of load charges is generally to *avoid the following types of funds:*

Load funds—4 to 9 percent load charges at purchase

Back-end load funds with contingent deferred sales charges—4 to 6 percent charges (declining over time) at redemption

12b-1 funds—up to 1.25 percent charge per year

On the other hand, *the following types of funds are generally eligible for purchase* because they have no load charges, 12b-1 fees, or, at most, small redemption or other fees:

"True" no-load funds—no load or other charges or fees (not necessarily those categorized in the marketplace as "no-load")

No-load funds—no load or other charges and small redemption fees limited to 1 percent

Miscellaneous-load funds—limited to nominal dollar charges or fees of any kind

Finally, there is one type of load fund that is to be given at least some consideration—low-load funds. Historically, these funds usually began as no-load funds and were later able to impose low-load charges because of their high performance records. Thus, *the following type of fund is normally eligible for purchase depending on the fund's long-term rate of return:*

Low-load funds—up to 2 to 3 percent load charges at purchase, with no other charges

Portfolio manager for at least five consecutive years.   One of the attributes of a well-managed mutual fund portfolio is the ability to earn superior returns in both rising and declining markets. For example, since late 1976, there have been three periods of declining stock prices (1976–1978, 1980–1982, and 1983–1984), and there have been three periods of rising prices (1978–1980, 1982–1983, and 1984–1987). The person largely responsible for the fund's investment performance relative to the overall market is the portfolio manager, and five years is normally long enough to gauge this person's performance. Thus, the investor should purchase only a fund that has a portfolio manager with at least five consecutive years' experience with that fund. In that period of time, the manager should have established and sharpened his or her approaches to portfolio management. The manager should also have experienced both good and bad markets, providing the needed wisdom to go along with the ability the individual might possess. For example, of the twenty-three funds on the *Forbes* 1986 "Honor Roll," only four of them had portfolio managers who had been in this position for less than five consecutive years (Table 10.1). Information about the tenure of the portfolio manager can also be obtained directly from the fund. In some cases persistence may be needed.

Furthermore, funds meeting this criterion also meet, or are likely to meet, investor concerns requiring (1) a minimum fund asset size (e.g., $5 million) to avoid erratic performance; (2) a maximum fund asset size (e.g., $80 million) to avoid loss of portfolio flexibility and liquidity due to large holdings of stocks; (3) a performance track record of at least one year to avoid undue risk; and (4) availability of a daily NAV quote in the newspaper to avoid an information gap.[5] Those funds reported in the press have at least 1,200 shareholders, which excludes the smaller funds. More important than this criterion to the concerns over minimum and maximum fund asset size is the finding (Chapter 9) that fund size was not related to risk-adjusted performance.

Portfolio policies.   Funds should focus on the attainment of their basic investment objectives without attempting to do so by acquiring portfolio assets or engaging in financing practices, investment strategies, and contracts, which may add to the inherent risk of the securities portfolio. An exception to this general rule is funds that include these investment strategies and contracts in their investment objectives (e.g., options/income funds, discussed in Chapter 3). More specifically, *investors should generally be wary of funds that are significantly involved in the purchase of securities on margin, bank or other borrowing, purchase of letter stock, short sales of securities, and so on.*[6] Judgment is required to determine whether a fund is less desirable because of any of these potential risks. (The securities aspects of these policies are discussed in standard investments texts.) Reference to the prospectus is absolutely necessary when making this decision.

The following basic portfolio policies from the prospectus of a leading

TABLE 10.1 The 1986 Annual Mutual Funds Survey: The Honor Roll

Some people pick funds the way they do horses. They bet on the one that finished first last time out. But buying the fund that was up the most last year is a prescription for trouble. Many a fund that buys high-risk, fast-moving stocks looks brilliant in a bull market but loses its investors huge sums in the inevitable bear market that follows. It is almost axiomatic that people lose more money in hot-performing funds than they gain. Why? Because the hot performance brings in a flood of new money, where-upon—almost inevitably—the hot performance turns cool or cold.

So how does a mutual fund get on the FORBES honor roll? Not by coming in first in any year, but by doing respectably well in all kinds of races, in up as well as down markets. Since one cannot predict the future, one wants a fund that will do well, come what may, not one that will glisten only when the sun shines. Alas, no announcement is made on Wall Street when the market is about to change direction. Thus the FORBES rating system demands that a fund earn a B or better grade in both bull markets and bear markets before it can qualify for the honor roll. It isn't hard at all to win a B in only up or only down markets—Bs go to the top 45% of funds in each group. Earning a B in both kinds of markets, however, is something only the most skilled can do.

Consistency, then, is key. We also demand excellent performance over the long haul—a period that we define as 9¾ years, covering three market cycles (*see chart on following page*). Our 23 honor roll funds have delivered a 20% or better compound annual return for that period.

To further narrow the list, we have added this year a new crite-rion. Honor roll members had to do well enough after taxes and sales charges to have turned $10,000 into at least $50,000 over the 9¾-year period if the investor reinvested all dividends. The aftertax results are shown in the column headed "hypothetical investment results." FORBES assumes tax rates that would have applied to someone with $100,000 of gross income in constant 1984 dollars, deductions equal to 20% of income and four exemptions. Loads, if any, were applied at 1986 rates. No deduc-

tion is made for the additional taxes that would be due if the investor cashed out his shares at the end of the period.

The rule on investment results penalizes funds paying out hefty income and capital gains distributions (better that fund shareholders simply see the fund's price per share go up, untaxed). The rule also penal-izes funds with loads. In short, FORBES' rules for the honor roll simulate real life.

This year's honor roll boasts several newcomers: Partners, Shearson Appreciation, Sigma Capital and Value Line Leveraged Growth. We have dropped honor roll members that are closed to new investors. That knocks off the list the excellent Vanguard Explorer, Loomis-Sayles Capital Devel-opment and Pennsylvania Mutual.

The "portfolio turnover" column tells whether the manager's style runs to in-and-out trading. Since trading costs money, not only in commissions but in the spread between bid and ask prices, shareholders should keep an eye on it. Some—repeat, some—managers can achieve superior results in spite of heavy transaction costs. For the group below, "average" turnover means turnover in the vicinity of 60% a year.

What about changes in fund management? Last year we received a letter from a portfolio management executive noting that Howard Schow, the man responsible for much of Amcap's long-term success, left the fund in 1983 and is now managing Vanguard's Primecap. "It's not the ships, but the men who sail them," he said. True enough.

So how does the investor make sure that the manager of an honor roll fund is the same one who achieved the honor roll results? We have allowed for that by telling readers how long their managers have reigned—shown in the third column below. The managers of Amcap, American Capital Venture and Growth Fund of America are new to the top spot. One should be alert to the possibility that the managers who created the honor roll performance are no longer in charge.—Eva Pomice

(*continued*)

103

TABLE 10.1 (*continued*)

Fund/distributor	Performance UP	Performance DOWN	Manager (consecutive years as manager)	Net assets 6/30/86 (millions)	Maximum load	Annual expenses per $100 assets
Acorn Fund/Acorn	B	A	Ralph Wanger [16]	$ 425	none	$0.78
Amcap Fund/American Funds	B	A	Michael Shanahan [1]	1,506	8.50%	0.54
American Capital Pace Fund/American Cap	B	A+	John Roche [1]	2,229	8.50	0.60
American Capital Venture Fund/American Cap	B	A	Robert Meyer [1]	415	8.50	0.68
Claremont Capital Corp/closed end	B	A+	Erik Bergstrom [10]	61	NA	1.06
Evergreen Fund/Lieber	A+	B	Stephen Lieber [15]	714	none	1.08
Fidelity Destiny Portfolio I/Fidelity	B	A	George Vanderheiden [6]	1,166	NA5	0.60
Fidelity Magellan Fund/Fidelity	A+	A	Peter Lynch [9]	7,412	3.00	1.08
Growth Fund of America/American Funds	A	A	William Newton [1]	829	8.50	0.69
Janus Fund/Janus	B	A	Thomas Bailey [17]	542	none	1.01‡
Mass Capital Development Fund/Mass Financial	A	B	William Harris [16]	1,035	7.25	0.71
NEL Growth Fund/NEL	A	B	Kenneth Heebner [10]	313	8.00	0.83
Nicholas Fund/Nicholas	B	A+	Albert Nicholas [17]	1,084	none	0.86
Over-the-Counter Securities Fund/Review	B	A	Binkley Shorts [5]	263	8.00	1.25
Partners Fund/Neuberger	B	A	Philip Steckler [11]6	431	none	0.93‡
Scudder Development Fund/Scudder	B	B	Edmund Swanberg [15]	359	none	1.30
Shearson Appreciation/Shearson	B	B	Harold Williamson [5]	279	5.00	1.10
Sigma Capital Shares/Sigma	B	B	Richard King [19]	102	8.50	1.01‡
Sigma Venture Shares/Sigma	A	B	Richard King [16]	93	8.50	0.95‡
Tudor Fund/Weiss, Peck	A	B	Melville Strauss [13]	191	none	0.95
Twentieth Century Select Investors/Twentieth Century	A+	B	James E. Stowers [15]	1,987	none	1.01
United Vanguard Fund/Waddell & Reed	B	B	Henry Herrmann [10]	525	8.50	1.05‡
Value Line Leveraged Growth Investors/Value Line	B	A	Mark Tavel [14]	306	none	0.80

Minimum investment[1]	Weighted average P/E[2]	% of assets in cash	Portfolio turnover[3]	Average annual total return	Hypothetical investment results[4]	Fund (consecutive years on honor roll)
$1,000	28.3	10.0%	low	21.8%	$55,990	Acorn Fund (3)
1,000	24.7	17.1	low	22.3	54,889	Amcap Fund (8)
500	24.6	19.1	average	27.1	78,222	American Capital Pace Fund (5)
500	28.1	2.4	high	24.2	59,307	American Capital Venture Fund (4)
none	20.9	24.7	very low	25.0	75,735	Claremont Capital Corp (3)
2,000	17.9	10.0	average	27.9	92,297	Evergreen Fund (2)
NA[5]	16.3	1.2	average	24.1	50,420	Fidelity Destiny Portfolio I (4)
1,000	18.8	1.0	average	35.1	151,684	Fidelity Magellan Fund (5)
1,000	35.8	11.7	low	23.4	62,987	Growth Fund of America (4)
1,000	31.1	28.9	very high	21.9	50,934	Janus Fund (5)
250	23.1	1.5	high	24.1	61,688	Mass Capital Development Fund (2)
250	33.4	0.5	very high	23.8	61,248	NEL Growth Fund (2)
500	19.6	37.7	very low	25.1	75,700	Nicholas Fund (5)
500	20.6	7.0	low	24.5	62,745	Over-the-Counter Securities Fund (5)
500	15.1	15.2	very high	21.8	50,716	Partners Fund
1,000	25.8	2.8	low	21.7	61,805	Scudder Development Fund (2)
500	21.1	15.4	average	20.7	54,754	Shearson Appreciation
none	21.3	26.6	very low	20.9	52,544	Sigma Capital Shares
none	26.2	10.0	very low	23.7	66,823	Sigma Venture Shares (2)
1,000	29.0	1.5	high	23.1	72,130	Tudor Fund (2)
none	22.2	1.0	high	29.6	108,588	Twentieth Century Select Investors (8)
500	26.6	15.3	very high	22.1	52,104	United Vanguard Fund (2)
1,000	22.7	5.5	high	24.3	61,769	Value Line Leveraged Growth Investors

[1]Most plans have lower minimum investment requirements for IRAs. [2]Average of price-to-earnings ratios for stocks in portfolio, weighted by size of holding as of 3/31/86. [3]Greater of security sales or purchases, divided by average net assets. A measure of trading activity. [4]Value on 6/30/86 of $10,000 invested 9/30/76, after taxes, for hypothetical upper-income investor *(see text for details)*. [5]Monthly contractual plans only. [6]Second manager, Dietrich Weismann, has two year's tenure. ‡Fund has 12b-1 plan (hidden loan) pending or in force. NA: Not available or not applicable.

Source: "Annual Mutual Funds Survey," *Forbes* (September 8, 1986), pp. 110–111.

fund provide *reasonable guidelines* for investors in selecting funds (italics added):

> The primary objective of the Fund is long-term capital appreciation. Consistent with this objective, the Fund invests in, among other securities, common stocks or securities convertible to common stock. The Fund's overall investment objective policy and defensive investment strategy are further described in the Prospectus.
>
> Consistent with the goal of long-term capital appreciation, the Fund will follow the following fundamental policies, which may not be changed without the approval of holders of the majority of outstanding voting securities:
>
> 1. The Fund *will not buy securities on margin*.
>
> 2. *Borrowing or other issuance of senior securities are limited* to bank loans not exceeding 12½% of the value of the Fund's assets, and such loans may be secured by not more than 25% of the value of its assets. (Under presently applicable state restrictions the effective limit is 10%.)
>
> 3. The Fund will not underwrite securities of other issuers.
>
> 4. The Fund will not invest in companies for the purpose of exercising control, or acquire more than 10% of the voting securities of any company (3% in the case of other investment companies).
>
> 5. The Fund will not purchase or sell interests in real estate, including interests in real estate investment trusts.
>
> 6. The Fund will not purchase or sell commodities or commodity contracts.
>
> 7. The Fund *will not purchase securities whose sale would not be permitted without registration under the Securities Act* of 1933 [*letter stock*].
>
> 8. The Fund will not make loans to other persons. The purchase of a portion of an issue of publicly distributed bonds, debentures or other securities, whether or not the purchase was made upon the original issuance of the securities, is not to be considered the making of a loan by the Fund.
>
> 9. The Fund *will not make short sales of securities unless* at the time of such short sale it owns or has the right to acquire, as a result of the ownership of convertible or exchangeable securities and without the payment of further consideration, or if it is entitled, subject to approval by a vote of shareholders of the companies involved, to receive as a result of a pending merger or acquisition, an approximately equal amount of such securities, and it will retain securities so long as it is in a short position as to them. In the event that any such merger or acquisition shall fail as a result of non-approval by shareholders, the Fund will cover the short position at the soonest possible time consistent with prudence.

10. Investments will be limited to not more than the following percentages of the Fund's total assets, taken at market value at the time of investment:

Securities of companies in the same industry	25%
Securities of one issuer (except United States Government obligations)	5%
Securities of other investment companies	10%

11. The Fund will not invest in oil, gas, or other mineral exploration or development programs.

12. The Fund *will not purchase put or call options* or combinations thereof.

13. The Fund will not invest more than 5% of its total assets in securities of unseasoned issuers which, including their predecessors, have been in operation for less than three years, and equity securities of issuers which are not readily marketable.

14. The Fund *will not invest more than 5% of its total assets in puts, calls, straddles, spreads, and any combination thereof.*

Buying securities on margin involves *borrowing* part of the purchase price from the broker. The securities are collateral for the loan. The Federal Reserve establishes the percentage that must be paid in cash—the initial margin requirement. After the purchase, the broker requires a minimum maintenance margin to provide adequate collateral for the loan made to the investor. The investor's maintenance margin varies as the price of the securities varies. If the price increases, the investor's margin increases as a proportion of the total value of the stock, and vice versa. If the stock price falls to the point where the maintenance margin is not being met, then the investor must provide additional securities collateral or the broker will sell the securities and repay the investor's loan. Thus, buying on margin provides the advantages and risks of financial leverage (borrowing money). The lower the margin, the greater the amount borrowed and the greater the percentage gain or loss on the investor's margin when the stock price increases or decreases. Thus, the use of margin adds financing risk to the inherent risks of the securities purchased on margin.

Some funds borrow money secured (collateralized) by their securities. This is done to purchase additional securities expected to provide a higher return than the rate of interest on the borrowed funds. Borrowing thus provides the advantages and risks of financial leverage and is called *leverage*. If the return on the additional securities is, in fact, larger than the borrowing rate, then the return on portfolio is greater than it would have been without the loan. In the case where the return on the additional securities is less than the borrowing rate, then the portfolio return is smaller than it otherwise would have been. Thus, borrowing also adds risk to the inherent risks of securities.

Letter stock is stock purchased directly from a corporation and that normally cannot be sold for two years. This restriction can only be avoided if the issuer registers the stock with the Securities and Exchange Commission or finds a buyer who is willing to hold the stock for the remainder of the two-year period. This lack of liquidity is inconsistent with usual investor expectations concerning ease of redemption of mutual fund shares. It adds an element of risk to those inherent in securities.

Short selling is the sale of stock that the investor does not own. This can be done by borrowing the stock from a broker and making delivery to the purchaser. The proceeds of the sale are deposited to the account of the customer who lent the stock through the broker. The motivation behind a short sale is the expectation of buying the stock later at a lower (hopefully) price. Subsequently, the investor purchases the stock and it is placed back in the account of the customer who originally lent it. The investor then receives the proceeds of the original short sale which is netted against the purchase price of the stock. The risk of a short sale is that the stock price will increase rather than decrease. Because prices sometimes rise dramatically, the risk can be significant.

Puts and calls are stock option contracts that give the purchaser the right either to buy or sell 100 shares of a security at a specified price during a designated period of time. Call options give the purchaser the right to purchase the shares, and put options give the purchaser the right to sell the shares. Sellers of call options are obligated to sell the stock if requested, and sellers of puts are obligated to buy the stock if requested.

Options provide a wide range of risk/return possibilities (e.g., straddle and spread strategies ranging from speculative to hedged positions). For example, the returns from the purchase of call options can range from very high to complete losses. In contrast, the sale of calls "covered" by stock held in the portfolio provides supplemental income and some downside protection against decreases in stock prices. Although the sale of covered options reduces the variability in the returns on common stock, most funds do not use them or other types of options, whether used for speculative or risk-reduction uses. However, as discussed in Chapter 3, there are option/income funds that seek high current income by investing primarily in stocks on which call options are traded. The investor should, therefore, evaluate these and other funds on the appropriateness of their objectives to the investor's risk/return preference and other selection criteria.

Litigation.   Mutual funds are sometimes sued for reasons that have little or no substance in law. On the other hand, pending legal action against a fund may have potentially significant implications for the fund and its shareholders. *If a fund's prospectus reveals any pending litigation, that fund* *should be avoided unless it can be determined that the litigation is without probable merit, has insignificant potential financial implications, or raises no probable ethical issues.*

SEC registration. SEC registration means that the fund is registered with the Securities and Exchange Commission. This is a legal requirement for the sale of fund shares in the United States. The SEC regulates mutual funds and provides that they disclose relevant information in their prospectuses and that they do not engage in unfair or illegal practices. If there is any reason to doubt that a fund is registered with the SEC, then the investor should avoid it. This is not normally a problem because those funds with price quotations in the major newspapers (e.g., *Wall Street Journal*) and periodicals (e.g., *Forbes*) are registered. However, "offshore" funds are not registered with the SEC. They operate in countries where fund regulation and regulatory enforcement is less restrictive than in the United States, and these funds are to be avoided.

State blue-sky laws. Most funds satisfy the blue sky laws that exist in each state for the protection of investors. These laws vary from state to state, but most funds meet the requirements of most or all states. In those cases in which a fund does not meet state legal requirements, residents of that state may not purchase shares in that fund. No-load funds do not mail literature to investors in those states in which the funds do not qualify under state law. Also, load funds are not sold in states in which they do not legally qualify. This criterion is not generally a problem for those funds with their NAVs listed in financial newspapers and periodicals. Nonetheless, there may be a substantive reason why a particular fund is not legally qualified, and this fund should be avoided.

INVESTOR RISK-PREFERENCE CRITERION

The risk-preference criterion discussed in this section helps the investor select the mutual fund objective that is consistent with the way he or she feels about risk (risk tolerance). It helps the investor to determine the importance of current income to the individual and the amount of risk he or she can tolerate. This forces the individual to acknowledge that investment decision making is a risk/return tradeoff process. There are no "free lunches"—the desire for higher returns normally carries with it a commensurately higher amount of risk. This approach has two parts. The first determines the investor's tolerance for risk, and the second describes investments that match this tolerance.

An investor's risk tolerance is probably dependent on three basic factors: psychological makeup, environmental factors, and socioeconomic characteristics. These factors help explain why we are as we are. Some investors are entrepreneurs and others are employees. Some investors purchase gold stocks and others hold bank deposits. Some investors purchase aggressive growth stock funds and others hold money market funds. The list could go on and on. These differences represent the fact that we were all born genetically unique and that we spend the rest of our lives illustrating that point. In addition, our psychological makeup has been influenced by the environmental factors to which we have been subjected. Some investors have had the cultural and educational benefits of affluence and others have not. Some investors have had a supportive and stable family structure and others have not. This list could also go on and on.

The investor's "life cycle," as defined by age, is usually presumed to influence the selection of an investment objective that is consistent with the individual's risk tolerance. In other words, the cycle is usually discussed in terms of overall investment objectives for family units in various age categories.

However, research has found that the life-cycle concept also includes other socioeconomic attributes that affect investor behavior.[7] The analysis revealed that major differences in investors' perceptions of their needs revolve around three variables: dividends, future expectations, and financial stability. It was found that age and family income levels were the key attributes differentiating the degree of investor interest in *dividends* (e.g., dividend distributions). The investor who was identified as being most interested in dividends is age forty-five or older, is separated, widowed, or divorced, and has a family income under $20,000. It was also found that investor interest in *future expectations* concerning the future outlook and stock growth potential was related primarily to dollar holdings of common stock, education, and occupation. The investor with common-stock holdings of less than $10,000 who earns $10,000 or more in a nonprofessional occupation (including retired and nonemployed) was most concerned with future expectations (e.g., capital gains distributions). Finally, it was found that investor interest in the *financial stability* of share values was related first to age and then to a number of other socioeconomic variables, but especially gender and education. The investor who was identified as being most concerned with financial stability is age fifty-five or older, is separated, divorced, or widowed, and is not a college graduate. Furthermore, the single female investor under age fifty-five with common-stock holdings of $5,000 and over is also interested in financial stability. Thus, the research suggests that an investor's selection of his or her investment objective is not simply a matter of age but is influenced by a combination of socioeconomic attributes. Ultimately, the risk tolerance is reflected in the investor's choice of investment objective.

As indicated by the above study, socioeconomic characteristics influence investor behavior. In another study, individual socioeconomic attributes were found to influence the way investors feel about the risk and return characteristics of common stock (as defined by their expected dividend yield, expected price appreciation, market risk, share marketability, and share price stability.[8] It was found that these risk and return characteristics are influenced by age, gender, decision orientation (degree of independent decision making), marital status, education, and income. More specifically, the results suggest that:

1. Expected dividend yield is more important to older than to younger investors.

2. Expected price appreciation is more important to younger than to older investors.

3. The marketability of shares is more important to older than to younger investors.

4. Expected dividend yield is more important to male rather than to female investors.

5. There is a tendency for price stability to be more important to female than to male investors.

6. Expected dividend yield is more important to investors who obtain assistance in making their stock decisions than to those who make their own decisions.

7. Expected price appreciation is more important to investors who usually make their own stock decisions than to those who obtain assistance in making decisions.

8. Expected dividend yield is more important to separated, divorced, or widowed investors than to single or married investors.

9. Price stability is more important to investors with less education than to those with at least some college education.

10. Dividend yield is more important to investors with family income below $20,000 than to those with higher income.

You should compare your feelings to these to see how you compare to the investors who participated in this study. This comparison should be done to raise the level of your investment consciousness and, therefore, to help you gain more insight on your risk tolerance. There are no right or wrong feelings, except those that remain unexplored and, thus, hinder the clarity of your decision making.

To measure your tolerance for risk (that is, how much risk you feel comfortable with), you may find that the answers to several questions are helpful. These questions should be answered to reflect your *actual feelings*, and not how you think you *should feel*. Again, there are no right or wrong answers. Answer each of the following questions by placing a checkmark next to the phrase that best describes your feelings, and then sum the numbers next to your responses:[9]

A. Investment Time Frame
   (1) I am interested primarily in short-term investment results.
   (2) I am willing to adjust my portfolio at least once a year.
   (3) I am interested primarily in long-term investment results.

B. Need for Income
   (1) I rely on current income and must know what it will be.
   (2) Current income is one of several factors important to me.
   (3) Current income is not important to me.

C. Preservation of Capital
   (1) I cannot afford (or do not want) any loss of capital.
   (2) I cannot afford to lose 10 to 20 percent of my capital for a quarter or two.
   (3) I can afford to lose 50 percent or more of my capital.

D. Need to Protect Against Inflation
   (1) Preserving current income and my capital is more important than beating inflation.
   (2) I want current income, but I want to beat inflation too.
   (3) My investments must grow faster than inflation.

E. Need to Beat the Market
   (1) I do not care about beating the market.
   (2) I am willing to give up some certainty to get better returns.
   (3) Beating the market is essential to me.
_____ Total Score (Add the numbers next to each box you check.)

The next step is to identify the specific risk category implied by your total score:

TOTAL SCORE	RISK CATEGORY
5–7	Low Risk
8–10	Modest Risk
11–13	Moderate (Average) Risk
14–15	High Risk
Special Risk

To begin the selection process, you need to know the following types of investments/mutual funds (and their general risk/return characteristics) which are consistent with each risk category:

General Risk Category	General Risk/Return Characteristics	Appropriate Type of Investment/Mutual Fund
Low Risk	Emphasis on conservation of capital–no/slight risk of capital loss; current income	Insured deposits Certificates of deposit (insured) Money Market Funds
Modest Risk	Emphasis on conservation of capital—some risk of capital loss; current income	Balanced Funds Bond and Preferred Funds Municipal Bond Funds
Moderate Risk (Average)	Average risk of capital loss; capital appreciation and current income	Growth and Income Funds Growth Funds
High Risk	Significant risk of capital loss; high/maximum capital appreciation	Growth Funds Aggressive Growth Funds
Special Risk	Specific purpose nondiversified risk with significant risk of capital loss; capital appreciation	International Funds Metals Funds Sector Funds

These types of mutual funds are not categorized in the same way as those in Chapter 3. This categorization of funds and their following investment objectives (and policies) are necessary to be consistent with the data base used in the fund evaluation and selection process (discussed below):[10]

International Funds—invest primarily in securities of companies domiciled outside the United States and traded on foreign exchanges.

Aggressive Growth Funds—seek maximum capital appreciation by actively investing in stocks of small companies and high-growth situations. Emphasis on long-term growth with little income.

Growth Funds—seek long-term capital growth by investing in large, established companies. Emphasis on steady, long-term growth with little income.

Growth and Income Funds—seek combination of long-term capital growth and current income by investing in common stock of well established companies.

Municipal Bond Funds—invest in tax-exempt issues of municipalities. Emphasis on high current income and safety, but subject to price swings due to volatile interest rates.

Bond and Preferred Funds—invest in corporate and government debt securities and corporate preferred stock. Emphasis on high current income and safety, but subject to price swings due to volatile interest rates.

Balanced Funds—invest in combination of fixed-income securities (bonds) and equity (common and preferred stock) securities. Conservative portfolio with income securities of large, well-established companies.

Metals Funds—invest in precious metals securities. Volatile, with performance tied to individual metals industries.

Sector funds are included here, as appropriate. These funds, which specialize in one industry group, may be very volatile.

The determination of the investor's risk tolerance can also be used to determine how much the individual needs to save per month to reach the amount needed to meet his or her financial goal. As indicated below in Figure 10.1, the higher the risk tolerance, the higher the *average* rate of return it can be assumed that the savings will earn.

Most people stumble toward their financial goals with an assortment of investments chosen for all sorts of reasons. If, however, you really want to meet your goals, it's wise to shape your portfolio specifically to your ends. This worksheet should help you do that.

1. Amount of money needed for a single objective based on 198_ costs $_____

You may require either a lump sum, as for the down payment on a house, or an annual cash flow—tuition for four years of college, say. If it's the latter, record above the amount you will need at the time you want the cash to start flowing—a sum that may not be obvious. For payouts of $10,000 a year for four years, for example, you'll need to accumulate less than $40,000 by year one since some money will remain invested and continue to grow

until year four. To learn the total you will need to accumulate, multiply the annual amount by the appropriate factor from the table below, which assumes that your investments will yield 10%.

Number of years of cash flow	
4	3.49
5	4.17
10	6.76
15	8.37
20	9.36
25	9.98
30	10.37

Figure 10.1   Crafting Your Own Portfolio

2. Amount you will need,
   adjusted for inflation $_____

   Multiply line 1 by the
   appropriate factor from the
   following table, which assumes
   an annual inflation rate of 5%.

Years to goal	
5	1.28
10	1.63
15	2.08
20	2.65
25	3.39
30	4.32

Years to goal	10% (low risk)	15% (medium risk)	20% (high risk)
5	1.61	2.01	2.49
10	2.60	4.05	6.19
15	4.18	8.14	15.41
20	6.73	16.37	38.34
25	10.83	32.92	95.40
30	17.45	66.21	237.38

5. Total you need to raise to
   meet your goal $_____

   Subtract line 4 from line 2.

6. Amount you must put
   aside each month to reach
   the total $_____

   This too will depend on the rate
   of return you believe you can
   achieve. Multiply line 5 by the
   appropriate factor from the
   following table.

3. Current value of your
   savings and investments
   earmarked for this goal $_____

   Include bank accounts, stocks,
   bonds, mutual funds, precious
   metals, gems, collectibles and
   the value of real estate other
   than the house you live in.

Years to goal	Rate of return 10%	15%	20%
5	.013	.011	.010
10	.005	.004	.003
15	.002	.001	.0009
20	.001	.0007	.0003
25	.0008	.0003	.0001
30	.0004	.0001	.00004

4. What these savings and
   investments will be worth
   when you need them $_____

   Multiply line 3 by the
   appropriate factor from the
   following table, choosing a rate
   of return that you think you can
   achieve. Here you must assess
   your tolerance for risk. The
   higher your return, the greater
   your risk.

Figure 10.1   (*continued*)

If the amount on line 6 is more than you can easily manage, you may want to repeat the calculation using a higher rate of return. Or, if you don't feel you can comfortably assume more risk, you may elect to adjust your present budget to permit increased savings. You may, however, have no choice: your starting amount may be too modest, your goal too ambitious. If this is the case, you'll have to rethink your goal.

Once you arrive at a compromise between your levels of savings and safety, the final step is to match your risk tolerance with the investments in the table below. Remember: the higher you aim, the harder it is to hit the target.

| | Annual return targets | |
5% to 10%	10% to 15%	15% to 20%
▶ Treasury issues ▶ High-grade bond funds ▶ CDs ▶ Money-market investments ▶ Annuities ▶ Savings deposits	▶ High-yield bond funds ▶ High-yield stocks ▶ Growth and income funds ▶ Growth stocks ▶ Growth funds ▶ Income-oriented limited partnerships ▶ Real estate (direct ownership)	▶ Options ▶ Emerging growth stocks ▶ Aggressive growth funds ▶ Junk bonds ▶ Growth-oriented limited partnerships

Figure 10.1   (*continued*)

Source: Patricia A. Dreyfus, "Crafting Your Own Portfolio," *Money* (October 1985), pp. 74–75.

FUND PERFORMANCE CRITERION: RATES OF RETURN COMPONENT

The evaluation of mutual funds on the basis of their consistent long-run rates of return also requires consideration of the risks that relate to the size of the returns. These risks include measures of total risk, systematic risk (relative to the overall market), degree of diversification (also a risk measure), and portfolio management skills (the risk of poor management). The fund evaluation and selection process requires that these measures be applied to a data base.

    If the investor can perform this evaluation and selection by using sufficiently complete and reasonably priced computer-based mutual fund performance data, then so much the better for savings in time and money in the collection and analysis of fund data. CDA Investment Technologies provides such a service. These performance data, for the period ending December 31, 1986, are included as the Appendix.[11] These are the data used here for the evaluation and selection of funds. While these performance data are most useful, there are also other useful sources of related data (Figure 10.2).

The beginning of the Appendix includes the (1) summary of the major elements of the CDA Mutual Fund Report; (2) abbreviations and definitions of the informational elements used in the monthly alphabetic listing of funds; (3) the "top 50" funds ranked by six different performance criteria; (4) the "top 50" funds ranked by the "CDA Rating" (discussed below) within each category of investment objective; (5) abbreviations and definitions of the informational elements used in the quarterly alphabetic listing of funds; (6) abbreviations and definitions of the elements used in the annual alphabetic listing of funds, and (7) directory of mutual fund management companies. The investor should become familiar with this material information in order to comprehend the following discussion and example of the fund evaluation and selection process.

To begin the process, let us assume that the investor has evaluated his or her risk preference and that it totals 14 points. This places the individual in the Aggressive Risk category, which includes both Aggressive Growth Funds and Growth Funds. The funds in the latter category are somewhat less aggressive in their investment stance. With a point total of 14, it may be assumed that the investor feels most comfortable investing in Growth Funds.

The next step is to evaluate the *rate-of-return performance* ("returns") of Growth Funds. As discussed previously, consistent rate-of-return performance over a long period of time offers hope as a predictor of future performance. In this regard, the investor should refer to the CDA Rating of Growth Funds, which gives preference to those funds that have done relatively well in both up and down markets, that have comparatively stable performance over varying time periods, and that have strong recent performance.

The CDA Rating is the percentile rank of each fund (1 = highest, 99 = lowest) based on its relative total rate-of-return performance over each of five periods of time: latest two down-market cycles, latest two up-market cycles, and latest twelve-month period. Market cycles are defined by a 10 percent or more change in the S&P 500 Index from month-end to month-end. For example, for a fund to be in the first percentile, it has to be among the top 1 percent of all funds ranked by their CDA Rating over the five periods of time. If these four market cycles are not available for a particular fund, a minimum of one down-market cycle and one up-market cycle is used.

The percentile total is adjusted downward for the amount of variability in the fund's percentile over these periods because variability in rates of return is defined as risk in the investments literature. Thus, a fund in the first percentile of the CDA Rating has the highest, *consistent* average rate of return

"Annual Mutual Funds Survey," *Forbes.* New York: Forbes, Inc. (annual survey issue).

Barron's. New York: Dow Jones & Co. (quarterly mutual funds section).

"The Best Mutual Funds" (Special Report). *Business Week*, February 24, 1986, pp. 54–85.

CDA Mutual Fund Report. Silver Spring, Md.: CDA Investment Technologies, Inc. (quarterly).

"Directory of Mutual Funds," *Mutual Fund Forecaster.* Fort Lauderdale, Fla.: Institute for Economic Research (monthly).

Donohue's Mutual Funds Almanac. Holliston, Mass.: Donohue Organization, Inc. (annual).

William G. Dromes and Peter D. Herrwagen. *Dow Jones-Irwin No-Load Mutual Funds.* Homewood, Ill.: Dow Jones-Irwin (annual).

Growth Fund Guide. Rapid City, S.D.: Growth Fund Resources, Inc. (monthly).

The Handbook for No-Load Investors. Hastings-on-Hudson, N.Y.: No-Load Fund Investors, Inc. (annual).

The Hulbert Financial Digest. Washington, D.C.: Mark Hulbert (monthly).*

"Investment Company Performance Comparisons," *United Mutual Fund Selector.* Boston: United Business Service Co. (bimonthly).

Investor's Directory: Your Guide to Mutual Funds. New York: No-Load Mutual Fund Association (annual).

Money Guide: Mutual Funds. New York: Time, Inc. (annual).

Mutual Fund Quarterly Performance Review. Gaithersburg, Md.: Schabacker Investment Management (quarterly).

The Mutual Fund Specialist. Eau Claire, Wis.: Royal R. LeMeir & Co. (monthly).

The Mutual Fund Strategist. Burlington, Vt.: Progressive Investing, Inc. (monthly)**

No Load Fund*X. San Francisco: Peter Dag and Associates (monthly).

No Load Fund*X Directory. San Francisco: Peter Dag and Associates, Inc. (annual).

Gerald W. Perritt and L. Kay Shannon. *The Individual Investor's Guide to No-Load Mutual Funds.* Chicago: Investment Information Services Press, 1984.

PG Publications. Palos Verdes, Calif.: Performance Guide Publications, Inc. (monthly).

Switch Fund Advisory. Gaithersburg, Md.: Schabacker Investment Management (monthly).

Weisenberger Investment Companies Service. Boston: Warren, Gorham & Lamont, Inc. (annual with quarterly and monthly supplements).

Figure 10.2   Selected Sources of Mutual Fund Performance Data

*Included because it evaluates the records of stock advisory newsletters (Chapter 11).

**Included because it includes excerpts from mutual fund newsletters and has a good timing record (Chapter 11).

over the five time periods. This notion of high and stable returns is a very appealing one for investors.

Next, the investor should determine the Growth Fund with the highest average annual rates of return over both the last five-year and ten-year periods. This information is available in the CDA "top 50" ratings. This five-year period coincides with the criterion that any fund selected should have the same portfolio manager for at least the last five years. As discussed previously, information on the portfolio managers of top-performing funds is available annually in the *Forbes* "Honor Roll" (Table 10.1) and by telephone directly from the fund. For example, the Fidelity Magellan Fund is the Growth Fund with the highest (first percentile) five-year average annual rate of return. It is also ranked first (first percentile) over a ten-year period. However, in more recent periods its performance has waned a bit. It is in the fourth percentile for the last three years and in the tenth percentile for the year 1986. These more recent results suggest quarterly review because of their eventual implications for long-run performance.

The use of the CDA Rating and the five-year and ten-year average annual rates of return to select funds implicitly assumes that a fund's future will be a repeat of this particular pattern. Although the research discussed in Chapter 9 does not *generally* support this assumption, the use of these return measures along with the requirement for consistent portfolio management and the other criteria does give more weight to the validity of this approach, at least in special cases.

The "total rate-of-return" measure used assumes that all income and capital gains distributions are reinvested. It also includes both realized and unrealized capital gains. Moreover, this return does not include an adjustment for load charges because the focus here is on portfolio performance. However, the calculations are net of fund operating expenses because fund NAVs are computed net of such expenses.

The calculation of the total rate of return involves taking the month-end closing NAV and adding back that month's per share income and capital gains distributions, if any. This figure is used to determine the percentage change from the closing NAV of the preceding month. To compute rates of return for longer periods of time, it is necessary to link the monthly returns to allow for compounding.

Having identified the Fidelity Magellan Fund on the basis of its CDA Rating and rate-of-return performance, the investor should evaluate its *risk, diversification, and the skill of its portfolio management*. This can be done by using other CDA statistical measures discussed in the Appendix.[12] The investor should also determine specifically the risk of the fund. For example, what is its total risk, and what is its risk relative to the overall stock market? This can be found by reference to the Appendix's quarterly supplement.

The standard deviation is the measure of the fund's total risk. It includes both systematic risk and the fund's unique risk. A portfolio's total risk can be reduced through diversification, but it cannot be eliminated. The standard deviation measures the dispersion of fund rates of return around its average return, using monthly returns over the last three-year period. The larger the standard deviation for a given average return, the larger the fund's total risk. This is the recommended risk measure for fixed income funds (discussed later).

The Fidelity Magellan Fund has a standard deviation of 4.77 percent, meaning that 67 percent of the time its return ranged from plus or minus 4.77 percentage points of its average return. This is not an excessive amount of risk. As indicated in the summary of the quarterly supplement in the Appendix, the average Growth Fund has a standard deviation of 4.40 percent, the average mutual fund has a standard deviation of 3.76 percent, and the overall stock market (represented by the S&P 500 Index) has a standard deviation of 4.20 percent. Thus, considering its superior long-term rate-of-return performance, the Magellan Fund's total risk appears reasonable.

The *beta coefficient* is a measure of the fund's risk relative to the overall market. As discussed in Chapter 9, it is a measure of systematic risk—a risk that cannot be eliminated through diversification. This measure is not generally appropriate for fixed-income (bond) funds because their returns are usually not highly correlated with overall market returns. The beta is measured here by using monthly fund and market returns over the last three-year period, and it is stated as a number that can be compared to the defined market beta of 1.0. Thus, the beta coefficient indicates the sensitivity of the fund's rate of return to a change in the market's rate of return. This measure is also related to the standard deviation. For example, a fund with a small beta and a large standard deviation of returns suggests that its returns are not highly correlated with the market's returns and that they contain large amounts of unique risk. An international fund would likely have these characteristics.

The Fidelity Magellan Fund has a beta of 1.09, which means that its returns are 9 percent more sensitive than the market's returns. The fact that the fund's beta is greater than the market's beta is not surprising, given the fact that the fund has such a superior rate-of-return performance. The surprising thing is that its beta is not larger than it is because high risk and high return *generally* go hand in hand. As indicated in the quarterly supplement in the Appendix, the average Growth Fund has a beta of 0.96, the average mutual fund has a beta of 0.70, and of course the overall market has a beta of 1.0. Thus, the size of the Magellan Fund's beta appears reasonable for its high long-run rate-of-return performance.

Although the returns on bond funds are not highly correlated with overall market returns, they are correlated with the level and changes in interest rates. Income Funds hold long-term debt securities, such as bonds, which pay interest and are subject to increases or decreases in their market prices as interest rates decrease or increase. The level of bond interest rates is determined by the general economic forces that affect the so-called "riskless rate of return" in the market for debt, the expected rate of inflation, and each issue's "risk premium." A bond's risk premium reflects the risk of default, its term to maturity, and the specific provisions of the bond contract (e.g., any collateral).[13] When interest rates decline, the prices of bonds increase, thereby providing an increase in the bond's rate of return (interest received plus increase in the price of the bond). On the other hand, when interest rates increase, bond prices decline, thereby lowering the bond's rate of return (interest received less the decline in the price of the bond).

Several factors determine the volatility of bond prices: (1) par (face, dollar, or maturity) value of the bond; (2) coupon (stated) rate of interest on the bond; (3) remaining term to maturity (number of years to the date on which the bond will be paid off); and (4) the bond's current market rate of interest ("yield to maturity").[14] The yield to maturity is the promised compound annual rate of return offered by the bond at its current market price, assuming the investor holds the bond to maturity. Analysis of the relationship between changes in yield to maturity and bond prices indicates that (1) bond prices move inversely (opposite direction) to changes in bond yields; (2) bond price volatility is directly related to the term to maturity; (3) the percentage change in bond price increases at a decreasing rate as the term to maturity increases; (4) a decrease in yield to maturity increases bond prices by more than a corresponding increase in yield lowers bond prices; and (5) a bond's percentage price fluctuation is inversely related to the size of its coupon rate.

The *coefficient of determination* (R^2) is the measure of the fund's risk as related to the degree of its diversification. The R^2 is called *R-square*. It indicates the proportion of the variation in the fund's returns that is explained by variation in the market's returns. It is measured by using monthly fund and market data over the last three-year period. The more diversified the fund is, the closer it comes to eliminating unique risk. An R^2 of 100 percent means the fund is as diversified as the overall market. Thus, such a fund has only undiversifiable (systematic) risk. The R^2 is also directly related to the beta coefficient in that a fund that is perfectly diversified ($R^2 = 100\%$) has only systematic risk (beta = 1.0). Thus, a fund with an R^2 of 100 percent also has a beta of 1.0.

The Magellan Fund has an R^2 of 92 percent. This result is consistent with the fund's beta of 1.09 because if the R^2 is less than 100 percent, then the fund has unique risk as well as systematic risk. As indicated in the summary of the quarterly supplement in the Appendix, the average Growth Fund has an R^2 of 83 percent, and the average mutual fund has an R^2 of 63 percent. Thus, the Magellan Fund appears to be very well diversified for its high long-run rate-of-return performance. It has removed most all of its unique risk while having the highest long-term rate-of-return performance among Growth Funds.

The *alpha coefficient* is the statistical measure that indicates the difference between the fund's actual return and what it should be, based on its beta coefficient and the market's actual return. This measure is also generally not appropriate for fixed-income (bond) funds because of its dependence on the beta coefficient (as discussed earlier). The alpha is measured by using monthly data over the last three-year period, and it is stated as a compound annual percentage (plus or minus). A positive alpha means that the portfolio manager has been so successful at market timing and/or stock selection that the fund has earned a rate of return larger than expected for its systematic risk and the market's actual return. The reverse is true for a negative alpha coefficient. In other words, if a fund's actual return is larger (smaller) than its expected return, then the positive (negative) difference is assumed to be due to management skill (or relative lack thereof), as measured by the alpha coefficient.

The Magellan Fund has an alpha coefficient of +2.2 percent (36th percentile). A positive alpha is not unexpected given the fund's high long-term performance record. Its management is either doing something right or it has been very lucky for a long time. In any case, Magellan's alpha is not as large as one might think, based on its superior long-term rate-of-return performance. But perhaps this is because the alpha is a three-year measure, rather than a five-year or ten-year measure. As indicated in the summary of the quarterly supplement in the Appendix, the average Growth Fund has an alpha of −4.8 percent, and the average mutual fund has an alpha of −1.9 percent. Compared to these alphas, the Magellan Fund's portfolio management has done quite well. However, there are large differences in the average alpha coefficients among the various fund categories (from −12.9 percent to +8.5 percent).

FUND PERFORMANCE CRITERION: OTHER COMPONENTS

Thus far, the investor has matched his or her risk preference to fund investment and selected the Growth Fund category. Next, the analysis revealed that the Fidelity Magellan Fund best satisfies the performance criterion relating to consistent long-run rates of return. Other components of this criterion include the low expense ratio, low portfolio turnover, and large net cash inflow. The use of the Treynor risk/return measure is also introduced later to facilitate a *composite* and objective comparison of funds with different performance attributes.

A *low expense ratio* is defined to mean below-average expenses for the fund category. The expense ratio includes the annual management fees, operating expenses, and 12b-1 fees (if any) as a percentage of the average net assets of the fund. As stated previously, funds with 12b-1 fees should normally be avoided. *Only no-load funds and those low-load funds with superior performance should be considered* (unless there are none in a particular fund category). The quarterly supplement in the Appendix provides no information on the expense ratios of the Fidelity family of mutual funds. However, it does indicate that the average expense ratio is 1.16 percent for Growth Funds and 1.06 percent for all mutual funds. Based on information in its May 30, 1986, prospectus, the Magellan Fund's expense ratio for the year ended March 31, 1986, was 1.08 percent. Thus, the relatively small expense ratio appears to satisfy this criterion component, something that is not unexpected, given the fund's large size and the fixed nature of some fund expenses.

Low portfolio turnover is below-average turnover of the fund's portfolio. *Turnover* refers to the percentage of the fund's portfolio that has been replaced ("turned over") over a specified interval, usually one year (100 percent is one turn). In other words, it is a measure of the purchase and sale activity in the fund's portfolio. All things being equal, a small turnover ratio is preferable to a large one. Turnover information is available in the fund prospectus or in some publications. In the *Forbes* "Honor Roll" the Magellan Fund's portfolio turnover is considered average (Table 10.1). More specifically, according to its May 30, 1986, prospectus, the Magellan Fund's turnover rate was 96 percent for the year ended March 31, 1986. Also, its average turnover rate has declined over the years. For example, it was 277 percent in 1981 and 205 percent in 1977. Thus, the Magellan Fund does not appear to satisfy strictly this criterion component. However, it does appear to be improving its turnover rate based on its historical performance.

Large net cash inflow is above-average net cash flow into the fund. It is the difference between fund sales and redemptions over some period of time, usually a year. If investors are placing more cash into a fund than they are taking out, then the portfolio manager has the flexibility to take advantage of new investment opportunities without necessarily having to change the current portfolio holdings. For the portfolio manager to have this flexibility is especially important if this individual is to take advantage of opportunities in a rising market. It also provides him or her with cash for share redemptions without having to raise cash by selling part of the current portfolio. This cash is especially important if the portfolio appears properly structured for anticipated market conditions.

The existence of a net cash inflow can be determined by comparing the percentage change in NAV to the percentage change in total net assets. If the percentage change in total net assets exceeds the percentage change in NAV, then the fund has a net cash inflow. The dollar amount of net cash inflow equals the dollar amount of the increase in fund net assets less the dollar amount of capital appreciation (increase in NAV times the initial number of shares). For example, a $1,000,000 increase in fund net assets less $600,000 capital appreciation equals $400,000 net cash inflow.

Research suggests that if a fund's net cash inflow is 200 or more percent of its beginning net assets, then the fund should end up in the top 25 percent of funds in its category ranked by performance.[15] Also, if a fund's net cash inflow increases by more than 36 percent a year, then it is likely to outperform the average fund in its category, and vice versa if the net inflow is much less than 36 percent. Thus, an ample net cash inflow is required to meet this criterion component.

The Magellan Fund's prospectus for the year ending March 31, 1986, indicated that its net assets increased by $3,722,417,345 and that its capital appreciation was $1,106,937,400 ($55.34 − $37.69 × 62,716,000 shares). Thus, the fund had a net cash inflow of $2,615,479,945, which represents a 110.7 percentage increase in its net assets since the beginning of the year ($2,363,578,301). The Magellan Fund certainly satisfies this criterion component.

OTHER SELECTION CRITERIA

A third criterion for fund selection is *load charge*. According to the "top 50" supplement in the Appendix, the Magellan Fund has a 3 percent load charge. This represents a low-load charge, and, as discussed previously, funds with low-load charges are eligible for purchase subject to their long-term rate of return performance. In this case, the performance of the Magellan Fund is high enough to compensate for its load charges.

A fourth criterion is *portfolio manager for at least five consecutive years*. The investor should normally purchase only a fund with a portfolio manager who has had at least five consecutive years with the fund. Referring to Table 10.1, the Magellan Fund's portfolio manager has had nine consecutive years in this capacity. Thus, the Magellan Fund satisfies this criterion, and then some.

In a period of five years or more, the portfolio manager should have established a philosophy and sharpened his or her approaches to portfolio management in good times and bad. In the case of the Magellan Fund, the portfolio manager's strategy includes the following:

> As a capital appreciation fund, its sole objective is to make money over the *long term*—to beat the overall market by 5 to 6 percent a year.
>
> To remain *fully invested* at all times—never tries to predict the market, but selects the best securities available in growth companies, conservative companies, and special situations.
>
> To *research* companies constantly and visit hundreds of them annually—receptive to new ideas from regional and national investment companies.
>
> To be willing to take *risk* to enhance long-term performance—10 to 20 percent declines are common and provide the *opportunity* to purchase good stocks at lower prices.[16]

A fifth criterion is *portfolio policies*. The investor should be wary of those funds that engage in activities that have the potential for adding to the risk inherent in the fund's investment objective and portfolio policies. Reference to the notice of a special meeting of Magellan Fund shareholders on December 30, 1986, indicates several proposals for significant changes in its investment and borrowing policies. One proposal provides that the fund may purchase or sell futures contracts and make the margin payments in connection with the purchase or sale of futures contracts or options on futures contracts. The fund states it has no *current* intention of implementing any specific strategies in these areas, but that it wants the flexibility to take future advantage of potential investment and risk management opportunities and techniques where these actions are consistent with the fund's investment objective and policies.

A second proposal provides that the fund may increase the amount it may borrow from 10 percent to 33⅓ percent of its assets, limited only to bank borrowing. This is proposed to provide the fund with maximum flexibility in the event of any sudden needs for cash. For example, if redemptions exceed sales, then the fund would be able to choose between temporary borrowing and the sale of securities to raise the cash needed to avoid delaying payment of redemption proceeds.

A third proposal provides the elimination of fund restrictions on the pledging of assets to other parties. The current limits on pledging may conflict with the fund's ability to engage in futures contracts and options on futures contracts and the ability to borrow for extraordinary or emergency purposes.

Of these three proposals, the third is required to implement the first two. The first proposal is not a current issue (but it undoubtedly will be at some point), and the second is a risk-reduction proposal. Thus, at this time, the Magellan Fund satisfies the investment policies criterion, but developments in this area should be followed closely.

A sixth criterion is *litigation*. Reference to the Magellan Fund's May 30, 1986, prospectus reveals the settlement of a law suit. The U.S. District Court approved the settlement of and then dismissed a shareholder action on behalf of the fund against the management company. The plaintiff alleged that the advisory and service fees, transfer agent fees, and sales charges paid to the management company and its affiliated companies were legally excessive. The settlement requires that the advisory and service fees be revised, and that there be no increases in fees for a period of five years, during which all present services will be provided. The management company was ordered to pay the plaintiff's legal fees. Currently, there are no outstanding legal claims involving the Magellan Fund. Therefore, the fund satisfies this criterion, but with the caveat that the investor should be alert to any future legal claims.

The seventh and eight criteria are *SEC registration* and *state blue-sky laws*. The Magellan Fund is a registered investment company regulated by the Securities and Exchange Commission. It is also registered to sell shares in all fifty states.[17] Answers to both of these questions can also be obtained by calling the fund on its toll-free number. Thus, the fund satisfies both of these criteria.

TREYNOR MEASURE

A final measure is needed to compare (but not to predict) the composite risk/ return performance of funds.[18] Without such a measure it is difficult to select between two funds of the same type where, for example, one has high risk and return and the other has slightly lower risk and return. Which is objectively superior?

There are several well-known, but somewhat different, composite performance measures that can be used to answer this question. Because these measures provide almost identical fund rankings, the measure selected here has the advantage of being easy to use. The Treynor measure was the first *composite measure* of portfolio (fund) performance, and it was derived from the need for a measure of portfolio risk to evaluate the performance of portfolio managers.[19] Thus, it applies to all funds regardless of their risk levels. Portfolio risk was determined to be of two kinds: "market" risk from overall market fluctuations and "unique" risk from the unique fluctuations in the portfolio's securities.

To identify market risk, the "characteristic line" was introduced to specify the relationship between the fund's rates of return over time and the overall market's returns over this period. The slope of the characteristic line measures the sensitivity of fund returns relative to market returns—this slope is the beta coefficient (discussed earlier). The higher the slope, the larger the beta coefficient and the greater the fund's risk relative to the overall market. The deviations from the characteristic line represent unique portfolio returns due to unique stock returns in the portfolio. However, in a properly diversified portfolio these unique returns cancel out. As discussed previously, the higher the R^2 of the fund and market returns, the lower the unique risk and the higher the degree of diversification.

The Treynor measure (T) indicates the rate of return earned in excess of the risk-free rate (i.e., the "risk premium") in relation to the level of systematic risk during a specified period of time:

$$T_i = \frac{R_i - RFR}{B_i}$$

where

T_i = Treynor portfolio performance measure for fund i during a specified period of time

R_i = Average rate of return on fund i during the specified period of time

RFR = Average rate of return on a risk-free security during the specified period of time

B_i = Volatility of fund i rates of return relative to market returns (beta coefficient) during the specified period of time

Thus, the T-value expresses the fund's risk premium per unit of systematic risk. The larger the fund's T-value, the more investors prefer it, regardless of their risk preferences (assuming risk aversion). Although the T-value is affected by the size of the risk-free rate, fund rankings based on this rate *are not*. A T-value can be negative if R_i is less than RFR; it can also be negative if B_i is negative. In the former case, a negative T-value generally means poor management because the fund did not earn a return equal to the riskless rate of return.

Because B_i is a measure of systematic risk, the Treynor measure implicitly assumes that the fund is perfectly diversified and has no unique risk. As discussed in Chapter 9, this is a reasonable assumption because most funds appear to be well diversified. However, this would not be true for the narrowly based "sector" funds which specialize in a particular industry segment (e.g., healthcare).

As an example of the use of the Treynor measure, let us assume two mutual funds with the following risk/return characteristics:

FUND A

Total return, 198_	15.00%
Beta, 198_	1.00
Risk-free rate of return, 198_	5.00%

Treynor measure:

$$T = \frac{15 - 5}{1} = 10$$

FUND B

Total return, 198_	16.00%
Beta, 198_	1.20
Risk-free rate of return, 198_	5.00%

$$T = \frac{16 - 5}{1.2} = 9.2$$

Thus, Fund A has the higher composite risk/return performance. Even though it has a smaller rate of return than Fund B, it provides more return per unit of systematic risk.

Some of the data needed for the calculation of the Treynor measure are in the Appendix: the fund's rate of return for the previous twelve months and its beta coefficient. The average riskless rate of return is represented by the 1986 average 360-day Treasury bill rate. This rate is available in several sources, especially the table of interest rates in the monthly issues of the *Federal Reserve Bulletin* (available in a public library).

Applying the Treynor measure to the two Growth Stock funds with the highest 1986 CDA Ratings, it may be seen that the Fidelity Magellan Fund has a higher composite risk/return performance than the Twentieth Century Select Fund:

FIDELITY MAGELLAN FUND

$$T = \frac{23.6 - 6.1}{1.09} = 16.1$$

TWENTIETH CENTURY SELECT FUND

$$T = \frac{20.7 - 6.1}{1.2} = 12.2$$

Thus, the Magellan Fund also performs well on a composite performance basis.

A FINAL WORD

Based on the selection criteria and the Treynor measure, the analysis indicates that the Magellan Fund was the top 1986 year-end choice for those investors whose risk preferences suggested Growth Funds. *However, the results of this analysis do not represent current recommendation of the Magellan Fund; they are illustrative of the fund evaluation and selection process.*

A final reminder is needed before purchasing a fund. As discussed in Chapter 8, investors should normally purchase shares *after* the fund's ex-distribution date so the NAV paid per share has been reduced by the per share distribution. By doing so, the investor avoids an immediate taxable distribution, obtains more shares for the amount invested, and postpones the receipt of taxable income.

ENDNOTES

[1]Some of these selection criteria are discussed in Donald D. Rugg, *The Dow Jones-Irwin Guide to Mutual Funds*, 3rd ed. (Homewood, Ill.: Dow Jones-Irwin, 1986), Chapter 5; also, for a balanced discussion of fund selection, see Dan Jamieson, "Investigating Mutual Funds," *Personal Investor* (November 1986), pp. 43–47.

[2]For a more complete discussion of this treatment of the consistency of fund performance and related psychological errors in interpreting it, see Hersh M. Shefrin and Meir Statman, "How Not to Make Money in the Stock Market," *Psychology Today* (February 1986), pp. 53–57.

[3]For a more complete discussion of this treatment of the exceptions to efficient markets, see Arlene Hershman, "You Might Make Money in the Market Because. . . ," *Dun's Business Month* (October 1984), pp. 78–83.

[4]Computed from Investment Company Institute, *1986 Mutual Fund Fact Book* (Washington, D.C.: 1986).

[5]Rugg, pp. 69–72.

[6]Rugg, pp. 83–85.

[7]H. Kent Baker, Michael B. Hargrove, and John A. Haslem, "A Test of a Revised Theory of the Investment Life Cycle," *Baylor Business Studies 10* (May, June, July 1979), pp. 17–33.

[8]H. Kent Baker and John A. Haslem, "The Impact of Socioeconomic Characteristics on Risk and Return Preference," *Journal of Business Research 2* (October 1974), pp. 469–476.

[9]This questionnaire is adapted from *The Independent Investor's Personal Investing Newsletter 2* (November 1986), p. 172 (adapted from Lipper Analytical Services, Inc.).

[10]The fund objectives (and policies) are from Spiro L. Kripotos, *What You Should Know About Mutual Fund Performance* (Silver Spring, Md.: CDA Investment Technologies, n.d.), p. 9.

[11]*CDA Mutual Fund Report* (Silver Spring, Md: CDA Investment Technologies, December 31, 1986).

[12]These statistical measures are discussed in the *CDA Mutual Fund Report* and, more completely, in Kripotos, pp. 5–8.

[13]For a discussion of the principles of bond prices and interest rates, see Frank K. Reilly, *Investment Analysis and Portfolio Management*, 2nd ed. (New York: Dryden Press, 1985), Chapter 18.

[14]Burton G. Malkiel, "Expectations, Bond Prices, and the Term Structure of Interest Rates," *Quarterly Journal of Economics 76* (May 1962), pp. 197–218.

[15]For a discussion of this research and the above treatment of the cash flow criterion, see Rugg, pp. 77–80.

[16]"A Conversation with Peter Lynch." A memo published by Fidelity Investments, January 1987.

[17]*Mutual Fund Forecaster* (Fort Lauderdale, Fla.: Institute for Economic Research [monthly issue]).

[18]For a discussion of the approaches to the composite evaluation of portfolio performance, see Reilly, Chapter 22.

[19]Jack L. Treynor, "How to Rate Management of Investment Funds," *Harvard Business Review 43* (January–February 1985), pp. 63–75; also, for a discussion of this treatment of the Treynor measure, see Reilly, pp. 678–680.

11

Investor Fund Management

The criteria and the Treynor measure in Chapter 10 have been used to select the Magellan Fund. There are now two remaining major decisions that will eventually have to be made. First, the investor needs to know when and in what amount the fund shares should be redeemed and invested in a money market fund, and vice versa, due to changing market conditions. Second, the investor needs to know when to sell the fund and replace it with another, based on a current evaluation of their relative performances.

WHEN TO REBALANCE THE PORTFOLIO

The *first decision* involves what to do with the amount invested in the still top-performing fund when the overall market turns up or down by a specified amount. These market moves are important because, as discussed previously, even a completely diversified mutual fund has market (systematic) risk. There are two basic approaches to this decision. One is to follow a *buy-and-hold* strategy and the other is to follow a *timing* strategy. The latter strategy involves the use of technical analysis, which includes moving averages (discussed later).

As discussed in Chapter 9, the preponderance of the research indicates that there is little or no evidence that funds are able to time market changes and adjust their portfolios accordingly. In the absence of generally superior market forecasting ability, the research findings suggest that funds should minimize their management and transaction expenses by using a buy-and-hold strategy and maintaining a diversified portfolio with a constant level of systematic risk. In general, funds are not able to predict security prices well enough to outperform a market buy-and-hold strategy.

MARKET TIMING

Although there are undoubtedly those funds, investors, and timing services and newsletters that represent exceptions to the research findings concerning market timing, the major issue here is whether the investor can do so directly or through others on a generally *consistent* basis. It is unlikely! For example, during the week of July 30, 1984, the Dow Jones Industrial Average (DJIA) gained 87.5 points following a decline of 200 points since the first week in January. Of the sixty leading investment newsletters, only five correctly timed this turn.[1] This result is especially significant for investors when one considers the fees, potential tax liabilities, and higher transactions costs involved in the use of timing newsletters and services. Some of these firms recommend *many* switches a year. Whereas most serious investors appear to believe that a buy-and-hold strategy generally outperforms a timing strategy, many purchasers and sellers of investment advice believe that market timing *can* be the better approach.[2]

Fund market timing is widely practiced and marketed, and its use has become increasingly popular due to the increased volatility of the financial markets and the ease of implementing buy/redemption decisions. To facilitate transfers from one family fund to another, the investor has on file the required form that permits him or her to make transfers by telephone, letter, or wire. Funds frequently use fees and minimum holding periods to limit the number of transactions.

The flexibility of timing strategies is designed to help avoid major losses during adverse markets.[3] There are three basic methods of "switching" among mutual funds based on timing strategies. The first method is to buy *market-timing funds*. These funds adjust their portfolios rather aggressively in anticipation of market and/or interest rate changes. In a second method, the investor does his or her *own switching* based on personal analysis and/or the recommendations of a market-timing newsletter (often with a telephone hotline service). The funds included in this method should not, of course, be those that do their own timing. Fund management companies have made this method relatively easy to execute by creating families of different types of funds, including money market funds, and by allowing investors to use a toll-free number and switch among these funds at a minimal cost. Also, some brokers execute investor no-load fund purchase and redemption decisions for a small fee. These opportunities tend to encourage additional fund switching activity. A third method is for the investor to employ a *market-timing service* to manage his or her fund portfolio and to time portfolio purchase/redemption decisions. Before doing so, however, the investor should ask the service to provide documented evidence of its long-term (i.e., five years) performance. It should also provide regular account statements, newsletters, and a toll-free number.

One analysis of the performance of market timers found that eight of twelve services outperformed (*exclusive of costs*) an average growth fund over a five-year period.[4] These costs are not insignificant. The timing services require minimum fund portfolios of from zero to $150,000 and tend to invest in load funds and to charge fees of 2 to 3 percent of the assets they manage. This study is summarized in Table 11.1.

A more recent study of market timers during 1981 to 1986 found that twelve of eighteen sampled clients of these nine timers did better than if they had invested in an average growth fund.[5] They averaged 15.2 percent return per year versus 13.6 percent for the average growth stock. However, of the thirty market timers invited to participate in the study, only nine accepted, so it is likely that these participants included the better performing firms. In addition, the 15.2 percent return on market-timer accounts excluded the higher taxes due to switches, management fees, and, frequently, load charges. Thus, consistent with the research discussed in Chapter 9, the *net* returns earned by market timers appear to be no more than comparable to those of a buy-and-hold strategy.

Nonetheless, for those investors interested in market timers, there are newsletters that track the performance of mutual fund advisory services. The number of subscribers and years in business, the apparent usefulness of the information, and the clarity of the buy/sell recommendations may also be useful in selecting a market-timing service.[6] Care must be taken because, based on their performance records, the vast majority of these services are probably of little consistent value.

TECHNICAL ANALYSIS

In spite of the research findings on market timing, investors should not blindly follow a buy-and-hold policy, even if it is a generally better approach. This is because research (Chapter 9) does not indicate *general* consistency of individual fund performance (not to be confused with the fund performance criterion discussed in Chapter 10). There are many widely used technical approaches to time mutual fund and other investment decisions.[7] Some of the basic technical approaches and terms are illustrated and described in Figure 11.1. If the application of a method of technical analysis results in a changed market forecast, then an investor following this approach should move to a

TABLE 11.1 A Guide to 12 Top Market Timers

Timing Service	Years of Experience	Minimum Investment	Assets Under Management	Fee	Average Number of Moves Per Year	$10,000 Investment Grew to in 5 Years	5-yr Compounded Annual Rate of Return
Greenwich Monitrend Corp. 222 Bridge Plaza South Fort Lee, N.J. 07024 201-886-2300	13	None	$105 million	2% plus $200	4.4	$26,565	21.6%
PSM Investors 121 Judy Farm Rd. Carlisle, Mass. 01741 617-369-0033	10	$75,000	$25 million	2%	3.8	$25,995	21.0%
Lowry Management Corp. 350 Royal Palm Way Palm Beach, Fla. 33480 305-655-1511	16	$100,000	$120 million	.5% plus $500	2.6	$25,963	21.0%
Schield Management Co. 1610 Wynkeep St. Denver, Colo. 80202 303-592-1545	12	$2,000	$25 million	2%	3.2	$24,747	19.8%
Schabacker Investment Management 8943 Shady Grove Court Gaithersburg, Md. 20877 301-840-0301	7	$100,000	$25 million	2%	.60	$24,365	19.5%
Monitored Assets Corp. 2910 Westown Pkwy. W. Des Moines, Iowa 50265 800-356-2267	13	$2,000	$50 million	2.5%	3.8	$23,167	18.3%
Fabian Financial Services P.O. Box 2538 Huntington Beach, Calif. 92647 714-840-7878	14	$150,000	N.A.	3%	1.6	$23,010	18.1%

(continued)

TABLE 11.1 (continued)

Timing Service	Years of Experience	Minimum Investment	Assets Under Management	Fee	Average Number of Moves Per Year	$10,000 Investment Grew in 5 Years to	5-yr Compounded Annual Rate of Return
Smathers & Co. P.O. Box 2390 Long Beach, Calif. 90801 213-427-9993	14	None	$50 million	2% ($500 minimum)	4	$21,869	16.9%
Shoal P. Berer Associates 717 Grant St. Pittsburgh, Pa. 15230 412-471-6226	15	$2,000 IRA $10,000 taxable	$35 million	2%	4.4	$20,510	15.4%
Chicoine Halliburton & Shannon 567 San Nicolas Dr. Newport Beach, Calif. 92660 714-644-5885	7	$50,000	$30 million	2.5%	8.8	$20,421	15.3%
Covato Lipsitz 1910 Cechran Rd. Pittsburgh, Pa. 15220 412-341-1144	13	$25,000	$17 million	2%	3.2	$19,531	14.3%
Investment Timing Services 1035 Boyce Rd. Pittsburgh, Pa. 15241 412-257-0100	6	$10,000	$130 million	2%	3.2	$17,300	11.6%

This table lists a dozen of the most respected market-timing services—firms that periodically switch clients' money between stock and money-market funds, aiming to ride the stock market's big rises and duck its major drops. Fees decline for larger accounts, usually those of $100,000 or more. The table also shows how $10,000 invested with each timer on March 15, 1979 would have grown in five years, giving the equivalent compounded annual rate of return. Performance records, compiled for Money by MoniResearch of Portland, Ore., are based on the timing services' actual buy-and-sell signals during the period. Cash invested in stocks is assumed to have earned a rate of return equal to that of the Lipper Growth Fund index, a composite of returns on 30 growth-stock funds. Money held out of stocks is assumed to have earned a return equal to that of 90-day Treasury bills at the time. An investor who spread out his $10,000 among the funds in the Lipper index and left the money in those funds for the full five years would have earned 15.6% compounded annual return. His investment would have grown to $20,684.

Source: Robert Runde, "Services that Time Your Trends," *Money* (May 1984), pp. 72–73.

OMENS BRIGHT . . .

The start of a major stock market advance is usually marked by particular signals; technicians look for rapid increases in stock prices and a simultaneous upsurge in the number of
shares changing hands. Both these events occurred in 1982. Technicians knew that stock
prices had risen meaningfully when the Dow industrials crossed their own moving average,
since moving averages smooth out minor fluctuations. Further, in August the number of
shares traded each week on the New York Stock Exchange soared to nearly double the
weekly levels of earlier months. This indicated that investors who had been waiting out the
bear market were jumping in. By the time the bull market that began in 1982 was 44 months
old, stock prices had more than doubled.   (continued)

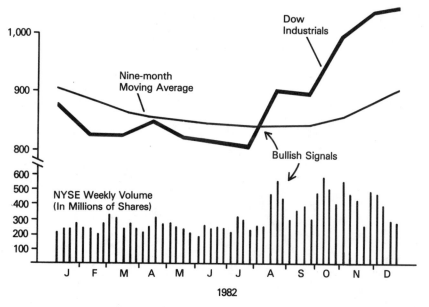

Figure 11.1   Technical Market Timing

fund with an investment objective more compatible with this forecast or to a
money market fund.

Because of the lack of research support for technical approaches such as
market timing, it may make more sense to use them after the fact *to confirm*,
rather than to forecast, developing market movements and trends. In other
words, it *may* make sense to use technical approaches to *indicate* change
(after a significant market move to minimize risk of a short-term reversal of
this apparent trend) rather than to *forecast* changes. After all, the research
on market "efficiency" suggests that, at the least, current security prices
already reflect all *historical* stock market information, including security
prices, price changes, trading volume, and other past market information.
This research underlies the Chapter 9 research findings on the general

. . . AND GLOOMY

During a healthy stock market advance, shares of all kinds should be going up together. If large numbers of stocks are falling even while some indexes are rising, it may be a sign of trouble to come. In late 1980, a new bull market appeared to have begun as both the Dow Jones industrial average and the S&P composite index marched steadily upward. But while the 30-stock Dow continued to a peak in March 1981, Standard & Poor's 500-stock index—which reflects a broader range of companies—didn't rise above its high of the previous November. Conclusion: even though a handful of Dow stocks were still moving higher, the average stock appeared to be weakening. Sure enough, during the next 15 months, the market turned down and stock prices fell nearly 25%.

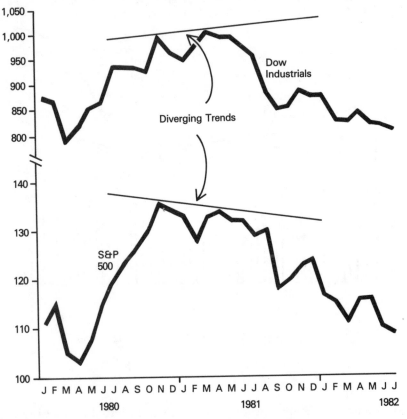

Technical Analysis: A method of making buy and sell decisions about a stock based upon market factors, such as trading volume and price behavior, rather than economic ones, such as sales and earnings.

Dow Theory: A technical system for identifying the primary trend of the stock market. A bull market is confirmed when both the Dow industrial and the Dow transportation indexes reach new highs.

Moving Average: A regularly updated figure calculated by averaging a fixed number of stock prices; as each new price is included, the oldest one is dropped and the average is recalculated.

Divergence: The comparative behavior of different groups of stocks. Two indexes diverge if one is rising while the other is falling.

Advance/Decline Line: A graph of a running tally calculated by adding the number of gainers in excess of losers in a given period, usually a day, or subtracting the number of losers in excess of gainers.

Figure 11.1 (*continued*)

Source: Michael Sivy, "Market Timing the Technical Way," *Money Guide: The Stock Market* (New York: Time, Inc., 1986) pp. 66–67.

inability of funds to time (forecast) changes in the market. Thus, market timing based on technical rules that use historical price and market data to predict future market and mutual fund price changes are generally unlikely to be of any value, especially on a consistent basis.

MOVING AVERAGES

Moving averages are methods of technical analysis; therefore, they are subject to the same problems discussed earlier (also, see Figure 11.1) Nonetheless, they are widely used and, for this reason, some discussion is merited. Also, moving averages can be an approach for validating, rather than forecasting, market movements and trends (also, as discussed earlier).

The *200-day moving average* is probably the most frequently used moving-average method. It is used to indicate future changes in the price of a particular stock or the overall stock market. The 200-day moving average is called this because it is the average of the previous 200 daily closing prices. Its advocates consider it a trend-detecting approach to market timing, which determines whether the trend of stock or market price is up or down. They believe its trend will continue until a reversal is indicated.

A moving average of past stock or market prices (e.g., DJIA) is computed to indicate the price trends. Next, the current price of the stock or market is compared to the moving average to see whether the relationship indicates a change in the price trend. If the market price trend has been upward, then the moving average would usually be below the current price, and vice versa. This is because the moving average has to move more slowly than the current price, because the moving average is an average of previous prices. If prices reverse and the current price breaks through the moving average from above on heavy volume, then this could be interpreted as a reversal in the upward long-run price trend, and vice versa.

A major danger with the use of moving averages, however, is that the investor can be "whipsawed" by fluctuating buy/sell signals. For example, a particular moving-average system might say that if the DJIA increases by more than 5 percent below its moving average, this is a "sell" signal.[8] When the DJIA fell by a then record amount on September 11, 1986, the moving-average systems signaled "sell." This sell signal came at the bottom of the downside move in the DJIA, and, as the DJIA subsequently moved upward, a "buy" signal was generated. The result was the redemption of shares near the short-term low in the DJIA and their subsequent repurchase near the short-term high—a large overall loss.

At the outside, the moving-average approach is probably only marginally (if at all) better than a buy-and-hold strategy, assuming away the costs of using the moving-average approach. This conclusion is supported by a study that investigated whether the use of moving averages produced superior returns relative to a buy-and-hold strategy.[9] Analysis of the performance of several monthly moving average plans (with and without reinvestment of dividends) and a buy-and-hold strategy found little evidence in a sample of 798 securities that investors would benefit from the use of monthly moving averages.

PORTFOLIO INSURANCE

A variation on the use of the moving average as an indicator of changes in the value of mutual funds is *portfolio insurance*.[10] This strategy does not prevent losses, but rather it limits them while allowing participation in rising markets. More specifically, it is not unlike the use of "stop-loss" orders to limit losses by placing sell orders under the current prices of stocks. The more successful the investor is in anticipating changes in the direction of the stock market, the more effectively this strategy can be applied. For this reason, some signals of forthcoming increases and decreases in the market are included in Figure 11.2. The portfolio strategy utilizes the mutual fund selected by the investor (Chapter 10) and a money market fund, preferably in the same family of funds for convenience. As stock prices decline, the investor uses predetermined decision rules to transfer money from the mutual fund to a money market fund, and vice versa as prices rise. These rules indicate when to transfer money, how much to transfer, to and from which funds to transfer, and the resulting fund portfolio mix. Thus, these rules attempt to remove psychological considerations from buy/sell decisions. However, as discussed below, the rules themselves do reflect investor risk preferences.

There are several portfolio insurance concepts, as applied here to funds:

1. *Floor*—the lowest total value of the portfolio that is acceptable to the investor

2. *Cushion*—margin of safety against a reduction in the *value* of the mutual fund, as measured by the total portfolio value less the floor

3. *Exposure*—amount invested at risk in the mutual fund (the money market fund is considered riskless)

4. *Multiple*—investor's fixed ratio of the exposure divided by the cushion, which is used to maintain the margin of safety relationship between the amount invested in the mutual fund and the cushion

5. *Tolerance*—percentage change in the cushion set by the investor to trigger a transfer between the types of funds in the portfolio

6. *Limit*—maximum acceptable percentage of the total portfolio value that can be invested at risk in the mutual fund

To test your own conclusions that stocks may be approaching a high or low point in a major market cycle, you should make a systematic review of economic trends, the state of the market and the mood of investors. You can do that by answering the questions in these two checklists. The information you'll need is available in the press, from brokers and from other sources described in the preceding article. When most of the checks line up in one of the "yes" columns, you can take it as a strong sign that a major turn is approaching—or may even have begun. Our own recent answers suggest that a buying opportunity is not far away.

THE TIME-TO-BUY CHECKLIST
("Yes" answers are favorable.)

The business cycle

1. Is business activity in a downtrend, and if so, do you foresee the end of that downtrend? — Yes ☑
2. Is inflation decelerating? — No ☑
3. If corporate profits have declined from their previous peak, do you expect them to start turning upward soon?

Monetary policy and interest rates

4. Are short-term interest rates starting to decline? — Yes ☑
5. Has the Federal Reserve Board given indications that it will ease restraints on growth of the money supply? — No ☑

Stock valuations

6. Has the price/earnings ratio of the Value Line composite index fallen to near or even below its level at the market's last cyclical low point? — Yes ☑

THE TIME-TO-SELL CHECKLIST
("Yes" answers are worrisome or bearish.)

1. Is there growing evidence that the business cycle has reached a peak? — No ☑
2. Is inflation accelerating? — No ☑☑
3. If corporate profits are rising, does the current rate of increase appear too strong to last?
4. Are short-term interest rates rising and are they as high as they were at the corresponding stage of the previous upturn? — No ☑
5. Has the Federal Reserve Board started to tighten monetary policy? — No ☑
6. Has the P/E ratio risen near or above its level at the market's last cyclical peak? — No ☑

Figure 11.2   How the Investment Signals Are Lining Up

(continued)

Sentiment indicators

7. Are mutual funds heavily in cash? ☑ ☐   7. Are the cash reserves of mutual funds low? ☑ ☐
8. Is the odd-lot short-sales ratio very high? ☑ ☐   8. Is the odd-lot short-sales ratio very low? ☑ ☐
9. Is the specialists' short-sales ratio exceptionally low? ☑ ☐   9. Is the specialists' short-sales ratio exceptionally high? ☑ ☐
10. Are your friends and business associates pessimistic or apathetic about the market? ☑ ☐   10. Are your friends and business associates talking about their winners and feeling euphoric about the market? ☑ ☐

State of the market

11. Has the market been declining for many months since its previous cyclical high? ☑ ☐   11. Has the market been advancing for many months since its previous cyclical low? ☑ ☐
12. Has the market registered a large percentage drop from its previous cyclical high? ☑ ☐   12. Has the market registered a large percentage gain from its previous cyclical low? ☑ ☐
13. Has the market recently accelerated its rate of decline, as it typically does in the final stages of bear markets? ☑ ☐   13. Is the advance/decline line underperforming the popular averages — an indication of deteriorating market strength? ☑ ☐
14. Has the market rebounded from its last major low point, dropped back to that low once or twice, and then advanced? ☑ ☐   14. Has the market dropped below its recent high and climbed back to it a couple of times or more, only to retreat again? ☑ ☐

The presidential election cycle

15. Is the next presidential election not much more than two years from now? ☑ ☐   15. Is this the year following a presidential election? ☑ ☐

Figure 11.2 (continued)

Source: "How the Investment Signals are Lining Up," Money (June 1982), p. 52.

140

Portfolio insurance provides a simple way to increase the expected returns of the investor's mutual fund portfolio while also limiting potential loss. This is done by setting the portfolio's initial exposure at a level greater than its cushion. As discussed earlier, the multiple is the fixed ratio of the exposure divided by the cushion as set by the investor. Each time the investor transfers monies between the mutual fund and the money market fund, the exposure is adjusted to an amount equal to the multiple times the new cushion.

This process may be initiated by placing all of the portfolio ($100) in the mutual fund—the limit is 100 percent and the initial exposure is $100. Assuming the investor sets a floor of $80, the cushion is $20; therefore, the multiple is five. The tolerance is set at 50 percent of the current amount of the cushion. Each time this amount is reached, the investor transfers monies within the portfolio to rebalance the exposure to maintain a multiple of five times the new cushion. The higher the multiple, the more the exposure is adjusted for a given change in the cushion, which equals the tolerance. For example, if the multiple is five, a $10 decline in the initial cushion (which equals the 50 percent tolerance) results in an adjusted *balance* (exposure) of $50 in the mutual fund. This process repeats itself each time the change in the cushion equals the tolerance (50 percent of the cushion) or, equivalently, 50 percent of the remaining distance to the floor.

If the value of the mutual fund in the portfolio continues to fall, then the cushion and the exposure approach zero as the total portfolio reaches its floor. This keeps the total portfolio value from falling below the floor, unless the market falls very sharply before the investor can transfer monies. On the other hand, if the value of the mutual fund continues to increase back toward its initial value, then the cushion and the exposure approach their maximum initial values as the total portfolio reaches its initial value.

As discussed previously, a decline in the cushion equal to the tolerance is met by adjusting the exposure to the defined multiple of the new cushion. This adjustment is called for *each time* a decline in the cushion equals the tolerance, which triggers the requisite transfer between the funds in the portfolio. The smaller the tolerance, the more directly it relates to changes in the cushion, and the higher the turnover of shares. This could mean higher back-load charges or redemption fees if "true" no-load funds are not used. These transactions also have tax implications for the capital gains or losses that result.

There are several other advantages of the portfolio insurance strategy, including (1) simplicity, (2) flexibility of response to market changes, and (3) custom-designed policies (the investor selects the policies that meet his or her risk preference and the changing conditions of the market). As mentioned earlier, this strategy can be easily managed on a weekly or, perhaps, monthly basis when the market is stable or on a daily basis when the market is quite volatile. It allows the investor to participate in the appreciation of his or her mutual fund assets while limiting its potential losses by shifting monies between the mutual fund (risky asset) and a money market fund (low-risk asset). The mutual fund selected has a high performance level for its investment objective (Chapter 10) and the money market fund has an acceptable rate of return on its short-term, money-market assets. As discussed earlier, the size and timing of portfolio shifts are determined by the investor's preference in setting policies for implementation of the strategy. The rules established by these policies should provide some decision discipline to those investors who have psychological hang-ups against realizing losses, even in the face of a significant downturn in the market.

As previously mentioned, the investor specifies the limit, exposure, floor, cushion, multiple, and tolerance in the portfolio insurance strategy. To the extent the investor does not already have strong preferences toward these variables, one recommended scenario is suggested. This scenario would appear to provide reasonable guidelines.

To be able to obtain maximum portfolio returns in an increasing market, the investor specifies the *exposure at its maximum dollar amount and the limit at 100 percent of the portfolio*. This limit means that all monies can be invested at risk in the mutual fund.

To avoid a loss of over 20 percent in a down market, the investor specifies a *floor of 80 percent*. This floor percentage reflects normal downside stock market risk and is also recommended to avoid portfolio losses due to "whipsawing" of the fund's value due to short-run market volatility. The higher the floor, the greater the risk of loss due to whipsawing (as with the moving-average strategy). A floor of 90 percent, for example, generates a large number of transfers in today's volatile market. A floor of 70 percent might be appropriate for an investor who wishes to avoid undue transfers, and who is not concerned about the occasional significant downturn. In any case, if no floor preference is revealed through introspection, a floor of 80 percent should be used, at least until the investor's "comfort zone" is determined through experience.

Having specified a floor of 80 percent, the investor automatically faces a *20 percent cushion* (100 percent total portfolio value less 80 percent floor). This cushion indicates how much the mutual fund can decline in value before the floor value of the portfolio is reached. The larger the dollar value of the cushion, the more the mutual fund can decline in value and not violate the floor.

Also, having specified the exposure and cushion levels, the investor faces the resulting *multiple of five*. A multiple of five means that the exposure will be maintained at an amount equal to five times the cushion. In this way, the cushion provides a *constant proportion* margin of safety relative to the amount of assets at risk (exposure).

The tolerance is specified relevant to the size of the cushion, which provides protection to the value of the portfolio in "down" markets and also increases its exposure in "up" markets. The mutual fund's beta is helpful in specifying the tolerance because it measures the sensitivity of its returns to the market's returns. It is suggested that a *tolerance of 50 percent of the current size of the cushion is reasonable*. This size tolerance is equivalent to 50 percent of the *remaining* distance to the floor or, equivalently, to a 10 percent decline in the value of the mutual fund at its maximum exposure. This size tolerance should avoid undue costs due to whipsawing, but these costs cannot be avoided entirely if the portfolio insurance strategy is to avoid significant portfolio losses. In a down market, the strategy takes a series of small losses to avoid a large loss (by maintaining a series of constant cushion multiples). In an up market, the strategy provides a series of small gains to maintain its cushion multiple and, thereby, limits the risk of missing a market reversal.

In this regard, the results of using portfolio insurance versus three buy-and-hold strategies for each of the years from 1974 to 1985 were analyzed.[11] In each year, the portfolio strategy initially assumed an exposure of 50 percent, a cushion of 20 percent, and a floor of 80 percent; the three buy-and-hold strategies initially assumed an exposure of 100 percent, a 50 percent exposure and 50 percent in Treasury bills, and a 20 percent exposure and 80 percent in Treasury bills, respectively. The 1985 results indicated that the 100 percent exposure buy-and-hold strategy ranked first, the portfolio insurance strategy ranked second, the 50 percent exposure buy-and-hold strategy ranked a close third, and the 20 percent exposure buy-and-hold strategy ranked fourth.

In general, insured portfolios *do not* outperform uninsured portfolios under all market conditions. For example, an insured portfolio would not outperform an all-stock portfolio in an up market. On the other hand, it would outperform a 100 percent exposure consecutive portfolio with riskless assets in an amount equal to the floor. The rate of return in a given year using portfolio insurance depends on the direction and volatility of the market and the policies impacting transfers within the portfolio. There are also costs involved in the transactions, such as tax liabilities, record keeping, possible load charges, etc.

For an example of how portfolio insurance works, see Table 11.2. This table initially (Scenario A) incorporates the following policy assumptions: (1) initial total portfolio value, $100; (2) limit (maximum percentage of total portfolio value invested in the mutual fund), 100 percent; (3) initial exposure (value of the mutual fund), $100; (4) initial (minimum) value of the money market fund, $0; (5) floor (minimum acceptable value of the total portfolio), $80; (6) initial cushion (initial total portfolio value less floor), $20; (7) multiple (exposure divided by cushion) of five, and (8) tolerance (50 percent of the current cushion). The investor specifies these assumptions, which are stated here at reasonable levels subject to investor preferences.

First, consider the portfolio rebalancing each time the cushion declines

TABLE 11.2 Illustration of Portfolio Insurance

Scenario A: Decrease in Value of Mutual Fund from Initial Value to Floor Value

Time Period	Change in Cushion	Mutual Fund Exposure Before Transfer	Cushion	Mutual Fund Exposure After Transfer	Value of Money Market Fund After Transfer	Portfolio Value	Floor
0	—	$100.00 100.00	$20.00	$100.00	$ 0.00	$100.00	$80.00
1	$ –10.00	90.00 50.00	10.00	50.00	40.00	90.00	80.00
2	– 5.00	45.00 25.00	5.00	25.00	60.00	85.00	80.00
3	– 2.50	22.50 12.50	2.50	12.50	70.00	82.50	80.00
4	– 1.25	11.25 6.25	1.25	6.25	75.00	81.25	80.00
5	– 0.625	5.62 3.12	0.62	3.12	77.50	80.62	80.00
6	– 0.3125	2.81	0.00*	0.00*	80.00*	80.00*	80.00

*Balance of Mutual Fund transferred to Money Market Fund to avoid subsequently smaller transfers.

Scenario B: Increase in Value of Mutual Fund to Initial Value Beginning at Floor Value

Time Period	Value of Money Market Fund Before Transfer	Change in Cushion	Cushion	Mutual Fund Exposure After Transfer	Value of Money Market Fund After Transfer	Portfolio Value	Floor
0	$80.00 80.00	—	$ 0.00	$ 0.00	$80.00	$ 80.00	$80.00
1	80.00 40.00	$ +10.00*	10.00	50.00	40.00	90.00	80.00
2	40.00 20.00	+ 5.00	15.00	75.00	20.00	95.00	80.00
3	20.00 10.00	+ 2.50	17.50	87.50	10.00	97.50	80.00
4	10.00 5.00	+ 1.25	18.75	93.75	5.00	98.75	80.00
5	5.00 2.50	+ 0.625	19.38	96.88	2.50	99.38	80.00
6	2.50	+ 0.3125	20.00**	100.00**	0.00**	100.00**	80.00

*See discussion for derivation of the initial cushion.

**Balance of Money Market Fund transferred to Mutual Fund to avoid subsequently smaller transfers.

Source: Adapted from Fischer Black and Robert Jones, "Simplifying Portfolio Insurance," *Portfolio Strategy* (August 1986), pp. 1–6.

50 percent of the distance to the floor. At time period 1, the cushion decreases by $10, which equals the tolerance. Thus, $40 is transferred from the mutual fund to the money market fund. This amount is transferred because a $10 decline in the cushion, which equals the tolerance, requires a $40 decline in the amount in the mutual fund, if the multiple of five is to be maintained (new exposure of $50 divided by the new cushion of $10). The floor, of course, remains constant at $80. This portfolio rebalancing process continues in an analogous fashion through time periods 2 through 5, except that the amounts of tolerance, cushion, and monies transferred decrease by 50 percent at each successive time period. In time period 6, the remaining amount in the mutual fund is transferred to avoid relatively small transfers in subsequent periods (assuming the value of the cushion continues to decline). Thus, at the end of this time period, all of the portfolio is invested in the money market fund (limit 0 percent), the cushion is zero, and the exposure is zero at the floor of $80 (no potential for further loss).

Next, starting at this position (Scenario B), consider the portfolio each time the cushion increases by 50 percent of the distance to its initial maximum of $20. At time period 1, the change in the value of the mutual fund is estimated using the fund's NAV as reported in the newspaper. A 10 percent increase in NAV since the time the investment in the fund became zero is assumed to be equivalent to 50 percent of the initial maximum cushion of $20 (i.e., $10). This assumption is needed (in this time period only) because there is no initial investment in the mutual fund. The $10 increase in the cushion can either be assumed for this and the subsequent calculations or represent additional actual investment. Thus, $40 is then transferred from the money market fund to the mutual fund. This amount is transferred because a $10 increase in the cushion (assumed or newly invested in the mutual fund) requires an additional $40 increase in the mutual fund, if the multiple of five is to be maintained (new exposure of $50 divided by the new cushion of $10). The floor remains at $80. This portfolio rebalancing process continues (including the initial assumed or actual $10 cushion) in an analogous fashion through time periods 2 through 5, except that the amounts of tolerance, cushion, and monies transferred decrease by 50 percent at each successive time period. In time period 6, the remaining amount in the money market fund is transferred to the mutual fund to avoid relatively small transfers in subsequent periods (assuming the cushion continues to increase). Thus, at the end of time period 6, all of the portfolio is invested in the mutual fund (limit 100 percent), the cushion is $20, and the exposure is $100 with potential for more appreciation. The floor, of course, remains at $80.

Because the use of portfolio insurance involves "switches" between the selected mutual fund and a money market fund, a family of funds (with different investment objectives under one management company) is most convenient to implement this strategy. Fund families simplify the use of portfolio insurance in funds by providing convenient in-house transfers and redemption services, among others.

To see how well the ten largest fund families provided services, information was collected on their 1986 overall investment performance, fees, and services.[12] The evaluation of their customer services included promptness of response to questions and requests for information, knowledge indicated by telephone service representatives, and speed and accuracy in responding to requests for switches and redemptions. All of the families were ranked at least "average" with respect to service. Thus, among the largest fund families, the investor should not have significant service problems switching between the selected mutual fund and a money market fund. A summary of the investment performance and service quality of each of these fund families is provided in Table 11.3.

TABLE 11.3 Service Ratings of Fund Families

Management Company	Service Rating		
	Below Average	Average	Above Average
American Capital Fund			
Assets: $15.9 billion			
Number of Funds: 30			
Performance	x		
Service		x	
Capital Research and Management			
Assets: $14.9 billion			
Number of Funds: 24			
Performance			x
Service			x
Dreyfus Corp.			
Assets: $33 billion			
Number of Funds: 25			
Performance		x	
Service			x
Fidelity Management Research			
Assets: $53 billion			
Number of Funds: 75			
Performance			x
Service			x
Franklin Group			
Assets: $28 billion			
Number of Funds: 24			
Performance		x	
Service			x

(continued)

TABLE 11.3 *(continued)*

Management Company	Below Average	Average	Above Average
IDS Financial Services Assets: $15.2 billion Number of Funds: 26			
Performance			x
Service	x		
Kemper Financial Services Assets: $32 billion Number of Funds: 21			
Performance		x	
Service			x
Putnam Financial Services Assets: $20.6 billion Number of Funds: 30			
Performance		x	
Service		x	
T. Rowe Price Associates Assets: $12.7 billion Number of Funds: 23			
Performance		x	
Service			x
Vanguard Group of Investment Companies Assets: $23 billion Number of Funds: 42			
Performance		x	
Service			x

Source: Excerpted from Leslie N. Vreeland, "A Guide to the 10 Biggest Fund Families," *Money* (November 1986), pp. 215ff.

WHICH MONEY MARKET FUND?

As stock prices decline significantly enough, the portfolio insurance strategy requires that monies be transferred from the mutual fund to a money market fund. The investor must then decide which money market fund to use. Assuming the mutual fund is one in a family of funds, the investor's choice of money market fund should be determined by his or her risk preference.

As discussed in Chapter 3, there are three basic types of money market funds ("money" funds): (1) *U.S. Treasury Money Funds*, (2) *Diversified Money Market Funds*, and (3) *Tax-Exempt Money Funds*. The investor's risk preference will be appropriately matched by one of these basic types of money funds. Although money market funds have an excellent record of providing safety of principal (low portfolio default risk), the three types of funds do reflect inherent differences in risk. U.S. Treasury money funds hold securities of the highest credit quality, which are directly or indirectly secured by the taxing power of the federal government. The remaining types of money market funds have more default risk, the degree of which is determined by the composition of their portfolios. Portfolios dominated by bankers' acceptances and/or repurchase agreements have less default risk than those dominated by commercial paper and/or negotiable certificates of deposit, especially Eurodollar CDs. Portfolios dominated by municipal securities have the most default risk. Thus, it is recommended that the investor's risk preference with respect to mutual funds (Chapter 10) also be used to select the type of money market fund to be used for portfolio balancing.

The types of money market funds that are consistent with each risk category follow:

GENERAL RISK CATEGORY	APPROPRIATE TYPE OF MONEY MARKET FUND
Low Risk	U.S. Treasury Money Fund
Modest Risk	U.S. Treasury Money Fund Money Market Fund (emphasis on repurchase agreements and/or bankers' acceptances)
Moderate (Average) Risk	Money Market Fund (emphasis on commercial paper and/or CDs)
High Risk Special Risk	Tax-Exempt Money Fund

These categories reflect *small risk differences* relative to their use in Chapter 10.

If the mutual fund held is in a fund family that has the appropriate type of money market fund for the investor's risk preference, then the investor should select it for portfolio balancing purposes. If the mutual fund does not have an appropriate campanion money market fund, the investor should *select the money fund that has the highest current twelve month yield for its basic type and that also meets the following criteria*:

1. The prospectus describes the services that are desired by the investor and contains no unpleasant "surprises."
2. The fund has an appropriate investment objective.
3. The discussion in the annual report of the portfolio's composition, quality, and maturity diversification are appropriate to the investor's risk preference when compared to other high-yielding funds.
4. The fund has been in business for a minimum of five years.

In fact, it would be even more prudent to apply the yield and other criteria to the appropriate type of money fund in the same fund family to see how they compare to the highest-yielding money fund outside the family that also meets the criteria. The money fund in the family should be reasonably comparable, as well as more convenient.

WHEN TO SELL THE MUTUAL FUND

The *second decision* involves knowing when to sell the fund shares and buy others. This decision can be made relatively easily. Again, assume that on December 31, 1986, the Fidelity Magellan Fund is the Growth Fund that best meets the selection criteria. Henceforth, the investor should review his or her risk preference and the fund's performance at the end of each succeeding quarter, with weekly attention to its price behavior when the market is especially volatile. After all, the investor's risk preference will change over time, the fund can change its effective investment objective, its performance can decline, or, as discussed earlier, the market can decline.[13] Assuming no change in risk preference, the investor should use the components of the fund *performance criterion* (included in the *CDA Mutual Fund Report*) and the Treynor measure in this quarterly review.

At some future time, the investor will find that another fund has replaced the Magellan Fund on the basis of its performance, especially its consistent, long-run rates of return. This new fund will be in the top percentile of the CDA Rating over the five time periods of up and down markets. It will also likely have the highest average annual rate of return over the last five and, perhaps, ten years, a low expense ratio, low portfolio turnover, and a large net cash inflow.

At this point, and with this performance information, the investor should evaluate the fund by using the remaining *selection criteria*: load charges, portfolio manager for at least five consecutive years, portfolio policies, litigation, SEC registration, and state blue-sky laws. Assuming the fund satisfies these remaining criteria, the investor should redeem his or her Magellan shares and purchase shares in the other, higher-performing fund. Obviously, judgment is required in these decisions, especially where the results do not all favor one fund. The application of the selection criteria must also be tempered by short-run market conditions, any special features of the funds, and the investor's own personal situation (such as financial goals and tax considerations).

AN INTERNATIONAL FOOTNOTE

The discussion of mutual fund diversification emphasizes how systematic risk cannot be eliminated. However, the addition of an international fund to the investor's total portfolio can reduce the overall level of systematic risk and, thereby, reduce the variability of the portfolio's returns. This is because the computed measure of systematic risk (beta) was based on market returns, which omitted international securities.

Both foreign and domestic securities are necessary to obtain the maximum benefits of diversification because they tend to have low covariance—a measure of the degree of co-movement in the returns on foreign and domestic securities. This low covariance reflects that the determinants of the returns on securities are generally factors internal to each country. The weaker the relationship between the economies of any two countries, the more this is so. More specifically, the determinants of the low covariance include *differences* in economic growth rates, monetary policy, inflation rates, business risk, financial risk, and liquidity risk (see below). These factors tend to be independent among countries, which represents their internally derived nature.

This discussion is consistent with the research findings on the benefits of international diversification.[14] In summary, these studies found that:

1. There are substantial portfolio risk-reduction benefits from international diversification—reduced variability in portfolio returns for the level of return.
2. There is a smaller degree of correlation (association) between stock returns in *different* countries than between stock returns in the *same* countries.
3. The correlation between stock returns differs between countries depending on their level of economic development and the degree of economic interdependence; furthermore, the correlations are not stable over time.
4. The portfolio risk-reduction benefits of international diversification are gradually decreasing as the economies of countries become increasingly more interdependent.

If the investor seeks the benefits of international diversification, then the fund performance and other selection criteria (Chapter 10) should be applied to the international mutual funds included in the Appendix. The fund selected should be evaluated quarterly by using the data in the Appendix, and the portfolio insurance strategy should be used to prevent significant loss. Generally, a traditional, broad-based international fund, rather than a single country or regional fund, should be selected because it provides more diversified international risk. As a result, it requires less in the way of detailed selection analysis and evaluation time. These funds can also outperform domestic funds, such as they did in 1985.

Finally, the investor needs to determine the proportions of the total portfolio that should be held in the selected domestic and international funds.

Ideally, the answer would be the combination that provides the largest return for the overall risk of the portfolio. However, in general, foreign stocks have more limited trading and greater price volatility compared to domestic, exchange-listed securities. This behavior means that most foreign stocks have less *liquidity* than their domestic counterparts because they are less likely to be sold quickly and without risk of significant price change from the previous trade. There are also the risks of a declining market plus the *unique risks* of international investing, which include political and economic events, currency restrictions, and weak foreign currencies against the dollar (fewer dollars to the investor upon sale). Thus, unless the investor knows his or her "comfort zone" on the issue of foreign investing, a *10 to 20 percent investment in an international fund appears reasonable*, at least as a starting point.

ENDNOTES

[1] Arthur H. Rogoff, "Time Switching Among Different Mutual Funds: Should-Yous, How Tos," *Sylvia Porter's Personal Finance* (December 1984), pp. 8ff.

[2] For a discussion of timing, see Marion Gordon and Janice Horowicz, "Inside Moves: Market Timing with Mutual Funds," *Personal Investor* (July 1985), pp. 32ff.

[3] For a discussion of this treatment of timing methods, see Rogoff, pp. 8ff.

[4] Robert Runde, "Services that Time Your Trends," *Money* (May 1984), pp. 117ff.

[5] Jerry Edgerton, "Rating the New Market Timers," *Money* (March 1987), pp. 117–120, 122, 124.

[6] John R. Erickson and Albert J. Freedman, "Rating the Raters," *Financial Planning* (December 1984), pp. 193–197.

[7] Michael Sivy, "Market Timing the Technical Way," *Money Guide: The Stock Market* (New York: Time, Inc., 1986), pp. 65–68, 70.

[8] "Moving Average System Followers Lose 120 Points," *Mutual Fund Forecaster* (November 6, 1986), p. 3.

[9] F. E. James, "Monthly Moving Averages—An Effective Investment Tool?" *Journal of Financial and Quantitative Analysis 3* (September 1968), pp. 315–326.

[10] For a discussion of this treatment of portfolio insurance, see Fischer Black and Robert Jones, "Simplifying Portfolio Insurance," *Portfolio Strategy* (August 1986), pp. 1–6; also, Barbara Donnelly, "Portfolio-Insurance Strategies Can Limit Investors' Losses, but Price May Be High," *Wall Street Journal*, January 13, 1987.

[11] Black and Jones, pp. 3–4.

[12] Leslie N. Vreeland, "A Guide to the 10 Biggest Fund Families," *Money* (November 1986), pp. 215ff.

[13] For a useful discussion of these factors, see Eric Schurenberg, "When to Take the Money and Run," *Money* (November 1986), pp. 237–238, 240.

[14] For a discussion of these studies and the general question of international diversification, see Frank K. Reilly, *Investment Analysis and Portfolio Management*, 2nd ed. (New York: Dryden Press, 1985), Chapter 21.

Glossary of Mutual Fund Terms

Adviser   The organization employed by a mutual fund to give professional advice on the fund's investments and asset management practices (also called "investment adviser").

Asked or Offering Price   (As seen in some mutual fund newspaper listings.) The price at which a mutual fund's shares can be purchased. The asked or offering price means the current net asset value per share plus sales charge, if any.

Automatic Reinvestment   An option available to mutual fund shareholders in which fund dividends and capital gains distributions are automatically plowed back into the fund to buy new shares and thereby increase holdings.

Bid or Redemption Price   (As seen in some mutual fund newspaper listings.) The price at which a mutual fund's shares are redeemed (bought back) by the fund. The bid or redemption price usually equals the current net asset value per share.

Broker/Dealer (or Dealer)   A firm that buys and sells mutual fund shares and other securities to the public.

Capital Gains Distributions   Payments to mutual fund shareholders of profits realized on the sale of securities in the fund's portfolio. These amounts usually are distributed to shareholders annually.

Source: Investment Company Institute, *1987 Mutual Fund Fact Book*, pp. 53–55. Reprinted with permission.

Capital Growth   An increase in market value of a mutual fund's securities, as reflected in the net asset value of fund shares. This is a long-term objective of many mutual funds.

Closed-End Investment Company   Unlike mutual funds (known as "open-end" investment companies), closed-end companies issue a limited number of shares and do not redeem them (buy them back). Instead, closed-end shares are traded in the securities markets, with supply and demand determining the price.

Contractual Plan   A program for the accumulation of mutual fund shares in which the investor agrees to invest a fixed amount on a regular basis for a specified number of years. A substantial portion of the sales charge applicable to the total investment is usually deducted from early payments.

Custodian   The organization (usually a bank) that keeps custody of securities and other assets of a mutual fund.

Diversification   The mutual fund policy of spreading its investments among a number of different securities to reduce the risks inherent in investing. The average investor would find it difficult to amass a portfolio as diversified as that of a mutual fund.

Dollar-Cost Averaging   Investing equal amounts of money at regular intervals regardless of whether securities markets are moving up or down. This practice reduces average share costs to the investor who acquires more shares in periods of lower securities prices and fewer shares in periods of higher prices. Unlike a contractual plan, dollar-cost averaging is voluntary.

Exchange Privilege   Enables mutual fund shareholders to transfer their investment from one fund to another within the same fund family as shareholder needs or objectives change. Usually funds let investors use the exchange privilege several times a year for a low or no fee per exchange.

Income Dividends   Payments to mutual fund shareholders of dividends, interest and/or short-term capital gains earned on the fund's portfolio of securities after deducting operating expenses.

Investment Adviser   See Adviser.

Investment Company   A corporation, trust, or partnership which invests pooled funds of shareholders in securities appropriate to the fund's objective. Among the benefits of investment companies are professional management and diversification. Mutual funds ("open-end" investment companies) are the most popular type of investment company.

Investment Objective The goal—such as long-term capital growth, current income, growth and income, etc.—which an investor or a mutual fund pursues. Each fund's objective is stated in its prospectus.

Long-Term Funds An industry designation for all funds other than short-term funds (money market and short-term municipal bond). The two broad categories of long-term funds are equity (stock) and bond and income funds.

Management Fee The amount paid by mutual funds to their investment advisers. The average annual fee industrywide is about one-half of one percent of fund assets.

Mutual Fund An investment company that pools money from shareholders and invests in a variety of securities, including stocks, bonds, and money market securities. A mutual fund stands ready to buy back (redeem) its shares at their current net asset value. The value of the shares depends on the market value of the fund's portfolio securities at the time. Most mutual funds offer new shares continuously.

Net Asset Value Per Share The market worth of a mutual fund's total assets—securities, cash, and any accrued earnings—after deducting liabilities, divided by the number of shares outstanding.

Open-End Investment Company The statutory terminology for a mutual fund, indicating that it stands ready to redeem (buy back) its shares on demand.

Over-The-Counter Market The market for securities transactions conducted through a communications network connecting dealers in stocks and bonds. The rules of such trading are written and enforced by the National Association of Securities Dealers, Inc. (NASD), the same organization that provides self-policing of member firms in the distribution of mutual fund shares.

Payroll Deduction Plan An arrangement some employers offer whereby employees may accumulate shares in a mutual fund. Employees authorize their employer to deduct a specified amount from their salary at stated times and transfer the proceeds to the fund.

Periodic Payment Plan See Contractual Plan.

Prospectus The official booklet that describes a mutual fund. The prospectus contains information as required by the U.S. Securities and Exchange Commission on such subjects as the fund's investment objectives and policies, services, investment restrictions, officers and directors, how shares are bought and redeemed, fund fees and other charges and the fund's financial statements.

Redemption Price   The amount per share mutual fund shareholders receive when they liquidate their shares (also known as the "bid price").

Reinvestment Privilege   A service provided by most mutual funds for the automatic reinvestment of shareholder dividends and capital gains distributions into additional shares.

Sales Charge   An amount charged to purchase shares in many mutual funds sold by brokers or other members of a sales force. Typically the charge ranges from 4 to 8.5 percent of the initial investment. The charge is added to the net asset value per share when determining the offering price.

Short-Term Funds   An industry designation for money market and short-term municipal bond funds. Due to the special nature of these funds and the huge, continuous inflows and outflows of money they experience, they are rarely viewed in terms of sales figures, as long-term funds are. Tracking changes in total assets is usually the preferred method of following trends in short-term funds.

Transfer Agent   The organization employed by a mutual fund to prepare and maintain records relating to the accounts of its shareholders.

12b-1 Fee   Fee charged by some funds and named after the 1980 Securities and Exchange Commission rule that permits them. Such fees pay for distribution costs such as advertising or for commissions paid to brokers. The fund's prospectus details 12b-1 charges, if applicable.

Underwriter   The organization that acts as the distributor of a mutual fund's shares to broker-dealers and investors.

Unit Investment Trust   An investment company that purchases a fixed portfolio of income-producing securities. Units in the trust are sold to investors by brokers.

Variable Annuity   An investment contract sold to an investor by an insurance company. Capital is accumulated, often through investment in a mutual fund, and converted to an income stream at a future date, perhaps retirement. Income payments vary with the value of the account.

Withdrawal Plan   A program in which shareholders receive payments from their mutual fund investments at regular intervals. Typically, these payments are drawn from the fund's dividends and capital gains distributions, if any, and from principal, as needed. Many mutual funds offer these plans.

Glossary of Retirement Plans

Federal income tax laws permit the establishment of a number of types of retirement plans, each of which may be funded with mutual fund shares.

Individual Retirement Accounts   All wage-earners under the age of 70½ may set up an Individual Retirement Account (IRA). The individual may contribute as much as 100 percent of his or her compensation each year, up to $2,000. Earnings are tax-deferred until withdrawal. The amount contributed each year may be wholly or partially tax-deductible. Under the Tax Reform Act of 1986, all taxpayers not covered by employer-sponsored retirement plans can continue to take the full deduction for IRA contributions. Those who are covered or who are married to someone who is covered must have an adjusted gross income of no more than $25,000 (single) or $40,000 (married, filing jointly) to take the full deduction. The deduction is phased out for incomes between $25,000 and $35,000 (single) and $40,000 and $50,000 (married, filing jointly). An individual who qualifies for an IRA and has a spouse who either has no earnings or elects to be treated as having no earnings, may contribute up to 100 percent of his or her income or $2,250, whichever is less.

Simplified Employee Pensions (SEPs)   SEPs are employer-sponsored plans that may be viewed as an aggregation of separate IRAs. In a SEP, the employer contribution, limited to $30,000 or 15 percent of compensation, whichever is less, is made to an Individual Retirement Account maintained for the employee.

Source: Investment Company Institute, *1987 Mutual Fund Fact Book*, p. 43. Reprinted with permission.

Section 403(b) Plans   Section 403(b) of the Internal Revenue Code permits employees of certain charitable organizations and public school systems to establish tax-sheltered retirement programs. These plans may be invested in either annuity contracts or mutual fund shares.

Section 401(k) Plans   One particularly popular type of plan which may be offered by either corporate or noncorporate entities is the 401(k) plan. A 401(k) plan is a tax-qualified profit-sharing plan that includes a "cash or deferred" arrangement. The cash or deferred arrangement permits employees to have a portion of their compensation contributed to a tax-sheltered plan on their behalf or paid to them directly as additional taxable compensation. Thus an employee may elect to reduce his or her taxable compensation with contributions to a 401(k) plan where those amounts will accumulate tax-free. The Tax Reform Act of 1986 established new, tighter antidiscrimination requirements for 401(k) plans and has curtailed the amount of elective deferrals which may be made by all employees. Nevertheless, 401(k) plans remain excellent retirement savings vehicles.

Corporate and Self-Employed Retirement Plans   Tax-qualified pension and profit-sharing plans may be established by corporations or self-employed individuals. Changes in the tax laws have made retirement plans for employees of corporations and those for self-employed individuals essentially comparable. Contributions to a plan are tax-deductible and earnings accumulate on a tax-sheltered basis.

The maximum annual amount which may be contributed to a defined contribution plan on behalf of an individual is limited to the lesser of 25 percent of the individual's compensation or $30,000.

Glossary of Other Selected Terms Used in This Book

Accumulation Plan   A voluntary or contractual plan for the acquisition of fund shares.

Administrative Expenses   The fund expenses paid directly by the fund.

Advisory Contract   The contract between the fund and its investment adviser.

Advisory Fee   The fee paid by the fund to the investment adviser for managing the fund.

Alpha (Coefficient)   See Appendix.

Back-End Load Fund   A fund that imposes a contingent deferred sales charge upon share redemption.

Bankers' Acceptances   Defined in Chapter 3.

Bear Market   A market characterized by a downward trend in securities prices.

Benchmark Market Portfolio   A measure of the overall market's risk and return that permits comparison of a fund's return for the same risk class.

Beta (Coefficient)   See Appendix.

Bid-Ask Spread   The difference between the current highest bid (purchase) price for a security and the current lowest offer (sales) price for the security.

Many of the general terms are defined from the point of view of mutual funds.

Blue-Sky Laws   State securities laws that exist for investor protection.

Board of Directors   Those individuals elected by shareholders to be responsible for the fund's overall management.

Bonus Fee   An additional, contractural fee paid by a fund to its investment adviser for a high level of investment performance.

Book Entry Notation   The shareholder's shares are maintained as book entry notations by the fund's transfer agent rather than as certificates held by the shareholder.

Broker   An agent who buys/sells securities for funds.

Bull Market   A market characterized by an upward trend in securities prices.

Buy-and-Hold Strategy   A strategy using an "unmanaged" portfolio, with no effort to select undervalued securities or to forecast ("time") turns in market trends.

Capital Appreciation   An increase in the market value of a fund's portfolio.

Cash (Distribution) Option   The fund shareholder elects to receive both dividend (income) and capital gains distributions in cash.

CDA Rating   See Appendix.

Characteristic Line   A measure of fund systematic risk based on the relationship between fund returns and market returns.

Coefficient of Determination (R^2)   See Appendix.

Commercial Paper   Defined in Chapter 3.

Commingled Fund   Defined in Chapter 3.

Commingled Real Estate Fund (CREF)   See Chapter 2.

Common Stock   Owner shares in a fund that have a residual claim on income and assets.

Conservation of Principal   Use of conservative securities to guard against a decline in the value of a fund's portfolio.

Consumer Price Index (CPI)   A general cost-of-living index (measure) based on a representative "market basket" of goods.

Contingent Deferred Sales Charge   A moderate fund charge imposed by some funds on shares redeemed prior to a specified period since their purchase—the charges typically decline to zero over a specified number of years.

Corporate Bond   A marketable, long-term debt obligation of a corporation.

Corporation Account   A fund account registered in a corporation's name by a duly authorized officer.

Correlation   A measure of the degree of association in the returns on two fund portfolios.

Covariance   A measure of the degree of co-movement in the returns on two fund portfolios.

Current Income   Current dividend (income) distribution from a fund.

Defined Benefit Plan   A Keogh or corporate retirement plan that permits employers to contribute the estimated amount needed to fund a predetermined annual employee retirement benefit.

Defined Contribution Plan   A Keogh or corporate retirement plan that permits three plan contribution options: variable percentage, fixed percentage, and a combination of the variable and fixed options.

Degree of Diversification   See "Coefficient of Determination."

Distribution   A fund payment of realized net income to shareholders, which can include a dividend (income) distribution and/or a capital gains distribution.

Diversification (Types)   See Chapter 7.

Diversified Closed-End Fund   See Chapter 2.

Diversified Investment Company   A fund that meets the asset, diversification, and other criteria required under law.

Diversified Money Market Fund   A fund that invests from among several types of money market securities, especially commercial paper, U.S. Treasury securities, and repurchase agreements.

Dividend Distribution   See "Income Distribution."

Dow-Jones Industrial Average (DJIA)   The most well-known measure of the performance of the overall stock market as represented by an index of 30 "blue chip" stocks.

Dual-Purpose Fund   See Chapter 2.

Efficient Markets Hypothesis   The "semi-strong" version of this theory states that the market correctly prices securities based on known, relevant information; thus, there are no opportunities to buy securities for less than their true value.

Eurodollar CD   Defined in Chapter 3.

Ex-Dividend Date   The date after which the purchaser will not receive the current fund distribution.

Expense Ratio   A measure of fund expense performance computed by dividing total expenses by average annual net assets.

Face-Amount Certificate Company   See Chapter 2.

Family of Funds (Fund Family)   A group of diverse funds sponsored by one management company.

Front-End Load Fund   A fund that charges an upfront sales charge.

Full-Service Broker   A broker who offers investment advice and charges higher commissions than "discount" brokers.

Fund   An abbreviation for "mutual fund."

Fund Distributor   The organization responsible for selling fund shares to the public (no-load funds) or to securities dealers and others for resale to the public (load funds).

Fund Redemption   Shareholder "sale" of fund shares by use of any of several prearranged fund services, including "special" checks, telephone, electronic funds transfer, automatic redemption, and by written request.

GNMA-Backed Mortgage Security   A security issued by the Government National Mortgage Association which represents an investment in a pool of mortgages.

Gross Return   A fund's "Rate of Return" gross of fund expenses.

Income-Earned (Distribution) Option   The fund shareholder elects to receive dividend distributions in cash, and capital gains distributions are reinvested in additional shares.

Individual Ownership Account   A fund account owned by one individual.

Inefficient Portfolio   A fund portfolio that earns a smaller return than the overall market for the same risk class.

Institutional Investor   A large, professional manager of client and other portfolios (e.g., bank trust department).

International Diversification   The use of domestic and international funds in the investor's portfolio to reduce overall portfolio risk for the level of return.

Investor   A person seeking consistent, moderate securities profits ("returns") over time.

Joint Tenant Account   An account with joint ownership (e.g., man and wife) in which the deceased's ownership share reverts to his or her estate.

Joint Tenants with Right of Survivorship Account   An account with joint ownership in which full ownership of the account reverts to the surviving owner.

Keogh Plan   A qualifying retirement plan for persons with full or part-time self-employment income.

Letter Stock   See Chapter 10.

Leverage   See Chapter 10.

Liquidity   The ability to convert a security to cash quickly and without a significant price concession from the previous trade.

Load Fund   A mutual fund that uses brokerage firms and other sales organizations to sell its shares to the public at NAV plus a sales ("load") charge.

Low-Load Fund   A fund that charges a low upfront sales charge.

Management Advisory Fee   See "Management Fee."

Management Company   The firm that organized the fund and controls it through its role as investment adviser.

Margin   See Chapter 10.

Market Timing   A strategy in which portfolio management includes efforts to forecast turns in market trends.

Maturity Diversification   The weighted-average maturity (days) of the securities in a money market fund.

Miscellaneous Load Fund   A mutual fund that imposes only nominal dollar charges or fees of any kind.

Money Market   The market for low risk, highly-liquid, short-term debt securities.

Money Market (Mutual) Fund   A mutual fund that invests primarily in short-term instruments, such as Treasury bills, commercial paper, and certificates of deposit.

Moving Average   A method of technical analysis that uses, say, a 200-day moving average of stock or market prices to forecast future price movements.

Municipal Bond   A bond issued by a state or political subdivision, which generally offers interest income exempt from federal taxation.

Mutual Funds (Types)   The various types are defined in Chapters 3 and 10.

Negotiable Certificate of Deposit (CD)   Defined in Chapter 3.

Net Cash Inflow   A measure of a fund's cash position computed by the difference between fund sales and redemptions over a period of time.

Net Realized Capital Gains (Losses)   The gains (losses) from the sale of fund securities that have higher (lower) prices than their purchase cost.

Net Return   A fund's "Rate of Return" net of fund expenses.

No-Load Fund   A fund that sells its shares directly to the public at NAV, with no load charges, 12-bl fees, and no more than small redemption fees.

Odd Lot (opposite of "Round" Lot)   A trade of less than 100 shares of a stock.

Option Contract   The right either to buy or sell 100 shares of a particular security at a specified price for a specific period of time.

Overvalued Stock   A stock selling for more than its "intrinsic" value.

Performance   Refers to a fund's record in earning returns and meeting other investment criteria specified by the investor (Chapter 10).

Portfolio   A group of securities managed collectively.

Portfolio Composition   The types (and percentages) of securities in a money market fund portfolio.

Portfolio Diversification   See "Diversification."

Portfolio Insurance   A strategy for limiting fund losses in falling markets while allowing participation in rising markets.

Portfolio Insurance (various terms)   Defined in Chapter 11.

Portfolio Management   Review of the portfolio selected as needed to "best" meet investor objectives.

Portfolio Turnover   A measure of the average percentage sales/purchase activity of a fund's portfolio.

Price Concession   The amount below (for a sale) or above (for a purchase) the current bid-ask quotation that must be accepted to consummate a trade (transaction).

Professional Management   The professional securities analysts and portfolio managers used by investment advisers to manage fund portfolios.

Puts and Calls   See "Option Contract" and Chapter 10.

Qualified Retirement Plan   A plan that qualifies to offer several tax advantages by meeting IRS requirements.

Quality Diversification   The weighted-average credit quality of the securities in a money market fund.

Random Portfolio Selection   The use of chance to select the securities in an unmanaged portfolio.

Rate of Return (Total Return)   A fund's "total" return is calculated by taking the end-of-the period NAV per share, adding back any per share dividend (income) and capital gains distributions, and computing the percentage change from the beginning-of-the period NAV per share.

Real Estate Investment Trust (REIT)   See Chapter 2.

Realized Capital-Loss Carryforward   A capital loss that has been realized and that can be offset against a fund's future capital gains.

Redemption Fee   A small charge imposed by some funds on shares redeemed, typically to discourage frequent redemptions.

Registered Fund   A fund "registered" with the Securities and Exchange Commission (SEC) for the sale of shares in the United States.

Regulated Investment Company   A fund that meets the income and diversification criteria required under law to avoid corporate income taxation.

Repurchase Agreement (RP)   Defined in Chapter 3.

Return(s)   See "Rate of Return (Total Return)."

Reward-to-Variability Ratio   A fund performance measure (e.g., Treynor Measure) that relates the "excess" return (over the "risk-free" rate) to total or systematic risk.

Risk   The variability of a fund's returns—the greater the variability, the more the risk (and vice versa).

Risk-Adjusted Performance (Return)   A measure of a fund's return performance adjusted for risk.

Risk and Return Characteristics (Risk/Return Performance)   A description of fund or portfolio performance that incorporates both return and risk.

Risk Class   A category of securities or fund objectives with equal risk.

Risk-Free Rate   The rate on a short-term, default-free security (i.e., a Treasury bill).

Risk Preference (Tolerance)   The investor's feelings about risk, which are used to select a fund with a consistent objective.

Risk Premium   The fund rate of return earned in excess of the "risk-free" rate and that is related to the amount of portfolio risk undertaken.

Risk-Return Preference   The combination of fund risk and return characteristics that best meets the investor's needs.

Round Lot   A trade of 100 shares of stock or multiples thereof.

Sector Fund   A mutual fund that specializes in a narrow segment (type) of securities.

Securities and Exchange Commission (SEC)   The federal agency charged with the regulation of investment companies.

Security Analysis   Determination of the "intrinsic" (fundamental) value of a common stock to see if it is overvalued or undervalued relative to its market price.

Share (Distribution) Option   The fund shareholder elects to have both dividend (income) and capital gains distributions automatically reinvested in additional shares.

Shareholder Services   See Chapter 7.

Short Sale   See Chapter 10.

Specialized Closed-End Fund   See Chapter 2.

Speculator   An active securities trader who seeks profits from short-term price movements.

Standard & Poor's 500 Composite Index (S&P 500)   A measure of the performance of the overall stock market as represented by an index of 500 stocks.

Standard Deviation   See Appendix.

Superior Portfolio Management (Superior Portfolio Performance)   A level of fund portfolio management (performance) that provides returns exceeding those of the overall stock market or the market risk class equivalent to the fund's risk.

Superior Rate-of-Return (Superior Rate-of-Return Management or Performance)   A level of fund rate of return that is greater than the overall market for the same risk class.

Switch   Transfer of monies between funds in a fund "family."

Systematic Risk (Market-Related Risk)   The type of risk that cannot normally be eliminated through portfolio diversification—measured by the variability of portfolio returns relative to overall market returns.

Tax-Exempt Money Fund   A fund that invests in short-term, high-quality municipal securities, including municipal notes and bonds.

Tax Reform Act of 1986   A major tax-reform act that dramatically lowered marginal tax rates.

Tax Shelter   See Chapter 2.

Tax Terms (various)   See Chapter 6.

Taxable-Equivalent Yield   The yield on a tax-exempt security that is equivalent to the before-tax yield on a taxable security.

Technical Analysis   The analysis of past securities price and volume data as a means of predicting future price movements.

Total Risk   See "Standard Deviation."

Trading Cost   The cost of a security transaction which includes any brokerage commission and price concession.

Treasury Bill   Defined in Chapter 3.

Treynor Measure (of Portfolio Performance)   A measure of portfolio performance computed by taking its rate of return less the risk-free rate as a percentage of the portfolio's systematic risk.

True No-Load Fund   A fund that sells its shares directly to the public at NAV, with no load charges, 12-bl fees, or redemption fees.

Trust Account   A fiduciary account established and owned by the beneficiary's trustee (e.g., bank).

Undervalued Stock (opposite of "Overvalued")   A stock selling for less than its "intrinsic" value.

U.S. Agency Security   Defined in Chapter 3.

U.S. Federal Agency Security   A security issued by a government-sponsored or government-owned agency.

U.S. Treasury Bond   A marketable long-term debt obligation of the U.S. Treasury.

U.S. Treasury Money Fund   A money market fund that invests in short-term U.S. Treasury securities, securities guaranteed by the U.S. government, and high-quality repurchase agreements involving the above securities.

Unmanaged Portfolio (Portfolio Buy-and-Hold Strategy)   Use of a market index to represent a portfolio that does not reflect the ability to select undervalued securities or forecast turns in market trends.

Unsystematic Risk (Company-Related Risk)   The type of risk that can be effectively eliminated through efficient fund portfolio diversification.

Variable Life Insurance   See Chapter 2.

Whipsawing   Losses that occur when a technical indicator gives a "buy" or "sell" signal and the market reverses course (e.g., buy signal followed by market decline).

Yankee CD   Defined in Chapter 3.

Appendix

CDA Mutual Fund Report
12/31/86

This material is reproduced
with the permission of:
CDA Investment Technologies, Inc.
11501 Georgia Avenue
Silver Spring, MD 20902
(301/942-1700)

Preface

Overview

The **CDA MUTUAL FUND REPORT** is issued monthly, with supplemental information at the end of each calendar quarter and still further supplemental information at the end of each calendar year. Coverage at the end of 1986 was almost 900 funds with nearly $360 billion in assets. Virtually all equity and fixed income funds are included, but not money market funds. Reports are mailed to subscribers within a few days of each monthend.

Detailed contents of each report are presented below. Here's a recap of the key information which is provided:

I. Monthly
  A. An alphabetic listing showing each fund's management company affiliation, investment objective, asset size, net asset value per share, load fee, yield, and rates of return for 10 years, 5 years, 3 years, 1 year, current month, year-to-date, each of the prior 3 calendar years, an "up" market and a "down" market. Also included is our proprietary "CDA Rating" for each fund.

  B. Top 50 tables, showing the best funds by CDA Rating, 10-year performance, 5-year performance, 3-year performance, 12-month performance and year-to-date performance.

  C. Funds ranked by CDA Rating within each investment objective category.

II. Quarterly
  A. An alphabetic listing showing each fund's asset allocation (cash, bonds, preferred, common), latest quarter return (with and without income), modern portfolio theory statistics (risk, diversification, risk-adjusted return), and income and capital gains distributions for the latest 12 months as well as month-by-month for the latest quarter.

  B. A directory showing the address and phone number of each mutual fund, arranged by management company groups.

III. Annually
  An alphabetic listing showing each fund's performance quarter-by quarter for the latest calendar year, and year-by-year for the latest decade.

All performance statistics throughout the report are computed without regard to load fees and income taxes. Both income and capital gains distributions are assumed to be reinvested at the end of the month in which they are ex-dividend. Whenever the data for a specific calculation is not available, the notation "na" will appear on the report. More detailed column-by-column descriptions appear below.

Monthly Alphabetic Listing

MGT CO. A six-character code for each mutual fund management company. The names which correspond to these codes are furnished with our quarterly supplemental report.

IO. Investment objective code. We have divided the funds into eight groups. Initially, we accept the fund's own determination of where it should be classified. Semi-annually we review the classifications and revise them as dictated by portfolio composition, income yield, and risk measures. Our groups are:

> IN- International funds which invest primarily in the securities of companies domiciled outside of the U.S.

> AG- Aggressive Growth funds seeking maximum capital appreciation.

> G- Growth funds emphasizing long-term growth of capital.

> GI- Growth & Income funds seeking a combination of long-term growth and current income.

> MB- Municipal Bond funds which invest in tax-exempt issues of municipalities.

> BP- Bond & Preferred funds whose investments consist of government and corporate debt and corporate preferred stocks.

> B- Balanced funds which invest in both fixed income and equity securities.

> ME- Metals funds which concentrate in precious or strategic metals issues.

ASSETS MIL$. The total net assets of the fund, in millions of dollars, as of the prior quarterend.

NAV. Net asset value per share (i.e., bid price) at the most recent monthend.

MAX LOAD. Maximum front-end sales charge, expressed as a percent of the monthend offering price. An asterisk indicates that the fund also has a redemption fee or deferred sales charge.

% YLD. Yield: the sum of the latest 12 months income distributions as a percent of the monthend adjusted offering price. (The adjusted offering price is equal to the offering price, plus the latest 3 months capital gains distributions, plus half of the prior 6 months capital gains distributions.)

PCNT. The percent rate of return for the indicated period, assuming all income and capital gains distributions were reinvested. Returns for 3, 5 and 10 years are annualized. Returns for other periods are not annualized.

RK. A rank, from 1 to 99, assigned to each fund for each time period. The ranks may be thought of as percentiles. A rank of 1 signifies the highest return; 99 signifies the lowest.

UP MKT and DOWN MKT. Market cycles as defined by a swing in the S&P index of 10% or more from monthend-to-monthend. The dates of the cycles are printed on the last line of the Alphabetic Listing.

CDA RATING. A composite percentile rating, from 1 (best) to 99 (worst), based upon the fund's performance over past market cycles (2 up markets and 2 down markets if available, but not less than 1 up market and 1 down market). Extra weight is given to the most recent performance; and funds are penalized for inconsistency. The best-rated funds will be those who have done well in different market environments, whose recent performance continues strong, and whose comparative results haven't fluctuated wildly over varying time periods.

A **Summary by Investment Objective** appears at the botton of the Alphabetic Listing. We show the number of funds in each investment objective group, total assets of the group, and average yield, rates of return and ranks for each time period. (The averages are equal-weighted; i.e., every fund is given the same weight no matter what its asset size.) Also shown are the returns for the Standard & Poor 500-Stock Index, the Salomon Brothers High-Grade Corporate Bond Index and 30-day U.S. Treasury bills. The index returns are adjusted for reinvestment of all income.

Top 50 Tables

The format of the Top 50 Tables is exactly the same as the format of the Alphabetic Listing. However, the funds are printed in order of their performance instead of alphabetically. Six Top 50 Tables are included in our monthly report:

1. Top 50 Funds by CDA Rating
2. Top 50 Funds by 10-Year Performance
3. Top 50 Funds by 5-Year Performance
4. Top 50 Funds by 3-Year Performance
5. Top 50 Funds by 12-Month Performance
6. Top 50 Funds by Year-to-Date Performance

Funds Ranked by CDA Rating Within Investment Objective

The final table included in the monthly report shows all of the funds categorized within our eight investment objective groups. Opposite each fund is its CDA Rating; and the funds are printed in order of their rating from best-to-worst. If the CDA Rating for a fund is not available ("na"), the fund appears alphabetically at the bottom of the list.

This table is furnished for the convenience of those subscribers who may be searching for a fund with a particular investment objective (e.g., International). Once the better-rated funds in a particular group are identified, a more complete record of their performance is readily available from the Alphabetic Listing.

Quarterly Supplement

Immediately after the end of each calendar quarter, we furnish a supplementary alphabetic listing of all funds showing their asset mix, quarterly performance, modern portfolio theory statistics, and income and capital gains distributions. Additionally, we provide a directory which lists all of the mutual fund management company codes, their corresponding names, and the address and phone number of each fund in the group. The directory is sequenced by 6-character management company codes as the appear in the Monthly Alphabetic Listing.

The columnar information in the quarterly alphabetic supplement is explained below:

IO. Investment objective code. See the description above under Monthly Alphabetic Listing.

ASSETS (MIL$). The total net assets of the fund, in millions of dollars, as of the date indicated.

ANNL %EXP RATE. Annual management fees, operating expenses and 12b-1 fees (if applicable) as a percentage of the average net assets of the fund. An asterisk denotes that the fund has a 12b-1 plan for recovery of marketing and distribution expenses.

PERCENT OF ASSETS. Asset mix expressed in terms of the percentage commitment of: (1) cash; (2) non-convertible bonds; (3) non-convertible preferred stock; (4) convertible securities; and (5) common stock. The percentages are as of the prior quarterend date, and will sum to 100 except for rounding errors.

LATEST QTR ROR. The percent rate of return for the latest quarter. The TOTAL return assumes reinvestment of all income and capital gains distributions; while the PRINCIPAL return assumes reinvestment of capital gains only.

36 MONTH MPT STATISTICS. Modern Portfolio Theory statistics which measure each fund's diversification, risk, and risk-adjusted rate of return. For the statistically inclined, the various measures are based upon linear regression over the most recent 36-month period. The dependent variable is the fund's monthly return reduced by the risk-free return of Treasury bills, expressed in continuously compounded form. The independent variable is the monthly return for the S&P 500 (including income) reduced by the T-bill return, also expressed in continuously compounded form. The individual MPT statistics are computed and interpreted as follows:

R2. R-squared, known statistically as the coefficient of determination, is an indication of the fund's diversification. It measures the percentage of the fund's performance variation which can be traced to the overall market. R-squared ranges between 0 and 100. A fund which has an R-squared of 85, for example, is 85% as diversified as the S&P 500. This means that 85% of the fund's risk is market-related, and the other 15% is attributable to the fund's unique characteristics.

STD DEV. Standard deviation is a measure of the fund's total risk. Statistically, it reflects the dispersion of the dependent variable, converted to monthly compounding. If two funds each had a 36% return over 3 years, and one fund achieved the 36% at the rate of roughly 1% every month, while the second fund was + 12% the first month, then –8%, then + 14%, then –11%, etc., clearly the second fund is more risky than the first, and its standard deviation would be correspondingly higher. Generally, the standard deviation is used in a relative sense, to compare one fund's risk against another. But it also may be used in an absolute sense: If a fund's standard deviation were, let us say, 3.6%, then its return for about 2 out of every 3 months would fall within a range plus or minus 3.6 percentage points from the fund's average monthly return. And its return for about 19 out of 20 months would fall within a range plus or minus 7.2 percentage points from its average.

BETA. The beta coefficient is a measure of the fund's volatility relative to the S&P 500 index. Statistically, it is the regression coefficient, or slope of the regression line. If beta is 1.00, it means that the fund is approximately as volatile as the market. If beta is 1.50, the fund is one-and-a-half times as volatile; and if beta is .75, the fund is 3/4ths as volatile. Beta reflects only the market-related portion of the fund's risk. Accordingly, it is a narrower measure than standard deviation, which reflects total risk (both market-related and unique). On the other hand, an investor can reduce, even eliminate, the unique risk by combining his investment in the fund with an investment in other assets that behave dissimilarly (i.e., by diversifying). For example, if two assets both have very high standard deviations, but one asset always appreciates when the other depreciates, and vice-versa, then a portfolio of the two assets would be of much lower risk than either asset taken alone. Beta is the preferred measure of risk in this context, because it reflects that portion of the risk which can't be further reduced by additional diversification.

ALPHA. The alpha coefficient is a measure of risk-adjusted return. Statistically, it is the intercept of the regression line, expressed as an annually compounded return. Alpha is the difference between the fund's actual performance and the performance anticipated in light of the fund's risk and the market's behavior. To illustrate, suppose the S&P 500 was up 15%, risk-free T-bills earned 9%, and the fund advanced 18%. Suppose further that the fund had a beta of 1.25. Since the fund was 25% riskier than the market, it should have out-performed the market. More specifically, an investor in the overall stock market would have done 6 percentage points better than a risk-free return (i.e., 15% for the S&P 500 minus 9% for T-bills). If the market's "risk premium" was 6 percentage points, then the fund's risk premium should have been 1.25 x 6, or 7.5 percentage points. Actually, the fund out-paced T-bills by 9 percentage points (18% minus 9%). Accordingly, the fund did 1.5 points better than expected, and its alpha coefficient would have been 1.5%. We show the annual percent alpha under the PCNT column, and its percentile rank (1 equals highest, 99 equals lowest) under the RK column.

DISTRIBUTION INFORMATION. Nine columns of information are tabulated under this caption. First, we show the latest quarterend bid price, or net asset value per share (N.A.V.). Then we record the per-share income distributions each month during the prior quarter, as well as the total for the most recent 12 months. Finally, we show per-share capital gains distributions, also month-by-month for the latest quarter plus a 12-month total.

A **Summary by Investment Objective** appears at the bottom of the Quarterly Supplement. We show the number of funds in each investment objective group, total assets of the group, and the average asset mix, quarterly performance, and modern portfolio theory statistics. (The averages are equal-weighted; i.e., every fund is given the same weight no matter what its asset size.) Also shown are the quarterly return and MPT statistics for the S&P 500 index, adjusted for reinvested income.

Annual Supplement

During the first week of January each year, we provide another supplementary listing of all funds showing their quarter-by-quarter performance for the year just ended, as well as their year-by-year performance for each of the prior 10 years. The columnar information in the annual alphabetic supplement is explained below:

IO. Investment objective code. See the description above under Monthly Alphabetic Listing.

ASSETS (MIL$). The total net assets of the fund, in millions of dollars, as of the date indicated.

PCNT. The percent rate of return for the quarters and years indicated, assuming all income and capital gains distributions were reinvested.

RK. A rank, from 1 to 99, assigned to each fund for each time period. The ranks may be thought of as percentiles. A rank of 1 signifies the highest rank; 99 signifies the lowest.

A **Summary by Investment Objective** appears at the bottom of the Annual Supplement. We show the number of funds in each investment objective group, the total assets of the group, and the average rates of return and ranks for each time period. (The averages are equal-weighted; i.e., every fund is given the same weight no matter what its asset size.) Also shown are the returns for the S&P 500, the Salomon Brothers High-Grade Corporate Bond Index, 30-day U.S. Treasury bills and the Consumer Price Index. The market returns are adjusted for reinvestment of all income.

Monthly—Alphabetic

CDA MONTHLY ALPHABETIC LISTING – 12/31/86

FUND	MGT CO	IO	ASSETS MIL$	NAV	MAX LOAD	% YLD	10 YEARS PCNT RK	5 YEARS PCNT RK	3 YEARS PCNT RK
ABT EMERGING GROWTH	MIDWES	AG	34	8.77	8.5	0.0	na --	na --	17.8 19
ABT GROWTH & INCOME TR.	MIDWES	GI	116	11.34	8.5	3.0	13.4 53	16.0 61	15.8 33
ABT SECURITY INCOME	MIDWES	GI	18	11.10	8.5	0.8	na --	na --	9.7 76
ABT UTILITY INCOME FD	MIDWES	GI	124	14.98	8.5	5.3	na --	14.3 73	19.6 10
ACORN FUND	HARRIS	G	395	39.27	0.0	1.2	20.1 10	20.0 23	19.1 13
AFFILIATED FUND	LD-ABT	GI	3008	10.50	7.2	4.4	15.0 39	20.9 18	18.5 15
AFUTURE FUND	CARLIL	AG	19	12.49	0.0	0.9	12.1 68	5.8 96	-2.6 95
AGE HIGH INCOME FUND	FRNKRE	BP	1141	3.67	4.0	12.7	10.2 83	17.0 51	13.4 55
ALLIANCE CONVERTIBLE	ALLIAN	BP	62	9.48	5.5	na	na --	na --	na --
ALLIANCE COUNTERPOINT	ALLIAN	G	37	14.11	5.5	1.7	na --	na --	na --
ALLIANCE HIGH GRADE BOND	ALLIAN	BP	7	12.15	0.0	6.5	na --	na --	na --
ALLIANCE HIGH YIELD BOND	ALLIAN	BP	267	9.71	5.5	12.8	na --	na --	na --
ALLIANCE INTERNATIONAL	ALLIAN	IN	164	21.07	8.5	0.1	na --	na --	na --
ALLIANCE MORTGAGE SECS	ALLIAN	BP	737	9.74	5.5	10.3	na --	na --	na --
ALLIANCE TECHNOLOGY	ALLIAN	AG	133	23.11	8.5	0.0	na --	na --	5.7 88
ALPHA FUND	MONTAG	G	24	6.97	8.5	2.7	15.2 38	19.0 34	10.0 75
AMA GROWTH FUND, INC.	AMA	G	27	10.56	0.0	1.3	11.9 68	13.5 77	13.1 57
AMA INCOME FUND, INC.	AMA	BP	21	9.41	0.0	7.4	9.0 91	15.8 63	13.1 56
AMCAP FUND	CAPRES	G	1385	9.63	8.5	1.7	20.3 9	16.7 54	11.9 64
AMERICAN BALANCED FUND	CAPRES	B	162	10.83	8.5	5.0	13.1 58	20.0 23	18.2 17
AMERICAN CAPITAL CORP BD	AM-CAP	BP	118	7.29	8.5	10.2	9.2 90	18.2 43	15.3 38
AMERICAN CAP COMSTOCK	AM-CAP	G	896	14.60	8.5	2.2	20.3 9	18.4 40	10.2 74
AMERICAN CAP ENTERPRISE	AM-CAP	G	577	12.78	8.5	1.7	17.3 20	14.0 74	10.6 72
AMERICAN CAP GOV SECS	AM-CAP	BP	8068	11.69	6.7	7.3	na --	na --	na --
AMERICAN CAPITAL GROWTH	AM-CAP	AG	26	22.86	0.0	0.4	na --	9.4 91	1.1 93
AMERICAN CAPITAL HARBOR	AM-CAP	GI	267	13.43	8.5	5.4	15.7 33	19.6 27	10.6 72
AMERICAN CAPTL HIYLD INV	AM-CAP	BP	520	9.79	6.7	12.7	na --	16.9 52	13.2 56
AMERICAN CAPITAL PACE FD	AM-CAP	G	2133	22.56	8.5	2.6	25.0 1	19.1 33	10.4 73
AMERICAN CAPITAL OTC SEC	AM-CAP	G	95	8.30	8.5	0.2	na --	na --	-0.7 94
AMERICAN CAPITAL VENTURE	AM-CAP	AG	335	14.55	8.5	1.4	20.5 9	13.6 76	3.4 91
AMERICAN CAPITAL MUNI BD	AM-CAP	MB	159	21.23	4.7	7.0	na --	na --	na --
AMERICAN GROWTH FUND	INVSMT	GI	65	7.57	8.4	3.3	14.9 41	12.3 82	5.9 88
AMERICAN HERITAGE FUND	HERTGE	AG	1	1.42	0.0	0.0	3.5 98	-7.9 99	-21.2 99
AMERICAN INVESTORS FUND	AM-INV	AG	67	6.45	0.0	0.0	5.5 97	-6.7 99	-4.4 97
AMERICAN INVS INCOME	AM-INV	BP	22	8.85	0.0	12.5	9.8 86	11.4 85	6.3 87
AMERICAN LEADERS FUND	FEDRES	GI	116	12.49	0.0	3.8	na --	17.8 45	17.5 21
AMERICAN MUTUAL FUND	CAPRES	GI	1992	17.99	8.5	3.5	17.4 20	21.4 15	17.9 19
AMERICAN NATIONAL GROWTH	SECRES	AG	90	4.59	8.5	1.1	16.3 25	16.3 58	7.3 83
AMERICAN NATL INC FUND	SECRES	GI	60	19.11	8.5	3.4	na --	14.6 71	10.8 71
AMERICAN TELECOMM TR GR	SHEAR	G	40	77.36	0.0	2.5	na --	na --	na --
AMERICAN TELECOMM TR INC	SHEAR	GI	97	99.20	0.0	5.0	na --	na --	na --
AMEV CAPITAL FUND, INC.	AMEV	G	98	13.73	8.5	0.9	18.8 15	21.1 16	15.5 37
AMEV GROWTH FUND, INC.	AMEV	AG	149	16.37	8.5	0.9	22.5 4	19.6 27	14.2 49
AMEV SPECIAL FUND, INC.	AMEV	AG	23	24.80	0.0	0.6	na --	19.8 25	15.2 39
AMEV US GOV SECURITIES	AMEV	BP	63	10.36	4.5	9.2	9.9 86	15.4 65	14.3 48
AMWAY MUTUAL FUND	AMWAY	G	35	7.82	6.5	1.4	10.8 78	12.8 80	11.7 64
ANALYTIC OPTIONED EQUITY	ANALYT	GI	83	13.70	0.0	3.0	na --	12.6 81	11.2 68
ARMSTRONG ASSOCIATES	PORTFO	G	12	7.99	0.0	1.9	na --	8.8 92	6.0 88
AXE-HOUGHTON INCOME	EW-AXE	BP	46	5.60	0.0	8.9	11.3 73	19.0 35	19.2 12
AXE-HOUGHTON FUND B	EW-AXE	B	182	11.10	0.0	5.0	13.4 54	19.8 25	20.8 7

LATEST 12 MNTHS		THIS MONTH		1986 TO DATE		CALENDAR YEARS						CYCLES				CDA RATING
						1985		1984		1983		UP MKT		DOWN MKT			
PCNT	RK	PCNT	RK	PCNT	RK	PCNT	RK	PCNT	RK	PCNT	RK	PCNT	RK	PCNT	RK		
13.2	58	-5.9	98	13.2	58	46.0	3	-1.1	64	na	--	na	--	na	--	na
16.8	37	-3.4	92	16.8	37	32.9	15	0.1	60	20.5	34	133.9	44	-25.5	89	46
9.6	78	-2.1	73	9.6	78	12.3	93	7.2	36	na	--	na	--	na	--	na
18.3	26	-3.9	96	18.3	26	23.3	52	17.3	2	-2.1	99	121.5	53	-0.4	45	18
23.2	10	5.1	1	23.2	10	31.4	19	4.5	48	25.1	21	164.9	23	-14.7	70	6
22.9	10	-2.7	83	22.9	10	26.8	37	6.9	37	25.5	21	182.7	13	-9.3	61	44
-5.9	97	-4.2	96	-5.9	97	21.5	61	-19.2	95	12.2	69	42.6	96	2.0	39	85
12.8	61	0.4	18	12.8	61	18.8	77	8.7	29	17.9	45	103.3	66	11.9	20	59
na	--	1.2	6	na	--	na	--	na	--	na	--	na	--	na	--	na
20.2	17	-9.4	99	20.2	17	na	--	na	--	na	--	na	--	na	--	na
15.4	46	1.4	5	15.4	46	na	--	na	--	na	--	na	--	na	--	na
11.0	71	0.6	13	11.0	71	na	--	na	--	na	--	na	--	na	--	na
43.9	3	1.1	7	43.9	3	64.5	1	na	--	na	--	na	--	na	--	na
11.1	71	0.3	22	11.1	71	18.7	77	na	--	na	--	na	--	na	--	na
12.0	65	-2.0	71	12.0	65	26.2	40	-16.4	92	46.5	1	193.2	8	na	--	na
13.0	59	-3.4	93	13.0	59	25.1	45	-5.7	76	25.7	20	165.9	22	4.0	34	43
11.0	71	-2.5	80	11.0	71	23.5	51	5.4	44	7.5	89	120.1	53	-20.6	83	65
12.7	61	0.4	19	12.7	61	18.3	79	8.4	32	9.1	83	88.2	82	13.1	17	73
15.6	44	-1.3	56	15.6	44	22.2	58	-0.9	62	19.1	40	128.4	48	1.9	39	9
16.8	37	-0.8	47	16.8	37	29.1	28	9.4	26	16.2	51	148.0	33	6.4	29	36
11.4	70	0.7	13	11.4	70	26.2	40	9.2	27	11.0	74	101.5	67	11.6	20	72
13.5	57	-2.8	85	13.5	57	21.3	63	-2.6	68	18.4	43	125.6	50	14.4	14	10
10.2	76	-2.5	81	10.2	76	29.6	26	-5.2	75	20.0	37	132.8	44	-24.4	87	84
10.5	75	0.3	24	10.5	75	17.1	83	na	--	na	--	na	--	na	--	na
1.9	93	-4.1	96	1.9	93	19.3	75	-15.0	91	10.7	75	94.3	76	na	--	na
13.4	57	-1.3	57	13.4	57	24.0	48	-3.7	71	26.6	17	148.6	32	-9.7	62	28
6.7	87	0.0	33	6.7	87	25.0	45	8.7	30	16.3	51	99.5	70	na	--	na
10.8	73	-2.8	86	10.8	73	22.4	56	-0.7	62	19.4	39	137.7	41	22.3	5	9
-9.7	98	-5.5	98	-9.7	98	23.4	51	-12.1	88	na	--	na	--	na	--	na
4.4	91	-1.8	68	4.4	91	13.1	92	-6.3	78	14.9	58	95.0	75	19.5	6	40
16.3	40	0.3	22	16.3	40	23.0	53	na	--	na	--	na	--	na	--	na
6.3	88	-2.3	77	6.3	88	17.8	80	-5.1	75	17.0	49	98.9	71	-1.3	46	57
-24.6	99	-3.8	95	-24.6	99	-13.6	99	-25.0	96	8.6	85	-18.4	99	-28.6	92	95
-1.7	96	-3.7	95	-1.7	96	14.3	91	-22.4	95	-4.1	99	27.0	98	-43.1	98	96
7.0	86	-0.4	42	7.0	86	22.7	55	-8.4	82	26.9	16	83.3	86	-14.9	71	89
9.5	79	-2.5	81	9.5	79	28.1	31	15.5	4	16.8	49	134.6	43	1.2	41	58
18.4	26	-1.1	54	18.4	26	30.1	23	6.4	40	24.1	24	170.8	18	5.8	30	11
10.9	73	-2.1	73	10.9	73	32.1	17	-15.6	92	17.6	47	125.0	50	3.7	34	26
8.0	84	-2.3	76	8.0	84	27.9	32	-1.5	65	22.8	28	110.3	60	16.9	9	66
19.1	22	-1.8	68	19.1	22	31.9	18	na	--	na	--	na	--	na	--	na
21.1	15	-2.4	78	21.1	15	33.3	14	na	--	na	--	na	--	na	--	na
21.5	14	-2.1	72	21.5	14	31.2	20	-3.5	71	21.1	33	169.0	19	-2.9	48	23
19.5	20	-3.3	91	19.5	20	35.2	10	-7.7	81	23.4	26	161.9	24	-3.4	50	9
20.1	18	-3.0	88	20.1	18	39.3	5	-8.5	83	23.2	26	167.9	20	-11.0	64	14
12.3	64	0.5	17	12.3	64	20.9	65	10.0	23	4.6	96	79.7	87	26.8	2	76
16.1	41	-3.0	87	16.1	41	26.1	41	-4.7	74	19.3	39	109.9	61	-16.0	73	55
10.5	75	-1.4	58	10.5	75	16.5	85	6.8	39	19.2	40	95.9	74	-1.0	46	82
11.3	70	-3.4	92	11.3	70	21.0	65	-11.5	87	11.0	74	76.7	89	na	--	na
15.8	43	0.7	12	15.8	43	26.6	38	15.5	4	7.5	89	109.2	61	18.4	8	39
24.7	8	-1.4	60	24.7	8	32.9	15	6.3	40	11.1	73	145.1	36	-3.9	51	27

CDA MONTHLY ALPHABETIC LISTING – 12/31/86

FUND	MGT CO	IO	ASSETS MIL$	NAV	MAX LOAD	% YLD	ANNUALIZED ROR THRU 12/31/86 10 YEARS PCNT RK	5 YEARS PCNT RK	3 YEARS PCNT RK
AXE-HOUGHTON STOCK FUND	EW-AXE	AG	92	8.11	0.0	0.4	11.7 69	14.2 73	7.1 84
BABSON GROWTH FUND	JONES	G	236	12.95	0.0	3.5	11.4 73	15.7 63	16.0 32
BABSON BOND TRUST	JONES	BP	65	1.69	0.0	9.3	9.7 87	16.9 52	15.8 33
BABSON ENTERPRISE FUND	JONES	G	48	12.12	0.0	0.5	na --	na --	12.3 62
BABSON VALUE FD INC.	JONES	G	6	14.64	0.0	6.1	na --	na --	na --
BARTLETT BASIC VALUE FD	BARTCO	GI	67	12.20	0.0	6.1	na --	na --	15.3 38
BASCOM HILL INVESTORS	MADINV	GI	7	15.11	0.0	3.8	na --	19.1 34	15.0 41
BEACON HILL MUTUAL FUND	BEACON	G	3	24.65	0.0	0.0	11.4 73	14.1 74	13.7 52
BENHAM CALIF TF-INTERMED	BENHAM	MB	135	10.67	0.0	6.3	na --	na --	10.6 72
BENHAM CALIF TF-LONG TRM	BENHAM	MB	194	11.50	0.0	7.0	na --	na --	14.1 50
BENHAM GNMA INCOME FUND	BENHAM	BP	256	10.45	0.0	9.8	na --	na --	na --
BOND FUND OF AMERICA	CAPRES	BP	598	14.21	4.7	9.4	11.2 74	18.9 37	17.7 20
BOSTON CO. CAP. APPREC.	BOSADV	G	422	32.42	0.0	1.4	14.3 44	20.0 23	20.9 7
BOSTON CO. MANAGED INC.	BOSADV	BP	37	11.91	0.0	12.0	na --	na --	16.2 29
BOSTON CO. SPEC GROWTH	BOSADV	G	40	17.21	0.0	1.5	na --	na --	8.9 79
BOWSER GROWTH FUND	COMCAP	G	3	1.82	0.0	0.0	na --	na --	na --
BRUCE FUND	BRUCE	AG	3	109.39	0.0	1.2	na --	22.2 11	23.5 3
BULL & BEAR CAP GROWTH	BULLBR	G	63	10.37	0.0	1.4	14.1 46	10.5 88	8.2 81
BULL & BEAR EQUITY INC.	BULLBR	B	9	11.03	0.0	3.2	13.1 58	16.3 57	17.2 22
BULL & BEAR HIGH YIELD	BULLBR	BP	151	13.57	0.0	13.6	na --	na --	11.0 70
BULLOCK AGGRES GROWTH SH	BULOCK	AG	6	9.41	8.5	0.0	na --	na --	-3.4 96
BULLOCK BALANCED SHARES	BULOCK	B	79	14.81	8.5	4.1	12.9 60	21.7 14	22.6 3
BULLOCK DIVIDEND SHARES	BULOCK	GI	345	3.53	8.5	2.9	13.2 56	21.1 17	19.4 12
BULLOCK GROWTH SHARES	BULOCK	G	159	7.74	8.5	1.2	12.6 64	15.6 64	13.8 52
BULLOCK HIGH INCOME SHS	BULOCK	BP	204	9.93	7.2	13.0	na --	13.9 74	8.8 79
BULLOCK MONTHLY INC SHS	BULOCK	BP	45	12.62	8.5	8.5	9.2 90	19.8 24	17.1 23
BULLOCK TAX-FREE SHARES	BULOCK	MB	111	11.19	4.7	7.2	na --	na --	14.8 43
CALVERT EQUITY	CALVER	G	8	19.89	0.0	0.8	na --	na --	8.0 82
CALVERT INCOME	CALVER	BP	21	16.98	0.0	8.6	na --	na --	16.6 27
CALVERT MANAGED GROWTH	CALVER	B	88	23.48	4.5	2.5	na --	na --	16.9 25
CANADIAN FUND	BULOCK	G	23	7.14	8.5	1.9	10.1 84	8.9 92	4.6 90
CAPITAL PRESERVATION TNT	BENHAM	BP	36	11.04	0.0	8.1	na --	na --	15.2 39
CARNEGIE CAPPIELLO GROW	CARCAP	G	48	14.01	4.5	2.5	na --	na --	na --
CARDINAL FUND	OHIO	G	85	14.64	8.5	2.2	na --	na --	18.5 16
CARDINAL GOVERNMENT GTD	OHIO	BP	127	9.35	4.7	na	na --	na --	na --
CASHMAN FARRELL VALUE FD	TAMCO	G	6	10.01	7.5	na	na --	na --	na --
CENTURY SHARES TRUST	CENSHS	G	150	18.30	0.0	2.7	15.0 38	19.4 30	21.7 5
CHARTER FUND	AIM	G	79	6.22	4.6	2.0	17.8 18	13.9 75	11.7 65
CHEAPSIDE DOLLAR FD LTD	SCHROD	G	46	12.45	0.0	1.9	na --	9.9 89	10.8 71
CHEMICAL FUND	ALLIAN	G	677	6.87	8.5	1.0	11.5 72	13.0 79	11.3 68
CIGNA AGGRESSIVE GROWTH	CIGNA	AG	17	12.10	4.7	0.6	na --	na --	na --
CIGNA GROWTH FUND	CIGNA	G	214	12.91	5.0	2.2	13.0 60	15.4 65	12.2 62
CIGNA HIGH YIELD	CIGNA	BP	246	10.54	5.0	11.1	na --	19.2 32	16.1 30
CIGNA INCOME FUND	CIGNA	BP	254	8.20	5.0	7.4	10.3 82	18.7 38	17.9 19
CIGNA MUNICIPAL BOND FD	CIGNA	MB	258	8.41	5.0	6.6	na --	18.9 36	16.9 25
CIGNA VALUE FUND	CIGNA	G	44	12.26	5.0	3.1	na --	na --	na --
CLIPPER FUND, INC.	PACFIN	GI	67	41.55	0.0	0.0	na --	na --	na --
COLONIAL ADV STRAT GOLD	COLONL	ME	29	17.99	6.7	0.8	na --	na --	na --
COLONIAL EQUITY INC TR	COLONL	G	11	15.81	6.7	2.5	na --	18.9 36	14.6 45
COLONIAL GOV MORTGAGE	COLONL	BP	27	14.36	4.7	6.9	na --	na --	na --

LATEST 12 MNTHS PCNT RK	THIS MONTH PCNT RK	1986 TO DATE PCNT RK	CALENDAR YEARS 1985 PCNT RK	1984 PCNT RK	1983 PCNT RK	CYCLES UP MKT PCNT RK	DOWN MKT PCNT RK	CDA RATING
10.9 72	-3.5 94	10.9 72	31.1 20	-15.5 91	23.7 25	147.7 33	-24.6 87	89
20.1 18	-1.6 62	20.1 18	29.7 25	0.2 59	15.9 52	146.3 34	-21.7 84	75
13.9 54	0.6 15	13.9 54	20.7 67	12.9 11	9.6 81	94.0 77	16.5 10	64
7.5 85	-0.8 48	7.5 85	38.6 6	-5.0 74	na --	na --	na --	na
20.7 16	-2.7 83	20.7 16	26.5 39	na --	na --	na --	na --	na
12.8 61	-2.0 71	12.8 61	25.3 45	8.4 32	na --	na --	na --	na
16.3 40	-1.7 64	16.3 40	31.5 19	-0.5 61	17.7 46	146.3 34	14.5 14	5
6.0 88	-1.4 59	6.0 88	33.5 14	3.8 49	16.6 50	118.6 54	-6.9 55	75
12.6 62	-0.5 43	12.6 62	14.0 91	5.4 43	na --	na --	na --	na
19.4 21	0.4 20	19.4 21	17.8 80	5.7 42	na --	na --	na --	na
11.5 68	0.4 18	11.5 68	na --	na --	na --	na --	na --	na
15.1 47	0.9 10	15.1 47	26.5 38	11.9 15	9.4 82	105.4 64	20.5 6	45
22.5 11	-1.3 57	22.5 11	35.0 10	6.9 37	24.0 24	196.1 8	-20.2 81	52
15.1 47	0.7 13	15.1 47	21.8 60	12.0 15	na --	na --	na --	na
7.7 84	-1.2 56	7.7 84	34.7 11	-10.9 86	na --	na --	na --	na
-23.2 99	-6.7 99	-23.2 99	-6.1 98	na --	na --	na --	na --	na
29.6 6	-4.8 98	29.6 6	37.0 7	6.2 41	17.7 47	213.5 5	-10.6 64	8
3.6 92	-3.1 89	3.6 92	27.8 33	-4.3 73	15.5 55	113.3 57	-28.8 93	83
18.7 25	-1.6 62	18.7 25	25.8 42	7.9 34	11.9 69	121.9 52	-11.3 64	33
6.0 88	0.7 12	6.0 88	21.0 64	6.5 39	na --	na --	na --	na
21.4 14	-1.5 61	21.4 14	10.2 95	-32.6 99	na --	na --	na --	na
19.0 23	-1.6 63	19.0 23	34.2 12	15.5 4	14.5 60	179.8 14	1.6 40	40
21.3 14	-1.7 64	21.3 14	31.0 21	7.0 37	21.0 33	182.9 13	-6.9 55	56
15.7 44	-2.9 86	15.7 44	27.1 36	0.3 59	15.7 53	139.1 40	-10.0 62	57
4.6 91	0.1 29	4.6 91	15.9 87	6.4 40	19.6 38	85.8 84	na --	na
14.0 54	1.3 6	14.0 54	22.4 57	15.2 5	10.0 78	114.7 57	13.4 17	55
16.1 41	-0.4 40	16.1 41	19.4 74	9.1 28	na --	na --	na --	na
12.1 65	-4.1 96	12.1 65	23.6 50	-9.1 84	9.0 84	na --	na --	na
10.1 77	0.4 19	10.1 77	24.0 48	16.0 3	5.1 95	na --	na --	na
18.1 28	-1.3 56	18.1 28	26.7 37	6.7 39	11.2 72	na --	na --	na
2.7 93	0.6 15	2.7 93	14.9 89	-2.9 69	25.0 22	89.6 81	-23.9 86	92
15.5 45	0.2 26	15.5 45	18.1 79	12.1 14	5.0 95	75.9 90	na --	na
12.7 61	-3.3 91	12.7 61	20.1 70	na --	na --	na --	na --	na
19.3 22	-2.7 84	19.3 22	34.1 12	4.0 48	26.6 17	196.8 8	na --	na
na --	0.6 14	na --	na --	na --	na --	na --	na --	na
na --	-1.6 62	na --	na --	na --	na --	na --	na --	na
9.4 80	-2.2 75	9.4 80	42.6 4	15.6 3	21.2 32	228.2 3	4.7 32	70
17.6 31	-1.8 66	17.6 31	25.5 44	-5.7 76	19.4 39	108.8 61	-5.7 54	17
11.9 66	-3.7 95	11.9 66	23.7 50	-1.7 66	8.5 86	107.4 63	-46.4 99	94
11.4 69	-2.9 87	11.4 69	31.0 20	-5.7 76	10.2 77	121.8 52	-17.1 76	86
0.3 95	-3.8 95	0.3 95	26.2 40	na --	na --	na --	na --	na
12.6 62	-2.6 82	12.6 62	27.6 33	-1.7 66	20.1 36	144.8 36	-18.5 78	77
15.9 43	-0.6 45	15.9 43	23.3 52	9.7 25	17.4 47	120.0 53	13.3 17	15
18.0 29	0.6 14	18.0 29	24.3 47	11.7 16	7.1 90	112.1 59	15.8 11	39
21.1 15	-0.3 38	21.1 15	22.2 57	8.1 33	6.5 92	95.2 75	3.6 34	31
8.7 82	-2.1 74	8.7 82	22.7 54	na --	na --	na --	na --	na
18.8 24	-2.3 77	18.8 24	26.4 39	na --	na --	na --	na --	na
30.2 5	3.7 2	30.2 5	na --	na --	na --	na --	na --	na
17.5 32	0.3 23	17.5 32	25.9 41	1.7 56	24.2 24	163.0 24	na --	na
8.8 81	0.0 31	8.8 81	na --	na --	na --	na --	na --	na

CDA MONTHLY ALPHABETIC LISTING − 12/31/86

FUND	MGT CO	IO	ASSETS MIL$	NAV	MAX LOAD	% YLD	ANNUALIZED ROR THRU 12/31/86 10 YEARS PCNT RK	5 YEARS PCNT RK	3 YEARS PCNT RK
COLONIAL FUND	COLONL	B	159	17.80	6.7	3.9	13.3 55	19.9 24	18.4 16
COLONIAL CORP CASH I	COLONL	B	407	49.16	2.0	8.7	na --	12.8 80	13.3 55
COLONIAL CORP CASH II	COLONL	B	318	47.71	2.0	7.2	na --	na --	na --
COLONIAL GOV SEC PLUS TR	COLONL	BP	2800	12.72	6.7	7.1	na --	na --	na --
COLONIAL GROWTH SHARES	COLONL	G	75	13.20	6.7	0.6	13.7 49	16.2 59	13.9 51
COLONIAL INCOME	COLONL	BP	153	7.23	4.7	10.7	9.4 89	17.5 47	14.9 42
COLONIAL OPTION INC I	COLONL	GI	1113	7.58	6.7	2.0	na --	12.1 83	9.5 77
COLONIAL OPTION INC II	COLONL	GI	200	10.47	6.7	2.4	na --	na --	na --
COLONIAL HIGH YIELD SECS	COLONL	BP	401	7.69	4.7	11.6	10.6 79	18.2 42	15.6 36
COLONIAL TAX EXEMPT HIYD	COLONL	MB	1258	13.73	4.7	6.8	na --	na --	10.3 74
COLONIAL TAX EX INSURED	COLONL	MB	87	7.94	4.7	6.5	na --	na --	na --
COLUMBIA FIXED INCOME FD	CLMBIA	BP	115	13.37	0.0	9.2	na --	na --	14.9 42
COLUMBIA GROWTH FUND	CLMBIA	G	209	22.88	0.0	1.5	17.1 21	18.7 38	10.2 74
COLUMBIA MUNICIPAL BOND	CLMBIA	MB	100	11.75	0.0	7.1	na --	na --	na --
COLUMBIA SPECIAL FUND	CLMBIA	AG	21	26.97	0.0	0.0	na --	na --	na --
COMMERCE INCOME SHARES	CRITER	B	59	9.96	8.5	2.6	11.7 70	15.7 63	13.4 55
COMMONWEALTH - PLANS A&B	STDLEY	B	10	1.49	7.6	5.1	12.7 62	16.0 61	14.2 49
COMMONWEALTH - PLAN C	STDLEY	B	40	2.08	7.5	4.3	11.1 75	14.8 70	12.7 60
COMPANION FUND	CIGNA	G	77	13.37	0.0	2.8	13.6 51	15.5 64	12.4 62
COMPOSITE BOND & STOCK	COMPOS	B	76	10.02	4.0	5.4	11.6 71	15.3 66	12.7 60
COMPOSITE FUND	COMPOS	G	68	10.95	4.0	3.4	12.5 64	14.0 74	11.8 64
CONCORD FUND	CONCOR	GI	2	26.63	0.0	2.9	11.9 68	9.5 90	6.5 86
CONSTELLATION GROWTH	AIM	AG	76	21.16	4.7	0.0	19.5 12	14.8 69	11.7 65
CONTINENTAL MUTUAL INV.	FD-M&R	B	1	6.79	0.0	3.4	6.3 96	8.1 93	5.7 88
CONVERTIBLE YIELD	AIM	GI	18	11.73	4.7	5.3	na --	10.0 89	7.0 85
COPLEY TAX-MANAGED FUND	COPLEY	G	31	11.02	0.0	0.0	na --	19.5 29	22.1 4
COUNTRY CAPITAL GROWTH	CONTRY	G	67	15.92	7.5	3.2	11.7 69	15.5 64	12.4 61
CRITERION QUAL TX FR INS	CRITER	MB	128	11.40	4.5	6.6	na --	na --	15.3 39
DEAN WITTER CALIF TX FR	DWRI	MB	316	12.25	0.0	6.1	na --	na --	na --
DEAN WITTER DEVELOP GROW	DWRI	G	140	8.88	0.0	0.1	na --	na --	0.1 94
DEAN WITTER DIVIDEND GRO	DWRI	GI	1024	18.48	0.0	2.8	na --	21.2 16	19.5 12
DEAN WITTER HIGH YIELD	DWRI	BP	1391	14.08	5.5	12.1	na --	18.5 40	15.6 35
DEAN WITTER INDUSTRY VAL	DWRI	G	71	12.64	0.0	2.2	na --	12.7 81	11.5 66
DEAN WITTER OPTION INC	DWRI	GI	589	9.59	0.0	1.8	na --	na --	na --
DEAN WITTER NAT RESOURCE	DWRI	G	53	7.96	0.0	2.7	na --	3.6 97	3.5 91
DEAN WITTER NY TX FR INC	DWRI	MB	101	11.57	0.0	6.1	na --	na --	na --
DEAN WITTER TX ADVANTAGE	DWRI	BP	303	10.29	0.0	7.3	na --	na --	na --
DEAN WITTER TAX EX SECS	DWRI	MB	838	11.49	4.0	7.3	na --	19.4 30	16.1 32
DEAN WITTER US GOV TRUST	DWRI	BP	10291	10.33	0.0	9.7	na --	na --	na --
DEAN WITTER WORLDWIDE	DWRI	IN	346	15.44	0.0	0.5	na --	na --	21.7 5
DECATUR FUND INC-SER 1	DLAWRE	GI	1076	16.86	8.5	3.9	16.0 29	21.2 16	19.2 13
DELAWARE FUND	DLAWRE	G	394	18.34	8.5	2.3	15.1 38	19.3 31	14.0 51
DELAWARE GOV FD-USG SER	DLAWRE	BP	40	9.22	4.7	9.3	na --	na --	na --
DELAWARE GOV FD-GNMA SER	DLAWRE	BP	43	9.27	4.6	9.6	na --	na --	na --
DELAWARE TREAS RESERVES	DLAWRE	BP	59	9.97	0.0	8.4	na --	na --	na --
DELCHESTER BOND FUND	DLAWRE	BP	191	8.05	6.7	11.8	10.2 83	19.3 31	15.6 35
DELTA TREND FUND	DLAWRE	AG	75	7.18	8.5	0.0	15.6 34	14.4 72	2.6 92
DEPOSITORS FUND/BOSTON	ETN&HD	G	57	54.34	0.0	1.9	na --	15.1 68	13.8 51
DE VEGH MUTUAL FUND	WS&W	G	53	12.80	0.0	1.8	10.6 79	10.8 87	9.1 78
DFA FIXED INC PORTFOLIO	DIMEN	BP	312	101.90	0.0	7.4	na --	na --	11.0 70

LATEST 12 MNTHS	THIS MONTH	1986 TO DATE	CALENDAR YEARS 1985	1984	1983	CYCLES UP MKT	DOWN MKT	CDA RATING
PCNT RK	PCNT RK	PCNT RK	PCNT RK	PCNT RK	PCNT RK	PCNT RK	PCNT RK	
21.5 13	-2.1 74	21.5 13	26.6 38	8.0 33	25.1 21	164.1 23	-8.2 58	47
9.8 78	-1.3 58	9.8 78	17.6 81	12.5 13	13.1 66	85.6 84	na --	na
5.8 89	-0.9 51	5.8 89	15.9 87	na --	na --	na --	na --	na
15.6 44	0.2 25	15.6 44	19.8 72	na --	na --	na --	na --	na
19.1 22	-1.7 65	19.1 22	23.8 49	0.3 59	15.6 54	139.6 40	-19.6 80	71
12.2 65	0.5 16	12.2 65	21.1 64	11.6 17	10.2 77	96.8 73	16.4 10	70
4.5 91	-2.6 82	4.5 91	20.1 70	4.7 46	19.0 41	92.0 78	-4.1 51	91
7.0 86	-1.8 68	7.0 86	13.0 92	na --	na --	na --	na --	na
14.8 50	0.8 12	14.8 50	21.8 59	10.5 20	20.3 35	117.1 56	7.8 26	49
14.8 50	-0.4 42	14.8 50	20.4 69	-2.8 69	12.1 69	74.1 90	na --	na
16.8 38	-1.7 63	16.8 38	na --	na --	na --	na --	na --	na
8.7 82	0.4 20	8.7 82	24.4 47	12.2 14	na --	na --	na --	na
6.8 87	-2.2 74	6.8 87	32.0 17	-5.1 75	21.5 32	163.3 23	-9.7 62	59
17.1 34	0.0 31	17.1 34	na --	na --	na --	na --	na --	na
15.7 44	-2.7 83	15.7 44	na --	na --	na --	na --	na --	na
10.4 75	-1.3 57	10.4 75	23.6 50	6.8 39	9.4 82	102.0 67	7.0 28	74
13.9 54	-1.4 58	13.9 54	24.7 46	4.9 45	14.2 62	111.6 59	2.2 38	43
12.3 65	-1.4 59	12.3 65	21.8 59	4.6 47	13.3 65	100.9 68	0.6 43	69
12.6 63	-2.8 84	12.6 63	28.1 32	-1.6 66	22.1 30	150.1 31	-17.4 76	72
14.1 53	-2.4 79	14.1 53	22.8 54	2.1 54	16.8 50	118.0 55	-2.7 47	51
19.7 20	-2.6 83	19.7 20	27.4 34	-8.3 82	15.2 57	111.3 60	9.3 24	56
-0.2 95	-1.7 64	-0.2 95	14.5 90	5.6 43	18.1 45	84.5 85	-9.6 61	85
27.8 7	-1.0 53	27.8 7	28.6 29	-15.2 91	24.6 23	183.3 12	-42.4 98	48
11.7 67	-0.9 50	11.7 67	13.0 92	-6.3 78	7.4 89	48.9 95	-12.5 67	93
4.6 91	-1.2 55	4.6 91	21.0 65	-3.3 70	11.7 70	78.6 88	1.2 41	95
17.7 30	-3.1 89	17.7 30	24.6 46	23.9 1	11.6 70	166.2 21	2.1 38	4
8.2 83	-3.4 92	8.2 83	29.9 24	1.1 57	19.5 38	141.2 39	-15.0 71	86
17.0 35	0.3 25	17.0 35	22.2 58	7.1 37	na --	na --	na --	na
16.6 38	-1.0 53	16.6 38	19.0 76	na --	na --	na --	na --	na
1.0 94	-3.7 95	1.0 94	17.2 83	-15.4 91	na --	na --	na --	na
19.3 22	-2.2 74	19.3 22	31.9 18	8.4 31	20.2 36	167.3 21	na --	na
16.5 38	0.4 19	16.5 38	23.0 53	7.9 34	12.5 67	106.0 63	na --	na
16.1 41	-2.1 74	16.1 41	29.7 26	-8.1 82	10.7 75	115.6 57	na --	na
7.5 86	-1.9 70	7.5 86	na --	na --	na --	na --	na --	na
11.2 70	-1.8 68	11.2 70	13.5 92	-12.0 87	15.0 57	63.0 93	na --	na
16.6 38	-0.7 46	16.6 38	na --	na --	na --	na --	na --	na
6.3 88	-0.8 49	6.3 88	14.7 90	na --	na --	na --	na --	na
17.9 29	-1.8 66	17.9 29	21.2 63	9.3 27	11.9 70	101.0 68	10.6 22	22
8.1 83	0.3 22	8.1 83	14.0 91	na --	na --	na --	na --	na
31.5 5	0.9 11	31.5 5	38.3 6	-1.0 63	na --	na --	na --	na
21.9 13	-2.4 78	21.9 13	27.0 36	9.4 26	23.1 27	166.7 21	3.0 36	17
11.0 72	-2.8 86	11.0 72	30.4 22	2.5 53	14.6 59	149.7 31	14.7 13	53
9.8 77	0.4 20	9.8 77	na --	na --	na --	na --	na --	na
10.3 76	0.4 20	10.3 76	na --	na --	na --	na --	na --	na
7.9 84	0.3 23	7.9 84	na --	na --	na --	na --	na --	na
16.8 36	1.0 8	16.8 36	21.8 60	8.6 31	14.1 62	113.2 58	12.6 18	42
5.3 90	-5.2 98	5.3 90	28.0 32	-19.8 95	37.8 4	107.2 63	24.2 3	53
13.9 54	0.6 13	13.9 54	30.2 23	-0.5 61	12.3 68	139.3 40	na --	na
8.2 83	-3.7 94	8.2 83	28.6 29	-6.7 78	17.0 49	90.6 80	-21.4 83	91
8.9 81	0.5 16	8.9 81	10.5 95	13.6 9	na --	na --	na --	na

CDA MONTHLY ALPHABETIC LISTING – 12/31/86

FUND	MGT CO	IO	ASSETS MIL$	NAV	MAX LOAD	% YLD	ANNUALIZED ROR THRU 12/31/86 10 YEARS PCNT RK	5 YEARS PCNT RK	3 YEARS PCNT RK
DFA SMALL CO. PORTFOLIO	DIMEN	G	927	8.70	0.0	1.1	na --	na --	7.3 84
DIVERSIFICATION FUND	ETN&HD	G	60	89.37	0.0	1.8	na --	16.5 56	12.8 59
DIVIDEND/GROWTH FD., INC	AMERIN	GI	4	24.79	0.0	6.1	na --	12.4 81	11.3 67
DMC TAX FREE-PA	DLAWRE	MB	304	8.05	4.7	7.0	na --	19.0 35	15.5 36
DMC TAX FREE-USA	DLAWRE	MB	265	11.78	4.7	7.0	na --	na --	na --
DMC TAX FREE-INSURED	DLAWRE	MB	36	10.90	4.7	6.6	na --	na --	na --
DODGE & COX BALANCED	DGE&CX	B	26	32.62	0.0	4.7	12.9 61	19.5 28	18.3 17
DODGE & COX STOCK	DGE&CX	GI	43	31.66	0.0	2.9	15.7 32	21.7 14	19.9 9
DOUBLE EXEMPT FLEX FUND	VOYAGR	MB	89	11.85	4.0	7.1	na --	na --	na --
DREXEL BURNHAM FUND	DREXEL	GI	133	21.28	3.5	3.3	15.3 36	18.9 37	20.1 8
DREXEL ST GOV SECURITIES	DREXEL	BP	334	10.70	0.0	9.3	na --	na --	na --
DREXEL ST OPTION INC FD	DREXEL	GI	36	10.12	0.0	3.8	na --	na --	na --
DREXEL ST EMERG GROWTH	DREXEL	G	38	12.63	0.0	0.0	na --	na --	na --
DREXEL ST GROWTH	DREXEL	G	22	11.80	0.0	4.6	na --	na --	na --
DREYFUS A BONDS PLUS	DRYFUS	BP	241	14.99	0.0	8.8	10.3 81	16.4 56	16.4 28
DREYFUS CALIF TAX EXEMPT	DRYFUS	MB	1158	15.47	0.0	7.0	na --	na --	13.4 54
DREYFUS CONVERTIBLE SECS	DRYFUS	B	172	8.87	0.0	5.9	13.0 58	18.6 38	18.3 16
DREYFUS FUND	DRYFUS	GI	2316	12.55	8.5	4.0	14.8 41	15.4 65	14.6 45
DREYFUS GNMA	DRYFUS	BP	1936	15.70	0.0	9.3	na --	na --	na --
DREYFUS GROWTH OPPORTUN.	DRYFUS	G	416	10.50	0.0	1.6	16.1 28	12.6 81	10.0 75
DREYFUS INSURED TAX EX	DRYFUS	MB	177	18.40	0.0	6.9	na --	na --	na --
DREYFUS INTERMDIATE MUNI	DRYFUS	MB	1060	14.12	0.0	7.0	na --	na --	12.9 58
DREYFUS LEVERAGE	DRYFUS	GI	486	16.23	8.5	2.3	17.2 21	18.4 40	18.8 14
DREYFUS MASS TAX EXEMPT	DRYFUS	MB	68	16.75	0.0	6.9	na --	na --	na --
DREYFUS NY TAX EXEMPT	DRYFUS	MB	1424	15.89	0.0	7.0	na --	na --	15.1 40
DREYFUS TAX EXEMPT BOND	DRYFUS	MB	3540	13.01	0.0	7.4	na --	18.8 37	15.0 41
DREYFUS THIRD CENTURY	DRYFUS	GI	156	6.51	0.0	4.4	15.7 33	11.6 84	11.2 68
EAGLE GROWTH SHARES	FAHNST	G	4	6.83	8.5	0.1	na --	4.2 96	-0.9 95
EATON & HOWARD STOCK	ETN&HD	GI	80	13.49	7.2	3.7	12.6 64	18.6 39	19.3 12
EATON VANCE GROWTH FD	ETN&HD	G	73	6.84	8.5	1.8	16.1 29	16.4 57	13.7 52
EATON VANCE GOV OBLIGATN	ETN&HD	BP	384	12.36	6.7	9.0	na --	na --	na --
EATON VANCE HIGH YIELD	ETN&HD	BP	32	5.32	6.7	10.5	9.7 87	18.3 41	16.9 24
EATON VANCE INC FD/BOST	ETN&HD	B	43	10.23	6.7	9.5	11.8 69	18.2 42	18.1 18
EATON VANCE INVESTORS FD	ETN&HD	B	219	7.64	8.5	5.3	13.3 54	16.5 55	14.2 49
EATON VANCE MUNICIPAL BD	ETN&HD	MB	49	9.25	3.7	7.1	na --	20.4 21	16.4 28
EATON VANCE SPL EQUITIES	ETN&HD	G	40	16.15	7.2	0.3	14.1 45	9.2 91	2.0 93
EATON VANCE TOTAL RETURN	ETN&HD	GI	570	10.67	4.7	3.2	na --	25.3 3	28.9 1
ELFUN TRUSTS	ELFUN	GI	480	27.49	0.0	3.3	16.4 24	19.6 28	18.1 18
ENERGY FUND	NEUBER	GI	376	18.47	0.0	4.6	13.6 50	11.8 83	12.3 62
EQUITEC SIEBEL TOTAL RET	SIEBEL	GI	76	13.32	0.0	1.5	na --	na --	na --
EUROPACIFIC GROWTH FUND	CAPRES	IN	160	24.58	8.5	0.6	na --	na --	na --
EVERGREEN FUND	SAXON	AG	639	12.47	0.0	1.0	24.3 3	19.1 34	15.3 38
EVERGREEN TOTAL RETURN	SAXON	B	794	19.18	0.0	5.4	na --	24.2 5	21.8 4
EXPLORER FUND	VGUARD	AG	266	27.66	0.0	0.1	17.4 19	8.9 92	-3.4 96
EXPLORER II	VGUARD	AG	34	18.99	0.0	0.2	na --	na --	na --
FAIRFIELD FUND	NATSEC	AG	44	8.28	8.5	0.9	12.8 61	11.2 86	7.3 84
FAIRMONT FUND	SACHS	G	72	49.50	0.0	1.1	na --	24.8 3	18.6 14
FARM BUREAU GROWTH FUND	PFS	G	42	14.19	0.0	2.7	11.0 76	10.7 88	9.6 77
FEDERATED CORP CASH TR	FEDRES	BP	131	10.66	0.0	6.8	na --	na --	na --
FEDERATED GNMA	FEDRES	BP	1348	11.43	0.0	9.8	na --	na --	14.7 45

LATEST 12 MNTHS		THIS MONTH		1986 TO DATE		CALENDAR YEARS						CYCLES				CDA RATING
						1985		1984		1983		UP MKT		DOWN MKT		
PCNT	RK	PCNT	RK	PCNT	RK	PCNT	RK	PCNT	RK	PCNT	RK	PCNT	RK	PCNT	RK	
6.8	87	-2.6	83	6.8	87	24.4	47	-7.1	79	40.2	3	148.9	32	na	--	na
8.9	81	-1.0	52	8.9	81	27.9	32	2.9	52	18.5	43	144.2	37	na	--	na
8.7	82	-3.4	93	8.7	82	13.9	91	11.4	17	15.1	57	72.4	91	24.8	3	90
18.9	24	0.8	11	18.9	24	17.3	82	10.4	21	13.4	65	100.5	69	-0.1	43	32
21.9	13	0.7	13	21.9	13	22.2	57	na	--	na	--	na	--	na	--	na
18.6	25	0.0	33	18.6	25	na	--	na	--	na	--	na	--	na	--	na
19.1	22	-0.4	42	19.1	22	32.5	16	4.8	46	17.0	49	140.8	40	-3.3	49	44
18.8	24	-1.6	62	18.8	24	37.7	7	5.4	44	26.7	17	191.3	10	-12.1	66	48
15.8	43	0.9	9	15.8	43	18.8	77	na	--	na	--	na	--	na	--	na
22.0	12	-0.7	46	22.0	12	32.2	17	7.3	36	12.1	69	151.8	30	-10.3	64	32
10.7	74	0.2	26	10.7	74	na	--	na	--	na	--	na	--	na	--	na
10.3	75	-1.5	61	10.3	75	na	--	na	--	na	--	na	--	na	--	na
-4.5	96	-6.2	98	-4.5	96	na	--	na	--	na	--	na	--	na	--	na
11.6	68	-1.4	60	11.6	68	na	--	na	--	na	--	na	--	na	--	na
13.9	54	1.0	9	13.9	54	23.1	53	12.4	13	7.6	88	90.6	80	19.9	6	64
17.6	31	0.1	27	17.6	31	18.1	80	5.0	45	na	--	na	--	na	--	na
24.3	9	0.9	10	24.3	9	23.7	50	7.7	35	21.1	33	143.8	37	-6.6	55	23
16.3	40	-2.0	71	16.3	40	25.2	45	3.3	50	19.7	37	132.5	44	-7.0	56	33
9.6	79	0.5	16	9.6	79	na	--	na	--	na	--	na	--	na	--	na
15.9	42	-0.6	45	15.9	42	30.7	22	-12.1	88	31.5	8	125.4	50	-34.9	96	41
17.0	35	-0.1	35	17.0	35	na	--	na	--	na	--	na	--	na	--	na
15.2	47	-0.1	36	15.2	47	16.1	87	7.5	36	na	--.	na	--	na	--	na
18.7	24	-0.4	42	18.7	24	30.1	24	8.6	30	17.3	48	156.6	27	-20.6	83	17
17.8	30	0.0	34	17.8	30	na	--	na	--	na	--	na	--	na	--	na
17.0	36	-0.3	39	17.0	36	20.7	66	8.1	33	na	--	na	--	na	--	na
17.3	33	-0.1	36	17.3	33	19.5	74	8.6	30	11.6	71	94.9	76	na	--	na
4.6	91	-3.3	91	4.6	91	29.5	26	1.6	56	20.2	35	111.8	59	-28.4	92	77
-9.1	98	-2.0	71	-9.1	98	16.0	87	-7.8	81	20.2	36	44.0	96	-17.2	76	99
15.6	44	-1.4	59	15.6	44	31.7	18	11.6	17	14.7	59	164.9	22	-14.9	71	67
10.5	75	0.0	32	10.5	75	30.3	22	2.3	54	17.0	49	145.3	35	-7.0	55	38
13.3	58	1.5	5	13.3	58	12.1	93	na	--	na	--	na	--	na	--	na
14.3	52	0.6	15	14.3	52	21.8	60	15.0	5	8.8	85	101.0	68	15.8	11	57
14.9	49	0.6	15	14.9	49	24.9	46	14.7	6	11.4	71	117.7	55	6.3	29	40
8.9	81	-0.7	47	8.9	81	25.4	44	9.0	29	14.6	59	130.1	46	1.1	42	60
18.5	26	0.1	31	18.5	26	21.4	62	9.6	25	8.2	86	103.2	66	4.0	33	24
-7.8	98	-0.9	51	-7.8	98	16.8	84	-1.5	65	10.2	77	74.8	90	7.0	28	87
31.9	5	-3.5	94	31.9	5	40.2	5	15.8	3	13.3	65	226.7	3	na	--	na
14.9	49	-1.2	56	14.9	49	34.9	10	6.2	41	17.7	47	168.9	19	-7.5	56	28
10.1	77	-2.0	71	10.1	77	22.6	55	4.8	46	22.1	30	111.2	60	-29.7	93	78
13.1	59	-1.4	59	13.1	59	na	--	na	--	na	--	na	--	na	--	na
40.0	3	4.7	1	40.0	3	35.2	9	na	--	na	--	na	--	na	--	na
13.2	58	-2.5	81	13.2	58	34.6	11	0.6	58	29.9	11	192.9	9	-16.9	75	16
20.2	18	-2.0	70	20.2	18	31.5	19	14.4	7	30.3	9	219.5	4	1.2	41	2
-8.7	98	-2.9	87	-8.7	98	22.4	56	-19.5	95	20.3	34	73.3	91	-8.2	58	78
-7.3	97	-2.5	80	-7.3	97	na	--	na	--	na	--	na	--	na	--	na
3.5	92	-3.2	90	3.5	92	43.3	3	-16.7	92	9.6	81	121.7	52	-26.9	91	94
14.0	53	-1.0	53	14.0	53	32.1	17	10.8	19	35.0	6	217.0	5	na	--	na
9.5	79	-2.5	81	9.5	79	25.5	44	-4.2	72	13.3	65	85.6	84	-9.9	62	84
3.4	93	-1.6	63	3.4	93	18.2	79	na	--	na	--	na	--	na	--	na
10.9	72	0.4	18	10.9	72	19.5	74	13.7	9	7.3	90	78.9	88	na	--	na

CDA MONTHLY ALPHABETIC LISTING – 12/31/86

FUND	MGT CO	IO	ASSETS MIL$	NAV	MAX LOAD	% YLD	10 YEARS PCNT RK	5 YEARS PCNT RK	3 YEARS PCNT RK
FEDERATED GROWTH TRUST	FEDRES	G	59	15.38	0.0	1.6	na --	na --	na --
FEDERATED HIGH INCOME	FEDRES	BP	360	12.32	4.0	11.7	na --	18.0 43	14.8 44
FEDERATED HIGH YIELD TR.	FEDRES	BP	159	10.91	0.0	12.0	na --	na --	na --
FEDERATED INCOME TRUST	FEDRES	BP	568	10.74	0.0	9.7	na --	na --	13.7 52
FEDERATED INTERM. GOV.	FEDRES	BP	1412	10.24	0.0	8.6	na --	na --	na --
FEDERATED INTMED MUNI TR	FEDRES	MB	70	10.51	0.0	6.0	na --	na --	na --
FEDERATED SH-INTERM GOV	FEDRES	BP	3696	10.44	0.0	8.4	na --	na --	na --
FEDERATED SH-INTERM MUNI	FEDRES	MB	461	10.38	0.0	5.4	na --	7.4 94	7.0 85
FEDERATED STOCK & BOND	FEDRES	B	68	15.34	0.0	5.5	13.0 59	19.4 30	15.6 36
FEDERATED STOCK TRUST	FEDRES	GI	450	21.60	0.0	2.9	na --	na --	20.8 7
FEDERATED TAX FR INCOME	FEDRES	MB	305	10.72	0.0	7.1	na --	19.5 28	14.8 43
FIDELITY AGGRESS TAX FR	FIDEL	MB	308	11.53	0.0	8.1	na --	na --	na --
FIDELITY CALIF TAX FREE	FIDEL	MB	446	11.80	0.0	6.8	na --	na --	na --
FIDELITY CONGRESS STREET	FIDEL	G	52	83.60	0.0	2.5	16.8 22	22.4 10	21.2 6
FIDELITY CONTRAFUND	FIDEL	G	82	11.29	0.0	2.0	11.6 71	13.5 76	9.5 78
FIDELITY CORP TR-ARP	FIDEL	BP	297	10.40	0.0	7.3	na --	na --	na --
FIDELITY DESTINY	FIDEL	G	1074	12.43	0.0	2.3	21.6 5	24.8 3	16.7 27
FIDELITY EQUITY INCOME	FIDEL	GI	3100	27.29	2.0	5.8	19.9 11	22.8 8	17.3 22
FIDELITY EXCHANGE FUND	FIDEL	G	140	62.94	0.0	2.5	13.8 48	19.1 33	18.0 18
FIDELITY FLEXIBLE BOND	FIDEL	BP	290	7.36	0.0	9.5	9.4 89	16.4 57	15.5 37
FIDELITY FREEDOM FUND	FIDEL	G	816	16.31	0.0	2.1	na --	na --	14.7 44
FIDELITY FUND	FIDEL	GI	760	16.05	0.0	3.6	14.8 42	19.5 28	14.3 47
FIDELITY GOVT SECS	FIDEL	BP	573	10.28	0.0	8.9	na --	15.0 68	14.6 46
FIDELITY GROWTH FUND	FIDEL	AG	169	14.11	3.0	0.4	na --	na --	14.3 47
FIDELITY GROWTH & INCOME	FIDEL	GI	460	13.33	0.0	1.2	na --	na --	na --
FIDELITY LTD TERM MUNS	FIDEL	MB	471	9.58	0.0	6.5	na --	15.5 64	14.1 50
FIDELITY MASS TAX FREE	FIDEL	MB	589	11.66	0.0	7.1	na --	na --	na --
FIDELITY MORTGAGE SECS	FIDEL	BP	660	10.58	0.0	9.5	na --	na --	na --
FIDELITY MUNI BOND FD	FIDEL	MB	1041	8.28	0.0	6.7	5.7 97	19.0 35	16.1 31
FIDELITY OVERSEAS FUND	FIDEL	IN	2561	28.68	3.0	0.0	na --	na --	na --
FIDELITY SEL AMER GOLD	FIDEL	ME	85	11.83	2.0	0.0	na --	na --	na --
FIDELITY SEL BIOTECH	FIDEL	AG	33	10.35	2.0	0.0	na --	na --	na --
FIDELITY HIGH YIELD MUNI	FIDEL	MB	2065	13.29	0.0	7.3	na --	19.5 28	16.7 27
FIDELITY HIGH INCOME FD	FIDEL	BP	1460	9.72	0.0	11.2	na --	21.4 15	17.9 19
FIDELITY SEL CHEMICAL	FIDEL	G	21	15.66	2.0	0.0	na --	na --	na --
FIDELITY MAGELLAN FUND	FIDEL	G	6555	48.69	3.0	0.8	32.8 1	30.2 1	22.1 4
FIDELITY PURITAN FD	FIDEL	B	2458	13.34	0.0	6.7	16.2 27	22.6 9	19.7 10
FIDELITY OTC PORTFOLIO	FIDEL	G	588	16.47	3.0	0.1	na --	na --	na --
FIDELITY QUALIFIED DIVD	FIDEL	B	214	14.97	0.0	7.1	na --	22.3 11	22.5 4
FIDELITY SEL DEF & AERO	FIDEL	G	9	14.79	2.0	0.2	na --	na --	na --
FIDELITY SELECT ENERGY	FIDEL	G	71	11.53	2.0	0.0	na --	6.1 95	8.4 80
FIDELITY SEL LEISURE ENT	FIDEL	G	114	20.51	2.0	0.0	na --	na --	na --
FIDELITY SELECT FINL SVC	FIDEL	G	120	31.56	2.0	0.6	na --	26.9 2	24.2 3
FIDELITY SELECT HEALTH	FIDEL	AG	217	32.78	2.0	0.0	na --	26.1 2	24.4 3
FIDELITY SEL PREC MET&MN	FIDEL	ME	241	11.15	2.0	0.8	na --	6.8 95	-4.2 97
FIDELITY SELECT TECHNLGY	FIDEL	AG	241	20.27	2.0	0.0	na --	14.5 72	-6.2 98
FIDELITY SEL UTILITIES	FIDEL	GI	195	27.31	2.0	0.8	na --	23.9 6	25.4 2
FIDELITY SPEC SITUATIONS	FIDEL	AG	54	16.21	3.0	0.5	na --	na --	na --
FIDELITY SEL BROKERAGE	FIDEL	G	11	12.12	2.0	0.1	na --	na --	na --
FIDELITY SEL ELECTRONICS	FIDEL	AG	3	8.46	2.0	0.0	na --	na --	na --

LATEST 12 MNTHS PCNT RK	THIS MONTH PCNT RK	1986 TO DATE PCNT RK	CALENDAR YEARS 1985 PCNT RK	1984 PCNT RK	1983 PCNT RK	CYCLES UP MKT PCNT RK	DOWN MKT PCNT RK	CDA RATING
24.1 9	-2.5 82	24.1 9	34.7 11	na --	na --	na --	na --	na
12.4 64	1.0 9	12.4 64	21.5 61	10.7 19	14.3 61	105.0 64	na --	na
15.9 42	1.1 7	15.9 42	22.2 58	na --	na --	na --	na --	na
9.8 78	0.8 11	9.8 78	17.0 84	14.4 7	7.8 88	74.4 90	na --	na
11.9 66	0.2 26	11.9 66	15.5 88	na --	na --	na --	na --	na
11.7 67	0.4 21	11.7 67	na --	na --	na --	na --	na --	na
9.5 79	0.4 21	9.5 79	12.0 93	na --	na --	na --	na --	na
7.6 85	0.5 16	7.6 85	6.5 97	6.9 38	5.6 94	32.6 97	na --	na
13.8 55	-1.2 56	13.8 55	19.3 75	13.8 9	21.2 32	138.2 41	7.0 28	38
13.8 55	-6.3 99	13.8 55	33.5 14	16.0 3	31.2 9	215.9 5	na --	na
20.4 16	0.1 28	20.4 16	18.3 78	6.2 40	10.8 74	98.6 71	2.0 39	29
17.5 32	-0.4 40	17.5 32	na --	na --	na --	na --	na --	na
17.1 35	0.3 24	17.1 35	16.6 85	na --	na --	na --	na --	na
27.1 7	-1.7 65	27.1 7	31.7 18	6.4 40	28.4 13	213.4 5	-10.1 63	35
12.8 61	-1.2 55	12.8 61	27.0 36	-8.3 82	23.2 27	119.2 54	-9.0 60	80
6.6 87	-0.7 46	6.6 87	16.4 86	na --	na --	na --	na --	na
17.6 31	-1.9 70	17.6 31	29.1 27	4.7 46	38.8 3	228.4 3	-0.1 43	4
16.8 37	-1.3 58	16.8 37	25.0 46	10.5 20	29.2 11	186.5 11	6.7 28	5
20.5 16	-1.7 65	20.5 16	31.1 20	4.0 49	20.1 36	170.8 18	-14.5 70	56
13.7 56	0.8 11	13.7 56	21.1 64	11.8 16	6.6 91	87.8 82	18.7 8	69
13.7 56	-3.6 94	13.7 56	28.5 30	3.4 50	na --	na --	na --	na
15.4 46	-2.3 77	15.4 46	27.7 33	1.4 57	22.4 29	159.8 25	-7.2 56	41
14.7 50	0.3 23	14.7 50	17.7 81	11.3 18	6.0 93	79.9 87	36.6 1	54
12.9 60	-2.0 71	12.9 60	39.8 5	-5.3 75	na --	na --	na --	na
34.9 4	-1.9 70	34.9 4	na --	na --	na --	na --	na --	na
15.2 47	-0.5 44	15.2 47	17.3 82	10.0 23	9.9 79	75.9 90	8.4 25	68
16.9 36	0.1 28	16.9 36	19.6 73	na --	na --	na --	na --	na
11.0 72	0.3 22	11.0 72	18.6 78	na --	na --	na --	na --	na
19.6 20	0.1 30	19.6 20	20.1 70	9.0 28	9.3 83	93.1 77	3.1 36	65
68.9 1	4.7 1	68.9 1	78.6 1	na --	na --	na --	na --	na
18.1 28	-0.2 36	18.1 28	na --	na --	na --	na --	na --	na
3.5 92	-6.4 99	3.5 92	na --	na --	na --	na --	na --	na
19.0 23	0.0 34	19.0 23	21.4 62	9.9 24	12.7 67	99.2 70	5.9 30	25
18.1 28	0.4 21	18.1 28	25.5 44	10.5 20	18.5 43	132.1 45	13.9 15	5
26.9 7	-1.8 68	26.9 7	na --	na --	na --	na --	na --	na
23.6 10	-1.4 60	23.6 10	42.9 4	3.0 52	38.6 4	291.0 1	13.5 16	1
20.8 15	0.3 23	20.8 15	28.5 30	10.5 19	25.6 20	172.7 17	11.3 21	19
11.2 70	-1.7 65	11.2 70	69.0 1	na --	na --	na --	na --	na
21.1 15	-2.6 82	21.1 15	25.6 43	20.8 1	15.5 54	169.3 18	na --	na
4.9 90	-4.7 97	4.9 90	26.4 39	na --	na --	na --	na --	na
5.5 89	0.7 13	5.5 89	17.9 80	2.4 53	20.3 35	81.6 86	na --	na
15.7 44	-4.4 97	15.7 44	56.5 2	na --	na --	na --	na --	na
15.1 48	-2.5 80	15.1 48	41.2 4	18.0 2	37.1 5	301.0 4	na --	na
22.0 12	-2.2 75	22.0 12	59.4 1	-1.1 63	14.1 62	234.7 2	na --	na
32.8 4	-0.7 46	32.8 4	-10.5 99	-26.1 97	2.6 97	52.8 94	na --	na
-7.4 97	-2.1 73	-7.4 97	7.4 96	-16.9 93	52.4 1	108.6 62	na --	na
24.0 9	-3.5 93	24.0 9	31.7 18	20.9 1	20.0 37	218.5 4	na --	na
27.9 6	-2.1 73	27.9 6	37.4 7	na --	na --	na --	na --	na
9.6 79	-3.2 90	9.6 79	na --	na --	na --	na --	na --	na
-23.9 99	-1.7 65	-23.9 99	na --	na --	na --	na --	na --	na

CDA MONTHLY ALPHABETIC LISTING – 12/31/86

FUND	MGT CO	IO	ASSETS MIL$	NAV	MAX LOAD	% YLD	10 YEARS PCNT RK	5 YEARS PCNT RK	3 YEARS PCNT RK
FIDELITY SEL PROPTY/CAS	FIDEL	G	8	10.97	2.0	0.0	na --	na --	na --
FIDELITY SEL COMPUTER	FIDEL	AG	3	12.21	2.0	0.0	na --	na --	na --
FIDELITY SEL FOOD/AGRI	FIDEL	G	9	14.10	2.0	0.0	na --	na --	na --
FIDELITY SEL SAVINGS/LN	FIDEL	G	23	12.88	2.0	0.0	na --	na --	na --
FIDELITY SEL SOFTWARE	FIDEL	AG	6	12.65	2.0	0.0	na --	na --	na --
FIDELITY SEL TELECOMM	FIDEL	G	7	13.18	2.0	0.0	na --	na --	na --
FIDELITY TREND	FIDEL	G	680	39.83	0.0	1.3	12.6 63	15.5 64	12.5 61
FIDELITY THRIFT TRUST	FIDEL	BP	324	11.55	0.0	5.6	11.5 72	16.1 60	15.8 33
FIDELITY VALUE FUND	FIDEL	G	119	23.06	0.0	0.0	na --	18.0 43	8.7 80
FIDUCIARY CAPITAL GROWTH	FIDMAN	G	52	17.90	0.0	4.6	na --	18.3 41	7.4 83
FINANCIAL BD-HIYLD PORT	FIF	BP	44	8.38	0.0	11.8	na --	na --	na --
FINANCIAL BD-SELECT INC	FIF	BP	20	7.10	0.0	9.2	na --	na --	15.3 37
FINANCIAL DYNAMICS FUND	FIF	AG	63	7.06	0.0	0.7	13.7 49	12.8 80	5.6 89
FINANCIAL INDUST. FUND	FIF	G	367	3.96	0.0	2.2	14.5 43	16.9 52	11.1 69
FINANCIAL INDUST. INCOME	FIF	GI	339	8.00	0.0	3.5	15.2 37	21.3 15	17.6 21
FINANCIAL TAX FR INC SHS	FIF	MB	117	15.59	0.0	7.1	na --	na --	17.9 19
FIRST INVEST. BND APPREC	FSTINV	BP	190	12.94	7.2	9.5	na --	12.8 80	11.1 69
FIRST INVEST. DISCOVERY	FSTINV	AG	33	9.03	8.5	1.2	8.7 92	7.0 94	-12.8 99
FIRST INVEST. FD. GROWTH	FSTINV	AG	53	5.70	8.5	0.0	7.9 94	4.0 96	-10.3 98
FIRST INVEST. FD. INCOME	FSTINV	BP	1675	5.94	8.5	11.6	9.5 88	13.0 79	10.8 71
FIRST INVEST. GOV FUND	FSTINV	BP	179	12.19	7.2	8.0	na --	na --	na --
FIRST INVEST. INTL SECS.	FSTINV	IN	29	16.53	8.5	0.1	na --	na --	11.4 66
FIRST INVEST. NATURL RES	FSTINV	AG	12	3.63	8.5	0.5	-4.0 99	-10.3 99	-17.9 99
FIRST INVEST. NY TAX FR	FSTINV	MB	71	14.25	7.2	6.2	na --	na --	na --
FIRST INVEST. NINETY-TEN	FSTINV	GI	10	12.50	8.5	4.9	na --	na --	4.0 90
FIRST INVEST. OPTION	FSTINV	GI	194	4.68	7.2	2.1	na --	7.7 93	6.8 85
FIRST INVEST. TAX EXEMPT	FSTINV	MB	644	10.14	7.2	6.9	na --	18.6 39	14.7 44
FLAGSHIP CORPORATE CASH	FLAGSP	BP	325	45.91	0.0	7.8	na --	na --	na --
FLAGSHIP MICHIGAN DBL TX	FLAGSP	MB	67	10.77	4.2	6.5	na --	na --	na --
FLAGSHIP OHIO DOUBLE TAX	FLAGSP	MB	116	10.60	4.2	6.8	na --	na --	na --
FLEX FD-RETIRE GR SERIES	MEEDER	GI	59	10.91	0.0	3.4	na --	na --	7.5 83
FORTY-FOUR WALL ST EQTY	FTY-FR	AG	8	5.75	1.0	0.0	na --	0.9 98	-4.2 97
FORTY-FOUR WALL ST FUND	FTY-FR	AG	22	3.09	0.0	0.0	-0.7 99	-20.0 99	-34.8 99
FOUNDATION GROWTH STOCK	FD-M&R	GI	1	5.03	8.5	3.3	6.6 96	7.9 93	6.0 88
FOUNDERS EQUITY INCOME	FNDRS	B	12	15.30	0.0	4.1	12.6 64	13.4 77	12.9 57
FOUNDERS GROWTH FUND	FNDRS	G	56	8.30	0.0	4.1	16.1 28	14.6 71	11.0 70
FOUNDERS MUTUAL FUND	FNDRS	GI	175	7.87	0.0	2.6	11.6 71	19.4 29	16.0 32
FOUNDERS SPECIAL FUND	FNDRS	AG	96	27.98	0.0	0.9	16.9 21	14.1 73	6.4 87
FPA CAPITAL FUND	FSTPAC	G	47	11.08	8.0	2.8	10.2 83	13.1 78	10.2 75
FPA NEW INCOME	FSTPAC	BP	6	9.50	5.0	8.4	na --	16.3 58	16.2 30
FPA PARAMOUNT FD INC	FSTPAC	GI	116	12.44	8.5	3.6	15.8 32	21.5 14	11.3 67
FPA PERENNIAL FUND	FSTPAC	G	60	18.47	8.5	2.4	na --	na --	na --
FRANKLIN CALIF TAX FREE	FRNKRE	MB	6889	7.22	4.0	7.9	na --	na --	14.4 47
FRANKLIN CORP CASH TR	FRNKRE	BP	70	8.82	0.0	6.7	na --	na --	na --
FRANKLIN DYNATECH	FRNKRE	G	32	9.95	4.0	2.4	13.7 49	12.3 82	-0.2 94
FRANKLIN EQUITY FUND	FRNKRE	G	145	6.25	4.0	1.3	16.3 25	19.2 32	19.8 9
FRANKLIN FEDERAL TAX FR	FRNKRE	MB	1506	12.06	4.0	8.0	na --	na --	na --
FRANKLIN GOLD FUND	FRNKRE	ME	126	8.99	4.0	3.6	21.8 5	6.8 95	-4.5 97
FRANKLIN GROWTH	FRNKRE	G	43	15.95	4.0	1.6	12.6 63	20.2 22	13.5 54
FRANKLIN INCOME	FRNKRE	B	227	2.24	4.0	9.3	16.2 27	19.9 24	16.5 27

LATEST 12 MNTHS PCNT RK	THIS MONTH PCNT RK	1986 TO DATE PCNT RK	CALENDAR YEARS 1985 PCNT RK	1984 PCNT RK	1983 PCNT RK	CYCLES UP MKT PCNT RK	DOWN MKT PCNT RK	CDA RATING
7.7 85	-0.9 50	7.7 85	na --	na --	na --	na --	na --	na
7.9 84	0.4 19	7.9 84	na --	na --	na --	na --	na --	na
22.5 11	-2.7 83	22.5 11	na --	na --	na --	na --	na --	na
27.5 7	0.2 26	27.5 7	na --	na --	na --	na --	na --	na
13.9 55	-2.2 76	13.9 55	na --	na --	na --	na --	na --	na
19.8 19	-1.4 60	19.8 19	na --	na --	na --	na --	na --	na
13.5 57	-2.2 76	13.5 57	28.2 31	-2.3 67	26.6 17	152.8 29	-24.1 87	81
13.1 59	0.5 16	13.1 59	20.8 66	13.5 10	9.4 82	86.9 83	25.7 3	66
15.1 47	-4.3 97	15.1 47	22.1 59	-8.7 83	31.9 8	156.2 27	1.2 41	12
-0.4 95	-6.0 98	-0.4 95	29.9 24	-4.2 72	28.9 11	153.2 29	na --	na
14.5 51	-0.3 40	14.5 51	26.4 40	na --	na --	na --	na --	na
18.8 24	0.7 13	18.8 24	22.7 55	5.2 44	5.1 95	78.6 88	na --	na
5.8 89	-1.7 65	5.8 89	29.1 27	-13.8 90	13.1 67	82.6 86	-0.2 44	74
8.1 83	-3.4 92	8.1 83	28.4 30	-1.1 64	14.5 60	117.6 55	-14.2 70	60
13.3 58	-3.2 90	13.3 58	30.7 21	9.7 25	23.5 26	168.6 20	-6.0 54	30
22.1 12	0.0 34	22.1 12	22.9 54	9.1 28	8.0 87	98.4 72	na --	na
11.5 68	-0.8 49	11.5 68	20.6 67	2.0 55	12.4 68	80.0 87	10.0 23	82
-14.7 99	-5.6 98	-14.7 99	15.0 89	-32.5 99	47.3 1	50.4 95	0.6 42	95
-5.3 96	-3.4 92	-5.3 96	5.3 97	-27.6 98	27.8 15	39.4 96	-25.4 89	96
11.3 70	0.6 15	11.3 70	19.7 73	2.0 54	13.1 66	76.4 89	7.7 26	79
11.1 71	0.2 27	11.1 71	17.9 80	na --	na --	na --	na --	na
44.8 2	4.0 1	44.8 2	10.7 94	-13.7 89	na --	na --	na --	na
-18.7 99	-0.5 44	-18.7 99	4.6 97	-34.8 99	-2.5 99	-23.4 99	-31.8 94	99
17.0 35	0.4 21	17.0 35	19.9 71	na --	na --	na --	na --	na
4.3 92	0.2 27	4.3 92	5.1 97	2.7 53	na --	na --	na --	na
6.1 88	-2.4 79	6.1 88	15.6 88	-0.7 62	14.3 61	54.3 94	na --	na
15.5 45	1.0 8	15.5 45	20.7 66	8.4 32	13.5 64	95.4 75	5.1 31	47
4.5 91	-0.5 43	4.5 91	13.7 92	5.7 43	na --	na --	na --	na
20.3 17	0.3 24	20.3 17	na --	na --	na --	na --	na --	na
17.6 31	0.3 23	17.6 31	na --	na --	na --	na --	na --	na
10.2 77	-1.9 69	10.2 77	14.1 91	-1.3 65	18.7 42	na --	na --	na
16.9 36	-2.9 86	16.9 36	22.4 57	-38.4 99	7.6 88	39.0 96	-33.6 95	98
-16.3 99	-11.7 99	-16.3 99	-20.1 99	-58.6 99	9.7 80	-48.7 99	-44.6 99	95
10.1 77	-0.8 48	10.1 77	11.6 94	-3.1 69	8.5 86	46.6 95	-12.6 67	92
14.5 51	-2.4 79	14.5 51	12.7 93	11.5 17	15.4 56	102.8 66	10.1 22	51
19.3 21	-2.2 75	19.3 21	28.8 28	-11.1 86	18.9 41	134.9 43	-7.5 57	35
16.8 37	-1.8 66	16.8 37	31.3 20	1.7 56	25.0 22	181.8 14	-19.7 81	78
18.9 24	-2.4 78	18.9 24	15.2 89	-12.2 88	23.2 27	122.0 52	-22.3 84	23
12.6 63	-3.2 90	12.6 63	29.0 28	-7.9 81	18.4 44	99.5 70	-13.7 69	86
11.1 71	1.0 9	11.1 71	21.3 62	16.4 3	6.2 93	87.3 83	na --	na
5.5 89	-3.0 88	5.5 89	18.8 77	10.1 23	31.3 8	145.5 35	0.0 43	50
10.2 76	-1.6 62	10.2 76	20.4 69	na --	na --	na --	na --	na
16.5 39	0.5 17	16.5 39	16.9 84	9.9 24	5.3 95	na --	na --	na
1.5 94	-1.6 63	1.5 94	13.9 91	na --	na --	na --	na --	na
-5.8 97	-3.0 88	-5.8 97	15.3 88	-8.5 83	32.8 8	104.2 65	-19.2 79	84
18.9 23	-3.3 92	18.9 23	32.9 15	8.9 29	18.7 42	171.4 18	-22.7 85	20
18.8 24	0.5 17	18.8 24	20.6 67	na --	na --	na --	na --	na
30.7 5	-0.8 48	30.7 5	-11.0 99	-25.0 97	8.9 85	52.0 94	-42.8 98	58
14.7 50	-0.9 50	14.7 50	26.5 38	0.9 58	17.8 46	147.2 34	-8.6 59	58
19.3 21	0.0 33	19.3 21	14.8 90	15.5 4	15.3 56	117.1 55	8.4 25	14

CDA MONTHLY ALPHABETIC LISTING – 12/31/86

FUND	MGT CO	IO	ASSETS MIL$	NAV	MAX LOAD	% YLD	10 YEARS PCNT RK	5 YEARS PCNT RK	3 YEARS PCNT RK
							ANNUALIZED ROR THRU 12/31/86		
FRANKLIN NEW YORK TAX FR	FRNKRE	MB	2126	11.64	4.0	7.8	na --	na --	16.1 30
FRANKLIN OPTION FUND	FRNKRE	G	27	5.93	4.0	1.9	12.7 63	11.6 84	11.1 69
FRANKLIN U.S. GOVT. SEC.	FRNKRE	BP	14367	7.42	4.0	10.9	7.4 95	16.5 56	14.3 48
FRANKLIN UTILITIES	FRNKRE	GI	327	8.18	4.0	6.6	14.5 43	22.8 8	22.5 3
FREEDOM GOLD & GOV TRUST	TUCKER	ME	47	16.03	0.0	6.8	na --	na --	na --
FREEDOM REGIONAL BANK FD	TUCKER	G	53	10.92	0.0	2.4	na --	na --	na --
FT INTERNATIONAL	FEDRES	IN	104	21.60	0.0	0.4	na --	na --	na --
FTP-EQ PORTFOLIO-GROWTH	FIDEL	G	58	11.92	0.0	0.5	na --	na --	11.0 70
FTP-EQ PORTFOLIO INCOME	FIDEL	GI	501	12.52	0.0	5.9	na --	na --	17.7 20
FTP-FIXED INC. LTD PORT.	FIDEL	BP	377	11.07	0.0	9.1	na --	na --	na --
FUND FOR U.S. GOVT. SEC.	FEDRES	BP	979	8.62	0.0	10.0	8.3 94	17.3 48	12.6 60
FUND OF AMERICA	AM-CAP	GI	145	10.49	8.5	2.5	16.1 28	19.4 29	7.8 82
FUND OF THE SOUTHWEST	TAMCO	AG	15	9.33	7.5	0.4	na --	na --	-1.2 95
FUNDAMENTAL INVESTORS	CAPRES	G	488	14.21	8.5	2.4	14.8 41	23.2 7	18.8 14
FUNDTRUST AGGRESSIVE	FURSEL	AG	40	13.27	0.0	1.1	na --	na --	na --
FUNDTRUST GROWTH	FURSEL	G	30	13.08	0.0	2.3	na --	na --	na --
FUNDTRUST GROWTH & INC	FURSEL	GI	46	12.88	0.0	2.5	na --	na --	na --
FUNDTRUST INCOME	FURSEL	BP	30	10.62	0.0	8.5	na --	na --	na --
G. T. PACIFIC GROWTH FD	GTCAP	IN	67	29.98	0.0	0.0	na --	17.3 48	21.7 5
GABELLI ASSET FUND	GABCO	G	41	11.29	0.0	na	na --	na --	na --
GATEWAY GROWTH PLUS FUND	GATEWY	AG	3	10.04	0.0	na	na --	na --	na --
GATEWAY OPTION INCOME	GATEWY	GI	36	14.63	0.0	2.2	na --	11.3 85	10.7 71
GENERAL ELEC S&S LT BOND	GENELC	BP	608	12.41	0.0	8.6	na --	19.4 29	18.5 15
GENL ELEC S&S PROGRAM	GENELC	GI	815	35.47	0.0	3.7	11.5 72	17.8 45	15.6 35
GENERAL SECURITIES	CRAHAL	GI	16	11.57	0.0	2.8	13.2 56	16.3 58	14.5 46
GIBRALTAR FUND, INC.	DAYTON	G	1	13.45	0.0	1.2	na --	na --	12.8 59
GINTEL CAP APPRECIATION	GINTEL	AG	21	11.00	0.0	0.0	na --	na --	na --
GINTEL ERISA	GINTEL	GI	79	45.23	0.0	2.7	na --	na --	15.7 34
GINTEL FUND	GINTEL	G	119	66.62	0.0	1.7	na --	20.3 21	11.9 63
GOLCONDA INVESTORS	GOLCON	ME	32	12.86	0.0	0.2	na --	2.1 97	1.2 93
GRADISON ESTABLISHED GR.	GRADSN	G	33	15.21	0.0	2.0	na --	na --	18.0 18
GRADISON OPPORTUNITY GR	GRADSN	AG	17	11.64	0.0	0.3	na --	na --	11.9 64
GREENWAY FUND	AIM	AG	19	10.11	4.7	0.5	na --	10.8 87	10.0 75
GROWTH FUND OF AMERICA	CAPRES	G	741	15.76	8.5	1.6	21.3 6	17.1 50	11.5 66
GROWTH FD OF WASHINGTON	JL	G	51	11.12	5.0	1.2	na --	na --	na --
GROWTH INDUSTRY SHARES	WMBLR	G	69	9.10	0.0	2.0	15.4 35	13.3 78	8.8 79
GUARDIAN MUTUAL FUND	NEUBER	GI	519	38.13	0.0	3.5	16.2 28	19.4 29	14.6 45
GUARDIAN PARK AVE FUND	GUARD	G	119	20.74	8.5	1.4	19.3 12	23.4 6	20.9 6
HAMILTON FUNDS	OPPEN	G	242	6.76	8.5	4.3	10.3 81	15.4 66	14.9 42
HANCOCK (JOHN) BOND	HANCOK	BP	1108	15.89	8.5	8.8	8.7 92	17.4 48	15.9 32
HANCOCK (JOHN) GLOBAL	HANCOK	IN	72	14.76	8.5	0.1	na --	na --	na --
HANCOCK (JOHN) GNMA	HANCOK	BP	371	10.72	8.5	8.7	na --	na --	na --
HANCOCK (JOHN) GROWTH	HANCOK	AG	85	14.03	8.5	1.0	13.5 53	15.0 68	12.8 58
HANCOCK (JOHN) SPECIAL	HANCOK	G	13	5.71	8.5	0.4	na --	na --	na --
HANCOCK (JOHN) TX EX DIV	HANCOK	MB	321	11.10	4.8	6.4	na --	16.9 51	15.9 32
HANCOCK (JOHN) US GOV	HANCOK	BP	182	9.71	8.5	7.8	8.9 92	14.6 71	15.3 38
HARTWELL GROWTH FUND	HARTWL	AG	10	12.01	0.0	0.5	18.9 14	12.8 80	7.8 82
HARTWELL LEVERAGE FUND	HARTWL	AG	25	16.15	0.0	0.0	17.4 19	8.0 93	1.2 93
HAWAIIAN TAX-FREE TRUST	HTC	MB	130	11.09	4.0	6.8	na --	na --	na --
HEARTLAND VALUE FUND	MILWCO	G	26	14.01	4.5	0.6	na --	na --	na --

LATEST 12 MNTHS PCNT RK	THIS MONTH PCNT RK	1986 TO DATE PCNT RK	CALENDAR YEARS 1985 PCNT RK	1984 PCNT RK	1983 PCNT RK	CYCLES UP MKT PCNT RK	DOWN MKT PCNT RK	CDA RATING
17.6 31	0.5 17	17.6 31	22.3 57	8.8 29	na --	na --	na --	na
7.6 85	-1.5 61	7.6 85	23.9 49	2.9 52	16.5 51	100.5 68	-9.3 61	83
10.4 75	0.5 16	10.4 75	19.8 72	12.8 12	8.1 87	88.0 82	19.2 7	87
23.7 9	-3.5 93	23.7 9	22.7 55	21.2 1	15.8 52	175.4 16	37.1 1	10
15.9 42	0.2 26	15.9 42	na --	na --	na --	na --	na --	na
20.2 18	-1.9 69	20.2 18	na --	na --	na --	na --	na --	na
55.2 2	3.7 2	55.2 2	61.2 1	na --	na --	na --	na --	na
15.0 49	-2.0 71	15.0 49	41.5 4	-16.0 92	na --	na --	na --	na
17.5 32	-1.4 59	17.5 32	25.7 43	10.4 21	na --	na --	na --	na
14.4 52	0.5 18	14.4 52	20.2 70	na --	na --	na --	na --	na
8.6 82	1.1 7	8.6 82	16.6 85	12.8 12	11.1 73	89.4 81	14.7 13	88
6.6 87	-2.4 78	6.6 87	15.8 88	1.5 56	28.2 14	142.4 38	-9.3 60	66
-1.6 96	-4.6 97	-1.6 96	16.0 87	-15.5 91	20.4 34	62.5 93	na --	na
21.8 13	-1.9 69	21.8 13	30.1 23	5.8 42	26.2 19	190.7 10	-3.2 49	43
11.9 66	-0.8 49	11.9 66	25.7 42	na --	na --	na --	na --	na
13.4 58	-0.8 49	13.4 58	25.0 46	na --	na --	na --	na --	na
14.5 51	-0.7 46	14.5 51	23.7 50	na --	na --	na --	na --	na
8.6 82	0.6 15	8.6 82	16.8 84	na --	na --	na --	na --	na
70.0 1	5.3 1	70.0 1	9.3 96	-3.0 69	37.0 5	182.2 13	-0.7 46	2
na --	-2.8 86	na --	na --	na --	na --	na --	na --	na
na --	-1.7 64	na --	na --	na --	na --	na --	na --	na
12.6 62	-0.4 41	12.6 62	16.0 87	4.0 49	14.9 58	76.9 89	-0.1 44	83
19.1 22	0.6 14	19.1 22	18.6 78	18.0 2	6.7 91	113.1 58	na --	na
17.6 31	-1.7 65	17.6 31	25.7 43	4.7 47	20.3 35	150.6 30	-16.4 74	74
9.0 81	-1.2 55	9.0 81	38.8 6	-0.9 62	10.6 76	143.2 38	-10.8 64	80
13.2 58	-1.5 61	13.2 58	27.5 34	-0.6 61	na --	na --	na --	na
na --	1.3 6	na --	na --	na --	na --	na --	na --	na
21.8 13	1.3 6	21.8 13	24.0 48	2.4 53	27.5 15	136.1 42	na --	na
19.9 19	0.9 10	19.9 19	19.9 72	-2.5 68	34.8 6	136.1 42	na --	na
35.0 4	1.9 4	35.0 4	2.6 97	-25.2 97	0.6 98	18.5 98	-39.4 97	97
22.0 12	-0.9 51	22.0 12	28.8 28	4.5 48	na --	na --	na --	na
13.0 60	-4.0 96	13.0 60	28.1 32	-3.2 70	na --	na --	na --	na
9.7 78	-2.2 76	9.7 78	32.9 15	-8.8 83	9.0 83	130.0 47	-34.3 96	93
16.0 42	-1.3 56	16.0 42	26.7 38	-5.6 76	27.1 16	130.3 46	-2.3 47	9
14.9 49	-0.9 51	14.9 49	na --	na --	na --	na --	na --	na
9.1 80	-1.6 62	9.1 80	23.4 51	-4.2 73	13.4 64	118.4 54	-9.4 61	68
11.9 66	-4.5 97	11.9 66	25.3 44	7.4 36	25.3 21	174.1 16	-13.3 68	50
18.1 28	-2.0 71	18.1 28	33.0 15	12.5 13	28.6 12	224.1 4	-5.5 53	8
19.8 19	-1.6 62	19.8 19	29.4 27	-2.2 67	9.9 79	130.6 46	-20.5 82	80
10.2 76	-1.9 69	10.2 76	22.3 57	15.4 5	9.0 84	102.3 67	16.4 10	75
26.8 7	0.9 10	26.8 7	na --	na --	na --	na --	na --	na
11.4 69	-0.5 43	11.4 69	na --	na --	na --	na --	na --	na
13.8 56	-3.2 90	13.8 56	28.3 31	-1.6 66	15.7 54	156.1 28	-32.5 95	84
-4.3 96	-6.2 99	-4.3 96	na --	na --	na --	na --	na --	na
17.2 33	0.0 33	17.2 33	21.5 62	9.2 27	7.6 88	86.2 84	3.2 35	55
14.5 51	0.2 26	14.5 51	18.0 80	13.4 10	6.4 92	79.3 87	3.1 36	79
24.4 9	-0.8 48	24.4 9	22.1 58	-17.6 93	25.5 21	146.4 34	-31.5 93	14
19.3 21	-0.4 40	19.3 21	27.0 36	-31.6 98	10.3 77	95.8 74	-32.1 94	49
15.0 48	0.1 29	15.0 48	na --	na --	na --	na --	na --	na
10.8 73	-2.4 78	10.8 73	41.4 4	na --	na --	na --	na --	na

CDA MONTHLY ALPHABETIC LISTING - 12/31/86

FUND	MGT CO	IO	ASSETS MIL$	NAV	MAX LOAD	% YLD	ANNUALIZED ROR THRU 12/31/86 10 YEARS PCNT RK	5 YEARS PCNT RK	3 YEARS PCNT RK
HIGH YIELD SECURITIES	AIM	BP	87	9.73	4.7	11.7	na --	16.2 59	10.9 71
HOME INVS GOV GTD INCOME	INTEGR	BP	184	10.67	0.0	8.3	na --	na --	na --
HORACE MANN GROWTH FUND	INA	G	75	21.29	0.0	4.6	12.8 62	16.8 53	12.9 58
HUTTON CAL MUNICIPAL FD	HUTTON	MB	162	11.08	4.0	7.1	na --	na --	14.8 43
HUTTON INV SER BASIC VAL	HUTTON	G	324	12.15	0.0	2.4	na --	na --	na --
HUTTON INV SER BOND/INC	HUTTON	BP	347	12.91	0.0	9.3	na --	na --	19.7 10
HUTTON INV SER SPL EQTY	HUTTON	AG	216	13.02	0.0	0.3	na --	na --	9.1 78
HUTTON INV SERIES GROWTH	HUTTON	G	1121	15.86	0.0	1.5	na --	na --	12.7 59
HUTTON INV SER GOV SECS	HUTTON	BP	5177	10.41	0.0	11.1	na --	na --	na --
HUTTON INV SER PRE METAL	HUTTON	ME	39	12.93	0.0	0.2	na --	na --	na --
HUTTON NATL MUNICIPAL FD	HUTTON	MB	951	11.97	4.0	7.1	na --	na --	18.5 15
HUTTON N.Y. MUNICIPAL FD	HUTTON	MB	224	11.32	4.0	7.0	na --	na --	15.7 34
HUTTON OPTION INCOME	HUTTON	GI	76	8.19	0.0	0.6	na --	na --	5.5 89
IDS BOND FUND	IDS	BP	1775	5.30	3.5	8.7	11.1 75	20.5 20	17.6 20
IDS DISCOVERY FUND	IDS	AG	268	7.45	5.0	1.6	na --	11.9 83	3.8 91
IDS EQUITY PLUS FD INC.	IDS	G	365	9.43	5.0	2.2	13.1 57	15.3 67	13.3 55
IDS EXTRA INCOME	IDS	BP	871	5.16	5.0	10.1	na --	na --	15.3 38
IDS GROWTH FUND	IDS	AG	708	20.35	5.0	0.6	21.1 6	14.8 69	9.9 76
IDS MUTUAL FUND	IDS	B	1242	12.45	5.0	5.9	13.1 58	20.9 18	19.9 9
IDS NEW DIMENSIONS FUND	IDS	G	510	8.52	5.0	1.7	19.2 13	20.2 22	16.1 30
IDS PROGRESSIVE FUND	IDS	GI	184	6.68	5.0	3.2	15.8 31	22.9 8	12.4 61
IDS SELECTIVE	IDS	BP	1111	9.08	5.0	8.4	10.6 79	20.3 21	17.0 24
IDS STOCK FUND	IDS	GI	1345	19.16	5.0	2.9	11.8 69	17.1 50	14.1 50
INCOME FUND OF AMERICA	CAPRES	B	601	12.03	8.5	7.9	14.2 45	22.3 11	19.5 11
INDUSTRY FUND OF AMERICA	HERTGE	AG	1	3.07	0.0	0.0	5.3 97	-6.0 98	-13.1 99
INTEGRATED CAPTL APPREC	INTEGR	G	126	13.17	0.0	2.1	na --	na --	na --
INTEGRATED INSD TAX FREE	INTEGR	MB	129	12.52	4.7	7.3	na --	na --	na --
INTERNATIONAL INVESTORS	VANECK	ME	865	12.04	8.5	3.0	24.5 2	11.0 86	0.6 94
INVEST. CO. OF AMERICA	CAPRES	GI	3487	13.19	8.5	2.9	16.3 25	22.5 9	19.9 9
INVEST. PORTFOLIOS-EQ	KEMPER	G	192	10.75	0.0	0.0	na --	na --	na --
INVEST. PORTFOLIOS-GOV +	KEMPER	BP	4528	8.53	0.0	7.9	na --	na --	na --
INVEST. PORTFOLIOS-HIYLD	KEMPER	BP	163	9.83	0.0	8.7	na --	na --	na --
INVEST. PORTFOLIOS-OP IN	KEMPER	GI	347	7.48	0.0	5.1	na --	na --	na --
INVEST. QUALITY INTEREST	CRITER	BP	128	10.14	4.5	8.4	na --	17.9 44	16.9 25
INVEST. TRUST OF BOSTON	MOSELY	G	65	11.98	7.0	2.5	11.1 75	14.9 69	13.2 56
INV TR/BOSTON HI IN PLUS	MOSELY	BP	22	14.11	6.7	9.8	na --	na --	na --
INVESTORS INCOME	TAMCO	BP	19	5.36	4.5	8.6	9.6 88	17.2 49	15.8 33
INVESTORS RESEARCH	INV-RE	G	59	5.15	8.5	0.4	18.8 15	22.6 9	14.1 49
IRI STOCK FUND	IRI	G	13	9.91	4.5	2.9	na --	na --	16.3 29
ISI GROWTH FUND	SIGMA	GI	13	6.48	8.5	1.3	10.1 85	9.8 90	6.4 87
ISI INCOME FUND	SIGMA	B	6	3.38	8.5	5.4	9.1 91	10.1 89	6.3 87
ISI TRUST FUND	SIGMA	B	102	10.22	8.5	5.2	9.9 86	11.5 84	9.8 76
ITB MASS TAX FREE	MOSELY	MB	45	16.83	4.2	6.5	na --	na --	na --
IVY GROWTH FUND	HMI	GI	165	13.44	0.0	2.8	17.8 19	23.0 7	17.7 20
IVY INSTITUTIONAL INV FD	HGM	G	131	125.53	0.0	4.1	na --	na --	na --
JANUS FUND	JANUS	GI	464	12.47	0.0	0.0	19.6 11	17.9 44	11.4 66
JANUS VALUE FUND	JANUS	G	11	12.07	0.0	6.4	na --	na --	na --
JANUS VENTURE FUND	JANUS	AG	28	27.45	0.0	5.2	na --	na --	na --
JP GROWTH FUND	JP-INV	GI	24	13.62	8.0	3.0	13.3 55	18.4 40	15.3 39
JP INCOME	JP-INV	BP	20	9.96	8.0	7.9	na --	19.1 34	19.0 13

LATEST 12 MNTHS PCNT RK	THIS MONTH PCNT RK	1986 TO DATE PCNT RK	CALENDAR YEARS 1985 PCNT RK	1984 PCNT RK	1983 PCNT RK	CYCLES UP MKT PCNT RK	DOWN MKT PCNT RK	CDA RATING
9.6 78	-0.3 38	9.6 78	17.9 80	5.5 43	19.3 40	97.2 73	11.3 21	76
9.1 80	0.1 29	9.1 80	na --	na --	na --	na --	na --	na
12.1 65	-2.1 73	12.1 65	25.9 41	1.9 55	22.3 29	156.4 27	-20.6 82	76
17.4 33	0.3 24	17.4 33	17.7 81	9.6 26	na --	na --	na --	na
13.7 56	-2.9 87	13.7 56	na --	na --	na --	na --	na --	na
19.8 19	1.0 7	19.8 19	25.3 45	14.2 8	7.8 88	na --	na --	na
7.0 86	-1.3 57	7.0 86	34.8 11	-10.0 85	na --	na --	na --	na
16.0 41	-0.8 48	16.0 41	22.0 59	1.1 57	22.5 28	na --	na --	na
13.1 59	-0.1 34	13.1 59	18.3 79	na --	na --	na --	na --	na
43.1 3	1.0 8	43.1 3	na --	na --	na --	na --	na --	na
22.4 11	0.3 23	22.4 11	20.6 68	12.9 11	na --	na --	na --	na
17.2 34	0.2 27	17.2 34	18.6 77	11.5 17	na --	na --	na --	na
1.7 94	-4.0 96	1.7 94	11.9 94	3.3 50	na --	na --	na --	na
20.3 17	1.1 7	20.3 17	24.0 48	9.1 28	14.6 59	126.9 49	11.9 19	28
5.4 90	-2.4 77	5.4 90	29.8 25	-18.3 94	21.4 32	97.2 72	na --	na
18.1 28	-1.2 55	18.1 28	30.7 22	-5.6 76	13.5 64	146.0 35	-11.6 65	52
16.4 39	0.9 9	16.4 39	20.5 68	9.2 27	na --	na --	na --	na
19.5 20	-3.2 90	19.5 20	36.2 8	-18.4 94	13.3 65	147.7 33	-8.8 59	8
23.2 10	1.0 8	23.2 10	23.3 52	13.6 10	15.4 56	146.4 34	-0.6 45	38
21.1 15	-2.5 81	21.1 15	35.4 9	-4.5 73	20.1 37	175.6 16	-6.5 55	16
13.3 58	-2.8 84	13.3 58	30.8 21	-4.1 72	18.0 45	143.3 37	-2.9 48	34
18.0 29	1.3 6	18.0 29	24.0 49	9.4 26	13.2 66	122.9 51	12.9 18	36
19.5 20	-1.7 64	19.5 20	21.6 61	2.2 54	15.9 52	128.0 48	-8.8 59	62
17.1 34	0.7 13	17.1 34	27.5 34	14.4 7	17.2 48	156.1 27	19.1 7	26
-14.2 99	-1.5 61	-14.2 99	-5.5 98	-19.1 94	19.6 38	-2.6 99	-33.7 96	97
17.0 36	-2.7 84	17.0 36	na --	na --	na --	na --	na --	na
11.4 69	0.5 17	11.4 69	na --	na --	na --	na --	na --	na
34.2 4	-0.7 47	34.2 4	-1.9 98	-22.6 96	8.9 84	79.2 88	-39.8 97	50
21.3 15	-0.8 47	21.3 15	32.9 15	6.8 38	20.2 36	186.8 11	-1.9 47	24
4.4 92	-3.1 89	4.4 92	22.6 55	na --	na --	na --	na --	na
11.6 68	0.1 30	11.6 68	10.5 95	na --	na --	na --	na --	na
18.6 25	1.0 8	18.6 25	20.0 71	na --	na --	na --	na --	na
1.5 94	-2.8 84	1.5 94	10.8 94	na --	na --	na --	na --	na
15.4 45	0.1 29	15.4 45	19.9 71	15.5 4	4.1 97	103.0 66	na --	na
11.9 66	-1.0 52	11.9 66	31.3 19	-1.1 64	9.8 79	124.8 50	-27.1 91	89
10.8 73	0.4 21	10.8 73	21.7 60	na --	na --	na --	na --	na
16.0 41	0.9 9	16.0 41	20.3 69	11.2 18	12.3 68	93.3 77	17.3 9	64
28.3 6	-2.7 83	28.3 6	19.5 74	-3.0 69	26.3 18	196.8 7	-24.9 88	15
15.8 44	-2.0 71	15.8 44	36.5 8	-0.3 60	13.8 63	na --	na --	na
-1.3 95	-2.3 76	-1.3 95	17.1 83	4.2 48	3.8 97	68.5 92	6.5 29	88
-4.5 96	-2.3 76	-4.5 96	9.7 95	14.5 7	4.4 96	52.0 94	13.3 17	90
6.1 88	-0.2 38	6.1 88	11.4 94	12.1 15	6.5 92	58.7 94	10.0 22	88
15.8 43	-0.3 40	15.8 43	18.0 80	na --	na --	na --	na --	na
16.8 38	-1.5 61	16.8 38	29.4 26	7.9 34	30.1 10	192.6 9	3.2 35	34
19.0 23	-1.8 67	19.0 23	37.5 7	na --	na --	na --	na --	na
11.2 70	-0.3 38	11.2 70	24.5 47	-0.1 60	26.1 19	141.3 39	4.7 32	16
11.5 68	0.5 17	11.5 68	na --	na --	na --	na --	na --	na
20.2 17	-1.8 66	20.2 17	na --	na --	na --	na --	na --	na
13.9 55	-2.1 73	13.9 55	25.1 45	7.5 36	16.1 52	134.5 43	2.0 39	63
16.4 39	0.5 17	16.4 39	26.1 41	14.9 5	4.2 97	113.1 58	na --	na

CDA MONTHLY ALPHABETIC LISTING - 12/31/86

FUND	MGT CO	IO	ASSETS MIL$	NAV	MAX LOAD	% YLD	ANNUALIZED ROR THRU 12/31/86 10 YEARS PCNT RK	5 YEARS PCNT RK	3 YEARS PCNT RK
KEMPER CALIF TAX FREE	KEMPER	MB	186	14.59	4.5	6.9	na --	na --	15.9 32
KEMPER GROWTH FUND	KEMPER	G	275	10.06	8.5	0.7	16.5 24	16.4 56	9.6 76
KEMPER HIGH YIELD FD	KEMPER	BP	323	11.45	5.5	10.4	na --	21.3 15	17.0 24
KEMPER INC & CAP PRESERV	KEMPER	BP	199	9.08	5.5	9.7	9.7 88	18.4 41	16.1 31
KEMPER INTL FD	KEMPER	IN	185	19.30	8.5	1.0	na --	21.9 13	26.9 2
KEMPER MUNI BOND FD LTD	KEMPER	MB	905	9.81	4.5	7.0	na --	21.0 17	16.7 26
KEMPER OPTION INCOME FD	KEMPER	GI	621	9.70	8.5	8.9	na --	10.9 87	7.7 83
KEMPER SUMMIT FUND	KEMPER	G	274	5.11	8.5	0.0	19.1 14	16.2 59	10.2 74
KEMPER TOTAL RETURN FD	KEMPER	GI	614	15.25	8.5	3.0	16.6 23	17.0 51	14.2 48
KEMPER US GOVT SECS	KEMPER	BP	2379	9.90	4.5	10.0	na --	17.4 48	16.8 26
KEYSTONE INTL FUND	KEYSTN	IN	90	7.16	0.0	0.7	14.1 46	19.3 32	23.7 3
KEYSTONE B-1	KEYSTN	BP	316	17.65	0.0	9.1	10.3 81	17.8 45	15.2 39
KEYSTONE B-2	KEYSTN	BP	575	19.89	0.0	10.0	11.0 77	16.7 53	13.9 51
KEYSTONE B-4	KEYSTN	BP	1500	7.77	0.0	12.3	11.1 76	16.0 60	11.3 67
KEYSTONE K-1	KEYSTN	B	439	8.67	0.0	5.9	11.7 70	17.0 51	13.5 54
KEYSTONE K-2	KEYSTN	G	288	7.64	0.0	1.4	12.8 62	19.1 33	14.8 44
KEYSTONE PRECIOUS METALS	KEYSTN	ME	65	14.59	0.0	2.5	na --	4.6 96	-3.2 96
KEYSTONE S-1	KEYSTN	G	106	19.77	0.0	1.7	8.5 93	13.7 75	10.0 75
KEYSTONE S-3	KEYSTN	G	230	7.93	0.0	1.4	13.6 52	15.1 68	8.6 80
KEYSTONE S-4	KEYSTN	AG	543	5.98	0.0	0.2	14.7 42	10.6 88	3.2 92
KEYSTONE TAX FREE	KEYSTN	MB	975	8.84	0.0	7.7	na --	na --	15.2 40
KIDDER P. EQUITY INCOME	WEBSTR	GI	42	17.49	0.0	2.6	na --	na --	na --
KIDDER P. GOVT INCOME	WEBSTR	BP	145	15.11	0.0	7.6	na --	na --	na --
KIDDER P. SPECIAL GROWTH	WEBSTR	AG	31	13.92	0.0	1.7	na --	na --	na --
KIDDER P. NATL TX-FR INC	WEBSTR	MB	19	15.89	4.0	6.9	na --	na --	na --
KIDDER P. N.Y. TX-FR INC	WEBSTR	MB	10	15.64	4.0	6.7	na --	na --	na --
LEGG MASON VALUE TRUST	LEGG	G	607	26.10	0.0	1.5	na --	na --	17.7 20
LEHMAN CAPITAL FUND	LEHMAN	G	103	17.87	0.0	1.3	24.6 2	22.0 12	11.7 65
LEHMAN INVESTORS FD, INC	LEHMAN	G	405	17.37	0.0	2.7	15.3 36	18.5 39	13.2 55
LEHMAN OPPORTUNITY FUND	LEHMAN	G	103	22.60	0.0	2.8	na --	22.9 7	16.2 30
LEPERCQ-ISTEL TRUST	LEPERQ	GI	26	13.29	0.0	4.5	11.0 76	8.4 92	7.3 84
LEVERAGE FUND OF BOSTON	ETN&HD	AG	25	7.26	0.0	0.0	na --	na --	0.6 94
LEXINGTON GOLDFUND	LEXGTN	ME	22	4.49	0.0	0.4	na --	na --	4.4 90
LEXINGTON GROWTH FUND	LEXGTN	G	28	11.80	0.0	1.7	13.7 50	9.5 90	10.3 73
LEXINGTON GNMA NEW INC	LEXGTN	BP	129	8.22	0.0	9.1	7.7 95	14.8 70	13.6 52
LEXINGTON RESEARCH FUND	LEXGTN	G	123	19.16	0.0	3.5	13.6 51	15.9 62	13.3 55
LG US GOV SECURITIES	MIDWES	BP	48	10.77	4.0	9.6	na --	na --	na --
LIBERTY FUND	NEUBER	BP	10	4.73	0.0	7.6	8.7 93	16.5 56	14.9 42
LINDNER DIVIDEND FUND	LINDNR	GI	62	23.74	0.0	8.2	22.3 4	25.0 3	17.5 21
LINDNER FUND	LINDNR	GI	361	16.12	0.0	7.9	na --	19.4 30	15.3 38
LMH FUND, LTD.	HEINE	GI	84	24.01	0.0	4.2	na --	na --	15.2 39
LOOMIS-SAYLES CAP. DEV.	LOOMIS	AG	208	23.12	0.0	0.6	23.6 3	28.8 1	20.0 9
LOOMIS-SAYLES MUTUAL	LOOMIS	GI	174	22.86	0.0	3.9	13.8 48	22.6 9	21.3 5
LORD ABBETT BOND-DEBEN.	LD-ABT	BP	610	10.28	8.5	10.6	10.9 77	15.9 62	12.0 63
LORD ABBETT DEV GROWTH	LD-ABT	AG	239	7.88	8.5	0.0	na --	7.7 93	-3.6 96
LORD ABBETT TX FREE NATL	LD-ABT	MB	184	11.23	4.8	7.2	na --	na --	na --
LORD ABBETT TX FREE NY	LD-ABT	MB	94	11.29	4.8	6.9	na --	na --	na --
LORD ABBETT US GOV SECS	LD-ABT	BP	269	3.27	6.7	9.8	11.0 77	17.5 47	16.7 26
LORD ABBETT VALUE APPREC	LD-ABT	G	299	12.69	8.5	1.7	na --	na --	15.6 36
LOWRY MARKET TIMING FD	CRITER	AG	69	8.52	8.5	3.8	na --	na --	0.9 94

LATEST 12 MNTHS		THIS MONTH		1986 TO DATE		CALENDAR YEARS						CYCLES				CDA RATING
						1985		1984		1983		UP MKT		DOWN MKT		
PCNT	RK	PCNT	RK	PCNT	RK	PCNT	RK	PCNT	RK	PCNT	RK	PCNT	RK	PCNT	RK	
18.2	27	0.0	33	18.2	27	21.9	59	8.0	33	na	--	na	--	na	--	na
12.4	64	-2.0	72	12.4	64	26.5	39	-7.2	79	26.0	20	144.6	36	-24.8	87	57
18.2	27	1.1	7	18.2	27	23.2	52	10.1	22	17.5	47	122.7	52	20.7	5	7
14.5	51	0.1	31	14.5	51	21.7	60	12.2	14	11.4	71	107.5	62	16.4	10	52
44.7	2	2.8	3	44.7	2	55.3	2	-9.1	84	28.1	14	201.7	7	na	--	na
19.0	23	-0.4	41	19.0	23	21.1	64	10.3	22	14.2	61	110.8	60	2.5	37	19
2.5	93	-2.8	85	2.5	93	15.1	89	5.9	42	16.4	51	78.2	88	-0.3	44	96
13.9	54	-0.8	48	13.9	54	27.3	35	-7.6	80	24.4	24	152.9	29	-19.1	79	22
17.5	32	-1.9	69	17.5	32	28.2	31	-1.0	63	19.7	37	140.4	40	-9.1	60	14
16.2	41	0.2	27	16.2	41	22.2	58	12.2	14	8.9	85	98.4	72	13.8	15	31
47.9	2	5.9	1	47.9	2	38.6	6	-7.5	80	13.5	64	162.2	24	-16.6	74	35
13.8	56	0.9	10	13.8	56	21.5	62	10.7	19	8.7	85	99.4	70	18.4	8	57
12.5	63	0.1	28	12.5	63	23.1	53	6.8	38	10.3	76	97.5	72	14.1	15	61
9.6	79	-0.7	47	9.6	79	20.2	70	4.7	46	15.5	54	88.7	81	15.4	12	77
16.0	42	-1.1	54	16.0	42	22.2	57	3.1	51	18.7	42	119.7	54	-0.2	44	40
21.3	14	-1.4	59	21.3	14	32.5	16	-5.9	77	24.1	24	164.8	23	-21.2	83	51
39.9	3	3.0	3	39.9	3	-9.7	99	-28.3	98	0.3	98	32.7	97	na	--	na
16.4	40	-1.6	63	16.4	40	24.0	48	-7.8	81	14.4	60	111.1	60	-22.3	84	89
15.0	49	-2.5	80	15.0	49	22.8	54	-9.3	84	26.0	20	147.7	33	-22.3	84	54
7.6	85	-2.6	82	7.6	85	28.2	31	-20.4	95	25.0	22	112.8	58	-39.9	98	79
17.1	34	-0.4	41	17.1	34	20.0	71	8.7	30	9.5	82	92.2	78	na	--	na
16.4	40	-1.7	64	16.4	40	na	--	na	--	na	--	na	--	na	--	na
6.9	87	0.1	27	6.9	87	na	--	na	--	na	--	na	--	na	--	na
5.1	90	-2.9	87	5.1	90	-9.0	98	na	--	na	--	na	--	na	--	na
18.5	25	0.3	24	18.5	25	na	--	na	--	na	--	na	--	na	--	na
15.9	43	-0.2	37	15.9	43	na	--	na	--	na	--	na	--	na	--	na
9.4	79	-1.8	67	9.4	79	31.8	18	12.9	11	42.7	2	238.1	2	na	--	na
13.9	54	-3.0	88	13.9	54	27.2	35	-3.9	72	38.2	4	184.5	12	5.3	30	3
14.6	51	-2.8	86	14.6	51	26.3	40	0.3	59	23.8	25	153.4	28	-5.5	53	48
6.4	87	-3.6	94	6.4	87	32.8	15	11.0	19	38.9	3	234.7	2	-13.8	69	76
8.2	83	-1.8	67	8.2	83	20.0	71	-4.9	74	17.1	48	87.4	83	-28.3	91	92
-11.1	98	-10.3	99	-11.1	98	32.1	17	-13.1	89	16.1	52	91.6	79	na	--	na
32.7	5	1.8	5	32.7	5	13.0	92	-24.0	96	-6.4	99	66.8	92	na	--	na
20.6	16	-2.4	79	20.6	16	26.7	37	-12.0	87	9.9	79	108.2	62	-28.0	91	37
11.9	66	0.7	13	11.9	66	17.2	83	11.9	15	7.6	89	73.4	91	11.2	22	85
20.2	17	-2.8	85	20.2	17	26.3	40	-4.3	73	28.7	12	147.4	33	-11.7	65	46
10.2	76	0.5	18	10.2	76	19.2	75	na	--	na	--	na	--	na	--	na
18.2	27	0.9	11	18.2	27	20.9	65	6.1	42	16.7	50	93.1	77	3.1	35	87
20.8	15	-0.3	40	20.8	15	17.0	83	14.9	5	43.8	2	173.3	17	39.1	1	3
13.8	55	-0.1	35	13.8	55	19.3	75	12.8	12	24.6	23	132.3	45	35.8	1	16
14.1	53	-1.4	60	14.1	53	22.7	55	9.4	27	na	--	na	--	na	--	na
27.5	7	-2.5	81	27.5	7	46.2	2	-7.3	80	15.4	56	241.8	2	15.7	12	2
24.8	8	-0.5	44	24.8	8	34.4	12	6.4	40	10.0	78	174.6	16	6.5	29	36
10.5	74	-0.3	39	10.5	74	20.7	67	5.3	44	16.9	49	96.0	74	9.9	23	71
0.4	95	-0.8	47	0.4	95	15.0	89	-22.4	96	24.8	23	63.5	92	-9.4	61	99
21.4	14	0.1	29	21.4	14	19.6	74	na	--	na	--	na	--	na	--	na
18.1	29	0.0	33	18.1	29	20.4	68	na	--	na	--	na	--	na	--	na
15.0	48	0.0	34	15.0	48	22.4	56	13.0	11	10.0	78	99.0	71	23.8	4	53
15.9	43	-2.6	82	15.9	43	34.7	11	-1.0	63	na	--	na	--	na	--	na
-9.3	98	0.4	21	-9.3	98	19.2	76	-5.0	74	na	--	na	--	na	--	na

CDA MONTHLY ALPHABETIC LISTING – 12/31/86

FUND	MGT CO	IO	ASSETS MIL$	NAV	MAX LOAD	% YLD	10 YEARS PCNT RK	5 YEARS PCNT RK	3 YEARS PCNT RK
							ANNUALIZED ROR THRU 12/31/86		
LUTHERAN BROTHER. FUND	FEDRES	GI	186	16.96	5.0	3.6	12.5 65	18.2 42	13.6 53
LUTHERAN BROTHER. INCOME	FEDRES	BP	504	8.97	5.0	9.5	10.0 85	15.8 63	13.6 53
LUTHERAN BROTHER. MUN BD	FEDRES	MB	210	8.34	5.0	6.8	na --	19.0 34	15.1 40
MACKENZIE INDUSTRIAL AM	MIM	G	7	8.75	8.5	0.9	na --	na --	na --
MACKENZIE INDUSTRIAL GOV	MIM	BP	20	9.33	6.7	9.0	na --	na --	na --
MACKENZIE INDUSTRIAL OPT	MIM	GI	75	8.83	8.5	14.5	na --	na --	na --
MANHATTAN FUND	NEUBER	G	241	8.95	0.0	0.8	16.6 23	22.9 8	19.8 10
MASS. CAPITAL DEVEL.	MASFIN	G	858	11.21	7.2	1.3	21.3 5	16.0 61	5.9 88
MASS. FINANCIAL BOND	MASFIN	BP	327	14.66	7.2	8.4	10.2 83	19.2 32	17.6 20
MASS. FINANCIAL DEVEL.	MASFIN	G	193	10.89	7.2	1.6	16.1 29	16.5 55	11.2 68
MASS. FINL EMERG. GWTH.	MASFIN	AG	233	16.82	7.2	0.0	na --	21.5 14	9.6 77
MASS. FINL GOV SEC HIYLD	MASFIN	BP	367	9.76	4.7	7.5	na --	na --	na --
MASS. FINL HI INCOME	MASFIN	BP	1000	6.92	7.2	12.5	na --	19.9 24	13.2 56
MASS. FINL INTL TRUST BD	MASFIN	BP	134	11.46	7.2	5.9	na --	19.4 30	20.0 8
MASS. FINANCIAL SPECIAL	MASFIN	AG	111	8.59	7.2	0.8	na --	na --	8.1 81
MASS. FINL TOTAL RETURN	MASFIN	B	285	10.19	7.2	5.1	13.7 49	20.6 20	18.6 14
MASS. FINL SECTORS FUND	MASFIN	G	124	9.57	4.7	na	na --	na --	na --
MASS. INV. GROWTH STOCK	MASFIN	G	893	9.44	7.2	1.5	13.5 53	15.0 68	10.7 72
MASS. INV. TRUST	MASFIN	GI	1188	12.09	7.2	2.7	12.3 66	16.7 54	14.7 45
MFS GOVT GUARANTEED	MASFIN	BP	432	10.32	4.7	9.1	na --	na --	na --
MFS GOV SECURITIES HIYLD	MASFIN	BP	367	9.76	4.7	6.9	na --	na --	na --
MFS MGD MUNI-BOND HIYLD	MASFIN	MB	383	10.31	4.7	9.4	na --	na --	na --
MFS MGD MUNI-BD TRUST	MASFIN	MB	801	10.63	4.7	6.7	na --	20.2 22	16.2 29
MFS MDG MULTI-ST MASS.	MASFIN	MB	183	11.02	4.7	6.6	na --	na --	na --
MFS MGD MULTI-ST N.C.	MASFIN	MB	83	11.53	4.7	6.4	na --	na --	na --
MFS MGD MULTI-ST VA	MASFIN	MB	149	11.12	4.7	6.5	na --	na --	na --
MATHERS FUND	MATHRS	G	149	16.96	0.0	4.2	16.7 22	13.4 78	12.0 63
MEDICAL TECHNOLOGY FUND	AMA	AG	66	13.38	0.0	0.0	na --	14.0 74	11.9 63
MEESCHAERT CAP. ACCUM.	MEESCH	G	30	25.87	0.0	2.9	10.3 82	10.4 88	9.8 76
MERRILL L. BASIC VALUE	MERRIL	GI	799	17.06	6.5	3.1	na --	22.5 10	18.2 17
MERRILL L. CALIF TAX-EX	MERRIL	MB	497	11.63	0.0	6.5	na --	na --	na --
MERRILL L. CORP DIV FUND	MERRIL	BP	253	10.90	2.0	7.9	na --	na --	na --
MERRILL L. BOND-INTERMED	MERRIL	BP	100	11.87	2.0	8.6	na --	16.7 53	16.1 31
MERRILL L. FEDERAL SECS	MERRIL	BP	6651	9.87	6.2	8.1	na --	na --	na --
MERRILL L. INTERNATIONAL	MERRIL	IN	278	14.28	8.5	1.8	na --	na --	na --
MERRILL L. CAPITAL FUND	MERRIL	GI	547	24.40	6.5	1.6	16.3 26	19.9 23	19.0 13
MERRILL L. EQUI-BOND I	MERRIL	B	16	13.24	4.0	4.2	na --	15.9 62	14.9 43
MERRILL L. HIGH INC BOND	MERRIL	BP	597	8.34	4.0	11.2	na --	na --	14.2 48
MERRILL L. PACIFIC FUND	MERRIL	IN	445	34.20	6.5	0.3	na --	29.6 1	37.9 1
MERRILL L. PHOENIX	MERRIL	B	118	12.39	6.5	4.3	na --	na --	18.7 14
MERRILL L. MUNI-BD HIYLD	MERRIL	MB	1557	10.67	4.0	7.3	na --	19.1 33	16.5 28
MERRILL L. MUNI-BD INSD	MERRIL	MB	2039	8.18	4.0	6.9	na --	17.9 44	14.9 42
MERRILL L. MUNI-LTD MAT	MERRIL	MB	668	9.90	1.0	5.6	na --	7.0 94	7.0 84
MERRILL L. SPECIAL VALUE	MERRIL	AG	97	13.97	6.5	0.3	na --	11.7 84	7.9 82
MERRILL L. NAT RESOURCE	MERRIL	G	259	12.71	0.0	0.9	na --	na --	na --
MERRILL L. HIGH QUAL BD	MERRIL	BP	225	11.95	4.0	8.6	na --	na --	17.1 23
MERRILL L. NY MUNI BOND	MERRIL	MB	487	11.24	0.0	6.3	na --	na --	na --
MERRILL L. FUND FOR TOM	MERRIL	G	607	15.18	0.0	0.7	na --	na --	na --
MERRILL L. RETIRE BEN IN	MERRIL	B	2066	11.03	0.0	2.2	na --	na --	na --
MERRILL L. RETIRE/INCOME	MERRIL	BP	1430	9.98	0.0	na	na --	na --	na --

LATEST 12 MNTHS PCNT RK	THIS MONTH PCNT RK	1986 TO DATE PCNT RK	CALENDAR YEARS 1985 PCNT RK	1984 PCNT RK	1983 PCNT RK	CYCLES UP MKT PCNT RK	DOWN MKT PCNT RK	CDA RATING
7.3 86	-2.6 82	7.3 86	19.4 74	14.5 6	25.0 22	142.5 38	1.3 40	85
10.3 76	0.8 12	10.3 76	17.3 82	13.3 10	10.7 75	88.1 82	12.5 19	81
20.6 16	0.1 28	20.6 16	18.4 78	6.8 39	9.0 84	95.8 74	2.4 37	32
-5.3 96	-0.6 45	-5.3 96	na --	na --	na --	na --	na --	na
7.9 84	0.4 19	7.9 84	na --	na --	na --	na --	na --	na
12.4 64	1.9 4	12.4 64	na --	na --	na --	na --	na --	na
17.0 35	-3.1 89	17.0 35	37.1 7	7.1 36	26.8 17	208.6 6	-16.5 74	58
6.1 88	-2.5 80	6.1 88	26.2 40	-11.4 87	26.5 18	137.2 42	-7.6 57	34
15.5 45	-0.8 49	15.5 45	25.2 45	12.6 12	9.9 79	112.3 59	13.9 15	45
13.0 59	-2.0 72	13.0 59	28.6 29	-5.4 75	22.4 29	153.4 28	-17.5 77	44
12.6 62	-3.4 93	12.6 62	25.8 42	-7.0 79	30.2 9	184.7 12	na --	na
na --	0.6 14	na --	na --	na --	na --	na --	na --	na
10.8 73	0.5 16	10.8 73	23.2 52	6.2 41	26.4 18	122.8 51	13.6 16	41
38.0 4	2.7 3	38.0 4	22.5 56	2.3 54	16.6 51	108.9 61	na --	na
18.0 29	-1.9 70	18.0 29	23.8 49	-13.6 89	na --	na --	na --	na
19.8 19	-1.1 54	19.8 19	30.2 23	6.9 37	19.1 40	162.9 24	1.3 40	21
na --	-4.5 97	na --	na --	na --	na --	na --	na --	na
12.5 63	-2.6 82	12.5 63	25.7 43	-4.2 72	15.5 55	127.0 48	-13.1 68	73
17.5 32	-1.3 58	17.5 32	24.5 47	3.0 52	20.9 33	149.7 31	-17.5 77	73
9.1 80	0.3 24	9.1 80	16.4 86	na --	na --	na --	na --	na
na --	0.6 14	na --	na --	na --	na --	na --	na --	na
12.2 65	-0.7 45	12.2 65	16.7 85	na --	na --	na --	na --	na
18.0 29	-0.5 42	18.0 29	20.4 69	10.5 20	12.7 67	105.5 64	16.2 11	15
17.5 32	0.1 30	17.5 32	na --	na --	na --	na --	na --	na
17.1 34	-0.2 37	17.1 34	na --	na --	na --	na --	na --	na
15.3 47	0.1 29	15.3 47	na --	na --	na --	na --	na --	na
12.9 60	-3.1 89	12.9 60	27.5 34	-2.4 67	16.1 52	130.1 47	-23.9 86	39
15.3 47	-2.8 86	15.3 47	39.0 5	-12.5 88	-0.6 98	117.5 55	-8.9 60	40
6.0 88	-7.6 99	6.0 88	18.4 78	5.4 43	9.5 81	90.3 80	-2.0 47	83
17.2 34	-1.4 60	17.2 34	32.0 18	6.8 38	30.1 10	201.7 7	-8.0 58	11
17.7 30	0.1 27	17.7 30	na --	na --	na --	na --	na --	na
12.4 63	-0.2 36	12.4 63	17.4 82	na --	na --	na --	na --	na
14.6 51	0.6 16	14.6 51	19.8 72	14.0 8	9.6 80	90.5 80	25.4 3	47
12.8 61	0.0 31	12.8 61	19.2 75	na --	na --	na --	na --	na
30.3 5	1.6 5	30.3 5	35.9 9	na --	na --	na --	na --	na
19.5 21	-0.8 49	19.5 21	29.7 25	8.7 30	23.1 27	167.9 20	4.9 31	29
11.3 70	-0.8 49	11.3 70	26.2 41	7.9 34	11.1 73	105.8 64	na --	na
12.9 60	0.6 14	12.9 60	21.7 60	8.5 31	18.3 44	100.0 69	na --	na
77.9 1	6.5 1	77.9 1	42.1 4	3.8 49	38.7 3	340.0 1	3.0 36	1
16.8 37	-0.7 46	16.8 37	30.2 23	9.9 24	31.0 9	na --	na --	na
19.0 23	-0.2 37	19.0 23	20.7 66	10.0 23	14.0 62	99.9 69	9.0 24	22
17.0 35	-0.2 38	17.0 35	19.5 74	8.5 31	12.2 68	91.6 79	2.1 38	51
7.5 86	0.4 21	7.5 86	6.7 96	6.9 38	5.6 94	32.4 97	14.2 14	93
1.7 94	-4.1 96	1.7 94	33.1 15	-7.3 79	22.3 29	129.0 47	-24.9 88	97
31.6 5	1.0 9	31.6 5	na --	na --	na --	na --	na --	na
14.3 52	1.1 7	14.3 52	22.4 56	15.0 5	9.4 82	95.4 75	na --	na
16.7 38	-0.2 38	16.7 38	na --	na --	na --	na --	na --	na
14.9 50	-3.7 95	14.9 50	25.7 42	na --	na --	na --	na --	na
13.5 57	-0.8 49	13.5 57	na --	na --	na --	na --	na --	na
na --	0.0 34	na --	na --	na --	na --	na --	na --	na

CDA MONTHLY ALPHABETIC LISTING – 12/31/86

FUND	MGT CO	IO	ASSETS MIL$	NAV	MAX LOAD	% YLD	10 YEARS PCNT RK	5 YEARS PCNT RK	3 YEARS PCNT RK
MIDAMERICA HIGH GROWTH	LIFINV	G	11	4.34	8.5	1.2	11.4 73	11.1 86	6.4 87
MIDAMERICA MUTUAL FUND	LIFINV	GI	32	5.98	8.5	3.0	13.3 54	16.8 53	13.4 54
MIDWEST INC-INTERMED TRM	MIDWES	BP	53	10.76	2.0	7.9	na --	na --	12.4 62
MONITREND VALUE FUND	MTREND	G	26	18.73	3.5	1.9	na --	na --	na --
MORGAN (W.L.) GROWTH	VGUARD	G	633	11.50	0.0	3.2	15.6 34	16.6 54	9.8 76
MUTUAL BEACON GROWTH FD	HSC	G	62	18.64	0.0	1.6	10.2 84	13.5 76	12.5 61
MUTUAL BENEFIT FUND	M-B-F	G	15	13.66	8.5	2.0	12.4 66	19.3 31	16.5 28
MUTUAL OF OMAHA AMERICA	OMAHA	BP	40	10.65	0.0	8.6	na --	12.2 82	13.2 56
MUTUAL OF OMAHA GROWTH	OMAHA	G	31	7.09	8.0	1.2	10.0 85	14.8 70	13.0 57
MUTUAL OF OMAHA INCOME	OMAHA	GI	105	8.94	8.0	8.0	9.4 89	14.4 72	14.4 47
MUTUAL QUALIFIED INCOME	HSC	B	517	20.04	0.0	5.2	na --	21.0 17	18.6 14
MUTUAL SHARES CORP.	HSC	B	1293	60.39	0.0	4.0	20.8 7	21.2 16	19.0 13
NAESS & THOMAS SPECIAL	VGUARD	AG	31	35.10	0.0	0.0	na --	9.6 90	-3.0 96
NATL AVIATION & TECH	AMFDA	G	84	11.02	8.5	1.9	na --	13.4 77	10.4 73
NATL FEDERAL SECURITIES	NATSEC	BP	1178	11.22	6.7	9.9	na --	na --	na --
NATIONAL INDUSTRIES FUND	COLE	G	27	11.64	0.0	2.9	8.4 94	6.7 95	5.9 88
NATL SECURITIES BALANCED	NATSEC	B	2	13.85	7.2	5.3	12.9 61	20.1 22	17.8 19
NATL SECURITIES BOND	NATSEC	BP	520	3.16	7.2	13.6	9.0 91	15.9 62	12.8 58
NATL SECURITIES CAL TX E	NATSEC	MB	74	13.20	5.2	7.1	na --	na --	na --
NATL SECURITIES GROWTH	NATSEC	G	66	11.01	7.2	1.7	9.0 92	9.8 89	7.3 83
NATL SECURITIES PREFERED	NATSEC	BP	4	8.50	7.2	8.1	11.6 70	20.4 21	18.4 16
NATL SECS REAL ESTATE	NATSEC	GI	13	9.82	7.7	2.6	na --	na --	na --
NATL SECURITIES STOCK	NATSEC	GI	255	8.99	7.2	3.8	13.2 56	16.1 60	17.1 23
NATL SECURITIES TOT INC	NATSEC	B	76	7.84	7.2	5.3	15.6 34	21.3 15	20.1 8
NATL SECURITIES TOT RET	NATSEC	GI	259	7.42	7.2	4.7	16.2 27	19.7 26	17.4 22
NATL SECURITIES TX EX BD	NATSEC	MB	78	10.26	5.2	7.0	na --	19.7 26	17.0 24
NATL TELECOMMUNICATIONS	AMFDA	G	59	13.80	8.5	1.1	na --	na --	2.3 92
NATIONWIDE FUND	NATFIN	GI	344	13.47	7.5	2.5	11.3 74	19.2 32	19.4 12
NATIONWIDE GROWTH FUND	NATFIN	G	162	8.56	7.5	2.9	16.4 25	23.1 7	19.6 11
NATIONWIDE BOND FUND	NATFIN	BP	20	10.21	7.5	8.2	na --	16.3 58	15.3 38
NAUTILUS FUND	ETN&HD	AG	18	12.15	4.7	0.0	na --	5.9 95	-9.8 98
NEL EQUITY FUND	LOOMIS	GI	30	20.60	8.0	2.8	14.6 43	18.6 39	15.6 35
NEL GOVERNMENT SEC TR	NEL	BP	174	13.48	6.5	7.3	na --	na --	na --
NEL GROWTH FUND	LOOMIS	AG	286	26.65	8.0	0.7	22.0 4	24.3 5	14.6 46
NEL INCOME	NEL	BP	50	11.65	8.0	7.3	8.5 93	16.0 61	15.0 41
NEL RETIREMENT EQUITY	LOOMIS	G	95	26.18	8.0	1.5	16.6 23	19.9 24	18.6 15
NEL TAX EXEMPT	NEL	MB	105	7.75	4.5	8.0	na --	20.9 19	17.3 22
NEUWIRTH FUND	WS&W	AG	26	13.27	0.0	0.3	13.3 55	14.7 70	10.9 71
NEW ECONOMY FUND	CAPRES	G	719	19.41	8.5	1.7	na --	na --	17.9 18
NEW PERSPECTIVE FUND	CAPRES	G	870	9.99	8.5	1.8	18.1 17	20.5 20	19.2 12
NEWPORT FAR EAST	COMCAP	IN	3	20.15	0.0	0.0	na --	na --	na --
NEW YORK VENTURE FUND	VENADV	G	147	9.20	8.5	0.9	21.1 7	22.3 11	21.1 6
NEWTON GROWTH FUND	M&I	G	34	20.74	0.0	4.2	14.9 40	16.7 54	8.8 79
NEWTON INCOME FUND	M&I	BP	12	8.47	0.0	8.6	7.1 96	14.9 69	11.4 67
NICHOLAS FUND	NICHOL	G	1053	34.87	0.0	2.5	22.8 3	21.7 13	16.8 26
NICHOLAS II	NICHOL	G	299	16.22	0.0	2.5	na --	na --	19.9 9
NICHOLAS INCOME FUND	NICHOL	BP	56	4.01	0.0	9.5	7.7 94	18.2 42	15.0 42
NICHOLSON GROWTH FUND	COMCAP	G	0	15.00	0.0	0.0	na --	na --	na --
NODDING CALAMOS INCOME	NODCAL	BP	16	11.23	0.0	4.6	na --	na --	na --
NOMURA PACIFIC BASIN FD	NOMURA	IN	53	21.13	0.0	1.4	na --	na --	na --

| LATEST 12 MNTHS | | THIS MONTH | | 1986 TO DATE | | CALENDAR YEARS | | | | | | CYCLES | | | | CDA RATING |
| | | | | | | 1985 | | 1984 | | 1983 | | UP MKT | | DOWN MKT | | |
PCNT	RK	PCNT	RK	PCNT	RK	PCNT	RK	PCNT	RK	PCNT	RK	PCNT	RK	PCNT	RK	
8.7	82	-0.7	46	8.7	82	20.4	69	-8.0	81	14.5	60	85.4	85	2.3	37	82
11.7	67	-2.8	85	11.7	67	24.9	46	4.5	47	15.4	55	127.0	48	2.2	38	47
11.3	70	0.1	30	11.3	70	14.5	90	11.4	18	4.7	96	na	--	na	--	na
9.1	81	-0.3	38	9.1	81	20.5	68	na	--	na	--	na	--	na	--	na
7.8	84	-1.6	63	7.8	84	29.5	26	-5.1	74	28.0	15	142.4	38	-12.5	66	55
15.4	46	0.4	18	15.4	46	23.3	51	0.0	60	13.7	63	100.2	69	-20.0	81	77
22.3	11	-1.1	55	22.3	11	28.8	28	0.3	58	26.6	17	163.5	23	-4.3	52	55
11.1	71	0.3	24	11.1	71	16.9	84	11.7	16	6.2	93	60.0	93	21.0	5	85
15.9	42	-0.3	39	15.9	42	28.8	28	-3.3	70	15.6	54	116.5	56	-12.3	66	80
9.3	80	-0.6	45	9.3	80	24.0	48	10.4	20	7.5	89	81.2	87	12.4	19	87
16.0	42	0.6	16	16.0	42	25.5	44	14.7	6	34.9	6	158.0	26	19.9	6	3
16.5	39	0.0	31	16.5	39	26.5	38	14.5	7	37.1	5	175.9	15	-2.8	47	6
0.1	95	-1.8	67	0.1	95	21.7	61	-25.1	97	17.9	45	77.1	89	-13.0	67	98
15.3	46	-2.7	84	15.3	46	21.2	63	-3.6	71	6.5	92	102.2	67	-14.2	70	69
9.6	79	-1.1	55	9.6	79	14.9	89	na	--	na	--	na	--	na	--	na
9.7	78	0.1	29	9.7	78	10.6	95	-2.3	67	11.3	72	67.8	92	-25.4	88	95
14.9	49	-0.3	39	14.9	49	27.3	35	11.8	16	15.5	55	152.6	29	4.4	32	43
5.4	90	-0.3	40	5.4	90	23.7	50	10.1	22	11.1	74	96.7	73	10.5	22	86
17.9	30	1.1	7	17.9	30	19.7	73	na	--	na	--	na	--	na	--	na
15.5	45	-1.0	52	15.5	45	23.6	50	-13.4	89	4.9	96	79.8	87	-18.5	78	90
18.2	27	-1.7	65	18.2	27	26.5	39	11.1	18	15.5	55	138.0	41	14.3	14	25
17.6	31	-3.3	92	17.6	31	na	--	na	--	na	--	na	--	na	--	na
15.3	46	-1.6	63	15.3	46	28.5	30	8.3	32	9.1	83	131.6	45	-12.3	66	52
22.2	11	-4.4	97	22.2	11	26.7	37	12.1	15	17.2	48	168.6	19	8.7	25	9
19.2	22	-0.7	47	19.2	22	24.4	47	9.0	28	17.8	46	160.7	25	-4.3	52	13
20.3	16	-0.7	46	20.3	16	21.2	63	9.8	24	9.9	78	103.6	65	-0.1	43	24
2.9	93	-2.3	76	2.9	93	17.2	83	-11.4	86	na	--	na	--	na	--	na
17.5	32	-2.1	72	17.5	32	36.4	8	6.2	41	15.8	53	151.8	30	-0.6	45	71
18.2	27	0.2	25	18.2	27	33.3	14	8.4	32	21.8	31	189.2	10	-3.3	49	27
12.8	61	1.0	8	12.8	61	19.1	76	14.1	8	6.0	94	88.3	81	15.0	13	64
-8.8	98	-0.4	41	-8.8	98	8.4	96	-25.8	97	34.9	6	44.3	95	32.0	2	97
21.9	13	-1.3	57	21.9	13	23.1	53	3.0	51	14.6	60	131.1	45	7.7	26	32
12.3	64	0.3	22	12.3	64	na	--	na	--	na	--	na	--	na	--	na
18.3	27	-2.5	81	18.3	27	34.9	10	-5.7	77	11.4	71	188.2	11	16.3	11	5
14.7	50	-0.1	35	14.7	50	18.6	78	11.9	15	5.4	94	87.2	83	19.2	7	70
23.4	10	-1.4	60	23.4	10	35.7	9	-0.5	61	16.7	50	163.6	23	9.2	24	20
21.2	15	0.0	32	21.2	15	21.9	59	9.4	26	7.3	89	109.6	61	11.2	21	12
8.1	84	-3.0	88	8.1	84	39.4	5	-9.5	84	14.3	61	148.4	32	-26.6	90	76
13.5	57	-1.3	57	13.5	57	38.6	6	4.3	48	na	--	na	--	na	--	na
26.8	7	2.3	4	26.8	7	33.8	13	-0.2	60	23.7	25	160.5	25	-6.3	54	10
73.4	1	5.0	1	73.4	1	16.2	86	na	--	na	--	na	--	na	--	na
22.8	11	0.0	32	22.8	11	38.1	6	4.7	46	23.0	28	218.5	4	-17.7	77	11
9.1	81	-1.5	61	9.1	81	28.7	29	-8.2	82	23.5	26	133.3	44	-17.0	75	66
9.0	81	0.4	21	9.0	81	12.8	93	12.2	14	11.6	70	84.2	85	8.9	24	90
11.7	67	-1.8	68	11.7	67	29.7	26	9.9	24	23.9	25	184.3	12	4.1	33	7
10.3	76	-2.1	72	10.3	76	33.8	13	16.9	2	na	--	na	--	na	--	na
11.5	68	0.0	32	11.5	68	21.2	63	12.6	12	12.4	68	99.1	70	16.3	11	82
6.2	88	-0.4	41	6.2	88	-5.9	98	na	--	na	--	na	--	na	--	na
16.1	41	-0.4	42	16.1	41	na	--	na	--	na	--	na	--	na	--	na
74.4	1	2.0	4	74.4	1	na	--	na	--	na	--	na	--	na	--	na

CDA MONTHLY ALPHABETIC LISTING - 12/31/86

FUND	MGT CO	IO	ASSETS MIL$	NAV	MAX LOAD	% YLD	ANNUALIZED ROR THRU 12/31/86 10 YEARS PCNT RK	5 YEARS PCNT RK	3 YEARS PCNT RK
NORTH STAR APOLLO FUND	INVADV	G	21	10.18	0.0	1.8	na --	na --	2.0 93
NORTH STAR BOND	INVADV	BP	36	10.39	0.0	8.6	na --	16.7 54	14.8 43
NORTH STAR REGIONAL FUND	INVADV	G	84	18.42	0.0	1.8	na --	21.6 14	18.5 15
NORTH STAR STOCK FUND	INVADV	G	65	14.25	0.0	2.4	na --	18.2 42	13.0 57
NORTHEAST INV GROWTH	NIT	G	18	18.36	0.0	0.7	na --	17.4 48	20.9 7
NORTHEAST INV. TRUST	NIT	BP	313	13.70	0.0	10.7	11.1 75	21.0 17	19.6 10
NOVA FUND INC	NOVA	AG	23	14.38	0.0	0.2	na --	13.2 78	8.7 80
NUVEEN MUNICIPAL BOND FD	NUVEEN	MB	668	8.96	4.0	6.4	na --	18.0 43	16.3 29
OLD DOMINION INVTS TR	INVSEC	GI	6	24.98	8.5	4.7	na --	15.2 67	14.7 45
OLYMPIC TRUST SERIES B	H&W	G	4	15.57	0.0	1.4	na --	na --	na --
OLYMPIC TRUST TOT RETURN	H&W	B	1	14.40	0.0	2.5	na --	na --	na --
OMEGA FUND	ENDOW	G	32	13.44	0.0	1.8	12.0 68	10.9 87	14.2 49
ONE HUNDRED FUND	BERGER	AG	11	19.71	0.0	0.0	12.1 67	9.9 89	6.4 86
ONE HUNDRED ONE FUND	BERGER	GI	3	14.98	0.0	3.3	12.5 65	17.7 46	13.6 53
OPPENHEIMER A.I.M. FUND	OPPEN	IN	373	26.99	8.5	0.5	19.6 11	19.7 26	19.5 11
OPPENHEIMER DIRECTORS	OPPEN	G	210	21.92	8.5	0.0	na --	12.9 79	2.3 92
OPPENHEIMER EQUITY INC.	OPPEN	GI	420	8.46	8.5	4.9	16.2 26	22.3 10	16.1 31
OPPENHEIMER FUND	OPPEN	AG	236	9.88	8.5	0.9	10.1 84	9.1 91	5.4 89
OPPENHEIMER GOLD & SPEC.	OPPEN	ME	40	8.45	8.5	1.5	na --	na --	-1.6 95
OPPENHEIMER HIGH YIELD	OPPEN	BP	636	16.73	6.7	12.5	na --	14.7 70	10.5 73
OPPENHEIMER PREMIUM INC	OPPEN	GI	375	18.26	8.5	4.2	na --	10.4 88	6.6 85
OPPENHEIMER NY TX EXEMPT	OPPEN	MB	51	12.68	4.7	6.2	na --	na --	na --
OPPENHEIMER REGENCY	OPPEN	AG	147	15.63	8.5	1.2	na --	na --	3.1 92
OPPENHEIMER SPECIAL FUND	OPPEN	G	709	18.90	8.5	4.4	18.3 16	13.4 77	6.5 86
OPPENHEIMER SELECT STOCK	OPPEN	G	10	12.22	8.5	1.8	na --	na --	na --
OPPENHEIMER RETR-GOV SEC	OPPEN	BP	12	10.42	8.5	8.8	na --	na --	na --
OPPENHEIMER TARGET FUND	OPPEN	G	119	20.49	8.5	1.7	na --	na --	5.2 89
OPPENHEIMER TAX FREE BD	OPPEN	MB	120	9.81	4.7	6.5	na --	na --	16.9 25
OPPENHEIMER TIME FUND	OPPEN	G	230	16.21	8.5	2.8	20.2 10	20.6 20	12.7 59
OVER-THE-COUNTER SEC.	REVIEW	G	237	16.99	8.0	0.3	21.3 6	16.3 57	11.4 67
PBHG GROWTH FUND	TAMCO	AG	18	12.32	7.5	0.5	na --	na --	na --
PACIFIC HORIZON AGGRE GR	SECPAC	AG	64	25.48	0.0	0.2	na --	na --	na --
PACIFIC HORIZON CAL TAX	SECPAC	MB	86	14.45	0.0	6.6	na --	na --	na --
PACIFIC HORIZON HIYLD BD	SECPAC	BP	27	16.41	0.0	11.1	na --	na --	na --
PAINE WEBBER AMERICA FD	PAINE	GI	91	15.04	8.5	5.8	na --	na --	na --
PAINE WEBBER ATLAS FD	PAINE	IN	224	15.94	8.5	5.1	na --	na --	na --
PAINE WEBBER CALIF TX-EX	PAINE	MB	136	11.18	4.2	6.7	na --	na --	na --
PAINE WEBBER FI INVT GR	PAINE	BP	331	10.75	4.2	10.7	na --	na --	na --
PAINE WEBBER GNMA	PAINE	BP	2907	10.21	4.2	11.1	na --	na --	na --
PAINE WEBBER HIGH YIELD	PAINE	BP	675	10.36	4.2	12.9	na --	na --	na --
PAINE WEBBER OLYMPUS FD	PAINE	G	109	10.86	8.5	0.0	na --	na --	na --
PAINE WEBBER TAX-EX INC	PAINE	MB	313	11.39	4.3	6.8	na --	na --	na --
PARTNERS FUND	NEUBER	GI	444	17.37	0.0	2.4	20.1 10	19.9 23	18.1 17
PAX WORLD FUND	PAX	IN	49	13.19	0.0	3.8	na --	13.2 78	13.5 53
PENN SQUARE MUTUAL FUND	PENN	GI	195	9.21	0.0	4.0	12.9 60	17.5 47	12.9 58
PENNSYLVANIA MUTUAL FUND	QUEST	G	346	6.98	0.0	1.7	20.8 7	22.1 12	13.2 56
PERMANENT PORTFOLIO	WORLD	G	71	13.18	0.0	0.0	na --	na --	3.5 91
PHILADELPHIA FUND	FAHNST	G	107	6.70	8.5	2.2	13.6 51	11.9 83	8.5 80
PHOENIX BALANCED FD SER	PIC	B	153	12.75	8.5	4.5	na --	23.9 5	21.0 6
PHOENIX GROWTH FUND SER	PIC	GI	242	16.40	8.5	1.6	19.2 13	26.2 2	20.4 8

LATEST 12 MNTHS		THIS MONTH		1986 TO DATE		CALENDAR YEARS						CYCLES				CDA RATING
						1985		1984		1983		UP MKT		DOWN MKT		
PCNT	RK	PCNT	RK	PCNT	RK	PCNT	RK	PCNT	RK	PCNT	RK	PCNT	RK	PCNT	RK	
2.0	93	-2.6	82	2.0	93	12.7	93	-7.6	80	na	--	na	--	na	--	na
9.2	80	0.5	17	9.2	80	20.1	70	15.5	4	8.0	87	91.9	78	na	--	na
22.8	11	-1.7	64	22.8	11	38.4	6	-2.1	67	13.1	67	181.6	14	-8.0	57	7
12.9	60	-0.4	41	12.9	60	23.2	52	3.7	50	19.4	39	143.6	37	-5.9	54	37
24.3	9	-1.1	54	24.3	9	36.7	8	3.9	49	9.6	80	161.3	25	na	--	na
20.4	16	0.9	10	20.4	16	25.6	43	13.1	11	11.2	72	124.3	51	16.6	9	26
7.7	85	-1.7	64	7.7	85	27.1	36	-6.2	78	16.7	50	101.7	67	na	--	na
19.1	22	-0.2	37	19.1	22	21.4	62	8.7	29	9.9	79	94.7	76	3.1	36	37
17.2	34	-3.1	89	17.2	34	27.0	36	1.3	57	22.3	29	125.8	49	-3.5	50	21
9.5	79	-1.7	66	9.5	79	na	--	na	--	na	--	na	--	na	--	na
9.9	77	-2.4	78	9.9	77	na	--	na	--	na	--	na	--	na	--	na
12.2	65	-2.4	79	12.2	65	32.3	16	0.2	59	22.0	30	130.5	46	-35.9	97	75
20.0	18	-1.9	70	20.0	18	25.7	42	-20.1	95	17.8	46	96.4	73	-15.8	73	49
15.0	48	-0.9	50	15.0	48	29.1	27	-1.2	64	35.2	6	178.6	15	-13.6	69	48
46.4	2	2.5	3	46.4	2	49.1	2	-21.7	95	26.3	19	180.2	14	-29.4	93	33
4.5	91	-3.5	93	4.5	91	23.3	52	-16.9	93	25.2	21	124.6	50	na	--	na
15.8	44	-1.4	59	15.8	44	30.9	21	3.2	51	34.3	6	193.4	8	-5.5	53	30
2.2	93	-2.2	74	2.2	93	34.1	12	-14.5	90	22.3	30	105.4	64	-33.4	95	97
36.7	4	0.0	33	36.7	4	-4.5	98	-27.0	98	na	--	na	--	na	--	na.
9.7	78	-0.5	43	9.7	78	18.8	77	3.5	50	14.6	59	81.4	86	9.9	23	88
1.2	94	-3.7	95	1.2	94	17.1	83	2.4	53	16.3	51	68.4	92	13.5	17	96
17.2	34	0.1	30	17.2	34	na	--	na	--	na	--	na	--	na	--	na
7.9	84	-0.9	50	7.9	84	31.6	19	-22.9	96	58.1	1	na	--	na	--	na
15.1	47	-0.4	40	15.1	47	16.8	85	-10.2	85	28.0	14	99.9	70	-16.6	74	37
13.9	54	-3.2	91	13.9	54	na	--	na	--	na	--	na	--	na	--	na
8.3	83	0.5	17	8.3	83	na	--	na	--	na	--	na	--	na	--	na
8.2	83	-6.4	99	8.2	83	29.8	24	-17.2	93	22.9	28	160.7	25	na	--	na
19.6	20	0.0	32	19.6	20	21.1	63	10.3	22	17.1	48	118.9	54	na	--	na
19.1	22	-3.7	95	19.1	22	33.2	14	-9.7	84	27.9	15	173.6	17	-15.3	72	7
5.4	90	-2.2	74	5.4	90	34.9	10	-2.6	68	39.1	3	158.7	26	-5.6	53	29
23.9	9	-2.2	75	23.9	9	na	--	na	--	na	--	na	--	na	--	na
20.1	18	-2.8	85	20.1	18	37.5	7	na	--	na	--	na	--	na	--	na
18.3	26	0.0	32	18.3	26	18.3	79	na	--	na	--	na	--	na	--	na
15.1	48	0.6	14	15.1	48	24.8	46	na	--	na	--	na	--	na	--	na
14.1	53	-0.8	48	14.1	53	20.6	68	na	--	na	--	na	--	na	--	na
38.9	4	2.3	4	38.9	4	65.6	1	na	--	na	--	na	--	na	--	na
19.0	23	0.1	28	19.0	23	na	--	na	--	na	--	na	--	na	--	na
14.4	52	0.9	9	14.4	52	22.7	54	na	--	na	--	na	--	na	--	na
11.1	71	0.3	22	11.1	71	19.9	72	na	--	na	--	na	--	na	--	na
14.1	53	0.1	29	14.1	53	21.7	61	na	--	na	--	na	--	na	--	na
7.5	85	-3.5	93	7.5	85	na	--	na	--	na	--	na	--	na	--	na
17.2	33	-0.3	38	17.2	33	19.0	76	na	--	na	--	na	--	na	--	na
17.3	33	-2.7	84	17.3	33	29.8	24	8.2	33	19.1	41	148.4	32	7.1	27	2
8.4	82	-2.4	79	8.4	82	25.5	43	7.5	35	15.4	56	130.2	46	-23.4	85	91
12.9	60	-1.6	62	12.9	60	26.6	38	0.5	58	29.2	11	148.8	32	-8.7	59	65
10.9	72	-0.5	43	10.9	72	26.7	37	3.1	51	40.6	2	199.1	7	-13.7	69	24
13.6	56	-0.1	35	13.6	56	12.2	93	-12.9	88	5.4	94	na	--	na	--	na
8.4	83	-1.4	59	8.4	83	22.0	59	-3.5	70	18.3	44	94.2	76	-16.2	74	78
19.8	19	-1.2	55	19.8	19	29.8	25	13.9	8	18.1	45	176.8	15	6.9	28	1
20.3	17	-1.9	70	20.3	17	31.9	18	10.0	23	28.6	12	210.7	5	-3.4	50	19

CDA MONTHLY ALPHABETIC LISTING – 12/31/86

FUND	MGT CO	IO	ASSETS MIL$	NAV	MAX LOAD	% YLD	10 YEARS PCNT RK	5 YEARS PCNT RK	3 YEARS PCNT RK
PHOENIX CONVERTIBLE FUND	PIC	GI	100	17.44	8.5	4.3	na --	20.8 19	14.5 46
PHOENIX HIGH YIELD	PIC	BP	103	9.64	7.0	11.5	na --	17.2 49	14.8 43
PHOENIX STOCK FUND SER	PIC	G	95	12.67	8.5	1.5	na --	24.7 3	17.3 22
PHOENIX TOTAL RETURN FD	PIC	GI	5	12.38	0.0	3.4	na --	16.6 55	9.3 78
PILGRIM ADJUSTABLE RATE	PILCAP	BP	883	22.01	1.5	7.5	na --	na --	7.8 82
PILGRIM GNMA	PILCAP	BP	260	15.33	1.5	10.3	na --	na --	na --
PILGRIM HIGH YIELD FD	PILCAP	BP	17	8.00	1.5	11.8	10.4 80	16.1 60	12.6 60
PILGRIM MAGNACAP FUND	PILCAP	GI	181	9.81	7.2	2.3	15.5 35	19.7 26	22.3 4
PILGRIM PREFERRED	PILCAP	BP	198	25.04	1.5	8.4	na --	na --	na --
PILOT FUND	CRITER	AG	64	9.47	8.5	0.0	12.7 62	15.3 66	7.0 85
PINE STREET FUND	WS&W	GI	61	12.50	0.0	3.6	13.0 60	17.6 47	16.3 29
PIONEER BOND FUND	PIONER	BP	37	9.60	4.5	9.2	na --	16.4 57	14.2 49
PIONEER FUND	PIONER	GI	1377	19.72	8.5	2.6	14.0 47	14.6 72	11.7 65
PIONEER II	PIONER	G	2842	18.14	8.5	2.5	19.6 12	18.0 44	12.6 60
PIONEER THREE	PIONER	G	543	15.18	8.5	2.0	na --	na --	12.9 57
PRICE (ROWE) EQUITY INC	PRICE	GI	71	12.96	0.0	4.9	na --	na --	na --
PRICE (ROWE) GROWTH&INC.	PRICE	GI	376	12.98	0.0	5.1	na --	na --	9.6 77
PRICE (ROWE) GROWTH STK.	PRICE	G	1278	16.96	0.0	1.9	10.8 78	16.3 59	17.6 21
PRICE (ROWE) HI YLD BOND	PRICE	BP	703	10.87	0.0	11.8	na --	na --	na --
PRICE (ROWE) INTERNATL.	PRICE	IN	753	25.78	0.0	0.8	na --	24.6 4	30.0 1
PRICE (ROWE) NEW AMERICA	PRICE	G	76	13.14	0.0	0.7	na --	na --	na --
PRICE (ROWE) NEW ERA	PRICE	G	494	17.76	0.0	2.5	15.4 36	13.7 75	13.9 51
PRICE (ROWE) NEW HORIZ.	PRICE	AG	1089	12.38	0.0	0.6	16.2 27	11.0 87	4.7 89
PRICE (ROWE) NEW INCOME	PRICE	BP	946	9.13	0.0	8.4	10.4 80	15.3 66	14.4 47
PRICE (ROWE) TAX FR HIYD	PRICE	MB	226	11.92	0.0	7.3	na --	na --	na --
PRICE (ROWE) TX FREE INC	PRICE	MB	1411	10.07	0.0	7.0	na --	16.0 61	14.5 46
PRICE (ROWE) TXFR SH-INT	PRICE	MB	242	5.27	0.0	5.7	na --	na --	8.4 80
PRIMECAP FUND	VGUARD	G	105	42.57	0.0	1.3	na --	na --	na --
PRINCOR CAP ACCUMULATION	PIMC	GI	55	17.16	8.5	2.7	14.7 42	18.8 37	17.0 24
PRINCOR GOV SECS INCOME	PIMC	BP	52	10.97	5.5	9.8	na --	na --	na --
PRINCOR GROWTH FD, INC.	PIMC	G	24	18.47	8.5	1.5	14.2 45	14.3 73	10.8 71
PROVIDENT FD. FOR INCOME	AM-CAP	B	102	4.59	7.2	5.6	13.2 56	19.3 31	11.4 66
PRU-BACHE ADJ RATE PFD	PRUBAC	BP	284	23.07	0.0	8.1	na --	na --	na --
PRU-BACHE EQUITY FUND	PRUBAC	AG	279	9.04	0.0	0.6	na --	na --	17.0 24
PRU-BACHE GLOBAL FUND	PRUBAC	IN	401	9.64	0.0	0.1	na --	na --	na --
PRU-BACHE GOV SECURITIES	PRUBAC	BP	702	10.84	0.0	9.1	na --	na --	14.8 44
PRU-BACHE HIGH YIELD	PRUBAC	BP	1589	10.66	0.0	9.7	na --	17.7 46	15.1 41
PRU-BACHE HIYLD MUNI	PRUBAC	MB	981	16.18	0.0	7.0	na --	na --	na --
PRU-BACHE GR OPPORTUNITY	PRUBAC	AG	88	11.40	0.0	0.0	na --	13.6 76	9.6 77
PRU-BACHE INCOMEVERTIBLE	PRUBAC	BP	281	10.94	0.0	5.3	na --	na --	na --
PRU-BACHE OPTION GROWTH	PRUBAC	G	72	8.72	0.0	1.7	na --	na --	13.3 55
PRU-BACHE GNMA FUND	PRUBAC	BP	270	15.94	0.0	8.5	na --	na --	14.1 50
PRU-BACHE RESEARCH FUND	PRUBAC	GI	174	12.24	0.0	1.4	na --	na --	15.3 37
PRU-BACHE UTILITY FUND	PRUBAC	GI	1212	14.78	0.0	5.1	na --	22.4 10	24.9 2
PUTNAM CALIF TAX EX	PUTNAM	MB	810	15.96	4.7	7.0	na --	na --	na --
PUTNAM CCT ARP	PUTNAM	BP	597	46.04	2.5	8.1	na --	na --	na --
PUTNAM CCT DSP	PUTNAM	B	412	48.89	2.5	10.3	na --	na --	na --
PUTNAM CONVERT INC-GR TR	PUTNAM	GI	755	16.24	8.5	5.4	16.0 30	18.1 43	15.8 33
PUTNAM ENERGY RESOURCES	PUTNAM	AG	36	11.25	8.5	2.4	na --	-2.0 98	2.1 92
PUTNAM INFOR SCIENCES	PUTNAM	AG	119	14.08	8.5	0.2	na --	na --	4.1 90

LATEST 12 MNTHS PCNT RK	THIS MONTH PCNT RK	1986 TO DATE PCNT RK	CALENDAR YEARS 1985 PCNT RK	1984 PCNT RK	1983 PCNT RK	CYCLES UP MKT PCNT RK	DOWN MKT PCNT RK	CDA RATING
17.3 33	-0.8 47	17.3 33	21.6 61	5.2 44	26.0 19	142.0 38	12.7 18	4
15.9 43	-0.4 41	15.9 43	21.1 64	7.9 34	13.4 64	100.0 69	14.2 15	28
17.4 33	-1.2 55	17.4 33	27.1 35	8.1 33	31.1 9	195.3 8	1.9 40	4
15.4 45	-1.2 56	15.4 45	16.3 86	-2.6 68	10.7 75	106.2 63	0.9 42	36
4.0 92	-1.1 53	4.0 92	14.6 90	5.1 45	na --	na --	na --	na
6.5 87	0.6 15	6.5 87	15.9 87	na --	na --	na --	na --	na
11.7 67	0.0 32	11.7 67	14.5 90	11.5 17	12.6 67	91.1 79	15.7 12	71
16.8 37	-2.4 78	16.8 37	34.8 10	16.1 3	22.6 28	204.3 6	4.1 33	42
na --	-0.2 37	na --	na --	na --	na --	na --	na --	na
10.6 74	-2.1 72	10.6 74	17.7 81	-5.9 77	18.8 42	117.6 55	-13.4 68	66
14.3 52	-2.3 76	14.3 52	30.7 22	5.2 45	19.1 41	157.4 26	-19.4 80	59
10.8 73	0.4 19	10.8 73	20.1 71	11.8 16	9.3 82	89.7 80	na --	na
11.7 67	-2.5 81	11.7 67	25.7 42	-0.7 62	25.0 22	140.8 40	-23.2 85	59
12.3 64	-1.6 63	12.3 64	31.2 20	-3.2 70	30.2 10	151.9 30	-4.5 52	17
10.9 72	-1.2 55	10.9 72	24.0 49	4.8 45	na --	na --	na --	na
26.6 7	-0.9 50	26.6 7	na --	na --	na --	na --	na --	na
7.9 84	-2.7 83	7.9 84	19.7 73	2.0 55	32.3 8	na --	na --	na
21.7 13	-1.0 53	21.7 13	35.1 10	-1.1 63	12.3 68	151.4 30	-26.1 89	74
14.9 49	0.3 24	14.9 49	na --	na --	na --	na --	na --	na
60.5 1	3.6 2	60.5 1	45.2 3	-5.8 77	28.6 12	225.0 3	-12.2 66	8
14.3 52	-3.0 88	14.3 52	na --	na --	na --	na --	na --	na
16.2 41	-1.8 67	16.2 41	22.9 54	3.5 50	26.4 18	145.4 35	-38.6 97	69
-0.1 95	-2.2 75	-0.1 95	24.0 49	-7.4 80	19.7 37	115.7 57	-24.0 86	73
13.9 55	0.4 20	13.9 55	17.6 82	11.7 16	9.8 80	83.5 85	19.4 7	65
20.3 17	-0.5 43	20.3 17	na --	na --	na --	na --	na --	na
19.8 19	0.2 26	19.8 19	16.9 84	7.2 36	7.0 90	87.6 82	7.2 27	38
9.6 78	-0.2 36	9.6 78	8.9 96	6.8 38	na --	na --	na --	na
23.5 10	-2.8 85	23.5 10	na --	na --	na --	na --	na --	na
11.8 66	-3.5 93	11.8 66	36.2 9	5.1 45	36.7 5	182.3 13	-0.7 45	42
11.6 68	0.2 25	11.6 68	na --	na --	na --	na --	na --	na
13.0 59	-3.5 93	13.0 59	31.6 19	-8.4 82	28.3 14	158.5 26	-24.9 87	49
12.4 64	-0.5 43	12.4 64	17.8 81	4.6 47	21.9 31	141.7 39	14.7 13	41
na --	-0.9 49	na --	na --	na --	na --	na --	na --	na
14.4 51	-3.1 89	14.4 51	32.4 16	5.9 42	28.2 14	168.4 20	na --	na
43.6 3	1.4 5	43.6 3	44.5 3	na --	na --	na --	na --	na
13.1 59	-0.5 43	13.1 59	17.0 84	14.3 8	6.2 93	na --	na --	na
14.9 49	0.3 23	14.9 49	20.4 68	10.1 22	15.6 54	104.5 65	9.7 23	33
18.7 25	0.1 28	18.7 25	na --	na --	na --	na --	na --	na
15.4 46	1.9 4	15.4 46	26.5 39	-9.7 84	15.0 57	123.3 51	na --	na
13.8 56	-3.3 91	13.8 56	na --	na --	na --	na --	na --	na
10.2 77	-3.5 94	10.2 77	34.1 12	-1.4 65	na --	na --	na --	na
11.6 68	0.3 23	11.6 68	17.7 81	13.1 11	6.1 93	72.5 91	na --	na
24.6 8	-2.2 74	24.6 8	27.6 33	-3.5 71	na --	na --	na --	na
27.6 7	-2.9 87	27.6 7	33.4 14	14.5 7	11.6 70	165.7 22	na --	na
18.0 29	0.2 25	18.0 29	20.7 66	na --	na --	na --	na --	na
4.6 91	-1.2 56	4.6 91	16.2 86	na --	na --	na --	na --	na
12.7 61	-0.9 50	12.7 61	17.2 83	na --	na --	na --	na --	na
15.7 44	-0.4 42	15.7 44	27.0 36	5.7 43	13.8 63	134.9 43	4.9 31	19
-2.3 96	0.0 33	-2.3 96	19.1 76	-8.5 83	28.5 13	52.2 94	-57.6 99	99
10.7 74	-1.8 68	10.7 74	17.6 82	-13.2 89	na --	na --	na --	na

CDA MONTHLY ALPHABETIC LISTING - 12/31/86

| | | | ASSETS | | MAX | % | ANNUALIZED ROR THRU 12/31/86 | | | | | |
| | | | | | | | 10 YEARS | | 5 YEARS | | 3 YEARS | |
FUND	MGT CO	IO	MIL$	NAV	LOAD	YLD	PCNT	RK	PCNT	RK	PCNT	RK
PUTNAM INTL EQUITIES	PUTNAM	IN	372	30.39	8.5	0.4	19.3	13	26.3	2	31.7	1
PUTNAM (GEORGE) FD. BOS.	PUTNAM	B	355	14.66	8.5	5.0	13.2	57	18.7	38	14.8	43
PUTNAM FD FOR GROWTH/INC	PUTNAM	GI	1164	13.69	8.5	4.3	16.3	26	19.7	26	18.3	17
PUTNAM GNMA PLUS	PUTNAM	BP	584	11.38	4.7	na	na	--	na	--	na	--
PUTNAM HEALTH SCIENCES	PUTNAM	AG	241	17.44	8.5	0.9	na	--	na	--	16.1	31
PUTNAM HIGH INCOME GOV	PUTNAM	BP	5132	12.47	6.7	8.2	na	--	na	--	na	--
PUTNAM HIGH YIELD	PUTNAM	BP	2364	15.62	6.7	12.7	na	--	18.6	39	13.6	53
PUTNAM INCOME FUND	PUTNAM	BP	208	7.42	6.7	10.0	10.3	81	18.6	38	15.8	33
PUTNAM INVESTORS FUND	PUTNAM	G	960	11.62	8.5	1.6	14.4	43	17.1	50	14.2	48
PUTNAM NY TAX EXEMPT	PUTNAM	MB	701	17.37	4.7	7.1	na	--	na	--	na	--
PUTNAM VISTA FUND	PUTNAM	AG	194	17.52	8.5	2.9	17.9	18	19.8	25	11.2	68
PUTNAM OPTION INCOME I	PUTNAM	GI	1114	10.56	8.5	1.7	na	--	13.0	79	10.9	70
PUTNAM OPTION INCOME II	PUTNAM	GI	1173	10.82	8.5	3.2	na	--	na	--	na	--
PUTNAM TAX EXEMPT INC	PUTNAM	MB	624	26.27	4.7	6.6	9.5	88	22.2	11	16.3	29
PUTNAM US GOV SECURITIES	PUTNAM	BP	965	14.71	4.7	9.8	na	--	na	--	na	--
PUTNAM VOYAGER FUND	PUTNAM	AG	350	19.59	8.5	0.7	18.3	16	18.9	36	16.1	31
QUALIFIED DIVD PORTF I	VGUARD	B	177	17.07	0.0	6.7	20.5	8	28.9	1	25.6	2
QUALIFIED DIVD PORTF II	VGUARD	BP	136	9.52	0.0	8.9	11.0	77	20.9	18	21.3	6
QUALIFIED DIVD PORT III	VGUARD	BP	141	22.47	0.0	7.4	na	--	na	--	6.1	87
QUASAR ASSOCIATES	ALLIAN	AG	145	56.85	0.0	0.0	na	--	na	--	12.3	62
QUEST FOR VALUE FUND	OPPCAP	G	75	25.49	0.0	0.7	na	--	24.3	4	15.1	41
RAINBOW FUND	FURMAN	G	2	5.41	0.0	0.0	11.3	74	9.5	91	10.0	75
REA GRAHAM FUND	REA	B	43	15.14	8.5	2.7	na	--	na	--	15.2	40
RETIREMENT PLANNING-BOND	VENADV	BP	53	7.96	0.0	10.2	na	--	na	--	na	--
RETIREMENT PLANNING-EQ	VENADV	G	10	19.23	0.0	0.2	na	--	na	--	na	--
RIGHTIME FUND	RIGHT	G	134	29.89	0.0	0.2	na	--	na	--	na	--
ROCHESTER TAX MANAGED FD	FLDNG	G	29	10.61	8.5	0.0	na	--	8.8	92	3.9	91
ROYCE VALUE FUND, INC.	QUEST	G	149	8.33	0.0	0.4	na	--	na	--	10.6	72
SAFECO EQUITY FUND	SAFECO	GI	47	9.54	0.0	2.5	14.0	47	15.7	63	15.4	37
SAFECO GROWTH FUND	SAFECO	G	68	14.00	0.0	2.0	15.4	35	12.2	82	4.2	90
SAFECO INCOME FUND	SAFECO	B	102	15.28	0.0	4.8	16.0	30	21.9	12	19.8	10
SAFECO MUNICIPAL BOND FD	SAFECO	MB	170	13.97	0.0	7.1	na	--	na	--	17.0	23
SBSF FUND	SBSF	G	90	12.72	0.0	5.0	na	--	na	--	16.7	26
SCHIELD AGGRESS GROWTH	SMC	AG	11	10.37	4.0	0.0	na	--	na	--	na	--
SCHIELD VALUE PORTFOLIO	SMC	G	12	11.14	4.0	0.0	na	--	na	--	na	--
SCI-TECH HOLDINGS	MERRIL	G	273	11.94	8.5	0.8	na	--	na	--	10.5	73
SCUDDER CALIF TAX FREE	SCUDER	MB	152	11.01	0.0	6.3	na	--	na	--	na	--
SCUDDER CAPITAL GROWTH	SCUDER	G	414	15.59	0.0	1.3	na	--	na	--	17.0	24
SCUDDER DEVELOPMENT FUND	SCUDER	AG	278	20.71	0.0	0.0	18.3	17	9.6	90	5.0	89
SCUDDER GLOBAL	SCUDER	IN	11	12.43	0.0	na	na	--	na	--	na	--
SCUDDER GOV MORTGAGE SEC	SCUDER	BP	214	15.50	0.0	9.1	na	--	na	--	na	--
SCUDDER GROWTH & INCOME	SCUDER	GI	367	15.02	0.0	4.3	13.6	50	16.2	59	15.1	40
SCUDDER INCOME FUND	SCUDER	BP	217	13.41	0.0	9.1	9.3	90	17.7	46	16.1	30
SCUDDER INTERNATIONAL FD	SCUDER	IN	686	39.79	0.0	1.1	17.8	18	23.8	6	30.6	1
SCUDDER NEW YORK TAX FR	SCUDER	MB	111	11.30	0.0	6.4	na	--	na	--	13.0	57
SCUDDER MANAGED MUNI BD	SCUDER	MB	630	8.93	0.0	6.5	7.2	95	19.0	36	14.8	44
SCUDDER TX FR TARGT 1990	SCUDER	MB	81	10.34	0.0	5.9	na	--	na	--	9.5	78
SCUDDER TX FR TARGT 1993	SCUDER	MB	95	11.04	0.0	6.1	na	--	na	--	11.2	68
SECURITY ACTION FD	SECRTY	G	77	9.69	8.5	2.4	na	--	na	--	11.8	64
SECURITY INC FD-CORP BD	SECRTY	BP	45	8.32	4.7	10.9	na	--	16.3	58	15.2	40

LATEST 12 MNTHS PCNT RK	THIS MONTH PCNT RK	1986 TO DATE PCNT RK	CALENDAR YEARS 1985 PCNT RK	1984 PCNT RK	1983 PCNT RK	CYCLES UP MKT PCNT RK	DOWN MKT PCNT RK	CDA RATING
38.0 4	1.0 8	38.0 4	64.4 1	0.8 58	27.9 15	269.8 1	-13.3 68	18
18.8 24	-1.3 58	18.8 24	29.8 24	-1.9 66	14.9 58	134.4 43	7.9 26	44
21.9 12	-1.1 54	21.9 12	28.3 30	5.7 43	21.6 31	153.9 28	-8.2 59	19
na --	-0.1 35	na --	na --	na --	na --	na --	na --	na
15.2 47	-1.1 54	15.2 47	40.7 4	-3.5 71	-2.5 99	110.9 60	na --	na
13.3 58	0.3 22	13.3 58	na --	na --	na --	na --	na --	na
13.5 57	1.1 7	13.5 57	19.8 72	7.7 35	15.5 55	103.4 66	15.1 12	39
12.6 62	0.8 12	12.6 62	20.4 69	14.5 6	11.4 71	104.8 65	21.3 5	60
15.0 48	-2.5 81	15.0 48	29.3 27	0.3 59	10.5 76	146.0 35	-16.9 75	61
18.4 26	0.0 34	18.4 26	21.1 64	na --	na --	na --	na --	na
19.4 21	-3.0 88	19.4 21	28.6 29	-10.4 85	15.3 57	166.0 21	4.3 33	13
11.7 67	-2.3 77	11.7 67	20.1 70	1.8 55	14.2 61	91.4 79	-4.4 52	79
8.6 82	-1.3 57	8.6 82	na --	na --	na --	na --	na --	na
21.9 12	-0.2 37	21.9 12	23.6 51	4.5 47	13.2 66	116.6 56	12.7 18	35
11.0 72	0.7 12	11.0 72	16.6 85	na --	na --	na --	na --	na
20.2 17	-1.0 52	20.2 17	37.6 7	-5.4 75	14.9 58	174.6 16	-15.1 72	13
21.6 13	0.9 10	21.6 13	30.1 24	25.4 1	32.9 7	238.8 2	29.1 2	6
24.7 8	-0.9 51	24.7 8	29.7 25	10.4 21	7.9 88	121.8 52	18.2 8	26
4.2 92	-0.5 44	4.2 92	11.5 94	2.9 52	na --	na --	na --	na
11.4 69	-2.3 77	11.4 69	41.8 4	-10.3 85	35.9 5	na --	na --	na
14.3 52	-2.3 76	14.3 52	27.4 34	4.8 45	38.2 4	190.3 10	32.2 2	3
15.8 43	-3.0 88	15.8 43	20.7 67	-4.9 74	22.2 30	95.4 75	-23.6 86	64
11.0 71	2.2 4	11.0 71	29.4 26	6.3 40	11.3 72	na --	na --	na
10.4 75	0.2 26	10.4 75	15.7 88	na --	na --	na --	na --	na
12.6 63	0.0 31	12.6 63	36.7 8	na --	na --	na --	na --	na
10.8 73	-1.8 68	10.8 73	na --	na --	na --	na --	na --	na
2.1 93	-2.1 73	2.1 93	6.3 97	3.2 51	18.7 42	84.0 85	4.8 31	93
6.3 87	-1.4 60	6.3 87	27.5 34	-0.2 60	43.0 2	na --	na --	na
12.6 62	-2.4 77	12.6 62	32.6 16	2.8 52	21.1 33	153.7 28	-19.3 79	46
1.8 94	-1.8 66	1.8 94	19.6 73	-7.0 79	31.3 9	126.6 49	-20.5 82	70
19.9 19	-1.3 57	19.9 19	31.4 19	9.1 28	28.2 14	193.1 9	-3.3 49	21
19.7 20	0.3 22	19.7 20	21.6 61	10.1 22	10.5 76	101.4 67	na --	na
19.4 21	0.8 11	19.4 21	19.0 76	11.8 15	na --	na --	na --	na
-1.3 95	-3.9 96	-1.3 95	na --	na --	na --	na --	na --	na
4.3 92	-5.0 98	4.3 92	na --	na --	na --	na --	na --	na
17.9 30	0.9 10	17.9 30	22.1 58	-6.3 78	na --	na --	na --	na
16.7 38	-0.1 36	16.7 38	18.3 79	na --	na --	na --	na --	na
16.5 39	-2.1 73	16.5 39	36.8 8	0.5 58	22.1 30	136.0 42	na --	na
7.7 85	-1.8 67	7.7 85	19.8 72	-10.3 85	18.2 44	86.9 83	-7.5 57	62
na --	2.1 4	na --	na --	na --	na --	na --	na --	na
11.3 70	0.5 18	11.3 70	na --	na --	na --	na --	na --	na
17.8 30	-1.4 58	17.8 30	34.5 11	-3.7 71	13.3 65	133.4 44	-16.8 75	51
14.6 51	0.4 20	14.6 51	21.7 60	12.3 13	10.8 74	106.2 63	13.8 16	56
50.5 2	3.7 2	50.5 2	48.9 2	-0.7 62	29.2 11	227.4 3	-17.8 77	22
14.0 53	0.1 30	14.0 53	16.0 87	9.2 27	na --	na --	na --	na
16.8 38	-0.6 44	16.8 38	17.5 82	10.2 22	40.6 3	92.1 78	7.1 27	67
9.4 80	-0.1 35	9.4 80	11.0 94	8.1 33	na --	na --	na --	na
10.9 73	-0.8 48	10.9 73	14.4 91	8.4 31	na --	na --	na --	na
13.4 57	-2.2 75	13.4 57	29.3 27	-4.6 73	28.5 13	na --	na --	na
10.9 72	-0.1 35	10.9 72	21.4 62	13.4 10	9.2 83	93.0 78	na --	na

CDA MONTHLY ALPHABETIC LISTING – 12/31/86

FUND	MGT CO	IO	ASSETS MIL$	NAV	MAX LOAD	% YLD	ANNUALIZED ROR THRU 12/31/86					
							10 YEARS PCNT	RK	5 YEARS PCNT	RK	3 YEARS PCNT	RK
SECURITY EQUITY FUND	SECRTY	GI	235	5.23	8.5	2.8	14.9	39	16.2	59	12.5	61
SECURITY INVESTMENT FUND	SECRTY	GI	101	8.92	8.5	5.5	12.2	67	11.4	85	9.0	79
SECURITY OMNI FUND	SECRTY	AG	23	2.91	8.5	na	na	--	na	--	na	--
SECURITY ULTRA FUND	SECRTY	GI	100	6.71	8.5	3.8	18.1	17	15.0	69	11.1	69
SELECTED AMERICAN SHARES	PAM	GI	144	12.65	0.0	3.5	13.4	53	22.0	12	21.4	5
SELECTED SPECIAL SHARES	PAM	G	35	17.83	0.0	3.3	10.2	84	13.7	75	8.3	81
SELIGMAN CAPITAL FUND	SELIG	AG	192	12.72	8.5	0.0	18.9	14	19.6	27	9.9	76
SELIGMAN CALIF TAX EX HI	SELIG	MB	51	6.57	4.5	6.7	na	--	na	--	na	--
SELIGMAN CAL TAX EX QUAL	SELIG	MB	53	6.78	4.5	6.4	na	--	na	--	na	--
SELIGMAN COMMUNICATIONS	SELIG	AG	41	11.39	8.5	0.6	na	--	na	--	12.2	63
SELIGMAN COMMON STOCK FD	SELIG	GI	523	13.03	7.2	3.1	15.6	34	21.2	16	17.5	21
SELIGMAN GROWTH FD	SELIG	G	602	5.25	7.2	1.5	12.5	66	15.1	67	11.5	65
SELIGMAN GOV GUARANTEED	SELIG	BP	77	8.15	4.7	7.0	na	--	na	--	na	--
SELIGMAN HIGH YIELD BOND	SELIG	BP	63	7.83	4.7	11.1	na	--	na	--	na	--
SELIGMAN INCOME FD	SELIG	B	143	13.44	4.7	7.4	13.2	57	18.4	41	18.6	15
SELIGMAN SECURED MTG	SELIG	BP	47	7.33	4.7	7.8	na	--	na	--	na	--
SELIGMAN TX EX LOUISIANA	SELIG	MB	45	7.98	4.7	6.9	na	--	na	--	na	--
SELIGMAN TAX EX MARYLAND	SELIG	MB	46	7.76	4.7	6.5	na	--	na	--	na	--
SELIGMAN TAX EX MASS	SELIG	MB	132	8.03	4.7	6.7	na	--	na	--	na	--
SELIGMAN TAX EX MICH	SELIG	MB	99	8.37	4.7	6.7	na	--	na	--	na	--
SELIGMAN TAX EX MINN	SELIG	MB	108	7.90	4.7	6.8	na	--	na	--	na	--
SELIGMAN TAX EX NATL	SELIG	MB	110	8.34	4.7	7.0	na	--	na	--	na	--
SELIGMAN TAX EX NEW YORK	SELIG	MB	65	8.24	4.7	6.7	na	--	na	--	na	--
SELIGMAN TAX EX OHIO	SELIG	MB	114	8.15	4.7	6.9	na	--	na	--	na	--
SENTINEL BALANCED FUND	NATLIF	B	41	12.35	8.5	4.9	13.6	52	21.8	13	20.5	8
SENTINEL BOND	NATLIF	BP	21	6.58	8.5	8.2	na	--	16.8	53	15.7	34
SENTINEL COMMON STOCK FD	NATLIF	GI	466	23.61	8.5	3.1	16.0	30	23.0	7	21.7	5
SENTINEL GROWTH FUND	NATLIF	G	51	13.96	8.5	1.6	16.0	31	19.8	25	13.1	57
SENTRY FUND	SENTRY	G	40	12.70	8.0	2.1	14.9	40	12.2	82	15.8	33
SEQUOIA FUND	RC	GI	690	39.29	0.0	3.6	20.5	8	23.2	6	19.5	11
SHEARSON AGGRESSIVE GRTH	SHEAR	AG	91	15.00	5.0	0.0	na	--	na	--	11.5	66
SHEARSON APPRECIATION	SHEAR	G	263	26.16	5.0	0.0	19.4	12	20.1	22	18.1	17
SHEARSON CALIF MUNICIPAL	SHEAR	MB	156	16.18	5.0	6.7	na	--	na	--	na	--
SHEARSON FUNDAMENTAL VAL	SHEAR	G	102	6.31	5.0	4.3	na	--	na	--	11.1	69
SHEARSON GLOBAL OPPORT	SHEAR	G	263	30.07	5.0	0.4	na	--	na	--	na	--
SHEARSON HIGH YIELD	SHEAR	BP	513	18.89	5.0	11.2	na	--	na	--	13.4	54
SHEARSON LG-TRM GOV SECS	SHEAR	BP	1481	9.23	0.0	6.4	na	--	na	--	na	--
SHEARSON MANAGED GOVTS	SHEAR	BP	1439	13.34	5.0	8.4	na	--	na	--	na	--
SHEARSON MANAGED MUNI BD	SHEAR	MB	628	15.58	5.0	7.0	na	--	na	--	16.6	27
SHEARSON SPEC EQTY GR	SHEAR	G	137	14.12	0.0	na	na	--	na	--	na	--
SHEARSON NEW YORK MUNI	SHEAR	MB	191	16.71	5.0	6.7	na	--	na	--	na	--
SHEARSON SPEC INTL EQ	SHEAR	IN	169	19.89	0.0	na	na	--	na	--	na	--
SHEARSON SPEC EQTY PLUS	SHEAR	AG	24	14.59	0.0	na	na	--	na	--	na	--
SHEARSON SPEC INTERM GOV	SHEAR	BP	44	11.76	0.0	6.3	na	--	na	--	na	--
SHEARSON SPEC TAX EX INC	SHEAR	MB	383	17.20	0.0	6.6	na	--	na	--	na	--
SHEARSON SPL OPTION INC	SHEAR	GI	615	14.09	0.0	2.4	na	--	na	--	na	--
SHERMAN, DEAN FUND	SHERMN	AG	2	5.23	0.0	0.0	5.1	98	-7.5	99	-9.8	98
SIERRA GROWTH FUND	COLE	AG	5	11.05	0.0	0.0	na	--	2.6	97	-3.6	96
SIGMA CAPITAL SHARES	SIGMA	G	89	8.66	8.5	1.6	18.3	16	22.1	12	16.4	29
SIGMA INCOME SHARES	SIGMA	BP	36	9.05	8.5	8.9	na	--	19.0	35	18.0	18

LATEST 12 MNTHS		THIS MONTH		1986 TO DATE		CALENDAR YEARS 1985		1984		1983		CYCLES UP MKT		DOWN MKT		CDA RATING
PCNT	RK	PCNT	RK	PCNT	RK	PCNT	RK	PCNT	RK	PCNT	RK	PCNT	RK	PCNT	RK	
13.1	59	-2.8	85	13.1	59	26.5	39	-0.6	61	19.6	38	150.4	31	-28.6	92	59
11.6	67	-1.5	60	11.6	67	20.4	69	-3.6	71	10.1	77	85.5	84	-15.6	72	72
na	--	-3.3	91	na	--	na	--	na	--	na	--	na	--	na	--	na
5.1	90	-3.2	90	5.1	90	28.7	29	1.4	57	11.2	73	124.9	50	-32.0	94	81
17.0	36	0.1	30	17.0	36	33.2	14	14.9	5	21.6	31	182.5	13	-4.2	51	45
7.4	86	-3.3	91	7.4	86	23.5	51	-4.2	72	28.0	15	141.8	39	-26.1	90	92
18.3	27	-2.1	72	18.3	27	30.8	21	-14.1	90	23.1	27	186.5	11	-15.9	73	15
23.4	10	0.4	20	23.4	10	na	--	na	--	na	--	na	--	na	--	na
18.1	28	0.4	21	18.1	28	na	--	na	--	na	--	na	--	na	--	na
17.6	31	-0.9	51	17.6	31	34.2	12	-10.6	86	na	--	na	--	na	--	na
22.1	12	-1.2	56	22.1	12	30.7	21	1.8	56	27.2	16	183.6	12	-10.2	63	34
16.5	39	-0.6	45	16.5	39	29.3	27	-7.8	81	14.9	58	138.5	41	-25.0	88	72
15.4	46	-0.7	47	15.4	46	na	--	na	--	na	--	na	--	na	--	na
15.8	43	0.2	25	15.8	43	na	--	na	--	na	--	na	--	na	--	na
17.0	35	-0.1	35	17.0	35	26.5	38	12.6	12	10.7	75	129.1	47	11.2	21	27
7.3	86	-0.6	45	7.3	86	na	--	na	--	na	--	na	--	na	--	na
16.7	38	-0.4	42	16.7	38	na	--	na	--	na	--	na	--	na	--	na
13.5	57	0.0	34	13.5	57	na	--	na	--	na	--	na	--	na	--	na
16.0	42	0.0	31	16.0	42	18.3	79	na	--	na	--	na	--	na	--	na
18.3	26	-0.4	41	18.3	26	21.0	65	na	--	na	--	na	--	na	--	na
16.2	40	-0.6	45	16.2	40	18.5	78	na	--	na	--	na	--	na	--	na
21.3	14	0.0	34	21.3	14	20.3	69	na	--	na	--	na	--	na	--	na
17.8	30	0.4	19	17.8	30	20.8	66	na	--	na	--	na	--	na	--	na
17.1	35	-0.6	44	17.1	35	18.7	77	na	--	na	--	na	--	na	--	na
19.0	23	-1.0	53	19.0	23	28.0	32	14.7	6	14.4	60	158.0	26	12.5	19	23
15.9	42	0.7	12	15.9	42	18.5	78	12.6	12	9.0	84	93.4	77	na	--	na
23.7	9	-2.4	79	23.7	9	29.8	25	12.4	13	20.3	35	192.4	9	4.4	32	21
12.9	60	-2.7	84	12.9	60	35.8	9	-5.7	77	26.3	18	168.7	19	-10.0	63	61
15.1	48	-2.5	80	15.1	48	32.4	16	1.8	55	5.4	95	125.6	49	-15.5	72	31
12.6	62	-2.8	85	12.6	62	27.7	33	18.7	2	27.0	16	173.6	17	26.6	3	13
25.7	8	-1.0	52	25.7	8	27.4	34	-13.4	89	na	--	na	--	na	--	na
20.0	18	-1.8	67	20.0	18	34.8	11	1.8	55	23.1	27	165.6	22	-3.6	51	18
18.1	29	0.3	24	18.1	29	19.3	75	na	--	na	--	na	--	na	--	na
4.7	91	-1.8	67	4.7	91	19.7	73	9.6	25	25.6	20	na	--	na	--	na
30.6	5	0.9	9	30.6	5	na	--	na	--	na	--	na	--	na	--	na
11.5	69	-0.2	36	11.5	69	19.2	76	9.8	24	14.8	58	98.4	72	na	--	na
10.5	75	0.1	27	10.5	75	na	--	na	--	na	--	na	--	na	--	na
10.6	74	0.1	28	10.6	74	17.7	81	na	--	na	--	na	--	na	--	na
18.7	25	0.1	29	18.7	25	20.9	65	10.5	20	na	--	na	--	na	--	na
na	--	-1.9	69	na	--	na	--	na	--	na	--	na	--	na	--	na
18.1	28	0.1	30	18.1	28	21.0	65	na	--	na	--	na	--	na	--	na
na	--	1.2	6	na	--	na	--	na	--	na	--	na	--	na	--	na
na	--	-2.9	86	na	--	na	--	na	--	na	--	na	--	na	--	na
10.7	74	0.5	18	10.7	74	na	--	na	--	na	--	na	--	na	--	na
16.8	37	0.2	26	16.8	37	na	--	na	--	na	--	na	--	na	--	na
15.3	46	-0.1	35	15.3	46	na	--	na	--	na	--	na	--	na	--	na
-4.7	96	-2.8	85	-4.7	96	13.1	92	-32.0	98	-3.8	99	-9.8	99	-36.5	97	94
-6.9	97	-5.3	98	-6.9	97	15.4	88	-16.6	92	9.7	80	37.5	97	-31.5	94	99
11.4	69	-0.6	44	11.4	69	39.3	5	1.5	56	28.7	12	191.7	9	-3.9	51	30
13.7	56	0.0	33	13.7	56	27.6	33	13.2	10	8.1	86	115.3	57	11.6	20	31

CDA MONTHLY ALPHABETIC LISTING - 12/31/86

| | | | ASSETS | | MAX | % | ANNUALIZED ROR THRU 12/31/86 | | | | | |
| | | | | | | | 10 YEARS | | 5 YEARS | | 3 YEARS | |
FUND	MGT CO	IO	MIL$	NAV	LOAD	YLD	PCNT	RK	PCNT	RK	PCNT	RK
SIGMA INVESTMENT SHARES	SIGMA	GI	78	9.89	8.5	2.8	14.4	44	19.0	36	19.5	11
SIGMA SPECIAL FUND	SIGMA	G	18	9.21	8.5	1.2	14.9	40	15.4	65	14.6	45
SIGMA TRUST SHARES	SIGMA	B	40	13.63	8.5	4.9	13.0	59	19.0	35	18.5	15
SIGMA VENTURE SHARES	SIGMA	AG	59	11.06	8.5	0.4	20.1	10	13.8	75	8.1	81
SIGMA WORLD	SIGMA	IN	8	15.75	8.5	0.0	na	--	na	--	na	--
SMITH, BARNEY EQUITY	SM-BAR	G	70	13.98	4.0	2.5	15.3	36	16.5	55	14.5	46
SMITH, BARNEY INC. & GR.	SM-BAR	B	310	11.40	5.7	5.5	16.9	22	20.5	21	19.4	12
SOGEN INTERNATIONAL FUND	SOGEN	IN	66	17.71	4.2	3.1	18.5	15	22.9	8	19.6	10
SOUTHEASTERN GROWTH FUND	WHEAT	G	86	12.59	0.0	2.4	na	--	na	--	na	--
SOVEREIGN INVESTORS	HOPPER	GI	32	24.73	5.3	4.0	15.0	39	20.8	19	20.9	6
STATE BOND COMMON STOCK	ST-B&M	G	29	6.35	8.5	1.3	9.3	90	11.9	83	11.4	67
STATE BOND DIVERSIFIED	ST-B&M	GI	15	7.42	8.5	2.9	11.6	71	18.4	41	17.5	21
STATE BOND PROGRESS FUND	ST-B&M	AG	7	10.10	8.5	1.2	12.2	67	11.1	86	6.4	86
STATE FARM BALANCED	STFARM	GI	43	17.29	0.0	4.1	14.3	44	18.0	44	17.7	19
STATE FARM GROWTH FUND	STFARM	G	243	11.95	0.0	2.8	15.6	33	16.5	55	14.1	50
STATE STREET GROWTH	ST-ST	G	247	70.51	0.0	2.6	na	--	15.4	65	14.1	50
STATE STREET INV. CORP.	ST-ST	G	536	75.42	0.4	2.7	13.8	47	15.3	66	14.4	47
STEADMAN AMERICAN INDUS.	STDMAN	G	6	2.32	0.0	0.0	1.0	99	-5.7	98	-12.7	99
STEADMAN ASSOCIATED	STDMAN	GI	20	0.89	0.0	3.9	6.3	96	9.2	91	4.5	90
STEADMAN INVESTMENT	STDMAN	G	8	1.60	0.0	0.0	3.8	98	3.9	97	1.2	93
STEADMAN OCEANOGRAPHIC	STDMAN	AG	4	4.48	0.0	0.0	1.3	99	-5.9	98	-12.2	98
STEIN R&F CAPITAL OPPOR.	SR&F	AG	164	26.75	0.0	0.7	17.0	21	11.1	86	6.6	85
STEINROE DISCOVERY FUND	SR&F	AG	73	10.56	0.0	0.4	na	--	na	--	6.5	86
STEINROE HIGH-YIELD BOND	SR&F	BP	59	9.96	0.0	na	na	--	na	--	na	--
STEINROE HIGH-YIELD MUNI	SR&F	MB	194	12.06	0.0	7.7	na	--	na	--	na	--
STEINROE INTERMED MUNI	SR&F	MB	88	10.77	0.0	6.1	na	--	na	--	na	--
STEINROE MANAGED BOND FD	SR&F	BP	193	9.26	0.0	8.4	na	--	na	--	16.7	26
STEIN R&F STOCK	SR&F	AG	220	16.97	0.0	1.3	13.0	59	15.3	67	10.2	74
STEINROE SPECIAL FUND	SR&F	G	235	16.95	0.0	1.7	na	--	21.7	13	13.6	53
STEINROE MANAGED MUNI FD	SR&F	MB	477	9.22	0.0	6.9	na	--	21.0	17	17.1	23
STEIN R&F TOTAL RETURN	SR&F	B	145	25.07	0.0	5.1	10.9	78	16.9	52	15.6	35
STEINROE UNIVERSE FUND	SR&F	AG	94	17.48	0.0	1.0	na	--	14.4	72	7.3	83
STRATEGIC CAPITAL GAINS	SD	AG	7	6.54	8.5	0.0	na	--	na	--	-5.0	97
STRATEGIC INVESTMENTS	SD	ME	96	4.65	8.5	5.9	19.0	14	-0.2	98	-15.8	99
STRATEGIC SILVER	SD	ME	22	3.95	8.5	0.0	na	--	na	--	na	--
STRATTON GROWTH FUND	STRMGT	G	18	20.02	0.0	1.3	13.8	48	17.7	46	10.4	73
STRATTON MONTHLY DIV SHS	STRMGT	B	43	29.21	0.0	7.7	na	--	20.5	20	23.6	3
STRONG INCOME FUND	STRONG	GI	72	12.65	0.0	5.5	na	--	na	--	na	--
STRONG INVESTMENT FUND	STRONG	B	319	22.18	1.0	5.4	na	--	24.4	4	15.5	36
STRONG OPPORTUNITY FUND	STRONG	AG	32	15.99	2.0	0.0	na	--	na	--	na	--
STRONG TOTAL RETURN FUND	STRONG	B	452	21.61	1.0	5.8	na	--	25.5	2	18.4	16
SUMMIT INVESTOR FD INC.	AIM	AG	62	6.68	4.7	0.7	na	--	na	--	11.5	66
SUNBELT GROWTH FUND	CRITER	G	76	18.43	8.5	0.8	na	--	na	--	9.6	77
SURVEYOR FUND	ALLIAN	AG	90	11.51	8.4	0.2	13.6	52	11.6	84	9.1	78
TAX EXEMPT BD FD/AMERICA	CAPRES	MB	260	11.48	4.7	6.6	na	--	na	--	15.6	36
TECHNOLOGY FUND	KEMPER	G	557	11.12	8.5	1.4	14.9	40	14.6	71	11.1	69
TELEPHONE INCOME SHARES	ALEX	GI	99	15.67	0.0	6.0	na	--	na	--	na	--
TEMPLETON FOREIGN FUND	TEMPLE	IN	184	15.41	8.5	2.0	na	--	na	--	17.2	22
TEMPLETON GROWTH FUND	TEMPLE	G	1813	12.87	8.5	2.8	18.2	17	18.4	40	16.5	28
TEMPLETON GLOBAL I	TEMPLE	G	301	40.81	0.0	2.5	na	--	23.9	5	15.7	34

LATEST 12 MNTHS		THIS MONTH		1986 TO DATE		CALENDAR YEARS						CYCLES				CDA RATING
						1985		1984		1983		UP MKT		DOWN MKT		
PCNT	RK	PCNT	RK	PCNT	RK	PCNT	RK	PCNT	RK	PCNT	RK	PCNT	RK	PCNT	RK	
25.3	8	-1.1	54	25.3	8	24.5	47	9.4	26	20.1	36	168.7	19	-5.0	53	36
16.5	39	-2.9	87	16.5	39	33.5	13	-3.4	70	21.9	31	146.3	35	-19.6	80	49
18.3	26	-0.8	48	18.3	26	26.9	37	11.0	19	17.9	45	149.6	31	-3.4	49	24
5.3	90	-0.2	37	5.3	90	35.5	9	-11.5	87	20.6	34	116.8	56	-11.5	65	53
43.7	3	3.7	2	43.7	3	na	--	na	--	na	--	na	--	na	--	na
16.2	40	-1.4	59	16.2	40	32.5	16	-2.4	68	19.0	41	143.5	37	-20.3	82	45
21.3	14	-1.0	53	21.3	14	27.1	36	10.3	21	17.3	48	161.7	24	13.6	16	11
25.1	8	1.3	6	25.1	8	32.7	16	3.1	51	25.0	23	166.8	21	9.4	24	7
15.4	45	-3.4	92	15.4	45	na	--	na	--	na	--	na	--	na	--	na
21.9	12	-2.2	75	21.9	12	30.6	22	11.2	18	19.6	38	178.7	15	4.5	32	32
13.9	54	-1.9	70	13.9	54	28.6	29	-5.6	76	7.0	91	104.6	65	-19.4	80	89
20.0	19	-2.2	75	20.0	19	27.3	35	6.2	41	19.3	40	161.4	25	-19.6	80	68
12.5	63	-3.5	94	12.5	63	28.3	30	-16.5	92	8.1	87	96.1	73	-14.1	70	74
14.9	49	-1.6	63	14.9	49	36.3	8	4.1	48	14.0	62	151.9	30	-12.8	67	34
12.9	60	-3.2	90	12.9	60	33.9	13	-1.6	66	15.7	53	136.1	42	-15.1	71	42
12.1	65	-3.5	94	12.1	65	34.1	12	-1.1	64	15.0	57	142.9	38	na	--	na
12.0	66	-1.7	64	12.0	66	32.0	17	1.3	57	20.8	34	147.3	33	-18.6	78	68
-19.7	99	-3.7	95	-19.7	99	7.8	96	-23.2	96	7.1	90	5.0	98	-30.8	93	98
2.8	93	-0.5	44	2.8	93	21.5	62	-8.6	83	7.0	90	69.4	92	-1.6	46	91
10.3	75	0.6	14	10.3	75	5.3	97	-10.9	86	8.7	85	33.0	97	-19.8	81	94
-11.3	98	-2.6	82	-11.3	98	-14.3	99	-10.9	86	10.2	77	2.8	98	-32.8	95	98
16.8	37	-1.0	53	16.8	37	24.6	46	-16.8	93	11.9	69	121.4	53	-34.5	96	46
-5.3	97	-3.2	90	-5.3	97	45.3	3	-12.2	88	na	--	na	--	na	--	na
na	--	0.2	25	na	--	na	--	na	--	na	--	na	--	na	--	na
17.6	31	-0.9	51	17.6	31	21.1	64	na	--	na	--	na	--	na	--	na
13.0	59	-0.3	39	13.0	59	na	--	na	--	na	--	na	--	na	--	na
16.3	40	-0.3	39	16.3	40	22.9	54	11.1	18	4.4	97	86.1	84	na	--	na
17.4	33	-1.0	53	17.4	33	26.5	39	-9.8	85	14.0	62	122.8	51	-25.8	89	80
14.8	50	-0.7	46	14.8	50	29.4	27	-1.2	64	32.9	7	202.7	7	-22.4	85	54
17.4	33	-1.0	52	17.4	33	22.6	55	11.5	17	10.9	74	108.4	62	8.0	26	20
16.9	36	-0.4	40	16.9	36	25.6	43	5.3	44	13.5	64	128.8	48	-19.0	79	78
18.7	24	2.7	3	18.7	24	28.3	31	-18.8	94	20.5	34	112.3	58	na	--	na
-21.4	99	2.2	4	-21.4	99	24.2	48	-12.3	88	14.4	61	47.1	95	na	--	na
28.3	6	-3.1	89	28.3	6	-29.5	99	-34.1	99	-1.9	98	-3.6	99	-49.6	99	63
-9.8	98	-4.4	97	-9.8	98	na	--	na	--	na	--	na	--	na	--	na
10.7	73	-1.0	52	10.7	73	27.5	34	-4.6	73	26.4	18	156.4	27	-15.6	72	53
20.4	16	-1.7	65	20.4	16	29.7	25	21.0	1	11.8	70	177.1	15	na	--	na
29.9	6	0.7	12	29.9	6	na	--	na	--	na	--	na	--	na	--	na
17.5	32	-0.8	49	17.5	32	19.4	75	9.8	24	45.1	1	171.7	18	na	--	na
59.9	1	-4.4	97	59.9	1	na	--	na	--	na	--	na	--	na	--	na
20.0	18	-1.8	68	20.0	18	25.4	44	10.4	21	41.3	2	188.9	10	na	--	na
14.0	53	-2.9	87	14.0	53	30.2	23	-6.7	78	9.9	78	na	--	na	--	na
14.1	53	-1.3	58	14.1	53	16.6	85	-1.0	63	10.4	76	114.1	57	na	--	na
14.0	53	-2.4	78	14.0	53	28.6	29	-11.5	87	18.2	44	129.2	47	-26.1	90	60
18.7	25	-0.2	37	18.7	25	19.7	73	8.7	30	8.6	86	na	--	na	--	na
14.2	52	-1.9	70	14.2	52	25.8	42	-4.5	73	19.1	40	131.9	45	-27.8	91	63
24.8	8	-1.3	57	24.8	8	29.0	28	na	--	na	--	na	--	na	--	na
28.7	6	3.4	2	28.7	6	26.8	37	-1.3	65	36.5	5	na	--	na	--	na
21.2	15	0.8	11	21.2	15	27.8	32	2.1	54	32.9	7	165.3	22	-18.2	78	12
18.6	25	-0.6	44	18.6	25	30.3	22	0.3	59	38.7	4	194.9	8	na	--	na

CDA MONTHLY ALPHABETIC LISTING - 12/31/86

| | | | | | | | ANNUALIZED ROR THRU 12/31/86 | | |
| | | | ASSETS | | MAX | % | 10 YEARS | 5 YEARS | 3 YEARS |
FUND	MGT CO	IO	MIL$	NAV	LOAD	YLD	PCNT RK	PCNT RK	PCNT RK
TEMPLETON GLOBAL II	TEMPLE	G	498	12.72	8.5	2.2	na --	na --	12.7 59
TEMPLETON WORLD FUND	TEMPLE	G	3213	14.74	8.5	2.5	na --	20.7 19	17.1 23
THOMSON MCKINNON GROWTH	THOMSN	G	191	13.28	0.0	2.3	na --	na --	na --
THOMSON MCKINNON INCOME	THOMSN	BP	332	10.21	0.0	10.8	na --	na --	na --
THOMSON MCKINNON OPPORT.	THOMSN	AG	52	12.41	0.0	0.0	na --	na --	na --
TRANSATLANTIC FUND INC.	KLEIN	IN	100	22.92	0.0	0.0	16.0 30	17.7 46	26.1 2
TRUSTEES COMM EQ-INTL	VGUARD	IN	634	38.65	0.0	2.3	na --	na --	28.0 2
TRUSTEES COMM EQ-US PORT	VGUARD	GI	165	28.68	0.0	3.3	na --	16.9 52	10.6 73
TUDOR FUND	WEISS	AG	159	20.08	0.0	0.3	20.5 8	20.6 20	11.1 69
TWENTIETH CENTURY GIFTR	INVRES	G	6	6.75	0.5	0.0	na --	na --	19.5 11
TWENTIETH CENTURY GROWTH	INVRES	AG	888	14.06	0.0	1.0	24.8 2	14.3 73	12.8 58
TWENTIETH CENTURY SELECT	INVRES	G	1832	31.61	0.0	1.5	26.6 1	22.5 9	14.3 48
TWENTIETH CENTURY ULTRA	INVRES	AG	300	8.92	0.5	0.1	na --	13.2 78	4.1 90
TWENTIETH CENTURY US GOV	INVRES	BP	237	100.93	0.0	8.1	na --	na --	12.2 62
TWENTIETH CENTURY VISTA	INVRES	AG	144	5.95	0.5	0.0	na --	na --	9.0 79
UMB BOND FUND	JONES	BP	23	11.37	0.0	7.5	na --	na --	14.1 51
UMB STOCK FUND	JONES	GI	32	12.78	0.0	3.8	na --	na --	11.9 64
UNIFIED GROWTH FUND	UNIFID	G	24	22.20	0.0	1.5	na --	17.0 51	15.5 36
UNIFIED INCOME FUND	UNIFID	B	13	12.65	0.0	7.0	na --	na --	9.5 78
UNIFIED MUNI FD-GENERAL	UNIFID	MB	6	9.27	0.0	6.1	na --	na --	na --
UNIFIED MUNI FD-INDIANA	UNIFID	MB	10	9.33	0.0	6.1	na --	na --	na --
UNIFIED MUTUAL SHARES	UNIFID	GI	18	17.07	0.0	3.4	12.5 65	17.8 45	16.5 27
UNITED ACCUMULATIVE FUND	WADDEL	G	678	7.78	8.5	2.6	15.7 32	20.9 18	16.4 28
UNITED CONTL. INCOME FD.	WADDEL	GI	241	19.31	8.5	3.4	15.2 37	24.1 5	21.7 5
UNITED BOND FUND	WADDEL	BP	335	6.42	8.5	8.0	9.8 86	19.8 25	17.4 22
UNITED GOLD & GOVERNMENT	WADDEL	ME	9	6.83	8.5	2.9	na --	na --	na --
UNITED GOV SECURITIES FD	WADDEL	BP	147	5.65	4.0	7.8	na --	na --	na --
UNITED HIGH INCOME FUND	WADDEL	BP	1229	13.95	8.5	11.3	na --	18.6 39	15.7 34
UNITED INCOME FUND	WADDEL	G	792	17.03	8.5	2.4	14.8 42	24.6 4	20.2 8
UNITED INTL. GROWTH FUND	WADDEL	IN	205	7.13	8.5	1.5	17.4 20	22.4 10	20.2 8
UNITED MUNICIPAL BOND FD	WADDEL	MB	402	7.18	4.0	6.7	5.9 97	19.6 27	18.4 16
UNITED MUNI HIGH INCOME	WADDEL	MB	28	5.30	3.9	7.4	na --	na --	na --
UNITED NEW CONCEPTS FUND	WADDEL	G	60	6.14	8.5	1.0	na --	na --	10.6 72
UNITED RETIREMENT SHARES	WADDEL	B	94	6.05	8.5	3.8	12.4 66	17.6 47	13.8 52
UNITED SCIENCE & ENERGY	WADDEL	G	173	10.00	8.5	2.0	14.0 47	16.1 60	12.8 59
UNITED VANGUARD FUND	WADDEL	GI	494	6.26	8.5	2.2	20.7 8	19.6 27	12.0 63
U.S. GOV GUARANTEED SECS	CAPRES	BP	189	14.96	4.7	9.4	na --	na --	na --
U.S. TREND FUND, INC.	TAMCO	G	79	10.72	7.5	2.1	17.7 19	12.6 81	8.2 81
US GOVT HIGH YIELD TRUST	CRITER	BP	2308	9.67	6.7	7.8	na --	na --	na --
US GOLD SHARES FUND	UNITED	ME	307	4.63	0.0	6.3	21.1 6	4.0 97	-11.0 98
US GOOD AND BAD TIMES FD	UNITED	G	21	16.68	0.0	0.0	na --	13.4 77	11.0 70
US GROWTH FUND	UNITED	AG	7	8.82	0.0	0.0	na --	na --	-0.7 95
US INCOME FUND	UNITED	GI	3	10.43	0.0	3.6	na --	na --	6.4 86
US LOCAP FUND	UNITED	AG	2	6.83	0.0	0.0	na --	na --	na --
US NEW PROSPECTOR FUND	UNITED	ME	46	1.31	0.0	0.0	na --	na --	na --
US PROSPECTOR FUND	UNITED	ME	72	0.72	0.0	0.0	na --	na --	-6.1 97
USAA MUTUAL FD GROWTH	USAA	G	174	14.76	0.0	1.2	10.6 79	11.2 85	6.8 85
USAA MUTUAL FD INCOME	USAA	BP	213	11.98	0.0	10.6	10.3 82	17.2 49	15.7 34
USAA SUNBELT ERA FUND	USAA	AG	118	17.10	0.0	0.4	na --	na --	2.1 92
USAA TAX EX HIGH YIELD	USAA	MB	779	13.79	0.0	8.0	na --	na --	15.6 35

LATEST 12 MNTHS		THIS MONTH		1986 TO DATE		CALENDAR YEARS						CYCLES				CDA RATING
						1985		1984		1983		UP MKT		DOWN MKT		
PCNT	RK	PCNT	RK	PCNT	RK	PCNT	RK	PCNT	RK	PCNT	RK	PCNT	RK	PCNT	RK	
10.2	76	-0.3	39	10.2	76	27.7	33	1.8	55	na	--	na	--	na	--	na
17.9	29	-1.5	62	17.9	29	30.3	23	4.6	47	34.0	7	188.8	10	-8.2	58	11
23.0	10	-2.9	86	23.0	10	30.5	22	na	--	na	--	na	--	na	--	na
10.6	74	0.0	32	10.6	74	19.1	76	na	--	na	--	na	--	na	--	na
4.2	92	-1.0	51	4.2	92	29.8	25	na	--	na	--	na	--	na	--	na
51.7	2	2.9	3	51.7	2	54.2	2	-14.4	90	32.9	7	185.1	11	-33.2	95	15
49.9	2	4.0	2	49.9	2	40.3	5	-0.3	61	na	--	na	--	na	--	na
15.5	45	-2.9	87	15.5	45	20.5	68	-2.9	69	29.1	11	135.9	42	-3.4	50	20
12.4	63	-2.3	77	12.4	63	31.2	20	-7.2	79	28.4	13	173.4	17	5.2	30	10
28.3	6	-3.1	89	28.3	6	55.3	2	-14.3	90	na	--	na	--	na	--	na
19.4	21	2.9	3	19.4	21	33.9	13	-10.2	85	24.4	23	167.7	20	-28.5	92	13
20.7	16	-3.2	91	20.7	16	33.8	13	-7.6	80	30.0	10	209.2	6	-10.0	63	1
10.3	76	-3.9	96	10.3	76	26.2	41	-18.9	94	26.9	16	144.7	36	na	--	na
11.4	69	1.4	5	11.4	69	12.9	92	12.3	14	7.0	91	na	--	na	--	na
26.5	8	-4.9	98	26.5	8	22.5	56	-16.3	92	na	--	na	--	na	--	na
12.6	62	0.4	18	12.6	62	16.2	86	13.5	10	4.8	96	na	--	na	--	na
12.3	65	-2.5	80	12.3	65	20.7	66	3.4	50	23.7	26	na	--	na	--	na
13.5	57	-1.1	54	13.5	57	26.0	41	7.6	35	11.3	72	144.5	36	na	--	na
9.8	77	-0.9	50	9.8	77	20.5	68	-0.8	62	17.9	46	na	--	na	--	na
17.8	30	-0.3	39	17.8	30	na	--	na	--	na	--	na	--	na	--	na
19.5	20	0.0	32	19.5	20	na	--	na	--	na	--	na	--	na	--	na
11.6	68	-1.5	61	11.6	68	30.8	21	8.4	31	21.7	31	152.3	29	-17.4	76	63
17.5	32	-1.8	66	17.5	32	25.6	43	7.0	37	25.9	20	180.8	14	-7.4	56	27
18.5	26	-1.5	61	18.5	26	33.8	13	13.8	9	24.7	23	209.6	6	-2.9	48	25
15.1	48	1.0	8	15.1	48	25.2	45	12.3	13	11.2	73	116.9	56	16.6	9	47
41.3	3	3.6	2	41.3	3	na	--	na	--	na	--	na	--	na	--	na
16.9	36	0.3	23	16.9	36	23.5	51	na	--	na	--	na	--	na	--	na
14.7	50	0.4	19	14.7	50	23.2	52	9.7	25	13.9	63	108.5	62	11.9	19	29
22.3	11	-2.0	72	22.3	11	33.9	13	6.1	42	31.6	8	212.7	5	-0.5	45	30
28.8	6	3.5	2	28.8	6	38.5	6	-2.7	68	28.4	13	183.2	13	3.9	34	17
21.8	13	0.0	33	21.8	13	24.0	49	9.9	23	8.5	86	103.6	65	0.9	42	54
na	--	0.6	14	na	--	na	--	na	--	na	--	na	--	na	--	na
15.1	48	-1.8	66	15.1	48	26.0	41	-6.7	78	na	--	na	--	na	--	na
13.8	55	0.8	11	13.8	55	24.2	48	4.2	48	13.1	66	129.0	47	3.0	37	45
18.1	28	-2.2	74	18.1	28	23.1	53	-1.4	65	18.5	43	121.5	53	-20.2	82	61
17.7	30	-1.1	54	17.7	30	23.0	53	-3.1	69	20.9	33	141.6	39	7.6	27	5
12.4	64	0.7	12	12.4	64	na	--	na	--	na	--	na	--	na	--	na
9.4	80	-3.2	91	9.4	80	22.7	55	-5.6	76	22.5	29	126.6	49	-18.1	78	50
5.9	89	0.1	28	5.9	89	na	--	na	--	na	--	na	--	na	--	na
37.5	4	-0.9	50	37.5	4	-27.0	99	-29.7	98	0.9	98	26.7	98	-51.0	99	61
8.9	81	-3.4	92	8.9	81	22.5	56	2.7	53	11.1	73	95.6	74	na	--	na
10.7	74	-2.1	73	10.7	74	20.0	71	-26.4	97	na	--	na	--	na	--	na
0.6	94	-1.9	69	0.6	94	15.3	88	3.9	49	na	--	na	--	na	--	na
-6.8	97	-2.7	84	-6.8	97	na	--	na	--	na	--	na	--	na	--	na
41.5	3	1.5	5	41.5	3	na	--	na	--	na	--	na	--	na	--	na
30.9	5	2.9	3	30.9	5	0.0	98	-36.8	99	na	--	na	--	na	--	na
9.8	77	-1.9	69	9.8	77	19.9	71	-7.5	80	15.8	53	107.5	62	-22.6	85	91
12.6	62	0.5	17	12.6	62	20.6	67	13.9	9	4.5	96	95.1	75	23.3	4	68
5.6	89	-3.5	94	5.6	89	23.0	53	-18.1	94	23.9	25	112.1	59	na	--	na
17.0	35	1.2	6	17.0	35	19.7	73	10.4	21	11.4	71	87.8	82	na	--	na

CDA MONTHLY ALPHABETIC LISTING − 12/31/86

FUND	MGT CO	IO	ASSETS MIL$	NAV	MAX LOAD	% YLD	10 YEARS PCNT	RK	5 YEARS PCNT	RK	3 YEARS PCNT	RK
USAA TAX EX INTERMEDIATE	USAA	MB	284	12.35	0.0	7.5	na	--	na	--	12.8	59
USAA TAX EX SH-TERM FD	USAA	MB	211	10.71	0.0	6.5	na	--	na	--	8.7	80
VALLEY FORGE FUND	VALMGT	GI	10	10.67	0.0	4.3	15.8	31	13.5	76	7.5	83
VALUE LINE FUND	BRNHRD	AG	203	14.68	0.0	1.5	16.5	24	11.2	85	10.2	74
VALUE LINE INCOME	BRNHRD	B	154	6.81	0.0	5.8	15.8	32	15.2	67	13.7	52
VALUE LINE LEVER. GROWTH	BRNHRD	G	239	22.79	0.0	1.3	22.0	4	14.6	71	12.5	61
VALUE LINE SPECIAL SIT.	BRNHRD	AG	194	15.07	0.0	0.3	15.2	37	6.9	94	-1.8	95
VALUE LINE US GOV SECS	BRNHRD	BP	117	12.77	0.0	10.2	na	--	na	--	15.1	40
VAN KAMPEN MERRITT-GOV	AMPORT	BP	3538	16.57	4.9	10.4	na	--	na	--	na	--
VANCE, SANDERS SPECIAL	ETN&HD	G	83	10.63	8.5	0.7	14.2	45	5.2	96	-2.5	95
VANGUARD CONVERTIBLE SEC	VGUARD	GI	40	9.68	0.0	na	na	--	na	--	na	--
VANGUARD FIXED INC HIYLD	VGUARD	BP	1158	9.20	0.0	11.2	na	--	17.7	45	15.0	41
VANGUARD FIXED INC INVT	VGUARD	BP	517	8.73	0.0	10.3	10.4	80	17.1	50	16.9	25
VANGUARD FIXED INC GNMA	VGUARD	BP	1853	10.05	0.0	10.0	na	--	17.3	49	15.4	37
VANGUARD FI SECS-SH TERM	VGUARD	BP	315	10.82	0.0	8.3	na	--	na	--	13.5	54
VANGUARD INDEX TRUST	VGUARD	GI	474	24.27	0.0	3.4	13.3	55	19.3	31	18.1	17
VANGUARD CALIF INS TX FR	VGUARD	MB	46	10.51	0.0	na	na	--	na	--	na	--
VANGUARD PENNA INS TX FR	VGUARD	MB	84	10.23	0.0	na	na	--	na	--	na	--
VANGUARD MUNI HIGH YIELD	VGUARD	MB	782	10.67	0.0	7.7	na	--	19.1	33	16.9	25
VANGUARD MUNI INSURED LT	VGUARD	MB	728	11.86	0.0	7.4	na	--	na	--	na	--
VANGUARD MUNI INTERM-TRM	VGUARD	MB	833	12.29	0.0	7.1	na	--	15.8	62	14.3	48
VANGUARD MUNI LONG-TERM	VGUARD	MB	627	11.12	0.0	7.5	na	--	18.9	37	16.1	31
VANGUARD MUNI SHORT-TERM	VGUARD	MB	940	15.44	0.0	5.6	na	--	7.3	94	7.1	84
VANGUARD SPEC PORT-ENRGY	VGUARD	G	14	11.18	0.0	3.9	na	--	na	--	na	--
VANGUARD SPEC PORT-GOLD	VGUARD	ME	54	9.22	0.0	2.3	na	--	na	--	na	--
VANGUARD SPC PORT-HEALTH	VGUARD	AG	43	17.64	0.0	0.7	na	--	na	--	na	--
VANGUARD SPEC-SVC ECON	VGUARD	G	49	17.59	0.0	0.9	na	--	na	--	na	--
VANGUARD SPEC PORT-TECH	VGUARD	AG	13	11.93	0.0	0.7	na	--	na	--	na	--
VANGUARD STAR FUND	VGUARD	B	416	11.34	0.0	7.3	na	--	na	--	na	--
VANGUARD WORLD-INTL GR	VGUARD	IN	411	11.26	0.0	0.6	na	--	29.7	1	34.4	1
VANGUARD WORLD-US GR	VGUARD	G	167	10.32	0.0	2.5	15.1	38	17.2	49	14.1	50
VENTURE INCOME PLUS	VENADV	BP	62	9.87	8.5	14.4	na	--	na	--	11.8	64
VENTURE MUNI PLUS	VENADV	MB	27	10.20	0.0	9.2	na	--	na	--	na	--
WALL STREET FUND	WALL	AG	9	6.96	5.5	0.7	9.8	87	12.9	79	11.6	65
WASHINGTON AREA GROWTH	CALVER	G	17	18.45	0.0	0.0	na	--	na	--	na	--
WASH. MUTUAL INVESTORS	CAPRES	GI	1568	12.30	8.5	3.7	16.6	23	24.4	4	20.5	7
WEALTH MONITORS FUND	WEALTH	G	5	8.32	8.5	na	na	--	na	--	na	--
WEINGARTEN EQUITY FUND	AIM	AG	160	17.63	4.7	0.8	24.3	2	21.7	13	16.7	26
WELLESLEY INCOME FUND	VGUARD	B	399	16.27	0.0	7.9	13.6	51	20.8	19	20.7	7
WELLINGTON FUND	VGUARD	B	1025	15.85	0.0	5.8	14.1	46	20.9	18	18.9	13
WESTERGAARD FUND INC.	EQ-RE	AG	15	9.57	8.5	1.8	na	--	na	--	-3.7	97
WINDSOR FUND	VGUARD	GI	4839	13.95	0.0	5.1	18.9	15	23.8	6	22.5	4
WINDSOR II	VGUARD	GI	730	12.39	0.0	3.3	na	--	na	--	na	--
WORLD OF TECHNOLOGY FUND	FIF	IN	8	9.68	0.0	0.0	na	--	na	--	4.0	91
WORLD TRENDS	VANECK	IN	58	13.41	7.5	1.0	na	--	na	--	na	--
WPG FUND	WEISS	G	39	20.64	0.0	2.8	na	--	17.2	50	12.6	60
YES FUND	SIS	BP	168	7.76	3.7	10.4	na	--	na	--	8.2	81

LATEST 12 MNTHS PCNT RK	THIS MONTH PCNT RK	1986 TO DATE PCNT RK	CALENDAR YEARS 1985 PCNT RK	1984 PCNT RK	1983 PCNT RK	CYCLES UP MKT PCNT RK	DOWN MKT PCNT RK	CDA RATING
13.4 58	0.8 11	13.4 58	16.3 86	8.8 29	9.6 81	70.5 91	na --	na
9.1 80	1.3 6	9.1 80	9.5 95	7.6 35	6.3 92	39.7 96	na --	na
5.5 89	0.6 15	5.5 89	10.5 95	6.7 39	17.9 46	82.0 86	17.1 9	67
16.8 37	-0.4 42	16.8 37	34.6 11	-14.7 90	-1.3 98	76.8 89	3.3 35	22
15.4 46	-0.1 36	15.4 46	23.7 50	2.9 52	6.7 91	94.0 77	20.8 5	30
23.3 10	-2.2 75	23.3 10	27.1 35	-9.1 83	7.9 87	100.8 68	22.5 4	3
5.1 90	-1.9 69	5.1 90	21.1 64	-25.5 97	19.5 39	63.2 93	-13.4 68	82
10.7 74	0.4 20	10.7 74	21.2 63	13.7 9	6.0 93	91.8 79	na --	na
13.8 55	0.2 25	13.8 55	22.3 57	na --	na --	na --	na --	na
-5.5 97	-0.9 51	-5.5 97	15.2 89	-14.8 91	19.3 39	60.3 93	-7.9 57	81
na --	-0.3 39	na --	na --	na --	na --	na --	na --	na
16.1 41	0.4 20	16.1 41	21.9 59	7.5 35	15.7 53	98.9 71	18.9 7	25
14.3 52	1.0 8	14.3 52	22.1 58	14.6 6	6.7 91	91.0 80	22.8 4	62
11.8 66	0.6 15	11.8 66	20.7 67	14.0 8	9.7 80	89.5 81	na --	na
11.4 69	0.4 19	11.4 69	14.9 89	14.2 8	9.1 83	na --	na --	na
18.2 27	-2.5 79	18.2 27	31.2 20	6.2 41	21.3 32	176.0 15	-17.0 76	67
na --	0.9 10	na --	na --	na --	na --	na --	na --	na
na --	-0.1 36	na --	na --	na --	na --	na --	na --	na
19.7 20	-0.2 37	19.7 20	21.7 61	9.7 25	10.4 76	98.9 71	3.7 34	28
18.6 25	-0.2 38	18.6 25	19.4 75	na --	na --	na --	na --	na
16.2 40	-0.5 43	16.2 40	17.4 82	9.5 26	6.5 92	76.7 89	2.1 38	70
19.4 21	0.1 30	19.4 21	20.8 66	8.5 31	9.5 81	94.7 76	1.5 40	38
7.4 86	0.2 25	7.4 86	7.0 96	6.8 38	5.1 95	31.7 97	14.8 13	93
12.5 63	1.6 5	12.5 63	14.4 90	na --	na --	na --	na --	na
49.5 2	3.0 3	49.5 2	-5.1 98	na --	na --	na --	na --	na
21.5 14	-1.7 65	21.5 14	45.7 3	na --	na --	na --	na --	na
12.8 60	-2.5 80	12.8 60	43.6 3	na --	na --	na --	na --	na
5.7 89	-2.1 72	5.7 89	14.0 91	na --	na --	na --	na --	na
13.8 55	-1.0 52	13.8 55	na --	na --	na --	na --	na --	na
56.6 1	4.4 1	56.6 1	56.9 2	-1.1 64	43.1 2	310.2 1	na --	na
7.6 85	-1.8 67	7.6 85	36.5 8	1.2 57	24.2 24	171.6 18	-15.7 73	72
1.1 94	0.1 31	1.1 94	28.2 31	7.9 34	18.8 42	98.2 72	na --	na
12.3 64	0.1 27	12.3 64	na --	na --	na --	na --	na --	na
11.1 71	-1.0 52	11.1 71	28.2 31	-2.3 67	13.9 63	132.4 45	-26.4 90	87
16.9 36	-2.6 83	16.9 36	na --	na --	na --	na --	na --	na
22.5 11	-2.4 79	22.5 11	32.1 17	8.3 32	26.2 19	206.9 6	5.5 30	26
na --	-2.5 80	na --	na --	na --	na --	na --	na --	na
24.4 9	-2.4 78	24.4 9	36.1 9	-6.1 77	28.9 12	221.3 4	-25.6 89	6
18.4 26	-0.4 41	18.4 26	27.4 35	16.6 3	18.6 43	154.1 28	11.4 20	18
18.2 27	-1.4 58	18.2 27	28.5 30	10.8 19	23.4 26	168.3 20	-2.8 48	43
-7.2 97	-3.0 88	-7.2 97	11.8 94	-13.9 90	na --	na --	na --	na
20.2 18	-0.6 45	20.2 18	28.0 32	19.5 2	30.1 10	225.2 3	8.8 25	12
21.4 14	-2.3 77	21.4 14	na --	na --	na --	na --	na --	na
16.5 39	0.1 28	16.5 39	16.5 85	-17.2 93	na --	na --	na --	na
40.6 3	1.8 5	40.6 3	na --	na --	na --	na --	na --	na
11.5 69	-1.8 66	11.5 69	30.2 23	-1.6 66	18.4 43	139.1 41	-11.8 65	62
8.5 82	0.3 22	8.5 82	7.2 96	8.8 29	na --	na --	na --	na

CDA MONTHLY ALPHABETIC LISTING – 12/31/86

FUND	MGT CO	IO	ASSETS MIL$	NAV	MAX LOAD	% YLD	ANNUALIZED ROR THRU 12/31/86 10 YEARS PCNT RK	5 YEARS PCNT RK	3 YEARS PCNT RK
SUMMARY BY INVESTMENT OBJECTIVE									
32 INTERNATIONAL		IN	9271			1.0	17.5 22	22.2 21	23.2 16
115 AGGRESSIVE GROWTH		AG	13500			0.5	14.4 44	11.0 72	4.9 77
236 GROWTH		G	62547			1.7	15.1 43	16.1 54	12.2 56
135 GROWTH & INCOME		GI	57333			3.7	14.8 43	17.9 42	14.9 41
120 MUNICIPAL BOND		MB	57394			6.9	7.1 94	17.8 40	14.6 42
183 BOND & PREFERRED		BP	138076			9.4	9.8 84	17.3 48	14.8 42
58 BALANCED		B	17523			5.5	13.4 55	19.0 35	16.9 30
18 METALS		ME	2197			2.1	21.6 7	5.0 95	-4.0 96
897 TOTAL FUNDS			357834			4.3	14.0 50	16.4 50	12.7 50
STANDARD & POOR 500							13.8	19.8	18.4
SALOMON BROS. CORP. BONDS							9.9	22.4	22.0
U.S. TREASURY BILLS							9.0	8.5	7.6

UP MARKET DATES: 7/31/82 – 8/31/86

* INDICATES THAT FUND CHARGES A REDEMPTION FEE OR DEFERRED SALES CHARGE

LATEST 12 MNTHS		THIS MONTH		1986 TO DATE		CALENDAR YEARS						CYCLES				CDA RATING
						1985		1984		1983		UP MKT		DOWN MKT		
PCNT	RK	PCNT	RK	PCNT	RK	PCNT	RK	PCNT	RK	PCNT	RK	PCNT	RK	PCNT	RK	RATING
45.2	7	2.8	7	45.2	7	42.1	20	-4.7	70	29.3	18	212.6	12	-11.8	63	23
8.6	63	-2.4	72	8.6	63	25.6	42	-14.4	86	19.0	46	109.8	57	-17.5	71	61
13.2	54	-2.0	68	13.2	54	27.7	37	-1.9	63	21.3	38	144.0	40	-12.4	65	52
14.8	48	-1.8	66	14.8	48	25.6	44	5.6	41	20.3	39	146.1	38	-3.4	50	47
17.1	35	0.0	31	17.1	35	18.9	73	8.5	30	10.6	77	89.8	75	5.9	30	41
12.4	62	0.3	24	12.4	62	20.0	68	10.8	21	10.9	74	97.7	72	15.1	14	57
16.0	41	-0.9	49	16.0	41	24.7	47	9.9	26	18.1	50	141.4	40	4.4	34	37
31.6	13	0.7	28	31.6	13	-7.6	98	-27.9	97	1.7	95	40.7	95	-44.5	98	66
14.9	50	-1.0	50	14.9	50	24.3	50	1.2	50	17.8	50	127.7	50	-4.5	50	50
18.6		-2.6		18.6		31.7		6.2		22.5		181.6		-16.5		
19.3		0.7		19.3		30.1		16.9		6.3		137.2		13.0		
5.8		0.4		5.8		7.3		9.8		8.9		38.1		23.8		

DOWN MARKET DATES: 11/30/80 - 7/31/82

Top 50 Tables

TOP 50 FUNDS BY CDA RATING – 12/31/86

			ASSETS		MAX	%	ANNUALIZED ROR THRU 12/31/86					
							10 YEARS		5 YEARS		3 YEARS	
FUND	MGT CO	IO	MIL$	NAV	LOAD	YLD	PCNT	RK	PCNT	RK	PCNT	RK
FIDELITY MAGELLAN FUND	FIDEL	G	6555	48.69	3.0	0.8	32.8	1	30.2	1	22.1	4
MERRILL L. PACIFIC FUND	MERRIL	IN	445	34.20	6.5	0.3	na	--	29.6	1	37.9	1
PHOENIX BALANCED FD SER	PIC	B	153	12.75	8.5	4.5	na	--	23.9	5	21.0	6
TWENTIETH CENTURY SELECT	INVRES	G	1832	31.61	0.0	1.5	26.6	1	22.5	9	14.3	48
EVERGREEN TOTAL RETURN	SAXON	B	794	19.18	0.0	5.4	na	--	24.2	5	21.8	4
G. T. PACIFIC GROWTH FD	GTCAP	IN	67	29.98	0.0	0.0	na	--	17.3	48	21.7	5
LOOMIS-SAYLES CAP. DEV.	LOOMIS	AG	208	23.12	0.0	0.6	23.6	3	28.8	1	20.0	9
PARTNERS FUND	NEUBER	GI	444	17.37	0.0	2.4	20.1	10	19.9	23	18.1	17
LEHMAN CAPITAL FUND	LEHMAN	G	103	17.87	0.0	1.3	24.6	2	22.0	12	11.7	65
MUTUAL QUALIFIED INCOME	HSC	B	517	20.04	0.0	5.2	na	--	21.0	17	18.6	14
LINDNER DIVIDEND FUND	LINDNR	GI	62	23.74	0.0	8.2	22.3	4	25.0	3	17.5	21
QUEST FOR VALUE FUND	OPPCAP	G	75	25.49	0.0	0.7	na	--	24.3	4	15.1	41
VALUE LINE LEVER. GROWTH	BRNHRD	G	239	22.79	0.0	1.3	22.0	4	14.6	71	12.5	61
FIDELITY DESTINY	FIDEL	G	1074	12.43	0.0	2.3	21.6	5	24.8	3	16.7	27
COPLEY TAX-MANAGED FUND	COPLEY	G	31	11.02	0.0	0.0	na	--	19.5	29	22.1	4
PHOENIX STOCK FUND SER	PIC	G	95	12.67	8.5	1.5	na	--	24.7	3	17.3	22
PHOENIX CONVERTIBLE FUND	PIC	GI	100	17.44	8.5	4.3	na	--	20.8	19	14.5	46
NEL GROWTH FUND	LOOMIS	AG	286	26.65	8.0	0.7	22.0	4	24.3	5	14.6	46
FIDELITY EQUITY INCOME	FIDEL	GI	3100	27.29	2.0	5.8	19.9	11	22.8	8	17.3	22
BASCOM HILL INVESTORS	MADINV	GI	7	15.11	0.0	3.8	na	--	19.1	34	15.0	41
UNITED VANGUARD FUND	WADDEL	GI	494	6.26	8.5	2.2	20.7	8	19.6	27	12.0	63
FIDELITY HIGH INCOME FD	FIDEL	BP	1460	9.72	0.0	11.2	na	--	21.4	15	17.9	19
ACORN FUND	HARRIS	G	395	39.27	0.0	1.2	20.1	10	20.0	23	19.1	13
QUALIFIED DIVD PORTF I	VGUARD	B	177	17.07	0.0	6.7	20.5	8	28.9	1	25.6	2
MUTUAL SHARES CORP.	HSC	B	1293	60.39	0.0	4.0	20.8	7	21.2	16	19.0	13
WEINGARTEN EQUITY FUND	AIM	AG	160	17.63	4.7	0.8	24.3	2	21.7	13	16.7	26
KEMPER HIGH YIELD FD	KEMPER	BP	323	11.45	5.5	10.4	na	--	21.3	15	17.0	24
OPPENHEIMER TIME FUND	OPPEN	G	230	16.21	8.5	2.8	20.2	10	20.6	20	12.7	59
SOGEN INTERNATIONAL FUND	SOGEN	IN	66	17.71	4.2	3.1	18.5	15	22.9	8	19.6	10
NICHOLAS FUND	NICHOL	G	1053	34.87	0.0	2.5	22.8	3	21.7	13	16.8	26
NORTH STAR REGIONAL FUND	INVADV	G	84	18.42	0.0	1.8	na	--	21.6	14	18.5	15
PRICE (ROWE) INTERNATL.	PRICE	IN	753	25.78	0.0	0.8	na	--	24.6	4	30.0	1
BRUCE FUND	BRUCE	AG	3	109.39	0.0	1.2	na	--	22.2	11	23.5	3
IDS GROWTH FUND	IDS	AG	708	20.35	5.0	0.6	21.1	6	14.8	69	9.9	76
GUARDIAN PARK AVE FUND	GUARD	G	119	20.74	8.5	1.4	19.3	12	23.4	6	20.9	6
AMEV GROWTH FUND, INC.	AMEV	AG	149	16.37	8.5	0.9	22.5	4	19.6	27	14.2	49
AMCAP FUND	CAPRES	G	1385	9.63	8.5	1.7	20.3	9	16.7	54	11.9	64
AMERICAN CAPITAL PACE FD	AM-CAP	G	2133	22.56	8.5	2.6	25.0	1	19.1	33	10.4	73
GROWTH FUND OF AMERICA	CAPRES	G	741	15.76	8.5	1.6	21.3	6	17.1	50	11.5	66
NATL SECURITIES TOT INC	NATSEC	B	76	7.84	7.2	5.3	15.6	34	21.3	15	20.1	8
NEW PERSPECTIVE FUND	CAPRES	G	870	9.99	8.5	1.8	18.1	17	20.5	20	19.2	12
FRANKLIN UTILITIES	FRNKRE	GI	327	8.18	4.0	6.6	14.5	43	22.8	8	22.5	3
TUDOR FUND	WEISS	AG	159	20.08	0.0	0.3	20.5	8	20.6	20	11.1	69
AMERICAN CAP COMSTOCK	AM-CAP	G	896	14.60	8.5	2.2	20.3	9	18.4	40	10.2	74
TEMPLETON WORLD FUND	TEMPLE	G	3213	14.74	8.5	2.5	na	--	20.7	19	17.1	23
AMERICAN MUTUAL FUND	CAPRES	GI	1992	17.99	8.5	3.5	17.4	20	21.4	15	17.9	19
MERRILL L. BASIC VALUE	MERRIL	GI	799	17.06	6.5	3.1	na	--	22.5	10	18.2	17
SMITH, BARNEY INC. & GR.	SM-BAR	B	310	11.40	5.7	5.5	16.9	22	20.5	21	19.4	12
NEW YORK VENTURE FUND	VENADV	G	147	9.20	8.5	0.9	21.1	7	22.3	11	21.1	6
NEL TAX EXEMPT	NEL	MB	105	7.75	4.5	8.0	na	--	20.9	19	17.3	22

LATEST 12 MNTHS PCNT RK	THIS MONTH PCNT RK	1986 TO DATE PCNT RK	CALENDAR YEARS 1985 PCNT RK	1984 PCNT RK	1983 PCNT RK	CYCLES UP MKT PCNT RK	DOWN MKT PCNT RK	CDA RATING
23.6 10	-1.4 60	23.6 10	42.9 4	3.0 52	38.6 4	291.0 1	13.5 16	1
77.9 1	6.5 1	77.9 1	42.1 4	3.8 49	38.7 3	340.0 1	3.0 36	1
19.8 19	-1.2 55	19.8 19	29.8 25	13.9 8	18.1 45	176.8 15	6.9 28	1
20.7 16	-3.2 91	20.7 16	33.8 13	-7.6 80	30.0 10	209.2 6	-10.0 63	1
20.2 18	-2.0 70	20.2 18	31.5 19	14.4 7	30.3 9	219.5 4	1.2 41	2
70.0 1	5.3 1	70.0 1	9.3 96	-3.0 69	37.0 5	182.2 13	-0.7 46	2
27.5 7	-2.5 81	27.5 7	46.2 2	-7.3 80	15.4 56	241.8 2	15.7 12	2
17.3 33	-2.7 84	17.3 33	29.8 24	8.2 33	19.1 41	148.4 32	7.1 27	2
13.9 54	-3.0 88	13.9 54	27.2 35	-3.9 72	38.2 4	184.5 12	5.3 30	3
16.0 42	0.6 16	16.0 42	25.5 44	14.7 6	34.9 6	158.0 26	19.9 6	3
20.8 15	-0.3 40	20.8 15	17.0 83	14.9 5	43.8 2	173.3 17	39.1 1	3
14.3 52	-2.3 76	14.3 52	27.4 34	4.8 45	38.2 4	190.3 10	32.2 2	3
23.3 10	-2.2 75	23.3 10	27.1 35	-9.1 83	7.9 87	100.8 68	22.5 4	3
17.6 31	-1.9 70	17.6 31	29.1 27	4.7 46	38.8 3	228.4 3	-0.1 43	4
17.7 30	-3.1 89	17.7 30	24.6 46	23.9 1	11.6 70	166.2 21	2.1 38	4
17.4 33	-1.2 55	17.4 33	27.1 35	8.1 33	31.1 9	195.3 8	1.9 40	4
17.3 33	-0.8 47	17.3 33	21.6 61	5.2 44	26.0 19	142.0 38	12.7 18	4
18.3 27	-2.5 81	18.3 27	34.9 10	-5.7 77	11.4 71	188.2 11	16.3 11	5
16.8 37	-1.3 58	16.8 37	25.0 46	15.5 20	29.2 11	186.5 11	6.7 28	5
16.3 40	-1.7 64	16.3 40	31.5 19	-0.5 61	17.7 46	146.3 34	14.5 14	5
17.7 30	-1.1 54	17.7 30	23.0 53	-3.1 69	20.9 33	141.6 39	7.6 27	5
18.1 28	0.4 21	18.1 28	25.5 44	10.5 20	18.5 43	132.1 45	13.9 15	5
23.2 10	5.1 1	23.2 10	31.4 19	4.5 48	25.1 21	164.9 23	-14.7 70	6
21.6 13	0.9 10	21.6 13	30.1 24	25.4 1	32.9 7	238.8 2	29.1 2	6
16.5 39	0.0 31	16.5 39	26.5 38	14.5 7	37.1 5	175.9 15	-2.8 47	6
24.4 9	-2.4 78	24.4 9	36.1 9	-6.1 77	28.9 12	221.3 4	-25.6 89	6
18.2 27	1.1 7	18.2 27	23.2 52	10.1 22	17.5 47	122.7 52	20.7 5	7
19.1 22	-3.7 95	19.1 22	33.2 14	-9.7 84	27.9 15	173.6 17	-15.3 72	7
25.1 8	1.3 6	25.1 8	32.7 16	3.1 51	25.0 23	166.8 21	9.4 24	7
11.7 67	-1.8 68	11.7 67	29.7 26	9.9 24	23.9 25	184.3 12	4.1 33	7
22.8 11	-1.7 64	22.8 11	38.4 6	-2.1 67	13.1 67	181.6 14	-8.0 57	7
60.5 1	3.6 2	60.5 1	45.2 3	-5.8 77	28.6 12	225.0 3	-12.2 66	8
29.6 6	-4.8 98	29.6 6	37.0 7	6.2 41	17.7 47	213.5 5	-10.6 64	8
19.5 20	-3.2 90	19.5 20	36.2 8	-18.4 94	13.3 65	147.7 33	-8.8 59	8
18.1 28	-2.0 71	18.1 28	33.0 15	12.5 13	28.6 12	224.1 4	-5.5 53	8
19.5 20	-3.3 91	19.5 20	35.2 10	-7.7 81	23.4 26	161.9 24	-3.4 50	9
15.6 44	-1.3 56	15.6 44	22.2 58	-0.9 62	19.1 40	128.4 48	1.9 39	9
10.8 73	-2.8 86	10.8 73	22.4 56	-0.7 62	19.4 39	137.7 41	22.3 5	9
16.0 42	-1.3 56	16.0 42	26.7 38	-5.6 76	27.1 16	130.3 46	-2.3 47	9
22.2 11	-4.4 97	22.2 11	26.7 37	12.1 15	17.2 48	168.6 19	8.7 25	9
26.8 7	2.3 4	26.8 7	33.8 13	-0.2 60	23.7 25	160.5 25	-6.3 54	10
23.7 9	-3.5 93	23.7 9	22.7 55	21.2 1	15.8 52	175.4 16	37.1 1	10
12.4 63	-2.3 77	12.4 63	31.2 20	-7.2 79	28.4 13	173.4 17	5.2 30	10
13.5 57	-2.8 85	13.5 57	21.3 63	-2.6 68	18.4 43	125.6 50	14.4 14	10
17.9 29	-1.5 62	17.9 29	30.3 23	4.6 47	34.0 7	188.8 10	-8.2 58	11
18.4 26	-1.1 54	18.4 26	30.1 23	6.4 40	24.1 24	170.8 18	5.8 30	11
17.2 34	-1.4 60	17.2 34	32.0 18	6.8 38	30.1 10	201.7 7	-8.0 58	11
21.3 14	-1.0 53	21.3 14	27.1 36	10.3 21	17.3 48	161.7 24	13.6 16	11
22.8 11	0.0 32	22.8 11	38.1 6	4.7 46	23.0 28	218.5 4	-17.7 77	11
21.2 15	0.0 32	21.2 15	21.9 59	9.4 26	7.3 89	109.6 61	11.2 21	12

TOP 50 FUNDS BY 10-YEAR PERFORMANCE – 12/31/86

FUND	MGT CO	IO	ASSETS MIL$	NAV	MAX LOAD	% YLD	10 YEARS PCNT	RK	5 YEARS PCNT	RK	3 YEARS PCNT	RK
FIDELITY MAGELLAN FUND	FIDEL	G	6555	48.69	3.0	0.8	32.8	1	30.2	1	22.1	4
TWENTIETH CENTURY SELECT	INVRES	G	1832	31.61	0.0	1.5	26.6	1	22.5	9	14.3	48
AMERICAN CAPITAL PACE FD	AM-CAP	G	2133	22.56	8.5	2.6	25.0	1	19.1	33	10.4	73
TWENTIETH CENTURY GROWTH	INVRES	AG	888	14.06	0.0	1.0	24.8	2	14.3	73	12.8	58
LEHMAN CAPITAL FUND	LEHMAN	G	103	17.87	0.0	1.3	24.6	2	22.0	12	11.7	65
INTERNATIONAL INVESTORS	VANECK	ME	865	12.04	8.5	3.0	24.5	2	11.0	86	0.6	94
WEINGARTEN EQUITY FUND	AIM	AG	160	17.63	4.7	0.8	24.3	2	21.7	13	16.7	26
EVERGREEN FUND	SAXON	AG	639	12.47	0.0	1.0	24.3	3	19.1	34	15.3	38
LOOMIS-SAYLES CAP. DEV.	LOOMIS	AG	208	23.12	0.0	0.6	23.6	3	28.8	1	20.0	9
NICHOLAS FUND	NICHOL	G	1053	34.87	0.0	2.5	22.8	3	21.7	13	16.8	26
AMEV GROWTH FUND, INC.	AMEV	AG	149	16.37	8.5	0.9	22.5	4	19.6	27	14.2	49
LINDNER DIVIDEND FUND	LINDNR	GI	62	23.74	0.0	8.2	22.3	4	25.0	3	17.5	21
VALUE LINE LEVER. GROWTH	BRNHRD	G	239	22.79	0.0	1.3	22.0	4	14.6	71	12.5	61
NEL GROWTH FUND	LOOMIS	AG	286	26.65	8.0	0.7	22.0	4	24.3	5	14.6	46
FRANKLIN GOLD FUND	FRNKRE	ME	126	8.99	4.0	3.6	21.8	5	6.8	95	-4.5	97
FIDELITY DESTINY	FIDEL	G	1074	12.43	0.0	2.3	21.6	5	24.8	3	16.7	27
MASS. CAPITAL DEVEL.	MASFIN	G	858	11.21	7.2	1.3	21.3	5	16.0	61	5.9	88
OVER-THE-COUNTER SEC.	REVIEW	G	237	16.99	8.0	0.3	21.3	6	16.3	57	11.4	67
GROWTH FUND OF AMERICA	CAPRES	G	741	15.76	8.5	1.6	21.3	6	17.1	50	11.5	66
IDS GROWTH FUND	IDS	AG	708	20.35	5.0	0.6	21.1	6	14.8	69	9.9	76
US GOLD SHARES FUND	UNITED	ME	307	4.63	0.0	6.3	21.1	6	4.0	97	-11.0	98
NEW YORK VENTURE FUND	VENADV	G	147	9.20	8.5	0.9	21.1	7	22.3	11	21.1	6
PENNSYLVANIA MUTUAL FUND	QUEST	G	346	6.98	0.0	1.7	20.8	7	22.1	12	13.2	56
MUTUAL SHARES CORP.	HSC	B	1293	60.39	0.0	4.0	20.8	7	21.2	16	19.0	13
UNITED VANGUARD FUND	WADDEL	GI	494	6.26	8.5	2.2	20.7	8	19.6	27	12.0	63
TUDOR FUND	WEISS	AG	159	20.08	0.0	0.3	20.5	8	20.6	20	11.1	69
SEQUOIA FUND	RC	GI	690	39.29	0.0	3.6	20.5	8	23.2	6	19.5	11
QUALIFIED DIVD PORTF I	VGUARD	B	177	17.07	0.0	6.7	20.5	8	28.9	1	25.6	2
AMERICAN CAPITAL VENTURE	AM-CAP	AG	335	14.55	8.5	1.4	20.5	9	13.6	76	3.4	91
AMERICAN CAP COMSTOCK	AM-CAP	G	896	14.60	8.5	2.2	20.3	9	18.4	40	10.2	74
AMCAP FUND	CAPRES	G	1385	9.63	8.5	1.7	20.3	9	16.7	54	11.9	64
OPPENHEIMER TIME FUND	OPPEN	G	230	16.21	8.5	2.8	20.2	10	20.6	20	12.7	59
PARTNERS FUND	NEUBER	GI	444	17.37	0.0	2.4	20.1	10	19.9	23	18.1	17
SIGMA VENTURE SHARES	SIGMA	AG	59	11.06	8.5	0.4	20.1	10	13.8	75	8.1	81
ACORN FUND	HARRIS	G	395	39.27	0.0	1.2	20.1	10	20.0	23	19.1	13
FIDELITY EQUITY INCOME	FIDEL	GI	3100	27.29	2.0	5.8	19.9	11	22.8	8	17.3	22
JANUS FUND	JANUS	GI	464	12.47	0.0	0.0	19.6	11	17.9	44	11.4	66
OPPENHEIMER A.I.M. FUND	OPPEN	IN	373	26.99	8.5	0.5	19.6	11	19.7	26	19.5	11
PIONEER II	PIONER	G	2842	18.14	8.5	2.5	19.6	12	18.0	44	12.6	60
CONSTELLATION GROWTH	AIM	AG	76	21.16	4.7	0.0	19.5	12	14.8	69	11.7	65
SHEARSON APPRECIATION	SHEAR	G	263	26.16	5.0	0.0	19.4	12	20.1	22	18.1	17
GUARDIAN PARK AVE FUND	GUARD	G	119	20.74	8.5	1.4	19.3	12	23.4	6	20.9	6
PUTNAM INTL EQUITIES	PUTNAM	IN	372	30.39	8.5	0.4	19.3	13	26.3	2	31.7	1
IDS NEW DIMENSIONS FUND	IDS	G	510	8.52	5.0	1.7	19.2	13	20.2	22	16.1	30
PHOENIX GROWTH FUND SER	PIC	GI	242	16.40	8.5	1.6	19.2	13	26.2	2	20.4	8
KEMPER SUMMIT FUND	KEMPER	G	274	5.11	8.5	0.0	19.1	14	16.2	59	10.2	74
STRATEGIC INVESTMENTS	SD	ME	96	4.65	8.5	5.9	19.0	14	-0.2	98	-15.8	99
SELIGMAN CAPITAL FUND	SELIG	AG	192	12.72	8.5	0.0	18.9	14	19.6	27	9.9	76
HARTWELL GROWTH FUND	HARTWL	AG	10	12.01	0.0	0.5	18.9	14	12.8	80	7.8	82
WINDSOR FUND	VGUARD	GI	4839	13.95	0.0	5.1	18.9	15	23.8	6	22.5	4

| LATEST 12 MNTHS | | THIS MONTH | | 1986 TO DATE | | CALENDAR YEARS | | | | | | CYCLES | | | | CDA RATING |
| | | | | | | 1985 | | 1984 | | 1983 | | UP MKT | | DOWN MKT | | |
PCNT	RK	PCNT	RK	PCNT	RK	PCNT	RK	PCNT	RK	PCNT	RK	PCNT	RK	PCNT	RK	
23.6	10	-1.4	60	23.6	10	42.9	4	3.0	52	38.6	4	291.0	1	13.5	16	1
20.7	16	-3.2	91	20.7	16	33.8	13	-7.6	80	30.0	10	209.2	6	-10.0	63	1
10.8	73	-2.8	86	10.8	73	22.4	56	-0.7	62	19.4	39	137.7	41	22.3	5	9
19.4	21	2.9	3	19.4	21	33.9	13	-10.2	85	24.4	23	167.7	20	-28.5	92	13
13.9	54	-3.0	88	13.9	54	27.2	35	-3.9	72	38.2	4	184.5	12	5.3	30	3
34.2	4	-0.7	47	34.2	4	-1.9	98	-22.6	96	8.9	84	79.2	88	-39.8	97	50
24.4	9	-2.4	78	24.4	9	36.1	9	-6.1	77	28.9	12	221.3	4	-25.6	89	6
13.2	58	-2.5	81	13.2	58	34.6	11	0.6	58	29.9	11	192.9	9	-16.9	75	16
27.5	7	-2.5	81	27.5	7	46.2	2	-7.3	80	15.4	56	241.8	2	15.7	12	2
11.7	67	-1.8	68	11.7	67	29.7	26	9.9	24	23.9	25	184.3	12	4.1	33	7
19.5	20	-3.3	91	19.5	20	35.2	10	-7.7	81	23.4	26	161.9	24	-3.4	50	9
20.8	15	-0.3	40	20.8	15	17.0	83	14.9	5	43.8	2	173.3	17	39.1	1	3
23.3	10	-2.2	75	23.3	10	27.1	35	-9.1	83	7.9	87	100.8	68	22.5	4	3
18.3	27	-2.5	81	18.3	27	34.9	10	-5.7	77	11.4	71	188.2	11	16.3	11	5
30.7	5	-0.8	48	30.7	5	-11.0	99	-25.0	97	8.9	85	52.0	94	-42.8	98	58
17.6	31	-1.9	70	17.6	31	29.1	27	4.7	46	38.8	3	228.4	3	-0.1	43	4
6.1	88	-2.5	80	6.1	88	26.2	40	-11.4	87	26.5	18	137.2	42	-7.6	57	34
5.4	90	-2.2	74	5.4	90	34.9	10	-2.6	68	39.1	3	158.7	26	-5.6	53	29
16.0	42	-1.3	56	16.0	42	26.7	38	-5.6	76	27.1	16	130.3	46	-2.3	47	9
19.5	20	-3.2	90	19.5	20	36.2	8	-18.4	94	13.3	65	147.7	33	-8.8	59	8
37.5	4	-0.9	50	37.5	4	-27.0	99	-29.7	98	0.9	98	26.7	98	-51.0	99	61
22.8	11	0.0	32	22.8	11	38.1	6	4.7	46	23.0	28	218.5	4	-17.7	77	11
10.9	72	-0.5	43	10.9	72	26.7	37	3.1	51	40.6	2	199.1	7	-13.7	69	24
16.5	39	0.0	31	16.5	39	26.5	38	14.5	7	37.1	5	175.9	15	-2.8	47	6
17.7	30	-1.1	54	17.7	30	23.0	53	-3.1	69	20.9	33	141.6	39	7.6	27	5
12.4	63	-2.3	77	12.4	63	31.2	20	-7.2	79	28.4	13	173.4	17	5.2	30	10
12.6	62	-2.8	85	12.6	62	27.7	33	18.7	2	27.0	16	173.6	17	26.6	3	13
21.6	13	0.9	10	21.6	13	30.1	24	25.4	1	32.9	7	238.8	2	29.1	2	6
4.4	91	-1.8	68	4.4	91	13.1	92	-6.3	78	14.9	58	95.0	75	19.5	6	40
13.5	57	-2.8	85	13.5	57	21.3	63	-2.6	68	18.4	43	125.6	50	14.4	14	10
15.6	44	-1.3	56	15.6	44	22.2	58	-0.9	62	19.1	40	128.4	48	1.9	39	9
19.1	22	-3.7	95	19.1	22	33.2	14	-9.7	84	27.9	15	173.6	17	-15.3	72	7
17.3	33	-2.7	84	17.3	33	29.8	24	8.2	33	19.1	41	148.4	32	7.1	27	2
5.3	90	-0.2	37	5.3	90	35.5	9	-11.5	87	20.6	34	116.8	56	-11.5	65	53
23.2	10	5.1	1	23.2	10	31.4	19	4.5	48	25.1	21	164.9	23	-14.7	70	6
16.8	37	-1.3	58	16.8	37	25.0	46	10.5	20	29.2	11	186.5	11	6.7	28	5
11.2	70	-0.3	38	11.2	70	24.5	47	-0.1	60	26.1	19	141.3	39	4.7	32	16
46.4	2	2.5	3	46.4	2	49.1	2	-21.7	95	26.3	19	180.2	14	-29.4	93	33
12.3	64	-1.6	63	12.3	64	31.2	20	-3.2	70	30.2	10	151.9	30	-4.5	52	17
27.8	7	-1.0	53	27.8	7	28.6	29	-15.2	91	24.6	23	183.3	12	-42.4	98	48
20.0	18	-1.8	67	20.0	18	34.8	11	1.8	55	23.1	27	165.6	22	-3.6	51	18
18.1	28	-2.0	71	18.1	28	33.0	15	12.5	13	28.6	12	224.1	4	-5.5	53	8
38.0	4	1.0	8	38.0	4	64.4	1	0.8	58	27.9	15	269.8	1	-13.3	68	18
21.1	15	-2.5	81	21.1	15	35.4	9	-4.5	73	20.1	37	175.6	16	-6.5	55	16
20.3	17	-1.9	70	20.3	17	31.9	18	10.0	23	28.6	12	210.7	5	-3.4	50	19
13.9	54	-0.8	48	13.9	54	27.3	35	-7.6	80	24.4	24	152.9	29	-19.1	79	22
28.3	6	-3.1	89	28.3	6	-29.5	99	-34.1	99	-1.9	98	-3.6	99	-49.6	99	63
18.3	27	-2.1	72	18.3	27	30.8	21	-14.1	90	23.1	27	186.5	11	-15.9	73	15
24.4	9	-0.8	48	24.4	9	22.1	58	-17.6	93	25.5	21	146.4	34	-31.5	93	14
20.2	18	-0.6	45	20.2	18	28.0	32	19.5	2	30.1	10	225.2	3	8.8	25	12

TOP 50 FUNDS BY 5-YEAR PERFORMANCE - 12/31/86

FUND	MGT CO	IO	ASSETS MIL$	NAV	MAX LOAD	% YLD	10 YEARS PCNT RK	5 YEARS PCNT RK	3 YEARS PCNT RK
FIDELITY MAGELLAN FUND	FIDEL	G	6555	48.69	3.0	0.8	32.8 1	30.2 1	22.1 4
VANGUARD WORLD-INTL GR	VGUARD	IN	411	11.26	0.0	0.6	na --	29.7 1	34.4 1
MERRILL L. PACIFIC FUND	MERRIL	IN	445	34.20	6.5	0.3	na --	29.6 1	37.9 1
QUALIFIED DIVD PORTF I	VGUARD	B	177	17.07	0.0	6.7	20.5 8	28.9 1	25.6 2
LOOMIS-SAYLES CAP. DEV.	LOOMIS	AG	208	23.12	0.0	0.6	23.6 3	28.8 1	20.0 9
FIDELITY SELECT FINL SVC	FIDEL	G	120	31.56	2.0	0.6	na --	26.9 2	24.2 3
PUTNAM INTL EQUITIES	PUTNAM	IN	372	30.39	8.5	0.4	19.3 13	26.3 2	31.7 1
PHOENIX GROWTH FUND SER	PIC	GI	242	16.40	8.5	1.6	19.2 13	26.2 2	20.4 8
FIDELITY SELECT HEALTH	FIDEL	AG	217	32.78	2.0	0.0	na --	26.1 2	24.4 3
STRONG TOTAL RETURN FUND	STRONG	B	452	21.61	1.0	5.8	na --	25.5 2	18.4 16
EATON VANCE TOTAL RETURN	ETN&HD	GI	570	10.67	4.7	3.2	na --	25.3 3	28.9 1
LINDNER DIVIDEND FUND	LINDNR	GI	62	23.74	0.0	8.2	22.3 4	25.0 3	17.5 21
FIDELITY DESTINY	FIDEL	G	1074	12.43	0.0	2.3	21.6 5	24.8 3	16.7 27
FAIRMONT FUND	SACHS	G	72	49.50	0.0	1.1	na --	24.8 3	18.6 14
PHOENIX STOCK FUND SER	PIC	G	95	12.67	8.5	1.5	na --	24.7 3	17.3 22
PRICE (ROWE) INTERNATL.	PRICE	IN	753	25.78	0.0	0.8	na --	24.6 4	30.0 1
UNITED INCOME FUND	WADDEL	G	792	17.03	8.5	2.4	14.8 42	24.6 4	20.2 8
WASH. MUTUAL INVESTORS	CAPRES	GI	1568	12.30	8.5	3.7	16.6 23	24.4 4	20.5 7
STRONG INVESTMENT FUND	STRONG	B	319	22.18	1.0	5.4	na --	24.4 4	15.5 36
QUEST FOR VALUE FUND	OPPCAP	G	75	25.49	0.0	0.7	na --	24.3 4	15.1 41
NEL GROWTH FUND	LOOMIS	AG	286	26.65	8.0	0.7	22.0 4	24.3 5	14.6 46
EVERGREEN TOTAL RETURN	SAXON	B	794	19.18	0.0	5.4	na --	24.2 5	21.8 4
UNITED CONTL. INCOME FD.	WADDEL	GI	241	19.31	8.5	3.4	15.2 37	24.1 5	21.7 5
TEMPLETON GLOBAL I	TEMPLE	G	301	40.81	0.0	2.5	na --	23.9 5	15.7 34
PHOENIX BALANCED FD SER	PIC	B	153	12.75	8.5	4.5	na --	23.9 5	21.0 6
FIDELITY SEL UTILITIES	FIDEL	GI	195	27.31	2.0	0.8	na --	23.9 6	25.4 2
WINDSOR FUND	VGUARD	GI	4839	13.95	0.0	5.1	18.9 15	23.8 6	22.5 4
SCUDDER INTERNATIONAL FD	SCUDER	IN	686	39.79	0.0	1.1	17.8 18	23.8 6	30.6 1
GUARDIAN PARK AVE FUND	GUARD	G	119	20.74	8.5	1.4	19.3 12	23.4 6	20.9 6
SEQUOIA FUND	RC	GI	690	39.29	0.0	3.6	20.5 8	23.2 6	19.5 11
FUNDAMENTAL INVESTORS	CAPRES	G	488	14.21	8.5	2.4	14.8 41	23.2 7	18.8 14
NATIONWIDE GROWTH FUND	NATFIN	G	162	8.56	7.5	2.9	16.4 25	23.1 7	19.6 11
IVY GROWTH FUND	HMI	GI	165	13.44	0.0	2.8	17.8 19	23.0 7	17.7 20
SENTINEL COMMON STOCK FD	NATLIF	GI	465	23.61	8.5	3.1	16.0 30	23.0 7	21.7 5
LEHMAN OPPORTUNITY FUND	LEHMAN	G	103	22.60	0.0	2.8	na --	22.9 7	16.2 30
MANHATTAN FUND	NEUBER	G	241	8.95	0.0	0.8	16.6 23	22.9 8	19.8 10
SOGEN INTERNATIONAL FUND	SOGEN	G	66	17.71	4.2	3.1	18.5 15	22.9 8	19.6 10
IDS PROGRESSIVE FUND	IDS	GI	184	6.68	5.0	3.2	15.8 31	22.9 8	12.4 61
FRANKLIN UTILITIES	FRNKRE	GI	327	8.18	4.0	6.6	14.5 43	22.8 8	22.5 3
FIDELITY EQUITY INCOME	FIDEL	GI	3100	27.29	2.0	5.8	19.9 11	22.8 8	17.3 22
FIDELITY PURITAN FD	FIDEL	B	2458	13.34	0.0	6.7	16.2 27	22.6 9	19.7 10
INVESTORS RESEARCH	INV-RE	G	59	5.15	8.5	0.4	18.8 15	22.6 9	14.1 49
LOOMIS-SAYLES MUTUAL	LOOMIS	GI	174	22.86	0.0	3.9	13.8 48	22.6 9	21.3 5
TWENTIETH CENTURY SELECT	INVRES	G	1832	31.61	0.0	1.5	26.6 1	22.5 9	14.3 48
INVEST. CO. OF AMERICA	CAPRES	GI	3487	13.19	8.5	2.9	16.3 25	22.5 9	19.9 9
MERRILL L. BASIC VALUE	MERRIL	GI	799	17.06	6.5	3.1	na --	22.5 10	18.2 17
UNITED INTL. GROWTH FUND	WADDEL	IN	205	7.13	8.5	1.5	17.4 20	22.4 10	20.2 8
PRU-BACHE UTILITY FUND	PRUBAC	GI	1212	14.78	0.0	5.1	na --	22.4 10	24.9 2
FIDELITY CONGRESS STREET	FIDEL	G	52	83.60	0.0	2.5	16.8 22	22.4 10	21.2 6
OPPENHEIMER EQUITY INC.	OPPEN	GI	420	8.46	8.5	4.9	16.2 26	22.3 10	16.1 31

LATEST 12 MNTHS		THIS MONTH		1986 TO DATE		CALENDAR YEARS						CYCLES				CDA RATING
						1985		1984		1983		UP MKT		DOWN MKT		
PCNT	RK	PCNT	RK	PCNT	RK	PCNT	RK	PCNT	RK	PCNT	RK	PCNT	RK	PCNT	RK	
23.6	10	-1.4	60	23.6	10	42.9	4	3.0	52	38.6	4	291.0	1	13.5	16	1
56.6	1	4.4	1	56.6	1	56.9	2	-1.1	64	43.1	2	310.2	1	na	--	na
77.9	1	6.5	1	77.9	1	42.1	4	3.8	49	38.7	3	340.0	1	3.0	36	1
21.6	13	0.9	10	21.6	13	30.1	24	25.4	1	32.9	7	238.8	2	29.1	2	6
27.5	7	-2.5	81	27.5	7	46.2	2	-7.3	80	15.4	56	241.8	2	15.7	12	2
15.1	48	-2.5	80	15.1	48	41.2	4	18.0	2	37.1	5	301.4	1	na	--	na
38.0	4	1.0	8	38.0	4	64.4	1	0.8	58	27.9	15	269.8	1	-13.3	68	18
20.3	17	-1.9	70	20.3	17	31.9	18	10.0	23	28.6	12	210.7	5	-3.4	50	19
22.0	12	-2.2	75	22.0	12	59.4	1	-1.1	63	14.1	62	234.7	2	na	--	na
20.0	18	-1.8	68	20.0	18	25.4	44	10.4	21	41.3	2	188.9	10	na	--	na
31.9	5	-3.5	94	31.9	5	40.2	5	15.8	3	13.3	65	226.7	3	na	--	na
20.8	15	-0.3	40	20.8	15	17.0	83	14.9	5	43.8	2	173.3	17	39.1	1	3
17.6	31	-1.9	70	17.6	31	29.1	27	4.7	46	38.8	3	228.4	3	-0.1	43	4
14.0	53	-1.0	53	14.0	53	32.1	17	10.8	19	35.0	6	217.0	5	na	--	na
17.4	33	-1.2	55	17.4	33	27.1	35	8.1	33	31.1	9	195.3	8	1.9	40	4
60.5	1	3.6	2	60.5	1	45.2	3	-5.8	77	28.6	12	225.0	3	-12.2	66	8
22.3	11	-2.0	72	22.3	11	33.9	13	6.1	42	31.6	8	212.7	5	-0.5	45	30
22.5	11	-2.4	79	22.5	11	32.1	17	8.3	32	26.2	19	206.9	6	5.5	30	26
17.5	32	-0.8	49	17.5	32	19.4	75	9.8	24	45.1	1	171.7	18	na	--	na
14.3	52	-2.3	76	14.3	52	27.4	34	4.8	45	38.2	4	190.3	10	32.2	2	3
18.3	27	-2.5	81	18.3	27	34.9	10	-5.7	77	11.4	71	188.2	11	16.3	11	5
20.2	18	-2.0	70	20.2	18	31.5	19	14.4	7	30.3	9	219.5	4	1.2	41	2
18.5	26	-1.5	61	18.5	26	33.8	13	13.8	9	24.7	23	209.6	6	-2.9	48	25
18.6	25	-0.6	44	18.6	25	30.3	22	0.3	59	38.7	4	194.9	8	na	--	na
19.8	19	-1.2	55	19.8	19	29.8	25	13.9	8	18.1	45	176.8	15	6.9	28	1
24.0	9	-3.5	93	24.0	9	31.7	18	20.9	1	20.0	37	218.5	4	na	--	na
20.2	18	-0.6	45	20.2	18	28.0	32	19.5	2	30.1	10	225.2	3	8.8	25	12
50.5	2	3.7	2	50.5	2	48.9	2	-0.7	62	29.2	11	227.4	3	-17.8	77	22
18.1	28	-2.0	71	18.1	28	33.0	15	12.5	13	28.6	12	224.1	4	-5.5	53	8
12.6	62	-2.8	85	12.6	62	27.7	33	18.7	2	27.0	16	173.6	17	26.6	3	13
21.8	13	-1.9	69	21.8	13	30.1	23	5.8	42	26.2	19	190.7	10	-3.2	49	43
18.2	27	0.2	25	18.2	27	33.3	14	8.4	32	21.8	31	189.2	10	-3.3	49	27
16.8	38	-1.5	61	16.8	38	29.4	26	7.9	34	30.1	10	192.6	9	3.2	35	34
23.7	9	-2.4	79	23.7	9	29.8	25	12.4	13	20.3	35	192.4	9	4.4	32	21
6.4	87	-3.6	94	6.4	87	32.8	15	11.0	19	38.9	3	234.7	2	-13.8	69	76
17.0	35	-3.1	89	17.0	35	37.1	7	7.1	36	26.8	17	208.6	6	-16.5	74	58
25.1	8	1.3	6	25.1	8	32.7	16	3.1	51	25.0	23	166.8	21	9.4	24	7
13.3	58	-2.8	84	13.3	58	30.8	21	-4.1	72	18.0	45	143.3	37	-2.9	48	34
23.7	9	-3.5	93	23.7	9	22.7	55	21.2	1	15.8	52	175.4	16	37.1	1	10
16.8	37	-1.3	58	16.8	37	25.0	46	10.5	20	29.2	11	186.5	11	6.7	28	5
20.8	15	0.3	23	20.8	15	28.5	30	10.5	19	25.6	20	172.7	17	11.3	21	19
28.3	6	-2.7	83	28.3	6	19.5	74	-3.0	69	26.3	18	196.8	7	-24.9	88	15
24.8	8	-0.5	44	24.8	8	34.4	12	6.4	40	10.0	78	174.6	16	6.5	29	36
20.7	16	-3.2	91	20.7	16	33.8	13	-7.6	80	30.0	10	209.2	6	-10.0	63	1
21.3	15	-0.8	47	21.3	15	32.9	15	6.8	38	20.2	36	186.8	11	-1.9	47	24
17.2	34	-1.4	60	17.2	34	32.0	18	6.8	38	30.1	10	201.7	7	-8.0	58	11
28.8	6	3.5	2	28.8	6	38.5	6	-2.7	68	28.4	13	183.2	13	3.9	34	17
27.6	7	-2.9	87	27.6	7	33.4	14	14.5	7	11.6	70	165.7	22	na	--	na
27.1	7	-1.7	65	27.1	7	31.7	18	6.4	40	28.4	13	213.4	5	-10.1	63	35
15.8	44	-1.4	59	15.8	44	30.9	21	3.2	51	34.3	6	193.4	8	-5.5	53	30

TOP 50 FUNDS BY 3-YEAR PERFORMANCE - 12/31/86

| | | | ASSETS | | MAX | % | ANNUALIZED ROR THRU 12/31/86 | | |
| | | | | | | | 10 YEARS | 5 YEARS | 3 YEARS |
FUND	MGT CO	IO	MIL$	NAV	LOAD	YLD	PCNT RK	PCNT RK	PCNT RK
MERRILL L. PACIFIC FUND	MERRIL	IN	445	34.20	6.5	0.3	na --	29.6 1	37.9 1
VANGUARD WORLD-INTL GR	VGUARD	IN	411	11.26	0.0	0.6	na --	29.7 1	34.4 1
PUTNAM INTL EQUITIES	PUTNAM	IN	372	30.39	8.5	0.4	19.3 13	26.3 2	31.7 1
SCUDDER INTERNATIONAL FD	SCUDER	IN	686	39.79	0.0	1.1	17.8 18	23.8 6	30.6 1
PRICE (ROWE) INTERNATL.	PRICE	IN	753	25.78	0.0	0.8	na --	24.6 4	30.0 1
EATON VANCE TOTAL RETURN	ETN&HD	GI	570	10.67	4.7	3.2	na --	25.3 3	28.9 1
TRUSTEES COMM EQ-INTL	VGUARD	IN	634	38.65	0.0	2.3	na --	na --	28.0 2
KEMPER INTL FD	KEMPER	IN	185	19.30	8.5	1.0	na --	21.9 13	26.9 2
TRANSATLANTIC FUND INC.	KLEIN	IN	100	22.92	0.0	0.0	16.0 30	17.7 46	26.1 2
QUALIFIED DIVD PORTF I	VGUARD	B	177	17.07	0.0	6.7	20.5 8	28.9 1	25.6 2
FIDELITY SEL UTILITIES	FIDEL	GI	195	27.31	2.0	0.8	na --	23.9 6	25.4 2
PRU-BACHE UTILITY FUND	PRUBAC	GI	1212	14.78	0.0	5.1	na --	22.4 10	24.9 2
FIDELITY SELECT HEALTH	FIDEL	AG	217	32.78	2.0	0.0	na --	26.1 2	24.4 3
FIDELITY SELECT FINL SVC	FIDEL	G	120	31.56	2.0	0.6	na --	26.9 2	24.2 3
KEYSTONE INTL FUND	KEYSTN	IN	90	7.16	0.0	0.7	14.1 46	19.3 32	23.7 3
STRATTON MONTHLY DIV SHS	STRMGT	B	43	29.21	0.0	7.7	na --	20.5 20	23.6 3
BRUCE FUND	BRUCE	AG	3	109.39	0.0	1.2	na --	22.2 11	23.5 3
BULLOCK BALANCED SHARES	BULOCK	B	79	14.81	8.5	4.1	12.9 60	21.7 14	22.6 3
FRANKLIN UTILITIES	FRNKRE	GI	327	8.18	4.0	6.6	14.5 43	22.8 8	22.5 3
WINDSOR FUND	VGUARD	GI	4839	13.95	0.0	5.1	18.9 15	23.8 6	22.5 4
FIDELITY QUALIFIED DIVD	FIDEL	B	214	14.97	0.0	7.1	na --	22.3 11	22.5 4
PILGRIM MAGNACAP FUND	PILCAP	GI	181	9.81	7.2	2.3	15.5 35	19.7 26	22.3 4
FIDELITY MAGELLAN FUND	FIDEL	G	6555	48.69	3.0	0.8	32.8 1	30.2 1	22.1 4
COPLEY TAX-MANAGED FUND	COPLEY	G	31	11.02	0.0	0.0	na --	19.5 29	22.1 4
EVERGREEN TOTAL RETURN	SAXON	B	794	19.18	0.0	5.4	na --	24.2 5	21.8 4
UNITED CONTL. INCOME FD.	WADDEL	GI	241	19.31	8.5	3.4	15.2 37	24.1 5	21.7 5
SENTINEL COMMON STOCK FD	NATLIF	GI	466	23.61	8.5	3.1	16.0 30	23.0 7	21.7 5
G. T. PACIFIC GROWTH FD	GTCAP	IN	67	29.98	0.0	0.0	na --	17.3 48	21.7 5
CENTURY SHARES TRUST	CENSHS	G	150	18.30	0.0	2.7	15.0 38	19.4 30	21.7 5
DEAN WITTER WORLDWIDE	DWRI	IN	346	15.44	0.0	0.5	na --	na --	21.7 5
SELECTED AMERICAN SHARES	PAM	GI	144	12.65	0.0	3.5	13.4 53	22.0 12	21.4 5
LOOMIS-SAYLES MUTUAL	LOOMIS	GI	174	22.86	0.0	3.9	13.8 48	22.6 9	21.3 5
QUALIFIED DIVD PORTF II	VGUARD	BP	136	9.52	0.0	8.9	11.0 77	20.9 18	21.3 6
FIDELITY CONGRESS STREET	FIDEL	G	52	83.60	0.0	2.5	16.8 22	22.4 10	21.2 6
NEW YORK VENTURE FUND	VENADV	G	147	9.20	8.5	0.9	21.1 7	22.3 11	21.1 6
PHOENIX BALANCED FD SER	PIC	B	153	12.75	8.5	4.5	na --	23.9 5	21.0 6
SOVEREIGN INVESTORS	HOPPER	GI	32	24.73	5.3	4.0	15.0 39	20.8 19	20.9 6
GUARDIAN PARK AVE FUND	GUARD	G	119	20.74	8.5	1.4	19.3 12	23.4 6	20.9 6
BOSTON CO. CAP. APPREC.	BOSADV	G	422	32.42	0.0	1.4	14.3 44	20.0 23	20.9 7
NORTHEAST INV GROWTH	NIT	G	18	18.36	0.0	0.7	na --	17.4 48	20.9 7
FEDERATED STOCK TRUST	FEDRES	GI	450	21.60	0.0	2.9	na --	na --	20.8 7
AXE-HOUGHTON FUND B	EW-AXE	B	182	11.10	0.0	5.0	13.4 54	19.8 25	20.8 7
WELLESLEY INCOME FUND	VGUARD	B	399	16.27	0.0	7.9	13.6 51	20.8 19	20.7 7
WASH. MUTUAL INVESTORS	CAPRES	GI	1568	12.30	8.5	3.7	16.6 23	24.4 4	20.5 7
SENTINEL BALANCED FUND	NATLIF	B	41	12.35	8.5	4.9	13.6 52	21.8 13	20.5 8
PHOENIX GROWTH FUND SER	PIC	GI	242	16.40	8.5	1.6	19.2 13	26.2 2	20.4 8
UNITED INCOME FUND	WADDEL	G	792	17.03	8.5	2.4	14.8 42	24.6 4	20.2 8
UNITED INTL. GROWTH FUND	WADDEL	IN	205	7.13	8.5	1.5	17.4 20	22.4 10	20.2 8
NATL SECURITIES TOT INC	NATSEC	B	76	7.84	7.2	5.3	15.6 34	21.3 15	20.1 8
DREXEL BURNHAM FUND	DREXEL	GI	133	21.28	3.5	3.3	15.3 36	18.9 37	20.1 8

LATEST 12 MNTHS		THIS MONTH		1986 TO DATE		CALENDAR YEARS						CYCLES				CDA RATING
						1985		1984		1983		UP MKT		DOWN MKT		
PCNT	RK	PCNT	RK	PCNT	RK	PCNT	RK	PCNT	RK	PCNT	RK	PCNT	RK	PCNT	RK	
77.9	1	6.5	1	77.9	1	42.1	4	3.8	49	38.7	3	340.0	1	3.0	36	1
56.6	1	4.4	1	56.6	1	56.9	2	-1.1	64	43.1	2	310.2	1	na	--	na
38.0	4	1.0	8	38.0	4	64.4	1	0.8	58	27.9	15	269.8	1	-13.3	68	18
50.5	2	3.7	2	50.5	2	48.9	2	-0.7	62	29.2	11	227.4	3	-17.8	77	22
60.5	1	3.6	2	60.5	1	45.2	3	-5.8	77	28.6	12	225.0	3	-12.2	66	8
31.9	5	-3.5	94	31.9	5	40.2	5	15.8	3	13.3	65	226.7	3	na	--	na
49.9	2	4.0	2	49.9	2	40.3	5	-0.3	61	na	--	na	--	na	--	na
44.7	2	2.8	3	44.7	2	55.3	2	-9.1	84	28.1	14	201.7	7	na	--	na
51.7	2	2.9	3	51.7	2	54.2	2	-14.4	90	32.9	7	185.1	11	-33.2	95	15
21.6	13	0.9	10	21.6	13	30.1	24	25.4	1	32.9	7	238.8	2	29.1	2	6
24.0	9	-3.5	93	24.0	9	31.7	18	20.9	1	20.0	37	218.5	4	na	--	na
27.6	7	-2.9	87	27.6	7	33.4	14	14.5	7	11.6	70	165.7	22	na	--	na
22.0	12	-2.2	75	22.0	12	59.4	1	-1.1	63	14.1	62	234.7	2	na	--	na
15.1	48	-2.5	80	15.1	48	41.2	4	18.0	2	37.1	5	301.4	1	na	--	na
47.9	2	5.9	1	47.9	2	38.6	6	-7.5	80	13.5	64	162.2	24	-16.6	74	35
20.4	16	-1.7	65	20.4	16	29.7	25	21.0	1	11.8	70	177.1	15	na	--	na
29.6	6	-4.8	98	29.6	6	37.0	7	6.2	41	17.7	47	213.5	5	-10.6	64	8
19.0	23	-1.6	63	19.0	23	34.2	12	15.5	4	14.5	60	179.8	14	1.6	40	40
23.7	9	-3.5	93	23.7	9	22.7	55	21.2	1	15.8	52	175.4	16	37.1	1	10
20.2	18	-0.6	45	20.2	18	28.0	32	19.5	2	30.1	10	225.2	3	8.8	25	12
21.1	15	-2.6	82	21.1	15	25.6	43	20.8	1	15.5	54	169.3	18	na	--	na
16.8	37	-2.4	78	16.8	37	34.8	10	16.1	3	22.6	28	204.3	6	4.1	33	42
23.6	10	-1.4	60	23.6	10	42.9	4	3.0	52	38.6	4	291.0	1	13.5	16	1
17.7	30	-3.1	89	17.7	30	24.6	46	23.9	1	11.6	70	166.2	21	2.1	38	4
20.2	18	-2.0	70	20.2	18	31.5	19	14.4	7	30.3	9	219.5	4	1.2	41	2
18.5	26	-1.5	61	18.5	26	33.8	13	13.8	9	24.7	23	209.6	6	-2.9	48	25
23.7	9	-2.4	79	23.7	9	29.8	25	12.4	13	20.3	35	192.4	9	4.4	32	21
70.0	1	5.3	1	70.0	1	9.3	96	-3.0	69	37.0	5	182.2	13	-0.7	46	2
9.4	80	-2.2	75	9.4	80	42.6	4	15.6	3	21.2	32	228.2	3	4.7	32	70
31.5	5	0.9	11	31.5	5	38.3	6	-1.0	63	na	--	na	--	na	--	na
17.0	36	0.1	30	17.0	36	33.2	14	14.9	5	21.6	31	182.5	13	-4.2	51	45
24.8	8	-0.5	44	24.8	8	34.4	12	6.4	40	10.0	78	174.6	16	6.5	29	36
24.7	8	-0.9	51	24.7	8	29.7	25	10.4	21	7.9	88	121.8	52	18.2	8	26
27.1	7	-1.7	65	27.1	7	31.7	18	6.4	40	28.4	13	213.4	5	-10.1	63	35
22.8	11	0.0	32	22.8	11	38.1	6	4.7	46	23.0	28	218.5	4	-17.7	77	11
19.8	19	-1.2	55	19.8	19	29.8	25	13.9	8	18.1	45	176.8	15	6.9	28	1
21.9	12	-2.2	75	21.9	12	30.6	22	11.2	18	19.6	38	178.7	15	4.5	32	32
18.1	28	-2.0	71	18.1	28	33.0	15	12.5	13	28.6	12	224.1	4	-5.5	53	8
22.5	11	-1.3	57	22.5	11	35.0	10	6.9	37	24.0	24	196.1	8	-20.2	81	52
24.3	9	-1.1	54	24.3	9	36.7	8	3.9	49	9.6	80	161.3	25	na	--	na
13.8	55	-6.3	99	13.8	55	33.5	14	16.0	3	31.2	9	215.9	5	na	--	na
24.7	8	-1.4	60	24.7	8	32.9	15	6.3	40	11.1	73	145.1	36	-3.9	51	27
18.4	26	-0.4	41	18.4	26	27.4	35	16.6	3	18.6	43	154.1	28	11.4	20	18
22.5	11	-2.4	79	22.5	11	32.1	17	8.3	32	26.2	19	206.9	6	5.5	30	26
19.0	23	-1.0	53	19.0	23	28.0	32	14.7	6	14.4	60	158.0	26	12.5	19	23
20.3	17	-1.9	70	20.3	17	31.9	18	10.0	23	28.6	12	210.7	5	-3.4	50	19
22.3	11	-2.0	72	22.3	11	33.9	13	6.1	42	31.6	8	212.7	5	-0.5	45	30
28.8	6	3.5	2	28.8	6	38.5	6	-2.7	68	28.4	13	183.2	13	3.9	34	17
22.2	11	-4.4	97	22.2	11	26.7	37	12.1	15	17.2	48	168.6	19	8.7	25	9
22.0	12	-0.7	46	22.0	12	32.2	17	7.3	36	12.1	69	151.8	30	-10.3	64	32

TOP 50 FUNDS BY 12-MONTH PERFORMANCE – 12/31/86

| | | | | | | | ANNUALIZED ROR THRU 12/31/86 | | | | | |
| | | | | | | | 10 YEARS | | 5 YEARS | | 3 YEARS | |
FUND	MGT CO	IO	ASSETS MIL$	NAV	MAX LOAD	% YLD	PCNT	RK	PCNT	RK	PCNT	RK
MERRILL L. PACIFIC FUND	MERRIL	IN	445	34.20	6.5	0.3	na	--	29.6	1	37.9	1
NOMURA PACIFIC BASIN FD	NOMURA	IN	53	21.13	0.0	1.4	na	--	na	--	na	--
NEWPORT FAR EAST	COMCAP	IN	3	20.15	0.0	0.0	na	--	na	--	na	--
G. T. PACIFIC GROWTH FD	GTCAP	IN	67	29.98	0.0	0.0	na	--	17.3	48	21.7	5
FIDELITY OVERSEAS FUND	FIDEL	IN	2561	28.68	3.0	0.0	na	--	na	--	na	--
PRICE (ROWE) INTERNATL.	PRICE	IN	753	25.78	0.0	0.8	na	--	24.6	4	30.0	1
STRONG OPPORTUNITY FUND	STRONG	AG	32	15.99	2.0	0.0	na	--	na	--	na	--
VANGUARD WORLD-INTL GR	VGUARD	IN	411	11.26	0.0	0.6	na	--	29.7	1	34.4	1
FT INTERNATIONAL	FEDRES	IN	104	21.60	0.0	0.4	na	--	na	--	na	--
TRANSATLANTIC FUND INC.	KLEIN	IN	100	22.92	0.0	0.0	16.0	30	17.7	46	26.1	2
SCUDDER INTERNATIONAL FD	SCUDER	IN	686	39.79	0.0	1.1	17.8	18	23.8	6	30.6	1
TRUSTEES COMM EQ-INTL	VGUARD	IN	634	38.65	0.0	2.3	na	--	na	--	28.0	2
VANGUARD SPEC PORT-GOLD	VGUARD	ME	54	9.22	0.0	2.3	na	--	na	--	na	--
KEYSTONE INTL FUND	KEYSTN	IN	90	7.16	0.0	0.7	14.1	46	19.3	32	23.7	3
OPPENHEIMER A.I.M. FUND	OPPEN	IN	373	26.99	8.5	0.5	19.6	11	19.7	26	19.5	11
FIRST INVEST. INTL SECS.	FSTINV	IN	29	16.53	8.5	0.1	na	--	na	--	11.4	66
KEMPER INTL FD	KEMPER	IN	185	19.30	8.5	1.0	na	--	21.9	13	26.9	2
ALLIANCE INTERNATIONAL	ALLIAN	IN	164	21.07	8.5	0.1	na	--	na	--	na	--
SIGMA WORLD	SIGMA	IN	8	15.75	8.5	0.0	na	--	na	--	na	--
PRU-BACHE GLOBAL FUND	PRUBAC	IN	401	9.64	0.0	0.1	na	--	na	--	na	--
HUTTON INV SER PRE METAL	HUTTON	ME	39	12.93	0.0	0.2	na	--	na	--	na	--
US NEW PROSPECTOR FUND	UNITED	ME	46	1.31	0.0	0.0	na	--	na	--	na	--
UNITED GOLD & GOVERNMENT	WADDEL	ME	9	6.83	8.5	2.9	na	--	na	--	na	--
WORLD TRENDS	VANECK	IN	58	13.41	7.5	1.0	na	--	na	--	na	--
EUROPACIFIC GROWTH FUND	CAPRES	IN	160	24.58	8.5	0.6	na	--	na	--	na	--
KEYSTONE PRECIOUS METALS	KEYSTN	ME	65	14.59	0.0	2.5	na	--	4.6	96	-3.2	96
PAINE WEBBER ATLAS FD	PAINE	IN	224	15.94	8.5	5.1	na	--	na	--	na	--
MASS. FINL INTL TRUST BD	MASFIN	BP	134	11.46	7.2	5.9	na	--	19.4	30	20.0	8
PUTNAM INTL EQUITIES	PUTNAM	IN	372	30.39	8.5	0.4	19.3	13	26.3	2	31.7	1
US GOLD SHARES FUND	UNITED	ME	307	4.63	0.0	6.3	21.1	6	4.0	97	-11.0	98
OPPENHEIMER GOLD & SPEC.	OPPEN	ME	40	8.45	8.5	1.5	na	--	na	--	-1.6	95
GOLCONDA INVESTORS	GOLCON	ME	32	12.86	0.0	0.2	na	--	2.1	97	1.2	93
FIDELITY GROWTH & INCOME	FIDEL	GI	460	13.33	0.0	1.2	na	--	na	--	na	--
INTERNATIONAL INVESTORS	VANECK	ME	865	12.04	8.5	3.0	24.5	2	11.0	86	0.6	94
FIDELITY SEL PREC MET&MN	FIDEL	ME	241	11.15	2.0	0.8	na	--	6.8	95	-4.2	97
LEXINGTON GOLDFUND	LEXGTN	ME	22	4.49	0.0	0.4	na	--	na	--	4.4	90
EATON VANCE TOTAL RETURN	ETN&HD	GI	570	10.67	4.7	3.2	na	--	25.3	3	28.9	1
MERRILL L. NAT RESOURCE	MERRIL	G	259	12.71	0.0	0.9	na	--	na	--	na	--
DEAN WITTER WORLDWIDE	DWRI	IN	346	15.44	0.0	0.5	na	--	na	--	21.7	5
US PROSPECTOR FUND	UNITED	ME	72	0.72	0.0	0.0	na	--	na	--	-6.1	97
FRANKLIN GOLD FUND	FRNKRE	ME	126	8.99	4.0	3.6	21.8	5	6.8	95	-4.5	97
SHEARSON GLOBAL OPPORT	SHEAR	G	263	30.07	5.0	0.4	na	--	na	--	na	--
MERRILL L. INTERNATIONAL	MERRIL	IN	278	14.28	8.5	1.8	na	--	na	--	na	--
COLONIAL ADV STRAT GOLD	COLONL	ME	29	17.99	6.7	0.8	na	--	na	--	na	--
STRONG INCOME FUND	STRONG	GI	72	12.65	0.0	5.5	na	--	na	--	na	--
BRUCE FUND	BRUCE	AG	3	109.39	0.0	1.2	na	--	22.2	11	23.5	3
UNITED INTL. GROWTH FUND	WADDEL	IN	205	7.13	8.5	1.5	17.4	20	22.4	10	20.2	8
TEMPLETON FOREIGN FUND	TEMPLE	IN	184	15.41	8.5	2.0	na	--	na	--	17.2	22
TWENTIETH CENTURY GIFTR	INVRES	G	6	6.75	0.5	0.0	na	--	na	--	19.5	11
STRATEGIC INVESTMENTS	SD	ME	96	4.65	8.5	5.9	19.0	14	-0.2	98	-15.8	99

LATEST 12 MNTHS		THIS MONTH		1986 TO DATE		CALENDAR YEARS						CYCLES				CDA RATING
						1985		1984		1983		UP MKT		DOWN MKT		
PCNT	RK	PCNT	RK	PCNT	RK	PCNT	RK	PCNT	RK	PCNT	RK	PCNT	RK	PCNT	RK	
77.9	1	6.5	1	77.9	1	42.1	4	3.8	49	38.7	3	340.0	1	3.0	36	1
74.4	1	2.0	4	74.4	1	na	--	na	--	na	--	na	--	na	--	na
73.4	1	5.0	1	73.4	1	16.2	86	na	--	na	--	na	--	na	--	na
70.0	1	5.3	1	70.0	1	9.3	96	-3.0	69	37.0	5	182.2	13	-0.7	46	2
68.9	1	4.7	1	68.9	1	78.6	1	na	--	na	--	na	--	na	--	na
60.5	1	3.6	2	60.5	1	45.2	3	-5.8	77	28.6	12	225.0	3	-12.2	66	8
59.9	1	-4.4	97	59.9	1	na	--	na	--	na	--	na	--	na	--	na
56.6	1	4.4	1	56.6	1	56.9	2	-1.1	64	43.1	2	310.2	1	na	--	na
55.2	2	3.7	2	55.2	2	61.2	1	na	--	na	--	na	--	na	--	na
51.7	2	2.9	3	51.7	2	54.2	2	-14.4	90	32.9	7	185.1	11	-33.2	95	15
50.5	2	3.7	2	50.5	2	48.9	2	-0.7	62	29.2	11	227.4	3	-17.8	77	22
49.9	2	4.0	2	49.9	2	40.3	5	-0.3	61	na	--	na	--	na	--	na
49.5	2	3.0	3	49.5	2	-5.1	98	na	--	na	--	na	--	na	--	na
47.9	2	5.9	1	47.9	2	38.6	6	-7.5	80	13.5	64	162.2	24	-16.6	74	35
46.4	2	2.5	3	46.4	2	49.1	2	-21.7	95	26.3	19	180.2	14	-29.4	93	33
44.8	2	4.0	1	44.8	2	10.7	94	-13.7	89	na	--	na	--	na	--	na
44.7	2	2.8	3	44.7	2	55.3	2	-9.1	84	28.1	14	201.7	7	na	--	na
43.9	3	1.1	7	43.9	3	64.5	1	na	--	na	--	na	--	na	--	na
43.7	3	3.7	2	43.7	3	na	--	na	--	na	--	na	--	na	--	na
43.6	3	1.4	5	43.6	3	44.5	3	na	--	na	--	na	--	na	--	na
43.1	3	1.0	8	43.1	3	na	--	na	--	na	--	na	--	na	--	na
41.5	3	1.5	5	41.5	3	na	--	na	--	na	--	na	--	na	--	na
41.3	3	3.6	2	41.3	3	na	--	na	--	na	--	na	--	na	--	na
40.6	3	1.8	5	40.6	3	na	--	na	--	na	--	na	--	na	--	na
40.0	3	4.7	1	40.0	3	35.2	9	na	--	na	--	na	--	na	--	na
39.9	3	3.0	3	39.9	3	-9.7	99	-28.3	98	0.3	98	32.7	97	na	--	na
38.9	4	2.3	4	38.9	4	65.6	1	na	--	na	--	na	--	na	--	na
38.0	4	2.7	3	38.0	4	22.5	56	2.3	54	16.6	51	108.9	61	na	--	na
38.0	4	1.0	8	38.0	4	64.4	1	0.8	58	27.9	15	269.8	1	-13.3	68	18
37.5	4	-0.9	50	37.5	4	-27.0	99	-29.7	98	0.9	98	26.7	98	-51.0	99	61
36.7	4	0.0	33	36.7	4	-4.5	98	-27.0	98	na	--	na	--	na	--	na
35.0	4	1.9	4	35.0	4	2.6	97	-25.2	97	0.6	98	18.5	98	-39.4	97	97
34.9	4	-1.9	70	34.9	4	na	--	na	--	na	--	na	--	na	--	na
34.2	4	-0.7	47	34.2	4	-1.9	98	-22.6	96	8.9	84	79.2	88	-39.8	97	50
32.8	4	-0.7	46	32.8	4	-10.5	99	-26.1	97	2.6	97	52.8	94	na	--	na
32.7	5	1.8	5	32.7	5	13.0	92	-24.0	96	-6.4	99	66.8	92	na	--	na
31.9	5	-3.5	94	31.9	5	40.2	5	15.8	3	13.3	65	226.7	3	na	--	na
31.6	5	1.0	9	31.6	5	na	--	na	--	na	--	na	--	na	--	na
31.5	5	0.9	11	31.5	5	38.3	6	-1.0	63	na	--	na	--	na	--	na
30.9	5	2.9	3	30.9	5	0.0	98	-36.8	99	na	--	na	--	na	--	na
30.7	5	-0.8	48	30.7	5	-11.0	99	-25.0	97	8.9	85	52.0	94	-42.8	98	58
30.6	5	0.9	9	30.6	5	na	--	na	--	na	--	na	--	na	--	na
30.3	5	1.6	5	30.3	5	35.9	9	na	--	na	--	na	--	na	--	na
30.2	5	3.7	2	30.2	5	na	--	na	--	na	--	na	--	na	--	na
29.9	6	0.7	12	29.9	6	na	--	na	--	na	--	na	--	na	--	na
29.6	6	-4.8	98	29.6	6	37.0	7	6.2	41	17.7	47	213.5	5	-10.6	64	8
28.8	6	3.5	2	28.8	6	38.5	6	-2.7	68	28.4	13	183.2	13	3.9	34	17
28.7	6	3.4	2	28.7	6	26.8	37	-1.3	65	36.5	5	na	--	na	--	na
28.3	6	-3.1	89	28.3	6	55.3	2	-14.3	90	na	--	na	--	na	--	na
28.3	6	-3.1	89	28.3	6	-29.5	99	-34.1	99	-1.9	98	-3.6	99	-49.6	99	63

TOP 50 FUNDS BY YEAR-TO-DATE PERFORMANCE – 12/31/86

| | | | | | | | ANNUALIZED ROR THRU 12/31/86 | | | | | |
| | | | ASSETS | | MAX | % | 10 YEARS | | 5 YEARS | | 3 YEARS | |
FUND	MGT CO	IO	MIL$	NAV	LOAD	YLD	PCNT	RK	PCNT	RK	PCNT	RK
MERRILL L. PACIFIC FUND	MERRIL	IN	445	34.20	6.5	0.3	na	--	29.6	1	37.9	1
NOMURA PACIFIC BASIN FD	NOMURA	IN	53	21.13	0.0	1.4	na	--	na	--	na	--
NEWPORT FAR EAST	COMCAP	IN	3	20.15	0.0	0.0	na	--	na	--	na	--
G. T. PACIFIC GROWTH FD	GTCAP	IN	67	29.98	0.0	0.0	na	--	17.3	48	21.7	5
FIDELITY OVERSEAS FUND	FIDEL	IN	2561	28.68	3.0	0.0	na	--	na	--	na	--
PRICE (ROWE) INTERNATL.	PRICE	IN	753	25.78	0.0	0.8	na	--	24.6	4	30.0	1
STRONG OPPORTUNITY FUND	STRONG	AG	32	15.99	2.0	0.0	na	--	na	--	na	--
VANGUARD WORLD-INTL GR	VGUARD	IN	411	11.26	0.0	0.6	na	--	29.7	1	34.4	1
FT INTERNATIONAL	FEDRES	IN	104	21.60	0.0	0.4	na	--	na	--	na	--
TRANSATLANTIC FUND INC.	KLEIN	IN	100	22.92	0.0	0.0	16.0	30	17.7	46	26.1	2
SCUDDER INTERNATIONAL FD	SCUDER	IN	686	39.79	0.0	1.1	17.8	18	23.8	6	30.6	1
TRUSTEES COMM EQ-INTL	VGUARD	IN	634	38.65	0.0	2.3	na	--	na	--	28.0	2
VANGUARD SPEC PORT-GOLD	VGUARD	ME	54	9.22	0.0	2.3	na	--	na	--	na	--
KEYSTONE INTL FUND	KEYSTN	IN	90	7.16	0.0	0.7	14.1	46	19.3	32	23.7	3
OPPENHEIMER A.I.M. FUND	OPPEN	IN	373	26.99	8.5	0.5	19.6	11	19.7	26	19.5	11
FIRST INVEST. INTL SECS.	FSTINV	IN	29	16.53	8.5	0.1	na	--	na	--	11.4	66
KEMPER INTL FD	KEMPER	IN	185	19.30	8.5	1.0	na	--	21.9	13	26.9	2
ALLIANCE INTERNATIONAL	ALLIAN	IN	164	21.07	8.5	0.1	na	--	na	--	na	--
SIGMA WORLD	SIGMA	IN	8	15.75	8.5	0.0	na	--	na	--	na	--
PRU-BACHE GLOBAL FUND	PRUBAC	IN	401	9.64	0.0	0.1	na	--	na	--	na	--
HUTTON INV SER PRE METAL	HUTTON	ME	39	12.93	0.0	0.2	na	--	na	--	na	--
US NEW PROSPECTOR FUND	UNITED	ME	46	1.31	0.0	0.0	na	--	na	--	na	--
UNITED GOLD & GOVERNMENT	WADDEL	ME	9	6.83	8.5	2.9	na	--	na	--	na	--
WORLD TRENDS	VANECK	IN	58	13.41	7.5	1.0	na	--	na	--	na	--
EUROPACIFIC GROWTH FUND	CAPRES	IN	160	24.58	8.5	0.6	na	--	na	--	na	--
KEYSTONE PRECIOUS METALS	KEYSTN	ME	65	14.59	0.0	2.5	na	--	4.6	96	-3.2	96
PAINE WEBBER ATLAS FD	PAINE	IN	224	15.94	8.5	5.1	na	--	na	--	na	--
MASS. FINL INTL TRUST BD	MASFIN	BP	134	11.46	7.2	5.9	na	--	19.4	30	20.0	8
PUTNAM INTL EQUITIES	PUTNAM	IN	372	30.39	8.5	0.4	19.3	13	26.3	2	31.7	1
US GOLD SHARES FUND	UNITED	ME	307	4.63	0.0	6.3	21.1	6	4.0	97	-11.0	98
OPPENHEIMER GOLD & SPEC.	OPPEN	ME	40	8.45	8.5	1.5	na	--	na	--	-1.6	95
GOLCONDA INVESTORS	GOLCON	ME	32	12.86	0.0	0.2	na	--	2.1	97	1.2	93
FIDELITY GROWTH & INCOME	FIDEL	GI	460	13.33	0.0	1.2	na	--	na	--	na	--
INTERNATIONAL INVESTORS	VANECK	ME	865	12.04	8.5	3.0	24.5	2	11.0	86	0.6	94
FIDELITY SEL PREC MET&MN	FIDEL	ME	241	11.15	2.0	0.8	na	--	6.8	95	-4.2	97
LEXINGTON GOLDFUND	LEXGTN	ME	22	4.49	0.0	0.4	na	--	na	--	4.4	90
EATON VANCE TOTAL RETURN	ETN&HD	GI	570	10.67	4.7	3.2	na	--	25.3	3	28.9	1
MERRILL L. NAT RESOURCE	MERRIL	G	259	12.71	0.0	0.9	na	--	na	--	na	--
DEAN WITTER WORLDWIDE	DWRI	IN	346	15.44	0.0	0.5	na	--	na	--	21.7	5
US PROSPECTOR FUND	UNITED	ME	72	0.72	0.0	0.0	na	--	na	--	-6.1	97
FRANKLIN GOLD FUND	FRNKRE	ME	126	8.99	4.0	3.6	21.8	5	6.8	95	-4.5	97
SHEARSON GLOBAL OPPORT	SHEAR	G	263	30.07	5.0	0.4	na	--	na	--	na	--
MERRILL L. INTERNATIONAL	MERRIL	IN	278	14.28	8.5	1.8	na	--	na	--	na	--
COLONIAL ADV STRAT GOLD	COLONL	ME	29	17.99	6.7	0.8	na	--	na	--	na	--
STRONG INCOME FUND	STRONG	GI	72	12.65	0.0	5.5	na	--	na	--	na	--
BRUCE FUND	BRUCE	AG	3	109.39	0.0	1.2	na	--	22.2	11	23.5	3
UNITED INTL. GROWTH FUND	WADDEL	IN	205	7.13	8.5	1.5	17.4	20	22.4	10	20.2	8
TEMPLETON FOREIGN FUND	TEMPLE	IN	184	15.41	8.5	2.0	na	--	na	--	17.2	22
TWENTIETH CENTURY GIFTR	INVRES	G	6	6.75	0.5	0.0	na	--	na	--	19.5	11
STRATEGIC INVESTMENTS	SD	ME	96	4.65	8.5	5.9	19.0	14	-0.2	98	-15.8	99

LATEST 12 MNTHS		THIS MONTH		1986 TO DATE		CALENDAR YEARS						CYCLES				CDA RATING
						1985		1984		1983		UP MKT		DOWN MKT		
PCNT	RK	PCNT	RK	PCNT	RK	PCNT	RK	PCNT	RK	PCNT	RK	PCNT	RK	PCNT	RK	
77.9	1	6.5	1	77.9	1	42.1	4	3.8	49	38.7	3	340.0	1	3.0	36	1
74.4	1	2.0	4	74.4	1	na	--	na	--	na	--	na	--	na	--	na
73.4	1	5.0	1	73.4	1	16.2	86	na	--	na	--	na	--	na	--	na
70.0	1	5.3	1	70.0	1	9.3	96	-3.0	69	37.0	5	182.2	13	-0.7	46	2
68.9	1	4.7	1	68.9	1	78.6	1	na	--	na	--	na	--	na	--	na
60.5	1	3.6	2	60.5	1	45.2	3	-5.8	77	28.6	12	225.0	3	-12.2	66	8
59.9	1	-4.4	97	59.9	1	na	--	na	--	na	--	na	--	na	--	na
56.6	1	4.4	1	56.6	1	56.9	2	-1.1	64	43.1	2	310.2	1	na	--	na
55.2	2	3.7	2	55.2	2	61.2	1	na	--	na	--	na	--	na	--	na
51.7	2	2.9	3	51.7	2	54.2	2	-14.4	90	32.9	7	185.1	11	-33.2	95	15
50.5	2	3.7	2	50.5	2	48.9	2	-0.7	62	29.2	11	227.4	3	-17.8	77	22
49.9	2	4.0	2	49.9	2	40.3	5	-0.3	61	na	--	na	--	na	--	na
49.5	2	3.0	3	49.5	2	-5.1	98	na	--	na	--	na	--	na	--	na
47.9	2	5.9	1	47.9	2	38.6	6	-7.5	80	13.5	64	162.2	24	-16.6	74	35
46.4	2	2.5	3	46.4	2	49.1	2	-21.7	95	26.3	19	180.2	14	-29.4	93	33
44.8	2	4.0	1	44.8	2	10.7	94	-13.7	89	na	--	na	--	na	--	na
44.7	2	2.8	3	44.7	2	55.3	2	-9.1	84	28.1	14	201.7	7	na	--	na
43.9	3	1.1	7	43.9	3	64.5	1	na	--	na	--	na	--	na	--	na
43.7	3	3.7	2	43.7	3	na	--	na	--	na	--	na	--	na	--	na
43.6	3	1.4	5	43.6	3	44.5	3	na	--	na	--	na	--	na	--	na
43.1	3	1.0	8	43.1	3	na	--	na	--	na	--	na	--	na	--	na
41.5	3	1.5	5	41.5	3	na	--	na	--	na	--	na	--	na	--	na
41.3	3	3.6	2	41.3	3	na	--	na	--	na	--	na	--	na	--	na
40.6	3	1.8	5	40.6	3	na	--	na	--	na	--	na	--	na	--	na
40.0	3	4.7	1	40.0	3	35.2	9	na	--	na	--	na	--	na	--	na
39.9	3	3.0	3	39.9	3	-9.7	99	-28.3	98	0.3	98	32.7	97	na	--	na
38.9	4	2.3	4	38.9	4	65.6	1	na	--	na	--	na	--	na	--	na
38.0	4	2.7	3	38.0	4	22.5	56	2.3	54	16.6	51	108.9	61	na	--	na
38.0	4	1.0	8	38.0	4	64.4	1	0.8	58	27.9	15	269.8	1	-13.3	68	18
37.5	4	-0.9	50	37.5	4	-27.0	99	-29.7	98	0.9	98	26.7	98	-51.0	99	61
36.7	4	0.0	33	36.7	4	-4.5	98	-27.0	98	na	--	na	--	na	--	na
35.0	4	1.9	4	35.0	4	2.6	97	-25.2	97	0.6	98	18.5	98	-39.4	97	97
34.9	4	-1.9	70	34.9	4	na	--	na	--	na	--	na	--	na	--	na
34.2	4	-0.7	47	34.2	4	-1.9	98	-22.6	96	8.9	84	79.2	88	-39.8	97	50
32.8	4	-0.7	46	32.8	4	-10.5	99	-26.1	97	2.6	97	52.8	94	na	--	na
32.7	5	1.8	5	32.7	5	13.0	92	-24.0	96	-6.4	99	66.8	92	na	--	na
31.9	5	-3.5	94	31.9	5	40.2	5	15.8	3	13.3	65	226.7	3	na	--	na
31.6	5	1.0	9	31.6	5	na	--	na	--	na	--	na	--	na	--	na
31.5	5	0.9	11	31.5	5	38.3	6	-1.0	63	na	--	na	--	na	--	na
30.9	5	2.9	3	30.9	5	0.0	98	-36.8	99	na	--	na	--	na	--	na
30.7	5	-0.8	48	30.7	5	-11.0	99	-25.0	97	8.9	85	52.0	94	-42.8	98	58
30.6	5	0.9	9	30.6	5	na	--	na	--	na	--	na	--	na	--	na
30.3	5	1.6	5	30.3	5	35.9	9	na	--	na	--	na	--	na	--	na
30.2	5	3.7	2	30.2	5	na	--	na	--	na	--	na	--	na	--	na
29.9	6	0.7	12	29.9	6	na	--	na	--	na	--	na	--	na	--	na
29.6	6	-4.8	98	29.6	6	37.0	7	6.2	41	17.7	47	213.5	5	-10.6	64	8
28.8	6	3.5	2	28.8	6	38.5	6	-2.7	68	28.4	13	183.2	13	3.9	34	17
28.7	6	3.4	2	28.7	6	26.8	37	-1.3	65	36.5	5	na	--	na	--	na
28.3	6	-3.1	89	28.3	6	55.3	2	-14.3	90	na	--	na	--	na	--	na
28.3	6	-3.1	89	28.3	6	-29.5	99	-34.1	99	-1.9	98	-3.6	99	-49.6	99	63

By Investment Objective

RANKED BY CDA RATING WITHIN
INVESTMENT OBJECTIVE – 12/31/86

INTERNATIONAL

1	MERRILL L. PACIFIC FUND
2	G. T. PACIFIC GROWTH FD
7	SOGEN INTERNATIONAL FUND
8	PRICE (ROWE) INTERNATL.
15	TRANSATLANTIC FUND INC.
17	UNITED INTL. GROWTH FUND
18	PUTNAM INTL EQUITIES
22	SCUDDER INTERNATIONAL FD
33	OPPENHEIMER A.I.M. FUND
35	KEYSTONE INTL FUND
91	PAX WORLD FUND
na	ALLIANCE INTERNATIONAL
na	DEAN WITTER WORLDWIDE
na	EUROPACIFIC GROWTH FUND
na	FIDELITY OVERSEAS FUND
na	FIRST INVEST. INTL SECS.
na	FT INTERNATIONAL
na	HANCOCK (JOHN) GLOBAL
na	KEMPER INTL FD
na	MERRILL L. INTERNATIONAL
na	NEWPORT FAR EAST
na	NOMURA PACIFIC BASIN FD
na	PAINE WEBBER ATLAS FD
na	PRU-BACHE GLOBAL FUND
na	SCUDDER GLOBAL
na	SHEARSON SPEC INTL EQ
na	SIGMA WORLD
na	TEMPLETON FOREIGN FUND
na	TRUSTEES COMM EQ-INTL
na	VANGUARD WORLD-INTL GR
na	WORLD OF TECHNOLOGY FUND
na	WORLD TRENDS

AGGRESSIVE GROWTH

2	LOOMIS-SAYLES CAP. DEV.
5	NEL GROWTH FUND
6	WEINGARTEN EQUITY FUND
8	BRUCE FUND
8	IDS GROWTH FUND
9	AMEV GROWTH FUND, INC.
10	TUDOR FUND
13	PUTNAM VISTA FUND
13	PUTNAM VOYAGER FUND
13	TWENTIETH CENTURY GROWTH
14	AMEV SPECIAL FUND, INC.
14	HARTWELL GROWTH FUND
15	SELIGMAN CAPITAL FUND
16	EVERGREEN FUND
22	VALUE LINE FUND
23	FOUNDERS SPECIAL FUND
26	AMERICAN NATIONAL GROWTH
40	MEDICAL TECHNOLOGY FUND
40	AMERICAN CAPITAL VENTURE
46	STEIN R&F CAPITAL OPPOR.
48	CONSTELLATION GROWTH
49	HARTWELL LEVERAGE FUND
49	ONE HUNDRED FUND

CONTINUED - AGGRESSIVE GROWTH

53	SIGMA VENTURE SHARES
53	DELTA TREND FUND
60	SURVEYOR FUND
62	SCUDDER DEVELOPMENT FUND
66	PILOT FUND
74	FINANCIAL DYNAMICS FUND
73	PRICE (ROWE) NEW HORIZ.
74	STATE BOND PROGRESS FUND
76	NEUWIRTH FUND
78	EXPLORER FUND
79	KEYSTONE S-4
80	STEIN R&F STOCK
82	VALUE LINE SPECIAL SIT.
84	HANCOCK (JOHN) GROWTH
85	AFUTURE FUND
87	WALL STREET FUND
89	AXE-HOUGHTON STOCK FUND
93	GREENWAY FUND
94	FAIRFIELD FUND
94	SHERMAN, DEAN FUND
95	FORTY-FOUR WALL ST FUND
95	FIRST INVEST. DISCOVERY
95	AMERICAN HERITAGE FUND
96	FIRST INVEST. FD. GROWTH
96	AMERICAN INVESTORS FUND
97	NAUTILUS FUND
97	OPPENHEIMER FUND
97	MERRILL L. SPECIAL VALUE
97	INDUSTRY FUND OF AMERICA
98	STEADMAN OCEANOGRAPHIC
98	FORTY-FOUR WALL ST EQTY
98	NAESS & THOMAS SPECIAL
99	LORD ABBETT DEV GROWTH
99	FIRST INVEST. NATURL RES
99	SIERRA GROWTH FUND
99	PUTNAM ENERGY RESOURCES
na	ABT EMERGING GROWTH
na	ALLIANCE TECHNOLOGY
na	AMERICAN CAPITAL GROWTH
na	BULLOCK AGGRES GROWTH SH
na	CIGNA AGGRESSIVE GROWTH
na	COLUMBIA SPECIAL FUND
na	EXPLORER II
na	FIDELITY GROWTH FUND
na	FIDELITY SEL BIOTECH
na	FIDELITY SELECT HEALTH
na	FIDELITY SELECT TECHNLGY
na	FIDELITY SPEC SITUATIONS
na	FIDELITY SEL ELECTRONICS
na	FIDELITY SEL COMPUTER
na	FIDELITY SEL SOFTWARE
na	FUND OF THE SOUTHWEST
na	FUNDTRUST AGGRESSIVE
na	GATEWAY GROWTH PLUS FUND
na	GINTEL CAP APPRECIATION
na	GRADISON OPPORTUNITY GR
na	HUTTON INV SER SPL EQTY
na	IDS DISCOVERY FUND

CONTINUED - AGGRESSIVE GROWTH

na	JANUS VENTURE FUND
na	KIDDER P. SPECIAL GROWTH
na	LEVERAGE FUND OF BOSTON
na	LOWRY MARKET TIMING FD
na	MASS. FINL EMERG. GWTH.
na	MASS. FINANCIAL SPECIAL
na	NOVA FUND INC
na	OPPENHEIMER REGENCY
na	PBHG GROWTH FUND
na	PACIFIC HORIZON AGGRE GR
na	PRU-BACHE EQUITY FUND
na	PRU-BACHE GR OPPORTUNITY
na	PUTNAM INFOR SCIENCES
na	PUTNAM HEALTH SCIENCES
na	QUASAR ASSOCIATES
na	SCHIELD AGGRESS GROWTH
na	SECURITY OMNI FUND
na	SELIGMAN COMMUNICATIONS
na	SHEARSON AGGRESSIVE GRTH
na	SHEARSON SPEC EQTY PLUS
na	STEINROE DISCOVERY FUND
na	STEINROE UNIVERSE FUND
na	STRATEGIC CAPITAL GAINS
na	STRONG OPPORTUNITY FUND
na	SUMMIT INVESTOR FD INC.
na	THOMSON MCKINNON OPPORT.
na	TWENTIETH CENTURY ULTRA
na	TWENTIETH CENTURY VISTA
na	US GROWTH FUND
na	US LOCAP FUND
na	USAA SUNBELT ERA FUND
na	VANGUARD SPC PORT-HEALTH
na	VANGUARD SPEC PORT-TECH
na	WESTERGAARD FUND INC.

GROWTH

1	FIDELITY MAGELLAN FUND
1	TWENTIETH CENTURY SELECT
3	LEHMAN CAPITAL FUND
3	QUEST FOR VALUE FUND
3	VALUE LINE LEVER. GROWTH
4	FIDELITY DESTINY
4	COPLEY TAX-MANAGED FUND
4	PHOENIX STOCK FUND SER
6	ACORN FUND
7	OPPENHEIMER TIME FUND
7	NICHOLAS FUND
7	NORTH STAR REGIONAL FUND
8	GUARDIAN PARK AVE FUND
9	AMCAP FUND
9	AMERICAN CAPITAL PACE FD
9	GROWTH FUND OF AMERICA
10	NEW PERSPECTIVE FUND
10	AMERICAN CAP COMSTOCK
11	TEMPLETON WORLD FUND
11	NEW YORK VENTURE FUND
12	FIDELITY VALUE FUND

CONTINUED - GROWTH

12	TEMPLETON GROWTH FUND
15	INVESTORS RESEARCH
16	IDS NEW DIMENSIONS FUND
17	CHARTER FUND
17	PIONEER II
18	SHEARSON APPRECIATION
20	NEL RETIREMENT EQUITY
20	FRANKLIN EQUITY FUND
22	KEMPER SUMMIT FUND
23	AMEV CAPITAL FUND, INC.
24	PENNSYLVANIA MUTUAL FUND
27	UNITED ACCUMULATIVE FUND
27	NATIONWIDE GROWTH FUND
29	OVER-THE-COUNTER SEC.
30	SIGMA CAPITAL SHARES
30	UNITED INCOME FUND
31	SENTRY FUND
34	MASS. CAPITAL DEVEL.
35	FOUNDERS GROWTH FUND
35	FIDELITY CONGRESS STREET
37	NORTH STAR STOCK FUND
37	OPPENHEIMER SPECIAL FUND
37	LEXINGTON GROWTH FUND
38	EATON VANCE GROWTH FD
39	MATHERS FUND
41	DREYFUS GROWTH OPPORTUN.
42	STATE FARM GROWTH FUND
43	FUNDAMENTAL INVESTORS
43	ALPHA FUND
44	MASS. FINANCIAL DEVEL.
45	SMITH, BARNEY EQUITY
46	LEXINGTON RESEARCH FUND
48	LEHMAN INVESTORS FD, INC
49	SIGMA SPECIAL FUND
49	PRINCOR GROWTH FD, INC.
50	U.S. TREND FUND, INC.
51	KEYSTONE K-2
52	IDS EQUITY PLUS FD INC.
52	BOSTON CO. CAP. APPREC.
53	DELAWARE FUND
53	STRATTON GROWTH FUND
54	STEINROE SPECIAL FUND
54	KEYSTONE S-3
55	MUTUAL BENEFIT FUND
55	MORGAN (W.L.) GROWTH
55	AMWAY MUTUAL FUND
56	FIDELITY EXCHANGE FUND
56	COMPOSITE FUND
57	KEMPER GROWTH FUND
57	BULLOCK GROWTH SHARES
58	MANHATTAN FUND
58	FRANKLIN GROWTH
59	COLUMBIA GROWTH FUND
60	FINANCIAL INDUST. FUND
61	PUTNAM INVESTORS FUND
61	UNITED SCIENCE & ENERGY
61	SENTINEL GROWTH FUND
62	WPG FUND

RANKED BY CDA RATING WITHIN
INVESTMENT OBJECTIVE – 12/31/86

CONTINUED - GROWTH

63	TECHNOLOGY FUND
64	RAINBOW FUND
65	AMA GROWTH FUND, INC.
66	NEWTON GROWTH FUND
68	GROWTH INDUSTRY SHARES
69	NATL AVIATION & TECH
68	STATE STREET INV. CORP.
69	PRICE (ROWE) NEW ERA
70	CENTURY SHARES TRUST
70	SAFECO GROWTH FUND
71	COLONIAL GROWTH SHARES
72	VANGUARD WORLD-US GR
72	SELIGMAN GROWTH FD
72	COMPANION FUND
73	MASS. INV. GROWTH STOCK
74	PRICE (ROWE) GROWTH STK.
75	OMEGA FUND
75	BEACON HILL MUTUAL FUND
75	BABSON GROWTH FUND
76	LEHMAN OPPORTUNITY FUND
76	HORACE MANN GROWTH FUND
77	MUTUAL BEACON GROWTH FD
77	CIGNA GROWTH FUND
78	PHILADELPHIA FUND
80	HAMILTON FUNDS
80	MUTUAL OF OMAHA GROWTH
80	FIDELITY CONTRAFUND
81	FIDELITY TREND
81	VANCE, SANDERS SPECIAL
82	MIDAMERICA HIGH GROWTH
83	BULL & BEAR CAP GROWTH
83	FRANKLIN OPTION FUND
83	MEESCHAERT CAP. ACCUM.
84	FARM BUREAU GROWTH FUND
84	FRANKLIN DYNATECH
84	AMERICAN CAP ENTERPRISE
86	CHEMICAL FUND
86	COUNTRY CAPITAL GROWTH
86	FPA CAPITAL FUND
87	EATON VANCE SPL EQUITIES
89	INVEST. TRUST OF BOSTON
89	KEYSTONE S-1
89	STATE BOND COMMON STOCK
90	NATL SECURITIES GROWTH
91	USAA MUTUAL FD GROWTH
91	DE VEGH MUTUAL FUND
92	CANADIAN FUND
92	SELECTED SPECIAL SHARES
93	ROCHESTER TAX MANAGED FD
94	STEADMAN INVESTMENT
94	CHEAPSIDE DOLLAR FD LTD
95	NATIONAL INDUSTRIES FUND
98	STEADMAN AMERICAN INDUS.
99	EAGLE GROWTH SHARES
na	ALLIANCE COUNTERPOINT
na	AMERICAN CAPITAL OTC SEC
na	AMERICAN TELECOMM TR GR
na	ARMSTRONG ASSOCIATES

CONTINUED - GROWTH

na	BABSON ENTERPRISE FUND
na	BABSON VALUE FD INC.
na	BOSTON CO. SPEC GROWTH
na	BOWSER GROWTH FUND
na	CALVERT EQUITY
na	CARNEGIE CAPPIELLO GROW
na	CARDINAL FUND
na	CASHMAN FARRELL VALUE FD
na	CIGNA VALUE FUND
na	COLONIAL EQUITY INC TR
na	DEAN WITTER DEVELOP GROW
na	DEAN WITTER INDUSTRY VAL
na	DEAN WITTER NAT RESOURCE
na	DEPOSITORS FUND/BOSTON
na	DFA SMALL CO. PORTFOLIO
na	DIVERSIFICATION FUND
na	DREXEL ST EMERG GROWTH
na	DREXEL ST GROWTH
na	FAIRMONT FUND
na	FEDERATED GROWTH TRUST
na	FIDELITY FREEDOM FUND
na	FIDELITY SEL CHEMICAL
na	FIDELITY OTC PORTFOLIO
na	FIDELITY SEL DEF & AERO
na	FIDELITY SELECT ENERGY
na	FIDELITY SEL LEISURE ENT
na	FIDELITY SELECT FINL SVC
na	FIDELITY SEL BROKERAGE
na	FIDELITY SEL PROPTY/CAS
na	FIDELITY SEL FOOD/AGRI
na	FIDELITY SEL SAVINGS/LN
na	FIDELITY SEL TELECOMM
na	FIDUCIARY CAPITAL GROWTH
na	FPA PERENNIAL FUND
na	FREEDOM REGIONAL BANK FD
na	FTP-EQ PORTFOLIO-GROWTH
na	FUNDTRUST GROWTH
na	GABELLI ASSET FUND
na	GIBRALTAR FUND, INC.
na	GINTEL FUND
na	GRADISON ESTABLISHED GR.
na	GROWTH FD OF WASHINGTON
na	HANCOCK (JOHN) SPECIAL
na	HEARTLAND VALUE FUND
na	HUTTON INV SER BASIC VAL
na	HUTTON INV SERIES GROWTH
na	INTEGRATED CAPTL APPREC
na	INVEST. PORTFOLIOS-EQ
na	IRI STOCK FUND
na	IVY INSTITUTIONAL INV FD
na	JANUS VALUE FUND
na	LEGG MASON VALUE TRUST
na	LORD ABBETT VALUE APPREC
na	MACKENZIE INDUSTRIAL AM
na	MASS. FINL SECTORS FUND
na	MERRILL L. NAT RESOURCE
na	MERRILL L. FUND FOR TOM
na	MONITREND VALUE FUND

CONTINUED - GROWTH

na	NATL TELECOMMUNICATIONS
na	NEW ECONOMY FUND
na	NICHOLAS II
na	NICHOLSON GROWTH FUND
na	NORTH STAR APOLLO FUND
na	NORTHEAST INV GROWTH
na	OLYMPIC TRUST SERIES B
na	OPPENHEIMER DIRECTORS
na	OPPENHEIMER SELECT STOCK
na	OPPENHEIMER TARGET FUND
na	PAINE WEBBER OLYMPUS FD
na	PERMANENT PORTFOLIO
na	PIONEER THREE
na	PRICE (ROWE) NEW AMERICA
na	PRIMECAP FUND
na	PRU-BACHE OPTION GROWTH
na	RETIREMENT PLANNING-EQ
na	RIGHTIME FUND
na	ROYCE VALUE FUND, INC.
na	SBSF FUND
na	SCHIELD VALUE PORTFOLIO
na	SCI-TECH HOLDINGS
na	SCUDDER CAPITAL GROWTH
na	SECURITY ACTION FD
na	SHEARSON FUNDAMENTAL VAL
na	SHEARSON GLOBAL OPPORT
na	SHEARSON SPEC EQTY GR
na	SOUTHEASTERN GROWTH FUND
na	STATE STREET GROWTH
na	SUNBELT GROWTH FUND
na	TEMPLETON GLOBAL I
na	TEMPLETON GLOBAL II
na	THOMSON MCKINNON GROWTH
na	TWENTIETH CENTURY GIFTR
na	UNIFIED GROWTH FUND
na	UNITED NEW CONCEPTS FUND
na	US GOOD AND BAD TIMES FD
na	VANGUARD SPEC PORT-ENRGY
na	VANGUARD SPEC-SVC ECON
na	WASHINGTON AREA GROWTH
na	WEALTH MONITORS FUND

GROWTH & INCOME

2	PARTNERS FUND
3	LINDNER DIVIDEND FUND
4	PHOENIX CONVERTIBLE FUND
5	FIDELITY EQUITY INCOME
5	BASCOM HILL INVESTORS
5	UNITED VANGUARD FUND
10	FRANKLIN UTILITIES
11	AMERICAN MUTUAL FUND
11	MERRILL L. BASIC VALUE
12	WINDSOR FUND
13	SEQUOIA FUND
13	NATL SECURITIES TOT RET
14	KEMPER TOTAL RETURN FD
16	LINDNER FUND

CONTINUED - GROWTH & INCOME

16	JANUS FUND
17	DECATUR FUND INC-SER 1
17	DREYFUS LEVERAGE
18	ABT UTILITY INCOME FD
19	PUTNAM FD FOR GROWTH/INC
19	PUTNAM CONVERT INC-GR TR
19	PHOENIX GROWTH FUND SER
20	TRUSTEES COMM EQ-US PORT
21	OLD DOMINION INVTS TR
21	SENTINEL COMMON STOCK FD
24	INVEST. CO. OF AMERICA
25	UNITED CONTL. INCOME FD.
26	WASH. MUTUAL INVESTORS
28	AMERICAN CAPITAL HARBOR
28	ELFUN TRUSTS
29	MERRILL L. CAPITAL FUND
30	OPPENHEIMER EQUITY INC.
30	FINANCIAL INDUST. INCOME
32	SOVEREIGN INVESTORS
32	DREXEL BURNHAM FUND
32	NEL EQUITY FUND
33	DREYFUS FUND
34	IVY GROWTH FUND
34	STATE FARM BALANCED
34	SELIGMAN COMMON STOCK FD
34	IDS PROGRESSIVE FUND
36	PHOENIX TOTAL RETURN FD
36	SIGMA INVESTMENT SHARES
36	LOOMIS-SAYLES MUTUAL
41	FIDELITY FUND
42	PRINCOR CAP ACCUMULATION
42	PILGRIM MAGNACAP FUND
44	AFFILIATED FUND
45	SELECTED AMERICAN SHARES
46	ABT GROWTH & INCOME TR.
46	SAFECO EQUITY FUND
47	MIDAMERICA MUTUAL FUND
48	DODGE & COX STOCK
48	ONE HUNDRED ONE FUND
50	GUARDIAN MUTUAL FUND
50	FPA PARAMOUNT FD INC
51	SCUDDER GROWTH & INCOME
52	NATL SECURITIES STOCK
56	BULLOCK DIVIDEND SHARES
57	AMERICAN GROWTH FUND
58	AMERICAN LEADERS FUND
59	PINE STREET FUND
59	SECURITY EQUITY FUND
59	PIONEER FUND
62	IDS STOCK FUND
63	JP GROWTH FUND
63	UNIFIED MUTUAL SHARES
65	PENN SQUARE MUTUAL FUND
66	FUND OF AMERICA
66	AMERICAN NATL INC FUND
67	VANGUARD INDEX TRUST
67	EATON & HOWARD STOCK
67	VALLEY FORGE FUND

RANKED BY CDA RATING WITHIN
INVESTMENT OBJECTIVE – 12/31/86

CONTINUED - GROWTH & INCOME

68	STATE BOND DIVERSIFIED
71	NATIONWIDE FUND
72	SECURITY INVESTMENT FUND
73	MASS. INV. TRUST
74	GENL ELEC S&S PROGRAM
77	DREYFUS THIRD CENTURY
78	ENERGY FUND
78	FOUNDERS MUTUAL FUND
79	PUTNAM OPTION INCOME I
80	GENERAL SECURITIES
81	SECURITY ULTRA FUND
82	ANALYTIC OPTIONED EQUITY
83	GATEWAY OPTION INCOME
85	CONCORD FUND
85	LUTHERAN BROTHER. FUND
87	MUTUAL OF OMAHA INCOME
88	ISI GROWTH FUND
90	DIVIDEND/GROWTH FD., INC
91	STEADMAN ASSOCIATED
91	COLONIAL OPTION INC I
92	FOUNDATION GROWTH STOCK
92	LEPERCQ-ISTEL TRUST
95	CONVERTIBLE YIELD
96	OPPENHEIMER PREMIUM INC
96	KEMPER OPTION INCOME FD
na	ABT SECURITY INCOME
na	AMERICAN TELECOMM TR INC
na	BARTLETT BASIC VALUE FD
na	CLIPPER FUND, INC.
na	COLONIAL OPTION INC II
na	DEAN WITTER DIVIDEND GRO
na	DEAN WITTER OPTION INC
na	DREXEL ST OPTION INC FD
na	EATON VANCE TOTAL RETURN
na	EQUITEC SIEBEL TOTAL RET
na	FEDERATED STOCK TRUST
na	FIDELITY GROWTH & INCOME
na	FIDELITY SEL UTILITIES
na	FIRST INVEST. NINETY-TEN
na	FIRST INVEST. OPTION
na	FLEX FD-RETIRE GR SERIES
na	FTP-EQ PORTFOLIO INCOME
na	FUNDTRUST GROWTH & INC
na	GINTEL ERISA
na	HUTTON OPTION INCOME
na	INVEST. PORTFOLIOS-OP IN
na	KIDDER P. EQUITY INCOME
na	LMH FUND, LTD.
na	MACKENZIE INDUSTRIAL OPT
na	NATL SECS REAL ESTATE
na	PAINE WEBBER AMERICA FD
na	PRICE (ROWE) EQUITY INC
na	PRICE (ROWE) GROWTH&INC.
na	PRU-BACHE RESEARCH FUND
na	PRU-BACHE UTILITY FUND
na	PUTNAM OPTION INCOME II
na	SHEARSON SPL OPTION INC
na	STRONG INCOME FUND

CONTINUED - GROWTH & INCOME

na	TELEPHONE INCOME SHARES
na	UMB STOCK FUND
na	US INCOME FUND
na	VANGUARD CONVERTIBLE SEC
na	WINDSOR II

MUNICIPAL BOND

12	NEL TAX EXEMPT
15	MFS MGD MUNI-BD TRUST
19	KEMPER MUNI BOND FD LTD
20	STEINROE MANAGED MUNI FD
22	MERRILL L. MUNI-BD HIYLD
22	DEAN WITTER TAX EX SECS
24	EATON VANCE MUNICIPAL BD
24	NATL SECURITIES TX EX BD
25	FIDELITY HIGH YIELD MUNI
28	VANGUARD MUNI HIGH YIELD
29	FEDERATED TAX FR INCOME
31	CIGNA MUNICIPAL BOND FD
32	LUTHERAN BROTHER. MUN BD
32	DMC TAX FREE-PA
35	PUTNAM TAX EXEMPT INC
37	NUVEEN MUNICIPAL BOND FD
38	PRICE (ROWE) TX FREE INC
38	VANGUARD MUNI LONG-TERM
47	FIRST INVEST. TAX EXEMPT
51	MERRILL L. MUNI-BD INSD
54	UNITED MUNICIPAL BOND FD
55	HANCOCK (JOHN) TX EX DIV
65	FIDELITY MUNI BOND FD
67	SCUDDER MANAGED MUNI BD
68	FIDELITY LTD TERM MUNS
70	VANGUARD MUNI INTERM-TRM
93	VANGUARD MUNI SHORT-TERM
93	MERRILL L. MUNI-LTD MAT
na	AMERICAN CAPITAL MUNI BD
na	BENHAM CALIF TF-INTERMED
na	BENHAM CALIF TF-LONG TRM
na	BULLOCK TAX-FREE SHARES
na	COLONIAL TAX EXEMPT HIYD
na	COLONIAL TAX EX INSURED
na	COLUMBIA MUNICIPAL BOND
na	CRITERION QUAL TX FR INS
na	DEAN WITTER CALIF TX FR
na	DEAN WITTER NY TX FR INC
na	DMC TAX FREE-USA
na	DMC TAX FREE-INSURED
na	DOUBLE EXEMPT FLEX FUND
na	DREYFUS CALIF TAX EXEMPT
na	DREYFUS INSURED TAX EX
na	DREYFUS INTERMDIATE MUNI
na	DREYFUS MASS TAX EXEMPT
na	DREYFUS NY TAX EXEMPT
na	DREYFUS TAX EXEMPT BOND
na	FEDERATED INTMED MUNI TR
na	FEDERATED SH-INTERM MUNI
na	FIDELITY AGGRESS TAX FR

CONTINUED - MUNICIPAL BOND

na FIDELITY CALIF TAX FREE
na FIDELITY MASS TAX FREE
na FINANCIAL TAX FR INC SHS
na FIRST INVEST. NY TAX FR
na FLAGSHIP MICHIGAN DBL TX
na FLAGSHIP OHIO DOUBLE TAX
na FRANKLIN CALIF TAX FREE
na FRANKLIN FEDERAL TAX FR
na FRANKLIN NEW YORK TAX FR
na HAWAIIAN TAX-FREE TRUST
na HUTTON CAL MUNICIPAL FD
na HUTTON NATL MUNICIPAL FD
na HUTTON N.Y. MUNICIPAL FD
na INTEGRATED INSD TAX FREE
na ITB MASS TAX FREE
na KEMPER CALIF TAX FREE
na KEYSTONE TAX FREE
na KIDDER P. NATL TX-FR INC
na KIDDER P. N.Y. TX-FR INC
na LORD ABBETT TX FREE NATL
na LORD ABBETT TX FREE NY
na MFS MGD MUNI-BOND HIYLD
na MFS MDG MULTI-ST MASS.
na MFS MGD MULTI-ST N.C.
na MFS MGD MULTI-ST VA
na MERRILL L. CALIF TAX-EX
na MERRILL L. NY MUNI BOND
na NATL SECURITIES CAL TX E
na OPPENHEIMER NY TX EXEMPT
na OPPENHEIMER TAX FREE BD
na PACIFIC HORIZON CAL TAX
na PAINE WEBBER CALIF TX-EX
na PAINE WEBBER TAX-EX INC
na PRICE (ROWE) TAX FR HIYD
na PRICE (ROWE) TXFR SH-INT
na PRU-BACHE HIYLD MUNI
na PUTNAM CALIF TAX EX
na PUTNAM NY TAX EXEMPT
na SAFECO MUNICIPAL BOND FD
na SCUDDER CALIF TAX FREE
na SCUDDER NEW YORK TAX FR
na SCUDDER TX FR TARGT 1990
na SCUDDER TX FR TARGT 1993
na SELIGMAN CALIF TAX EX HI
na SELIGMAN CAL TAX EX QUAL
na SELIGMAN TX EX LOUISIANA
na SELIGMAN TAX EX MARYLAND
na SELIGMAN TAX EX MASS
na SELIGMAN TAX EX MICH
na SELIGMAN TAX EX MINN
na SELIGMAN TAX EX NATL
na SELIGMAN TAX EX NEW YORK
na SELIGMAN TAX EX OHIO
na SHEARSON CALIF MUNICIPAL
na SHEARSON MANAGED MUNI BD
na SHEARSON NEW YORK MUNI
na SHEARSON SPEC TAX EX INC
na STEINROE HIGH-YIELD MUNI

CONTINUED - MUNICIPAL BOND

na STEINROE INTERMED MUNI
na TAX EXEMPT BD FD/AMERICA
na UNIFIED MUNI FD-GENERAL
na UNIFIED MUNI FD-INDIANA
na UNITED MUNI HIGH INCOME
na USAA TAX EX HIGH YIELD
na USAA TAX EX INTERMEDIATE
na USAA TAX EX SH-TERM FD
na VANGUARD CALIF INS TX FR
na VANGUARD PENNA INS TX FR
na VANGUARD MUNI INSURED LT
na VENTURE MUNI PLUS

BOND & PREFERRED

5   FIDELITY HIGH INCOME FD
7   KEMPER HIGH YIELD FD
15 CIGNA HIGH YIELD
25 NATL SECURITIES PREFERED
25 VANGUARD FIXED INC HIYLD
26 QUALIFIED DIVD PORTF II
26 NORTHEAST INV. TRUST
28 PHOENIX HIGH YIELD
28 IDS BOND FUND
29 UNITED HIGH INCOME FUND
31 KEMPER US GOVT SECS
31 SIGMA INCOME SHARES
33 PRU-BACHE HIGH YIELD
36 IDS SELECTIVE
39 PUTNAM HIGH YIELD
39 CIGNA INCOME FUND
39 AXE-HOUGHTON INCOME
41 MASS. FINL HI INCOME
42 DELCHESTER BOND FUND
45 BOND FUND OF AMERICA
45 MASS. FINANCIAL BOND
47 UNITED BOND FUND
47 MERRILL L. BOND-INTERMED
49 COLONIAL HIGH YIELD SECS
52 KEMPER INC & CAP PRESERV
53 LORD ABBETT US GOV SECS
54 FIDELITY GOVT SECS
55 BULLOCK MONTHLY INC SHS
56 SCUDDER INCOME FUND
57 EATON VANCE HIGH YIELD
57 KEYSTONE B-1
59 AGE HIGH INCOME FUND
60 PUTNAM INCOME FUND
61 KEYSTONE B-2
62 VANGUARD FIXED INC INVT
64 INVESTORS INCOME
64 NATIONWIDE BOND FUND
64 BABSON BOND TRUST
64 DREYFUS A BONDS PLUS
65 PRICE (ROWE) NEW INCOME
66 FIDELITY THRIFT TRUST
68 USAA MUTUAL FD INCOME
69 FIDELITY FLEXIBLE BOND

RANKED BY CDA RATING WITHIN
INVESTMENT OBJECTIVE – 12/31/86

CONTINUED - BOND & PREFERRED

70	NEL INCOME
70	COLONIAL INCOME
71	PILGRIM HIGH YIELD FD
71	LORD ABBETT BOND-DEBEN.
72	AMERICAN CAPITAL CORP BD
73	AMA INCOME FUND, INC.
75	HANCOCK (JOHN) BOND
76	AMEV US GOV SECURITIES
76	HIGH YIELD SECURITIES
77	KEYSTONE B-4
79	HANCOCK (JOHN) US GOV
79	FIRST INVEST. FD. INCOME
81	LUTHERAN BROTHER. INCOME
82	FIRST INVEST. BND APPREC
82	NICHOLAS INCOME FUND
85	MUTUAL OF OMAHA AMERICA
85	LEXINGTON GNMA NEW INC
86	NATL SECURITIES BOND
87	FRANKLIN U.S. GOVT. SEC.
87	LIBERTY FUND
88	FUND FOR U.S. GOVT. SEC.
88	OPPENHEIMER HIGH YIELD
89	AMERICAN INVS INCOME
90	NEWTON INCOME FUND
na	ALLIANCE CONVERTIBLE
na	ALLIANCE HIGH GRADE BOND
na	ALLIANCE HIGH YIELD BOND
na	ALLIANCE MORTGAGE SECS
na	AMERICAN CAP GOV SECS
na	AMERICAN CAPTL HIYLD INV
na	BENHAM GNMA INCOME FUND
na	BOSTON CO. MANAGED INC.
na	BULL & BEAR HIGH YIELD
na	BULLOCK HIGH INCOME SHS
na	CALVERT INCOME
na	CAPITAL PRESERVATION TNT
na	CARDINAL GOVERNMENT GTD
na	COLONIAL GOV MORTGAGE
na	COLONIAL GOV SEC PLUS TR
na	COLUMBIA FIXED INCOME FD
na	DEAN WITTER HIGH YIELD
na	DEAN WITTER TX ADVANTAGE
na	DEAN WITTER US GOV TRUST
na	DELAWARE GOV FD-USG SER
na	DELAWARE GOV FD-GNMA SER
na	DELAWARE TREAS RESERVES
na	DFA FIXED INC PORTFOLIO
na	DREXEL ST GOV SECURITIES
na	DREYFUS GNMA
na	EATON VANCE GOV OBLIGATN
na	FEDERATED CORP CASH TR
na	FEDERATED GNMA
na	FEDERATED HIGH INCOME
na	FEDERATED HIGH YIELD TR.
na	FEDERATED INCOME TRUST
na	FEDERATED INTERM. GOV.
na	FEDERATED SH-INTERM GOV
na	FIDELITY CORP TR-ARP

CONTINUED - BOND & PREFERRED

na	FIDELITY MORTGAGE SECS
na	FINANCIAL BD-HIYLD PORT
na	FINANCIAL BD-SELECT INC
na	FIRST INVEST. GOV FUND
na	FLAGSHIP CORPORATE CASH
na	FPA NEW INCOME
na	FRANKLIN CORP CASH TR
na	FTP-FIXED INC. LTD PORT.
na	FUNDTRUST INCOME
na	GENERAL ELEC S&S LT BOND
na	HANCOCK (JOHN) GNMA
na	HOME INVS GOV GTD INCOME
na	HUTTON INV SER BOND/INC
na	HUTTON INV SER GOV SECS
na	IDS EXTRA INCOME
na	INVEST. PORTFOLIOS-GOV +
na	INVEST. PORTFOLIOS-HIYLD
na	INVEST. QUALITY INTEREST
na	INV TR/BOSTON HI IN PLUS
na	JP INCOME
na	KIDDER P. GOVT INCOME
na	LG US GOV SECURITIES
na	MACKENZIE INDUSTRIAL GOV
na	MASS. FINL GOV SEC HIYLD
na	MASS. FINL INTL TRUST BD
na	MFS GOVT GUARANTEED
na	MFS GOV SECURITIES HIYLD
na	MERRILL L. CORP DIV FUND
na	MERRILL L. FEDERAL SECS
na	MERRILL L. HIGH INC BOND
na	MERRILL L. HIGH QUAL BD
na	MERRILL L. RETIRE/INCOME
na	MIDWEST INC-INTERMED TRM
na	NATL FEDERAL SECURITIES
na	NEL GOVERNMENT SEC TR
na	NODDING CALAMOS INCOME
na	NORTH STAR BOND
na	OPPENHEIMER RETR-GOV SEC
na	PACIFIC HORIZON HIYLD BD
na	PAINE WEBBER FI INVT GR
na	PAINE WEBBER GNMA
na	PAINE WEBBER HIGH YIELD
na	PILGRIM ADJUSTABLE RATE
na	PILGRIM GNMA
na	PILGRIM PREFERRED
na	PIONEER BOND FUND
na	PRICE (ROWE) HI YLD BOND
na	PRINCOR GOV SECS INCOME
na	PRU-BACHE ADJ RATE PFD
na	PRU-BACHE GOV SECURITIES
na	PRU-BACHE INCOMEVERTIBLE
na	PRU-BACHE GNMA FUND
na	PUTNAM CCT ARP
na	PUTNAM GNMA PLUS
na	PUTNAM HIGH INCOME GOV
na	PUTNAM US GOV SECURITIES
na	QUALIFIED DIVD PORT III
na	RETIREMENT PLANNING-BOND

CONTINUED - BOND & PREFERRED

na	SCUDDER GOV MORTGAGE SEC
na	SECURITY INC FD-CORP BD
na	SELIGMAN GOV GUARANTEED
na	SELIGMAN HIGH YIELD BOND
na	SELIGMAN SECURED MTG
na	SENTINEL BOND
na	SHEARSON HIGH YIELD
na	SHEARSON LG-TRM GOV SECS
na	SHEARSON MANAGED GOVTS
na	SHEARSON SPEC INTERM GOV
na	STEINROE HIGH-YIELD BOND
na	STEINROE MANAGED BOND FD
na	THOMSON MCKINNON INCOME
na	TWENTIETH CENTURY US GOV
na	UMB BOND FUND
na	UNITED GOV SECURITIES FD
na	U.S. GOV GUARANTEED SECS
na	US GOVT HIGH YIELD TRUST
na	VALUE LINE US GOV SECS
na	VAN KAMPEN MERRITT-GOV
na	VANGUARD FIXED INC GNMA
na	VANGUARD FI SECS-SH TERM
na	VENTURE INCOME PLUS
na	YES FUND

BALANCED

1	PHOENIX BALANCED FD SER
2	EVERGREEN TOTAL RETURN
3	MUTUAL QUALIFIED INCOME
6	QUALIFIED DIVD PORTF I
6	MUTUAL SHARES CORP.
9	NATL SECURITIES TOT INC
11	SMITH, BARNEY INC. & GR.
14	FRANKLIN INCOME
18	WELLESLEY INCOME FUND
19	FIDELITY PURITAN FD
21	SAFECO INCOME FUND
21	MASS. FINL TOTAL RETURN
23	SENTINEL BALANCED FUND
23	DREYFUS CONVERTIBLE SECS
24	SIGMA TRUST SHARES
26	INCOME FUND OF AMERICA
27	SELIGMAN INCOME FD
27	AXE-HOUGHTON FUND B
30	VALUE LINE INCOME
33	BULL & BEAR EQUITY INC.
36	AMERICAN BALANCED FUND
38	IDS MUTUAL FUND
38	FEDERATED STOCK & BOND
40	BULLOCK BALANCED SHARES
40	KEYSTONE K-1
40	EATON VANCE INC FD/BOST
41	PROVIDENT FD. FOR INCOME
43	WELLINGTON FUND
43	NATL SECURITIES BALANCED
43	COMMONWEALTH - PLANS A&B
44	PUTNAM (GEORGE) FD. BOS.

CONTINUED - BALANCED

44	DODGE & COX BALANCED
45	UNITED RETIREMENT SHARES
47	COLONIAL FUND
51	COMPOSITE BOND & STOCK
51	FOUNDERS EQUITY INCOME
60	EATON VANCE INVESTORS FD
69	COMMONWEALTH - PLAN C
74	COMMERCE INCOME SHARES
78	STEIN R&F TOTAL RETURN
88	ISI TRUST FUND
90	ISI INCOME FUND
93	CONTINENTAL MUTUAL INV.
na	CALVERT MANAGED GROWTH
na	COLONIAL CORP CASH I
na	COLONIAL CORP CASH II
na	FIDELITY QUALIFIED DIVD
na	MERRILL L. EQUI-BOND I
na	MERRILL L. PHOENIX
na	MERRILL L. RETIRE BEN IN
na	OLYMPIC TRUST TOT RETURN
na	PUTNAM CCT DSP
na	REA GRAHAM FUND
na	STRATTON MONTHLY DIV SHS
na	STRONG INVESTMENT FUND
na	STRONG TOTAL RETURN FUND
na	UNIFIED INCOME FUND
na	VANGUARD STAR FUND

METALS

50	INTERNATIONAL INVESTORS
58	FRANKLIN GOLD FUND
61	US GOLD SHARES FUND
63	STRATEGIC INVESTMENTS
97	GOLCONDA INVESTORS
na	COLONIAL ADV STRAT GOLD
na	FIDELITY SEL AMER GOLD
na	FIDELITY SEL PREC MET&MN
na	FREEDOM GOLD & GOV TRUST
na	HUTTON INV SER PRE METAL
na	KEYSTONE PRECIOUS METALS
na	LEXINGTON GOLDFUND
na	OPPENHEIMER GOLD & SPEC.
na	STRATEGIC SILVER
na	UNITED GOLD & GOVERNMENT
na	US NEW PROSPECTOR FUND
na	US PROSPECTOR FUND
na	VANGUARD SPEC PORT-GOLD

Quarterly Supplement

CDA QUARTERLY SUPPLEMENT – 12/31/86

FUND	IO	ASSETS (MIL$) 9/86	ANNL %EXP RATE	CASH	NON BOND	CVT PREF	CVTS	COMM STKS	TOTAL	PRINCIPAL
				PERCENT OF ASSETS					LATEST QTR ROR 9/86 – 12/86	
ABT EMERGING GROWTH	AG	34	1.40	3	0	0	0	97	-1.5	-1.5
ABT GROWTH & INCOME TR.	GI	116	1.35*	0	0	0	1	98	5.2	4.1
ABT SECURITY INCOME	GI	18	1.80	13	0	0	0	87	2.8	2.8
ABT UTILITY INCOME FD	GI	124	1.25*	1	0	2	0	97	1.5	0.2
ACORN FUND	G	395	na	8	2	0	5	85	8.6	8.6
AFFILIATED FUND	GI	3,008	0.32	3	0	0	7	90	6.3	5.2
AFUTURE FUND	AG	19	0.67	12	0	0	0	88	-2.2	-2.2
AGE HIGH INCOME FUND	BP	1,141	na	7	93	0	0	0	2.1	-1.1
ALLIANCE CONVERTIBLE	BP	62	na	na	na	na	na	na	2.1	0.5
ALLIANCE COUNTERPOINT	G	37	na	na	na	na	na	na	1.9	1.1
ALLIANCE HIGH GRADE BOND	BP	7	na	0	0	0	0	0	5.5	4.1
ALLIANCE HIGH YIELD BOND	BP	267	na	6	94	0	0	0	3.8	0.6
ALLIANCE INTERNATIONAL	IN	164	na	1	0	0	0	99	2.9	2.9
ALLIANCE MORTGAGE SECS	BP	737	na	0	100	0	0	0	3.2	0.6
ALLIANCE TECHNOLOGY	AG	133	na	15	0	0	0	84	9.6	9.6
ALPHA FUND	G	24	1.50	1	0	0	3	96	4.5	4.5
AMA GROWTH FUND, INC.	G	27	1.34	18	0	0	0	82	3.8	3.4
AMA INCOME FUND, INC.	BP	21	1.47	55	30	0	15	0	4.0	2.1
AMCAP FUND	G	1,385	0.52	19	0	0	0	80	4.8	4.8
AMERICAN BALANCED FUND	B	162	0.68	9	39	0	0	52	4.4	3.0
AMERICAN CAPITAL CORP BD	BP	118	0.72	3	95	0	2	0	3.7	0.8
AMERICAN CAP COMSTOCK	G	896	0.58	13	0	0	0	87	5.0	5.0
AMERICAN CAP ENTERPRISE	G	577	0.61	3	0	0	1	96	3.5	3.5
AMERICAN CAP GOV SECS	BP	8,068	0.67*	2	98	0	0	0	3.0	1.3
AMERICAN CAPITAL GROWTH	AG	26	0.91	0	0	0	3	97	-4.3	-4.3
AMERICAN CAPITAL HARBOR	GI	267	0.63	10	0	0	56	34	2.0	0.6
AMERICAN CAPTL HIYLD INV	BP	520	0.66	5	91	1	3	0	1.5	-1.7
AMERICAN CAPITAL PACE FD	G	2,133	0.58	9	1	0	0	90	3.9	3.9
AMERICAN CAPITAL OTC SEC	G	95	1.19	2	0	0	4	94	-5.0	-5.1
AMERICAN CAPITAL VENTURE	AG	335	0.71	13	0	0	16	71	1.4	0.0
AMERICAN CAPITAL MUNI BD	MB	159	0.72	4	96	0	0	0	4.5	2.6
AMERICAN GROWTH FUND	GI	65	na	50	0	0	0	50	1.2	1.2
AMERICAN HERITAGE FUND	AG	1	na	28	0	0	0	72	-4.3	-4.3
AMERICAN INVESTORS FUND	AG	67	na	4	0	0	5	91	0.7	0.7
AMERICAN INVS INCOME	BP	22	na	2	85	1	12	0	1.9	-1.1
AMERICAN LEADERS FUND	GI	116	1.00	27	0	0	0	73	3.1	2.2
AMERICAN MUTUAL FUND	GI	1,992	0.45	33	2	0	1	64	4.3	3.3
AMERICAN NATIONAL GROWTH	AG	90	0.95	9	0	0	0	91	5.3	4.6
AMERICAN NATL INC FUND	GI	60	0.90	28	0	0	8	64	2.2	1.4
AMERICAN TELECOMM TR GR	G	40	0.90	1	0	0	1	99	4.0	4.0
AMERICAN TELECOMM TR INC	GI	97	0.87	2	0	0	19	79	1.6	0.7
AMEV CAPITAL FUND, INC.	G	98	0.90	17	0	0	0	83	3.7	3.5
AMEV GROWTH FUND, INC.	AG	149	0.86	15	0	0	0	85	2.5	2.5
AMEV SPECIAL FUND, INC.	AG	23	1.10	9	0	0	0	91	3.5	3.5
AMEV US GOV SECURITIES	BP	63	1.13	12	88	0	0	0	2.4	0.1
AMWAY MUTUAL FUND	G	35	1.10	6	0	0	0	94	4.5	3.7
ANALYTIC OPTIONED EQUITY	GI	83	1.23	14	0	0	0	86	4.7	4.0
ARMSTRONG ASSOCIATES	G	12	2.00	5	0	0	0	95	0.0	-1.7
AXE-HOUGHTON INCOME	BP	46	1.49*	4	96	0	0	0	5.1	2.8
AXE-HOUGHTON FUND B	B	182	1.19*	18	38	0	0	44	6.0	4.6

| 36 MONTH MPT STATISTICS | | | | | DISTRIBUTION INFORMATION | | | | | | | | |
R2	STD DEV	BETA	ALPHA PCNT	RK	12/86 N.A.V.	INCOME OCT	NOV	DEC	12 MON	CAPITAL GAIN OCT	NOV	DEC	12 MON
78	6.06	1.27	-3.0	59	8.77				0.000				0.000
84	3.86	0.85	-0.8	50	11.34		.160		0.460		2.70		2.700
68	2.60	0.52	-3.0	59	11.10				0.100				0.760
45	4.05	0.65	4.5	23	14.98		.190		0.870		.110		0.330
73	3.72	0.76	3.0	32	39.27				0.500			4.10	6.320
96	4.00	0.94	0.7	43	10.50		.130		0.550		1.14		1.140
83	5.09	1.10	-18.5	96	12.49				0.108				0.000
38	1.62	0.24	2.9	33	3.67	.041	.041	.036	0.487				0.000
na	na	na	na	na	9.48			.151	na				na
na	na	na	na	na	14.11	.123			0.263	.315			0.315
na	na	na	na	na	12.15	.056	.054	.054	0.792				0.000
na	na	na	na	na	9.71	.103	.103	.103	1.324				0.094
na	na	na	na	na	21.07				0.033				2.752
na	na	na	na	na	9.74	.084	.084	.084	1.063				0.205
72	7.26	1.45	-14.5	93	23.11				0.012				0.000
79	4.23	0.90	-6.1	74	6.97				0.226			.620	0.923
90	4.28	0.97	-4.2	65	10.56	.045			0.155	1.78			1.785
39	1.50	0.23	2.8	33	9.41	.175			0.695				0.000
86	4.28	0.95	-5.1	70	9.63				0.190			.600	1.250
94	3.01	0.70	2.7	34	10.83		.160		0.640			.920	2.020
32	1.92	0.26	4.5	23	7.29	.068	.068	.068	0.816				0.000
87	4.14	0.92	-6.2	74	14.60				0.383			1.30	1.788
93	5.37	1.23	-8.5	83	12.78				0.268			1.01	2.650
na	na	na	na	na	11.69	.060	.065	.065	0.933	.085	.035	.035	0.603
76	5.19	1.08	-15.2	94	22.86				0.098				5.783
88	3.42	0.77	-4.5	67	13.43		.210		0.840			.930	1.560
33	1.90	0.26	2.5	35	9.79	.108	.108	.108	1.338	.010			0.010
92	4.19	0.96	-6.4	75	22.56				0.650				0.835
75	5.74	1.17	-17.5	96	8.30		.015		0.015		.905		0.905
87	5.09	1.12	-13.7	92	14.55	.225			0.225	.295			0.295
na	na	na	na	na	21.23	.130	.130	.130	1.560				0.000
58	4.12	0.75	-8.4	82	7.57				0.290				1.090
43	5.32	0.83	-32.4	99	1.42				0.000			.360	0.360
89	5.55	1.24	-21.1	98	6.45				0.000			.600	0.600
40	2.37	0.37	-4.6	67	8.85			.270	1.110				0.000
85	3.36	0.74	1.7	38	12.49		.120		0.500			.621	0.621
93	3.55	0.82	1.3	40	17.99	.190			0.740			1.22	2.080
88	5.58	1.24	-11.4	89	4.59		.034		0.061		.439		0.439
84	3.74	0.82	-4.8	68	19.11		.156		0.752				2.030
na	na	na	na	na	77.36				2.270			13.82	23.700
na	na	na	na	na	99.20	.450		.450	4.940				0.000
86	4.69	1.04	-2.8	58	13.73			.015	0.130				1.060
87	5.29	1.17	-5.1	70	16.37				0.154				0.590
88	5.55	1.23	-4.8	68	24.80				0.140				1.230
16	1.58	0.15	4.7	21	10.36	.080	.080	.080	1.002				0.000
94	4.44	1.03	-5.9	73	7.82			.060	0.120				0.000
93	2.52	0.59	-2.3	56	13.70			.100	0.449			1.51	2.195
83	3.93	0.86	-9.2	85	7.99	.160			0.160	.510			0.510
28	2.61	0.33	7.3	5	5.60	.125			0.500				0.000
77	3.40	0.72	4.8	21	11.10	.180			0.660			2.08	2.940

CDA QUARTERLY SUPPLEMENT – 12/31/86

FUND	IO	ASSETS (MIL$) 9/86	ANNL %EXP RATE	CASH	NON CVT BOND	PREF	CVTS	COMM STKS	TOTAL	PRINCIPAL
AXE-HOUGHTON STOCK FUND	AG	92	1.40*	5	0	0	0	95	4.8	4.8
BABSON GROWTH FUND	G	236	na	2	0	0	0	98	5.3	4.2
BABSON BOND TRUST	BP	65	na	5	95	0	0	0	3.5	1.2
BABSON ENTERPRISE FUND	G	48	na	5	0	0	0	95	2.2	1.7
BABSON VALUE FD INC.	G	6	na	7	4	0	1	88	4.2	0.5
BARTLETT BASIC VALUE FD	GI	67	1.56	9	12	0	0	79	-0.8	-1.8
BASCOM HILL INVESTORS	GI	7	1.20	32	2	0	5	61	2.6	2.6
BEACON HILL MUTUAL FUND	G	3	3.50	8	0	0	0	92	4.7	4.7
BENHAM CALIF TF-INTERMED	MB	135	0.01	3	97	0	0	0	2.4	0.9
BENHAM CALIF TF-LONG TRM	MB	194	0.01	2	98	0	0	0	3.6	1.9
BENHAM GNMA INCOME FUND	BP	256	0.75	1	99	0	0	0	3.3	1.1
BOND FUND OF AMERICA	BP	598	0.60	6	94	0	0	0	4.9	2.4
BOSTON CO. CAP. APPREC.	G	422	na	2	14	0	1	82	6.3	5.7
BOSTON CO. MANAGED INC.	BP	37	0.50	2	98	0	0	0	3.3	0.8
BOSTON CO. SPEC GROWTH	G	40	0.10	0	0	0	9	91	2.1	2.1
BOWSER GROWTH FUND	G	3	3.31	12	0	0	0	88	-9.9	-9.9
BRUCE FUND	AG	3	2.60	6	48	0	0	46	-0.4	-0.4
BULL & BEAR CAP GROWTH	G	63	2.41*	5	0	0	1	94	2.0	2.0
BULL & BEAR EQUITY INC.	B	9	3.14*	1	12	0	46	41	3.1	2.4
BULL & BEAR HIGH YIELD	BP	151	1.88*	1	99	0	0	0	0.0	-3.1
BULLOCK AGGRES GROWTH SH	AG	6	na	10	0	0	1	89	3.5	3.5
BULLOCK BALANCED SHARES	B	79	na	17	29	1	0	53	2.2	1.2
BULLOCK DIVIDEND SHARES	GI	345	na	9	0	0	5	86	5.2	4.3
BULLOCK GROWTH SHARES	G	159	na	3	0	0	0	97	0.7	0.5
BULLOCK HIGH INCOME SHS	BP	204	na	1	99	0	0	0	0.9	-2.5
BULLOCK MONTHLY INC SHS	BP	45	na	6	94	0	0	0	5.1	2.9
BULLOCK TAX-FREE SHARES	MB	111	na	3	97	0	0	0	3.7	1.8
CALVERT EQUITY	G	8	na	11	0	0	0	89	-0.1	-0.9
CALVERT INCOME	BP	21	na	2	95	0	0	3	2.1	0.2
CALVERT MANAGED GROWTH	B	88	na	16	21	0	0	63	3.2	1.9
CANADIAN FUND	G	23	na	7	0	0	2	91	3.4	3.2
CAPITAL PRESERVATION TNT	BP	36	0.50	4	96	0	0	0	3.6	2.1
CARNEGIE CAPPIELLO GROW	G	48	1.46	7	0	0	4	89	1.3	1.3
CARDINAL FUND	G	85	na	18	0	0	0	82	2.5	1.2
CARDINAL GOVERNMENT GTD	BP	127	na	6	94	0	0	0	2.1	-0.4
CASHMAN FARRELL VALUE FD	G	6	1.50	38	3	0	3	56	0.1	-0.9
CENTURY SHARES TRUST	G	150	0.38	4	2	0	0	94	-1.8	-3.2
CHARTER FUND	G	79	1.10*	25	0	0	0	75	3.8	3.8
CHEAPSIDE DOLLAR FD LTD	G	46	1.30	2	0	0	0	98	3.1	3.1
CHEMICAL FUND	G	677	0.63	2	0	1	0	96	3.5	3.5
CIGNA AGGRESSIVE GROWTH	AG	17	1.18	10	0	0	0	90	6.0	6.0
CIGNA GROWTH FUND	G	214	1.06*	10	0	0	0	90	2.7	2.7
CIGNA HIGH YIELD	BP	246	1.15*	4	96	0	0	0	1.7	-1.1
CIGNA INCOME FUND	BP	254	0.87*	7	91	0	2	0	4.1	2.2
CIGNA MUNICIPAL BOND FD	MB	258	0.80*	5	95	0	0	0	4.5	2.7
CIGNA VALUE FUND	G	44	1.06*	13	0	0	0	87	4.5	4.5
CLIPPER FUND, INC.	GI	67	na	4	46	0	0	50	3.5	3.5
COLONIAL ADV STRAT GOLD	ME	29	1.28*	7	20	0	0	73	4.8	4.8
COLONIAL EQUITY INC TR	G	11	1.50	15	11	0	0	74	3.5	2.9
COLONIAL GOV MORTGAGE	BP	27	na	30	70	0	0	0	2.4	1.0

36 MONTH MPT STATISTICS					DISTRIBUTION INFORMATION								
	STD		ALPHA		12/86	INCOME				CAPITAL GAIN			
R2	DEV	BETA	PCNT	RK	N.A.V.	OCT	NOV	DEC	12 MON	OCT	NOV	DEC	12 MON
88	5.62	1.25	-11.6	90	8.11				0.040			1.74	1.800
93	4.25	0.98	-1.8	54	12.95		.150		0.503			.600	1.973
22	1.30	0.15	6.1	9	1.69		.038		0.158				0.000
71	5.09	1.02	-5.3	71	12.12		.068		0.068			1.26	1.530
na	na	na	na	na	14.64		.565		0.905		.135		0.145
60	2.25	0.42	2.9	33	12.20		.130		0.780			.550	0.980
78	2.99	0.64	0.6	44	15.11				0.695			3.14	4.958
83	4.23	0.92	-3.2	60	24.65				0.000				0.000
19	1.64	0.18	1.0	42	10.67	.054	.050	.050	0.672				0.000
27	2.52	0.32	2.9	33	11.50	.066	.063	.063	0.803				0.087
na	na	na	na	na	10.45	.076	.076	.076	1.025				0.000
35	1.73	0.25	6.8	6	14.21	.120	.120	.120	1.440			.400	0.400
93	3.88	0.89	3.2	31	32.42	.200			0.500			2.74	5.780
25	1.35	0.17	6.3	8	11.91	.101	.098	.098	1.424				0.140
80	5.23	1.11	-8.9	84	17.21				0.310			3.50	4.960
na	na	na	na	na	1.82				0.000				0.000
42	5.85	0.90	5.3	15	109.39				1.290				0.000
91	4.98	1.13	-9.7	86	10.37				0.200			4.22	5.910
85	2.58	0.58	3.1	32	11.03			.080	0.380			.740	2.010
30	1.68	0.22	0.9	43	13.57	.146	.147	.148	1.841				0.015
59	4.96	0.91	-17.7	96	9.41				0.000				0.000
84	2.90	0.64	7.3	5	14.81		.150		0.670				0.530
97	3.85	0.91	1.7	38	3.53	.035			0.125	.400			0.400
93	4.30	0.99	-3.7	63	7.74		.030		0.130		2.84		2.840
17	1.48	0.15	-0.3	47	9.93	.121	.104	.120	1.395				0.000
23	2.25	0.26	6.1	9	12.62	.090	.090	.090	1.170				0.000
29	2.15	0.28	3.8	27	11.19	.071	.064	.070	0.851				0.000
87	4.64	1.03	-9.0	84	19.89	.174			0.174	2.14			2.140
20	2.44	0.26	5.6	12	16.98	.094	.127	.100	1.467	.086			0.086
82	2.94	0.64	2.2	37	23.48	.289			0.629	.218			0.218
32	3.62	0.49	-7.3	79	7.14		.020		0.170		1.20		1.200
21	1.51	0.17	5.3	15	11.04	.056	.054	.054	0.956			.543	0.853
na	na	na	na	na	14.01				0.380				0.690
92	3.66	0.84	1.6	39	14.64	.190			0.370	1.08			1.080
na	na	na	na	na	9.35	.084	.080	.076	na				na
na	na	na	na	na	10.01		.100		na		.040		na
71	5.07	1.01	2.7	34	18.30		.270		0.510			.400	1.110
91	4.33	0.99	-5.5	72	6.22				0.170			1.86	2.375
94	5.04	1.16	-7.8	81	12.45				0.240				0.730
95	5.16	1.19	-7.7	80	6.87				0.095			2.03	5.163
na	na	na	na	na	12.10				0.075			.220	0.490
96	4.23	0.99	-5.1	70	12.91				0.350			2.46	3.520
30	1.41	0.19	6.0	10	10.54	.100	.100	.100	1.235				0.000
38	1.98	0.29	6.5	7	8.20	.050	.050	.050	0.643				0.000
32	2.25	0.31	5.5	14	8.41	.050	.048	.048	0.601			.260	0.260
na	na	na	na	na	12.26				0.430			1.02	1.320
na	na	na	na	na	41.55				0.000			1.41	1.410
na	na	na	na	na	17.99				0.148				0.432
86	4.24	0.94	-2.7	58	15.81		.100		0.490			1.60	3.210
na	na	na	na	na	14.36	.070	.065	.065	1.055	.070	.075		0.465

CDA QUARTERLY SUPPLEMENT – 12/31/86

FUND	IO	ASSETS (MIL$) 9/86	ANNL %EXP RATE	CASH	NON CVT BOND	PREF	CVTS	COMM STKS	TOTAL	PRINCIPAL
COLONIAL FUND	B	159	1.05	2	16	0	0	82	3.6	2.5
COLONIAL CORP CASH I	B	407	1.03*	5	0	25	0	70	2.5	0.6
COLONIAL CORP CASH II	B	318	1.17*	5	0	77	0	18	1.1	-0.4
COLONIAL GOV SEC PLUS TR	BP	2,800	1.14*	7	93	0	0	0	3.5	1.8
COLONIAL GROWTH SHARES	G	75	1.25	9	0	0	1	90	4.9	4.5
COLONIAL INCOME	BP	153	0.94	3	97	0	0	0	3.3	0.4
COLONIAL OPTION INC I	GI	1,113	0.93	3	0	0	0	97	4.1	3.7
COLONIAL OPTION INC II	GI	200	1.03	8	14	0	0	78	5.5	4.9
COLONIAL HIGH YIELD SECS	BP	401	1.08	5	95	0	0	0	3.2	0.4
COLONIAL TAX EXEMPT HIYD	MB	1,258	1.11*	4	96	0	0	0	3.1	1.1
COLONIAL TAX EX INSURED	MB	87	0.86*	3	96	0	0	0	2.3	0.6
COLUMBIA FIXED INCOME FD	BP	115	0.79	4	96	0	0	0	4.1	1.9
COLUMBIA GROWTH FUND	G	209	0.99	5	0	0	0	95	4.7	4.7
COLUMBIA MUNICIPAL BOND	MB	100	0.64	3	97	0	0	0	2.5	0.9
COLUMBIA SPECIAL FUND	AG	21	na	1	0	0	0	99	-1.1	-1.1
COMMERCE INCOME SHARES	B	59	0.83*	6	32	0	0	62	4.7	4.7
COMMONWEALTH - PLANS A&B	B	10	na	3	27	0	7	63	4.4	2.9
COMMONWEALTH - PLAN C	B	40	na	5	30	0	6	59	3.9	2.6
COMPANION FUND	G	77	0.49	10	0	0	0	90	2.5	2.5
COMPOSITE BOND & STOCK	B	76	na	4	50	0	0	45	1.5	0.2
COMPOSITE FUND	G	68	na	19	21	0	0	60	1.8	0.9
CONCORD FUND	GI	2	na	24	0	0	0	76	-1.2	-3.9
CONSTELLATION GROWTH	AG	76	1.18	0	0	0	0	100	9.7	9.7
CONTINENTAL MUTUAL INV.	B	1	na	0	0	0	0	0	1.8	1.8
CONVERTIBLE YIELD	GI	18	1.50	3	0	0	96	0	0.1	-1.4
COPLEY TAX-MANAGED FUND	G	31	1.40	15	0	0	15	70	0.2	0.2
COUNTRY CAPITAL GROWTH	G	67	0.95	13	0	0	0	87	4.0	4.0
CRITERION QUAL TX FR INS	MB	128	na	na	na	na	na	na	4.4	2.2
DEAN WITTER CALIF TX FR	MB	316	na	0	0	0	0	0	2.7	1.3
DEAN WITTER DEVELOP GROW	G	140	1.80*	15	1	0	0	84	3.8	3.6
DEAN WITTER DIVIDEND GRO	GI	1,024	1.46*	6	13	0	0	81	4.0	3.2
DEAN WITTER HIGH YIELD	BP	1,391	na	0	0	0	0	0	3.1	-0.1
DEAN WITTER INDUSTRY VAL	G	71	1.34*	5	11	0	1	83	4.2	3.6
DEAN WITTER OPTION INC	GI	589	na	0	0	0	0	0	5.2	5.0
DEAN WITTER NAT RESOURCE	G	53	1.68*	12	0	0	0	88	4.2	4.2
DEAN WITTER NY TX FR INC	MB	101	na	0	0	0	0	0	3.5	2.0
DEAN WITTER TX ADVANTAGE	BP	303	na	0	0	0	0	0	0.7	-1.0
DEAN WITTER TAX EX SECS	MB	838	na	0	0	0	0	0	2.6	0.7
DEAN WITTER US GOV TRUST	BP	10,291	na	0	0	0	0	0	2.3	0.1
DEAN WITTER WORLDWIDE	IN	346	na	0	0	0	0	0	5.8	5.8
DECATUR FUND INC-SER 1	GI	1,076	0.62	6	2	4	4	84	5.9	4.8
DELAWARE FUND	G	394	0.67	9	2	2	0	87	0.8	0.0
DELAWARE GOV FD-USG SER	BP	40	na	2	98	0	0	0	2.6	0.2
DELAWARE GOV FD-GNMA SER	BP	43	na	0	100	0	0	0	2.2	-0.3
DELAWARE TREAS RESERVES	BP	59	0.93	0	100	0	0	0	1.3	-0.6
DELCHESTER BOND FUND	BP	191	0.79	11	89	0	0	0	3.5	0.4
DELTA TREND FUND	AG	75	1.09	13	0	5	0	82	2.0	2.0
DEPOSITORS FUND/BOSTON	G	57	0.77	4	0	0	0	95	8.0	7.5
DE VEGH MUTUAL FUND	G	53	0.63*	9	0	0	0	91	2.4	1.5
DFA FIXED INC PORTFOLIO	BP	312	na	44	56	0	0	0	1.7	0.0

R2	STD DEV	BETA	ALPHA PCNT	RK	12/86 N.A.V.	OCT	NOV	DEC	12 MON	OCT	NOV	DEC	12 MON
93	2.90	0.67	3.2	31	17.80		.200		0.800		1.32		1.317
72	1.85	0.38	1.5	39	49.16	.230	.340	.350	4.403	.200	.100	.060	0.570
na	na	na	na	na	47.71	.240	.240	.240	3.540	.070	.070	.070	0.310
na	na	na	na	na	12.72	.075	.070	.070	0.995	.125	.030	.020	0.545
88	4.67	1.05	-4.2	65	13.20	.050			0.090				0.536
23	1.67	0.19	4.8	21	7.23			.210	0.810				0.000
89	3.60	0.81	-5.8	73	7.58		.030		0.170		.245		0.930
na	na	na	na	na	10.47			.070	0.280			.310	1.240
21	1.37	0.16	5.8	11	7.69	.075	.070	.070	0.935				0.000
22	2.80	0.32	-0.6	48	13.73	.088	.088	.088	0.981				0.000
na	na	na	na	na	7.94	.045	.045	.045	0.540				0.000
15	1.77	0.16	5.1	18	13.37	.094	.094	.094	1.230				0.000
93	5.19	1.19	-8.5	83	22.88				0.400			3.92	6.480
na	na	na	na	na	11.75	.066	.063	.063	0.834				0.000
na	na	na	na	na	26.97				0.000			.740	0.740
76	3.41	0.71	-1.6	53	9.96				0.300				0.880
94	3.12	0.73	-1.0	51	1.49	.024			0.091			.167	0.260
92	2.95	0.68	-1.9	54	2.08	.027			0.105			.168	0.291
95	4.24	0.99	-4.9	69	13.37				0.380				1.250
76	2.51	0.53	-0.4	48	10.02		.140		0.600		.710		0.710
70	3.66	0.73	-3.1	60	10.95	.110			0.450	1.21		.460	1.670
58	1.85	0.34	-4.2	65	26.63		.760		0.760				0.000
82	7.09	1.52	-10.2	87	21.16				0.000		6.75		6.750
61	2.30	0.44	-5.7	73	6.79				0.234				0.000
83	3.26	0.71	-7.1	78	11.73		.180		0.660		.120		0.490
50	3.09	0.52	7.9	4	11.02				0.000				0.000
91	4.72	1.07	-5.6	72	15.92				0.600				2.850
34	2.59	0.36	3.4	29	11.40	.060	.060	.119	0.793				0.000
na	na	na	na	na	12.25	.066	.051	.051	0.749				0.235
84	4.94	1.08	-16.1	95	8.88	.012			0.012				0.000
95	3.24	0.76	3.3	31	18.48			.130	0.520			.330	0.476
41	1.54	0.24	5.0	19	14.08	.150	.150	.150	1.800				0.000
92	4.43	1.02	-6.0	73	12.64	.080			0.315			1.74	1.745
na	na	na	na	na	9.59	.020			0.185	.253			1.073
56	4.64	0.83	-11.1	89	7.96				0.216				0.000
na	na	na	na	na	11.57	.062	.055	.055	0.708				0.008
na	na	na	na	na	10.29	.066	.055	.055	0.748				0.000
23	2.47	0.28	4.9	20	11.49	.072	.072	.072	0.873				0.288
na	na	na	na	na	10.33	.082	.072	.074	1.007				0.000
54	3.48	0.62	6.6	6	15.44				0.089			1.48	1.976
92	3.71	0.85	2.1	37	16.86		.200		0.800			2.00	2.000
86	4.24	0.94	-3.1	60	18.34			.160	0.550		4.31		4.310
na	na	na	na	na	9.22	.072	.075	.075	0.903				0.080
na	na	na	na	na	9.27	.075	.077	.077	0.940				0.045
na	na	na	na	na	9.97	.065	.061	.061	0.833				0.000
28	1.82	0.23	5.0	19	8.05	.083	.083	.083	1.018				0.000
74	6.08	1.23	-15.2	94	7.18				0.000				0.000
90	4.34	0.98	-3.7	63	54.34	.250			1.040				0.000
90	4.91	1.10	-8.8	83	12.80	.130			0.274			1.60	2.890
2	0.48	0.02	2.9	33	101.90	.570	.580	.530	7.620			.790	0.790

CDA QUARTERLY SUPPLEMENT - 12/31/86

FUND	IO	ASSETS (MIL$) 9/86	ANNL %EXP RATE	PERCENT OF ASSETS					LATEST QTR ROR 9/86 - 12/86	
				CASH	BOND	NON CVT PREF	CVTS	COMM STKS	TOTAL	PRINCIPAL
DFA SMALL CO. PORTFOLIO	G	927	na	2	0	0	0	98	0.4	-0.7
DIVERSIFICATION FUND	G	60	0.77	4	0	0	0	96	4.8	4.4
DIVIDEND/GROWTH FD., INC	GI	4	na	2	0	0	0	98	5.1	4.2
DMC TAX FREE-PA	MB	304	0.07	0	100	0	0	0	3.8	2.0
DMC TAX FREE-USA	MB	265	0.08	0	100	0	0	0	5.4	3.6
DMC TAX FREE-INSURED	MB	36	na	na	na	na	na	na	3.8	2.2
DODGE & COX BALANCED	B	26	na	5	29	0	0	66	6.4	5.2
DODGE & COX STOCK	GI	43	na	4	0	0	0	96	7.5	6.8
DOUBLE EXEMPT FLEX FUND	MB	89	0.88	1	99	0	0	0	3.8	2.0
DREXEL BURNHAM FUND	GI	133	1.00	11	18	0	8	62	6.6	5.7
DREXEL ST GOV SECURITIES	BP	334	na	4	95	0	0	1	4.1	2.4
DREXEL ST OPTION INC FD	GI	36	2.99*	16	0	0	12	72	5.6	5.3
DREXEL ST EMERG GROWTH	G	38	na	12	0	0	0	88	-5.7	-5.7
DREXEL ST GROWTH	G	22	na	5	0	0	0	95	6.8	6.2
DREYFUS A BONDS PLUS	BP	241	0.87	3	97	0	0	0	4.2	2.1
DREYFUS CALIF TAX EXEMPT	MB	1,158	0.72	8	92	0	0	0	4.1	2.4
DREYFUS CONVERTIBLE SECS	B	172	0.85	31	25	0	21	23	2.1	0.8
DREYFUS FUND	GI	2,316	0.75	27	9	0	0	64	3.0	2.4
DREYFUS GNMA	BP	1,936	1.16*	0	100	0	0	0	3.2	1.0
DREYFUS GROWTH OPPORTUN.	G	416	0.98	2	0	0	0	98	3.8	3.8
DREYFUS INSURED TAX EX	MB	177	0.93*	3	97	0	0	0	3.3	1.7
DREYFUS INTERMDIATE MUNI	MB	1,060	0.75	2	98	0	0	0	3.9	2.2
DREYFUS LEVERAGE	GI	486	0.94	18	2	0	0	80	4.7	2.1
DREYFUS MASS TAX EXEMPT	MB	68	0.26	4	96	0	0	0	3.5	1.9
DREYFUS NY TAX EXEMPT	MB	1,424	0.71	2	98	0	0	0	4.0	2.3
DREYFUS TAX EXEMPT BOND	MB	3,540	0.68	4	96	0	0	0	4.2	2.4
DREYFUS THIRD CENTURY	GI	156	0.97	31	0	1	0	68	1.2	1.2
EAGLE GROWTH SHARES	G	4	na	23	0	0	0	77	0.4	0.3
EATON & HOWARD STOCK	GI	80	0.86	9	0	0	0	91	3.9	3.0
EATON VANCE GROWTH FD	G	73	0.91	1	0	0	0	99	4.6	4.6
EATON VANCE GOV OBLIGATN	BP	384	1.58	0	100	0	0	0	3.3	0.8
EATON VANCE HIGH YIELD	BP	32	0.98	7	93	0	0	0	3.8	0.9
EATON VANCE INC FD/BOST	B	43	1.18	7	70	0	0	23	4.8	2.2
EATON VANCE INVESTORS FD	B	219	0.89	7	31	0	0	62	2.5	1.2
EATON VANCE MUNICIPAL BD	MB	49	0.81	5	95	0	0	0	4.3	2.4
EATON VANCE SPL EQUITIES	G	40	0.96	2	0	0	0	98	1.0	1.0
EATON VANCE TOTAL RETURN	GI	570	1.54	0	0	0	0	100	2.6	1.4
ELFUN TRUSTS	GI	480	na	9	4	0	5	82	4.9	4.9
ENERGY FUND	GI	376	na	8	15	0	0	77	2.8	2.8
EQUITEC SIEBEL TOTAL RET	GI	76	2.50*	25	10	0	0	64	2.8	2.4
EUROPACIFIC GROWTH FUND	IN	160	1.57*	25	3	0	1	70	8.4	8.4
EVERGREEN FUND	AG	639	1.04	2	0	0	0	98	-0.6	-0.6
EVERGREEN TOTAL RETURN	B	794	na	10	0	0	14	76	1.6	0.4
EXPLORER FUND	AG	266	0.80	0	0	0	2	98	1.6	1.6
EXPLORER II	AG	34	1.06	10	0	0	0	90	0.0	-0.2
FAIRFIELD FUND	AG	44	na	0	0	0	0	100	7.8	7.8
FAIRMONT FUND	G	72	na	2	0	0	0	98	3.9	3.4
FARM BUREAU GROWTH FUND	G	42	0.99	7	0	0	0	93	6.8	6.8
FEDERATED CORP CASH TR	BP	131	0.90*	1	0	99	0	0	0.5	-1.0
FEDERATED GNMA	BP	1,348	0.51	0	100	0	0	0	2.7	0.3

| 36 MONTH MPT STATISTICS | | | | | DISTRIBUTION INFORMATION | | | | | | | | |
R2	STD DEV	BETA	ALPHA PCNT	RK	12/86 N.A.V.	INCOME OCT	NOV	DEC	12 MON	CAPITAL GAIN OCT	NOV	DEC	12 MON
83	4.24	0.92	-8.7	83	8.70		.102		0.102		.652		0.652
88	4.12	0.92	-4.0	64	89.37			.370	1.570				0.000
91	3.80	0.86	-4.7	68	24.79		.200		1.500				1.680
29	1.80	0.24	4.9	20	8.05	.048	.047	.047	0.591				0.000
na	na	na	na	na	11.78	.059	.072	.072	0.874				0.263
na	na	na	na	na	10.90	.058	.058	.058	0.757				0.000
93	3.03	0.70	2.7	34	32.62		.380		1.615		1.76		3.555
95	4.19	0.98	1.5	39	31.66		.220		0.940		1.30		3.900
na	na	na	na	na	11.85	.074	.064	.070	0.881				0.086
93	3.22	0.75	3.9	27	21.28	.200			0.800			2.18	4.234
na	na	na	na	na	10.70	.060	.060	.060	1.015	.090			0.255
na	na	na	na	na	10.12	.040			0.410	.260		.220	1.060
na	na	na	na	na	12.63				0.000				0.170
na	na	na	na	na	11.80	.070			0.560			.500	0.690
24	1.94	0.23	5.8	11	14.99	.108	.105	.105	1.334			.250	0.250
13	2.29	0.20	3.4	30	15.47	.094	.080	.080	1.082				0.000
59	2.33	0.44	5.5	14	8.87	.040	.035	.040	0.550			.200	0.850
87	3.70	0.83	-1.6	53	12.55	.070			0.590			.950	2.700
na	na	na	na	na	15.70	.106	.106	.115	1.466				0.000
72	3.84	0.79	-5.2	70	10.50				0.205			1.50	2.700
na	na	na	na	na	18.40	.105	.094	.094	1.268				0.000
34	1.47	0.21	2.8	34	14.12	.083	.072	.072	0.983				0.000
80	3.36	0.72	3.1	32	16.23		.520		0.520		4.73		4.730
na	na	na	na	na	16.75	.093	.085	.085	1.152				0.000
32	2.26	0.31	3.8	27	15.89	.093	.083	.083	1.112				0.000
31	1.96	0.27	4.2	25	13.01	.080	.072	.072	0.963				0.000
82	3.80	0.82	-4.5	66	6.51				0.310				0.960
69	4.14	0.82	-14.9	94	6.83			.010	0.010			.080	0.080
94	3.70	0.86	2.2	37	13.49	.130			0.580			1.15	2.640
89	4.47	1.01	-4.0	64	6.84				0.140				0.800
na	na	na	na	na	12.36	.100	.100	.100	1.200	.050			0.250
24	1.69	0.20	6.6	6	5.32	.150			0.600				0.000
54	1.80	0.32	6.4	8	10.23			.260	1.040				0.000
93	2.97	0.69	-0.6	49	7.64		.100		0.470			.550	1.510
27	2.39	0.30	5.1	19	9.25	.055	.055	.055	0.681				0.000
76	5.32	1.10	-14.6	94	16.15				0.050		1.85		1.850
38	4.76	0.70	12.0	2	10.67	.140			0.400		1.12		1.145
96	4.11	0.96	0.1	46	27.49				0.990		2.55		4.190
75	3.43	0.71	-2.5	57	18.47				0.880				1.660
na	na	na	na	na	13.32			.050	0.205				0.019
na	na	na	na	na	24.58				0.170		.700		1.250
86	3.91	0.87	-1.4	52	12.47				0.140		1.00		1.657
79	2.80	0.60	6.9	5	19.18	.082	.079	.080	1.081			.350	1.109
61	4.91	0.91	-17.7	96	27.66		.020		0.020		3.27		3.270
na	na	na	na	na	18.99		.040		0.040		.470		0.470
83	6.75	1.45	-13.1	92	8.28				0.090				2.680
81	4.25	0.91	1.0	41	49.50			.300	0.585		5.56		11.556
93	4.64	1.06	-8.0	82	14.19				0.400				1.730
na	na	na	na	na	10.66	.054	.054	.055	0.727				0.000
6	1.71	0.10	5.5	14	11.43	.090	.090	.091	1.121				0.025

CDA QUARTERLY SUPPLEMENT – 12/31/86

FUND	IO	ASSETS (MIL$) 9/86	ANNL %EXP RATE	CASH	NON BOND	CVT PREF	CVTS	COMM STKS	TOTAL	PRINCIPAL
FEDERATED GROWTH TRUST	G	59	1.00*	4	0	0	0	95	5.4	5.0
FEDERATED HIGH INCOME	BP	360	1.04	5	95	0	0	0	1.7	-1.2
FEDERATED HIGH YIELD TR.	BP	159	0.75*	5	95	0	0	0	2.8	-0.1
FEDERATED INCOME TRUST	BP	568	0.53	2	98	0	0	0	2.8	0.5
FEDERATED INTERM. GOV.	BP	1,412	0.45	3	97	0	0	0	2.3	0.3
FEDERATED INTMED MUNI TR	MB	70	0.42	2	97	0	0	0	4.0	2.5
FEDERATED SH-INTERM GOV	BP	3,696	0.45	2	98	0	0	0	1.6	-0.4
FEDERATED SH-INTERM MUNI	MB	461	0.46	73	27	0	0	0	2.1	0.9
FEDERATED STOCK & BOND	B	68	1.00	15	49	0	0	36	2.9	1.6
FEDERATED STOCK TRUST	GI	450	0.92*	2	0	0	0	98	0.6	-0.1
FEDERATED TAX FR INCOME	MB	305	0.95	1	99	0	0	0	3.8	2.0
FIDELITY AGGRESS TAX FR	MB	308	na	5	95	0	0	0	3.9	1.9
FIDELITY CALIF TAX FREE	MB	446	na	10	90	0	0	0	3.7	2.0
FIDELITY CONGRESS STREET	G	52	na	2	0	0	0	98	8.1	6.8
FIDELITY CONTRAFUND	G	82	na	2	0	0	2	96	5.4	4.3
FIDELITY CORP TR-ARP	BP	297	na	4	0	92	3	1	1.2	-0.4
FIDELITY DESTINY	G	1,074	na	5	2	1	1	91	4.5	4.5
FIDELITY EQUITY INCOME	GI	3,100	na	6	9	8	16	61	3.9	1.6
FIDELITY EXCHANGE FUND	G	140	na	2	0	0	0	98	6.8	6.8
FIDELITY FLEXIBLE BOND	BP	290	na	0	100	0	0	0	3.8	1.4
FIDELITY FREEDOM FUND	G	816	na	5	0	0	1	94	2.2	2.2
FIDELITY FUND	GI	760	na	10	4	2	10	74	2.7	1.3
FIDELITY GOVT SECS	BP	573	na	1	99	0	0	0	3.3	1.2
FIDELITY GROWTH FUND	AG	169	na	1	0	0	1	98	4.0	4.0
FIDELITY GROWTH & INCOME	GI	460	na	na	na	na	na	na	3.1	2.3
FIDELITY LTD TERM MUNS	MB	471	na	10	90	0	0	0	3.0	1.4
FIDELITY MASS TAX FREE	MB	589	na	7	93	0	0	0	3.2	1.5
FIDELITY MORTGAGE SECS	BP	660	na	5	95	0	0	0	2.9	0.7
FIDELITY MUNI BOND FD	MB	1,041	na	12	88	0	0	0	4.2	2.5
FIDELITY OVERSEAS FUND	IN	2,561	na	8	0	0	0	92	0.0	0.0
FIDELITY SEL AMER GOLD	ME	85	na	16	0	0	2	82	0.0	0.0
FIDELITY SEL BIOTECH	AG	33	na	0	0	0	0	100	-1.7	-1.7
FIDELITY HIGH YIELD MUNI	MB	2,065	na	6	94	0	0	0	3.7	1.9
FIDELITY HIGH INCOME FD	BP	1,460	na	9	90	1	0	0	3.8	0.9
FIDELITY SEL CHEMICAL	G	21	na	0	0	0	0	100	6.0	6.0
FIDELITY MAGELLAN FUND	G	6,555	na	1	0	0	2	97	4.8	4.8
FIDELITY PURITAN FD	B	2,458	na	15	24	1	18	42	4.1	2.5
FIDELITY OTC PORTFOLIO	G	588	na	1	0	0	0	99	1.4	1.3
FIDELITY QUALIFIED DIVD	B	214	na	4	0	25	2	69	1.2	-0.4
FIDELITY SEL DEF & AERO	G	9	na	1	0	0	0	99	-0.3	-0.3
FIDELITY SELECT ENERGY	G	71	na	5	0	0	1	94	5.5	5.5
FIDELITY SEL LEISURE ENT	G	114	na	2	0	2	0	96	-0.8	-0.8
FIDELITY SELECT FINL SVC	G	120	na	2	0	0	2	96	-1.3	-1.3
FIDELITY SELECT HEALTH	AG	217	na	0	0	0	0	100	4.7	4.7
FIDELITY SEL PREC MET&MN	ME	241	na	10	0	0	0	90	-0.1	-0.1
FIDELITY SELECT TECHNLGY	AG	241	na	0	0	0	0	100	7.6	7.6
FIDELITY SEL UTILITIES	GI	195	na	1	0	0	0	99	1.9	1.9
FIDELITY SPEC SITUATIONS	AG	54	na	22	11	0	0	67	3.2	2.7
FIDELITY SEL BROKERAGE	G	11	na	0	0	0	10	90	2.1	2.1
FIDELITY SEL ELECTRONICS	AG	3	na	2	0	0	1	97	-1.4	-1.4

| 36 MONTH MPT STATISTICS | | | | | DISTRIBUTION INFORMATION | | | | | | | | |
| | STD | | ALPHA | | 12/86 | INCOME | | | | CAPITAL GAIN | | | |
R2	DEV	BETA	PCNT	RK	N.A.V.	OCT	NOV	DEC	12 MON	OCT	NOV	DEC	12 MON
na	na	na	na	na	15.38			.062	0.264			.618	0.776
23	1.42	0.16	5.0	19	12.32	.120	.120	.120	1.505				0.000
na	na	na	na	na	10.91	.107	.107	.103	1.309				0.031
6	1.81	0.10	4.6	22	10.74	.085	.083	.081	1.045				0.072
na	na	na	na	na	10.24	.070	.066	.068	0.879				0.062
na	na	na	na	na	10.51	.050	.048	.048	0.627				0.000
na	na	na	na	na	10.44	.070	.064	.068	0.881				0.004
8	0.43	0.03	-0.9	50	10.38	.044	.043	.043	0.557				0.000
71	2.47	0.50	2.4	36	15.34		.200		0.860			.350	1.063
92	4.19	0.96	2.5	36	21.60			.142	0.638			.076	0.761
30	2.43	0.32	3.4	29	10.72	.062	.063	.061	0.764				0.000
na	na	na	na	na	11.53	.076	.076	.076	0.938				0.000
na	na	na	na	na	11.80	.066	.066	.063	0.806				0.000
92	4.48	1.02	2.2	37	83.60	1.05			2.100				0.560
84	4.79	1.04	-7.8	81	11.29			.130	0.250			1.20	2.150
na	na	na	na	na	10.40	.057	.057	.057	0.762				0.020
94	4.61	1.06	-2.0	55	12.43				0.320				2.540
88	3.11	0.70	2.0	38	27.29			.650	1.700			1.30	3.080
97	4.33	1.02	-0.5	48	62.94				1.600			1.36	2.530
20	1.83	0.20	5.2	17	7.36	.057	.058	.058	0.702				0.000
91	4.84	1.10	-4.0	64	16.31				0.350				0.980
90	4.12	0.94	-2.8	58	16.05			.240	0.660		2.10		4.080
23	1.64	0.19	4.5	23	10.28	.071	.071	.070	0.916				0.000
83	5.69	1.23	-5.5	72	14.11				0.070		2.90		4.650
na	na	na	na	na	13.33	.050		.060	0.160				0.000
23	1.81	0.21	3.9	26	9.58	.051	.051	.048	0.620				0.000
na	na	na	na	na	11.66	.069	.069	.063	0.828				0.000
na	na	na	na	na	10.58	.079	.077	.076	1.002				0.000
30	2.41	0.32	4.6	22	8.28	.046	.046	.046	0.556				0.000
na	na	na	na	na	28.68				0.000			2.14	2.140
na	na	na	na	na	11.83				0.000				0.000
na	na	na	na	na	10.35				0.000				0.000
27	2.16	0.27	5.6	12	13.29	.084	.084	.077	1.006			.400	0.440
36	2.02	0.29	6.5	7	9.72	.092	.092	.095	1.112			.180	0.310
na	na	na	na	na	15.66				0.000				0.060
92	4.77	1.09	2.2	36	48.69				0.460		2.85		6.840
80	2.46	0.53	5.8	11	13.34	.200			0.920				0.760
na	na	na	na	na	16.47	.020			0.020	1.27			1.270
48	2.64	0.44	9.2	3	14.97	.091	.091	.079	1.112			.720	1.940
na	na	na	na	na	14.79				0.025				0.200
29	4.84	0.62	-5.0	69	11.53				0.000				0.000
na	na	na	na	na	20.51				0.010				0.040
77	4.67	0.97	5.3	16	31.56				0.205				0.330
81	6.38	1.35	1.6	39	32.78				0.000				0.360
0	10.27	0.08	-11.7	90	11.15				0.095				0.000
29	8.94	1.13	-21.7	98	20.27				0.000				0.080
49	4.03	0.67	9.3	3	27.31				0.215				0.140
na	na	na	na	na	16.21		.090		0.090		.970		0.970
na	na	na	na	na	12.12				0.015				0.020
na	na	na	na	na	8.46				0.000				0.000

CDA QUARTERLY SUPPLEMENT – 12/31/86

FUND	IO	ASSETS (MIL$) 9/86	ANNL %EXP RATE	PERCENT OF ASSETS					LATEST QTR ROR 9/86 - 12/86	
				CASH	NON BOND	CVT PREF	CVTS	COMM STKS	TOTAL	PRINCIPAL
FIDELITY SEL PROPTY/CAS	G	8	na	1	0	0	0	99	-5.2	-5.2
FIDELITY SEL COMPUTER	AG	3	na	4	0	0	0	96	11.0	11.0
FIDELITY SEL FOOD/AGRI	G	9	na	0	0	0	0	100	0.6	0.6
FIDELITY SEL SAVINGS/LN	G	23	na	14	0	0	0	86	5.8	5.8
FIDELITY SEL SOFTWARE	AG	6	na	2	0	0	0	98	9.2	9.2
FIDELITY SEL TELECOMM	G	7	na	6	0	0	4	90	5.4	5.4
FIDELITY TREND	G	680	na	3	0	0	0	97	4.4	3.1
FIDELITY THRIFT TRUST	BP	324	na	6	94	0	0	0	2.9	2.9
FIDELITY VALUE FUND	G	119	na	11	0	2	2	85	-1.1	-1.1
FIDUCIARY CAPITAL GROWTH	G	52	1.30	7	0	0	1	92	-5.2	-9.1
FINANCIAL BD-HIYLD PORT	BP	44	0.93	4	95	1	0	0	0.5	-2.3
FINANCIAL BD-SELECT INC	BP	20	0.97	4	96	0	0	0	4.0	1.6
FINANCIAL DYNAMICS FUND	AG	63	0.90	9	0	0	4	87	6.6	6.6
FINANCIAL INDUST. FUND	G	367	0.74	9	8	0	0	83	2.3	1.8
FINANCIAL INDUST. INCOME	GI	339	0.71	10	13	1	13	63	0.7	0.7
FINANCIAL TAX FR INC SHS	MB	117	0.68	2	98	0	0	0	4.9	3.2
FIRST INVEST. BND APPREC	BP	190	na	2	55	8	34	1	1.2	-2.0
FIRST INVEST. DISCOVERY	AG	33	na	6	0	0	0	94	-2.5	-2.5
FIRST INVEST. FD. GROWTH	AG	53	na	11	0	0	0	89	1.4	1.4
FIRST INVEST. FD. INCOME	BP	1,675	na	7	85	5	2	1	2.6	-0.3
FIRST INVEST. GOV FUND	BP	179	na	9	91	0	0	0	3.2	1.5
FIRST INVEST. INTL SECS.	IN	29	na	0	0	0	0	100	9.7	9.7
FIRST INVEST. NATURL RES	AG	12	na	13	0	1	4	82	2.5	2.5
FIRST INVEST. NY TAX FR	MB	71	na	2	98	0	0	0	4.1	1.8
FIRST INVEST. NINETY-TEN	GI	10	na	100	0	0	0	0	0.6	-1.6
FIRST INVEST. OPTION	GI	194	na	4	0	3	1	92	3.2	2.7
FIRST INVEST. TAX EXEMPT	MB	644	na	2	98	0	0	0	4.2	1.5
FLAGSHIP CORPORATE CASH	BP	325	0.80	0	0	100	0	0	0.1	-1.7
FLAGSHIP MICHIGAN DBL TX	MB	67	0.75	0	100	0	0	0	4.0	2.3
FLAGSHIP OHIO DOUBLE TAX	MB	116	0.75	0	100	0	0	0	4.1	2.2
FLEX FD-RETIRE GR SERIES	GI	59	1.43	100	0	0	0	0	-1.2	-1.2
FORTY-FOUR WALL ST EQTY	AG	8	na	0	0	0	0	100	17.1	17.1
FORTY-FOUR WALL ST FUND	AG	22	na	0	0	0	0	100	-4.9	-4.9
FOUNDATION GROWTH STOCK	GI	1	na	0	0	0	0	0	1.8	1.8
FOUNDERS EQUITY INCOME	B	12	1.75*	15	21	0	0	64	3.7	2.6
FOUNDERS GROWTH FUND	G	56	1.42*	16	0	0	0	84	3.0	-1.0
FOUNDERS MUTUAL FUND	GI	175	0.95*	7	0	0	0	93	4.5	3.8
FOUNDERS SPECIAL FUND	AG	96	na	9	0	0	0	91	3.9	3.0
FPA CAPITAL FUND	G	47	0.90	1	0	0	5	94	3.9	3.9
FPA NEW INCOME	BP	6	1.52	7	83	0	10	0	3.0	0.7
FPA PARAMOUNT FD INC	GI	116	1.02	12	0	0	2	86	-0.7	-0.7
FPA PERENNIAL FUND	G	60	1.24	20	9	0	10	61	1.5	1.5
FRANKLIN CALIF TAX FREE	MB	6,889	na	4	96	0	0	0	4.0	2.1
FRANKLIN CORP CASH TR	BP	70	na	4	0	96	0	0	0.4	-1.1
FRANKLIN DYNATECH	G	32	na	6	0	0	0	94	3.9	3.9
FRANKLIN EQUITY FUND	G	145	na	1	0	0	0	99	5.4	5.4
FRANKLIN FEDERAL TAX FR	MB	1,506	na	0	100	0	0	0	4.5	2.3
FRANKLIN GOLD FUND	ME	126	na	6	1	0	0	93	0.2	0.2
FRANKLIN GROWTH	G	43	na	10	1	0	0	89	6.6	6.6
FRANKLIN INCOME	B	227	na	9	25	2	0	64	2.9	0.4

R2	STD DEV	BETA	ALPHA PCNT	RK	12/86 N.A.V.	OCT	NOV	DEC	12 MON	OCT	NOV	DEC	12 MON
na	na	na	na	na	10.97				0.000				0.000
na	na	na	na	na	12.21				0.000				0.040
na	na	na	na	na	14.10				0.000				0.000
na	na	na	na	na	12.88				0.000				0.000
na	na	na	na	na	12.65				0.000				0.000
na	na	na	na	na	13.18				0.000				0.000
91	5.04	1.14	-6.3	75	39.83			.610	0.610			7.43	10.640
20	1.76	0.19	5.6	13	11.55				0.660			.220	0.220
82	4.38	0.94	-7.7	80	23.06				0.000			1.99	1.990
75	4.91	1.01	-9.3	85	17.90	.953			0.953	2.83			2.834
na	na	na	na	na	8.38			.240	1.010			.170	0.170
29	2.10	0.27	4.4	24	7.10			.170	0.680			.320	0.320
78	5.80	1.21	-12.5	91	7.06				0.060			.850	2.090
90	4.40	1.00	-6.1	74	3.96		.020		0.100				1.020
95	3.50	0.81	1.1	41	8.00				0.330			.510	2.400
17	2.92	0.29	6.5	7	15.59	.100	.087	.085	1.170			.580	1.383
41	1.72	0.27	0.6	44	12.94	.100	.100	.220	1.320				0.240
53	6.20	1.07	-26.8	99	9.03				0.120				0.800
58	6.80	1.22	-25.8	98	5.70				0.000				0.410
26	1.49	0.19	1.1	41	5.94	.055	.055	.065	0.750				0.000
na	na	na	na	na	12.19	.060	.060	.090	1.070	.040		.110	0.270
23	5.83	0.66	-2.8	58	16.53				0.010				1.440
5	8.73	0.46	-27.0	99	3.63				0.021				0.000
na	na	na	na	na	14.25	.070	.180	.070	0.950				0.000
16	1.40	0.13	-4.6	67	12.50	.270			0.670				0.000
78	2.96	0.63	-6.5	76	4.68			.020	0.110			.180	0.510
31	1.72	0.24	4.2	24	10.14	.055	.155	.055	0.755				0.012
2	1.31	0.05	-0.2	47	45.91	.289	.252	.270	3.601				0.000
na	na	na	na	na	10.77	.059	.057	.059	0.729				0.081
na	na	na	na	na	10.60	.070	.060	.060	0.757				0.066
56	3.53	0.63	-6.0	74	10.91				0.417			1.27	1.266
67	13.45	2.51	-29.9	99	5.75				0.000				0.000
64	11.83	2.18	-50.8	99	3.09				0.000				0.000
64	1.93	0.38	-5.0	69	5.03				0.181				0.000
67	2.27	0.45	0.5	44	15.30	.180			0.660	.880			0.880
86	4.79	1.06	-6.8	76	8.30		.386		0.386		1.06		1.059
95	4.43	1.03	-2.3	56	7.87	.073			0.288	2.59		.628	3.215
85	4.93	1.08	-10.8	88	27.98			.285	0.285			3.47	3.467
83	4.99	1.08	-7.6	80	11.08				0.370			.450	1.470
6	1.83	0.10	6.9	6	9.50		.210		0.840		.030		0.030
63	2.67	0.51	-1.4	53	12.44				0.530			.930	0.930
na	na	na	na	na	18.47				0.510			1.10	1.700
31	1.63	0.22	4.1	25	7.22	.045	.045	.045	0.595				0.000
na	na	na	na	na	8.82	.050	.043	.043	0.592				0.000
81	4.92	1.05	-16.1	95	9.95				0.250				0.000
92	4.48	1.02	1.0	42	6.25				0.090			.150	0.601
na	na	na	na	na	12.06	.084	.084	.084	1.009			.022	0.022
0	10.29	0.09	-12.0	90	8.99				0.340				0.000
88	3.89	0.87	-3.0	59	15.95				0.260			.057	0.239
30	2.26	0.30	5.2	17	2.24		.055		0.220		.020		0.020

CDA QUARTERLY SUPPLEMENT - 12/31/86

FUND	IO	ASSETS (MIL$) 9/86	ANNL %EXP RATE	PERCENT OF ASSETS					LATEST QTR ROR 9/86 - 12/86	
				CASH	NON CVT BOND	PREF	CVTS	COMM STKS	TOTAL	PRINCIPAL
FRANKLIN NEW YORK TAX FR	MB	2,126	na	4	96	0	0	0	4.4	2.3
FRANKLIN OPTION FUND	G	27	na	10	0	0	0	90	5.6	4.9
FRANKLIN U.S. GOVT. SEC.	BP	14,367	na	2	98	0	0	0	2.7	0.1
FRANKLIN UTILITIES	GI	327	na	22	0	0	0	78	1.5	-0.2
FREEDOM GOLD & GOV TRUST	ME	47	1.45	12	74	0	0	14	2.2	0.6
FREEDOM REGIONAL BANK FD	G	53	1.33	4	0	0	6	90	-2.8	-3.2
FT INTERNATIONAL	IN	104	1.00*	1	0	0	0	99	6.9	6.9
FTP-EQ PORTFOLIO-GROWTH	G	58	na	0	0	0	1	99	4.3	3.9
FTP-EQ PORTFOLIO INCOME	GI	501	na	8	11	8	12	61	4.1	2.6
FTP-FIXED INC. LTD PORT.	BP	377	na	5	95	0	0	0	3.1	0.9
FUND FOR U.S. GOVT. SEC.	BP	979	0.95	3	97	0	0	0	2.4	0.1
FUND OF AMERICA	GI	145	0.76	3	4	0	2	91	4.4	3.9
FUND OF THE SOUTHWEST	AG	15	na	3	0	0	0	97	-0.8	-0.8
FUNDAMENTAL INVESTORS	G	488	0.63	10	0	0	0	90	6.8	6.1
FUNDTRUST AGGRESSIVE	AG	40	na	na	na	na	na	na	3.9	3.9
FUNDTRUST GROWTH	G	30	na	na	na	na	na	na	4.5	3.9
FUNDTRUST GROWTH & INC	GI	46	na	na	na	na	na	na	4.0	3.0
FUNDTRUST INCOME	BP	30	na	na	na	na	na	na	2.4	0.1
G. T. PACIFIC GROWTH FD	IN	67	1.40	8	0	0	4	88	-3.2	-3.2
GABELLI ASSET FUND	G	41	na	25	0	0	0	75	0.0	0.0
GATEWAY GROWTH PLUS FUND	AG	3	na	9	0	0	0	91	3.5	3.5
GATEWAY OPTION INCOME	GI	36	1.50	2	0	0	0	98	5.4	4.8
GENERAL ELEC S&S LT BOND	BP	608	na	5	95	0	0	0	3.8	1.7
GENL ELEC S&S PROGRAM	GI	815	na	7	0	0	4	89	4.8	4.8
GENERAL SECURITIES	GI	16	1.50	35	39	0	0	26	1.7	1.6
GIBRALTAR FUND, INC.	G	1	na	52	0	0	0	48	1.5	1.5
GINTEL CAP APPRECIATION	AG	21	2.50*	20	0	0	0	80	6.0	6.0
GINTEL ERISA	GI	79	1.30	27	0	0	0	73	10.8	10.8
GINTEL FUND	G	119	1.20	26	0	0	0	74	9.4	9.4
GOLCONDA INVESTORS	ME	32	2.82*	5	1	3	0	91	1.1	1.1
GRADISON ESTABLISHED GR.	G	33	1.60*	19	0	0	0	81	6.9	6.3
GRADISON OPPORTUNITY GR	AG	17	1.70*	20	0	0	0	80	-5.8	-6.1
GREENWAY FUND	AG	19	1.83	4	0	0	0	96	3.8	3.8
GROWTH FUND OF AMERICA	G	741	0.67	14	5	0	0	81	5.0	3.3
GROWTH FD OF WASHINGTON	G	51	na	13	0	0	1	86	1.8	1.2
GROWTH INDUSTRY SHARES	G	69	0.95	16	0	0	0	83	5.9	5.5
GUARDIAN MUTUAL FUND	GI	519	na	3	13	0	0	84	1.6	-0.1
GUARDIAN PARK AVE FUND	G	119	na	1	0	0	17	82	4.7	4.7
HAMILTON FUNDS	G	242	0.86	15	0	0	7	78	3.2	1.0
HANCOCK (JOHN) BOND	BP	1,108	0.70	2	98	0	0	0	0.9	-1.4
HANCOCK (JOHN) GLOBAL	IN	72	na	na	na	na	na	na	6.9	6.9
HANCOCK (JOHN) GNMA	BP	371	na	na	na	na	na	na	3.5	1.0
HANCOCK (JOHN) GROWTH	AG	85	1.01	6	0	0	9	85	2.7	2.7
HANCOCK (JOHN) SPECIAL	G	13	na	na	na	na	na	na	0.8	0.8
HANCOCK (JOHN) TX EX DIV	MB	321	na	na	na	na	na	na	4.5	2.8
HANCOCK (JOHN) US GOV	BP	182	0.90	4	96	0	0	0	3.4	1.3
HARTWELL GROWTH FUND	AG	10	na	6	0	0	0	94	8.8	8.8
HARTWELL LEVERAGE FUND	AG	25	na	5	0	0	0	95	8.1	8.1
HAWAIIAN TAX-FREE TRUST	MB	130	na	0	100	0	0	0	3.6	1.9
HEARTLAND VALUE FUND	G	26	2.00*	5	0	0	0	95	2.8	2.8

| 36 MONTH MPT STATISTICS | | | | | DISTRIBUTION INFORMATION | | | | | | | | | |
R2	STD DEV	BETA	ALPHA PCNT	RK	12/86 N.A.V.	INCOME OCT	NOV	DEC	12 MON	CAPITAL GAIN OCT	NOV	DEC	12 MON
28	2.02	0.26	5.2	17	11.64	.080	.080	.080	0.960			.180	0.180
86	3.55	0.79	-4.2	65	5.93	.035			0.125	.135			1.005
6	1.66	0.10	5.1	18	7.42	.070	.060	.060	0.840				0.000
37	3.60	0.52	8.3	4	8.18			.140	0.560			.011	0.011
na	na	na	na	na	16.03	.250			1.110	.050			0.610
na	na	na	na	na	10.92	.060			0.290		1.00		1.480
na	na	na	na	na	21.60				0.083			1.83	2.170
78	6.49	1.36	-9.3	85	11.92	.050			0.070			1.00	1.330
85	3.00	0.66	2.7	35	12.52	.050	.080	.070	0.780			.750	1.090
na	na	na	na	na	11.07	.084	.082	.081	1.024			.140	0.160
4	1.51	0.07	3.9	26	8.62	.065	.063	.063	0.863				0.000
79	3.68	0.78	-7.0	78	10.49			.055	0.320			1.21	1.330
75	5.33	1.09	-17.3	95	9.33				0.050		1.85		1.850
90	4.62	1.04	0.0	46	14.21		.100		0.400		1.24		2.750
na	na	na	na	na	13.27				0.150	.370			0.370
na	na	na	na	na	13.08	.070			0.310	.240			0.240
na	na	na	na	na	12.88	.130			0.330	.360			0.360
na	na	na	na	na	10.62	.080	.080	.080	0.910	.050			0.050
5	5.82	0.32	9.6	3	29.98				0.010				0.000
na	na	na	na	na	11.29				na				na
na	na	na	na	na	10.04				na				na
84	2.03	0.45	-1.4	53	14.63	.080			0.340	.370			1.460
25	1.82	0.22	7.8	4	12.41	.089	.081	.085	1.082			.150	0.318
98	4.00	0.95	-1.8	54	35.47				1.570			7.15	10.110
72	4.37	0.89	-2.2	55	11.57		.021		0.381		2.13		2.129
62	2.68	0.51	-0.2	47	13.45				0.170				0.300
na	na	na	na	na	11.00				0.000			.910	0.910
73	4.00	0.82	-0.6	48	45.23				1.200				1.350
66	4.34	0.84	-4.0	64	66.62				1.680			28.97	32.060
0	7.15	0.04	-6.4	76	12.86				0.030				0.000
89	4.17	0.94	0.3	45	15.21		.090		0.330		.650		1.180
73	4.86	0.99	-5.4	71	11.64		.040		0.040		.450		0.800
75	5.71	1.17	-8.6	83	10.11				0.055			.350	0.975
87	4.96	1.10	-6.7	76	15.76	.280			0.280	.790			0.790
na	na	na	na	na	11.12			.070	0.140			.459	0.459
82	4.98	1.07	-8.7	83	9.10	.045			0.213			1.53	3.518
93	3.80	0.87	-2.0	55	38.13	.760			1.510	4.50			4.500
89	4.56	1.02	1.9	38	20.74				0.330			1.56	3.813
85	3.92	0.87	-1.7	53	6.76			.170	0.365			1.03	1.030
26	2.04	0.25	5.1	18	15.89	.128	.128	.128	1.536				0.000
na	na	na	na	na	14.76				0.023				0.024
na	na	na	na	na	10.72		.270		1.034	.163			0.172
85	5.12	1.12	-5.8	73	14.03				0.168			1.43	2.200
na	na	na	na	na	5.71				0.028			.048	0.055
37	2.25	0.33	4.3	24	11.10	.063	.063	.063	0.756			.226	0.226
21	1.71	0.19	5.2	17	9.71	.070	.070	.060	0.830				0.000
72	6.23	1.25	-11.1	89	12.01				0.070			.890	1.950
74	7.93	1.60	-19.3	97	16.15				0.000				0.000
na	na	na	na	na	11.09	.066	.059	.059	0.782				0.007
na	na	na	na	na	14.01				0.085			.605	0.827

CDA QUARTERLY SUPPLEMENT - 12/31/86

FUND	IO	ASSETS (MIL$) 9/86	ANNL %EXP RATE	CASH	NON BOND	CVT PREF	CVTS	COMM STKS	TOTAL	PRINCIPAL
HIGH YIELD SECURITIES	BP	87	na	9	90	0	1	0	1.3	-1.6
HOME INVS GOV GTD INCOME	BP	184	na	0	100	0	0	0	3.1	1.2
HORACE MANN GROWTH FUND	G	75	na	6	0	0	0	94	5.8	3.8
HUTTON CAL MUNICIPAL FD	MB	162	na	2	98	0	0	0	3.7	1.8
HUTTON INV SER BASIC VAL	G	324	na	26	0	0	2	72	1.8	1.1
HUTTON INV SER BOND/INC	BP	347	na	1	99	0	0	0	4.8	2.5
HUTTON INV SER SPL EQTY	AG	216	na	22	0	0	2	76	3.1	3.1
HUTTON INV SERIES GROWTH	G	1,121	na	34	0	0	1	65	5.8	5.4
HUTTON INV SER GOV SECS	BP	5,177	na	15	85	0	0	0	2.7	0.0
HUTTON INV SER PRE METAL	ME	39	na	22	0	0	0	78	4.9	4.9
HUTTON NATL MUNICIPAL FD	MB	951	na	3	97	0	0	0	4.9	2.9
HUTTON N.Y. MUNICIPAL FD	MB	224	na	1	99	0	0	0	4.2	2.3
HUTTON OPTION INCOME	GI	76	na	7	0	0	0	93	0.3	0.3
IDS BOND FUND	BP	1,775	0.72*	6	85	2	7	0	5.1	2.9
IDS DISCOVERY FUND	AG	268	0.61*	13	1	1	4	81	3.9	3.9
IDS EQUITY PLUS FD INC.	G	365	0.47*	7	1	0	3	89	4.0	3.4
IDS EXTRA INCOME	BP	871	0.80*	4	93	1	2	0	3.8	1.2
IDS GROWTH FUND	AG	708	0.61*	11	0	0	0	89	5.1	5.1
IDS MUTUAL FUND	B	1,242	0.60*	2	36	0	2	60	7.1	5.6
IDS NEW DIMENSIONS FUND	G	510	0.69*	23	2	0	0	75	4.4	4.4
IDS PROGRESSIVE FUND	GI	184	0.67*	6	11	0	0	83	-0.3	-0.3
IDS SELECTIVE	BP	1,111	0.73*	7	89	1	3	0	5.0	2.8
IDS STOCK FUND	GI	1,345	0.52*	7	6	0	2	85	5.2	4.2
INCOME FUND OF AMERICA	B	601	0.55	16	41	0	2	41	5.4	2.1
INDUSTRY FUND OF AMERICA	AG	1	na	60	0	0	0	40	0.2	0.2
INTEGRATED CAPTL APPREC	G	126	0.99	15	0	0	0	85	4.7	3.1
INTEGRATED INSD TAX FREE	MB	129	0.73	6	94	0	0	0	2.8	1.0
INTERNATIONAL INVESTORS	ME	865	0.81	3	0	0	5	92	0.2	-0.6
INVEST. CO. OF AMERICA	GI	3,487	0.42	20	4	0	0	76	5.2	4.4
INVEST. PORTFOLIOS-EQ	G	192	2.03*	6	0	0	0	94	2.2	2.2
INVEST. PORTFOLIOS-GOV +	BP	4,528	1.92*	10	90	0	0	0	3.2	0.8
INVEST. PORTFOLIOS-HIYLD	BP	163	1.97*	4	95	1	0	0	4.3	1.8
INVEST. PORTFOLIOS-OP IN	GI	347	1.99*	7	0	0	0	93	2.8	-0.7
INVEST. QUALITY INTEREST	BP	128	1.01*	11	89	0	0	0	2.8	1.1
INVEST. TRUST OF BOSTON	G	65	na	4	0	0	9	87	5.0	4.3
INV TR/BOSTON HI IN PLUS	BP	22	na	4	70	3	18	4	2.6	0.1
INVESTORS INCOME	BP	19	1.50	13	87	0	0	0	4.2	1.9
INVESTORS RESEARCH	G	59	0.81	63	0	0	0	37	2.6	2.1
IRI STOCK FUND	G	13	0.10	0	35	0	0	65	4.5	4.5
ISI GROWTH FUND	GI	13	1.50	18	1	0	0	81	-3.0	-3.0
ISI INCOME FUND	B	6	1.59	78	22	0	0	0	-4.4	-6.1
ISI TRUST FUND	B	102	1.12	69	0	0	0	31	2.1	2.1
ITB MASS TAX FREE	MB	45	na	2	98	0	0	0	3.0	1.3
IVY GROWTH FUND	GI	165	1.25	15	35	0	0	50	2.5	2.5
IVY INSTITUTIONAL INV FD	G	131	1.24	8	2	0	0	90	5.5	5.5
JANUS FUND	GI	464	1.01	51	4	0	0	45	3.1	3.1
JANUS VALUE FUND	G	11	2.00	1	0	0	0	99	2.0	2.0
JANUS VENTURE FUND	AG	28	1.90	43	0	0	0	57	-0.2	-5.0
JP GROWTH FUND	GI	24	0.86	20	0	0	0	80	3.6	3.6
JP INCOME	BP	20	0.90	13	87	0	0	0	3.6	1.4

| | 36 MONTH MPT STATISTICS | | | | DISTRIBUTION INFORMATION | | | | | | | | |
| | STD | | ALPHA | | 12/86 | INCOME | | | | CAPITAL GAIN | | | |
R2	DEV	BETA	PCNT	RK	N.A.V.	OCT	NOV	DEC	12 MON	OCT	NOV	DEC	12 MON
39	1.08	0.17	1.4	40	9.73	.095	.095	.095	1.195				0.000
na	na	na	na	na	10.67	.076	.058	.058	0.891				0.096
96	4.33	1.01	-4.7	68	21.29			.490	1.170			3.96	6.160
20	2.64	0.29	3.8	27	11.08	.069	.069	.069	0.831			.110	0.194
na	na	na	na	na	12.15	.080			0.304			.380	0.515
29	2.70	0.35	7.5	4	12.91	.097	.097	.097	1.214			.180	0.180
83	4.58	1.00	-7.8	81	13.02				0.049			1.00	1.000
89	3.66	0.83	-3.2	61	15.86	.060			0.234			.115	1.673
na	na	na	na	na	10.41	.093	.093	.093	1.164				0.210
na	na	na	na	na	12.93				0.025			.220	0.220
20	2.44	0.26	7.4	4	11.97	.076	.076	.076	0.912			.330	0.563
30	2.30	0.30	4.5	23	11.32	.070	.070	.070	0.843			.200	0.277
79	3.27	0.70	-8.2	82	8.19				0.050	.225		.225	0.996
33	2.21	0.31	6.1	9	5.30	.038	.035	.039	0.485				0.212
78	5.24	1.10	-13.2	92	7.45				0.126				0.394
93	4.55	1.05	-4.7	67	9.43		.058		0.243	1.30			1.301
54	1.75	0.31	3.9	26	5.16	.044	.040	.048	0.555				0.146
74	6.18	1.26	-9.4	86	20.35				0.137				2.688
53	2.83	0.50	6.3	8	12.45			.175	0.807				1.342
81	4.62	0.99	-1.8	54	8.52				0.176				2.361
70	3.71	0.75	-2.7	58	6.68				0.245				1.179
32	2.09	0.29	5.7	11	9.08	.062	.058	.068	0.805				0.000
95	4.01	0.93	-3.0	59	19.16	.200			0.653	2.24			2.240
83	2.64	0.58	5.1	18	12.03	.200		.200	1.080	.590			0.590
46	4.58	0.74	-24.8	98	3.07				0.000			2.06	2.060
na	na	na	na	na	13.17	.220			0.290			.320	0.350
na	na	na	na	na	12.52	.077	.060	.080	0.954				0.000
0	9.24	0.09	-7.4	80	12.04	.100			0.400			.200	0.200
94	3.76	0.87	2.5	35	13.19			.110	0.440			.970	2.450
na	na	na	na	na	10.75				0.000				0.210
na	na	na	na	na	8.53	.070	.065	.065	0.680				0.190
na	na	na	na	na	9.83	.080	.080	.080	0.860				0.150
na	na	na	na	na	7.48	.090	.090	.085	0.395				0.700
15	2.66	0.25	6.1	9	10.14		.090	.090	0.935	.090		.150	0.850
91	4.83	1.10	-5.2	70	11.98			.080	0.340				1.050
na	na	na	na	na	14.11	.100	.130	.130	1.530	.460			0.460
31	1.42	0.19	5.6	13	5.36		.120		0.480				0.000
64	4.99	0.95	-3.1	60	5.15			.030	0.030			1.27	1.274
85	4.97	1.09	-2.5	57	9.91				0.300				0.879
69	3.18	0.63	-6.9	77	6.48				0.100			.400	0.400
2	1.77	0.06	-1.8	54	3.38			.060	0.200				0.000
42	1.35	0.21	0.0	46	10.22				0.600			.475	0.502
na	na	na	na	na	16.83	.098	.091	.094	1.149				0.046
86	3.02	0.67	2.6	35	13.44				0.460			3.14	4.480
na	na	na	na	na	125.53				6.150			26.09	40.670
85	3.31	0.73	-3.4	62	12.47				0.000			2.20	2.200
na	na	na	na	na	12.07				0.800				0.820
na	na	na	na	na	27.45	1.48			1.480	1.04			1.040
93	3.67	0.85	-1.2	52	13.62				0.500			2.13	3.770
25	2.62	0.31	7.3	5	9.96	.210			0.850				0.000

CDA QUARTERLY SUPPLEMENT – 12/31/86

FUND	IO	ASSETS (MIL$) 9/86	ANNL %EXP RATE	PERCENT OF ASSETS		NON CVT			COMM	LATEST QTR ROR 9/36 - 12/86	
				CASH	BOND	PREF	CVTS	STKS		TOTAL	PRINCIPAL
KEMPER CALIF TAX FREE	MB	186	na	4	96	0	0	0		4.4	2.6
KEMPER GROWTH FUND	G	275	na	12	0	0	0	88		4.2	4.2
KEMPER HIGH YIELD FD	BP	323	na	4	94	2	0	0		4.9	2.0
KEMPER INC & CAP PRESERV	BP	199	na	10	89	0	0	1		2.4	-0.1
KEMPER INTL FD	IN	185	1.05	6	8	0	3	83		5.8	4.7
KEMPER MUNI BOND FD LTD	MB	905	na	6	94	0	0	0		4.0	2.1
KEMPER OPTION INCOME FD	GI	621	na	2	0	0	98	0		3.2	0.9
KEMPER SUMMIT FUND	G	274	na	5	0	0	1	94		5.7	5.7
KEMPER TOTAL RETURN FD	GI	614	na	6	26	0	4	64		3.5	2.7
KEMPER US GOVT SECS	BP	2,379	na	9	91	0	0	0		3.6	1.0
KEYSTONE INTL FUND	IN	90	1.70	7	0	0	0	93		4.2	3.4
KEYSTONE B-1	BP	316	1.09	5	94	0	1	0		3.8	1.7
KEYSTONE B-2	BP	575	1.05	0	93	0	6	0		2.3	-0.2
KEYSTONE B-4	BP	1,500	0.86	1	90	0	8	1		1.7	-1.3
KEYSTONE K-1	B	439	0.86	5	36	0	1	58		4.5	2.9
KEYSTONE K-2	G	288	1.00	8	0	0	0	92		6.1	4.6
KEYSTONE PRECIOUS METALS	ME	65	1.44	7	0	0	0	93		6.2	4.9
KEYSTONE S-1	G	106	1.13	8	0	0	0	92		5.0	4.8
KEYSTONE S-3	G	230	1.04	7	0	0	0	93		3.1	1.6
KEYSTONE S-4	AG	543	0.83	10	0	0	0	90		5.7	5.7
KEYSTONE TAX FREE	MB	975	0.92	2	98	0	0	0		3.5	1.6
KIDDER P. EQUITY INCOME	GI	42	na	na	na	na	na	na		2.7	1.9
KIDDER P. GOVT INCOME	BP	145	na	na	na	na	na	na		3.2	1.3
KIDDER P. SPECIAL GROWTH	AG	31	2.30*	36	0	0	0	64		3.5	3.5
KIDDER P. NATL TX-FR INC	MB	19	na	na	na	na	na	na		3.5	1.8
KIDDER P. N.Y. TX-FR INC	MB	10	na	na	na	na	na	na		4.0	2.4
LEGG MASON VALUE TRUST	G	607	2.50*	9	0	0	1	89		-0.2	-0.5
LEHMAN CAPITAL FUND	G	103	1.13	15	0	0	0	85		5.4	5.4
LEHMAN INVESTORS FD, INC	G	405	na	6	0	0	0	94		4.4	3.7
LEHMAN OPPORTUNITY FUND	G	103	na	10	0	0	0	90		-1.6	-4.2
LEPERCQ-ISTEL TRUST	GI	26	1.50	1	20	0	0	79		2.3	2.3
LEVERAGE FUND OF BOSTON	AG	25	2.91	0	4	0	0	96		-7.3	-7.3
LEXINGTON GOLDFUND	ME	22	na	7	0	0	0	93		2.5	2.5
LEXINGTON GROWTH FUND	G	28	na	14	3	0	1	82		3.1	3.1
LEXINGTON GNMA NEW INC	BP	129	na	0	90	0	0	10		4.3	2.1
LEXINGTON RESEARCH FUND	G	123	na	15	2	0	4	79		3.4	2.6
LG US GOV SECURITIES	BP	48	na	6	94	0	0	0		3.6	1.4
LIBERTY FUND	BP	10	na	4	90	0	0	6		4.8	2.4
LINDNER DIVIDEND FUND	GI	62	na	22	11	17	13	37		5.7	5.7
LINDNER FUND	GI	361	0.58	31	3	0	6	60		4.0	4.0
LMH FUND, LTD.	GI	84	1.25	51	0	0	0	49		0.8	0.8
LOOMIS-SAYLES CAP. DEV.	AG	208	0.77	0	0	0	0	100		2.1	2.1
LOOMIS-SAYLES MUTUAL	GI	174	0.87	3	24	10	0	63		4.8	4.0
LORD ABBETT BOND-DEBEN.	BP	610	0.68	8	50	2	39	0		2.7	-0.1
LORD ABBETT DEV GROWTH	AG	239	0.87	3	0	0	2	95		7.9	7.9
LORD ABBETT TX FREE NATL	MB	184	0.66	3	97	0	0	0		4.9	3.0
LORD ABBETT TX FREE NY	MB	94	0.74	2	98	0	0	0		5.2	3.3
LORD ABBETT US GOV SECS	BP	269	1.01	3	97	0	0	0		3.3	0.6
LORD ABBETT VALUE APPREC	G	299	0.86	4	0	0	4	92		0.0	0.0
LOWRY MARKET TIMING FD	AG	69	1.46*	100	0	0	0	0		1.0	-3.0

| 36 MONTH MPT STATISTICS | | | | | DISTRIBUTION INFORMATION | | | | | | | | |
| | STD | | ALPHA | | 12/86 | INCOME | | | | CAPITAL GAIN | | | |
R2	DEV	BETA	PCNT	RK	N.A.V.	OCT	NOV	DEC	12 MON	OCT	NOV	DEC	12 MON
29	2.04	0.27	5.0	19	14.59	.090	.079	.079	1.056				0.000
91	4.18	0.95	-7.0	78	10.06				0.100	3.57			3.570
32	1.52	0.21	6.5	7	11.45	.105	.105	.105	1.260				0.000
29	1.53	0.20	5.8	11	9.08	.075	.075	.075	0.935				0.000
23	4.85	0.56	11.8	2	19.30	.240			0.280	6.32			6.320
28	2.03	0.26	5.7	11	9.81	.060	.060	.060	0.720				0.000
83	2.91	0.64	-5.8	73	9.70		.230		0.970		.120		0.460
91	4.63	1.05	-7.4	79	5.11				0.000	1.02			1.020
93	3.90	0.90	-2.6	57	15.25		.140		0.560		1.96		1.960
24	1.79	0.22	6.3	8	9.90	.085	.085	.085	1.040				0.000
15	4.64	0.43	10.3	3	7.16		.060		0.060		1.11		1.110
31	2.25	0.30	4.0	26	17.65	.110	.125	.125	1.620		.070		0.070
39	1.80	0.27	3.1	31	19.89	.500			2.000	.140			0.140
42	1.49	0.23	1.2	40	7.77			.230	0.960				0.070
85	2.85	0.63	-0.7	50	8.67		.140		0.560			.250	1.500
90	4.15	0.94	-2.5	57	7.64			.130	0.130		1.51		1.510
0	9.38	0.04	-10.5	88	14.59	.170			0.370				0.080
92	4.38	1.00	-7.1	78	19.77	.060			0.420	3.80	.720		4.520
94	4.73	1.09	-9.0	84	7.93	.140			0.140	1.72	.210		1.930
86	5.81	1.28	-15.1	94	5.98				0.010				0.880
27	2.10	0.27	4.3	24	8.84	.057	.056	.055	0.690		.170		0.170
na	na	na	na	na	17.49		.140		0.450				0.000
na	na	na	na	na	15.11	.098	.089	.089	1.159				0.160
na	na	na	na	na	13.92				0.240				0.000
na	na	na	na	na	15.89	.094	.084	.084	1.150				0.000
na	na	na	na	na	15.64	.089	.076	.076	1.090				0.000
88	4.08	0.91	0.3	46	26.10	.090			0.420		1.60		2.780
86	5.17	1.14	-6.9	77	17.87				0.250		1.50		4.035
96	4.29	1.00	-4.4	66	17.37	.150			0.535		2.50		4.550
86	3.75	0.83	-0.3	47	22.60		.705		0.705	2.66			2.660
86	4.26	0.94	-8.9	84	13.29				0.640		1.00		1.080
73	7.18	1.44	-18.5	96	7.26				0.000				0.680
0	7.70	-0.09	-2.1	55	4.49				0.017				0.000
82	4.62	1.00	-6.8	77	11.80				0.200				0.000
9	1.84	0.13	4.3	24	8.22	.058	.061	.057	0.750				0.000
86	4.20	0.93	-3.7	63	19.16		.150		0.665				2.325
na	na	na	na	na	10.77	.082	.074	.079	1.077				0.100
28	2.28	0.30	3.8	28	4.73	.110			0.360				0.000
46	1.79	0.29	6.2	8	23.74				2.170		2.70		3.258
77	1.59	0.34	3.7	28	16.12				1.495		1.50		4.086
76	2.88	0.60	1.1	41	24.01				1.099				4.415
78	6.01	1.26	-1.1	51	23.12				0.160				7.460
79	3.93	0.84	4.1	25	22.86	.200			0.940		1.60		2.750
52	1.74	0.31	1.0	42	10.28	.290			1.190		1.50		0.140
71	6.15	1.23	-20.3	97	7.88				0.000				0.390
na	na	na	na	na	11.23	.069	.070	.069	0.846				0.200
na	na	na	na	na	11.29	.068	.068	.068	0.824				0.140
22	1.63	0.18	6.5	7	3.27	.029	.029	.029	0.348			.040	0.040
84	5.26	1.14	-3.7	63	12.69				0.230				0.860
55	4.14	0.73	-12.6	91	8.52		.350		0.350				0.000

CDA QUARTERLY SUPPLEMENT - 12/31/86

FUND	IO	ASSETS (MIL$) 9/86	ANNL %EXP RATE	CASH	NON CVT BOND	PREF	CVTS	COMM STKS	LATEST QTR ROR 9/86 - 12/86 TOTAL	PRINCIPAL
LUTHERAN BROTHER. FUND	GI	186	1.11	27	0	0	0	72	3.0	2.1
LUTHERAN BROTHER. INCOME	BP	504	1.05	5	95	0	0	0	3.3	0.9
LUTHERAN BROTHER. MUN BD	MB	210	1.15	3	97	0	0	0	3.8	2.0
MACKENZIE INDUSTRIAL AM	G	7	na	0	0	0	0	0	-0.1	-0.1
MACKENZIE INDUSTRIAL GOV	BP	20	na	0	0	0	0	0	7.0	4.6
MACKENZIE INDUSTRIAL OPT	GI	75	na	0	0	0	0	0	4.8	0.8
MANHATTAN FUND	G	241	na	4	0	0	0	96	5.5	5.5
MASS. CAPITAL DEVEL.	G	858	0.71	7	0	0	0	93	4.6	4.6
MASS. FINANCIAL BOND	BP	327	0.79	22	78	0	0	0	5.3	3.2
MASS. FINANCIAL DEVEL.	G	193	0.82	0	0	0	1	99	4.7	3.8
MASS. FINL EMERG. GWTH.	AG	233	1.36	2	0	0	1	97	3.2	3.2
MASS. FINL GOV SEC HIYLD	BP	367	na	na	na	na	na	na	3.8	1.6
MASS. FINL HI INCOME	BP	1,000	0.80	9	85	1	3	2	2.7	-0.7
MASS. FINL INTL TRUST BD	BP	134	1.18	22	78	0	0	0	4.1	0.7
MASS. FINANCIAL SPECIAL	AG	111	1.39	6	0	0	0	94	7.3	7.3
MASS. FINL TOTAL RETURN	B	285	0.73	6	22	1	13	59	5.7	4.3
MASS. FINL SECTORS FUND	G	124	na	na	na	na	na	na	0.2	0.2
MASS. INV. GROWTH STOCK	G	893	0.50	10	0	0	0	90	3.8	3.4
MASS. INV. TRUST	GI	1,188	0.49	2	0	0	2	96	6.7	5.9
MFS GOVT GUARANTEED	BP	432	1.44*	3	97	0	0	0	2.3	0.1
MFS GOV SECURITIES HIYLD	BP	367	na	0	100	0	0	0	3.8	1.6
MFS MGD MUNI-BOND HIYLD	MB	383	0.67	9	91	0	0	0	2.2	-0.2
MFS MGD MUNI-BD TRUST	MB	801	0.67	13	87	0	0	0	3.7	2.0
MFS MDG MULTI-ST MASS.	MB	183	1.07*	15	85	0	0	0	3.1	1.5
MFS MGD MULTI-ST N.C.	MB	83	1.36*	9	91	0	0	0	3.4	1.8
MFS MGD MULTI-ST VA	MB	149	1.34*	17	83	0	0	0	2.9	1.3
MATHERS FUND	G	149	0.74	5	0	0	0	95	4.3	4.3
MEDICAL TECHNOLOGY FUND	AG	66	1.63*	0	0	0	0	100	5.4	5.4
MEESCHAERT CAP. ACCUM.	G	30	1.70	42	0	0	0	58	-4.3	-6.8
MERRILL L. BASIC VALUE	GI	799	na	15	0	1	0	84	4.0	4.0
MERRILL L. CALIF TAX-EX	MB	497	na	8	92	0	0	0	3.6	2.0
MERRILL L. CORP DIV FUND	BP	253	na	6	0	90	0	4	2.0	0.0
MERRILL L. BOND-INTERMED	BP	100	na	na	na	na	na	na	3.8	1.5
MERRILL L. FEDERAL SECS	BP	6,651	na	100	0	0	0	0	2.6	0.5
MERRILL L. INTERNATIONAL	IN	278	na	12	3	0	0	85	5.5	4.3
MERRILL L. CAPITAL FUND	GI	547	na	31	1	0	0	68	5.3	4.5
MERRILL L. EQUI-BOND I	B	16	na	7	58	0	0	35	3.1	1.0
MERRILL L. HIGH INC BOND	BP	597	na	11	88	0	0	1	3.7	0.7
MERRILL L. PACIFIC FUND	IN	445	na	9	1	0	0	90	4.6	4.6
MERRILL L. PHOENIX	B	118	na	39	17	2	0	42	2.2	0.1
MERRILL L. MUNI-BD HIYLD	MB	1,557	na	4	96	0	0	0	3.8	1.9
MERRILL L. MUNI-BD INSD	MB	2,039	na	8	92	0	0	0	3.6	1.7
MERRILL L. MUNI-LTD MAT	MB	668	na	59	41	0	0	0	1.6	0.3
MERRILL L. SPECIAL VALUE	AG	97	na	3	3	0	0	94	-2.7	-2.9
MERRILL L. NAT RESOURCE	G	259	na	15	0	0	0	85	6.6	6.6
MERRILL L. HIGH QUAL BD	BP	225	na	22	78	0	0	0	4.4	2.2
MERRILL L. NY MUNI BOND	MB	487	na	1	99	0	0	0	3.8	2.4
MERRILL L. FUND FOR TOM	G	607	na	13	0	0	0	87	2.4	2.4
MERRILL L. RETIRE BEN IN	B	2,066	na	26	32	0	0	42	3.0	1.3
MERRILL L. RETIRE/INCOME	BP	1,430	na	9	91	0	0	0	2.0	0.1

R2	STD DEV	BETA	ALPHA PCNT	RK	12/86 N.A.V.	INCOME OCT	NOV	DEC	12 MON	CAPITAL GAIN OCT	NOV	DEC	12 MON
72	3.45	0.70	-1.2	52	16.96		.150		0.650			.400	0.400
16	1.48	0.14	4.1	25	8.97	.070	.070	.070	0.897				0.000
27	2.45	0.31	3.9	27	8.34	.050	.050	.050	0.600				0.000
na	na	na	na	na	8.75				0.084				0.000
na	na	na	na	na	9.33	.070	.070	.070	0.899				0.000
na	na	na	na	na	8.83		.350		1.395				0.000
95	4.63	1.07	0.5	45	8.95				0.080		.650		1.240
90	4.85	1.09	-11.3	89	11.21				0.176		1.05		1.930
31	2.08	0.28	6.4	8	14.66	.100	.105	.105	1.360		.400		0.400
92	4.91	1.12	-7.1	79	10.89	.055		.052	0.227	2.44			2.445
79	5.95	1.25	-9.5	86	16.82				0.000		1.64		1.640
na	na	na	na	na	9.76	.075	.072	.068	0.772	.025	.028	.032	0.085
28	1.60	0.21	3.1	32	6.92	.078	.078	.078	0.936				0.099
0	3.63	0.05	11.0	2	11.46		.435		0.825			1.59	2.248
89	5.38	1.20	-10.5	88	8.59				0.079		.500		1.052
94	3.29	0.77	2.5	35	10.19		.137		0.581				0.883
na	na	na	na	na	9.57				na				na
93	4.76	1.09	-7.3	79	9.44		.057		0.197		2.98		2.978
96	4.19	0.98	-2.9	59	12.09			.100	0.400			1.75	1.751
na	na	na	na	na	10.32	.077	.077	.077	0.985				0.000
na	na	na	na	na	9.76	.075	.072	.068	0.716	.025	.028	.032	0.241
na	na	na	na	na	10.31	.083	.083	.081	1.019				0.077
28	2.01	0.26	5.3	15	10.63	.064	.061	.061	0.776		.388		0.388
na	na	na	na	na	11.02	.063	.058	.057	0.767				0.010
na	na	na	na	na	11.53	.064	.062	.060	0.770				0.161
na	na	na	na	na	11.12	.062	.057	.059	0.754				0.004
89	4.82	1.08	-6.1	74	16.96				0.810		2.37		7.380
86	6.35	1.39	-8.9	84	13.38				0.000				0.185
63	3.09	0.59	-3.6	62	25.87		.750		0.750				0.000
93	3.90	0.90	0.8	43	17.06				0.580				0.860
na	na	na	na	na	11.63	.070	.055	.056	0.761	.045			0.045
na	na	na	na	na	10.90	.072	.070	.073	0.877				0.000
29	1.52	0.20	5.8	10	11.87	.086	.086	.086	1.043				0.000
na	na	na	na	na	9.87	.078	.063	.063	0.868			.040	0.440
na	na	na	na	na	14.28		.160		0.300				1.270
92	3.56	0.82	2.3	36	24.40		.190		0.440				2.100
73	2.54	0.52	1.5	39	13.24		.300		0.610		.740		0.740
36	1.59	0.23	3.8	28	8.34	.085	.074	.083	0.973				0.000
10	6.05	0.45	22.7	1	34.20				0.110				0.190
82	2.39	0.52	4.9	20	12.39	.290			0.610	1.01			1.010
27	1.95	0.25	5.7	12	10.67	.072	.060	.070	0.822				0.178
27	2.19	0.28	4.0	26	8.18	.052	.043	.051	0.586				0.011
17	0.29	0.03	-0.9	50	9.90	.046	.040	.046	0.561				0.000
81	4.91	1.05	-9.3	85	13.97		.020		0.050				0.620
na	na	na	na	na	12.71				0.110				0.280
23	1.83	0.21	6.7	6	11.95	.090	.077	.085	1.068				0.000
ra	na	na	na	na	11.24	.054	.053	.053	0.712	.073			0.073
na	na	na	na	na	15.18				0.100				0.080
na	na	na	na	na	11.03	.190			0.250	.280			0.280
na	na	na	na	na	9.98	.059	.059	.066	na				na

CDA QUARTERLY SUPPLEMENT – 12/31/86

FUND	IO	ASSETS (MIL$) 9/86	ANNL %EXP RATE	CASH	NON CVT BOND	NON CVT PREF	CVTS	COMM STKS	LATEST QTR ROR 9/86 - 12/86 TOTAL	PRINCIPAL
MIDAMERICA HIGH GROWTH	G	11	na	16	0	0	0	84	6.4	5.0
MIDAMERICA MUTUAL FUND	GI	32	na	26	0	0	0	74	4.0	2.3
MIDWEST INC-INTERMED TRM	BP	53	1.20	15	85	0	0	0	2.3	0.5
MONITREND VALUE FUND	G	26	na	na	na	na	na	na	-0.2	-1.5
MORGAN (W.L.) GROWTH	G	633	0.60	2	0	0	0	98	4.3	2.8
MUTUAL BEACON GROWTH FD	G	62	1.40	8	5	5	6	76	5.3	3.6
MUTUAL BENEFIT FUND	G	15	0.70	13	0	0	0	86	6.4	6.4
MUTUAL OF OMAHA AMERICA	BP	40	0.75	13	87	0	0	0	2.5	0.6
MUTUAL OF OMAHA GROWTH	G	31	0.83	15	0	0	0	85	3.9	2.6
MUTUAL OF OMAHA INCOME	GI	105	0.58	6	62	1	2	29	3.9	1.8
MUTUAL QUALIFIED INCOME	B	517	0.70	9	8	8	8	68	4.3	1.0
MUTUAL SHARES CORP.	B	1,293	0.67	12	7	7	7	67	3.4	0.9
NAESS & THOMAS SPECIAL	AG	31	na	4	0	0	0	96	2.5	2.5
NATL AVIATION & TECH	G	84	na	4	3	0	8	85	2.0	2.0
NATL FEDERAL SECURITIES	BP	1,178	na	1	99	0	0	0	3.4	0.7
NATIONAL INDUSTRIES FUND	G	27	0.70	4	0	0	0	96	3.6	2.6
NATL SECURITIES BALANCED	B	2	1.22	18	29	0	4	49	4.3	2.7
NATL SECURITIES BOND	BP	520	0.94	8	92	0	0	0	0.5	-3.1
NATL SECURITIES CAL TX E	MB	74	0.46	3	97	0	0	0	4.0	2.1
NATL SECURITIES GROWTH	G	66	0.91	12	0	0	0	88	6.8	6.3
NATL SECURITIES PREFERED	BP	4	1.07	9	0	70	21	0	1.8	-0.5
NATL SECS REAL ESTATE	GI	13	na	13	0	0	2	85	0.0	-0.6
NATL SECURITIES STOCK	GI	255	na	19	1	0	4	76	3.5	2.5
NATL SECURITIES TOT INC	B	76	0.90	12	26	0	6	56	4.6	3.3
NATL SECURITIES TOT RET	GI	259	0.88	27	21	1	0	51	4.4	3.1
NATL SECURITIES TX EX BD	MB	78	0.79	3	97	0	0	0	4.3	2.5
NATL TELECOMMUNICATIONS	G	59	na	1	2	0	10	87	5.3	5.3
NATIONWIDE FUND	GI	344	0.65	6	0	0	0	94	6.5	5.9
NATIONWIDE GROWTH FUND	G	162	0.69	16	0	0	0	84	5.8	2.7
NATIONWIDE BOND FUND	BP	20	0.76	7	93	0	0	0	3.9	1.8
NAUTILUS FUND	AG	18	1.75	10	0	0	0	90	3.4	3.4
NEL EQUITY FUND	GI	30	1.25	7	24	2	0	67	6.1	6.1
NEL GOVERNMENT SEC TR	BP	174	na	4	96	0	0	0	3.1	1.4
NEL GROWTH FUND	AG	286	0.85	1	0	0	0	99	3.7	3.7
NEL INCOME	BP	50	0.93	7	93	0	0	0	2.9	0.8
NEL RETIREMENT EQUITY	G	95	0.92	1	0	0	0	99	5.3	5.3
NEL TAX EXEMPT	MB	105	na	11	89	0	0	0	4.2	2.5
NEUWIRTH FUND	AG	26	na	16	0	0	1	83	-1.1	-1.1
NEW ECONOMY FUND	G	719	0.67	26	0	0	0	74	3.8	1.9
NEW PERSPECTIVE FUND	G	870	0.68	18	4	0	1	77	8.2	6.9
NEWPORT FAR EAST	IN	3	na	na	na	na	na	na	6.7	6.7
NEW YORK VENTURE FUND	G	147	0.99	1	0	5	2	92	6.9	6.9
NEWTON GROWTH FUND	G	34	1.51*	16	4	0	0	80	3.0	1.5
NEWTON INCOME FUND	BP	12	1.75*	24	76	0	0	0	2.0	0.0
NICHOLAS FUND	G	1,053	0.86	38	1	0	1	60	1.7	1.7
NICHOLAS II	G	299	0.86	9	0	0	2	89	1.4	-1.1
NICHOLAS INCOME FUND	BP	56	1.00	13	82	2	0	3	2.3	0.0
NICHOLSON GROWTH FUND	G	0	4.04*	10	0	0	0	90	2.7	2.7
NODDING CALAMOS INCOME	BP	16	na	0	0	0	100	0	2.7	1.4
NOMURA PACIFIC BASIN FD	IN	53	1.48	23	0	0	1	77	7.6	7.6

36 MONTH MPT STATISTICS					DISTRIBUTION INFORMATION								
	STD		ALPHA		12/86	INCOME				CAPITAL GAIN			
R2	DEV	BETA	PCNT	RK	N.A.V.	OCT	NOV	DEC	12 MON	OCT	NOV	DEC	12 MON
82	5.09	1.10	-10.9	88	4.34			.070	0.070			.994	0.994
89	4.01	0.91	-3.3	61	5.98			.120	0.240			1.39	1.387
8	1.33	0.09	3.5	29	10.76	.066	.066	.068	0.866				0.000
na	na	na	na	na	18.73			.260	0.380			.710	0.780
80	4.85	1.03	-7.5	80	11.50			.200	0.430			1.75	2.880
70	2.92	0.59	-1.2	52	18.64		.310		0.310		.940		0.940
92	4.11	0.94	-1.1	51	13.66				0.315			1.05	1.660
17	1.73	0.17	3.4	29	10.65			.210	0.920				0.000
76	4.09	0.85	-3.2	60	7.09			.095	0.095			.420	0.420
57	2.23	0.41	2.3	36	8.94			.190	0.800			.272	0.272
63	2.14	0.41	6.0	10	20.04		.700		1.100			1.15	1.150
68	2.14	0.42	6.2	8	60.39		1.60		2.600			4.05	4.050
75	6.06	1.24	-19.9	97	35.10				0.000	5.67			5.670
64	4.42	0.85	-5.3	71	11.02				0.240			.520	0.930
na	na	na	na	na	11.22	.100	.100	.100	1.200		.065		0.290
86	4.22	0.93	-10.0	87	11.64			.130	0.380			1.32	1.820
86	2.46	0.55	3.9	27	13.85			.220	0.880		1.00		2.610
27	2.08	0.26	2.2	36	3.16	.038	.038	.039	0.465				0.000
na	na	na	na	na	13.20	.082	.082	.080	0.991				0.000
81	5.21	1.11	-10.3	87	11.01		.060		0.200				0.000
51	1.64	0.28	7.1	5	8.50	.190			0.760				0.330
na	na	na	na	na	9.82		.070		0.280		.120		0.430
91	3.43	0.78	1.0	43	8.99	.110			0.440		1.60		2.030
70	3.06	0.62	5.3	16	7.84		.110		0.460		.150		0.360
84	2.73	0.60	3.0	32	7.42			.095	0.380				0.080
27	2.38	0.30	5.6	13	10.26	.063	.060	.060	0.759				0.000
84	4.74	1.04	-13.9	93	13.80				0.160				0.000
95	4.05	0.94	1.4	40	13.47		.090		0.390		.810		0.810
83	4.57	0.99	1.1	41	8.56		.300		0.300		1.21		1.210
23	1.68	0.20	5.1	18	10.21		.210		0.910		.040		0.040
46	5.72	0.92	-23.2	98	12.15				0.000				0.000
90	4.37	0.99	-2.2	55	20.60				0.730			3.25	5.020
na	na	na	na	na	13.48	.075	.075	.075	1.055				0.047
85	5.65	1.24	-5.4	71	26.65				0.220			1.80	3.970
22	1.50	0.17	5.1	18	11.65	.080	.080	.080	0.930				0.000
84	4.98	1.09	-0.6	49	26.18				0.420				2.730
33	2.29	0.32	5.7	12	7.75	.046	.042	.042	0.678			.360	0.600
80	5.88	1.25	-8.5	82	13.27				0.044			2.01	3.213
88	4.09	0.92	0.4	45	19.41			.380	0.380			1.12	2.250
57	4.01	0.73	3.3	30	9.99	.130			0.220	1.25			1.250
na	na	na	na	na	20.15				0.000				0.000
88	4.03	0.90	3.2	31	9.20				0.100				1.680
74	4.22	0.87	-7.0	77	20.74			.350	1.059			4.27	11.733
8	0.99	0.07	2.8	33	8.47		.170		0.730				0.000
82	3.21	0.69	1.6	39	34.87				0.882				0.187
77	3.23	0.67	4.5	23	16.22	.420			0.420	.513			0.513
18	1.52	0.16	5.3	16	4.01	.092			0.382				0.000
na	na	na	na	na	15.00				0.000				0.000
na	na	na	na	na	11.23		.150		0.536			.400	0.534
na	na	na	na	na	21.13				0.300				0.060

CDA QUARTERLY SUPPLEMENT - 12/31/86

FUND	IO	ASSETS (MIL$) 9/86	ANNL %EXP RATE	CASH	NON CVT BOND	PREF	CVTS	COMM STKS	TOTAL	PRINCIPAL
NORTH STAR APOLLO FUND	G	21	na	17	0	3	0	80	2.3	1.5
NORTH STAR BOND	BP	36	na	9	91	0	0	0	2.7	0.5
NORTH STAR REGIONAL FUND	G	84	na	29	0	1	1	69	4.6	3.6
NORTH STAR STOCK FUND	G	65	na	18	0	3	0	79	5.5	4.3
NORTHEAST INV GROWTH	G	18	na	7	0	0	0	93	5.1	5.1
NORTHEAST INV. TRUST	BP	313	na	0	100	0	0	0	3.4	0.7
NOVA FUND INC	AG	23	1.50	9	0	0	0	91	8.7	8.7
NUVEEN MUNICIPAL BOND FD	MB	668	0.75	0	100	0	0	0	3.7	1.9
OLD DOMINION INVTS TR	GI	6	1.17	9	0	0	0	91	6.4	5.1
OLYMPIC TRUST SERIES B	G	4	na	2	0	0	0	98	2.6	1.4
OLYMPIC TRUST TOT RETURN	B	1	na	15	42	0	0	43	3.2	3.2
OMEGA FUND	G	32	1.65	3	7	0	7	83	5.1	5.1
ONE HUNDRED FUND	AG	11	1.70	4	0	0	0	96	3.4	3.4
ONE HUNDRED ONE FUND	GI	3	1.90	9	0	0	47	44	1.4	0.6
OPPENHEIMER A.I.M. FUND	IN	373	1.63	0	0	0	0	100	7.5	7.1
OPPENHEIMER DIRECTORS	G	210	1.04	1	3	0	0	96	1.2	1.2
OPPENHEIMER EQUITY INC.	GI	420	1.00	15	14	0	18	53	3.8	2.4
OPPENHEIMER FUND	AG	236	na	10	0	0	0	90	0.9	0.7
OPPENHEIMER GOLD & SPEC.	ME	40	1.50	0	0	0	0	100	2.1	2.1
OPPENHEIMER HIGH YIELD	BP	636	0.86	8	89	0	2	0	3.5	0.2
OPPENHEIMER PREMIUM INC	GI	375	0.89	0	0	0	0	100	6.2	5.9
OPPENHEIMER NY TX EXEMPT	MB	51	0.86	6	94	0	0	0	4.0	2.4
OPPENHEIMER REGENCY	AG	147	1.10	29	0	0	3	68	3.3	3.3
OPPENHEIMER SPECIAL FUND	G	709	0.84	33	24	1	0	42	3.1	3.1
OPPENHEIMER SELECT STOCK	G	10	1.50	15	0	0	0	85	3.3	3.0
OPPENHEIMER RETR-GOV SEC	BP	12	1.00	1	99	0	0	0	2.0	-0.3
OPPENHEIMER TARGET FUND	G	119	1.11	2	0	0	1	97	-5.7	-5.7
OPPENHEIMER TAX FREE BD	MB	120	0.78	5	95	0	0	0	4.1	2.5
OPPENHEIMER TIME FUND	G	230	0.90	6	0	0	0	94	2.5	2.5
OVER-THE-COUNTER SEC.	G	237	na	7	0	0	6	87	-0.7	-0.7
PBHG GROWTH FUND	AG	18	1.50	7	5	0	0	87	10.3	9.9
PACIFIC HORIZON AGGRE GR	AG	64	na	0	0	0	0	0	2.4	2.4
PACIFIC HORIZON CAL TAX	MB	86	na	0	0	0	0	0	4.0	2.4
PACIFIC HORIZON HIYLD BD	BP	27	na	0	0	0	0	0	3.1	0.4
PAINE WEBBER AMERICA FD	GI	91	1.34	8	15	2	40	35	0.3	-0.8
PAINE WEBBER ATLAS FD	IN	224	1.42	5	2	0	2	90	5.5	-0.3
PAINE WEBBER CALIF TX-EX	MB	136	na	0	100	0	0	0	3.8	2.1
PAINE WEBBER FI INVT GR	BP	331	0.70	9	91	0	0	0	4.6	1.7
PAINE WEBBER GNMA	BP	2,907	na	0	100	0	0	0	3.4	0.6
PAINE WEBBER HIGH YIELD	BP	675	0.74	2	96	0	1	0	1.7	-1.6
PAINE WEBBER OLYMPUS FD	G	109	1.06	5	0	0	0	94	-0.4	-0.4
PAINE WEBBER TAX-EX INC	MB	313	na	0	100	0	0	0	3.5	1.8
PARTNERS FUND	GI	444	na	1	27	0	0	72	3.8	3.8
PAX WORLD FUND	IN	49	1.40	6	12	0	0	82	2.4	2.4
PENN SQUARE MUTUAL FUND	GI	195	0.79	11	0	0	0	89	5.9	4.7
PENNSYLVANIA MUTUAL FUND	G	346	na	18	0	0	0	82	2.4	2.4
PERMANENT PORTFOLIO	G	71	na	45	10	0	0	45	0.3	0.3
PHILADELPHIA FUND	G	107	na	12	0	0	0	88	3.4	2.8
PHOENIX BALANCED FD SER	B	153	na	13	27	3	15	42	2.7	1.4
PHOENIX GROWTH FUND SER	GI	242	na	18	3	0	0	79	4.7	4.7

36 MONTH MPT STATISTICS					12/86	INCOME				CAPITAL GAIN			
R2	STD DEV	BETA	ALPHA PCNT	RK	N.A.V.	OCT	NOV	DEC	12 MON	OCT	NOV	DEC	12 MON
78	4.61	0.97	-13.6	92	10.18		.081		0.184				0.335
13	2.14	0.18	4.8	20	10.39	.230			0.896				0.000
83	4.13	0.90	1.0	42	18.42		.207		0.416			2.00	6.447
90	4.03	0.91	-3.7	63	14.25		.180		0.373			1.00	1.801
84	4.32	0.94	2.7	34	18.36				0.130			.314	0.523
22	1.67	0.19	9.1	3	13.70		.365		1.460				0.000
67	5.12	1.00	-8.2	82	14.38				0.040			2.00	2.280
28	1.84	0.24	5.6	13	8.96	.053	.050	.050	0.605				0.205
90	4.18	0.95	-2.6	57	24.98	.310			1.360	1.68			1.680
na	na	na	na	na	15.57			.180	0.225				0.000
na	na	na	na	na	14.40				0.360				0.255
88	4.81	1.07	-4.2	66	13.44				0.280			1.73	2.120
63	5.33	1.00	-10.1	87	19.71				0.000	1.16			1.160
40	3.44	0.52	0.4	45	14.98	.150			0.590	3.00			3.000
35	5.06	0.72	3.7	28	26.99	.110			0.170	3.08		.730	3.810
87	4.55	1.01	-13.7	93	21.92				0.000				0.000
87	3.05	0.69	1.0	42	8.46	.120			0.473			.090	0.610
84	5.56	1.21	-12.7	91	9.88	.020			0.100	.030			1.070
0	8.54	0.08	-9.3	85	8.45				0.137				0.000
44	1.73	0.28	0.0	46	16.73	.180	.180	.180	2.240				0.000
59	3.09	0.57	-6.2	74	18.26	.050			0.878	.550			1.892
na	na	na	na	na	12.68	.065	.060	.067	0.831		.135		0.225
77	5.40	1.13	-14.0	93	15.63				0.207				0.128
75	4.59	0.95	-9.6	86	18.90				1.000			.200	3.970
na	na	na	na	na	12.22	.030			0.237				0.658
na	na	na	na	na	10.42	.235			1.000				0.515
73	4.89	0.99	-11.1	88	20.49				0.380				0.000
31	2.14	0.29	5.7	12	9.81	.050	.052	.052	0.672				0.000
82	4.66	1.00	-4.8	68	16.21				0.520				1.620
68	3.66	0.72	-3.3	61	16.99				0.060			1.44	2.540
na	na	na	na	na	12.32		.040		0.070				0.000
na	na	na	na	na	25.48				0.053				0.000
na	na	na	na	na	14.45	.078	.072	.072	0.959				0.000
na	na	na	na	na	16.41	.149	.153	.146	1.822				0.000
na	na	na	na	na	15.04			.170	0.980				1.061
na	na	na	na	na	15.94	.991			0.991	2.14			2.140
na	na	na	na	na	11.18	.062	.062	.063	0.781				0.000
na	na	na	na	na	10.75	.100	.100	.100	1.201				0.013
na	na	na	na	na	10.21	.093	.093	.093	1.184				0.005
na	na	na	na	na	10.36	.118	.118	.118	1.400				0.025
na	na	na	na	na	10.86				0.000	.511			0.511
na	na	na	na	na	11.39	.066	.068	.059	0.814				0.000
94	3.42	0.80	1.7	38	17.37				0.440				2.250
86	3.23	0.72	-1.5	53	13.19				0.500				0.710
95	4.08	0.95	-4.2	66	9.21	.110			0.390			.620	1.250
83	2.93	0.64	-1.1	51	6.98				0.130			.720	1.110
25	2.46	0.30	-6.5	76	13.18				0.000				0.000
93	4.05	0.93	-7.8	81	6.70			.050	0.210			2.35	2.350
84	2.84	0.62	6.0	10	12.75			.190	0.685			1.39	2.071
92	3.66	0.84	3.3	31	16.40				0.335			2.14	2.912

CDA QUARTERLY SUPPLEMENT - 12/31/86

FUND	IO	ASSETS (MIL$) 9/86	ANNL %EXP RATE	CASH	NON CVT BOND	PREF	CVTS	COMM STKS	TOTAL	PRINCIPAL
PHOENIX CONVERTIBLE FUND	GI	100	na	25	0	0	58	17	3.7	2.6
PHOENIX HIGH YIELD	BP	103	na	4	96	0	0	0	3.2	0.1
PHOENIX STOCK FUND SER	G	95	na	19	4	0	0	77	6.8	6.8
PHOENIX TOTAL RETURN FD	GI	5	na	33	0	0	0	67	4.1	4.1
PILGRIM ADJUSTABLE RATE	BP	883	0.80*	6	0	92	1	0	0.2	-1.5
PILGRIM GNMA	BP	260	1.00*	0	100	0	0	0	2.6	0.3
PILGRIM HIGH YIELD FD	BP	17	1.50*	16	82	2	0	0	2.2	-0.7
PILGRIM MAGNACAP FUND	GI	181	1.40*	8	0	0	6	86	2.1	2.1
PILGRIM PREFERRED	BP	198	na	na	na	na	na	na	2.0	-0.8
PILOT FUND	AG	64	1.22*	13	0	0	0	87	4.9	4.9
PINE STREET FUND	GI	61	1.17	5	0	2	12	81	2.5	1.6
PIONEER BOND FUND	BP	37	1.00	23	77	0	0	0	2.9	0.6
PIONEER FUND	GI	1,377	0.68	1	0	0	4	96	4.5	3.8
PIONEER II	G	2,842	0.68	10	0	0	0	90	5.2	3.8
PIONEER THREE	G	543	0.75	9	0	0	1	90	3.2	2.1
PRICE (ROWE) EQUITY INC	GI	71	na	12	0	0	28	60	6.8	5.4
PRICE (ROWE) GROWTH&INC.	GI	376	1.01	5	16	0	3	76	2.2	0.8
PRICE (ROWE) GROWTH STK.	G	1,278	na	9	0	0	1	90	3.3	3.3
PRICE (ROWE) HI YLD BOND	BP	703	1.00	7	91	0	1	0	2.8	-0.1
PRICE (ROWE) INTERNATL.	IN	753	1.10	2	3	0	2	93	8.6	8.6
PRICE (ROWE) NEW AMERICA	G	76	na	4	0	0	0	96	4.4	4.4
PRICE (ROWE) NEW ERA	G	494	na	10	0	0	0	90	4.2	4.2
PRICE (ROWE) NEW HORIZ.	AG	1,089	0.72	4	0	0	1	95	3.3	3.3
PRICE (ROWE) NEW INCOME	BP	946	0.66	15	85	0	0	0	3.0	1.1
PRICE (ROWE) TAX FR HIYD	MB	226	1.00	3	97	0	0	0	3.8	2.0
PRICE (ROWE) TX FREE INC	MB	1,411	0.62	18	82	0	0	0	4.4	2.8
PRICE (ROWE) TXFR SH-INT	MB	242	0.79	22	78	0	0	0	2.1	0.8
PRIMECAP FUND	G	105	0.98	4	0	0	0	96	7.4	6.6
PRINCOR CAP ACCUMULATION	GI	55	1.01	2	5	1	0	92	4.0	3.4
PRINCOR GOV SECS INCOME	BP	52	0.96	0	100	0	0	0	4.8	2.7
PRINCOR GROWTH FD, INC.	G	24	1.07	3	0	0	0	97	4.6	4.6
PROVIDENT FD. FOR INCOME	B	102	0.72	3	34	0	1	62	5.3	3.8
PRU-BACHE ADJ RATE PFD	BP	284	na	na	na	na	na	na	0.2	-1.5
PRU-BACHE EQUITY FUND	AG	279	1.00	23	0	0	0	76	4.2	4.2
PRU-BACHE GLOBAL FUND	IN	401	na	na	na	na	na	na	1.1	1.1
PRU-BACHE GOV SECURITIES	BP	702	na	11	88	0	0	0	2.1	-0.1
PRU-BACHE HIGH YIELD	BP	1,589	na	10	90	0	0	0	2.7	0.9
PRU-BACHE HIYLD MUNI	MB	981	na	3	97	0	0	0	4.2	2.5
PRU-BACHE GR OPPORTUNITY	AG	88	na	15	0	0	0	85	9.0	9.0
PRU-BACHE INCOMEVERTIBLE	BP	281	na	na	na	na	na	na	1.7	0.3
PRU-BACHE OPTION GROWTH	G	72	na	15	5	0	4	76	-1.0	-1.8
PRU-BACHE GNMA FUND	BP	270	na	3	96	0	0	0	3.5	1.6
PRU-BACHE RESEARCH FUND	GI	174	na	23	1	0	0	76	3.7	3.7
PRU-BACHE UTILITY FUND	GI	1,212	na	17	1	0	0	83	3.5	2.2
PUTNAM CALIF TAX EX	MB	810	na	0	100	0	0	0	4.2	2.3
PUTNAM CCT ARP	BP	597	na	100	0	0	0	0	0.4	-1.3
PUTNAM CCT DSP	B	412	na	2	0	67	0	31	2.0	-0.2
PUTNAM CONVERT INC-GR TR	GI	755	na	4	0	0	83	13	3.5	2.0
PUTNAM ENERGY RESOURCES	AG	36	na	8	0	0	19	74	5.4	3.6
PUTNAM INFOR SCIENCES	AG	119	na	5	0	0	0	95	8.0	7.7

| 36 MONTH MPT STATISTICS | | | | | DISTRIBUTION INFORMATION | | | | | | | | |
R2	STD DEV	BETA	ALPHA PCNT	RK	12/86 N.A.V.	INCOME OCT	NOV	DEC	12 MON	CAPITAL GAIN OCT	NOV	DEC	12 MON
88	2.62	0.59	0.6	44	17.44	.200			0.893			1.72	2.383
33	1.45	0.20	4.6	22	9.64	.100	.100	.100	1.195				0.000
87	4.40	0.98	-0.7	49	12.67				0.249			2.59	3.518
79	3.43	0.73	-5.3	71	12.38				0.425				0.000
4	1.70	0.08	-0.6	49	22.01	.140	.125	.125	1.685				0.000
na	na	na	na	na	15.33	.120	.117	.117	1.599				0.000
15	1.76	0.17	2.9	33	8.00	.080	.080	.080	0.960				0.000
85	3.29	0.72	6.1	9	9.81				0.250				0.340
na	na	na	na	na	25.04	.240	.240	.225	2.145				0.000
74	5.81	1.18	-11.2	89	9.47				0.000			1.00	1.000
94	3.98	0.92	-1.0	51	12.50			.120	0.518			1.10	3.062
24	1.37	0.16	4.4	24	9.60	.075	.070	.070	0.920				0.000
92	4.17	0.95	-5.2	71	19.72	.160			0.670			3.74	5.250
87	4.36	0.97	-4.6	67	18.14	.260			0.520	1.03			1.030
84	3.77	0.83	-3.0	60	15.18	.180			0.360	1.16			1.165
na	na	na	na	na	12.96	.170			0.650			.250	0.260
85	3.94	0.87	-6.2	75	12.98	.200			0.710			.880	1.570
82	4.24	0.92	0.1	46	16.96				0.380			3.00	4.180
na	na	na	na	na	10.87	.116	.099	.099	1.282				0.130
20	4.92	0.53	14.8	1	25.78				0.220			2.50	2.750
na	na	na	na	na	13.14				0.100			.300	0.300
83	4.03	0.88	-2.6	57	17.76				0.500			2.40	3.250
79	5.66	1.19	-13.1	92	12.38				0.090			2.22	2.640
32	1.12	0.16	4.7	21	9.13	.064	.055	.055	0.771				0.000
na	na	na	na	na	11.92	.076	.067	.067	0.868				0.000
29	1.77	0.23	4.1	26	10.07	.059	.050	.050	0.701				0.000
23	0.77	0.09	-0.1	47	5.27	.026	.022	.022	0.299				0.000
na	na	na	na	na	42.57			.320	0.560			.630	0.730
87	4.11	0.91	-0.3	48	17.16	.103			0.523				1.804
na	na	na	na	na	10.97	.077	.073	.073	1.147				0.284
88	5.16	1.15	-7.7	81	18.47				0.321				1.895
80	2.86	0.62	-2.4	56	4.59			.075	0.300			.370	0.440
na	na	na	na	na	23.07	.141	.131	.140	1.861				0.000
92	4.93	1.13	-2.3	56	9.04				0.060			.580	1.220
na	na	na	na	na	9.64				0.010			.950	1.100
20	1.33	0.14	5.2	17	10.84	.080	.080	.075	0.986				0.160
38	1.36	0.20	4.8	20	10.66	.095	.090		1.045			.090	0.110
na	na	na	na	na	16.18	.092	.089	.087	1.174			.600	0.780
77	5.58	1.17	-8.8	83	11.40				0.000	2.87		.500	3.370
na	na	na	na	na	10.94			.160	0.580				0.000
86	4.17	0.92	-3.5	62	8.72	.075			0.160				1.055
9	1.40	0.10	5.0	19	15.94	.100	.100	.100	1.365			.190	0.380
76	3.88	0.81	-0.8	50	12.24				0.175			.500	0.500
28	3.63	0.46	11.1	2	14.78			.200	0.800			.810	0.810
na	na	na	na	na	15.96	.090	.098	.098	1.174				0.000
na	na	na	na	na	46.04	.264	.263	.263	3.809				0.000
na	na	na	na	na	48.89	.392	.361	.361	5.189				0.000
92	2.98	0.69	0.8	43	16.24		.240		0.960				0.440
34	5.90	0.81	-12.2	90	11.25		.200		0.300				0.000
75	6.09	1.25	-14.1	93	14.08	.030			0.030				0.000

CDA QUARTERLY SUPPLEMENT – 12/31/86

FUND	IO	ASSETS (MIL$) 9/86	ANNL %EXP RATE	CASH	NON CVT BOND	PREF	CVTS	COMM STKS	TOTAL	PRINCIPAL
PUTNAM INTL EQUITIES	IN	372	na	15	0	0	1	84	5.8	5.8
PUTNAM (GEORGE) FD. BOS.	B	355	na	9	27	0	1	63	5.6	4.2
PUTNAM FD FOR GROWTH/INC	GI	1,164	na	16	7	0	19	58	5.1	3.9
PUTNAM GNMA PLUS	BP	584	na	100	0	0	0	0	2.7	-0.1
PUTNAM HEALTH SCIENCES	AG	241	na	5	0	0	2	94	5.3	4.3
PUTNAM HIGH INCOME GOV	BP	5,132	na	100	0	0	0	0	3.7	1.7
PUTNAM HIGH YIELD	BP	2,364	na	5	92	3	0	0	4.1	0.9
PUTNAM INCOME FUND	BP	208	na	28	72	0	0	0	3.8	1.1
PUTNAM INVESTORS FUND	G	960	na	4	0	0	0	96	4.7	4.2
PUTNAM NY TAX EXEMPT	MB	701	na	0	100	0	0	0	4.1	2.3
PUTNAM VISTA FUND	AG	194	na	0	0	0	0	100	5.0	5.0
PUTNAM OPTION INCOME I	GI	1,114	na	0	0	0	0	100	4.8	4.7
PUTNAM OPTION INCOME II	GI	1,173	na	5	0	0	0	95	4.8	3.9
PUTNAM TAX EXEMPT INC	MB	624	na	100	0	0	0	0	5.3	3.6
PUTNAM US GOV SECURITIES	BP	965	na	100	0	0	0	0	3.2	0.7
PUTNAM VOYAGER FUND	AG	350	na	4	0	0	0	96	8.1	8.1
QUALIFIED DIVD PORTF I	B	177	0.56	20	0	2	21	57	4.6	1.5
QUALIFIED DIVD PORTF II	BP	136	0.59	4	0	96	0	0	4.2	1.6
QUALIFIED DIVD PORT III	BP	141	na	6	0	94	0	0	0.8	-0.9
QUASAR ASSOCIATES	AG	145	na	0	0	0	0	100	0.7	0.7
QUEST FOR VALUE FUND	G	75	2.18	25	0	0	1	74	2.5	2.5
RAINBOW FUND	G	2	3.46	9	0	0	0	91	4.6	4.6
REA GRAHAM FUND	B	43	na	19	24	0	0	57	4.1	4.1
RETIREMENT PLANNING-BOND	BP	53	2.40*	9	91	0	0	0	3.1	0.6
RETIREMENT PLANNING-EQ	G	10	2.54*	2	0	6	0	92	6.4	6.4
RIGHTIME FUND	G	134	2.30*	6	0	0	0	94	4.3	4.3
ROCHESTER TAX MANAGED FD	G	29	na	0	0	0	20	80	-0.1	-0.1
ROYCE VALUE FUND, INC.	G	149	na	22	0	0	0	78	0.3	0.3
SAFECO EQUITY FUND	GI	47	0.86	3	0	0	3	94	1.3	0.8
SAFECO GROWTH FUND	G	68	0.85	13	0	0	3	84	1.8	1.0
SAFECO INCOME FUND	B	102	0.96	4	0	0	36	60	4.3	3.2
SAFECO MUNICIPAL BOND FD	MB	170	na	3	97	0	0	0	4.6	2.9
SBSF FUND	G	90	na	23	0	0	1	77	2.2	-0.3
SCHIELD AGGRESS GROWTH	AG	11	na	13	0	0	0	87	-7.8	-7.8
SCHIELD VALUE PORTFOLIO	G	12	na	11	0	0	0	89	-6.4	-6.4
SCI-TECH HOLDINGS	G	273	na	16	0	1	0	83	3.2	2.8
SCUDDER CALIF TAX FREE	MB	152	0.88	5	95	0	0	0	3.9	2.3
SCUDDER CAPITAL GROWTH	G	414	0.87	6	0	2	0	91	6.1	4.8
SCUDDER DEVELOPMENT FUND	AG	278	1.25	7	0	0	0	93	5.6	5.6
SCUDDER GLOBAL	IN	11	na	na	na	na	na	na	8.9	8.9
SCUDDER GOV MORTGAGE SEC	BP	214	na	na	na	na	na	na	3.4	1.3
SCUDDER GROWTH & INCOME	GI	367	0.77	8	0	1	33	58	4.8	3.7
SCUDDER INCOME FUND	BP	217	0.86	7	76	2	1	13	4.2	1.9
SCUDDER INTERNATIONAL FD	IN	686	0.99	3	6	0	0	91	9.4	9.4
SCUDDER NEW YORK TAX FR	MB	111	0.88	4	96	0	0	0	4.2	2.6
SCUDDER MANAGED MUNI BD	MB	630	0.62	3	97	0	0	0	4.0	2.2
SCUDDER TX FR TARGT 1990	MB	81	1.24	8	92	0	0	0	2.4	1.0
SCUDDER TX FR TARGT 1993	MB	95	1.21	4	96	0	0	0	3.0	1.6
SECURITY ACTION FD	G	77	na	na	na	na	na	na	0.7	0.7
SECURITY INC FD-CORP BD	BP	45	1.40*	3	97	0	0	0	1.7	-0.8

| | 36 MONTH MPT STATISTICS | | | | DISTRIBUTION INFORMATION | | | | | | | | |
| | STD | | ALPHA | | 12/86 | INCOME | | | | CAPITAL GAIN | | | |
R2	DEV	BETA	PCNT	RK	N.A.V.	OCT	NOV	DEC	12 MON	OCT	NOV	DEC	12 MON
49	4.23	0.71	14.4	1	30.39				0.140				1.580
87	3.49	0.78	-1.0	50	14.66		.200		0.800				0.110
93	3.12	0.72	2.6	35	13.69		.150		0.650				1.130
na	na	na	na	na	11.38	.107	.107	.107	na				na
84	5.88	1.27	-4.5	67	17.44	.200			0.200	2.74			2.740
na	na	na	na	na	12.47	.085	.080	.080	1.115	.115	.020	.020	0.385
26	1.69	0.21	3.4	29	15.62	.165	.165	.165	2.120				0.000
24	1.77	0.21	5.5	14	7.42	.066	.066	.066	0.792				0.000
92	4.97	1.13	-4.7	68	11.62		.050		0.200				1.770
na	na	na	na	na	17.37	.105	.107	.105	1.300			.140	0.140
88	5.45	1.21	-7.9	82	17.52				0.590				2.840
86	3.47	0.77	-4.2	66	10.56	.020			0.204	.400			1.506
na	na	na	na	na	10.82		.100		0.400		.350		1.400
36	2.29	0.34	4.7	21	26.27	.140	.147	.145	1.862	.220		.250	0.610
na	na	na	na	na	14.71	.120	.120	.120	1.507				0.010
84	5.74	1.25	-4.2	65	19.59				0.150				2.730
64	2.94	0.56	10.7	2	17.07		.610		1.360		3.29		3.290
28	2.54	0.33	9.2	3	9.52		.250		0.850				0.000
3	1.67	0.07	-2.1	55	22.47	.127	.132	.127	1.660				0.000
77	6.07	1.26	-7.4	80	56.85				0.000		9.21		9.210
84	2.98	0.66	0.5	45	25.49				0.198			.770	2.592
75	3.72	0.77	-5.1	69	5.41				0.000				0.000
32	2.72	0.37	3.3	30	15.14				0.470				1.830
na	na	na	na	na	7.96	.065	.065	.065	0.815				0.000
na	na	na	na	na	19.23				0.050			1.00	2.200
na	na	na	na	na	29.89				0.050			1.95	1.950
81	3.15	0.68	-9.5	86	10.61				0.000				0.000
74	3.39	0.70	-3.8	64	8.33				0.040			.580	0.880
93	4.24	0.98	-2.3	56	9.54	.059			0.294	2.03			2.034
88	4.39	0.98	-11.8	90	14.00	.129			0.311	1.58			1.585
94	3.33	0.77	3.4	30	15.28	.172			0.776	.727			0.727
30	2.36	0.31	5.5	13	13.97	.083	.074	.078	1.005				0.207
53	3.24	0.56	2.8	34	12.72			.350	0.690			1.21	1.740
na	na	na	na	na	10.37				0.000				0.000
na	na	na	na	na	11.14				0.000				0.000
61	4.25	0.80	-4.9	69	11.94		.050		0.100				0.530
na	na	na	na	na	11.01	.058	.056	.056	0.704				0.296
86	4.54	1.01	-1.2	52	15.59		.230		0.230		2.46		2.460
79	5.41	1.14	-12.5	91	20.71				0.000				1.330
na	na	na	na	na	12.43				na				na
na	na	na	na	na	15.50	.106	.115	.100	1.416				0.075
90	4.22	0.96	-2.4	56	15.02		.170		0.680			850	2.276
36	1.79	0.26	5.3	16	13.41		.300		1.220				0.000
24	4.24	0.50	15.7	1	39.79				0.492			4.25	5.934
29	2.41	0.31	2.0	38	11.30	.062	.057	.057	0.731				0.149
27	2.55	0.32	3.5	29	8.93	.057	.049	.049	0.600			.240	0.240
16	1.34	0.13	0.5	44	10.34	.052	.047	.047	0.612				0.000
18	1.78	0.19	1.5	40	11.04	.058	.051	.051	0.670				0.000
81	3.83	0.82	-3.9	64	9.69				0.250				0.270
22	1.67	0.19	5.1	19	8.32	.070	.070	.070	0.949				0.000

CDA QUARTERLY SUPPLEMENT – 12/31/86

FUND	IO	ASSETS (MIL$) 9/86	ANNL %EXP RATE	CASH	NON BOND	CVT PREF	CVTS	COMM STKS	LATEST QTR ROR 9/86 - 12/86 TOTAL	PRINCIPAL
SECURITY EQUITY FUND	GI	235	0.77	14	1	0	0	85	4.1	2.6
SECURITY INVESTMENT FUND	GI	101	0.79	9	5	0	40	46	2.4	0.9
SECURITY OMNI FUND	AG	23	na	na	na	na	na	na	-3.8	-8.7
SECURITY ULTRA FUND	GI	100	0.82	45	0	0	0	55	-0.9	-4.7
SELECTED AMERICAN SHARES	GI	144	0.87	3	0	0	0	97	3.7	3.7
SELECTED SPECIAL SHARES	G	35	1.23	10	0	0	17	73	-0.4	-0.4
SELIGMAN CAPITAL FUND	AG	192	0.82	14	0	0	0	86	2.3	2.3
SELIGMAN CALIF TAX EX HI	MB	51	0.66	5	94	0	0	0	7.4	5.5
SELIGMAN CAL TAX EX QUAL	MB	53	0.67	10	90	0	0	0	4.3	2.6
SELIGMAN COMMUNICATIONS	AG	41	na	6	0	0	0	94	5.1	5.1
SELIGMAN COMMON STOCK FD	GI	523	0.58	3	8	0	4	85	6.6	5.6
SELIGMAN GROWTH FD	G	602	0.59	12	0	0	0	88	8.1	7.2
SELIGMAN GOV GUARANTEED	BP	77	0.66*	12	88	0	0	0	1.9	0.8
SELIGMAN HIGH YIELD BOND	BP	63	0.79*	6	94	0	0	0	2.6	-0.1
SELIGMAN INCOME FD	B	143	na	3	45	0	13	39	3.5	1.3
SELIGMAN SECURED MTG	BP	47	0.64*	0	100	0	0	0	2.5	1.3
SELIGMAN TX EX LOUISIANA	MB	45	na	4	96	0	0	0	3.5	1.7
SELIGMAN TAX EX MARYLAND	MB	46	na	7	93	0	0	0	3.8	2.3
SELIGMAN TAX EX MASS	MB	132	na	2	98	0	0	0	3.4	1.7
SELIGMAN TAX EX MICH	MB	99	na	3	97	0	0	0	3.1	1.4
SELIGMAN TAX EX MINN	MB	108	na	11	89	0	0	0	3.3	1.5
SELIGMAN TAX EX NATL	MB	110	na	4	96	0	0	0	4.0	2.2
SELIGMAN TAX EX NEW YORK	MB	65	na	11	89	0	0	0	4.7	3.0
SELIGMAN TAX EX OHIO	MB	114	na	10	90	0	0	0	3.9	2.2
SENTINEL BALANCED FUND	B	41	na	15	36	0	0	49	5.3	3.9
SENTINEL BOND	BP	21	na	7	93	0	0	0	4.0	1.7
SENTINEL COMMON STOCK FD	GI	466	na	8	0	0	0	92	6.5	5.6
SENTINEL GROWTH FUND	G	51	na	15	0	0	0	85	5.7	4.8
SENTRY FUND	G	40	2.00	13	0	0	0	87	4.1	2.9
SEQUOIA FUND	GI	690	1.00	51	0	0	0	49	0.2	0.2
SHEARSON AGGRESSIVE GRTH	AG	91	na	2	0	0	0	98	7.6	7.6
SHEARSON APPRECIATION	G	263	na	20	0	0	0	80	6.2	6.2
SHEARSON CALIF MUNICIPAL	MB	156	na	0	100	0	0	0	4.5	2.6
SHEARSON FUNDAMENTAL VAL	G	102	na	5	1	2	2	90	1.3	-2.9
SHEARSON GLOBAL OPPORT	G	263	1.50	1	0	2	0	97	6.7	6.7
SHEARSON HIGH YIELD	BP	513	na	11	87	0	1	1	2.3	-0.5
SHEARSON LG-TRM GOV SECS	BP	1,481	2.77*	30	70	0	0	0	3.4	1.8
SHEARSON MANAGED GOVTS	BP	1,439	na	15	85	0	0	0	3.7	1.6
SHEARSON MANAGED MUNI BD	MB	628	na	0	100	0	0	0	4.2	2.3
SHEARSON SPEC EQTY GR	G	137	na	59	0	1	0	40	-0.4	-0.4
SHEARSON NEW YORK MUNI	MB	191	na	0	100	0	0	0	4.4	2.5
SHEARSON SPEC INTL EQ	IN	169	2.50*	0	0	2	2	96	5.7	5.7
SHEARSON SPEC EQTY PLUS	AG	24	2.50*	11	0	1	3	85	-0.7	-0.7
SHEARSON SPEC INTERM GOV	BP	44	1.60	24	76	0	0	0	2.4	0.9
SHEARSON SPEC TAX EX INC	MB	383	1.65*	3	97	0	0	0	4.7	3.0
SHEARSON SPL OPTION INC	GI	615	2.07*	17	1	0	1	81	4.1	3.6
SHERMAN, DEAN FUND	AG	2	2.61*	4	1	0	0	95	-8.6	-8.6
SIERRA GROWTH FUND	AG	5	na	0	0	0	0	0	1.4	1.4
SIGMA CAPITAL SHARES	G	89	1.01*	21	0	0	0	79	3.1	3.1
SIGMA INCOME SHARES	BP	36	0.82*	12	82	1	5	0	3.0	1.0

| | 36 MONTH MPT STATISTICS | | | | DISTRIBUTION INFORMATION | | | | | | | | |
| | STD | | ALPHA | | 12/86 | INCOME | | | | CAPITAL GAIN | | | |
R2	DEV	BETA	PCNT	RK	N.A.V.	OCT	NOV	DEC	12 MON	OCT	NOV	DEC	12 MON
86	3.89	0.86	-3.8	63	5.23	.080			0.180	.320			1.090
84	3.37	0.74	-5.6	73	8.92			.140	0.560			.420	0.420
na	na	na	na	na	2.91	.240			na	1.32			na
80	3.24	0.70	-3.4	62	6.71		.350		0.350		1.88		1.880
85	3.11	0.69	5.7	12	12.65				0.480			1.18	2.290
80	3.93	0.84	-7.1	78	17.83				0.640			1.75	3.450
84	5.58	1.22	-9.0	84	12.72				0.000			2.36	2.430
na	na	na	na	na	6.57	.043	.037	.037	0.496	.529			0.529
na	na	na	na	na	6.78	.040	.035	.035	0.464	.126			0.126
79	5.58	1.18	-6.8	77	11.39				0.080			.350	0.350
93	4.25	0.98	-0.5	48	13.03			.140	0.500			2.03	3.370
86	5.22	1.15	-7.1	78	5.25			.050	0.100			1.14	1.700
na	na	na	na	na	8.15	.048	.041		0.615	.052	.059	.058	0.530
na	na	na	na	na	7.83	.076	.069	.069	0.916				0.000
59	2.38	0.44	5.6	13	13.44			.300	1.090			.590	0.850
na	na	na	na	na	7.33	.051	.043		0.609	.029	.037	.036	0.353
na	na	na	na	na	7.98	.050	.045	.045	0.586	.083			0.083
na	na	na	na	na	7.76	.043	.038	.038	0.528	.002			0.002
na	na	na	na	na	8.03	.049	.043	.043	0.580	.180			0.180
na	na	na	na	na	8.37	.052	.046	.046	0.609	.290			0.290
na	na	na	na	na	7.90	.052	.043	.043	0.579	.214			0.214
na	na	na	na	na	8.34	.054	.046	.046	0.637	.325			0.325
na	na	na	na	na	8.24	.050	.044	.044	0.594	.246			0.246
na	na	na	na	na	8.15	.051	.044	.044	0.602	.117			0.117
84	2.94	0.65	5.3	17	12.35		.175		0.675			.406	0.406
26	1.69	0.21	5.4	15	6.58	.051	.051	.050	0.617			.349	0.349
93	4.10	0.94	3.4	30	23.61		.217		0.827			1.08	1.083
88	5.01	1.12	-5.5	72	13.96		.149		0.279			2.64	2.644
89	4.46	1.00	-2.2	55	12.70			.170	0.320			1.21	1.210
70	2.58	0.51	5.7	12	39.29				1.610		4.85		8.540
79	6.73	1.41	-9.3	85	15.00				0.000			.370	0.840
94	4.04	0.94	0.4	45	26.16				0.000			1.10	1.650
na	na	na	na	na	16.18	.107	.086	.102	1.159			.200	0.330
84	3.20	0.70	-3.4	62	6.31		.316		0.316		.536	.200	0.736
na	na	na	na	na	30.07				0.152			3.25	6.031
28	1.48	0.19	3.5	29	18.89	.180	.180	.170	2.230				0.000
na	na	na	na	na	9.23	.048	.040	.053	0.602	.025	.020	.020	0.290
na	na	na	na	na	13.34	.100	.083	.095	1.203	.015	.158	.020	0.218
24	2.48	0.29	5.3	16	15.58	.109	.086	.102	1.176			.140	0.430
na	na	na	na	na	14.12				na				na
na	na	na	na	na	16.71	.114	.087	.102	1.202			.190	0.280
na	na	na	na	na	19.89				na				na
na	na	na	na	na	14.59				na				na
na	na	na	na	na	11.76	.061	.047	.063	0.743	.076			0.146
na	na	na	na	na	17.20	.101	.080	.096	1.127				0.000
na	na	na	na	na	14.09	.030	.030	.010	0.360	.020	.275		1.495
9	7.74	0.56	-20.6	98	5.23				0.000				0.000
70	5.90	1.17	-19.9	97	11.05				0.000				0.000
79	4.19	0.89	-0.6	49	8.66				0.158			.250	0.475
15	2.10	0.20	7.5	4	9.05	.060	.059	.059	0.885				0.000

CDA QUARTERLY SUPPLEMENT – 12/31/86

FUND	IO	ASSETS (MIL$) 9/86	ANNL %EXP RATE	CASH	NON CVT BOND	PREF	CVTS	COMM STKS	LATEST QTR ROR 9/86 - 12/86 TOTAL	PRINCIPAL
SIGMA INVESTMENT SHARES	GI	78	0.89*	8	0	0	6	86	7.2	6.4
SIGMA SPECIAL FUND	G	18	1.17*	0	0	0	0	100	4.5	4.5
SIGMA TRUST SHARES	B	40	0.92*	13	23	0	6	58	2.4	1.1
SIGMA VENTURE SHARES	AG	59	0.95*	1	0	0	0	99	5.1	5.1
SIGMA WORLD	IN	8	na	na	na	na	na	na	9.3	9.3
SMITH, BARNEY EQUITY	G	70	na	20	0	0	4	76	6.0	5.4
SMITH, BARNEY INC. & GR.	B	310	na	11	0	0	14	74	4.2	0.7
SOGEN INTERNATIONAL FUND	IN	66	1.39	13	24	0	5	58	4.4	4.4
SOUTHEASTERN GROWTH FUND	G	86	2.20	14	0	0	3	82	1.3	-1.1
SOVEREIGN INVESTORS	GI	32	1.00	13	0	0	14	73	3.3	2.2
STATE BOND COMMON STOCK	G	29	1.01	5	0	0	0	95	7.1	6.3
STATE BOND DIVERSIFIED	GI	15	0.87	12	0	0	2	86	4.8	3.9
STATE BOND PROGRESS FUND	AG	7	1.11	8	0	0	5	87	3.4	3.4
STATE FARM BALANCED	GI	43	na	13	18	0	9	60	4.2	2.1
STATE FARM GROWTH FUND	G	243	na	14	2	0	0	84	4.4	2.9
STATE STREET GROWTH	G	247	na	3	0	0	0	96	3.7	3.7
STATE STREET INV. CORP.	G	536	na	6	0	1	0	93	5.6	4.2
STEADMAN AMERICAN INDUS.	G	6	na	0	0	0	0	0	-1.7	-1.7
STEADMAN ASSOCIATED	GI	20	na	0	0	0	0	0	6.5	4.7
STEADMAN INVESTMENT	G	8	na	0	0	0	0	0	3.2	3.2
STEADMAN OCEANOGRAPHIC	AG	4	na	0	0	0	0	0	-2.4	-2.4
STEIN R&F CAPITAL OPPOR.	AG	164	0.96	8	0	0	6	86	4.4	4.4
STEINROE DISCOVERY FUND	AG	73	1.29	13	0	0	0	87	-0.4	-0.4
STEINROE HIGH-YIELD BOND	BP	59	2.01	0	100	0	0	0	4.8	0.5
STEINROE HIGH-YIELD MUNI	MB	194	0.77	9	91	0	0	0	4.2	2.2
STEINROE INTERMED MUNI	MB	88	1.07	0	100	0	0	0	4.2	2.0
STEINROE MANAGED BOND FD	BP	193	0.69	9	91	0	0	0	3.9	1.8
STEIN R&F STOCK	AG	220	0.67	3	0	0	0	97	6.3	5.9
STEINROE SPECIAL FUND	G	235	0.91	4	9	0	1	86	7.1	7.1
STEINROE MANAGED MUNI FD	MB	477	0.65	14	86	0	0	0	3.9	2.1
STEIN R&F TOTAL RETURN	B	145	0.80	17	22	0	26	35	4.1	2.8
STEINROE UNIVERSE FUND	AG	94	1.20	28	0	0	0	72	8.0	8.0
STRATEGIC CAPITAL GAINS	AG	7	na	5	0	0	0	95	-6.4	-6.4
STRATEGIC INVESTMENTS	ME	96	na	5	0	0	0	95	-5.9	-5.9
STRATEGIC SILVER	ME	22	na	5	0	0	0	95	-10.4	-10.4
STRATTON GROWTH FUND	G	18	1.49	4	0	0	8	88	1.3	1.3
STRATTON MONTHLY DIV SHS	B	43	na	10	0	0	34	56	-0.2	-2.0
STRONG INCOME FUND	GI	72	na	na	na	na	na	na	3.5	1.2
STRONG INVESTMENT FUND	B	319	na	47	0	0	0	53	2.4	2.4
STRONG OPPORTUNITY FUND	AG	32	na	na	na	na	na	na	0.8	0.8
STRONG TOTAL RETURN FUND	B	452	1.60	3	36	2	1	58	3.5	3.5
SUMMIT INVESTOR FD INC.	AG	62	1.28	3	0	0	0	97	4.3	4.3
SUNBELT GROWTH FUND	G	76	1.25*	21	0	0	0	79	5.5	5.3
SURVEYOR FUND	AG	90	na	7	0	0	1	92	2.9	2.7
TAX EXEMPT BD FD/AMERICA	MB	260	0.61	10	90	0	0	0	4.2	2.4
TECHNOLOGY FUND	G	557	na	5	0	0	0	95	6.2	6.2
TELEPHONE INCOME SHARES	GI	99	0.87*	9	4	0	9	78	3.5	2.0
TEMPLETON FOREIGN FUND	IN	184	0.90	23	3	0	0	74	7.4	5.0
TEMPLETON GROWTH FUND	G	1,813	0.73	23	13	0	0	64	5.6	4.0
TEMPLETON GLOBAL I	G	301	0.83	19	7	0	0	74	3.1	0.6

| 36 MONTH MPT STATISTICS | | | | | DISTRIBUTION INFORMATION | | | | | | | | |
R2	STD DEV	BETA	ALPHA PCNT	RK	12/86 N.A.V.	INCOME OCT	NOV	DEC	12 MON	CAPITAL GAIN OCT	NOV	DEC	12 MON
88	4.00	0.90	2.0	37	9.89	.075			0.318			.720	1.150
93	4.60	1.06	-3.8	64	9.21				0.134			.730	0.796
84	2.44	0.54	4.6	22	13.63	.173			0.765			.610	1.108
70	5.31	1.05	-9.2	85	11.06				0.048			.670	0.973
na	na	na	na	na	15.75				0.000			.650	0.650
94	4.17	0.97	-2.9	59	13.98	.100			0.420			2.35	4.180
86	2.80	0.62	4.5	22	11.40	.140		.250	0.670				0.130
65	2.83	0.55	5.4	14	17.71				0.600				2.220
na	na	na	na	na	12.59			.300	0.300				0.210
86	3.72	0.82	3.9	26	24.73			.280	1.100			1.73	1.730
88	4.95	1.10	-6.8	76	6.35		.050		0.100			.506	0.707
92	3.64	0.84	0.8	43	7.42		.070		0.250			.548	0.846
83	5.41	1.17	-11.6	89	10.10				0.140				0.355
89	3.44	0.78	1.5	40	17.29		.380		0.735			.715	0.715
90	4.34	0.98	-3.4	62	11.95		.190		0.360			.925	0.925
92	4.31	0.99	-3.5	62	70.51				1.820				0.000
94	4.28	0.99	-3.2	61	75.42			1.05	2.250			7.50	7.500
66	5.30	1.02	-26.4	99	2.32				0.000				0.000
77	5.06	1.05	-12.2	90	0.89			.015	0.035				0.035
63	4.53	0.86	-13.3	92	1.60				0.000				0.000
67	6.72	1.29	-27.8	99	4.48				0.000				0.000
74	6.10	1.24	-12.0	90	26.75				0.200			.850	0.850
75	7.10	1.44	-13.7	93	10.56				0.040				0.030
na	na	na	na	na	9.96	.250	.084	.084	na				na
na	na	na	na	na	12.06	.230			0.933				0.000
na	na	na	na	na	10.77	.142	.046	.046	0.659				0.000
15	2.49	0.23	6.1	10	9.26	.204			0.836	.740			0.740
85	5.06	1.11	-7.9	81	16.97		.060		0.250			3.01	3.219
85	4.97	1.09	-4.8	69	16.95				0.340			3.23	3.806
20	3.11	0.34	5.3	15	9.22	.170			0.676			.540	0.540
88	2.86	0.64	1.0	42	25.07		.340		1.350			1.64	2.700
76	5.16	1.07	-9.9	87	17.48				0.210			.850	4.470
10	8.81	0.64	-17.0	95	6.54				0.000				0.000
1	15.89	-0.28	-19.7	97	4.65				0.300				0.000
na	na	na	na	na	3.95				0.000				0.000
85	4.84	1.06	-7.2	79	20.02				0.280			.650	2.070
39	3.34	0.50	9.6	3	29.21	.190	.190	.190	2.280			.500	0.500
na	na	na	na	na	12.65	.290			0.700				0.000
59	2.20	0.41	3.2	31	22.18				1.220				0.150
na	na	na	na	na	15.99				0.000				0.000
70	2.90	0.58	4.1	25	21.61				1.270				0.470
85	4.80	1.05	-6.3	75	6.68				0.050			.380	0.660
80	4.45	0.95	-6.9	77	18.43			.030	0.160				0.000
81	6.21	1.32	-10.6	88	11.51		.040		0.040	4.48			4.480
31	2.15	0.29	4.4	24	11.48	.068	.066	.065	0.805		.090		0.121
93	4.44	1.02	-6.3	75	11.12				0.210	2.68			2.680
na	na	na	na	na	15.67	.090	.090	.090	1.080			2.23	3.090
36	3.50	0.51	3.8	28	15.41	.360			0.360	1.07			1.070
69	3.29	0.66	1.7	38	12.87			.190	0.400				0.480
79	3.21	0.59	0.7	43	40.81	1.09			1.090	2.20			2.200

CDA QUARTERLY SUPPLEMENT – 12/31/86

FUND	IO	ASSETS (MIL$) 9/86	ANNL %EXP RATE	CASH	NON CVT BOND	PREF	CVTS	COMM STKS	TOTAL	PRINCIPAL
TEMPLETON GLOBAL II	G	498	1.00	24	1	0	0	74	1.7	-0.7
TEMPLETON WORLD FUND	G	3,213	0.71	22	7	0	0	71	3.0	0.3
THOMSON MCKINNON GROWTH	G	191	na	17	6	1	0	76	3.4	2.8
THOMSON MCKINNON INCOME	BP	332	na	2	97	1	0	0	3.4	0.7
THOMSON MCKINNON OPPORT.	AG	52	na	7	2	0	0	91	3.9	3.9
TRANSATLANTIC FUND INC.	IN	100	1.50	5	0	0	6	89	4.6	4.6
TRUSTEES COMM EQ-INTL	IN	634	0.56	0	0	0	0	100	12.4	11.5
TRUSTEES COMM EQ-US PORT	GI	165	0.48	2	0	0	0	98	3.4	2.4
TUDOR FUND	AG	159	0.95	7	0	0	0	92	3.1	3.1
TWENTIETH CENTURY GIFTR	G	6	1.01	0	0	0	0	100	7.4	7.4
TWENTIETH CENTURY GROWTH	AG	888	1.01	1	0	0	0	99	6.7	6.7
TWENTIETH CENTURY SELECT	G	1,832	1.01	1	0	0	0	99	5.0	5.0
TWENTIETH CENTURY ULTRA	AG	300	1.01	1	0	0	0	99	6.7	6.7
TWENTIETH CENTURY US GOV	BP	237	1.01	11	89	0	0	0	3.2	1.3
TWENTIETH CENTURY VISTA	AG	144	1.01	0	0	0	0	100	4.4	4.4
UMB BOND FUND	BP	23	na	20	80	0	0	0	2.6	2.6
UMB STOCK FUND	GI	32	na	14	0	0	8	78	3.2	3.2
UNIFIED GROWTH FUND	G	24	na	24	0	0	0	76	3.8	3.8
UNIFIED INCOME FUND	B	13	na	22	14	0	33	31	1.4	-1.9
UNIFIED MUNI FD-GENERAL	MB	6	na	2	98	0	0	0	3.8	0.4
UNIFIED MUNI FD-INDIANA	MB	10	na	2	98	0	0	0	4.1	1.1
UNIFIED MUTUAL SHARES	GI	18	na	35	0	0	3	62	3.5	3.5
UNITED ACCUMULATIVE FUND	G	678	0.60	15	0	0	1	84	1.9	1.9
UNITED CONTL. INCOME FD.	GI	241	0.83	6	22	1	3	68	2.3	1.2
UNITED BOND FUND	BP	335	0.53	2	88	0	10	0	4.5	2.4
UNITED GOLD & GOVERNMENT	ME	9	0.48	9	35	2	2	52	10.3	9.7
UNITED GOV SECURITIES FD	BP	147	0.87	5	95	0	0	0	3.0	1.1
UNITED HIGH INCOME FUND	BP	1,229	0.81	5	94	1	0	0	3.2	0.1
UNITED INCOME FUND	G	792	0.63	11	0	0	1	88	6.4	5.7
UNITED INTL. GROWTH FUND	IN	205	1.09	12	0	1	0	87	3.6	3.6
UNITED MUNICIPAL BOND FD	MB	402	0.61	0	100	0	0	0	4.4	2.6
UNITED MUNI HIGH INCOME	MB	28	0.52	1	99	0	0	0	3.5	1.5
UNITED NEW CONCEPTS FUND	G	60	1.47	25	0	0	1	74	5.1	5.1
UNITED RETIREMENT SHARES	B	94	0.92	7	23	0	0	70	4.1	3.2
UNITED SCIENCE & ENERGY	G	173	0.67	13	0	0	0	87	9.8	9.8
UNITED VANGUARD FUND	GI	494	0.98	21	0	1	3	75	5.5	4.3
U.S. GOV GUARANTEED SECS	BP	189	na	na	na	na	na	na	4.1	1.6
U.S. TREND FUND, INC.	G	79	na	11	0	0	0	89	4.2	2.6
US GOVT HIGH YIELD TRUST	BP	2,308	0.93*	7	93	0	0	0	1.9	-0.5
US GOLD SHARES FUND	ME	307	na	2	0	0	0	98	-0.6	-0.6
US GOOD AND BAD TIMES FD	G	21	na	17	0	0	0	83	5.7	5.7
US GROWTH FUND	AG	7	na	4	0	0	0	96	4.4	4.4
US INCOME FUND	GI	3	na	0	0	0	19	81	-3.5	-5.1
US LOCAP FUND	AG	2	na	5	0	0	0	95	-2.3	-2.3
US NEW PROSPECTOR FUND	ME	46	na	10	0	0	0	90	6.4	6.4
US PROSPECTOR FUND	ME	72	na	4	0	0	0	96	5.9	5.9
USAA MUTUAL FD GROWTH	G	174	1.09	8	0	0	4	88	3.6	2.4
USAA MUTUAL FD INCOME	BP	213	0.65	4	80	0	0	16	3.4	-0.4
USAA SUNBELT ERA FUND	AG	118	1.05	6	0	0	7	87	1.2	0.9
USAA TAX EX HIGH YIELD	MB	779	0.50	0	100	0	0	0	4.1	2.1

| | 36 MONTH MPT STATISTICS | | | | DISTRIBUTION INFORMATION | | | | | | | | |
| | STD | | ALPHA | | 12/86 | INCOME | | | | CAPITAL GAIN | | | |
R2	DEV	BETA	PCNT	RK	N.A.V.	OCT	NOV	DEC	12 MON	OCT	NOV	DEC	12 MON
79	3.53	0.75	-2.5	57	12.72	.320			0.320	.430			0.430
85	3.48	0.77	1.1	41	14.74	.440			0.440	1.28			1.280
na	na	na	na	na	13.28	.080			0.350	1.92			1.920
na	na	na	na	na	10.21	.092	.092	.092	1.107				0.000
na	na	na	na	na	12.41				0.000	1.27			1.270
17	5.46	0.53	11.3	2	22.92				0.000			3.80	4.180
21	3.79	0.41	14.3	1	38.65		.350		1.030			6.55	6.550
86	4.56	1.01	-6.7	76	28.68		.330		1.160			6.15	6.150
84	5.17	1.13	-7.3	79	20.08				0.070			3.00	5.480
81	6.91	1.46	-3.3	61	6.75				0.000			1.25	1.420
80	5.55	1.18	-6.3	75	14.06				0.182			5.08	5.076
90	5.31	1.20	-5.3	71	31.61				0.515			3.46	3.462
84	6.96	1.50	-16.2	95	8.92				0.010				0.000
10	0.91	0.07	3.6	28	100.93	.695	.612	.600	8.320			1.55	2.112
78	7.72	1.60	-13.0	91	5.95				0.000			.651	0.651
18	1.33	0.14	4.6	22	11.37				0.850				0.025
95	3.62	0.84	-4.0	65	12.78				0.510		.400		1.010
89	4.15	0.93	-1.8	54	22.20				0.350		1.60		1.600
72	2.28	0.47	-2.7	58	12.65	.430			0.890				0.000
na	na	na	na	na	9.27	.310			0.570				0.020
na	na	na	na	na	9.33	.270			0.570				0.000
90	3.56	0.81	0.3	45	17.07				0.590				0.170
88	3.98	0.89	-0.6	49	7.78				0.250			1.19	2.180
80	3.40	0.73	5.5	14	19.31			.200	0.750				1.520
28	2.31	0.29	6.1	9	6.42	.044	.043	.043	0.559				0.000
na	na	na	na	na	6.83			.040	0.220		.080		0.080
na	na	na	na	na	5.65	.037	.034	.038	0.480				0.513
35	1.53	0.22	5.3	16	13.95	.141	.140	.140	1.729				0.083
88	4.63	1.03	1.2	40	17.03			.120	0.490			1.57	2.280
29	3.42	0.45	7.0	5	7.13				0.130				1.620
32	2.29	0.31	6.8	6	7.18	.045	.041	.039	0.544	.685			0.685
na	na	na	na	na	5.30	.037	.033	.034	0.408				0.000
70	4.21	0.84	-5.2	70	6.14				0.070				0.260
78	3.00	0.63	-0.5	48	6.05	.050			0.270				0.940
84	4.36	0.95	-4.3	66	10.00				0.240			1.23	1.520
78	3.46	0.73	-3.0	59	6.26		.090		0.170		.965		0.965
na	na	na	na	na	14.96	.126	.126	.120	1.482	.020			0.058
91	5.14	1.16	-10.0	87	10.72		.220		0.330		3.76		3.760
na	na	na	na	na	9.67	.100	.054	.071	0.817		.046		0.370
0	15.06	-0.05	-16.9	95	4.63				0.290				0.000
83	4.20	0.91	-5.4	72	16.68				0.000				0.000
76	5.36	1.11	-17.0	95	8.82				0.000				0.000
47	2.89	0.47	-5.5	72	10.43			.180	0.390			.300	0.300
na	na	na	na	na	6.83				0.000				0.000
na	na	na	na	na	1.31				0.000			.020	0.020
0	7.95	0.07	-13.4	92	0.72				0.000				0.000
89	4.80	1.08	-10.4	88	14.76		.190		0.190		1.59		1.590
22	1.82	0.21	5.4	15	11.98	.270	.090	.090	1.280		.060		0.060
79	5.96	1.25	-15.8	94	17.10		.070		0.070		.350		0.350
18	2.51	0.26	4.8	20	13.79			.257	1.097				0.040

CDA QUARTERLY SUPPLEMENT - 12/31/86

FUND	IO	ASSETS (MIL$) 9/86	ANNL %EXP RATE	CASH	NON BOND	CVT PREF	CVTS	COMM STKS	TOTAL	PRINCIPAL
USAA TAX EX INTERMEDIATE	MB	284	0.57	0	100	0	0	0	2.6	0.9
USAA TAX EX SH-TERM FD	MB	211	0.65	0	100	0	0	0	2.1	0.7
VALLEY FORGE FUND	GI	10	1.40	84	5	1	0	9	1.9	1.9
VALUE LINE FUND	AG	203	0.73	3	2	0	0	96	7.4	7.0
VALUE LINE INCOME	B	154	0.78	3	45	1	2	48	3.8	2.1
VALUE LINE LEVER. GROWTH	G	239	0.84	0	0	0	0	100	7.3	7.3
VALUE LINE SPECIAL SIT.	AG	194	1.01	1	5	0	0	94	6.0	6.0
VALUE LINE US GOV SECS	BP	117	0.76	13	87	0	0	0	2.9	0.3
VAN KAMPEN MERRITT-GOV	BP	3,538	na	0	100	0	0	0	4.1	1.3
VANCE, SANDERS SPECIAL	G	83	0.92	6	0	0	0	94	-0.7	-0.7
VANGUARD CONVERTIBLE SEC	GI	40	na	10	0	0	90	0	3.1	2.1
VANGUARD FIXED INC HIYLD	BP	1,158	0.60	4	95	0	1	0	3.2	0.3
VANGUARD FIXED INC INVT	BP	517	0.55	2	98	0	0	0	4.8	2.3
VANGUARD FIXED INC GNMA	BP	1,853	0.50	0	100	0	0	0	3.8	1.4
VANGUARD FI SECS-SH TERM	BP	315	na	na	na	na	na	na	2.3	0.5
VANGUARD INDEX TRUST	GI	474	0.28	0	0	0	0	100	5.7	4.3
VANGUARD CALIF INS TX FR	MB	46	na	0	100	0	0	0	4.8	3.1
VANGUARD PENNA INS TX FR	MB	84	na	0	100	0	0	0	4.2	2.5
VANGUARD MUNI HIGH YIELD	MB	782	0.33	0	100	0	0	0	4.5	2.6
VANGUARD MUNI INSURED LT	MB	728	0.33	0	100	0	0	0	4.0	2.2
VANGUARD MUNI INTERM-TRM	MB	833	0.33	0	100	0	0	0	3.4	1.7
VANGUARD MUNI LONG-TERM	MB	627	0.33	0	100	0	0	0	4.6	2.7
VANGUARD MUNI SHORT-TERM	MB	940	0.33	0	100	0	0	0	1.5	0.2
VANGUARD SPEC PORT-ENRGY	G	14	na	5	0	5	2	88	7.2	7.2
VANGUARD SPEC PORT-GOLD	ME	54	0.73	13	3	0	0	84	7.0	7.0
VANGUARD SPC PORT-HEALTH	AG	43	0.83	3	0	0	0	97	2.3	2.3
VANGUARD SPEC-SVC ECON	G	49	0.57	1	0	0	2	97	2.6	2.6
VANGUARD SPEC PORT-TECH	AG	13	0.72	5	0	0	0	95	4.8	4.8
VANGUARD STAR FUND	B	416	na	12	25	0	0	63	3.7	3.7
VANGUARD WORLD-INTL GR	IN	411	0.78	4	0	0	1	95	8.0	8.0
VANGUARD WORLD-US GR	G	167	0.81	0	0	0	19	81	2.0	2.0
VENTURE INCOME PLUS	BP	62	1.25	5	84	10	0	1	2.9	-0.9
VENTURE MUNI PLUS	MB	27	2.75*	4	96	0	0	0	3.3	1.1
WALL STREET FUND	AG	9	2.00	2	3	0	5	91	5.2	5.2
WASHINGTON AREA GROWTH	G	17	na	12	0	0	3	85	4.4	4.4
WASH. MUTUAL INVESTORS	GI	1,568	0.51	4	0	0	0	95	5.7	4.7
WEALTH MONITORS FUND	G	5	2.00	0	18	0	0	82	-6.9	-6.9
WEINGARTEN EQUITY FUND	AG	160	0.77	2	0	0	0	98	5.8	5.8
WELLESLEY INCOME FUND	B	399	0.60	0	62	0	1	37	4.3	1.3
WELLINGTON FUND	B	1,025	0.64	0	37	0	1	62	4.3	1.9
WESTERGAARD FUND INC.	AG	15	2.25	23	0	0	0	77	-0.7	-0.7
WINDSOR FUND	GI	4,839	0.53	16	1	0	0	83	2.6	-0.7
WINDSOR II	GI	730	0.80	6	0	0	0	94	5.1	3.2
WORLD OF TECHNOLOGY FUND	IN	8	1.50	2	0	0	7	91	7.4	7.4
WORLD TRENDS	IN	58	na	23	0	0	23	53	2.3	2.3
WPG FUND	G	39	1.21	7	0	1	0	92	4.5	4.5
YES FUND	BP	168	na	0	100	0	0	0	3.6	1.0

| | 36 MONTH MPT STATISTICS | | | | DISTRIBUTION INFORMATION | | | | | | | | |
| | STD | | ALPHA | | 12/86 | INCOME | | | | CAPITAL GAIN | | | |
R2	DEV	BETA	PCNT	RK	N.A.V.	OCT	NOV	DEC	12 MON	OCT	NOV	DEC	12 MON
16	1.76	0.17	3.1	32	12.35			.212	0.932				0.000
2	0.91	0.03	0.7	44	10.71			.151	0.691				0.000
41	0.88	0.14	-1.4	52	10.67				0.460				0.590
87	5.81	1.29	-9.4	86	14.68			.070	0.240			1.75	1.750
82	3.23	0.70	-1.2	52	6.81		.120		0.420			.480	0.911
90	5.49	1.24	-7.0	78	22.79				0.340			2.60	2.600
87	6.32	1.40	-20.1	97	15.07				0.039				0.000
10	1.95	0.15	5.4	15	12.77	.330			1.320			.230	0.376
na	na	na	na	na	16.57	.150	.150	.150	1.813				0.000
68	4.97	0.98	-17.4	96	10.63				0.080				1.040
na	na	na	na	na	9.68			.090	na				na
27	1.70	0.22	4.7	21	9.20	.086	.087	.087	1.032				0.000
20	1.87	0.20	6.6	7	8.73	.069	.069	.068	0.895				0.000
11	1.72	0.14	5.9	10	10.05	.079	.078	.077	1.003				0.000
17	0.90	0.09	4.6	22	10.82	.068	.068	.065	0.895				0.000
100	4.19	1.00	-0.2	47	24.27			.350	0.890			2.02	2.020
na	na	na	na	na	10.51	.058	.055	.055	na				na
na	na	na	na	na	10.23	.058	.058	.056	na				na
30	2.52	0.33	5.2	17	10.67	.068	.066	.066	0.836				0.390
na	na	na	na	na	11.86	.073	.071	.071	0.887				0.170
20	1.91	0.21	4.1	25	12.29	.072	.070	.070	0.873				0.020
30	2.51	0.33	4.5	23	11.12	.069	.067	.067	0.837				0.190
19	0.30	0.04	-0.9	50	15.44	.070	.068	.058	0.869				0.010
na	na	na	na	na	11.18				0.440				0.050
na	na	na	na	na	9.22				0.210				0.000
na	na	na	na	na	17.64				0.130		.700		0.800
na	na	na	na	n3	17.59				0.160		.600		0.700
na	na	na	na	na	11.93				0.080		.300		0.300
na	na	na	na	na	11.34				0.860		.440		0.710
22	5.11	0.58	18.2	1	11.26				0.070				0.800
89	4.29	0.96	-3.3	61	10.32				0.280				1.940
17	1.71	0.17	2.2	37	9.87	.125	.125	.125	1.555				0.000
na	na	na	na	na	10.20	.075	.075	.075	0.935				0.000
88	5.40	1.20	-7.5	80	6.96				0.060			1.80	3.060
na	na	na	na	na	18.45				0.006	.720			0.720
97	4.00	0.94	2.4	36	12.30		.130		0.510			.210	0.660
na	na	na	na	na	8.32				na				na
86	5.95	1.31	-4.2	66	17.63				0.170		3.75		4.780
63	2.42	0.46	7.3	5	16.27			.490	1.330			.470	0.470
94	2.99	0.70	3.4	30	15.85		.400		0.940		.340		0.340
62	5.66	1.05	-19.0	97	9.57				0.190				0.260
85	3.45	0.76	5.9	10	13.95	.550			0.850	2.59			2.590
na	na	na	na	na	12.39	.230			0.430	.520			0.520
59	5.79	1.05	-12.6	91	9.68				0.000				0.000
na	na	na	na	na	13.41				0.150			.050	0.050
89	4.44	1.00	-4.8	69	20.64				0.680			3.75	6.020
12	1.92	0.16	-1.1	51	7.76	.065	.065	.065	0.838				0.000

CDA QUARTERLY SUPPLEMENT – 12/31/86

FUND	IO	ASSETS (MIL$) 9/86	ANNL %EXP RATE	CASH	NON CVT BOND	PREF	CVTS	COMM STKS	TOTAL	PRINCIPAL
					PERCENT OF ASSETS				LATEST QTR ROR 9/86 - 12/86	

SUMMARY BY INVESTMENT OBJECTIVE

FUND	IO	ASSETS (MIL$) 9/86	ANNL %EXP RATE	CASH	BOND	PREF	CVTS	STKS	TOTAL	PRINCIPAL
32 INTERNATIONAL	IN	9,271	1.31	8	2	0	2	84	5.8	5.4
115 AGGRESSIVE GROWTH	AG	13,500	1.26	9	1	0	1	87	3.0	2.8
236 GROWTH	G	62,547	1.16	10	1	0	1	86	3.3	2.8
135 GROWTH & INCOME	GI	57,333	1.04	14	5	1	8	69	3.5	2.6
120 MUNICIPAL BOND	MB	57,394	0.74	6	91	0	0	0	3.8	2.0
183 BOND & PREFERRED	BP	138,076	0.99	9	80	5	2	0	3.0	0.6
58 BALANCED	B	17,523	1.01	13	25	4	6	51	3.4	1.9
18 METALS	ME	2,197	1.31	8	7	0	0	84	2.0	1.8
897 TOTAL FUNDS		357,834	1.06	10	31	1	2	52	3.4	2.2
STANDARD & POOR 500									5.6	4.7

* Includes 12b-1 fees

| 36 MONTH MPT STATISTICS | | | | | DISTRIBUTION INFORMATION | | | | | | | | | |
R2	STD DEV	BETA	ALPHA PCNT	RK	12/86 N.A.V.	INCOME OCT	NOV	DEC	12 MON	CAPITAL GAIN OCT	NOV	DEC	12 MON
33	4.57	0.57	8.5	16									
73	6.01	1.19	-12.9	85									
83	4.40	0.96	-4.8	65									
81	3.50	0.75	-0.6	48									
26	2.06	0.25	3.9	24									
24	1.75	0.20	4.6	20									
73	2.69	0.55	3.0	29									
0	10.15	0.01	-10.9	84									
63	3.76	0.70	-1.9	50									
100	4.20	1.00	0.0										

Annual Supplement

CDA ANNUAL SUPPLEMENT – 12/31/86

FUND	IO	ASSETS (MIL$) 9/86	1986 QUARTERLY RETURNS 1st PCNT RK	2nd PCNT RK	3rd PCNT RK	4th PCNT RK
ABT EMERGING GROWTH	AG	34	17.8 12	12.5 4	-13.3 88	-1.5 96
ABT GROWTH & INCOME TR.	GI	116	8.9 66	4.9 30	-2.9 50	5.2 18
ABT SECURITY INCOME	GI	18	4.4 89	1.0 68	1.2 35	2.8 67
ABT UTILITY INCOME FD	GI	124	12.7 41	1.0 67	2.4 25	1.5 84
ACORN FUND	G	395	13.9 35	6.6 19	-6.7 64	8.6 3
AFFILIATED FUND	GI	3,008	16.1 19	3.6 41	-4.0 54	6.3 10
AFUTURE FUND	AG	19	11.7 48	6.4 20	-19.0 98	-2.2 96
AGE HIGH INCOME FUND	BP	1,141	6.4 81	3.8 40	0.1 40	2.1 78
ALLIANCE CONVERTIBLE	BP	62	na --	3.4 44	-3.2 52	2.1 77
ALLIANCE COUNTERPOINT	G	37	16.2 19	8.8 9	-6.7 64	1.9 80
ALLIANCE HIGH GRADE BOND	BP	7	7.3 75	-1.8 94	3.8 17	5.5 15
ALLIANCE HIGH YIELD BOND	BP	267	6.4 80	2.7 51	-2.2 47	3.8 44
ALLIANCE INTERNATIONAL	IN	164	21.6 4	7.9 13	6.6 4	2.9 65
ALLIANCE MORTGAGE SECS	BP	737	3.7 91	0.0 79	3.8 17	3.2 58
ALLIANCE TECHNOLOGY	AG	133	9.6 61	8.0 12	-13.6 89	9.6 2
ALPHA FUND	G	24	16.6 17	7.2 17	-13.5 89	4.5 27
AMA GROWTH FUND, INC.	G	27	16.1 19	5.3 27	-12.5 87	3.8 47
AMA INCOME FUND, INC.	BP	21	7.0 77	0.8 70	0.4 39	4.0 40
AMCAP FUND	G	1,385	11.6 48	4.8 31	-5.6 61	4.8 22
AMERICAN BALANCED FUND	B	162	11.8 47	2.7 52	-2.5 48	4.4 31
AMERICAN CAPITAL CORP BD	BP	118	6.4 80	1.9 57	-1.0 44	3.7 49
AMERICAN CAP COMSTOCK	G	896	13.7 36	0.5 73	-5.4 60	5.0 21
AMERICAN CAP ENTERPRISE	G	577	18.7 10	3.5 43	-13.3 88	3.5 51
AMERICAN CAP GOV SECS	BP	8,068	3.6 92	1.6 60	2.0 30	3.0 64
AMERICAN CAPITAL GROWTH	AG	26	15.4 23	5.3 27	-12.4 86	-4.3 97
AMERICAN CAPITAL HARBOR	GI	267	12.4 43	5.2 28	-6.0 62	2.0 79
AMERICAN CAPTL HIYLD INV	BP	520	6.5 79	3.2 46	-4.5 56	1.5 83
AMERICAN CAPITAL PACE FD	G	2,133	13.0 40	-0.4 83	-5.2 59	3.9 42
AMERICAN CAPITAL OTC SEC	G	95	15.1 26	2.2 55	-19.2 98	-5.0 98
AMERICAN CAPITAL VENTURE	AG	335	11.9 47	7.3 16	-14.3 91	1.4 84
AMERICAN CAPITAL MUNI BD	MB	159	12.3 44	-0.6 84	-0.3 42	4.5 29
AMERICAN GROWTH FUND	GI	65	15.7 20	-2.0 95	-7.4 67	1.2 86
AMERICAN HERITAGE FUND	AG	1	5.9 83	-18.0 99	-9.3 76	-4.3 98
AMERICAN INVESTORS FUND	AG	67	17.4 14	-3.4 97	-13.9 90	0.7 88
AMERICAN INVS INCOME	BP	22	6.4 80	-1.1 90	-0.2 42	1.9 80
AMERICAN LEADERS FUND	GI	116	10.8 52	-2.6 96	-1.6 45	3.1 62
AMERICAN MUTUAL FUND	GI	1,992	12.7 41	4.0 38	-3.2 51	4.3 32
AMERICAN NATIONAL GROWTH	AG	90	14.4 31	3.2 46	-10.8 83	5.3 17
AMERICAN NATL INC FUND	GI	60	6.9 78	4.8 32	-5.7 61	2.2 76
AMERICAN TELECOMM TR GR	G	40	15.5 23	8.8 9	-8.9 75	4.0 39
AMERICAN TELECOMM TR INC	GI	97	10.9 51	11.0 5	-3.2 52	1.6 83
AMEV CAPITAL FUND, INC.	G	98	17.3 15	13.7 3	-12.1 86	3.7 49
AMEV GROWTH FUND, INC.	AG	149	18.1 11	13.3 3	-12.9 87	2.5 71
AMEV SPECIAL FUND, INC.	AG	23	17.5 14	13.6 3	-13.0 88	3.5 52
AMEV US GOV SECURITIES	BP	63	5.4 85	0.4 74	3.6 19	2.4 72
AMWAY MUTUAL FUND	G	35	14.6 30	4.0 39	-6.8 65	4.5 27
ANALYTIC OPTIONED EQUITY	GI	83	4.2 90	4.0 38	-2.7 49	4.7 24
ARMSTRONG ASSOCIATES	G	12	12.4 43	0.0 79	-1.0 44	0.0 91
AXE-HOUGHTON INCOME	BP	46	8.7 68	1.2 66	0.2 40	5.1 19
AXE-HOUGHTON FUND B	B	182	17.9 12	4.1 37	-4.1 54	6.0 11

TEN YEARS OF ANNUAL RETURNS

1986		1985		1984		1983		1982		1981		1980		1979		1978		1977	
PCNT	RK	PCNT	RK	PCNT	RK	PCNT	RK	PCNT	RK	PCNT	RK	PCNT	RK	PCNT	RK	PCNT	RK	PCNT	RK
13.2	58	46.0	3	-1.1	64	na	--	na	--	na	--	na	--	na	--	na	--	na	--
16.8	37	32.9	15	0.1	60	20.5	34	12.0	88	-13.9	94	48.8	11	33.0	24	0.4	88	-1.9	67
9.6	78	12.3	93	7.2	36	na	--	na	--	na	--	na	--	na	--	na	--	na	--
18.3	26	23.3	52	17.3	2	-2.1	99	16.5	79	2.8	38	1.8	87	na	--	na	--	na	--
23.2	10	31.4	19	4.5	48	25.1	21	17.5	78	-7.3	79	30.7	39	50.4	7	16.9	18	18.0	8
22.9	10	26.8	37	6.9	37	25.5	21	23.8	61	0.0	50	24.6	55	29.3	31	3.6	69	-6.6	89
-5.9	97	21.5	61	-19.2	95	12.2	69	27.7	48	-1.8	58	38.5	23	40.3	16	20.0	13	3.6	39
12.8	61	18.8	77	8.7	29	17.9	45	27.5	49	6.9	21	2.1	87	3.9	84	-3.2	95	10.3	16
na	--	na	--	na	--	na	--	na	--	na	--	na	--	na	--	na	--	na	--
20.2	17	na	--	na	--	na	--	na	--	na	--	na	--	na	--	na	--	na	--
15.4	46	na	--	na	--	na	--	na	--	na	--	na	--	na	--	na	--	na	--
11.0	71	na	--	na	--	na	--	na	--	na	--	na	--	na	--	na	--	na	--
43.9	3	64.5	1	na	--	na	--	na	--	na	--	na	--	na	--	na	--	na	--
11.1	71	18.7	77	na	--	na	--	na	--	na	--	na	--	na	--	na	--	na	--
12.0	65	26.2	40	-16.4	92	46.5	1	na	--	na	--	na	--	na	--	na	--	na	--
13.0	59	25.1	45	-5.7	76	25.7	20	42.7	8	11.5	8	17.0	70	24.1	45	10.5	36	-4.1	79
11.0	71	23.5	51	5.4	44	7.5	89	21.2	69	-8.8	84	15.8	71	24.8	43	15.2	22	7.4	21
12.7	61	18.3	79	8.4	32	9.1	83	31.7	31	4.3	31	0.2	90	-1.9	96	3.6	68	6.8	23
15.6	44	22.2	58	-0.9	62	19.1	40	29.6	40	6.2	23	27.6	47	51.9	5	22.3	9	16.6	9
16.8	37	29.1	28	9.4	26	16.2	51	29.7	39	4.1	32	14.3	74	7.7	79	6.3	56	0.7	55
11.4	70	26.2	40	9.2	27	11.0	74	35.3	20	1.6	43	-2.5	92	-1.9	95	1.3	84	6.6	25
13.5	57	21.3	63	-2.6	68	18.4	43	46.5	5	8.0	15	32.3	35	47.8	8	13.7	26	13.9	12
10.2	76	29.6	26	-5.2	75	20.0	37	18.4	77	-12.9	92	72.8	3	51.2	6	21.3	10	-6.8	89
10.5	75	17.1	83	na	--	na	--	na	--	na	--	na	--	na	--	na	--	na	--
1.9	93	19.3	75	-15.0	91	10.7	75	36.8	16	na	--	na	--	na	--	na	--	na	--
13.4	57	24.0	48	-3.7	71	26.6	17	43.1	8	-5.4	71	33.0	33	24.1	45	8.9	42	2.9	42
6.7	87	25.0	45	8.7	30	16.3	51	29.5	40	na	--	na	--	na	--	na	--	na	--
10.8	73	22.4	56	-0.7	62	19.4	39	49.4	3	16.9	4	44.3	14	44.5	10	23.5	7	28.6	2
-9.7	98	23.4	51	-12.1	88	na	--	na	--	na	--	na	--	na	--	na	--	na	--
4.4	91	13.1	92	-6.3	78	14.9	58	48.6	4	12.7	7	28.9	43	47.7	8	26.5	5	25.9	3
16.3	40	23.0	53	na	--	na	--	na	--	na	--	na	--	na	--	na	--	na	--
6.3	88	17.8	80	-5.1	75	17.0	49	28.8	43	4.2	32	18.6	68	50.9	6	7.3	49	11.6	15
-24.6	99	-13.6	99	-25.0	96	8.6	85	24.6	58	-11.1	89	27.5	47	53.4	5	5.9	58	16.0	10
-1.7	96	14.3	91	-22.4	95	-4.1	99	-15.5	99	-6.3	75	47.3	12	63.6	3	1.6	80	5.1	31
7.0	86	22.7	55	-8.4	82	26.9	16	12.6	87	-4.6	67	18.3	68	15.2	69	3.0	72	10.7	15
9.5	79	28.1	31	15.5	4	16.8	49	20.1	73	1.9	42	na	--	na	--	na	--	na	--
18.4	26	30.1	23	6.4	40	24.1	24	29.6	40	7.8	17	25.4	52	21.5	53	12.7	29	2.0	49
10.9	73	32.1	17	-15.6	92	17.6	47	46.1	5	2.5	39	18.1	69	29.4	30	19.8	14	13.4	13
8.0	84	27.9	32	-1.5	65	22.8	28	18.5	76	15.1	5	na	--	na	--	na	--	na	--
19.1	22	31.9	18	na	--	na	--	na	--	na	--	na	--	na	--	na	--	na	--
21.1	15	33.3	14	na	--	na	--	na	--	na	--	na	--	na	--	na	--	na	--
21.5	14	31.2	20	-3.5	71	21.1	33	39.7	11	-0.8	54	57.1	7	29.2	31	15.4	21	-7.7	93
19.5	20	35.2	10	-7.7	81	23.4	26	33.2	26	1.0	46	63.5	5	42.6	13	28.2	3	2.7	44
20.1	18	39.3	5	-8.5	83	23.2	26	30.7	35	-5.0	69	na	--	na	--	na	--	na	--
12.3	64	20.9	65	10.0	23	4.6	96	31.1	33	12.5	7	5.8	82	-1.3	95	2.4	74	4.2	36
16.1	41	26.1	41	-4.7	74	19.3	39	9.5	92	-4.6	67	13.0	75	24.1	45	2.8	72	11.8	15
10.5	75	16.5	85	6.8	39	19.2	40	10.3	90	7.0	20	20.3	64	17.8	61	na	--	na	--
11.3	70	21.0	65	-11.5	87	11.0	74	15.5	81	na	--	na	--	na	--	na	--	na	--
15.8	43	26.6	38	15.5	4	7.5	89	31.0	34	5.8	25	7.8	80	1.9	87	0.6	87	4.9	33
24.7	8	32.9	15	6.3	40	11.1	73	26.1	53	-1.4	57	22.1	60	11.2	75	4.3	66	1.8	50

CDA ANNUAL SUPPLEMENT – 12/31/86

FUND	IO	ASSETS (MIL$) 9/86	1986 QUARTERLY RETURNS							
			1st PCNT	RK	2nd PCNT	RK	3rd PCNT	RK	4th PCNT	RK
AXE-HOUGHTON STOCK FUND	AG	92	14.2	33	6.5	19	-13.0	87	4.8	23
BABSON GROWTH FUND	G	236	13.7	36	4.9	30	-4.5	56	5.3	17
BABSON BOND TRUST	BP	65	6.2	81	1.2	65	2.4	25	3.5	53
BABSON ENTERPRISE FUND	G	48	13.4	38	2.2	55	-9.2	76	2.2	76
BABSON VALUE FD INC.	G	6	16.4	18	1.8	59	-2.2	47	4.2	33
BARTLETT BASIC VALUE FD	GI	67	13.1	39	3.8	40	-3.1	51	-0.8	95
BASCOM HILL INVESTORS	GI	7	12.5	42	2.3	54	-1.6	45	2.6	69
BEACON HILL MUTUAL FUND	G	3	8.4	69	8.8	9	-14.2	91	4.7	25
BENHAM CALIF TF-INTERMED	MB	135	5.0	86	0.9	69	3.8	18	2.4	72
BENHAM CALIF TF-LONG TRM	MB	194	9.5	62	-0.7	85	6.0	5	3.6	50
BENHAM GNMA INCOME FUND	BP	256	3.5	93	0.0	79	4.3	15	3.3	57
BOND FUND OF AMERICA	BP	598	7.9	71	1.9	58	-0.2	41	4.9	21
BOSTON CO. CAP. APPREC.	G	422	16.8	17	4.4	35	-5.5	61	6.3	10
BOSTON CO. MANAGED INC.	BP	37	6.9	78	3.4	44	0.8	37	3.3	57
BOSTON CO. SPEC GROWTH	G	40	19.4	8	5.2	28	-16.0	94	2.1	77
BOWSER GROWTH FUND	G	3	5.1	86	-2.0	95	-17.2	96	-9.9	99
BRUCE FUND	AG	3	27.0	1	8.4	10	-5.6	61	-0.4	93
BULL & BEAR CAP GROWTH	G	63	15.7	21	3.6	42	-15.2	93	2.0	80
BULL & BEAR EQUITY INC.	B	9	14.9	27	2.8	50	-2.6	49	3.1	61
BULL & BEAR HIGH YIELD	BP	151	6.4	81	2.7	51	-2.9	50	0.0	92
BULLOCK AGGRES GROWTH SH	AG	6	12.5	42	15.6	2	-9.8	79	3.5	52
BULLOCK BALANCED SHARES	B	79	12.3	44	6.4	20	-2.5	48	2.2	77
BULLOCK DIVIDEND SHARES	GI	345	15.7	21	7.4	16	-7.1	66	5.2	18
BULLOCK GROWTH SHARES	G	159	19.1	9	7.0	17	-9.8	79	0.7	88
BULLOCK HIGH INCOME SHS	BP	204	4.8	88	1.4	62	-2.4	48	0.9	87
BULLOCK MONTHLY INC SHS	BP	45	7.0	77	0.2	76	1.1	36	5.1	19
BULLOCK TAX-FREE SHARES	MB	111	8.7	67	-1.5	93	4.5	14	3.7	48
CALVERT EQUITY	G	8	12.8	40	5.1	29	-5.3	60	-0.1	92
CALVERT INCOME	BP	21	8.6	68	0.4	75	-1.0	44	2.1	78
CALVERT MANAGED GROWTH	B	88	14.7	29	8.1	12	-7.7	69	3.2	60
CANADIAN FUND	G	23	4.3	89	-2.1	95	-2.8	49	3.4	55
CAPITAL PRESERVATION TNT	BP	36	8.4	69	0.8	71	2.1	28	3.6	50
CARNEGIE CAPPIELLO GROW	G	48	12.2	45	6.4	20	-6.9	65	1.3	85
CARDINAL FUND	G	85	15.9	20	6.9	18	-6.0	62	2.5	72
CARDINAL GOVERNMENT GTD	BP	127	na	--	0.6	72	3.2	21	2.1	77
CASHMAN FARRELL VALUE FD	G	6	na	--	1.3	63	0.1	40	0.1	91
CENTURY SHARES TRUST	G	150	20.0	7	0.8	71	-7.9	70	-1.8	96
CHARTER FUND	G	79	14.9	28	7.5	15	-8.2	72	3.8	46
CHEAPSIDE DOLLAR FD LTD	G	46	14.7	29	5.8	23	-10.6	82	3.1	61
CHEMICAL FUND	G	677	14.6	29	4.9	31	-10.5	82	3.5	51
CIGNA AGGRESSIVE GROWTH	AG	17	10.2	56	1.4	62	-15.3	93	6.0	11
CIGNA GROWTH FUND	G	214	12.5	42	5.9	23	-8.0	71	2.7	67
CIGNA HIGH YIELD	BP	246	7.2	75	4.6	33	1.6	32	1.7	82
CIGNA INCOME FUND	BP	254	10.2	56	1.6	60	1.1	36	4.1	36
CIGNA MUNICIPAL BOND FD	MB	258	11.8	47	-1.3	91	5.0	9	4.5	28
CIGNA VALUE FUND	G	44	9.6	61	0.6	72	-5.7	61	4.5	28
CLIPPER FUND, INC.	GI	67	17.2	15	-0.1	80	-1.9	46	3.5	54
COLONIAL ADV STRAT GOLD	ME	29	2.1	97	-2.1	95	24.3	2	4.8	24
COLONIAL EQUITY INC TR	G	11	14.1	33	1.8	59	-2.3	47	3.5	52
COLONIAL GOV MORTGAGE	BP	27	3.4	93	0.9	69	1.8	31	2.4	72

TEN YEARS OF ANNUAL RETURNS

1986		1985		1984		1983		1982		1981		1980		1979		1978		1977	
PCNT	RK	PCNT	RK	PCNT	RK	PCNT	RK	PCNT	RK	PCNT	RK	PCNT	RK	PCNT	RK	PCNT	RK	PCNT	RK
10.9	72	31.1	20	-15.5	91	23.7	25	27.8	47	-5.7	72	36.9	25	23.8	47	10.0	38	-11.2	99
20.1	18	29.7	25	0.2	59	15.9	52	14.5	83	-6.0	73	27.9	46	17.2	63	8.8	43	-7.4	92
13.9	54	20.7	67	12.9	11	9.6	81	28.1	46	5.9	25	2.9	86	2.3	86	0.7	87	2.9	43
7.5	85	38.6	6	-5.0	74	na	--	na	--	na	--	na	--	na	--	na	--	na	--
20.7	16	26.5	39	na	--	na	--	na	--	na	--	na	--	na	--	na	--	na	--
12.8	61	25.3	45	8.4	32	na	--	na	--	na	--	na	--	na	--	na	--	na	--
16.3	40	31.5	19	-0.5	61	17.7	46	33.7	24	13.8	6	23.0	57	19.0	58	na	--	na	--
6.0	88	33.5	14	3.8	49	16.6	50	12.7	87	1.9	42	26.6	49	8.3	79	8.4	44	0.8	54
12.6	62	14.0	91	5.4	43	na	--	na	--	na	--	na	--	na	--	na	--	na	--
19.4	21	17.8	80	5.7	42	na	--	na	--	na	--	na	--	na	--	na	--	na	--
11.5	68	na	--	na	--	na	--	na	--	na	--	na	--	na	--	na	--	na	--
15.1	47	26.5	38	11.9	15	9.4	82	33.0	27	6.5	22	3.5	85	3.1	85	2.0	77	5.1	30
22.5	11	35.0	10	6.9	37	24.0	24	13.6	84	-3.6	65	28.0	45	20.1	55	8.4	44	-5.1	83
15.1	47	21.8	60	12.0	15	na	--	na	--	na	--	na	--	na	--	na	--	na	--
7.7	84	34.7	11	-10.9	86	na	--	na	--	na	--	na	--	na	--	na	--	na	--
23.2	99	-6.1	98	na	--	na	--	na	--	na	--	na	--	na	--	na	--	na	--
29.6	6	37.0	7	6.2	41	17.7	47	22.7	64	0.3	50	na	--	na	--	na	--	na	--
3.6	92	27.8	33	-4.3	73	15.5	55	12.6	87	-12.1	91	51.3	9	54.6	4	3.2	70	6.8	24
18.7	25	25.8	42	7.9	34	11.9	69	18.3	77	-7.1	78	30.4	40	17.0	64	3.6	68	9.6	17
6.0	88	21.0	64	6.5	39	na	--	na	--	na	--	na	--	na	--	na	--	na	--
21.4	14	10.2	95	-32.6	99	na	--	na	--	na	--	na	--	na	--	na	--	na	--
19.0	23	34.2	12	15.5	4	14.5	60	26.2	52	3.5	36	13.2	75	9.8	76	1.5	81	-2.9	72
21.3	14	31.0	21	7.0	37	21.0	33	26.4	52	-0.4	52	23.0	57	12.5	73	5.1	63	-8.1	95
15.7	44	27.1	36	0.3	59	15.7	53	21.1	69	-0.7	54	24.8	54	24.3	44	8.7	43	-5.3	84
4.6	91	15.9	87	6.4	40	19.6	38	24.6	58	na	--	na	--	na	--	na	--	na	--
14.0	54	22.4	57	15.2	5	10.0	78	40.0	11	1.5	44	-4.0	93	-2.4	97	-0.1	90	2.6	44
16.1	41	19.4	74	9.1	28	na	--	na	--	na	--	na	--	na	--	na	--	na	--
12.1	65	23.6	50	-9.1	84	9.0	84	na	--	na	--	na	--	na	--	na	--	na	--
10.1	77	24.0	48	16.0	3	5.1	95	na	--	na	--	na	--	na	--	na	--	na	--
18.1	28	26.7	37	6.7	39	11.2	72	na	--	na	--	na	--	na	--	na	--	na	--
2.7	93	14.9	89	-2.9	69	25.0	22	7.1	94	-0.8	55	19.8	66	29.8	29	12.7	29	-1.4	64
15.5	45	18.1	79	12.1	14	5.0	95	na	--	na	--	na	--	na	--	na	--	na	--
12.7	61	20.1	70	na	--	na	--	na	--	na	--	na	--	na	--	na	--	na	--
19.3	22	34.1	12	4.0	48	26.6	17	na	--	na	--	na	--	na	--	na	--	na	--
na	--	na	--	na	--	na	--	na	--	na	--	na	--	na	--	na	--	na	--
na	--	na	--	na	--	na	--	na	--	na	--	na	--	na	--	na	--	na	--
9.4	80	42.6	4	15.6	3	21.2	32	11.0	89	20.5	3	6.0	81	21.2	53	10.4	36	-2.0	68
17.6	31	25.5	44	-5.7	76	19.4	39	15.5	82	1.0	47	34.0	31	43.2	12	31.8	2	5.3	30
11.9	66	23.7	50	-1.7	66	8.5	86	8.7	92	-31.8	99	54.0	8	na	--	na	--	na	--
11.4	69	31.0	20	-5.7	76	10.2	77	21.3	68	-4.3	67	30.8	38	24.8	43	11.9	31	-8.1	95
0.3	95	26.2	40	na	--	na	--	na	--	na	--	na	--	na	--	na	--	na	--
12.6	62	27.6	33	-1.7	66	20.1	36	20.6	71	-4.9	68	34.6	30	24.2	44	12.2	30	-7.4	92
15.9	43	23.3	52	9.7	25	17.4	47	30.7	36	7.2	19	na	--	na	--	na	--	na	--
18.0	29	24.3	47	11.7	16	7.1	90	34.2	22	5.4	27	3.2	85	-0.7	93	-1.1	92	5.9	26
21.1	15	22.2	57	8.1	33	6.5	92	39.6	12	-9.4	85	-11.8	96	-2.0	97	-3.7	96	na	--
8.7	82	22.7	54	na	--	na	--	na	--	na	--	na	--	na	--	na	--	na	--
18.8	24	26.4	39	na	--	na	--	na	--	na	--	na	--	na	--	na	--	na	--
30.2	5	na	--	na	--	na	--	na	--	na	--	na	--	na	--	na	--	na	--
17.5	32	25.9	41	1.7	56	24.2	24	27.2	50	na	--	na	--	na	--	na	--	na	--
8.8	81	na	--	na	--	na	--	na	--	na	--	na	--	na	--	na	--	na	--

CDA ANNUAL SUPPLEMENT – 12/31/86

		ASSETS (MIL$)	1986 QUARTERLY RETURNS							
			1st		2nd		3rd		4th	
FUND	IO	9/86	PCNT	RK	PCNT	RK	PCNT	RK	PCNT	RK
COLONIAL FUND	B	159	14.6	30	4.1	37	-1.7	46	3.6	50
COLONIAL CORP CASH I	B	407	4.8	87	0.5	73	1.6	32	2.5	71
COLONIAL CORP CASH II	B	318	3.6	91	-0.8	87	1.8	31	1.1	86
COLONIAL GOV SEC PLUS TR	BP	2,800	9.0	65	0.2	77	2.3	25	3.5	52
COLONIAL GROWTH SHARES	G	75	19.3	8	3.0	48	-7.6	68	4.9	21
COLONIAL INCOME	BP	153	4.9	87	2.0	56	1.5	33	3.3	56
COLONIAL OPTION INC I	GI	1,113	5.3	85	0.6	72	-5.2	59	4.1	38
COLONIAL OPTION INC II	GI	200	7.7	72	0.0	79	-5.8	62	5.5	15
COLONIAL HIGH YIELD SECS	BP	401	5.8	84	3.6	41	1.4	34	3.2	59
COLONIAL TAX EXEMPT HIYD	MB	1,258	7.1	76	-0.3	81	4.3	15	3.1	63
COLONIAL TAX EX INSURED	MB	87	11.4	49	-1.6	93	4.1	16	2.3	74
COLUMBIA FIXED INCOME FD	BP	115	0.4	98	0.8	71	3.3	21	4.1	38
COLUMBIA GROWTH FUND	G	209	15.1	26	3.6	42	-14.4	91	4.7	25
COLUMBIA MUNICIPAL BOND	MB	100	9.0	65	-1.3	91	6.1	5	2.5	71
COLUMBIA SPECIAL FUND	AG	21	22.7	3	13.3	3	-15.9	94	-1.1	95
COMMERCE INCOME SHARES	B	59	12.2	45	0.6	72	-6.7	64	4.7	24
COMMONWEALTH - PLANS A&B	B	10	12.0	46	3.4	44	-5.8	62	4.4	30
COMMONWEALTH - PLAN C	B	40	11.3	50	2.7	51	-5.4	60	3.9	42
COMPANION FUND	G	77	12.3	44	6.7	19	-8.4	73	2.5	71
COMPOSITE BOND & STOCK	B	76	8.3	69	3.9	39	-0.1	41	1.5	83
COMPOSITE FUND	G	68	12.4	43	6.1	22	-1.3	45	1.8	81
CONCORD FUND	GI	2	3.0	95	0.5	73	-2.4	48	-1.2	95
CONSTELLATION GROWTH	AG	76	21.8	4	13.2	4	-15.5	94	9.7	1
CONTINENTAL MUTUAL INV.	B	1	7.4	74	2.0	57	0.2	40	1.8	81
CONVERTIBLE YIELD	GI	18	12.6	42	4.2	36	-11.0	84	0.1	91
COPLEY TAX-MANAGED FUND	G	31	12.5	42	2.3	54	2.1	27	0.2	91
COUNTRY CAPITAL GROWTH	G	67	10.0	57	4.8	31	-9.7	78	4.0	40
CRITERION QUAL TX FR INS	MB	128	10.9	51	-1.5	92	2.6	24	4.4	30
DEAN WITTER CALIF TX FR	MB	316	9.1	64	-1.0	89	5.0	9	2.7	68
DEAN WITTER DEVELOP GROW	G	140	12.4	43	0.5	73	-13.8	89	3.8	47
DEAN WITTER DIVIDEND GRO	GI	1,024	12.3	44	5.7	24	-3.3	52	4.0	41
DEAN WITTER HIGH YIELD	BP	1,391	7.9	71	3.2	47	1.6	33	3.1	63
DEAN WITTER INDUSTRY VAL	G	71	14.0	34	6.7	19	-8.4	73	4.2	34
DEAN WITTER OPTION INC	GI	589	5.2	85	2.5	52	-5.3	60	5.2	18
DEAN WITTER NAT RESOURCE	G	53	3.1	95	-0.9	89	4.5	14	4.2	35
DEAN WITTER NY TX FR INC	MB	101	8.0	70	-0.5	84	4.8	11	3.5	51
DEAN WITTER TX ADVANTAGE	BP	303	3.9	90	-0.9	88	2.5	24	0.7	88
DEAN WITTER TAX EX SECS	MB	838	11.0	51	-1.3	91	5.0	9	2.6	70
DEAN WITTER US GOV TRUST	BP	10,291	2.0	97	0.7	71	2.8	23	2.3	75
DEAN WITTER WORLDWIDE	IN	346	15.7	21	8.3	11	-0.8	43	5.8	13
DECATUR FUND INC-SER 1	GI	1,076	13.0	39	4.0	38	-2.1	46	5.9	12
DELAWARE FUND	G	394	18.4	10	0.1	77	-7.2	67	0.8	87
DELAWARE GOV FD-USG SER	BP	40	3.2	94	1.0	68	2.7	23	2.6	69
DELAWARE GOV FD-GNMA SER	BP	43	3.5	92	0.9	69	3.3	20	2.2	77
DELAWARE TREAS RESERVES	BP	59	2.7	96	1.9	58	1.8	30	1.3	85
DELCHESTER BOND FUND	BP	191	7.4	74	3.8	40	1.3	35	3.5	52
DELTA TREND FUND	AG	75	18.2	11	10.5	6	-21.0	98	2.0	79
DEPOSITORS FUND/BOSTON	G	57	12.4	43	3.0	49	-8.9	75	8.0	3
DE VEGH MUTUAL FUND	G	53	14.7	29	3.2	46	-10.7	82	2.4	73
DFA FIXED INC PORTFOLIO	BP	312	2.8	96	2.0	57	2.1	28	1.7	82

TEN YEARS OF ANNUAL RETURNS

1986		1985		1984		1983		1982		1981		1980		1979		1978		1977	
PCNT	RK	PCNT	RK	PCNT	RK	PCNT	RK	PCNT	RK	PCNT	RK	PCNT	RK	PCNT	RK	PCNT	RK	PCNT	RK
21.5	13	26.6	38	8.0	33	25.1	21	19.2	75	-3.1	63	24.4	56	17.7	61	5.7	60	-5.8	86
9.8	78	17.6	81	12.5	13	13.1	66	11.1	89	na	--	na	--	na	--	na	--	na	--
5.8	89	15.9	87	na	--	na	--	na	--	na	--	na	--	na	--	na	--	na	--
15.6	44	19.8	72	na	--	na	--	na	--	na	--	na	--	na	--	na	--	na	--
19.1	22	23.8	49	0.3	59	15.6	54	23.7	61	-8.4	83	41.5	18	38.6	16	5.9	58	-10.1	97
12.2	65	21.1	64	11.6	17	10.2	77	34.0	24	4.3	31	-1.8	92	-1.1	94	1.4	83	6.6	24
4.5	91	20.1	70	4.7	46	19.0	41	13.5	85	1.0	47	na	--	na	--	na	--	na	--
7.0	86	13.0	92	na	--	na	--	na	--	na	--	na	--	na	--	na	--	na	--
14.8	50	21.8	59	10.5	20	20.3	35	24.4	59	6.4	22	0.6	89	7.6	80	4.6	64	-1.6	66
14.8	50	20.4	69	-2.8	69	12.1	69	na	--	na	--	na	--	na	--	na	--	na	--
16.8	38	na	--	na	--	na	--	na	--	na	--	na	--	na	--	na	--	na	--
8.7	82	24.4	47	12.2	14	na	--	na	--	na	--	na	--	na	--	na	--	na	--
6.8	87	32.0	17	-5.1	75	21.5	32	44.9	7	-2.9	62	39.2	22	40.6	15	8.0	47	-0.1	59
17.1	34	na	--	na	--	na	--	na	--	na	--	na	--	na	--	na	--	na	--
15.7	44	na	--	na	--	na	--	na	--	na	--	na	--	na	--	na	--	na	--
10.4	75	23.6	50	6.8	39	9.4	82	30.1	38	3.3	36	24.5	55	16.6	65	3.0	71	-5.8	85
13.9	54	24.7	46	4.9	45	14.2	62	23.3	62	0.8	47	25.3	53	21.0	54	4.5	65	-1.2	64
12.3	65	21.8	59	4.6	47	13.3	65	23.0	63	-0.7	54	24.6	55	15.4	68	3.0	71	-2.6	69
12.6	63	28.1	32	-1.6	66	22.1	30	18.5	76	-1.9	59	34.9	29	24.8	43	12.8	28	-6.3	87
14.1	53	22.8	54	2.1	54	16.8	50	22.1	65	4.5	30	17.4	69	19.9	56	1.8	79	-2.0	68
19.7	20	27.4	34	-8.3	82	15.2	57	19.6	74	14.9	5	18.3	69	23.2	48	5.5	61	-4.4	79
-0.2	95	14.5	90	5.6	43	18.1	45	10.3	90	2.4	40	25.5	52	32.1	25	1.6	80	13.6	12
27.8	7	28.6	29	-15.2	91	24.6	23	15.0	83	-17.5	96	74.5	2	76.8	2	21.2	11	-3.4	75
11.7	67	13.0	92	-6.3	78	7.4	89	16.2	80	-5.7	73	27.9	46	23.1	48	-8.2	99	-8.4	96
4.6	91	21.0	65	-3.3	70	11.7	70	17.8	78	4.7	30	34.5	30	16.2	66	na	--	na	--
17.7	30	24.6	46	23.9	1	11.6	70	19.9	73	4.1	32	16.0	71	na	--	na	--	na	--
8.2	83	29.9	24	1.1	57	19.5	38	20.9	70	-3.0	63	30.6	39	20.1	55	2.5	73	-5.3	84
17.0	35	22.2	58	7.1	37	na	--	na	--	na	--	na	--	na	--	na	--	na	--
16.8	38	19.0	76	na	--	na	--	na	--	na	--	na	--	na	--	na	--	na	--
1.0	94	17.2	83	-15.4	91	na	--	na	--	na	--	na	--	na	--	na	--	na	--
19.3	22	31.9	18	8.4	31	20.2	36	27.8	47	na	--	na	--	na	--	na	--	na	--
16.5	38	23.0	53	7.9	34	12.5	67	34.2	22	na	--	na	--	na	--	na	--	na	--
16.1	41	29.7	26	-8.1	82	10.7	75	18.5	76	na	--	na	--	na	--	na	--	na	--
7.5	86	na	--	na	--	na	--	na	--	na	--	na	--	na	--	na	--	na	--
11.2	70	13.5	92	-12.0	87	15.0	57	-6.3	98	na	--	na	--	na	--	na	--	na	--
16.6	38	na	--	na	--	na	--	na	--	na	--	na	--	na	--	na	--	na	--
6.3	88	14.7	90	na	--	na	--	na	--	na	--	na	--	na	--	na	--	na	--
17.9	29	21.2	63	9.3	27	11.9	70	38.7	13	-6.5	76	na	--	na	--	na	--	na	--
8.1	83	14.0	91	na	--	na	--	na	--	na	--	na	--	na	--	na	--	na	--
31.5	5	38.3	6	-1.0	63	na	--	na	--	na	--	na	--	na	--	na	--	na	--
21.9	13	27.0	36	9.4	26	23.1	27	25.6	56	5.4	28	24.4	56	24.0	46	2.7	73	1.4	52
11.0	72	30.4	22	2.5	53	14.6	59	42.4	9	8.9	12	25.8	50	23.8	46	2.3	75	-3.1	73
9.8	77	na	--	na	--	na	--	na	--	na	--	na	--	na	--	na	--	na	--
10.3	76	na	--	na	--	na	--	na	--	na	--	na	--	na	--	na	--	na	--
7.9	84	na	--	na	--	na	--	na	--	na	--	na	--	na	--	na	--	na	--
16.8	36	21.8	60	8.6	31	14.1	62	37.3	14	1.0	46	0.7	89	1.7	88	2.2	75	3.3	41
5.3	90	28.0	32	-19.8	95	37.8	4	31.5	32	20.3	3	28.8	44	29.2	31	2.6	73	6.0	26
13.9	54	30.2	23	-0.5	61	12.3	68	22.1	66	na	--	na	--	na	--	na	--	na	--
8.2	83	28.6	29	-6.7	78	17.0	49	10.1	91	-12.1	91	42.8	15	30.3	27	5.2	62	-4.4	80
8.9	81	10.5	95	13.6	9	na	--	na	--	na	--	na	--	na	--	na	--	na	--

CDA ANNUAL SUPPLEMENT – 12/31/86

FUND	IO	ASSETS (MIL$) 9/86	1986 QUARTERLY RETURNS 1st PCNT RK	2nd PCNT RK	3rd PCNT RK	4th PCNT RK
DFA SMALL CO. PORTFOLIO	G	927	13.6 37	4.5 34	-10.4 81	0.4 89
DIVERSIFICATION FUND	G	60	9.8 59	3.3 45	-8.3 72	4.8 23
DIVIDEND/GROWTH FD., INC	GI	4	10.7 53	2.5 52	-8.9 75	5.1 20
DMC TAX FREE-PA	MB	304	9.7 60	-0.2 81	4.6 14	3.8 44
DMC TAX FREE-USA	MB	265	10.5 54	-0.1 80	4.7 13	5.4 16
DMC TAX FREE-INSURED	MB	36	9.8 59	-0.3 81	4.4 15	3.8 46
DODGE & COX BALANCED	B	26	13.0 39	2.8 50	-3.6 53	6.4 9
DODGE & COX STOCK	GI	43	14.3 32	2.8 50	-6.0 62	7.5 4
DOUBLE EXEMPT FLEX FUND	MB	89	7.4 74	0.1 78	3.9 17	3.8 46
DREXEL BURNHAM FUND	GI	133	13.9 35	7.0 17	-6.1 63	6.6 8
DREXEL ST GOV SECURITIES	BP	334	5.6 84	-0.8 87	1.6 32	4.1 37
DREXEL ST OPTION INC FD	GI	36	6.5 80	3.4 44	-5.2 59	5.6 14
DREXEL ST EMERG GROWTH	G	38	15.1 26	14.6 2	-23.2 99	-5.7 98
DREXEL ST GROWTH	G	22	12.2 45	1.2 65	-8.0 71	6.8 7
DREYFUS A BONDS PLUS	BP	241	7.3 75	0.3 75	1.6 32	4.2 33
DREYFUS CALIF TAX EXEMPT	MB	1,158	9.2 63	-0.4 83	3.9 17	4.1 38
DREYFUS CONVERTIBLE SECS	B	172	12.5 42	8.2 11	0.0 40	2.1 78
DREYFUS FUND	GI	2,316	14.8 28	2.1 56	-3.6 53	3.0 65
DREYFUS GNMA	BP	1,936	3.6 91	-0.5 83	3.0 22	3.2 60
DREYFUS GROWTH OPPORTUN.	G	416	11.1 50	4.9 30	-4.2 55	3.8 45
DREYFUS INSURED TAX EX	MB	177	10.4 55	-1.1 89	3.7 18	3.3 57
DREYFUS INTERMDIATE MUNI	MB	1,060	6.7 79	0.2 76	3.7 18	3.9 42
DREYFUS LEVERAGE	GI	486	14.6 30	3.3 45	-4.2 54	4.7 25
DREYFUS MASS TAX EXEMPT	MB	68	10.7 53	-1.9 95	4.8 11	3.5 53
DREYFUS NY TAX EXEMPT	MB	1,424	8.9 66	-1.5 93	4.9 10	4.0 39
DREYFUS TAX EXEMPT BOND	MB	3,540	7.7 72	-0.1 80	4.6 14	4.2 34
DREYFUS THIRD CENTURY	GI	156	7.1 76	0.1 77	-3.7 53	1.2 86
EAGLE GROWTH SHARES	G	4	5.1 86	-2.9 96	-11.3 84	0.4 89
EATON & HOWARD STOCK	GI	80	10.9 51	5.1 28	-4.5 57	3.9 43
EATON VANCE GROWTH FD	G	73	11.6 48	5.2 27	-10.1 80	4.6 26
EATON VANCE GOV OBLIGATN	BP	384	7.5 73	-0.2 81	2.2 27	3.3 57
EATON VANCE HIGH YIELD	BP	32	5.7 84	1.9 57	2.1 27	3.8 45
EATON VANCE INC FD/BOST	B	43	5.9 83	3.0 47	0.5 38	4.8 23
EATON VANCE INVESTORS FD	B	219	7.5 73	3.6 41	-4.6 57	2.5 72
EATON VANCE MUNICIPAL BD	MB	49	9.8 60	-0.6 85	4.2 16	4.3 33
EATON VANCE SPL EQUITIES	G	40	5.0 86	5.9 23	-18.0 97	1.0 87
EATON VANCE TOTAL RETURN	GI	570	15.7 20	9.2 8	1.7 31	2.6 70
ELFUN TRUSTS	GI	480	14.4 31	4.5 34	-8.4 73	4.9 22
ENERGY FUND	GI	376	2.7 97	3.8 40	0.5 38	2.8 66
EQUITEC SIEBEL TOTAL RET	GI	76	12.9 40	4.3 35	-6.5 64	2.8 67
EUROPACIFIC GROWTH FUND	IN	160	18.3 10	6.5 19	2.5 24	8.4 3
EVERGREEN FUND	AG	639	16.7 17	7.3 16	-9.1 76	-0.6 94
EVERGREEN TOTAL RETURN	B	794	12.6 42	6.1 22	-1.0 44	1.6 83
EXPLORER FUND	AG	266	7.2 75	0.4 75	-16.5 95	1.6 83
EXPLORER II	AG	34	6.2 82	4.2 36	-16.2 95	0.0 92
FAIRFIELD FUND	AG	44	12.4 43	2.6 52	-16.8 96	7.8 4
FAIRMONT FUND	G	72	13.7 36	7.4 15	-10.1 80	3.9 42
FARM BUREAU GROWTH FUND	G	42	12.8 41	1.4 62	-10.3 81	6.8 7
FEDERATED CORP CASH TR	BP	131	3.4 94	-1.8 94	1.3 34	0.5 89
FEDERATED GNMA	BP	1,348	3.4 93	0.5 73	4.0 17	2.7 68

TEN YEARS OF ANNUAL RETURNS

1986		1985		1984		1983		1982		1981		1980		1979		1978		1977	
PCNT	RK	PCNT	RK	PCNT	RK	PCNT	RK	PCNT	RK	PCNT	RK	PCNT	RK	PCNT	RK	PCNT	RK	PCNT	RK
6.8	87	24.4	47	-7.1	79	40.2	3	na	--	na	--	na	--	na	--	na	--	na	--
8.9	81	27.9	32	2.9	52	18.5	43	26.0	54	na	--	na	--	na	--	na	--	na	--
8.7	82	13.9	91	11.4	17	15.1	57	13.2	86	13.9	5	na	--	na	--	na	--	na	--
18.9	24	17.3	82	10.4	21	13.4	65	36.9	15	-6.4	75	-19.4	99	0.0	92	-2.9	94	na	--
21.9	13	22.2	57	na	--	na	--	na	--	na	--	na	--	na	--	na	--	na	--
18.6	25	na	--	na	--	na	--	na	--	na	--	na	--	na	--	na	--	na	--
19.1	22	32.5	16	4.8	46	17.0	49	26.0	54	-2.5	61	21.6	61	13.7	71	6.1	57	-3.2	74
18.8	24	37.7	7	5.4	44	26.7	17	22.0	66	-2.5	61	33.1	33	21.1	54	9.6	40	-6.1	86
15.8	43	18.8	77	na	--	na	--	na	--	na	--	na	--	na	--	na	--	na	--
22.0	12	32.2	17	7.3	36	12.1	69	22.3	65	-2.6	61	33.9	31	23.5	47	12.9	28	-4.0	77
10.7	74	na	--	na	--	na	--	na	--	na	--	na	--	na	--	na	--	na	--
10.3	75	na	--	na	--	na	--	na	--	na	--	na	--	na	--	na	--	na	--
-4.5	96	na	--	na	--	na	--	na	--	na	--	na	--	na	--	na	--	na	--
11.6	68	na	--	na	--	na	--	na	--	na	--	na	--	na	--	na	--	na	--
13.9	54	23.1	53	12.4	13	7.6	88	26.0	54	9.1	11	5.2	82	6.0	82	1.3	83	1.4	51
17.6	31	18.1	80	5.0	45	na	--	na	--	na	--	na	--	na	--	na	--	na	--
24.3	9	23.7	50	7.7	35	21.1	33	17.2	78	1.2	45	14.8	73	15.8	67	1.5	81	6.2	26
16.3	40	25.2	45	3.3	50	19.7	37	13.9	84	5.4	27	30.3	40	25.6	41	12.3	29	0.1	58
9.6	79	na	--	na	--	na	--	na	--	na	--	na	--	na	--	na	--	na	--
15.9	42	30.7	22	-12.1	88	31.5	8	3.6	96	-15.1	95	52.9	8	46.7	9	20.5	12	7.1	22
17.0	35	na	--	na	--	na	--	na	--	na	--	na	--	na	--	na	--	na	--
15.2	47	16.1	87	7.5	36	na	--	na	--	na	--	na	--	na	--	na	--	na	--
18.7	24	30.1	24	8.6	30	17.3	48	18.4	76	-8.2	83	37.0	24	40.5	15	10.6	36	7.4	20
17.8	30	na	--	na	--	na	--	na	--	na	--	na	--	na	--	na	--	na	--
17.0	36	20.7	66	8.1	33	na	--	na	--	na	--	na	--	na	--	na	--	na	--
17.3	33	19.5	74	8.6	30	11.6	71	39.6	12	na	--	na	--	na	--	na	--	na	--
4.6	91	29.5	26	1.6	56	20.2	35	4.6	96	-11.1	89	40.5	19	59.8	3	10.2	37	13.1	13
-9.1	98	16.0	87	-7.8	81	20.2	36	5.0	95	6.2	24	na	--	na	--	na	--	na	--
15.6	44	31.7	18	11.6	17	14.7	59	20.3	72	-4.8	68	24.9	54	17.6	62	6.8	53	-6.7	89
10.5	75	30.3	22	2.3	54	17.0	49	24.0	61	0.8	48	32.4	34	23.5	47	22.8	8	2.8	43
13.3	58	12.1	93	na	--	na	--	na	--	na	--	na	--	na	--	na	--	na	--
14.3	52	21.8	60	15.0	5	8.8	85	33.1	27	1.7	43	1.3	88	-0.4	93	0.5	88	5.7	27
14.9	49	24.9	46	14.7	6	11.4	71	25.7	55	5.6	26	10.7	77	6.9	81	0.6	87	4.9	32
8.9	81	25.4	44	9.0	29	14.6	59	25.9	55	4.8	29	20.3	64	18.8	59	7.9	47	0.8	55
18.5	26	21.4	62	9.6	25	8.2	86	48.4	4	-10.7	88	-15.3	98	-0.8	94	na	--	na	--
-7.8	98	16.8	84	-1.5	65	10.2	77	32.9	28	7.1	19	42.9	15	34.7	20	15.0	23	1.9	49
31.9	5	40.2	5	15.8	3	13.3	65	27.5	49	na	--	na	--	na	--	na	--	na	--
14.9	49	34.9	10	6.2	41	17.7	47	26.1	53	1.3	44	30.1	41	25.6	41	14.2	25	-0.9	63
10.1	77	22.6	55	4.8	46	22.1	30	1.0	97	-10.2	86	41.7	17	49.3	7	5.5	60	2.5	45
13.1	59	na	--	na	--	na	--	na	--	na	--	na	--	na	--	na	--	na	--
40.0	3	35.2	9	na	--	na	--	na	--	na	--	na	--	na	--	na	--	na	--
13.2	58	34.6	11	0.6	58	29.9	11	20.3	72	-1.1	56	46.7	12	46.1	10	38.0	1	25.2	4
20.2	18	31.5	19	14.4	7	30.3	9	25.6	55	8.9	12	26.7	48	22.3	50	na	--	na	--
-8.7	98	22.4	56	-19.5	95	20.3	34	41.3	10	1.6	43	55.3	7	33.8	22	20.4	12	27.9	3
-7.3	97	na	--	na	--	na	--	na	--	na	--	na	--	na	--	na	--	na	--
3.5	92	43.3	3	-16.7	92	9.6	81	25.4	56	-6.2	74	60.6	6	29.0	32	10.7	35	-8.4	95
14.0	53	32.1	17	10.8	19	35.0	6	34.2	23	na	--	na	--	na	--	na	--	na	--
9.5	79	25.5	44	-4.2	72	13.3	65	11.4	89	3.1	37	27.8	46	19.5	57	5.4	61	2.7	43
3.4	93	18.2	79	na	--	na	--	na	--	na	--	na	--	na	--	na	--	na	--
10.9	72	19.5	74	13.7	9	7.3	90	na	--	na	--	na	--	na	--	na	--	na	--

CDA ANNUAL SUPPLEMENT – 12/31/86

FUND	IO	ASSETS (MIL$) 9/86	1st PCNT RK	2nd PCNT RK	3rd PCNT RK	4th PCNT RK
FEDERATED GROWTH TRUST	G	59	19.1 9	6.2 21	-6.9 65	5.4 17
FEDERATED HIGH INCOME	BP	360	6.0 82	3.4 43	0.8 37	1.7 82
FEDERATED HIGH YIELD TR.	BP	159	6.7 79	3.8 40	1.8 30	2.8 66
FEDERATED INCOME TRUST	BP	568	3.3 94	0.3 76	3.1 22	2.8 66
FEDERATED INTERM. GOV.	BP	1,412	4.9 87	1.4 62	2.8 23	2.3 75
FEDERATED INTMED MUNI TR	MB	70	4.6 88	-1.4 92	4.2 15	4.0 40
FEDERATED SH-INTERM GOV	BP	3,696	3.4 93	1.9 58	2.4 25	1.6 83
FEDERATED SH-INTERM MUNI	MB	461	2.8 96	1.4 63	1.1 36	2.1 77
FEDERATED STOCK & BOND	B	68	8.8 67	1.7 59	-0.1 41	2.9 65
FEDERATED STOCK TRUST	GI	450	14.4 31	2.1 56	-3.2 51	0.6 88
FEDERATED TAX FR INCOME	MB	305	11.8 47	-1.1 90	4.9 10	3.8 46
FIDELITY AGGRESS TAX FR	MB	308	9.6 61	-0.6 84	3.8 18	3.9 43
FIDELITY CALIF TAX FREE	MB	446	9.6 61	-1.6 93	4.7 12	3.7 48
FIDELITY CONGRESS STREET	G	52	18.8 9	7.5 15	-7.9 70	8.1 3
FIDELITY CONTRAFUND	G	82	15.1 26	0.2 77	-7.2 67	5.4 16
FIDELITY CORP TR-ARP	BP	297	4.0 90	-1.8 94	3.1 21	1.2 85
FIDELITY DESTINY	G	1,074	20.2 7	3.3 45	-9.4 77	4.5 27
FIDELITY EQUITY INCOME	GI	3,100	14.4 31	1.2 66	-2.9 49	3.9 42
FIDELITY EXCHANGE FUND	G	140	15.6 22	8.4 11	-9.9 79	6.8 7
FIDELITY FLEXIBLE BOND	BP	290	7.4 74	1.3 63	0.7 37	3.8 46
FIDELITY FREEDOM FUND	G	816	20.6 6	0.5 73	-8.2 72	2.2 76
FIDELITY FUND	GI	760	16.7 17	3.4 43	-6.9 66	2.7 68
FIDELITY GOVT SECS	BP	573	7.5 73	1.3 64	2.0 29	3.3 57
FIDELITY GROWTH FUND	AG	169	17.4 14	7.1 17	-13.6 89	4.0 40
FIDELITY GROWTH & INCOME	GI	460	29.7 1	6.9 18	-5.6 61	3.1 61
FIDELITY LTD TERM MUNS	MB	471	7.1 76	-0.1 80	4.6 13	3.0 64
FIDELITY MASS TAX FREE	MB	589	9.6 61	-1.5 93	4.9 10	3.2 58
FIDELITY MORTGAGE SECS	BP	660	4.0 90	0.5 73	3.2 21	2.9 65
FIDELITY MUNI BOND FD	MB	1,041	9.9 58	-0.8 86	5.3 8	4.2 35
FIDELITY OVERSEAS FUND	IN	2,561	38.5 1	7.6 14	13.3 3	0.0 91
FIDELITY SEL AMER GOLD	ME	85	3.0 95	-1.4 91	16.2 2	0.0 92
FIDELITY SEL BIOTECH	AG	33	25.7 2	12.5 4	-25.5 99	-1.7 96
FIDELITY HIGH YIELD MUNI	MB	2,065	9.4 63	-0.6 84	5.5 6	3.7 48
FIDELITY HIGH INCOME FD	BP	1,460	8.5 68	3.9 39	0.9 36	3.8 46
FIDELITY SEL CHEMICAL	G	21	22.5 4	5.7 24	-7.5 68	6.0 11
FIDELITY MAGELLAN FUND	G	6,555	22.4 4	6.0 22	-9.1 76	4.8 24
FIDELITY PURITAN FD	B	2,458	12.8 40	2.0 56	0.9 37	4.1 37
FIDELITY OTC PORTFOLIO	G	588	20.7 6	5.6 25	-13.9 90	1.4 85
FIDELITY QUALIFIED DIVD	B	214	11.8 47	4.4 35	2.6 24	1.2 86
FIDELITY SEL DEF & AERO	G	9	10.1 57	5.4 26	-9.3 77	-0.3 93
FIDELITY SELECT ENERGY	G	71	-9.4 99	5.2 28	5.0 9	5.5 15
FIDELITY SEL LEISURE ENT	G	114	23.2 3	12.3 4	-15.7 94	-0.8 95
FIDELITY SELECT FINL SVC	G	120	24.5 2	6.2 21	-11.8 85	-1.3 96
FIDELITY SELECT HEALTH	AG	217	22.2 4	14.7 2	-16.9 96	4.7 24
FIDELITY SEL PREC MET&MN	ME	241	15.2 25	-13.1 99	32.8 1	-0.1 92
FIDELITY SELECT TECHNLGY	AG	241	7.9 71	-4.5 97	-16.5 95	7.6 4
FIDELITY SEL UTILITIES	GI	195	13.7 36	8.0 12	-1.0 44	1.9 80
FIDELITY SPEC SITUATIONS	AG	54	21.4 5	5.6 25	-3.4 52	3.2 59
FIDELITY SEL BROKERAGE	G	11	22.6 3	0.1 78	-12.5 87	2.1 77
FIDELITY SEL ELECTRONICS	AG	3	1.0 98	-10.0 98	-15.0 92	-1.4 96

TEN YEARS OF ANNUAL RETURNS

1986		1985		1984		1983		1982		1981		1980		1979		1978		1977	
PCNT	RK	PCNT	RK	PCNT	RK	PCNT	RK	PCNT	RK	PCNT	RK	PCNT	RK	PCNT	RK	PCNT	RK	PCNT	RK
24.1	9	34.7	11	na	--	na	--	na	--	na	--	na	--	na	--	na	--	na	--
12.4	64	21.5	61	10.7	19	14.3	61	32.2	29	na	--	na	--	na	--	na	--	na	--
15.9	42	22.2	58	na	--	na	--	na	--	na	--	na	--	na	--	na	--	na	--
9.8	78	17.0	84	14.4	7	7.8	88	na	--	na	--	na	--	na	--	na	--	na	--
11.9	66	15.5	88	na	--	na	--	na	--	na	--	na	--	na	--	na	--	na	--
11.7	67	na	--	na	--	na	--	na	--	na	--	na	--	na	--	na	--	na	--
9.5	79	12.0	93	na	--	na	--	na	--	na	--	na	--	na	--	na	--	na	--
7.6	85	6.5	97	6.9	38	5.6	94	10.2	90	na	--	na	--	na	--	na	--	na	--
13.8	55	19.3	75	13.8	9	21.2	32	29.7	39	4.2	32	14.3	74	14.0	71	1.5	82	1.9	49
13.8	55	33.5	14	16.0	3	31.2	9	na	--	na	--	na	--	na	--	na	--	na	--
20.4	16	18.3	78	6.2	40	10.8	74	45.3	6	-10.4	87	-17.1	99	-3.5	98	-5.5	98	na	--
17.5	32	na	--	na	--	na	--	na	--	na	--	na	--	na	--	na	--	na	--
17.1	35	16.6	85	na	--	na	--	na	--	na	--	na	--	na	--	na	--	na	--
27.1	7	31.7	18	6.4	40	28.4	13	20.2	72	-0.9	55	27.1	47	17.0	64	26.2	5	-7.3	90
12.8	61	27.0	36	-8.3	82	23.2	27	16.6	79	3.1	37	29.5	42	26.2	39	5.9	58	-10.9	98
6.6	87	16.4	86	na	--	na	--	na	--	na	--	na	--	na	--	na	--	na	--
17.6	31	29.1	27	4.7	46	38.8	3	37.5	14	7.2	19	19.9	66	32.9	24	20.9	12	12.6	14
16.8	37	25.0	46	10.5	20	29.2	11	34.1	23	8.6	14	32.3	35	30.7	27	11.3	33	5.0	31
20.5	16	31.1	20	4.0	49	20.1	36	21.5	68	-4.2	66	29.6	42	23.7	47	7.2	50	-7.8	93
13.7	56	21.1	64	11.8	16	6.6	91	30.1	38	3.9	34	2.3	86	1.2	90	1.4	82	5.1	31
13.7	56	28.5	30	3.4	50	na	--	na	--	na	--	na	--	na	--	na	--	na	--
15.4	46	27.7	33	1.4	57	22.4	29	33.2	26	-3.3	64	33.9	31	18.6	60	9.4	41	-3.3	75
14.7	50	17.7	81	11.3	18	6.0	93	26.2	53	22.1	2	12.7	76	na	--	na	--	na	--
12.9	60	39.8	5	-5.3	75	na	--	na	--	na	--	na	--	na	--	na	--	na	--
34.9	4	na	--	na	--	na	--	na	--	na	--	na	--	na	--	na	--	na	--
15.2	47	17.3	82	10.0	23	9.9	79	25.9	55	-2.9	62	-6.5	94	0.5	91	-3.6	95	na	--
16.9	36	19.6	73	na	--	na	--	na	--	na	--	na	--	na	--	na	--	na	--
11.0	72	18.6	78	na	--	na	--	na	--	na	--	na	--	na	--	na	--	na	--
19.6	20	20.1	70	9.0	28	9.3	83	39.7	11	-10.2	87	-18.0	99	-1.9	96	-6.3	98	7.5	20
68.9	1	78.6	1	na	--	na	--	na	--	na	--	na	--	na	--	na	--	na	--
18.1	28	na	--	na	--	na	--	na	--	na	--	na	--	na	--	na	--	na	--
3.5	92	na	--	na	--	na	--	na	--	na	--	na	--	na	--	na	--	na	--
19.0	23	21.4	62	9.9	24	12.7	67	36.0	18	-6.2	74	-12.6	96	1.3	89	-0.1	90	na	--
18.1	28	25.5	44	10.5	20	18.5	43	35.7	19	6.9	21	4.4	84	4.7	83	4.0	67	na	--
26.9	7	na	--	na	--	na	--	na	--	na	--	na	--	na	--	na	--	na	--
23.6	10	42.9	4	3.0	52	38.6	4	48.4	4	17.1	4	70.0	4	51.8	6	31.6	2	14.4	11
20.8	15	28.5	30	10.5	19	25.6	20	28.6	44	11.2	9	20.2	65	14.8	69	4.5	65	0.8	54
11.2	70	69.0	1	na	--	na	--	na	--	na	--	na	--	na	--	na	--	na	--
21.1	15	25.6	43	20.8	1	15.5	54	28.7	43	na	--	na	--	na	--	na	--	na	--
4.9	90	26.4	39	na	--	na	--	na	--	na	--	na	--	na	--	na	--	na	--
5.5	89	17.9	80	2.4	53	20.3	35	-12.2	99	na	--	na	--	na	--	na	--	na	--
15.7	44	56.5	2	na	--	na	--	na	--	na	--	na	--	na	--	na	--	na	--
15.1	48	41.2	4	18.0	2	37.1	5	25.2	56	na	--	na	--	na	--	na	--	na	--
22.0	12	59.4	1	-1.1	63	14.1	62	45.3	6	na	--	na	--	na	--	na	--	na	--
32.8	4	-10.5	99	-26.1	97	2.6	97	54.1	2	na	--	na	--	na	--	na	--	na	--
-7.4	97	7.4	96	-16.9	93	52.4	1	56.3	2	na	--	na	--	na	--	na	--	na	--
24.0	9	31.7	18	20.9	1	20.0	37	23.1	62	na	--	na	--	na	--	na	--	na	--
27.9	6	37.4	7	na	--	na	--	na	--	na	--	na	--	na	--	na	--	na	--
9.6	79	na	--	na	--	na	--	na	--	na	--	na	--	na	--	na	--	na	--
-23.9	99	na	--	na	--	na	--	na	--	na	--	na	--	na	--	na	--	na	--

CDA ANNUAL SUPPLEMENT – 12/31/86

		ASSETS (MIL$)	1986 QUARTERLY RETURNS						
			1st		2nd		3rd		4th
FUND	IO	9/86	PCNT RK		PCNT RK		PCNT RK		PCNT RK
FIDELITY SEL PROPTY/CAS	G	8	21.6 4		1.9 58		-8.3 72		-5.2 98
FIDELITY SEL COMPUTER	AG	3	6.4 80		6.7 18		-14.4 91		11.0 1
FIDELITY SEL FOOD/AGRI	G	9	17.7 13		13.7 3		-9.1 76		0.6 88
FIDELITY SEL SAVINGS/LN	G	23	33.4 1		8.2 12		-16.5 95		5.8 12
FIDELITY SEL SOFTWARE	AG	6	10.0 58		10.9 6		-14.5 92		9.2 2
FIDELITY SEL TELECOMM	G	7	11.5 49		6.9 17		-4.7 57		5.4 16
FIDELITY TREND	G	680	19.7 7		1.9 58		-10.8 83		4.4 30
FIDELITY THRIFT TRUST	BP	324	7.1 76		0.9 69		1.8 31		2.9 65
FIDELITY VALUE FUND	G	119	17.7 13		2.8 50		-3.8 54		-1.1 95
FIDUCIARY CAPITAL GROWTH	G	52	14.2 33		7.8 13		-14.7 92		-5.2 98
FINANCIAL BD-HIYLD PORT	BP	44	7.5 73		3.3 44		2.6 24		0.5 89
FINANCIAL BD-SELECT INC	BP	20	11.1 51		0.8 71		2.0 29		4.0 40
FINANCIAL DYNAMICS FUND	AG	63	13.7 36		6.2 21		-17.7 97		6.6 8
FINANCIAL INDUST. FUND	G	367	15.1 26		-0.6 84		-7.6 69		2.3 75
FINANCIAL INDUST. INCOME	GI	339	14.4 31		4.8 31		-6.2 63		0.7 88
FINANCIAL TAX FR INC SHS	MB	117	12.1 46		-6.1 98		10.5 3		4.9 21
FIRST INVEST. BND APPREC	BP	190	8.5 68		4.4 34		-2.7 49		1.2 86
FIRST INVEST. DISCOVERY	AG	33	9.6 60		-5.3 97		-15.7 94		-2.5 97
FIRST INVEST. FD. GROWTH	AG	53	12.3 44		-2.7 96		-14.6 92		1.4 84
FIRST INVEST. FD. INCOME	BP	1,675	5.0 87		2.9 49		0.4 39		2.6 69
FIRST INVEST. GOV FUND	BP	179	2.9 96		0.6 72		4.0 17		3.2 59
FIRST INVEST. INTL SECS.	IN	29	16.4 18		3.6 41		9.5 4		9.7 1
FIRST INVEST. NATURL RES	AG	12	-14.9 99		-16.3 99		11.3 3		2.5 70
FIRST INVEST. NY TAX FR	MB	71	9.6 61		-0.1 80		2.7 23		4.1 38
FIRST INVEST. NINETY-TEN	GI	10	1.9 98		1.3 64		0.5 39		0.6 89
FIRST INVEST. OPTION	GI	194	4.4 88		2.2 55		-3.6 53		3.2 60
FIRST INVEST. TAX EXEMPT	MB	644	7.3 75		1.1 67		2.2 26		4.2 35
FLAGSHIP CORPORATE CASH	BP	325	2.1 97		-0.7 86		3.0 22		0.1 91
FLAGSHIP MICHIGAN DBL TX	MB	67	8.1 70		1.0 67		5.9 6		4.0 41
FLAGSHIP OHIO DOUBLE TAX	MB	116	7.4 74		0.4 74		4.8 12		4.1 38
FLEX FD-RETIRE GR SERIES	GI	59	16.5 17		5.8 23		-9.6 78		-1.2 95
FORTY-FOUR WALL ST EQTY	AG	8	18.5 10		10.1 7		-23.5 99		17.1 1
FORTY-FOUR WALL ST FUND	AG	22	8.4 69		5.2 27		-22.8 99		-4.9 98
FOUNDATION GROWTH STOCK	GI	1	6.6 79		1.6 60		-0.2 42		1.8 81
FOUNDERS EQUITY INCOME	B	12	6.0 82		3.6 41		0.5 38		3.7 48
FOUNDERS GROWTH FUND	G	56	20.6 6		8.1 12		-11.2 84		3.0 64
FOUNDERS MUTUAL FUND	GI	175	16.0 20		7.4 15		-10.2 81		4.5 28
FOUNDERS SPECIAL FUND	AG	96	19.8 7		7.1 17		-10.9 83		3.9 41
FPA CAPITAL FUND	G	47	15.5 23		3.4 43		-9.3 77		3.9 43
FPA NEW INCOME	BP	6	4.3 89		1.5 61		1.9 30		3.0 64
FPA PARAMOUNT FD INC	GI	116	5.0 87		-0.9 88		2.2 27		-0.7 94
FPA PERENNIAL FUND	G	60	5.8 83		3.5 42		-0.8 43		1.5 84
FRANKLIN CALIF TAX FREE	MB	6,889	7.0 77		0.7 71		3.9 17		4.0 39
FRANKLIN CORP CASH TR	BP	70	2.9 95		-1.9 94		0.1 40		0.4 89
FRANKLIN DYNATECH	G	32	7.6 73		2.4 53		-17.6 97		3.9 43
FRANKLIN EQUITY FUND	G	145	17.9 12		5.6 25		-9.4 77		5.4 16
FRANKLIN FEDERAL TAX FR	MB	1,506	9.1 65		-1.8 94		6.1 5		4.5 29
FRANKLIN GOLD FUND	ME	126	13.0 39		-14.0 99		34.2 1		0.2 90
FRANKLIN GROWTH	G	43	10.9 52		3.2 47		-5.9 62		6.6 9
FRANKLIN INCOME	B	227	9.9 59		0.3 76		5.3 8		2.9 65

TEN YEARS OF ANNUAL RETURNS

1986		1985		1984		1983		1982		1981		1980		1979		1978		1977	
PCNT	RK	PCNT	RK	PCNT	RK	PCNT	RK	PCNT	RK	PCNT	RK	PCNT	RK	PCNT	RK	PCNT	RK	PCNT	RK
7.7	85	na	--	na	--	na	--	na	--	na	--	na	--	na	--	na	--	na	--
7.9	84	na	--	na	--	na	--	na	--	na	--	na	--	na	--	na	--	na	--
22.5	11	na	--	na	--	na	--	na	--	na	--	na	--	na	--	na	--	na	--
27.5	7	na	--	na	--	na	--	na	--	na	--	na	--	na	--	na	--	na	--
13.9	55	na	--	na	--	na	--	na	--	na	--	na	--	na	--	na	--	na	--
19.8	19	na	--	na	--	na	--	na	--	na	--	na	--	na	--	na	--	na	--
13.5	57	28.2	31	-2.3	67	26.6	17	14.3	84	-5.4	70	25.9	50	26.4	39	9.7	40	-3.3	75
13.1	59	20.8	66	13.5	10	9.4	82	24.2	60	12.4	7	10.6	78	7.2	80	3.1	71	2.9	42
15.1	47	22.1	59	-8.7	83	31.9	8	35.2	20	6.8	21	28.8	43	na	--	na	--	na	--
-0.4	95	29.9	24	-4.2	72	28.9	11	45.1	7	na	--	na	--	na	--	na	--	na	--
14.5	51	26.4	40	na	--	na	--	na	--	na	--	na	--	na	--	na	--	na	--
18.8	24	22.7	55	5.2	44	5.1	95	na	--	na	--	na	--	na	--	na	--	na	--
5.8	89	29.1	27	-13.8	90	13.1	67	36.9	15	-0.5	53	21.9	60	42.4	13	6.2	56	7.8	19
8.1	83	28.4	30	-1.1	64	14.5	60	38.8	13	-14.2	94	29.4	42	38.3	17	11.3	33	3.5	40
13.3	58	30.7	21	9.7	25	23.5	26	30.9	34	-5.7	72	21.1	62	29.7	30	1.4	82	3.9	37
22.1	12	22.9	54	9.1	28	8.0	87	na	--	na	--	na	--	na	--	na	--	na	--
11.5	68	20.6	67	2.0	55	12.4	68	18.3	77	12.5	7	17.3	70	11.2	75	na	--	na	--
-14.7	99	15.0	89	-32.5	99	47.3	1	43.9	7	4.3	31	9.9	78	35.0	20	9.5	40	-3.3	74
-5.3	96	5.3	97	-27.6	98	27.8	15	31.9	30	-12.9	92	40.1	20	23.8	46	16.4	19	0.1	58
11.3	70	19.7	73	2.0	54	13.1	66	19.6	74	6.8	21	4.9	83	6.5	82	1.0	85	11.9	14
11.1	71	17.9	80	na	--	na	--	na	--	na	--	na	--	na	--	na	--	na	--
44.8	2	10.7	94	-13.7	89	na	--	na	--	na	--	na	--	na	--	na	--	na	--
-18.7	99	4.6	97	-34.8	99	-2.5	99	7.5	94	-4.1	66	11.7	77	5.0	83	1.1	85	0.3	57
17.0	35	19.9	71	na	--	na	--	na	--	na	--	na	--	na	--	na	--	na	--
4.3	92	5.1	97	2.7	53	na	--	na	--	na	--	na	--	na	--	na	--	na	--
6.1	88	15.6	88	-0.7	62	14.3	61	4.1	96	na	--	na	--	na	--	na	--	na	--
15.5	45	20.7	66	8.4	32	13.5	64	36.6	16	-5.4	70	-11.8	96	-0.1	92	na	--	na	--
4.5	91	13.7	92	5.7	43	na	--	na	--	na	--	na	--	na	--	na	--	na	--
20.3	17	na	--	na	--	na	--	na	--	na	--	na	--	na	--	na	--	na	--
17.6	31	na	--	na	--	na	--	na	--	na	--	na	--	na	--	na	--	na	--
10.2	77	14.1	91	-1.3	65	18.7	42	na	--	na	--	na	--	na	--	na	--	na	--
16.9	36	22.4	57	-38.4	99	7.6	88	10.5	90	-9.2	85	na	--	na	--	na	--	na	--
-16.3	99	-20.1	99	-58.6	99	9.7	80	7.7	94	-22.6	98	36.3	26	73.7	2	32.9	2	16.5	9
10.1	77	11.6	94	-3.1	69	8.5	86	13.4	85	-7.0	77	24.7	54	26.2	39	-5.4	97	-6.4	88
14.5	51	12.7	93	11.5	17	15.4	56	13.0	86	14.9	5	23.0	57	22.0	51	4.0	67	-3.0	72
19.3	21	28.8	28	-11.1	86	18.9	41	21.4	68	3.6	35	50.3	10	36.4	19	11.8	31	-4.8	81
16.8	37	31.3	20	1.7	56	25.0	22	24.6	58	-7.4	79	27.8	46	12.9	72	4.5	65	-11.9	99
18.9	24	15.2	89	-12.2	88	23.2	27	30.2	37	-12.9	92	51.6	9	53.4	5	6.9	53	14.0	12
12.6	63	29.0	28	-7.9	81	18.4	44	17.0	78	-5.6	72	34.7	29	12.8	73	7.3	50	-7.3	91
11.1	71	21.3	62	16.4	3	6.2	93	27.8	47	na	--	na	--	na	--	na	--	na	--
5.5	89	18.8	77	10.1	23	31.3	8	46.1	5	-10.3	87	22.9	58	27.9	34	13.2	27	2.4	46
10.2	76	20.4	69	na	--	na	--	na	--	na	--	na	--	na	--	na	--	na	--
16.5	39	16.9	84	9.9	24	5.3	95	na	--	na	--	na	--	na	--	na	--	na	--
1.5	94	13.9	91	na	--	na	--	na	--	na	--	na	--	na	--	na	--	na	--
-5.8	97	15.3	88	-8.5	83	32.8	8	35.2	20	-7.9	81	37.5	24	34.3	21	13.5	27	4.7	34
18.9	23	32.9	15	8.9	29	18.7	42	17.8	77	-9.6	85	35.5	27	30.2	28	7.6	49	9.8	16
18.8	24	20.6	67	na	--	na	--	na	--	na	--	na	--	na	--	na	--	na	--
30.7	5	-11.0	99	-25.0	97	8.9	85	46.7	5	-18.7	97	73.7	3	150.8	2	9.7	40	32.5	2
14.7	50	26.5	38	0.9	58	17.8	46	45.4	6	-5.0	69	14.9	73	8.7	79	15.8	21	-4.4	81
19.3	21	14.8	90	15.5	4	15.3	56	35.8	18	1.1	46	19.4	67	27.6	35	8.4	45	8.5	18

CDA ANNUAL SUPPLEMENT - 12/31/86

FUND	IO	ASSETS (MIL$) 9/86	1986 QUARTERLY RETURNS			
			1st PCNT RK	2nd PCNT RK	3rd PCNT RK	4th PCNT RK
FRANKLIN NEW YORK TAX FR	MB	2,126	10.0 57	-2.8 96	5.3 7	4.4 29
FRANKLIN OPTION FUND	G	27	7.5 73	2.7 51	-7.8 69	5.6 14
FRANKLIN U.S. GOVT. SEC.	BP	14,367	3.6 92	-0.1 80	3.8 17	2.7 67
FRANKLIN UTILITIES	GI	327	13.5 37	3.9 39	3.3 20	1.5 84
FREEDOM GOLD & GOV TRUST	ME	47	7.1 76	0.9 69	5.0 10	2.2 77
FREEDOM REGIONAL BANK FD	G	53	19.6 7	12.6 4	-8.2 72	-2.8 97
FT INTERNATIONAL	IN	104	21.0 5	12.7 4	6.5 4	6.9 6
FTP-EQ PORTFOLIO-GROWTH	G	58	18.1 11	8.4 10	-13.9 90	4.3 32
FTP-EQ PORTFOLIO INCOME	GI	501	15.0 27	1.0 67	-2.8 49	4.1 37
FTP-FIXED INC. LTD PORT.	BP	377	7.4 74	1.4 62	1.8 30	3.1 61
FUND FOR U.S. GOVT. SEC.	BP	979	2.8 96	0.2 77	2.9 22	2.4 74
FUND OF AMERICA	GI	145	10.9 52	-0.8 87	-7.1 67	4.4 30
FUND OF THE SOUTHWEST	AG	15	17.0 16	-1.7 94	-13.7 89	-0.8 94
FUNDAMENTAL INVESTORS	G	488	15.6 22	5.1 29	-6.1 63	6.8 7
FUNDTRUST AGGRESSIVE	AG	40	12.4 43	4.0 38	-7.9 70	3.9 43
FUNDTRUST GROWTH	G	30	10.7 53	2.4 53	-4.3 55	4.5 29
FUNDTRUST GROWTH & INC	GI	46	10.7 53	3.2 46	-3.6 53	4.0 41
FUNDTRUST INCOME	BP	30	4.8 87	1.2 65	0.0 40	2.4 73
G. T. PACIFIC GROWTH FD	IN	67	21.8 4	18.2 1	22.0 2	-3.2 97
GABELLI ASSET FUND	G	41	na --	7.4 15	0.7 38	0.0 91
GATEWAY GROWTH PLUS FUND	AG	3	na --	na --	-10.3 81	3.5 52
GATEWAY OPTION INCOME	GI	36	4.8 87	5.1 29	-2.9 50	5.4 17
GENERAL ELEC S&S LT BOND	BP	608	10.8 53	1.5 61	2.1 28	3.8 46
GENL ELEC S&S PROGRAM	GI	815	13.1 39	5.8 23	-6.3 63	4.8 23
GENERAL SECURITIES	GI	16	9.2 64	1.3 63	-3.1 51	1.7 82
GIBRALTAR FUND, INC.	G	1	9.8 59	6.5 19	-4.6 57	1.5 83
GINTEL CAP APPRECIATION	AG	21	na --	1.9 58	-5.2 59	6.0 11
GINTEL ERISA	GI	79	17.0 15	2.6 52	-8.4 73	10.8 1
GINTEL FUND	G	119	14.9 28	3.5 43	-7.8 69	9.4 2
GOLCONDA INVESTORS	ME	32	10.1 57	-5.0 97	27.8 2	1.1 86
GRADISON ESTABLISHED GR.	G	33	16.8 16	-0.6 84	-1.7 46	6.9 6
GRADISON OPPORTUNITY GR	AG	17	20.7 5	7.9 13	-7.9 70	-5.8 98
GREENWAY FUND	AG	19	12.4 43	4.0 38	-9.6 78	3.8 47
GROWTH FUND OF AMERICA	G	741	15.3 25	6.3 20	-9.9 79	5.0 20
GROWTH FD OF WASHINGTON	G	51	16.8 17	8.2 11	-10.7 82	1.8 81
GROWTH INDUSTRY SHARES	G	69	11.5 49	8.6 9	-14.9 92	5.9 12
GUARDIAN MUTUAL FUND	GI	519	11.6 48	5.5 26	-6.4 63	1.6 83
GUARDIAN PARK AVE FUND	G	119	19.3 8	7.2 16	-11.8 85	4.7 25
HAMILTON FUNDS	G	242	16.5 18	3.3 45	-3.6 53	3.2 58
HANCOCK (JOHN) BOND	BP	1,108	6.4 81	1.0 68	1.6 32	0.9 87
HANCOCK (JOHN) GLOBAL	IN	72	15.7 21	10.9 6	-7.6 68	6.9 7
HANCOCK (JOHN) GNMA	BP	371	3.4 93	0.8 70	3.3 20	3.5 53
HANCOCK (JOHN) GROWTH	AG	85	1? ? 15	12.0 5	-15.6 94	2.7 68
HANCOCK (JOHN) SPECIAL	G	13	' ; 42	6.5 19	-20.8 98	0.8 87
HANCOCK (JOHN) TX EX DIV	MB	321	8.0 71	-0.9 88	4.9 11	4.5 28
HANCOCK (JOHN) US GOV	BP	182	7.1 76	1.5 61	2.0 29	3.4 56
HARTWELL GROWTH FUND	AG	10	13.6 37	8.4 10	-7.1 67	8.8 2
HARTWELL LEVERAGE FUND	AG	25	21.0 5	8.6 9	-16.1 95	8.1 3
HAWAIIAN TAX-FREE TRUST	MB	130	7.8 71	-1.2 91	4.2 16	3.6 50
HEARTLAND VALUE FUND	G	26	14.7 29	4.8 32	-10.3 81	2.8 67

TEN YEARS OF ANNUAL RETURNS

1986		1985		1984		1983		1982		1981		1980		1979		1978		1977	
PCNT	RK	PCNT	RK	PCNT	RK	PCNT	RK	PCNT	RK	PCNT	RK	PCNT	RK	PCNT	RK	PCNT	RK	PCNT	RK
17.6	31	22.3	57	8.8	29	na	--	na	--	na	--	na	--	na	--	na	--	na	--
7.6	85	23.9	49	2.9	52	16.5	51	8.2	93	5.0	29	40.0	21	28.6	32	9.8	39	-7.9	94
10.4	75	19.8	72	12.8	12	8.1	87	32.8	28	7.1	19	-12.8	97	1.5	88	-1.2	93	1.8	50
23.7	9	22.7	55	21.2	1	15.8	52	31.2	32	21.0	3	6.2	81	-0.3	92	0.0	89	8.2	19
15.9	42	na	--	na	--	na	--	na	--	na	--	na	--	na	--	na	--	na	--
20.2	18	na	--	na	--	na	--	na	--	na	--	na	--	na	--	na	--	na	--
55.2	2	61.2	1	na	--	na	--	na	--	na	--	na	--	na	--	na	--	na	--
15.0	49	41.5	4	-16.0	92	na	--	na	--	na	--	na	--	na	--	na	--	na	--
17.5	32	25.7	43	10.4	21	na	--	na	--	na	--	na	--	na	--	na	--	na	--
14.4	52	20.2	70	na	--	na	--	na	--	na	--	na	--	na	--	na	--	na	--
8.6	82	16.6	85	12.8	12	11.1	73	40.1	11	-0.4	52	-3.5	93	1.2	90	1.7	79	1.3	52
6.6	87	15.8	88	1.5	56	28.2	14	51.3	3	-5.8	73	35.1	28	41.4	14	4.4	66	-2.6	70
-1.6	96	16.0	87	-15.5	91	20.4	34	na	--	na	--	na	--	na	--	na	--	na	--
21.8	13	30.1	23	5.8	42	26.2	19	34.0	23	-1.2	56	21.2	62	17.1	63	6.4	55	-5.8	86
11.9	66	25.7	42	na	--	na	--	na	--	na	--	na	--	na	--	na	--	na	--
13.4	58	25.0	46	na	--	na	--	na	--	na	--	na	--	na	--	na	--	na	--
14.5	51	23.7	50	na	--	na	--	na	--	na	--	na	--	na	--	na	--	na	--
8.6	82	16.8	84	na	--	na	--	na	--	na	--	na	--	na	--	na	--	na	--
70.0	1	9.3	96	-3.0	69	37.0	5	-10.1	99	10.0	10	35.2	28	na	--	na	--	na	--
na	--	na	--	na	--	na	--	na	--	na	--	na	--	na	--	na	--	na	--
na	--	na	--	na	--	na	--	na	--	na	--	na	--	na	--	na	--	na	--
12.6	62	16.0	87	4.0	49	14.9	58	9.5	92	4.4	30	16.5	71	15.4	68	5.9	58	na	--
19.1	22	18.6	78	18.0	2	6.7	91	36.7	16	na	--	na	--	na	--	na	--	na	--
17.6	31	25.7	43	4.7	47	20.3	35	21.9	66	-5.7	72	22.2	60	19.3	57	6.7	54	-10.4	98
9.0	81	38.8	6	-0.9	62	10.6	76	28.2	46	1.8	42	25.2	53	13.5	72	16.0	20	-2.9	71
13.2	58	27.5	34	-0.6	61	na	--	na	--	na	--	na	--	na	--	na	--	na	--
na	--	na	--	na	--	na	--	na	--	na	--	na	--	na	--	na	--	na	--
21.8	13	24.0	48	2.4	53	27.5	15	na	--	na	--	na	--	na	--	na	--	na	--
19.9	19	19.9	72	-2.5	68	34.8	6	33.5	25	na	--	na	--	na	--	na	--	na	--
35.0	4	2.6	97	-25.2	97	0.6	98	6.4	95	-17.8	97	42.4	16	na	--	na	--	na	--
22.0	12	28.8	28	4.5	48	na	--	na	--	na	--	na	--	na	--	na	--	na	--
13.0	60	28.1	32	-3.2	70	na	--	na	--	na	--	na	--	na	--	na	--	na	--
9.7	78	32.9	15	-8.8	83	9.0	83	15.4	82	-11.0	89	39.0	22	na	--	na	--	na	--
16.0	42	26.7	38	-5.6	76	27.1	16	25.0	57	0.5	49	40.1	20	45.9	10	26.6	4	19.8	7
14.9	49	na	--	na	--	na	--	na	--	na	--	na	--	na	--	na	--	na	--
9.1	80	23.4	51	-4.2	73	13.4	64	27.8	47	5.7	26	39.4	21	30.2	28	19.9	13	-2.7	70
11.9	66	25.3	44	7.4	36	25.3	21	28.7	43	-4.8	68	30.2	41	37.9	17	8.9	42	-0.9	63
18.1	28	33.0	15	12.5	13	28.6	12	26.0	54	5.2	28	21.5	61	29.1	31	14.6	24	8.1	19
19.8	19	29.4	27	-2.2	67	9.9	79	22.6	64	-8.0	82	25.3	52	16.2	66	5.8	59	-7.7	93
10.2	76	22.3	57	15.4	5	9.0	84	31.5	31	4.0	34	-1.2	92	-3.5	98	-0.1	90	4.4	35
26.8	7	na	--	na	--	na	--	na	--	na	--	na	--	na	--	na	--	na	--
11.4	69	na	--	na	--	na	--	na	--	na	--	na	--	na	--	na	--	na	--
13.8	56	28.3	31	-1.6	66	15.7	54	21.3	68	-17.1	96	58.3	6	34.0	22	15.8	20	-13.6	99
-4.3	96	na	--	na	--	na	--	na	--	na	--	na	--	na	--	na	--	na	--
17.2	33	21.5	62	9.2	27	7.6	88	30.6	36	-6.3	75	-17.5	99	-5.1	99	-5.1	97	na	--
14.5	51	18.0	80	13.4	10	6.4	92	21.2	69	-4.1	66	17.2	70	6.7	81	1.4	83	-2.1	68
24.4	9	22.1	58	-17.6	93	25.5	21	16.1	80	-7.0	77	69.9	4	40.6	15	18.9	16	16.9	8
19.3	21	27.0	36	-31.6	98	10.3	77	28.9	42	-13.4	93	93.9	1	55.4	4	11.3	33	16.6	9
15.0	48	na	--	na	--	na	--	na	--	na	--	na	--	na	--	na	--	na	--
10.8	73	41.4	4	na	--	na	--	na	--	na	--	na	--	na	--	na	--	na	--

CDA ANNUAL SUPPLEMENT - 12/31/86

FUND	IO	ASSETS (MIL$) 9/86	1st PCNT RK	2nd PCNT RK	3rd PCNT RK	4th PCNT RK
HIGH YIELD SECURITIES	BP	87	3.6 91	3.2 46	1.2 35	1.3 85
HOME INVS GOV GTD INCOME	BP	184	3.1 95	0.1 78	2.6 23	3.1 63
HORACE MANN GROWTH FUND	G	75	11.0 51	5.4 26	-9.5 77	5.8 12
HUTTON CAL MUNICIPAL FD	MB	162	9.0 65	-0.3 81	4.2 16	3.7 48
HUTTON INV SER BASIC VAL	G	324	12.9 40	3.6 41	-4.5 56	1.8 81
HUTTON INV SER BOND/INC	BP	347	13.5 38	-0.8 86	1.5 33	4.8 22
HUTTON INV SER SPL EQTY	AG	216	16.2 19	3.4 43	-13.7 89	3.1 62
HUTTON INV SERIES GROWTH	G	1,121	13.8 35	6.8 18	-9.7 78	5.8 13
HUTTON INV SER GOV SECS	BP	5,177	6.9 78	0.8 70	2.1 28	2.7 68
HUTTON INV SER PRE METAL	ME	39	10.0 57	-8.7 98	35.8 1	4.9 21
HUTTON NATL MUNICIPAL FD	MB	951	10.6 54	-0.3 82	5.9 5	4.9 22
HUTTON N.Y. MUNICIPAL FD	MB	224	8.3 69	-0.9 88	4.8 12	4.2 35
HUTTON OPTION INCOME	GI	76	7.0 77	-3.0 97	-2.3 47	0.3 90
IDS BOND FUND	BP	1,775	10.9 52	2.4 54	0.9 37	5.1 19
IDS DISCOVERY FUND	AG	268	9.5 62	7.5 14	-13.9 90	3.9 42
IDS EQUITY PLUS FD INC.	G	365	17.4 14	5.3 27	-8.1 71	4.0 39
IDS EXTRA INCOME	BP	871	8.9 66	3.0 48	0.0 41	3.8 46
IDS GROWTH FUND	AG	708	16.3 18	15.3 2	-15.2 93	5.1 20
IDS MUTUAL FUND	B	1,242	11.2 50	3.3 45	0.2 40	7.1 6
IDS NEW DIMENSIONS FUND	G	510	17.0 15	12.2 5	-11.7 85	4.4 30
IDS PROGRESSIVE FUND	GI	184	12.7 41	0.9 70	-0.1 41	-0.3 93
IDS SELECTIVE	BP	1,111	9.2 64	1.8 59	1.2 35	5.0 20
IDS STOCK FUND	GI	1,345	15.0 27	7.7 13	-8.3 72	5.2 19
INCOME FUND OF AMERICA	B	601	10.1 56	2.0 57	-1.1 44	5.4 16
INDUSTRY FUND OF AMERICA	AG	1	4.7 88	-10.9 98	-8.2 72	0.2 90
INTEGRATED CAPTL APPREC	G	126	15.1 25	8.6 9	-10.6 82	4.7 25
INTEGRATED INSD TAX FREE	MB	129	6.0 82	-2.0 95	4.3 15	2.8 66
INTERNATIONAL INVESTORS	ME	865	10.6 54	-7.7 98	31.2 1	0.2 90
INVEST. CO. OF AMERICA	AG	3,487	14.5 30	5.2 28	-4.3 55	5.2 18
INVEST. PORTFOLIOS-EQ	G	192	9.9 58	1.0 68	-8.0 70	2.2 76
INVEST. PORTFOLIOS-GOV +	BP	4,528	5.6 84	0.6 72	1.7 31	3.2 59
INVEST. PORTFOLIOS-HIYLD	BP	163	6.3 81	4.7 32	2.3 26	4.3 33
INVEST. PORTFOLIOS-OP IN	GI	347	3.1 94	0.6 72	-4.8 58	2.8 66
INVEST. QUALITY INTEREST	BP	128	10.3 56	0.3 75	1.5 33	2.8 66
INVEST. TRUST OF BOSTON	G	65	14.8 29	2.9 50	-9.8 78	5.0 21
INV TR/BOSTON HI IN PLUS	BP	22	7.0 77	1.2 65	-0.2 42	2.6 70
INVESTORS INCOME	BP	19	5.8 83	2.7 51	2.5 24	4.2 34
INVESTORS RESEARCH	G	59	24.5 2	23.2 1	-18.4 97	2.6 69
IRI STOCK FUND	G	13	23.9 2	-0.2 81	-10.4 81	4.5 27
ISI GROWTH FUND	GI	13	9.2 64	3.6 41	-10.1 80	-3.0 97
ISI INCOME FUND	B	6	1.3 98	1.9 58	-3.2 51	-4.4 98
ISI TRUST FUND	B	102	5.0 86	2.5 53	-3.4 52	2.1 78
ITB MASS TAX FREE	MB	45	7.8 71	-1.0 89	5.3 7	3.0 64
IVY GROWTH FUND	GI	165	10.1 56	2.7 51	0.8 37	2.5 71
IVY INSTITUTIONAL INV FD	G	131	14.1 33	2.5 53	-3.6 52	5.5 15
JANUS FUND	GI	464	14.4 31	4.6 33	-9.9 79	3.1 62
JANUS VALUE FUND	G	11	20.5 6	0.3 75	-9.6 78	2.0 79
JANUS VENTURE FUND	AG	28	15.6 22	13.2 4	-8.0 70	-0.2 93
JP GROWTH FUND	GI	24	14.2 32	4.5 34	-8.0 71	3.6 50
JP INCOME	BP	20	9.2 64	1.3 63	1.6 33	3.6 50

TEN YEARS OF ANNUAL RETURNS

1986		1985		1984		1983		1982		1981		1980		1979		1978		1977	
PCNT	RK	PCNT	RK	PCNT	RK	PCNT	RK	PCNT	RK	PCNT	RK	PCNT	RK	PCNT	RK	PCNT	RK	PCNT	RK
9.6	78	17.9	80	5.5	43	19.3	40	30.2	37	7.3	18	3.5	84	4.4	83	0.4	88	na	--
9.1	80	na	--	na	--	na	--	na	--	na	--	na	--	na	--	na	--	na	--
12.1	65	25.9	41	1.9	55	22.3	29	23.6	61	-7.5	80	36.4	25	25.0	42	4.1	67	-6.6	88
17.4	33	17.7	81	9.6	26	na	--	na	--	na	--	na	--	na	--	na	--	na	--
13.7	56	na	--	na	--	na	--	na	--	na	--	na	--	na	--	na	--	na	--
19.8	19	25.3	45	14.2	8	7.8	88	na	--	na	--	na	--	na	--	na	--	na	--
7.0	86	34.8	11	-10.0	85	na	--	na	--	na	--	na	--	na	--	na	--	na	--
16.0	41	22.0	59	1.1	57	22.5	28	na	--	na	--	na	--	na	--	na	--	na	--
13.1	59	18.3	79	na	--	na	--	na	--	na	--	na	--	na	--	na	--	na	--
43.1	3	na	--	na	--	na	--	na	--	na	--	na	--	na	--	na	--	na	--
22.4	11	20.6	68	12.9	11	na	--	na	--	na	--	na	--	na	--	na	--	na	--
17.2	34	18.6	77	11.5	17	na	--	na	--	na	--	na	--	na	--	na	--	na	--
1.7	94	11.9	94	3.3	50	na	--	na	--	na	--	na	--	na	--	na	--	na	--
20.3	17	24.0	48	9.1	28	14.6	59	36.3	17	3.7	35	1.4	87	1.0	90	2.4	75	3.6	39
5.4	90	29.8	25	-18.3	94	21.4	32	29.4	41	na	--	na	--	na	--	na	--	na	--
18.1	28	30.7	22	-5.6	76	13.5	64	23.1	63	0.7	48	31.6	37	22.2	51	10.1	38	-5.2	84
16.4	39	20.5	68	9.2	27	na	--	na	--	na	--	na	--	na	--	na	--	na	--
19.5	20	36.2	8	-18.4	94	13.3	65	32.8	28	8.1	15	76.5	2	39.8	16	17.7	17	8.5	18
23.2	10	23.3	52	13.6	10	15.4	56	29.9	38	-1.6	57	18.8	68	11.2	76	3.4	69	-1.5	65
21.1	15	35.4	9	-4.5	73	20.1	37	33.7	25	0.3	49	55.6	7	33.5	23	9.3	41	1.6	51
13.3	58	30.8	21	-4.1	72	18.0	45	67.1	1	-13.5	93	38.5	22	18.6	59	8.8	42	0.2	58
18.0	29	24.0	49	9.4	26	13.2	66	39.2	13	2.7	38	1.2	88	-0.2	92	2.3	75	2.6	44
19.5	20	21.6	61	2.2	54	15.9	52	27.7	48	-6.6	76	26.4	49	20.6	55	7.2	51	-9.1	96
17.1	34	27.5	34	14.4	7	17.2	48	36.4	17	11.3	9	9.9	78	7.6	80	5.1	63	-0.3	60
-14.2	99	-5.5	98	-19.1	94	19.6	38	-6.4	98	-2.9	62	29.0	43	57.6	4	14.9	23	0.7	55
17.0	36	na	--	na	--	na	--	na	--	na	--	na	--	na	--	na	--	na	--
11.4	69	na	--	na	--	na	--	na	--	na	--	na	--	na	--	na	--	na	--
34.2	4	-1.9	98	-22.6	96	8.9	84	51.8	3	-19.6	98	64.9	5	177.2	1	9.2	41	32.9	2
21.3	15	32.9	15	6.8	38	20.2	36	33.4	25	1.1	45	21.8	61	19.1	58	14.6	24	-2.6	69
4.4	92	22.6	55	na	--	na	--	na	--	na	--	na	--	na	--	na	--	na	--
11.6	68	10.5	95	na	--	na	--	na	--	na	--	na	--	na	--	na	--	na	--
18.6	25	20.0	71	na	--	na	--	na	--	na	--	na	--	na	--	na	--	na	--
1.5	94	10.8	94	na	--	na	--	na	--	na	--	na	--	na	--	na	--	na	--
15.4	45	19.9	71	15.5	4	4.1	97	36.9	15	na	--	na	--	na	--	na	--	na	--
11.9	66	31.3	19	-1.1	64	9.8	79	25.4	56	-18.7	97	44.6	13	18.6	59	11.4	33	-7.6	92
10.8	73	21.7	60	na	--	na	--	na	--	na	--	na	--	na	--	na	--	na	--
16.0	41	20.3	69	11.2	18	12.3	68	26.9	51	6.2	24	-4.5	94	2.1	87	8.1	46	0.9	54
28.3	6	19.5	74	-3.0	69	26.3	18	47.5	4	-17.4	96	73.1	3	17.5	62	14.3	25	5.6	29
15.8	44	36.5	8	-0.3	60	13.8	63	na	--	na	--	na	--	na	--	na	--	na	--
-1.3	95	17.1	83	4.2	48	3.8	97	27.7	48	-1.8	58	9.0	79	44.5	11	1.2	84	4.9	33
-4.5	96	9.7	95	14.5	7	4.4	96	29.3	41	-0.1	51	6.2	81	24.2	44	4.9	63	6.5	25
6.1	88	11.4	94	12.1	15	6.5	92	21.9	67	-0.8	54	7.9	80	20.6	54	7.8	48	7.5	20
15.8	43	18.0	80	na	--	na	--	na	--	na	--	na	--	na	--	na	--	na	--
16.8	38	29.4	26	7.9	34	30.1	10	32.9	27	5.9	24	34.7	30	31.1	26	4.9	63	-7.3	91
19.0	23	37.5	7	na	--	na	--	na	--	na	--	na	--	na	--	na	--	na	--
11.2	70	24.5	47	-0.1	60	26.1	19	30.6	36	7.1	20	52.2	8	34.6	21	15.9	20	3.5	40
11.5	68	na	--	na	--	na	--	na	--	na	--	na	--	na	--	na	--	na	--
20.2	17	na	--	na	--	na	--	na	--	na	--	na	--	na	--	na	--	na	--
13.9	55	25.1	45	7.5	36	16.1	52	30.9	35	1.0	47	27.7	47	17.7	62	7.5	49	-8.0	94
16.4	39	26.1	41	14.9	5	4.2	97	36.4	17	na	--	na	--	na	--	na	--	na	--

CDA ANNUAL SUPPLEMENT - 12/31/86

FUND	IO	ASSETS (MIL$) 9/86	1986 QUARTERLY RETURNS							
			1st		2nd		3rd		4th	
			PCNT	RK	PCNT	RK	PCNT	RK	PCNT	RK
KEMPER CALIF TAX FREE	MB	186	8.2	70	0.2	76	4.5	14	4.4	31
KEMPER GROWTH FUND	G	275	11.8	47	2.1	56	-5.5	61	4.2	34
KEMPER HIGH YIELD FD	BP	323	6.7	78	4.9	30	0.7	38	4.9	22
KEMPER INC & CAP PRESERV	BP	199	6.6	79	3.0	48	1.9	30	2.4	73
KEMPER INTL FD	IN	185	18.4	10	4.7	32	10.3	4	5.8	13
KEMPER MUNI BOND FD LTD	MB	905	9.0	65	-0.4	83	5.4	7	4.0	41
KEMPER OPTION INCOME FD	GI	621	3.3	94	0.3	75	-4.2	55	3.2	59
KEMPER SUMMIT FUND	G	274	15.0	27	4.0	38	-9.9	80	5.7	13
KEMPER TOTAL RETURN FD	GI	614	13.3	38	5.9	23	-5.4	60	3.5	54
KEMPER US GOVT SECS	BP	2,379	8.6	68	1.2	65	2.0	29	3.6	49
KEYSTONE INTL FUND	IN	90	13.4	38	9.6	8	14.2	3	4.2	34
KEYSTONE B-1	BP	316	7.8	72	0.5	73	1.3	35	3.8	47
KEYSTONE B-2	BP	575	7.1	76	2.2	55	0.4	39	2.3	74
KEYSTONE B-4	BP	1,500	6.1	82	3.0	48	-1.3	45	1.7	82
KEYSTONE K-1	B	439	12.5	42	3.6	41	-4.8	58	4.5	28
KEYSTONE K-2	G	288	14.6	29	5.2	27	-5.2	59	6.1	11
KEYSTONE PRECIOUS METALS	ME	65	12.8	40	-10.6	98	30.6	1	6.2	10
KEYSTONE S-1	G	106	15.7	21	6.5	19	-10.1	80	5.0	20
KEYSTONE S-3	G	230	17.2	15	4.6	33	-9.0	75	3.1	63
KEYSTONE S-4	AG	543	14.2	32	4.1	37	-14.4	91	5.7	14
KEYSTONE TAX FREE	MB	975	8.9	66	-1.1	89	5.0	9	3.5	53
KIDDER P. EQUITY INCOME	GI	42	14.1	33	2.1	56	-2.7	49	2.7	68
KIDDER P. GOVT INCOME	BP	145	3.0	95	-2.7	96	3.4	19	3.2	59
KIDDER P. SPECIAL GROWTH	AG	31	9.7	60	9.1	8	-15.1	93	3.5	53
KIDDER P. NATL TX-FR INC	MB	19	10.1	56	-0.9	88	4.9	10	3.5	53
KIDDER P. N.Y. TX-FR INC	MB	10	8.8	67	-1.6	94	4.2	16	4.0	39
LEGG MASON VALUE TRUST	G	607	15.4	24	2.0	57	-6.8	65	-0.2	93
LEHMAN CAPITAL FUND	G	103	13.9	35	9.7	7	-13.5	89	5.4	16
LEHMAN INVESTORS FD, INC	G	405	12.1	46	6.4	20	-8.0	71	4.4	29
LEHMAN OPPORTUNITY FUND	G	103	12.9	40	0.6	72	-4.7	58	-1.6	96
LEPERCQ-ISTEL TRUST	GI	26	9.2	64	1.9	58	-4.9	58	2.3	75
LEVERAGE FUND OF BOSTON	AG	25	7.0	77	3.0	49	-13.0	87	-7.3	99
LEXINGTON GOLDFUND	ME	22	9.3	63	-5.4	98	25.1	2	2.5	71
LEXINGTON GROWTH FUND	G	28	15.5	23	9.6	8	-7.7	69	3.1	61
LEXINGTON GNMA NEW INC	BP	129	3.5	93	0.0	79	3.6	19	4.3	32
LEXINGTON RESEARCH FUND	G	123	16.9	16	4.1	37	-4.5	56	3.4	55
LG US GOV SECURITIES	BP	48	3.6	92	-0.6	84	3.3	20	3.6	49
LIBERTY FUND	BP	10	8.2	70	-0.5	83	4.8	11	4.8	23
LINDNER DIVIDEND FUND	GI	62	7.1	76	4.1	37	2.5	25	5.7	13
LINDNER FUND	GI	361	7.3	75	2.9	49	-0.8	43	4.0	41
LMH FUND, LTD.	GI	84	9.2	64	3.4	43	0.1	40	0.8	87
LOOMIS-SAYLES CAP. DEV.	AG	208	25.0	2	7.7	14	-7.2	67	2.1	78
LOOMIS-SAYLES MUTUAL	GI	174	19.2	9	6.2	21	-5.9	62	4.8	22
LORD ABBETT BOND-DEBEN.	BP	610	7.9	71	2.3	54	-2.6	48	2.7	67
LORD ABBETT DEV GROWTH	AG	239	12.0	46	1.8	59	-18.4	97	7.9	4
LORD ABBETT TX FREE NATL	MB	184	10.7	53	-0.9	88	5.4	6	4.9	21
LORD ABBETT TX FREE NY	MB	94	8.4	69	-1.2	90	4.8	12	5.2	18
LORD ABBETT US GOV SECS	BP	269	7.5	73	-0.7	85	4.3	15	3.3	58
LORD ABBETT VALUE APPREC	G	299	17.5	14	5.7	24	-6.7	64	0.0	92
LOWRY MARKET TIMING FD	AG	69	10.3	55	-3.0	96	-16.1	95	1.0	87

TEN YEARS OF ANNUAL RETURNS

1986		1985		1984		1983		1982		1981		1980		1979		1978		1977	
PCNT	RK	PCNT	RK	PCNT	RK	PCNT	RK	PCNT	RK	PCNT	RK	PCNT	RK	PCNT	RK	PCNT	RK	PCNT	RK
18.2	27	21.9	59	8.0	33	na	--	na	--	na	--	na	--	na	--	na	--	na	--
12.4	64	26.5	39	-7.2	79	26.0	20	28.6	44	-11.8	91	44.2	14	40.3	15	17.8	17	2.3	47
18.2	27	23.2	52	10.1	22	17.5	47	39.2	12	8.6	13	-0.9	91	2.4	86	na	--	na	--
14.5	51	21.7	60	12.2	14	11.4	71	33.4	25	3.0	37	-2.7	93	2.1	87	3.2	70	2.3	46
44.7	2	55.3	2	-9.1	84	28.1	14	2.8	97	na	--	na	--	na	--	na	--	na	--
19.0	23	21.1	64	10.3	22	14.2	61	43.0	8	-9.7	86	-13.7	97	-2.0	96	na	--	na	--
2.5	93	15.1	89	5.9	42	16.4	51	15.2	82	2.6	39	25.0	53	17.0	64	5.5	60	na	--
13.9	54	27.3	35	-7.6	80	24.4	24	27.1	51	-2.1	59	46.1	13	41.3	14	18.7	16	12.6	14
17.5	32	28.2	31	-1.0	63	19.7	37	22.7	64	0.2	50	40.2	20	30.7	27	10.6	35	4.8	34
16.2	41	22.2	58	12.2	14	8.9	85	28.3	45	0.6	49	-0.9	91	na	--	na	--	na	--
47.9	2	38.6	6	-7.5	80	13.5	64	12.4	87	-2.3	60	21.1	62	25.0	42	6.4	55	-1.5	65
13.8	56	21.5	62	10.7	19	8.7	85	36.3	17	5.2	28	2.7	86	3.0	85	1.7	80	4.1	36
12.5	63	23.1	53	6.8	38	10.3	76	32.9	27	9.1	11	3.5	85	6.0	82	2.0	77	7.0	22
9.6	79	20.2	70	4.7	46	15.5	54	31.8	31	10.1	9	8.2	79	1.6	88	4.3	66	7.4	21
16.0	42	22.2	57	3.1	51	18.7	42	26.2	53	4.4	30	15.3	72	9.2	77	3.2	71	2.0	48
21.3	14	32.5	16	-5.9	77	24.1	24	27.7	48	-11.9	91	28.8	44	17.4	63	8.7	43	-3.9	77
39.9	3	-9.7	99	-28.3	98	0.3	98	38.1	14	na	--	na	--	na	--	na	--	na	--
16.4	40	24.0	48	-7.8	81	14.4	60	24.5	58	-14.0	94	21.9	60	16.0	66	6.9	52	-8.0	94
15.0	49	22.8	54	-9.3	84	26.0	20	25.1	57	-5.4	70	30.3	40	31.7	26	8.4	45	0.7	55
7.6	85	28.2	31	-20.4	95	25.0	22	20.5	71	-22.7	99	60.5	6	47.0	9	19.9	14	8.8	17
17.1	34	20.0	71	8.7	30	9.5	82	na	--	na	--	na	--	na	--	na	--	na	--
16.4	40	na	--	na	--	na	--	na	--	na	--	na	--	na	--	na	--	na	--
6.9	87	na	--	na	--	na	--	na	--	na	--	na	--	na	--	na	--	na	--
5.1	90	-9.0	98	na	--	na	--	na	--	na	--	na	--	na	--	na	--	na	--
18.5	25	na	--	na	--	na	--	na	--	na	--	na	--	na	--	na	--	na	--
15.9	43	na	--	na	--	na	--	na	--	na	--	na	--	na	--	na	--	na	--
9.4	79	31.8	18	12.9	11	42.7	2	na	--	na	--	na	--	na	--	na	--	na	--
13.9	54	27.2	35	-3.9	72	38.2	4	40.6	10	7.1	19	39.9	21	44.3	11	23.3	7	25.0	4
14.6	51	26.3	40	0.3	59	23.8	25	30.2	37	-0.1	51	28.2	45	29.3	30	11.5	32	-3.6	76
6.4	87	32.8	15	11.0	19	38.9	3	29.0	42	0.1	50	26.4	49	na	--	na	--	na	--
8.2	83	20.0	71	-4.9	74	17.1	48	3.6	96	-9.9	86	41.6	18	31.3	26	15.5	21	-1.7	66
-11.1	98	32.1	17	-13.1	89	16.1	52	na	--	na	--	na	--	na	--	na	--	na	--
32.7	5	13.0	92	-24.0	96	-6.4	99	na	--	na	--	na	--	na	--	na	--	na	--
20.6	16	26.7	37	-12.0	87	9.9	79	6.7	94	-5.9	73	31.4	37	26.4	38	30.8	2	11.6	15
11.9	66	17.2	83	11.9	15	7.6	89	26.1	53	1.6	43	-0.3	90	0.6	91	-0.7	91	3.8	38
20.2	17	26.3	40	-4.3	73	28.7	12	12.0	88	6.4	22	22.4	59	32.0	25	7.0	52	-7.1	90
10.2	76	19.2	75	na	--	na	--	na	--	na	--	na	--	na	--	na	--	na	--
18.2	27	20.9	65	6.1	42	16.7	50	21.1	69	0.3	49	1.5	87	10.4	76	2.4	74	-6.9	90
20.8	15	17.0	83	14.9	5	43.8	2	30.8	35	26.3	1	26.3	50	12.4	73	14.4	24	19.4	7
13.8	55	19.3	75	12.8	12	24.6	23	27.0	51	34.7	1	na	--	na	--	na	--	na	--
14.1	53	22.7	55	9.4	27	na	--	na	--	na	--	na	--	na	--	na	--	na	--
27.5	7	46.2	2	-7.3	80	15.4	56	77.5	1	3.8	35	42.6	16	27.4	35	24.9	6	-0.5	61
24.8	8	34.4	12	6.4	40	10.0	78	40.9	10	-0.1	51	14.9	73	13.7	71	4.9	64	-4.0	78
10.5	74	20.7	67	5.3	44	16.9	49	27.3	50	5.4	27	8.9	79	6.9	81	2.9	72	6.9	23
0.4	95	15.0	89	-22.4	96	24.8	23	29.6	40	7.7	17	32.1	36	na	--	na	--	na	--
21.4	14	19.6	74	na	--	na	--	na	--	na	--	na	--	na	--	na	--	na	--
18.1	29	20.4	68	na	--	na	--	na	--	na	--	na	--	na	--	na	--	na	--
15.0	48	22.4	56	13.0	11	10.0	78	27.9	47	13.5	6	3.6	84	3.7	85	1.0	85	2.8	43
15.9	43	34.7	11	-1.0	63	na	--	na	--	na	--	na	--	na	--	na	--	na	--
-9.3	98	19.2	76	-5.0	74	na	--	na	--	na	--	na	--	na	--	na	--	na	--

CDA ANNUAL SUPPLEMENT – 12/31/86

FUND	IO	ASSETS (MIL$) 9/86	1st PCNT RK	2nd PCNT RK	3rd PCNT RK	4th PCNT RK
LUTHERAN BROTHER. FUND	GI	186	4.6 88	1.0 68	-1.3 44	3.0 64
LUTHERAN BROTHER. INCOME	BP	504	3.3 94	0.8 70	2.4 25	3.3 57
LUTHERAN BROTHER. MUN BD	MB	210	12.1 46	-1.2 91	4.9 10	3.8 45
MACKENZIE INDUSTRIAL AM	G	7	-0.6 99	-0.4 82	-4.2 54	-0.1 92
MACKENZIE INDUSTRIAL GOV	BP	20	1.2 98	-0.8 87	0.5 38	7.0 6
MACKENZIE INDUSTRIAL OPT	GI	75	3.1 94	4.8 31	-0.8 43	4.8 23
MANHATTAN FUND	G	241	17.7 12	3.2 46	-8.7 74	5.5 15
MASS. CAPITAL DEVEL.	G	858	16.0 20	2.1 56	-14.3 91	4.6 26
MASS. FINANCIAL BOND	BP	327	6.6 79	2.4 53	0.4 39	5.3 17
MASS. FINANCIAL DEVEL.	G	193	18.5 10	5.0 29	-13.2 88	4.7 25
MASS. FINL EMERG. GWTH.	AG	233	18.9 9	10.7 6	-17.1 96	3.2 60
MASS. FINL GOV SEC HIYLD	BP	367	na --	1.1 66	1.8 31	3.8 44
MASS. FINL HI INCOME	BP	1,000	5.6 84	2.3 54	-0.1 41	2.7 69
MASS. FINL INTL TRUST BD	BP	134	18.0 11	5.8 23	6.1 5	4.1 37
MASS. FINANCIAL SPECIAL	AG	111	20.6 6	6.8 18	-14.6 92	7.3 5
MASS. FINL TOTAL RETURN	B	285	14.4 31	4.1 37	-4.7 58	5.7 13
MASS. FINL SECTORS FUND	G	124	na --	na --	-15.6 94	0.2 90
MASS. INV. GROWTH STOCK	G	893	16.5 18	4.2 36	-10.7 83	3.8 45
MASS. INV. TRUST	GI	1,188	15.4 24	4.5 34	-8.6 74	6.7 8
MFS GOVT GUARANTEED	BP	432	3.9 90	-0.8 87	3.5 19	2.3 74
MFS GOV SECURITIES HIYLD	BP	367	na --	1.1 66	1.8 31	3.8 44
MFS MGD MUNI-BOND HIYLD	MB	383	5.2 85	1.5 61	2.8 23	2.2 76
MFS MGD MUNI-BD TRUST	MB	801	9.2 63	-0.6 84	4.8 11	3.7 47
MFS MDG MULTI-ST MASS.	MB	183	8.6 68	-0.9 87	5.8 6	3.1 61
MFS MGD MULTI-ST N.C.	MB	83	8.8 67	-0.5 83	4.6 13	3.4 55
MFS MGD MULTI-ST VA	MB	149	7.5 74	-1.3 91	5.6 6	2.9 65
MATHERS FUND	G	149	12.3 44	1.5 61	-5.0 58	4.3 32
MEDICAL TECHNOLOGY FUND	AG	66	19.3 8	13.1 4	-19.0 98	5.4 16
MEESCHAERT CAP. ACCUM.	G	30	14.4 31	6.4 20	-9.1 75	-4.3 98
MERRILL L. BASIC VALUE	GI	799	14.6 30	1.6 61	-3.1 51	4.0 41
MERRILL L. CALIF TAX-EX	MB	497	10.7 53	-2.1 95	4.8 11	3.6 50
MERRILL L. CORP DIV FUND	BP	253	5.6 84	0.2 76	4.1 16	2.0 79
MERRILL L. BOND-INTERMED	BP	100	6.4 81	1.6 60	2.1 28	3.8 47
MERRILL L. FEDERAL SECS	BP	6,651	5.8 84	1.0 68	3.0 22	2.6 70
MERRILL L. INTERNATIONAL	IN	278	16.9 16	4.1 36	1.5 33	5.5 15
MERRILL L. CAPITAL FUND	GI	547	16.0 20	2.3 54	-4.4 56	5.3 17
MERRILL L. EQUI-BOND I	B	16	10.0 58	0.4 75	-2.3 47	3.1 62
MERRILL L. HIGH INC BOND	BP	597	6.6 79	2.8 50	-0.7 43	3.7 49
MERRILL L. PACIFIC FUND	IN	445	29.5 1	15.5 2	13.7 3	4.6 26
MERRILL L. PHOENIX	B	118	13.7 36	1.4 63	-0.9 43	2.2 76
MERRILL L. MUNI-BD HIYLD	MB	1,557	9.5 62	-1.0 89	5.6 6	3.8 44
MERRILL L. MUNI-BD INSD	MB	2,039	9.1 65	-0.8 87	4.5 14	3.6 51
MERRILL L. MUNI-LTD MAT	MB	668	2.9 96	1.4 62	1.4 34	1.6 82
MERRILL L. SPECIAL VALUE	AG	97	14.3 32	5.2 27	-13.1 88	-2.7 97
MERRILL L. NAT RESOURCE	G	259	6.4 80	1.3 63	14.5 3	6.6 8
MERRILL L. HIGH QUAL BD	BP	225	6.1 82	1.2 65	1.9 30	4.4 30
MERRILL L. NY MUNI BOND	MB	487	8.7 67	-0.9 88	4.4 15	3.8 44
MERRILL L. FUND FOR TOM	G	607	16.4 18	8.0 12	-10.8 83	2.4 73
MERRILL L. RETIRE BEN IN	B	2,066	10.5 54	1.2 64	-1.5 45	3.0 64
MERRILL L. RETIRE/INCOME	BP	1,430	na --	0.4 75	3.1 21	2.0 80

TEN YEARS OF ANNUAL RETURNS

1986		1985		1984		1983		1982		1981		1980		1979		1978		1977	
PCNT	RK	PCNT	RK	PCNT	RK	PCNT	RK	PCNT	RK	PCNT	RK	PCNT	RK	PCNT	RK	PCNT	RK	PCNT	RK
7.3	86	19.4	74	14.5	6	25.0	22	25.9	55	4.0	33	21.1	63	15.4	68	2.0	77	-5.1	83
10.3	76	17.3	82	13.3	10	10.7	75	28.5	45	4.0	33	7.0	80	3.8	85	2.2	76	5.3	30
20.6	16	18.4	78	6.8	39	9.0	84	43.8	7	-10.2	86	-15.7	98	-4.6	99	-5.1	97	na	--
-5.3	96	na	--	na	--	na	--	na	--	na	--	na	--	na	--	na	--	na	--
7.9	84	na	--	na	--	na	--	na	--	na	--	na	--	na	--	na	--	na	--
12.4	64	na	--	na	--	na	--	na	--	na	--	na	--	na	--	na	--	na	--
17.0	35	37.1	7	7.1	36	26.8	17	28.7	43	-7.1	78	36.8	25	33.7	22	7.2	51	-9.4	97
6.1	88	26.2	40	-11.4	87	26.5	18	39.9	11	0.0	51	56.9	7	52.9	5	19.6	14	14.7	11
15.5	45	25.2	45	12.6	12	9.9	79	34.3	22	1.2	45	0.7	89	1.5	88	2.0	77	4.5	35
13.0	59	28.6	29	-5.4	75	22.4	29	27.3	50	-7.4	79	41.4	18	37.6	18	11.6	32	3.0	42
12.6	62	25.8	42	-7.0	79	30.2	9	54.3	2	na	--	na	--	na	--	na	--	na	--
na	--	na	--	na	--	na	--	na	--	na	--	na	--	na	--	na	--	na	--
10.8	73	23.2	52	6.2	41	26.4	18	35.4	20	7.3	18	5.4	82	7.0	81	na	--	na	--
38.0	4	22.5	56	2.3	54	16.6	51	20.2	72	na	--	na	--	na	--	na	--	na	--
18.0	29	23.8	49	-13.6	89	na	--	na	--	na	--	na	--	na	--	na	--	na	--
19.8	19	30.2	23	6.9	37	19.1	40	28.6	44	3.8	34	19.5	67	11.2	75	0.8	86	1.8	49
na	--	na	--	na	--	na	--	na	--	na	--	na	--	na	--	na	--	na	--
12.5	63	25.7	43	-4.2	72	15.5	55	28.6	44	-6.2	74	40.1	20	26.6	38	13.6	26	-6.4	88
17.5	32	24.5	47	3.0	52	20.9	33	18.9	75	-4.9	69	30.6	39	22.0	51	8.3	45	-10.1	97
9.1	80	16.4	86	na	--	na	--	na	--	na	--	na	--	na	--	na	--	na	--
na	--	na	--	na	--	na	--	na	--	na	--	na	--	na	--	na	--	na	--
12.2	65	16.7	85	na	--	na	--	na	--	na	--	na	--	na	--	na	--	na	--
18.0	29	20.4	69	10.5	20	12.7	67	42.0	9	-1.8	58	-1.3	92	na	--	na	--	na	--
17.5	32	na	--	na	--	na	--	na	--	na	--	na	--	na	--	na	--	na	--
17.1	34	na	--	na	--	na	--	na	--	na	--	na	--	na	--	na	--	na	--
15.3	47	na	--	na	--	na	--	na	--	na	--	na	--	na	--	na	--	na	--
12.9	60	27.5	34	-2.4	67	16.1	52	14.7	83	-7.7	80	40.3	19	46.7	9	15.0	22	14.2	11
15.3	47	39.0	5	-12.5	88	-0.6	98	38.0	14	-7.9	82	48.7	11	na	--	na	--	na	--
6.0	88	18.4	78	5.4	43	9.5	81	13.3	85	2.4	40	13.4	75	28.1	33	6.8	53	2.0	48
17.2	34	32.0	18	6.8	38	30.1	10	28.3	45	1.3	45	na	--	na	--	na	--	na	--
17.7	30	na	--	na	--	na	--	na	--	na	--	na	--	na	--	na	--	na	--
12.4	63	17.4	82	na	--	na	--	na	--	na	--	na	--	na	--	na	--	na	--
14.6	51	19.8	72	14.0	8	9.6	80	26.5	52	11.5	8	na	--	na	--	na	--	na	--
12.8	61	19.2	75	na	--	na	--	na	--	na	--	na	--	na	--	na	--	na	--
30.3	5	35.9	9	na	--	na	--	na	--	na	--	na	--	na	--	na	--	na	--
19.5	21	29.7	25	8.7	30	23.1	27	19.7	74	11.3	9	24.6	55	26.7	37	11.7	32	-7.4	92
11.3	70	26.2	41	7.9	34	11.1	73	24.4	59	na	--	na	--	na	--	na	--	na	--
12.9	60	21.7	60	8.5	31	18.3	44	na	--	na	--	na	--	na	--	na	--	na	--
77.9	1	42.1	4	3.8	49	38.7	3	0.5	97	21.1	2	90.6	1	na	--	na	--	na	--
16.8	37	30.2	23	9.9	24	31.0	9	na	--	na	--	na	--	na	--	na	--	na	--
19.0	23	20.7	66	10.0	23	14.0	62	33.2	27	-3.8	65	na	--	na	--	na	--	na	--
17.0	35	19.5	74	8.5	31	12.2	68	33.9	24	-8.5	83	-11.4	95	-0.7	93	-3.7	95	na	--
7.5	86	6.7	96	6.9	38	5.6	94	8.5	93	9.7	10	na	--	na	--	na	--	na	--
1.7	94	33.1	15	-7.3	79	22.3	29	13.3	85	-7.0	77	na	--	na	--	na	--	na	--
31.6	5	na	--	na	--	na	--	na	--	na	--	na	--	na	--	na	--	na	--
14.3	52	22.4	56	15.0	5	9.4	82	na	--	na	--	na	--	na	--	na	--	na	--
16.7	38	na	--	na	--	na	--	na	--	na	--	na	--	na	--	na	--	na	--
14.9	50	25.7	42	na	--	na	--	na	--	na	--	na	--	na	--	na	--	na	--
13.5	57	na	--	na	--	na	--	na	--	na	--	na	--	na	--	na	--	na	--
na	--	na	--	na	--	na	--	na	--	na	--	na	--	na	--	na	--	na	--

CDA ANNUAL SUPPLEMENT - 12/31/86

		ASSETS (MIL$)	1986 QUARTERLY RETURNS							
			1st		2nd		3rd		4th	
FUND	IO	9/86	PCNT	RK	PCNT	RK	PCNT	RK	PCNT	RK
MIDAMERICA HIGH GROWTH	G	11	17.7	13	0.2	77	-13.3	88	6.4	10
MIDAMERICA MUTUAL FUND	GI	32	13.5	37	-0.6	85	-4.8	58	4.0	40
MIDWEST INC-INTERMED TRM	BP	53	5.0	87	1.3	64	2.3	26	2.3	74
MONITREND VALUE FUND	G	26	8.2	70	4.0	38	-3.0	50	-0.2	92
MORGAN (W.L.) GROWTH	G	633	11.0	51	3.2	46	-9.7	78	4.3	31
MUTUAL BEACON GROWTH FD	G	62	7.8	72	6.2	21	-4.2	55	5.3	18
MUTUAL BENEFIT FUND	G	15	16.2	19	6.4	20	-7.1	66	6.4	9
MUTUAL OF OMAHA AMERICA	BP	40	5.8	83	0.1	78	2.3	26	2.5	70
MUTUAL OF OMAHA GROWTH	G	31	14.5	30	8.5	10	-10.2	80	3.9	42
MUTUAL OF OMAHA INCOME	GI	105	7.6	72	2.4	53	-4.5	57	3.9	43
MUTUAL QUALIFIED INCOME	B	517	9.4	63	5.5	26	-3.6	53	4.3	32
MUTUAL SHARES CORP.	B	1,293	10.0	58	5.6	25	-3.0	50	3.4	55
NAESS & THOMAS SPECIAL	AG	31	14.6	30	6.9	18	-20.3	98	2.5	71
NATL AVIATION & TECH	G	84	15.3	24	0.9	69	-2.9	50	2.0	79
NATL FEDERAL SECURITIES	BP	1,178	3.6	91	0.9	69	1.3	34	3.4	54
NATIONAL INDUSTRIES FUND	G	27	12.7	41	7.5	14	-12.6	87	3.6	49
NATL SECURITIES BALANCED	B	2	10.2	56	6.1	22	-5.8	61	4.3	31
NATL SECURITIES BOND	BP	520	5.1	86	2.2	55	-2.2	47	0.5	89
NATL SECURITIES CAL TX E	MB	74	9.0	66	-0.4	82	4.4	14	4.0	39
NATL SECURITIES GROWTH	G	66	19.4	8	3.3	45	-12.3	86	6.8	7
NATL SECURITIES PREFERED	BP	4	10.6	54	5.2	28	-0.1	41	1.8	81
NATL SECS REAL ESTATE	GI	13	21.0	5	1.7	59	-4.6	57	0.0	91
NATL SECURITIES STOCK	GI	255	15.7	21	3.3	44	-6.8	65	3.5	51
NATL SECURITIES TOT INC	B	76	13.5	37	10.2	6	-6.7	64	4.6	26
NATL SECURITIES TOT RET	GI	259	12.8	41	6.9	18	-5.3	60	4.4	31
NATL SECURITIES TX EX BD	MB	78	10.3	55	-0.8	86	5.4	7	4.3	32
NATL TELECOMMUNICATIONS	G	59	9.1	65	1.1	67	-11.4	85	5.3	18
NATIONWIDE FUND	GI	344	14.3	32	5.7	24	-8.7	74	6.5	9
NATIONWIDE GROWTH FUND	G	162	15.8	20	4.7	32	-7.8	70	5.8	12
NATIONWIDE BOND FUND	BP	20	6.7	78	0.8	71	1.0	36	3.9	42
NAUTILUS FUND	AG	18	0.2	99	-2.4	96	-9.8	79	3.4	55
NEL EQUITY FUND	GI	30	20.3	6	4.6	33	-8.7	74	6.1	11
NEL GOVERNMENT SEC TR	BP	174	7.3	75	0.0	78	1.5	34	3.1	61
NEL GROWTH FUND	AG	286	17.9	12	7.2	16	-9.8	79	3.7	49
NEL INCOME	BP	50	7.2	76	1.0	67	3.0	22	2.9	66
NEL RETIREMENT EQUITY	G	95	19.3	8	7.5	14	-8.6	74	5.3	18
NEL TAX EXEMPT	MB	105	11.7	48	-1.4	92	5.6	6	4.2	35
NEUWIRTH FUND	AG	26	22.5	3	5.0	29	-15.1	93	-1.1	95
NEW ECONOMY FUND	G	719	11.5	49	5.5	26	-7.1	67	3.8	45
NEW PERSPECTIVE FUND	G	870	10.9	52	3.2	45	2.4	25	8.2	3
NEWPORT FAR EAST	IN	3	25.6	2	13.2	3	14.2	3	6.7	8
NEW YORK VENTURE FUND	G	147	17.9	12	1.8	59	-4.3	55	6.9	7
NEWTON GROWTH FUND	G	34	10.6	54	-2.2	96	-2.1	47	3.0	64
NEWTON INCOME FUND	BP	12	5.0	86	0.1	77	1.6	32	2.0	79
NICHOLAS FUND	G	1,053	9.6	61	5.2	28	-4.6	57	1.7	82
NICHOLAS II	G	299	10.5	54	7.6	14	-8.5	73	1.4	84
NICHOLAS INCOME FUND	BP	56	4.4	89	2.0	57	2.3	25	2.3	74
NICHOLSON GROWTH FUND	G	0	7.4	74	7.8	13	-10.7	82	2.7	68
NODDING CALAMOS INCOME	BP	16	13.7	36	3.5	42	-3.9	54	2.7	68
NOMURA PACIFIC BASIN FD	IN	53	26.7	1	16.0	2	10.3	4	7.6	4

TEN YEARS OF ANNUAL RETURNS

1986 PCNT RK	1985 PCNT RK	1984 PCNT RK	1983 PCNT RK	1982 PCNT RK	1981 PCNT RK	1980 PCNT RK	1979 PCNT RK	1978 PCNT RK	1977 PCNT RK
8.7 82	20.4 69	-8.0 81	14.5 60	22.8 64	9.2 10	13.8 74	23.1 49	8.2 46	5.0 32
11.7 67	24.9 46	4.5 47	15.4 55	29.3 41	-0.4 53	19.0 67	22.4 49	10.4 36	0.3 57
11.3 70	14.5 90	11.4 18	4.7 96	na --	na --	na --	na --	na --	na --
9.1 81	20.5 68	na --	na --	na --	na --	na --	na --	na --	na --
7.8 84	29.5 26	-5.1 74	28.0 15	27.2 50	-4.7 68	34.9 29	19.2 58	19.4 15	7.4 21
15.4 46	23.3 51	0.0 60	13.7 63	16.4 79	-7.5 80	31.4 37	16.7 65	2.1 76	-3.2 73
22.3 11	28.8 28	0.3 58	26.6 17	21.0 70	2.2 41	20.1 65	11.9 74	1.5 81	-4.7 81
11.1 71	16.9 84	11.7 16	6.2 93	15.4 82	12.9 6	na --	na --	na --	na --
15.9 42	28.8 28	-3.3 70	15.6 54	19.5 75	-7.1 78	31.1 38	16.2 65	2.1 76	-9.9 97
9.3 80	24.0 48	10.4 20	7.5 89	21.9 67	5.7 26	7.7 80	7.0 80	2.1 76	0.6 56
16.0 42	25.5 44	14.7 6	34.9 6	15.4 82	22.3 1	na --	na --	na --	na --
16.5 39	26.5 38	14.5 7	37.1 5	13.2 86	8.7 13	19.3 67	43.0 13	18.4 16	15.5 10
0.1 95	21.7 61	-25.1 97	17.9 45	47.3 5	-2.9 62	na --	na --	na --	na --
15.3 46	21.2 63	-3.6 71	6.5 92	30.9 34	-7.8 81	28.6 44	na --	na --	na --
9.6 79	14.9 89	na --	na --	na --	na --	na --	na --	na --	na --
9.7 78	10.6 95	-2.3 67	11.3 72	4.7 96	-10.7 88	35.2 28	26.5 38	8.3 46	-1.7 66
14.9 49	27.3 35	11.8 16	15.5 55	32.1 30	4.1 33	12.3 76	13.3 72	2.7 73	-0.9 62
5.4 90	23.7 50	10.1 22	11.1 74	31.4 32	3.8 35	-0.6 91	2.1 87	-0.2 90	7.4 21
17.9 30	19.7 73	na --	na --	na --	na --	na --	na --	na --	na --
15.5 45	23.6 50	-13.4 89	4.9 96	23.1 63	-8.7 83	39.3 22	14.6 70	7.6 49	-5.9 86
18.2 27	26.5 39	11.1 18	15.5 55	32.1 29	7.8 16	6.6 81	1.2 89	-0.4 91	2.3 47
17.6 31	na --	na --	na --	na --	na --	na --	na --	na --	na --
15.3 46	28.5 30	8.3 32	9.1 83	20.4 72	-3.6 64	33.0 34	26.0 40	5.4 62	-3.6 75
22.2 11	26.7 37	12.1 15	17.2 48	29.3 41	8.9 12	16.7 71	14.4 70	5.8 59	5.7 28
19.2 22	24.4 47	9.0 28	17.8 46	29.1 42	0.9 47	32.2 35	24.7 43	5.3 62	4.4 35
20.3 16	21.2 63	9.8 24	9.9 78	39.5 12	-11.5 90	-16.3 98	na --	na --	na --
2.9 93	17.2 83	-11.4 86	na --	na --	na --	na --	na --	na --	na --
17.5 32	36.4 8	6.2 41	15.8 53	22.1 65	1.9 41	17.9 69	9.8 76	0.8 86	-9.0 96
18.2 27	33.3 14	8.4 32	21.8 31	35.6 19	3.0 37	18.7 68	21.7 52	9.9 38	-0.9 63
12.8 61	19.1 76	14.1 8	6.0 94	31.1 33	2.2 41	na --	na --	na --	na --
-8.8 98	8.4 96	-25.8 97	34.9 6	34.5 22	2.4 40	135.6 1	na --	na --	na --
21.9 13	23.1 53	3.0 51	14.6 60	32.5 29	5.7 25	19.9 66	25.4 41	7.3 50	-2.7 71
12.3 64	na --	na --	na --	na --	na --	na --	na --	na --	na --
18.3 27	34.9 10	-5.7 77	11.4 71	77.3 1	2.9 38	47.7 11	27.4 36	26.9 4	-0.1 59
14.7 50	18.6 78	11.9 15	5.4 94	30.9 34	7.7 17	-3.7 93	-1.2 95	0.8 86	3.9 38
23.4 10	35.7 9	-0.5 61	16.7 50	27.3 49	9.2 11	25.6 51	18.5 60	20.7 12	-4.3 79
21.2 15	21.9 59	9.4 26	7.3 89	48.7 4	-6.0 74	-15.0 97	-4.1 99	-6.3 98	na --
8.1 84	39.4 5	-9.5 84	14.3 61	27.6 48	-13.1 93	49.0 10	25.2 42	10.1 37	-2.0 68
13.5 57	38.6 6	4.3 48	na --	na --	na --	na --	na --	na --	na --
26.8 7	33.8 13	-0.2 60	23.7 25	21.3 68	2.2 40	25.5 51	27.3 36	24.0 6	2.2 47
73.4 1	16.2 86	na --	na --	na --	na --	na --	na --	na --	na --
22.8 11	38.1 6	4.7 46	23.0 28	25.2 56	-0.8 55	44.2 14	38.5 17	19.5 14	4.6 34
9.1 81	28.7 29	-8.2 82	23.5 26	36.1 18	-1.8 58	36.3 26	25.0 42	8.4 45	2.1 47
9.0 81	12.8 93	12.2 14	11.6 70	30.2 37	1.6 43	3.5 84	-1.2 94	0.1 89	-5.2 83
11.7 67	29.7 26	9.9 24	23.9 25	35.5 20	8.5 14	35.4 27	31.0 27	25.5 6	20.4 6
10.3 76	33.8 13	16.9 2	na --	na --	na --	na --	na --	na --	na --
11.5 68	21.2 63	12.6 12	12.4 68	34.9 21	3.9 34	-2.7 93	-2.8 98	-2.3 94	-5.0 82
6.2 88	-5.9 98	na --	na --	na --	na --	na --	na --	na --	na --
16.1 41	na --	na --	na --	na --	na --	na --	na --	na --	na --
74.4 1	na --	na --	na --	na --	na --	na --	na --	na --	na --

CDA ANNUAL SUPPLEMENT – 12/31/86

FUND	IO	ASSETS (MIL$) 9/86	1st PCNT RK	2nd PCNT RK	3rd PCNT RK	4th PCNT RK
NORTH STAR APOLLO FUND	G	21	9.7 60	-0.6 85	-8.5 73	2.3 75
NORTH STAR BOND	BP	36	5.6 85	-1.4 92	2.1 28	2.7 67
NORTH STAR REGIONAL FUND	G	84	14.1 33	15.2 2	-10.7 82	4.6 26
NORTH STAR STOCK FUND	G	65	10.7 54	5.2 28	-8.2 71	5.5 15
NORTHEAST INV GROWTH	G	18	16.8 16	13.4 3	-10.7 82	5.1 19
NORTHEAST INV. TRUST	BP	313	8.7 67	4.1 37	2.9 22	3.4 56
NOVA FUND INC	AG	23	2.2 97	7.9 13	-10.2 81	8.7 2
NUVEEN MUNICIPAL BOND FD	MB	668	9.9 58	-0.8 86	5.3 7	3.7 49
OLD DOMINION INVTS TR	GI	6	11.4 49	4.4 34	-5.3 60	6.4 10
OLYMPIC TRUST SERIES B	G	4	12.1 46	12.3 4	-15.1 93	2.6 69
OLYMPIC TRUST TOT RETURN	B	1	6.5 80	3.2 47	-3.0 50	3.2 60
OMEGA FUND	G	32	18.0 12	-0.3 82	-9.2 76	5.1 20
ONE HUNDRED FUND	AG	11	17.2 15	16.6 2	-15.1 93	3.4 55
ONE HUNDRED ONE FUND	GI	3	2.0 97	19.3 1	-6.9 65	1.4 84
OPPENHEIMER A.I.M. FUND	IN	373	25.7 1	7.5 15	0.8 37	7.5 5
OPPENHEIMER DIRECTORS	G	210	10.1 57	2.7 51	-8.6 74	1.2 86
OPPENHEIMER EQUITY INC.	GI	420	12.2 45	2.1 56	-2.7 49	3.8 45
OPPENHEIMER FUND	AG	236	15.5 22	1.0 68	-13.2 88	0.9 87
OPPENHEIMER GOLD & SPEC.	ME	40	12.2 45	-9.2 98	31.5 1	2.1 78
OPPENHEIMER HIGH YIELD	BP	636	4.4 88	3.3 44	-1.7 46	3.5 53
OPPENHEIMER PREMIUM INC	GI	375	0.8 98	-0.7 85	-4.8 58	6.2 10
OPPENHEIMER NY TX EXEMPT	MB	51	8.9 66	-1.1 90	4.7 13	4.0 40
OPPENHEIMER REGENCY	AG	147	11.9 47	3.1 47	-9.6 77	3.3 57
OPPENHEIMER SPECIAL FUND	G	709	11.5 49	1.4 62	-1.2 44	3.1 62
OPPENHEIMER SELECT STOCK	G	10	14.6 30	3.6 42	-7.1 66	3.3 58
OPPENHEIMER RETR-GOV SEC	BP	12	3.4 93	0.5 73	2.3 26	2.0 79
OPPENHEIMER TARGET FUND	G	119	25.0 2	2.9 49	-10.7 83	-5.7 98
OPPENHEIMER TAX FREE BD	MB	120	10.8 53	-1.4 92	5.1 8	4.1 36
OPPENHEIMER TIME FUND	G	230	18.1 11	11.0 6	-11.4 85	2.5 71
OVER-THE-COUNTER SEC.	G	237	15.7 21	4.9 30	-12.6 87	-0.7 94
PBHG GROWTH FUND	AG	18	15.1 26	10.2 7	-11.4 84	10.3 1
PACIFIC HORIZON AGGRE GR	AG	64	21.2 5	18.6 1	-18.4 97	2.4 72
PACIFIC HORIZON CAL TAX	MB	86	10.0 58	-0.7 86	4.2 16	4.0 39
PACIFIC HORIZON HIVLD BD	BP	27	7.3 75	1.7 60	2.2 26	3.1 62
PAINE WEBBER AMERICA FD	GI	91	13.4 38	4.1 37	-3.7 53	0.3 90
PAINE WEBBER ATLAS FD	IN	224	19.6 8	8.4 10	1.6 33	5.5 16
PAINE WEBBER CALIF TX-EX	MB	136	10.6 54	-1.2 90	4.9 11	3.8 45
PAINE WEBBER FI INVT GR	BP	331	7.6 72	0.2 76	1.4 34	4.6 27
PAINE WEBBER GNMA	BP	2,907	3.5 92	0.1 78	3.7 18	3.4 56
PAINE WEBBER HIGH YIELD	BP	675	6.8 78	3.8 40	1.2 36	1.7 81
PAINE WEBBER OLYMPUS FD	G	109	17.6 13	6.0 22	-13.4 88	-0.4 93
PAINE WEBBER TAX-EX INC	MB	313	9.2 64	-0.9 88	4.6 13	3.5 52
PARTNERS FUND	GI	444	15.2 25	4.4 35	-6.0 62	3.8 47
PAX WORLD FUND	IN	49	8.7 67	5.4 26	-7.6 68	2.4 72
PENN SQUARE MUTUAL FUND	GI	195	12.6 41	2.4 53	-7.5 68	5.9 12
PENNSYLVANIA MUTUAL FUND	G	346	10.4 55	5.6 25	-7.0 66	2.4 73
PERMANENT PORTFOLIO	G	71	9.0 66	0.0 79	4.0 17	0.3 90
PHILADELPHIA FUND	G	107	12.3 44	2.2 55	-8.7 74	3.4 55
PHOENIX BALANCED FD SER	B	153	14.0 34	5.0 29	-2.6 48	2.7 67
PHOENIX GROWTH FUND SER	GI	242	15.6 22	4.3 35	-4.7 57	4.7 25

TEN YEARS OF ANNUAL RETURNS

1986		1985		1984		1983		1982		1981		1980		1979		1978		1977	
PCNT	RK	PCNT	RK	PCNT	RK	PCNT	RK	PCNT	RK	PCNT	RK	PCNT	RK	PCNT	RK	PCNT	RK	PCNT	RK
2.0	93	12.7	93	-7.6	80	na	--	na	--	na	--	na	--	na	--	na	--	na	--
9.2	80	20.1	70	15.5	4	8.0	87	32.1	30	na	--	na	--	na	--	na	--	na	--
22.8	11	38.4	6	-2.1	67	13.1	67	41.4	9	-3.3	64	na	--	na	--	na	--	na	--
12.9	60	23.2	52	3.7	50	19.4	39	33.9	24	-1.3	57	na	--	na	--	na	--	na	--
24.3	9	36.7	8	3.9	49	9.6	80	15.2	83	na	--	na	--	na	--	na	--	na	--
20.4	16	25.6	43	13.1	11	11.2	72	36.5	17	5.8	25	-0.1	90	-1.1	94	-0.9	91	6.6	25
7.7	85	27.1	36	-6.2	78	16.7	50	24.1	60	na	--	na	--	na	--	na	--	na	--
19.1	22	21.4	62	8.7	29	9.9	79	32.3	29	-7.1	78	-11.6	95	na	--	na	--	na	--
17.2	34	27.0	36	1.3	57	22.3	29	9.9	91	4.6	30	21.4	62	22.3	50	6.2	56	na	--
9.5	79	na	--	na	--	na	--	na	--	na	--	na	--	na	--	na	--	na	--
9.9	77	na	--	na	--	na	--	na	--	na	--	na	--	na	--	na	--	na	--
12.2	65	32.3	16	0.2	59	22.0	30	-7.5	98	-9.2	85	37.6	23	37.5	18	7.7	48	0.3	56
20.0	18	25.7	42	-20.1	95	17.8	46	13.0	86	-1.5	57	35.2	28	29.8	29	11.9	31	1.2	53
15.0	48	29.1	27	-1.2	64	35.2	6	13.8	84	3.2	36	20.2	65	15.5	67	0.0	89	0.4	56
46.4	2	49.1	2	-21.7	95	26.3	19	14.0	84	-11.8	90	62.1	5	50.5	7	13.4	27	-0.2	60
4.5	91	23.3	52	-16.9	93	25.2	21	36.9	15	na	--	na	--	na	--	na	--	na	--
15.8	44	30.9	21	3.2	51	34.3	6	30.5	36	5.3	28	21.4	62	24.1	46	6.3	55	-2.7	70
2.2	93	34.1	12	-14.5	90	22.3	30	7.8	93	-11.1	89	41.9	17	38.6	17	8.4	44	-10.4	98
36.7	4	-4.5	98	-27.0	98	na	--	na	--	na	--	na	--	na	--	na	--	na	--
9.7	78	18.8	77	3.5	50	14.6	59	28.5	45	6.3	23	1.2	88	4.3	84	na	--	na	--
1.2	94	17.1	83	2.4	53	16.3	51	16.0	81	13.8	6	14.5	74	11.6	74	6.8	53	na	--
17.2	34	na	--	na	--	na	--	na	--	na	--	na	--	na	--	na	--	na	--
7.9	84	31.6	19	-22.9	96	58.1	1	na	--	na	--	na	--	na	--	na	--	na	--
15.1	47	16.8	85	-10.2	85	28.0	14	21.3	69	-5.5	71	46.0	13	37.6	18	21.3	10	24.2	4
13.9	54	na	--	na	--	na	--	na	--	na	--	na	--	na	--	na	--	na	--
8.3	83	na	--	na	--	na	--	na	--	na	--	na	--	na	--	na	--	na	--
8.2	83	29.8	25	-17.2	93	22.9	28	na	--	na	--	na	--	na	--	na	--	na	--
19.6	20	21.1	63	10.3	22	17.1	48	na	--	na	--	na	--	na	--	na	--	na	--
19.1	22	33.2	14	-9.7	84	27.9	15	39.1	13	-10.4	87	40.7	19	41.9	14	19.4	15	15.4	10
5.4	90	34.9	10	-2.6	68	39.1	3	10.8	90	7.5	18	22.9	58	54.6	4	30.2	3	21.5	5
23.9	9	na	--	na	--	na	--	na	--	na	--	na	--	na	--	na	--	na	--
20.1	18	37.5	7	na	--	na	--	na	--	na	--	na	--	na	--	na	--	na	--
18.3	26	18.3	79	na	--	na	--	na	--	na	--	na	--	na	--	na	--	na	--
15.1	48	24.8	46	na	--	na	--	na	--	na	--	na	--	na	--	na	--	na	--
14.1	53	20.6	68	na	--	na	--	na	--	na	--	na	--	na	--	na	--	na	--
38.9	4	65.6	1	na	--	na	--	na	--	na	--	na	--	na	--	na	--	na	--
19.0	23	na	--	na	--	na	--	na	--	na	--	na	--	na	--	na	--	na	--
14.4	52	22.7	54	na	--	na	--	na	--	na	--	na	--	na	--	na	--	na	--
11.1	71	19.9	72	na	--	na	--	na	--	na	--	na	--	na	--	na	--	na	--
14.1	53	21.7	61	na	--	na	--	na	--	na	--	na	--	na	--	na	--	na	--
7.5	85	na	--	na	--	na	--	na	--	na	--	na	--	na	--	na	--	na	--
17.2	33	19.0	76	na	--	na	--	na	--	na	--	na	--	na	--	na	--	na	--
17.3	33	29.8	24	8.2	33	19.1	41	26.6	52	6.1	24	33.6	32	43.1	13	16.3	19	6.9	23
8.4	82	25.5	43	7.5	35	15.4	56	10.2	91	-6.9	77	na	--	na	--	na	--	na	--
12.9	60	26.6	38	0.5	58	29.2	11	20.7	70	1.2	45	25.5	52	21.7	51	4.1	67	-6.3	87
10.9	72	26.7	37	3.1	51	40.6	2	33.2	26	0.4	49	25.0	53	35.9	19	15.9	20	23.8	5
13.6	56	12.2	93	-12.9	88	5.4	94	na	--	na	--	na	--	na	--	na	--	na	--
8.4	83	22.0	59	-3.5	70	18.3	44	16.0	80	-8.8	84	36.2	26	26.9	37	24.8	6	3.9	38
19.8	19	29.8	24	13.9	8	18.1	45	39.4	12	0.0	51	19.9	66	4.1	84	-4.0	96	na	--
20.3	17	31.9	18	10.0	23	28.6	12	42.6	9	1.8	42	33.7	31	33.2	23	7.7	48	-7.3	91

CDA ANNUAL SUPPLEMENT – 12/31/86

		ASSETS (MIL$)	1986 QUARTERLY RETURNS							
			1st		2nd		3rd		4th	
FUND	IO	9/86	PCNT	RK	PCNT	RK	PCNT	RK	PCNT	RK
PHOENIX CONVERTIBLE FUND	GI	100	9.8	59	4.7	32	-1.6	45	3.7	48
PHOENIX HIGH YIELD	BP	103	7.7	72	3.7	40	0.5	38	3.2	58
PHOENIX STOCK FUND SER	G	95	14.1	33	5.8	23	-8.9	75	6.8	7
PHOENIX TOTAL RETURN FD	GI	5	13.0	40	6.5	20	-7.8	69	4.1	37
PILGRIM ADJUSTABLE RATE	BP	883	3.6	92	-2.0	95	2.3	25	0.2	90
PILGRIM GNMA	BP	260	1.2	98	-0.8	86	3.4	19	2.6	70
PILGRIM HIGH YIELD FD	BP	17	5.4	85	3.0	47	0.6	38	2.2	76
PILGRIM MAGNACAP FUND	GI	181	17.0	16	4.9	30	-6.7	64	2.1	78
PILGRIM PREFERRED	BP	198	na	--	2.5	53	1.3	34	2.0	80
PILOT FUND	AG	64	13.6	37	2.1	55	-9.2	76	4.9	21
PINE STREET FUND	GI	61	15.4	24	3.0	48	-6.1	63	2.5	72
PIONEER BOND FUND	BP	37	4.5	88	1.6	61	1.5	33	2.9	65
PIONEER FUND	GI	1,377	10.4	55	1.2	65	-4.4	56	4.5	28
PIONEER II	G	2,842	11.5	49	1.1	66	-5.3	60	5.2	18
PIONEER THREE	G	543	14.9	28	3.0	49	-9.2	76	3.2	59
PRICE (ROWE) EQUITY INC	GI	71	15.1	26	4.6	33	-1.5	45	6.8	7
PRICE (ROWE) GROWTH&INC.	GI	376	14.1	34	-2.4	96	-5.2	59	2.2	76
PRICE (ROWE) GROWTH STK.	G	1,278	16.4	18	4.5	34	-3.1	51	3.3	58
PRICE (ROWE) HI YLD BOND	BP	703	7.0	77	4.9	30	-0.4	42	2.8	66
PRICE (ROWE) INTERNATL.	IN	753	22.5	4	8.6	10	11.2	3	8.6	3
PRICE (ROWE) NEW AMERICA	G	76	20.8	5	5.4	26	-14.0	90	4.4	29
PRICE (ROWE) NEW ERA	G	494	12.3	44	1.3	64	-2.0	46	4.2	33
PRICE (ROWE) NEW HORIZ.	AG	1,089	10.9	52	4.8	31	-16.7	96	3.3	58
PRICE (ROWE) NEW INCOME	BP	946	7.0	77	1.4	62	1.8	30	3.0	63
PRICE (ROWE) TAX FR HIYD	MB	226	9.9	58	-0.4	83	6.0	5	3.8	47
PRICE (ROWE) TX FREE INC	MB	1,411	10.4	55	-1.2	90	5.2	8	4.4	30
PRICE (ROWE) TXFR SH-INT	MB	242	3.5	93	1.1	67	2.6	24	2.1	77
PRIMECAP FUND	G	105	15.5	23	3.0	48	-3.4	52	7.4	5
PRINCOR CAP ACCUMULATION	GI	55	13.2	38	5.7	24	-10.2	80	4.0	40
PRINCOR GOV SECS INCOME	BP	52	3.3	94	-0.3	82	3.4	19	4.8	22
PRINCOR GROWTH FD, INC.	G	24	14.8	28	4.9	30	-10.3	81	4.6	26
PROVIDENT FD. FOR INCOME	B	102	11.3	50	-1.8	94	-2.3	48	5.3	17
PRU-BACHE ADJ RATE PFD	BP	284	na	--	-1.6	93	0.4	39	0.2	90
PRU-BACHE EQUITY FUND	AG	279	15.0	27	3.3	44	-7.7	69	4.2	34
PRU-BACHE GLOBAL FUND	IN	401	24.4	2	10.1	7	3.7	18	1.1	86
PRU-BACHE GOV SECURITIES	BP	702	5.9	83	1.8	59	2.7	23	2.1	78
PRU-BACHE HIGH YIELD	BP	1,589	6.5	80	3.8	39	1.3	35	2.7	68
PRU-BACHE HIYLD MUNI	MB	981	9.6	61	-1.3	91	5.4	7	4.2	36
PRU-BACHE GR OPPORTUNITY	AG	88	16.2	19	3.4	44	-12.0	86	9.0	2
PRU-BACHE INCOMEVERTIBLE	BP	281	12.3	44	1.7	60	-2.1	47	1.7	82
PRU-BACHE OPTION GROWTH	G	72	10.2	56	3.0	48	-2.0	46	-1.0	95
PRU-BACHE GNMA FUND	BP	270	2.9	96	1.2	64	3.5	19	3.5	53
PRU-BACHE RESEARCH FUND	GI	174	19.8	7	9.7	7	-8.6	73	3.7	49
PRU-BACHE UTILITY FUND	GI	1,212	11.6	48	7.8	13	2.6	24	3.5	54
PUTNAM CALIF TAX EX	MB	810	8.4	69	0.2	77	4.4	15	4.2	36
PUTNAM CCT ARP	BP	597	4.0	90	-1.0	89	1.2	36	0.4	89
PUTNAM CCT DSP	B	412	6.7	78	1.5	61	2.0	29	2.0	79
PUTNAM CONVERT INC-GR TR	GI	755	11.6	48	5.5	26	-5.1	59	3.5	52
PUTNAM ENERGY RESOURCES	AG	36	-5.8	99	0.2	77	-1.8	46	5.4	16
PUTNAM INFOR SCIENCES	AG	119	7.7	72	6.9	17	-11.0	84	8.0	4

TEN YEARS OF ANNUAL RETURNS

1986		1985		1984		1983		1982		1981		1980		1979		1978		1977	
PCNT	RK	PCNT	RK	PCNT	RK	PCNT	RK	PCNT	RK	PCNT	RK	PCNT	RK	PCNT	RK	PCNT	RK	PCNT	RK
17.3	33	21.6	61	5.2	44	26.0	19	35.7	19	8.6	14	24.7	54	15.1	69	na	--	na	--
15.9	43	21.1	64	7.9	34	13.4	64	29.1	42	8.0	16	na	--	na	--	na	--	na	--
17.4	33	27.1	35	8.1	33	31.1	9	42.7	8	3.2	36	50.3	9	41.1	14	10.9	34	na	--
15.4	45	16.3	86	-2.6	68	10.7	75	48.9	3	-5.0	69	28.7	44	12.8	73	na	--	na	--
4.0	92	14.6	90	5.1	45	na	--	na	--	na	--	na	--	na	--	na	--	na	--
6.5	87	15.9	87	na	--	na	--	na	--	na	--	na	--	na	--	na	--	na	--
11.7	67	14.5	90	11.5	17	12.6	67	31.3	32	8.8	13	1.3	88	3.9	84	1.1	85	10.4	16
16.8	37	34.8	10	16.1	3	22.6	28	9.4	92	20.7	3	12.7	76	27.7	34	6.1	57	-6.2	87
na	--	na	--	na	--	na	--	na	--	na	--	na	--	na	--	na	--	na	--
10.6	74	17.7	81	-5.9	77	18.8	42	40.4	10	-8.1	82	36.4	26	26.5	38	4.4	66	-1.8	67
14.3	52	30.7	22	5.2	45	19.1	41	20.4	71	-7.7	81	33.7	32	20.1	56	5.8	59	-4.1	78
10.8	73	20.1	71	11.8	16	9.3	82	31.2	32	na	--	na	--	na	--	na	--	na	--
11.7	67	25.7	42	-0.7	62	25.0	22	13.3	85	-3.1	63	30.6	39	27.9	33	12.3	29	3.7	38
12.3	64	31.2	20	-3.2	70	30.2	10	22.9	63	8.0	15	28.7	44	32.8	24	15.0	22	23.6	5
10.9	72	24.0	49	4.8	45	na	--	na	--	na	--	na	--	na	--	na	--	na	--
26.6	7	na	--	na	--	na	--	na	--	na	--	na	--	na	--	na	--	na	--
7.9	84	19.7	73	2.0	55	32.3	8	na	--	na	--	na	--	na	--	na	--	na	--
21.7	13	35.1	10	-1.1	63	12.3	68	16.3	80	-12.5	91	29.8	42	11.3	75	11.7	32	-6.9	90
14.9	49	na	--	na	--	na	--	na	--	na	--	na	--	na	--	na	--	na	--
60.5	1	45.2	3	-5.8	77	28.6	12	6.2	95	-1.9	59	na	--	na	--	na	--	na	--
14.3	52	na	--	na	--	na	--	na	--	na	--	na	--	na	--	na	--	na	--
16.2	41	22.9	54	3.5	50	26.4	18	1.7	97	-15.5	96	51.4	9	59.7	3	12.1	30	-4.0	77
-0.1	95	24.0	49	-7.4	80	19.7	37	22.5	65	-7.9	82	57.1	7	35.5	20	20.9	11	12.8	13
13.9	55	17.6	82	11.7	16	9.8	80	24.0	60	7.6	17	2.9	86	8.1	79	4.6	64	5.7	28
20.3	17	na	--	na	--	na	--	na	--	na	--	na	--	na	--	na	--	na	--
19.8	19	16.9	84	7.2	36	7.0	90	30.8	35	-0.9	55	-5.2	94	na	--	na	--	na	--
9.6	78	8.9	96	6.8	38	na	--	na	--	na	--	na	--	na	--	na	--	na	--
23.5	10	na	--	na	--	na	--	na	--	na	--	na	--	na	--	na	--	na	--
11.8	66	36.2	9	5.1	45	36.7	5	8.0	93	4.1	32	36.8	25	14.4	70	3.9	68	-1.2	64
11.6	68	na	--	na	--	na	--	na	--	na	--	na	--	na	--	na	--	na	--
13.0	59	31.6	19	-8.4	82	28.3	14	11.8	88	-1.9	59	38.0	23	27.1	36	8.1	46	4.3	36
12.4	64	17.8	81	4.6	47	21.9	31	43.3	8	11.4	8	12.1	76	9.5	77	1.2	84	3.6	39
na	--	na	--	na	--	na	--	na	--	na	--	na	--	na	--	na	--	na	--
14.4	51	32.4	16	5.9	42	28.2	14	na	--	na	--	na	--	na	--	na	--	na	--
43.6	3	44.5	3	na	--	na	--	na	--	na	--	na	--	na	--	na	--	na	--
13.1	59	17.0	84	14.3	8	6.2	93	na	--	na	--	na	--	na	--	na	--	na	--
14.9	49	20.4	68	10.1	22	15.6	54	27.9	46	2.6	39	4.9	83	na	--	na	--	na	--
18.7	25	na	--	na	--	na	--	na	--	na	--	na	--	na	--	na	--	na	--
15.4	46	26.5	39	-9.7	84	15.0	57	25.1	57	na	--	na	--	na	--	na	--	na	--
13.8	56	na	--	na	--	na	--	na	--	na	--	na	--	na	--	na	--	na	--
10.2	77	34.1	12	-1.4	65	na	--	na	--	na	--	na	--	na	--	na	--	na	--
11.6	68	17.7	81	13.1	11	6.1	93	na	--	na	--	na	--	na	--	na	--	na	--
24.6	8	27.6	33	-3.5	71	na	--	na	--	na	--	na	--	na	--	na	--	na	--
27.6	7	33.4	14	14.5	7	11.6	70	26.4	52	na	--	na	--	na	--	na	--	na	--
18.0	29	20.7	66	na	--	na	--	na	--	na	--	na	--	na	--	na	--	na	--
4.6	91	16.2	86	na	--	na	--	na	--	na	--	na	--	na	--	na	--	na	--
12.7	61	17.2	83	na	--	na	--	na	--	na	--	na	--	na	--	na	--	na	--
15.7	44	27.0	36	5.7	43	13.8	63	29.8	39	7.8	17	38.3	23	19.8	56	8.8	43	-0.9	62
-2.3	96	19.1	76	-8.5	83	28.5	13	-33.8	99	-18.4	97	na	--	na	--	na	--	na	--
10.7	74	17.6	82	-13.2	89	na	--	na	--	na	--	na	--	na	--	na	--	na	--

CDA ANNUAL SUPPLEMENT – 12/31/86

| | | ASSETS (MIL$) | 1986 QUARTERLY RETURNS | | | | | | | |
| | | | 1st | | 2nd | | 3rd | | 4th | |
FUND	IO	9/86	PCNT	RK	PCNT	RK	PCNT	RK	PCNT	RK
PUTNAM INTL EQUITIES	IN	372	23.0	3	5.8	24	0.2	39	5.8	12
PUTNAM (GEORGE) FD. BOS.	B	355	12.2	45	4.6	33	-4.1	54	5.6	14
PUTNAM FD FOR GROWTH/INC	GI	1,164	13.8	35	4.8	31	-2.7	49	5.1	20
PUTNAM GNMA PLUS	BP	584	na	--	na	--	1.8	31	2.7	67
PUTNAM HEALTH SCIENCES	AG	241	15.6	22	16.1	2	-18.5	98	5.3	17
PUTNAM HIGH INCOME GOV	BP	5,132	6.7	79	0.4	74	2.0	29	3.7	47
PUTNAM HIGH YIELD	BP	2,364	5.6	84	3.3	45	-0.1	41	4.1	36
PUTNAM INCOME FUND	BP	208	5.1	86	1.6	60	1.6	32	3.8	45
PUTNAM INVESTORS FUND	G	960	15.0	27	6.9	18	-10.6	82	4.7	25
PUTNAM NY TAX EXEMPT	MB	701	9.5	62	-0.7	86	4.6	13	4.1	36
PUTNAM VISTA FUND	AG	194	15.0	26	6.2	21	-6.9	66	5.0	21
PUTNAM OPTION INCOME I	GI	1,114	6.8	78	2.8	51	-3.0	50	4.8	22
PUTNAM OPTION INCOME II	GI	1,173	6.0	82	3.0	48	-5.1	59	4.8	24
PUTNAM TAX EXEMPT INC	MB	624	11.1	50	-0.8	86	5.0	9	5.3	17
PUTNAM US GOV SECURITIES	BP	965	2.8	96	0.8	70	3.8	18	3.2	60
PUTNAM VOYAGER FUND	AG	350	16.9	16	11.5	5	-14.7	92	8.1	3
QUALIFIED DIVD PORTF I	B	177	10.9	52	2.2	55	2.6	23	4.6	26
QUALIFIED DIVD PORTF II	BP	136	13.1	39	-0.3	82	6.1	5	4.2	33
QUALIFIED DIVD PORT III	BP	141	3.0	95	-1.7	94	2.1	29	0.8	88
QUASAR ASSOCIATES	AG	145	21.0	5	8.9	9	-16.1	95	0.7	88
QUEST FOR VALUE FUND	G	75	14.2	33	4.1	37	-6.2	63	2.5	72
RAINBOW FUND	G	2	8.6	68	10.3	6	-7.5	68	4.6	26
REA GRAHAM FUND	B	43	3.9	90	1.1	67	1.5	33	4.1	36
RETIREMENT PLANNING-BOND	BP	53	4.3	89	-0.5	83	3.2	21	3.1	62
RETIREMENT PLANNING-EQ	G	10	14.2	33	2.2	55	-9.3	77	6.4	9
RIGHTIME FUND	G	134	14.8	28	5.7	24	-12.5	87	4.3	32
ROCHESTER TAX MANAGED FD	G	29	11.0	51	0.1	78	-8.0	71	-0.1	92
ROYCE VALUE FUND, INC.	G	149	9.3	63	5.6	25	-8.2	72	0.3	89
SAFECO EQUITY FUND	GI	47	13.8	35	7.1	17	-8.8	75	1.3	85
SAFECO GROWTH FUND	G	68	9.9	58	2.4	53	-11.1	84	1.8	81
SAFECO INCOME FUND	B	102	13.4	38	4.6	33	-3.1	51	4.3	33
SAFECO MUNICIPAL BOND FD	MB	170	9.8	59	-1.0	89	5.3	7	4.6	26
SBSF FUND	G	90	16.8	17	4.5	34	-4.3	55	2.2	76
SCHIELD AGGRESS GROWTH	AG	11	16.4	18	4.4	34	-12.0	86	-7.8	99
SCHIELD VALUE PORTFOLIO	G	12	17.5	14	3.5	42	-8.3	73	-6.4	99
SCI-TECH HOLDINGS	G	273	12.4	43	6.2	21	-4.3	55	3.2	59
SCUDDER CALIF TAX FREE	MB	152	7.5	73	-0.7	85	5.2	8	3.9	42
SCUDDER CAPITAL GROWTH	G	414	16.0	20	5.1	29	-9.9	79	6.1	11
SCUDDER DEVELOPMENT FUND	AG	278	13.2	39	8.6	10	-17.0	96	5.6	14
SCUDDER GLOBAL	IN	11	na	--	na	--	na	--	8.9	2
SCUDDER GOV MORTGAGE SEC	BP	214	3.0	95	0.7	72	3.8	18	3.4	54
SCUDDER GROWTH & INCOME	GI	367	15.4	24	4.7	32	-6.9	65	4.8	24
SCUDDER INCOME FUND	BP	217	6.7	79	1.1	67	2.0	29	4.2	35
SCUDDER INTERNATIONAL FD	IN	686	19.0	9	7.5	15	7.6	4	9.4	2
SCUDDER NEW YORK TAX FR	MB	111	6.0	82	-1.3	91	4.6	13	4.2	33
SCUDDER MANAGED MUNI BD	MB	630	5.7	84	1.1	66	5.1	8	4.0	41
SCUDDER TX FR TARGT 1990	MB	81	3.5	93	1.1	66	2.1	28	2.4	73
SCUDDER TX FR TARGT 1993	MB	95	3.8	90	0.3	75	3.3	20	3.0	63
SECURITY ACTION FD	G	77	14.9	27	6.8	18	-8.3	72	0.7	88
SECURITY INC FD-CORP BD	BP	45	5.5	85	1.3	64	2.1	28	1.7	82

TEN YEARS OF ANNUAL RETURNS

1986		1985		1984		1983		1982		1981		1980		1979		1978		1977	
PCNT	RK	PCNT	RK	PCNT	RK	PCNT	RK	PCNT	RK	PCNT	RK	PCNT	RK	PCNT	RK	PCNT	RK	PCNT	RK
38.0	4	64.4	1	0.8	58	27.9	15	9.9	91	-0.5	53	25.5	51	19.5	57	22.5	8	-0.8	62
18.8	24	29.8	24	-1.9	66	14.9	58	35.5	20	6.5	22	16.9	70	15.4	68	5.8	60	-3.6	76
21.9	12	28.3	30	5.7	43	21.6	31	22.1	66	-3.2	64	37.3	24	22.2	50	12.8	28	0.3	56
na	--	na	--	na	--	na	--	na	--	na	--	na	--	na	--	na	--	na	--
15.2	47	40.7	4	-3.5	71	-2.5	99	na	--	na	--	na	--	na	--	na	--	na	--
13.3	58	na	--	na	--	na	--	na	--	na	--	na	--	na	--	na	--	na	--
13.5	57	19.8	72	7.7	35	15.5	55	38.7	13	5.3	28	7.0	80	2.8	86	na	--	na	--
12.6	62	20.4	69	14.5	6	11.4	71	35.8	18	8.1	15	0.0	90	-1.9	96	1.6	80	5.5	29
15.0	48	29.3	27	0.3	59	10.5	76	33.6	25	-8.9	84	44.5	13	20.4	55	14.0	25	-3.2	73
18.4	26	21.1	64	na	--	na	--	na	--	na	--	na	--	na	--	na	--	na	--
19.4	21	28.6	29	-10.4	85	15.3	57	55.5	2	7.3	18	29.8	41	31.8	26	18.0	17	-2.5	69
11.7	67	20.1	70	1.8	55	14.2	61	18.2	77	-1.3	57	24.4	56	15.1	69	6.4	55	na	--
8.6	82	na	--	na	--	na	--	na	--	na	--	na	--	na	--	na	--	na	--
21.9	12	23.6	51	4.5	47	13.2	66	52.9	2	-4.7	68	-5.4	94	0.8	90	-6.7	99	6.9	22
10.9	72	16.6	85	na	--	na	--	na	--	na	--	na	--	na	--	na	--	na	--
20.2	17	37.6	7	-5.4	75	14.9	58	32.1	30	-3.8	65	41.6	18	37.1	19	14.2	25	5.8	27
21.6	13	30.1	24	25.4	1	32.9	7	34.9	21	22.3	2	13.8	74	16.9	64	5.8	59	5.6	29
24.7	8	29.7	25	10.4	21	7.9	88	34.1	23	5.6	26	1.1	89	-2.2	97	-1.9	93	6.9	23
4.2	92	11.5	94	2.9	52	na	--	na	--	na	--	na	--	na	--	na	--	na	--
11.4	69	41.8	4	-10.3	85	35.9	5	na	--	na	--	na	--	na	--	na	--	na	--
14.3	52	27.4	34	4.8	45	38.2	4	40.8	10	30.3	1	na	--	na	--	na	--	na	--
15.8	43	20.7	67	-4.9	74	22.2	30	-3.2	98	-3.1	63	20.7	64	31.8	25	0.0	89	19.9	6
11.0	71	29.4	26	6.3	40	11.3	72	na	--	na	--	na	--	na	--	na	--	na	--
10.4	75	15.7	88	na	--	na	--	na	--	na	--	na	--	na	--	na	--	na	--
12.6	63	36.7	8	na	--	na	--	na	--	na	--	na	--	na	--	na	--	na	--
10.8	73	na	--	na	--	na	--	na	--	na	--	na	--	na	--	na	--	na	--
2.1	93	6.3	97	3.2	51	18.7	42	14.6	83	18.9	3	na	--	na	--	na	--	na	--
6.3	87	27.5	34	-0.2	60	43.0	2	na	--	na	--	na	--	na	--	na	--	na	--
12.6	62	32.6	16	2.8	52	21.1	33	11.4	89	-5.1	70	28.1	45	26.6	37	11.0	34	5.0	32
1.8	94	19.6	73	-7.0	79	31.3	9	19.4	75	-2.3	60	31.0	38	34.8	20	18.1	16	16.2	10
19.9	19	31.4	19	9.1	28	28.2	14	22.1	66	6.5	22	22.4	59	21.0	54	1.7	79	2.4	46
19.7	20	21.6	61	10.1	22	10.5	76	na	--	na	--	na	--	na	--	na	--	na	--
19.4	21	19.0	76	11.8	15	na	--	na	--	na	--	na	--	na	--	na	--	na	--
-1.3	95	na	--	na	--	na	--	na	--	na	--	na	--	na	--	na	--	na	--
4.3	92	na	--	na	--	na	--	na	--	na	--	na	--	na	--	na	--	na	--
17.9	30	22.1	58	-6.3	78	na	--	na	--	na	--	na	--	na	--	na	--	na	--
16.7	38	18.3	79	na	--	na	--	na	--	na	--	na	--	na	--	na	--	na	--
16.5	39	36.8	8	0.5	58	22.1	30	na	--	na	--	na	--	na	--	na	--	na	--
7.7	85	19.8	72	-10.3	85	18.2	44	15.6	81	9.6	10	46.5	13	29.8	29	30.0	3	25.1	4
na	--	na	--	na	--	na	--	na	--	na	--	na	--	na	--	na	--	na	--
11.3	70	na	--	na	--	na	--	na	--	na	--	na	--	na	--	na	--	na	--
17.8	30	34.5	11	-3.7	71	13.3	65	22.6	65	-6.2	74	34.2	31	23.3	48	10.8	35	-1.5	65
14.6	51	21.7	60	12.3	13	10.8	74	30.1	38	4.0	33	1.6	87	1.3	89	0.8	86	0.3	57
50.5	2	48.9	2	-0.7	62	29.2	11	1.2	97	-2.7	61	26.9	48	19.2	58	21.2	10	-0.5	61
14.0	53	16.0	87	9.2	27	na	--	na	--	na	--	na	--	na	--	na	--	na	--
16.8	38	17.5	82	10.2	22	40.6	3	12.1	88	-10.8	88	-12.0	96	0.4	91	-2.4	94	9.1	17
9.4	80	11.0	94	8.1	33	na	--	na	--	na	--	na	--	na	--	na	--	na	--
10.9	73	14.4	91	8.4	31	na	--	na	--	na	--	na	--	na	--	na	--	na	--
13.4	57	29.3	27	-4.6	73	28.5	13	na	--	na	--	na	--	na	--	na	--	na	--
10.9	72	21.4	62	13.4	10	9.2	83	27.4	49	na	--	na	--	na	--	na	--	na	--

CDA ANNUAL SUPPLEMENT – 12/31/86

FUND	IO	ASSETS (MIL$) 9/86	1st PCNT	1st RK	2nd PCNT	2nd RK	3rd PCNT	3rd RK	4th PCNT	4th RK
SECURITY EQUITY FUND	GI	235	15.2	25	4.3	36	-9.5	77	4.1	37
SECURITY INVESTMENT FUND	GI	101	10.8	52	3.2	46	-4.7	57	2.4	73
SECURITY OMNI FUND	AG	23	na	--	na	--	-13.5	89	-3.8	97
SECURITY ULTRA FUND	GI	100	13.0	39	4.2	36	-10.0	80	-0.9	95
SELECTED AMERICAN SHARES	GI	144	12.1	46	7.7	14	-6.5	63	3.7	49
SELECTED SPECIAL SHARES	G	35	8.5	68	4.0	39	-4.4	56	-0.4	93
SELIGMAN CAPITAL FUND	AG	192	21.1	5	7.7	14	-11.4	85	2.3	75
SELIGMAN CALIF TAX EX HI	MB	51	9.8	59	-0.4	82	5.2	8	7.4	5
SELIGMAN CAL TAX EX QUAL	MB	53	9.4	63	-1.1	90	4.7	13	4.3	32
SELIGMAN COMMUNICATIONS	AG	41	15.3	24	10.9	6	-12.5	86	5.1	19
SELIGMAN COMMON STOCK FD	GI	523	17.6	13	6.3	20	-8.4	73	6.6	8
SELIGMAN GROWTH FD	G	602	18.2	11	9.4	8	-16.6	95	8.1	3
SELIGMAN GOV GUARANTEED	BP	77	13.3	38	0.4	74	-0.5	42	1.9	80
SELIGMAN HIGH YIELD BOND	BP	63	7.6	73	3.5	43	1.4	34	2.6	69
SELIGMAN INCOME FD	B	143	10.0	57	2.8	50	0.0	41	3.5	54
SELIGMAN SECURED MTG	BP	47	2.4	97	-0.3	82	2.5	24	2.5	71
SELIGMAN TX EX LOUISIANA	MB	45	9.7	60	-2.1	95	5.0	9	3.5	54
SELIGMAN TAX EX MARYLAND	MB	46	7.3	75	-3.1	97	5.1	8	3.8	44
SELIGMAN TAX EX MASS	MB	132	8.0	71	-1.4	92	5.3	7	3.4	54
SELIGMAN TAX EX MICH	MB	99	9.5	62	-1.0	89	5.8	6	3.1	61
SELIGMAN TAX EX MINN	MB	108	9.2	63	-1.5	93	4.6	14	3.3	57
SELIGMAN TAX EX NATL	MB	110	10.8	52	-0.1	80	5.4	7	4.0	40
SELIGMAN TAX EX NEW YORK	MB	65	7.8	71	-0.4	83	4.7	12	4.7	24
SELIGMAN TAX EX OHIO	MB	114	8.9	66	-1.6	93	5.1	8	3.9	41
SENTINEL BALANCED FUND	B	41	13.5	37	3.2	47	-3.4	52	5.3	17
SENTINEL BOND	BP	21	8.6	68	0.4	74	2.3	26	4.0	39
SENTINEL COMMON STOCK FD	GI	466	16.4	18	8.1	12	-7.8	69	6.5	9
SENTINEL GROWTH FUND	G	51	12.9	40	6.5	19	-11.2	84	5.7	14
SENTRY FUND	G	40	14.6	29	9.9	7	-12.3	86	4.1	36
SEQUOIA FUND	GI	690	8.4	69	7.2	16	-3.2	52	0.2	91
SHEARSON AGGRESSIVE GRTH	AG	91	20.4	6	13.4	3	-14.5	92	7.6	4
SHEARSON APPRECIATION	G	263	14.8	28	7.8	13	-8.7	74	6.2	10
SHEARSON CALIF MUNICIPAL	MB	156	9.5	62	-1.1	90	4.3	15	4.5	28
SHEARSON FUNDAMENTAL VAL	G	102	4.8	87	1.2	65	-2.7	49	1.3	85
SHEARSON GLOBAL OPPORT	G	263	19.2	9	3.6	41	-0.8	43	6.7	8
SHEARSON HIGH YIELD	BP	513	5.4	85	4.0	38	-0.7	42	2.3	75
SHEARSON LG-TRM GOV SECS	BP	1,481	4.6	88	0.5	74	1.7	31	3.4	56
SHEARSON MANAGED GOVTS	BP	1,439	3.7	91	-0.2	81	3.1	22	3.7	48
SHEARSON MANAGED MUNI BD	MB	628	9.5	62	-0.8	87	4.8	11	4.2	34
SHEARSON SPEC EQTY GR	G	137	na	--	1.3	64	-0.3	42	-0.4	94
SHEARSON NEW YORK MUNI	MB	191	9.3	63	-1.5	92	5.0	9	4.4	30
SHEARSON SPEC INTL EQ	IN	169	na	--	0.1	78	2.2	27	5.7	13
SHEARSON SPEC EQTY PLUS	AG	24	na	--	2.5	52	-16.7	96	-0.7	94
SHEARSON SPEC INTERM GOV	BP	44	4.3	89	1.6	60	2.0	29	2.4	73
SHEARSON SPEC TAX EX INC	MB	383	9.6	60	0.0	79	1.8	30	4.7	25
SHEARSON SPL OPTION INC	GI	615	8.1	70	5.0	30	-2.3	48	4.1	38
SHERMAN, DEAN FUND	AG	2	1.1	98	-15.0	99	21.2	2	-8.6	99
SIERRA GROWTH FUND	AG	5	4.2	90	2.8	50	-14.3	91	1.4	84
SIGMA CAPITAL SHARES	G	89	11.6	48	8.4	11	-10.7	83	3.1	61
SIGMA INCOME SHARES	BP	36	5.9	83	0.9	69	3.2	21	3.0	64

TEN YEARS OF ANNUAL RETURNS

1986		1985		1984		1983		1982		1981		1980		1979		1978		1977	
PCNT	RK	PCNT	RK	PCNT	RK	PCNT	RK	PCNT	RK	PCNT	RK	PCNT	RK	PCNT	RK	PCNT	RK	PCNT	RK
13.1	59	26.5	39	-0.6	61	19.6	38	24.4	59	-15.4	95	48.6	11	34.1	21	12.8	28	-0.1	59
11.6	67	20.4	69	-3.6	71	10.1	77	20.1	73	-4.1	66	33.4	33	32.2	24	1.2	84	7.9	19
na	--	na	--	na	--	na	--	na	--	na	--	na	--	na	--	na	--	na	--
5.1	90	28.7	29	1.4	57	11.2	73	31.9	30	-24.8	99	71.8	3	59.1	3	23.8	7	3.1	42
17.0	36	33.2	14	14.9	5	21.6	31	24.3	59	-0.9	55	21.6	61	8.9	78	3.5	69	-4.1	78
7.4	86	23.5	51	-4.2	72	28.0	15	16.8	78	-7.3	79	24.0	56	27.0	37	1.5	81	-6.6	88
18.3	27	30.8	21	-14.1	90	23.1	27	49.7	3	-3.4	64	43.2	15	37.2	18	15.2	21	5.7	28
23.4	10	na	--	na	--	na	--	na	--	na	--	na	--	na	--	na	--	na	--
18.1	28	na	--	na	--	na	--	na	--	na	--	na	--	na	--	na	--	na	--
17.6	31	34.2	12	-10.6	86	na	--	na	--	na	--	na	--	na	--	na	--	na	--
22.1	12	30.7	21	1.8	56	27.2	16	26.6	51	-2.2	59	30.4	40	25.6	41	6.3	56	-4.4	80
16.5	39	29.3	27	-7.8	81	14.9	58	26.9	51	-13.0	93	33.1	33	29.1	32	10.1	37	-2.8	71
15.4	46	na	--	na	--	na	--	na	--	na	--	na	--	na	--	na	--	na	--
15.8	43	na	--	na	--	na	--	na	--	na	--	na	--	na	--	na	--	na	--
17.0	35	26.5	38	12.6	12	10.7	75	26.0	54	9.1	11	15.2	72	9.1	77	3.2	70	4.8	33
7.3	86	na	--	na	--	na	--	na	--	na	--	na	--	na	--	na	--	na	--
16.7	38	na	--	na	--	na	--	na	--	na	--	na	--	na	--	na	--	na	--
13.5	57	na	--	na	--	na	--	na	--	na	--	na	--	na	--	na	--	na	--
16.0	42	18.3	79	na	--	na	--	na	--	na	--	na	--	na	--	na	--	na	--
18.3	26	21.0	65	na	--	na	--	na	--	na	--	na	--	na	--	na	--	na	--
16.2	40	18.5	78	na	--	na	--	na	--	na	--	na	--	na	--	na	--	na	--
21.3	14	20.3	69	na	--	na	--	na	--	na	--	na	--	na	--	na	--	na	--
17.8	30	20.8	66	na	--	na	--	na	--	na	--	na	--	na	--	na	--	na	--
17.1	35	18.7	77	na	--	na	--	na	--	na	--	na	--	na	--	na	--	na	--
19.0	23	28.0	32	14.7	6	14.4	60	34.1	23	5.5	27	11.3	77	13.9	71	-1.7	93	1.4	52
15.9	42	18.5	78	12.6	12	9.0	84	28.9	42	na	--	na	--	na	--	na	--	na	--
23.7	9	29.8	25	12.4	13	20.3	35	29.7	39	6.0	24	22.5	58	21.5	52	1.9	78	-2.4	69
12.9	60	35.8	9	-5.7	77	26.3	18	34.9	21	-4.6	67	41.9	17	26.2	40	10.4	37	-5.2	83
15.1	48	32.4	16	1.8	55	5.4	95	8.6	93	4.7	29	41.4	19	29.9	28	14.6	24	2.5	45
12.6	62	27.7	33	18.7	2	27.0	16	30.8	35	21.3	2	12.9	75	12.0	74	23.9	7	19.9	6
25.7	8	27.4	34	-13.4	89	na	--	na	--	na	--	na	--	na	--	na	--	na	--
20.0	18	34.8	11	1.8	55	23.1	27	23.5	61	2.0	41	36.0	27	44.8	10	21.2	11	-3.3	74
18.1	29	19.3	75	na	--	na	--	na	--	na	--	na	--	na	--	na	--	na	--
4.7	91	19.7	73	9.6	25	25.6	20	na	--	na	--	na	--	na	--	na	--	na	--
30.6	5	na	--	na	--	na	--	na	--	na	--	na	--	na	--	na	--	na	--
11.5	69	19.2	76	9.8	24	14.8	58	na	--	na	--	na	--	na	--	na	--	na	--
10.5	75	na	--	na	--	na	--	na	--	na	--	na	--	na	--	na	--	na	--
10.6	74	17.7	81	na	--	na	--	na	--	na	--	na	--	na	--	na	--	na	--
18.7	25	20.9	65	10.5	20	na	--	na	--	na	--	na	--	na	--	na	--	na	--
na	--	na	--	na	--	na	--	na	--	na	--	na	--	na	--	na	--	na	--
18.1	28	21.0	65	na	--	na	--	na	--	na	--	na	--	na	--	na	--	na	--
na	--	na	--	na	--	na	--	na	--	na	--	na	--	na	--	na	--	na	--
na	--	na	--	na	--	na	--	na	--	na	--	na	--	na	--	na	--	na	--
10.7	74	na	--	na	--	na	--	na	--	na	--	na	--	na	--	na	--	na	--
16.8	37	na	--	na	--	na	--	na	--	na	--	na	--	na	--	na	--	na	--
15.3	46	na	--	na	--	na	--	na	--	na	--	na	--	na	--	na	--	na	--
-4.7	96	13.1	92	-32.0	98	-3.8	99	-3.9	98	-0.1	52	35.0	29	36.4	19	28.4	3	2.4	45
-6.9	97	15.4	88	-16.6	92	9.7	80	15.6	81	-19.7	98	37.3	24	na	--	na	--	na	--
11.4	69	39.3	5	1.5	56	28.7	12	33.9	24	2.6	39	32.0	36	28.3	33	8.0	47	5.2	30
13.7	56	27.6	33	13.2	10	8.1	86	34.7	22	0.6	48	na	--	na	--	na	--	na	--

CDA ANNUAL SUPPLEMENT - 12/31/86

| | | ASSETS (MIL$) | 1986 QUARTERLY RETURNS | | | |
| | | | 1st | 2nd | 3rd | 4th |
FUND	IO	9/86	PCNT RK	PCNT RK	PCNT RK	PCNT RK
SIGMA INVESTMENT SHARES	GI	78	15.6 22	9.6 8	-7.7 69	7.2 6
SIGMA SPECIAL FUND	G	18	14.0 34	6.3 21	-7.9 70	4.5 27
SIGMA TRUST SHARES	B	40	9.4 62	5.3 27	0.3 39	2.4 73
SIGMA VENTURE SHARES	AG	59	15.1 26	7.3 16	-18.9 98	5.1 19
SIGMA WORLD	IN	8	13.9 35	11.6 5	3.4 20	9.3 2
SMITH, BARNEY EQUITY	G	70	14.0 34	5.1 29	-8.5 73	6.0 11
SMITH, BARNEY INC. & GR.	B	310	11.3 49	2.3 54	2.3 26	4.2 35
SOGEN INTERNATIONAL FUND	IN	66	15.7 20	5.0 29	-1.5 45	4.4 30
SOUTHEASTERN GROWTH FUND	G	86	22.7 3	3.5 42	-10.2 81	1.3 85
SOVEREIGN INVESTORS	GI	32	17.4 14	8.0 12	-6.9 66	3.3 57
STATE BOND COMMON STOCK	G	29	13.9 35	8.2 11	-13.7 89	7.1 6
STATE BOND DIVERSIFIED	GI	15	14.4 32	5.7 25	-5.3 60	4.8 23
STATE BOND PROGRESS FUND	AG	7	18.8 9	8.2 11	-15.4 93	3.4 56
STATE FARM BALANCED	GI	43	12.0 46	2.9 49	-4.4 56	4.2 34
STATE FARM GROWTH FUND	G	243	11.3 50	4.3 35	-6.9 65	4.4 29
STATE STREET GROWTH	G	247	13.7 36	4.7 32	-9.2 76	3.7 48
STATE STREET INV. CORP.	G	536	12.0 46	2.9 50	-7.9 70	5.6 14
STEADMAN AMERICAN INDUS.	G	6	6.2 81	3.3 45	-25.6 99	-1.7 96
STEADMAN ASSOCIATED	GI	20	11.8 47	11.8 5	-22.8 99	6.5 9
STEADMAN INVESTMENT	G	8	10.3 55	3.1 47	-6.1 62	3.2 58
STEADMAN OCEANOGRAPHIC	AG	4	17.0 15	4.6 33	-25.7 99	-2.4 97
STEIN R&F CAPITAL OPPOR.	AG	164	14.0 34	17.1 1	-16.2 95	4.4 29
STEINROE DISCOVERY FUND	AG	73	12.7 41	8.9 9	-22.6 99	-0.4 93
STEINROE HIGH-YIELD BOND	BP	59	na --	-0.2 81	2.2 27	4.8 24
STEINROE HIGH-YIELD MUNI	MB	194	9.1 64	-1.4 92	4.9 10	4.2 35
STEINROE INTERMED MUNI	MB	88	4.7 88	0.2 76	3.4 20	4.2 34
STEINROE MANAGED BOND FD	BP	193	8.9 66	1.5 61	1.3 35	3.9 43
STEIN R&F STOCK	AG	220	14.4 32	9.7 8	-11.9 86	6.3 10
STEINROE SPECIAL FUND	G	235	15.4 24	4.0 38	-10.7 83	7.1 6
STEINROE MANAGED MUNI FD	MB	477	12.2 45	-5.1 97	6.2 5	3.9 43
STEIN R&F TOTAL RETURN	B	145	12.2 45	4.3 35	-4.1 54	4.1 37
STEINROE UNIVERSE FUND	AG	94	17.5 13	11.4 5	-16.0 94	8.0 4
STRATEGIC CAPITAL GAINS	AG	7	-13.6 99	9.5 8	-11.2 84	-6.4 99
STRATEGIC INVESTMENTS	ME	96	15.1 25	-20.8 99	49.6 1	-5.9 99
STRATEGIC SILVER	ME	22	-4.6 99	-11.2 99	18.9 2	-10.4 99
STRATTON GROWTH FUND	G	18	18.0 12	1.4 62	-8.6 74	1.3 85
STRATTON MONTHLY DIV SHS	B	43	17.3 15	1.4 63	1.4 34	-0.2 93
STRONG INCOME FUND	GI	72	16.6 17	7.0 17	0.5 38	3.5 51
STRONG INVESTMENT FUND	B	319	15.5 23	3.2 47	-3.6 53	2.4 74
STRONG OPPORTUNITY FUND	AG	32	36.2 1	31.8 1	-11.6 85	0.8 87
STRONG TOTAL RETURN FUND	B	452	18.2 11	5.3 27	-6.8 65	3.5 53
SUMMIT INVESTOR FD INC.	AG	62	15.7 21	6.1 22	-10.9 83	4.3 33
SUNBELT GROWTH FUND	G	76	13.7 36	3.5 42	-8.1 71	5.5 15
SURVEYOR FUND	AG	90	17.7 13	9.9 7	-14.3 91	2.9 65
TAX EXEMPT BD FD/AMERICA	MB	260	10.4 55	-1.6 93	5.0 10	4.2 35
TECHNOLOGY FUND	G	557	14.0 34	2.0 57	-7.6 68	6.2 10
TELEPHONE INCOME SHARES	GI	99	11.1 50	11.8 5	-2.9 50	3.5 51
TEMPLETON FOREIGN FUND	IN	184	15.5 23	4.2 36	-0.5 42	7.4 5
TEMPLETON GROWTH FUND	G	1,813	15.5 23	0.4 74	-1.0 43	5.6 14
TEMPLETON GLOBAL I	G	301	13.5 38	5.9 23	-4.2 55	3.1 62

TEN YEARS OF ANNUAL RETURNS

1986		1985		1984		1983		1982		1981		1980		1979		1978		1977	
PCNT	RK	PCNT	RK	PCNT	RK	PCNT	RK	PCNT	RK	PCNT	RK	PCNT	RK	PCNT	RK	PCNT	RK	PCNT	RK
25.3	8	24.5	47	9.4	26	20.1	36	16.2	80	5.7	26	27.1	48	17.7	61	7.1	51	-4.8	81
16.5	39	33.5	13	-3.4	70	21.9	31	11.8	88	-1.3	56	14.7	73	49.1	8	17.6	18	-1.6	66
18.3	26	26.9	37	11.0	19	17.9	45	21.7	67	1.1	46	15.5	72	9.5	77	5.4	61	5.6	28
5.3	90	35.5	9	-11.5	87	20.6	34	25.1	57	2.3	40	41.0	19	34.0	22	21.5	10	40.0	2
43.7	3	na	--	na	--	na	--	na	--	na	--	na	--	na	--	na	--	na	--
16.2	40	32.5	16	-2.4	68	19.0	41	20.0	73	-6.4	75	42.6	16	27.7	34	13.3	27	0.2	58
21.3	14	27.1	36	10.3	21	17.3	48	27.3	49	11.8	8	33.6	32	21.3	53	1.8	79	1.6	51
25.1	8	32.7	16	3.1	51	25.0	23	31.0	34	8.0	16	32.3	34	24.1	44	7.2	50	2.4	45
15.4	45	na	--	na	--	na	--	na	--	na	--	na	--	na	--	na	--	na	--
21.9	12	30.6	22	11.2	18	19.6	38	21.8	67	7.9	16	20.2	65	23.2	48	3.6	68	-4.9	82
13.9	54	28.6	29	-5.6	76	7.0	91	18.7	76	-6.5	76	28.6	45	18.7	59	9.7	39	-11.4	99
20.0	19	27.3	35	6.2	41	19.3	40	20.1	73	-9.1	85	23.6	57	16.0	66	-1.2	92	-0.2	60
12.5	63	28.3	30	-16.5	92	8.1	87	30.0	38	-5.7	72	36.4	25	29.4	30	16.1	19	-3.1	73
14.9	49	36.3	8	4.1	48	14.0	62	22.9	64	-2.4	61	18.5	68	26.4	39	9.7	39	3.5	40
12.9	60	33.9	13	-1.6	66	15.7	53	24.5	59	-4.2	66	25.6	51	43.3	12	12.1	30	3.3	41
12.1	65	34.1	12	-1.1	64	15.0	57	19.6	74	na	--	na	--	na	--	na	--	na	--
12.0	66	32.0	17	1.3	57	20.8	34	12.8	87	-2.3	60	26.2	50	30.0	28	12.3	30	-0.8	62
-19.7	99	7.8	96	-23.2	96	7.1	90	4.8	95	-14.5	95	32.2	35	33.3	23	-0.9	92	-1.1	64
2.8	93	21.5	62	-8.6	83	7.0	90	27.3	50	-3.7	65	9.6	78	8.8	78	-1.3	93	4.6	34
10.3	75	5.3	97	-10.9	86	8.7	85	7.4	94	-11.5	90	28.9	43	21.6	52	-8.0	99	-5.7	85
-11.3	98	-14.3	99	-10.9	86	10.2	77	-1.4	98	-20.9	98	39.4	21	44.3	11	-2.6	94	-0.2	60
16.8	37	24.6	46	-16.8	93	11.9	69	24.9	57	-15.3	95	77.8	2	51.9	6	17.0	18	5.9	27
-5.3	97	45.3	3	-12.2	88	na	--	na	--	na	--	na	--	na	--	na	--	na	--
na	--	na	--	na	--	na	--	na	--	na	--	na	--	na	--	na	--	na	--
17.6	31	21.1	64	na	--	na	--	na	--	na	--	na	--	na	--	na	--	na	--
13.0	59	na	--	na	--	na	--	na	--	na	--	na	--	na	--	na	--	na	--
16.3	40	22.9	54	11.1	18	4.4	97	na	--	na	--	na	--	na	--	na	--	na	--
17.4	33	26.5	39	-9.8	85	14.0	62	33.4	26	-19.0	97	62.8	5	28.8	32	7.1	51	-8.6	96
14.8	50	29.4	27	-1.2	64	32.9	7	36.7	16	-11.1	89	na	--	na	--	na	--	na	--
17.4	33	22.6	55	11.5	17	10.9	74	46.0	6	-7.8	81	-15.3	97	-0.6	93	-3.4	95	na	--
16.9	36	25.6	43	5.3	44	13.5	64	24.2	60	-13.4	93	26.7	49	17.1	63	6.8	54	-5.7	85
18.7	24	28.3	31	-18.8	94	20.5	34	31.5	31	na	--	na	--	na	--	na	--	na	--
-21.4	99	24.2	48	-12.3	88	14.4	61	na	--	na	--	na	--	na	--	na	--	na	--
28.3	6	-29.5	99	-34.1	99	-1.9	98	69.0	1	-29.3	99	74.1	2	192.2	1	11.0	34	44.2	1
-9.8	98	na	--	na	--	na	--	na	--	na	--	na	--	na	--	na	--	na	--
10.7	73	27.5	34	-4.6	73	26.4	18	32.6	28	-6.7	76	31.9	36	18.2	60	7.1	52	3.3	40
20.4	16	29.7	25	21.0	1	11.8	70	20.5	71	na	--	na	--	na	--	na	--	na	--
29.9	6	na	--	na	--	na	--	na	--	na	--	na	--	na	--	na	--	na	--
17.5	32	19.4	75	9.8	24	45.1	1	33.2	26	na	--	na	--	na	--	na	--	na	--
59.9	1	na	--	na	--	na	--	na	--	na	--	na	--	na	--	na	--	na	--
20.0	18	25.4	44	10.4	21	41.3	2	32.5	29	na	--	na	--	na	--	na	--	na	--
14.0	53	30.2	23	-6.7	78	9.9	78	na	--	na	--	na	--	na	--	na	--	na	--
14.1	53	16.6	85	-1.0	63	10.4	76	na	--	na	--	na	--	na	--	na	--	na	--
14.0	53	28.6	29	-11.5	87	18.2	44	13.0	86	-6.9	76	46.6	12	29.8	29	14.8	23	1.2	53
18.7	25	19.7	73	8.7	30	8.6	86	na	--	na	--	na	--	na	--	na	--	na	--
14.2	52	25.8	42	-4.5	73	19.1	40	21.0	70	-14.2	94	48.8	10	32.1	25	22.3	9	-1.8	67
24.8	8	29.0	28	na	--	na	--	na	--	na	--	na	--	na	--	na	--	na	--
28.7	6	26.8	37	-1.3	65	36.5	5	na	--	na	--	na	--	na	--	na	--	na	--
21.2	15	27.8	32	2.1	54	32.9	7	10.8	89	-0.2	52	25.8	50	27.0	36	19.4	15	20.1	6
18.6	25	30.3	22	0.3	59	38.7	4	35.8	19	na	--	na	--	na	--	na	--	na	--

CDA ANNUAL SUPPLEMENT – 12/31/86

FUND	IO	ASSETS (MIL$) 9/86	1st PCNT RK	2nd PCNT RK	3rd PCNT RK	4th PCNT RK
TEMPLETON GLOBAL II	G	498	14.2 32	2.5 52	-7.5 68	1.7 82
TEMPLETON WORLD FUND	G	3,213	15.1 25	1.1 66	-1.7 46	3.0 63
THOMSON MCKINNON GROWTH	G	191	15.6 22	6.1 22	-3.0 51	3.4 56
THOMSON MCKINNON INCOME	BP	332	4.4 89	2.1 56	0.4 39	3.4 54
THOMSON MCKINNON OPPORT.	AG	52	11.7 48	9.5 8	-18.0 97	3.9 43
TRANSATLANTIC FUND INC.	IN	100	24.3 2	7.4 15	8.7 4	4.6 27
TRUSTEES COMM EQ-INTL	IN	634	19.2 8	8.3 11	3.3 20	12.4 1
TRUSTEES COMM EQ-US PORT	GI	165	10.7 53	2.5 52	-1.5 45	3.4 55
TUDOR FUND	AG	159	14.7 29	7.2 16	-11.3 84	3.1 62
TWENTIETH CENTURY GIFTR	G	6	23.2 3	18.6 1	-18.2 97	7.4 5
TWENTIETH CENTURY GROWTH	AG	888	17.5 14	11.6 5	-14.7 92	6.7 8
TWENTIETH CENTURY SELECT	G	1,832	19.9 7	8.4 10	-11.6 85	5.0 20
TWENTIETH CENTURY ULTRA	AG	300	18.5 10	5.5 26	-17.4 96	6.7 8
TWENTIETH CENTURY US GOV	BP	237	3.5 92	1.7 60	2.6 23	3.2 60
TWENTIETH CENTURY VISTA	AG	144	22.6 3	20.9 1	-18.3 97	4.4 29
UMB BOND FUND	BP	23	6.1 82	1.2 65	2.1 27	2.6 69
UMB STOCK FUND	GI	32	11.0 51	3.7 40	-5.5 61	3.2 59
UNIFIED GROWTH FUND	G	24	14.5 30	6.0 22	-10.0 80	3.8 44
UNIFIED INCOME FUND	B	13	8.2 70	1.2 64	-1.2 44	1.4 84
UNIFIED MUNI FD-GENERAL	MB	6	8.2 70	0.0 79	4.8 12	3.8 44
UNIFIED MUNI FD-INDIANA	MB	10	8.7 67	1.0 68	4.6 13	4.1 38
UNIFIED MUTUAL SHARES	GI	18	11.9 47	4.8 31	-8.1 71	3.5 52
UNITED ACCUMULATIVE FUND	G	678	15.4 24	7.5 14	-7.1 66	1.9 80
UNITED CONTL. INCOME FD.	GI	241	15.3 24	7.2 16	-6.2 63	2.3 75
UNITED BOND FUND	BP	335	9.4 62	-0.1 80	0.7 37	4.5 28
UNITED GOLD & GOVERNMENT	ME	9	18.1 11	-5.1 97	14.2 3	10.3 1
UNITED GOV SECURITIES FD	BP	147	10.0 57	-0.1 80	3.2 21	3.0 63
UNITED HIGH INCOME FUND	BP	1,229	6.4 81	3.6 42	0.9 36	3.2 60
UNITED INCOME FUND	G	792	21.9 4	1.9 58	-7.4 67	6.4 9
UNITED INTL. GROWTH FUND	IN	205	16.8 16	3.0 48	3.3 20	3.6 50
UNITED MUNICIPAL BOND FD	MB	402	11.3 50	-0.6 85	5.6 6	4.4 31
UNITED MUNI HIGH INCOME	MB	28	na --	2.2 54	4.7 12	3.5 51
UNITED NEW CONCEPTS FUND	G	60	18.6 10	8.7 9	-15.1 93	5.1 19
UNITED RETIREMENT SHARES	B	94	14.0 34	3.8 40	-7.6 68	4.1 37
UNITED SCIENCE & ENERGY	G	173	14.9 27	3.9 39	-9.9 79	9.8 1
UNITED VANGUARD FUND	GI	494	17.5 13	1.8 59	-6.7 64	5.5 15
U.S. GOV GUARANTEED SECS	BP	189	3.8 91	0.9 70	3.1 21	4.1 37
U.S. TREND FUND, INC.	G	79	15.1 25	0.8 71	-9.5 77	4.2 36
US GOVT HIGH YIELD TRUST	BP	2,308	3.1 94	-1.4 92	2.2 26	1.9 81
US GOLD SHARES FUND	ME	307	17.0 16	-18.8 99	45.8 1	-0.6 94
US GOOD AND BAD TIMES FD	G	21	15.0 27	4.3 35	-14.1 90	5.7 13
US GROWTH FUND	AG	7	14.3 32	8.5 10	-14.5 91	4.4 31
US INCOME FUND	GI	3	0.4 98	2.7 52	1.2 35	-3.5 97
US LOCAP FUND	AG	2	9.8 59	4.7 32	-17.1 96	-2.3 96
US NEW PROSPECTOR FUND	ME	46	6.4 81	-4.0 97	30.2 2	6.4 9
US PROSPECTOR FUND	ME	72	3.6 91	-7.0 98	28.3 2	5.9 12
USAA MUTUAL FD GROWTH	G	174	16.1 19	6.0 22	-13.8 90	3.6 51
USAA MUTUAL FD INCOME	BP	213	5.5 85	0.0 79	3.4 19	3.4 56
USAA SUNBELT ERA FUND	AG	118	15.1 25	9.8 7	-17.5 97	1.2 86
USAA TAX EX HIGH YIELD	MB	779	8.0 70	-0.9 88	5.0 9	4.1 38

TEN YEARS OF ANNUAL RETURNS

1986 PCNT RK	1985 PCNT RK	1984 PCNT RK	1983 PCNT RK	1982 PCNT RK	1981 PCNT RK	1980 PCNT RK	1979 PCNT RK	1978 PCNT RK	1977 PCNT RK
10.2 76	27.7 33	1.8 55	na --	na --	na --	na --	na --	na --	na --
17.9 29	30.3 23	4.6 47	34.0 7	19.3 75	6.2 23	20.8 63	28.1 33	21.5 9	na --
23.0 10	30.5 22	na --	na --	na --	na --	na --	na --	na --	na --
10.6 74	19.1 76	na --	na --	na --	na --	na --	na --	na --	na --
4.2 92	29.8 25	na --	na --	na --	na --	na --	na --	na --	na --
51.7 2	54.2 2	-14.4 90	32.9 7	-15.3 99	-14.5 95	49.3 10	15.5 67	25.6 5	5.9 27
49.9 2	40.3 5	-0.3 61	na --	na --	na --	na --	na --	na --	na --
15.5 45	20.5 68	-2.9 69	29.1 11	24.9 58	6.9 20	na --	na --	na --	na --
12.4 63	31.2 20	-7.2 79	28.4 13	45.3 6	8.8 13	43.2 15	27.6 35	20.0 13	6.4 25
28.3 6	55.3 2	-14.3 90	na --	na --	na --	na --	na --	na --	na --
19.4 21	33.9 13	-10.2 85	24.4 23	9.3 92	-5.5 71	70.7 4	74.2 2	47.2 1	13.8 12
20.7 16	33.8 13	-7.6 80	30.0 10	42.4 9	1.4 44	46.8 12	47.5 8	37.6 1	26.5 3
10.3 76	26.2 41	-18.9 94	26.9 16	29.7 40	na --	na --	na --	na --	na --
11.4 69	12.9 92	12.3 14	7.0 91	na --	na --	na --	na --	na --	na --
26.5 8	22.5 56	-16.3 92	na --	na --	na --	na --	na --	na --	na --
12.6 62	16.2 86	13.5 10	4.8 96	na --	na --	na --	na --	na --	na --
12.3 65	20.7 66	3.4 50	23.7 26	na --	na --	na --	na --	na --	na --
13.5 57	26.0 41	7.6 35	11.3 72	28.2 46	na --	na --	na --	na --	na --
9.8 77	20.5 68	-0.8 62	17.9 46	na --	na --	na --	na --	na --	na --
17.8 30	na --	na --	na --	na --	na --	na --	na --	na --	na --
19.5 20	na --	na --	na --	na --	na --	na --	na --	na --	na --
11.6 68	30.8 21	8.4 31	21.7 31	17.6 78	-7.0 78	22.9 58	22.4 49	6.6 54	-3.7 76
17.5 32	25.6 43	7.0 37	25.9 20	29.9 39	-1.1 56	34.7 30	17.7 62	9.8 38	-2.9 72
18.5 26	33.8 13	13.8 9	24.7 23	31.1 33	0.6 48	20.8 64	11.8 74	1.4 82	1.6 51
15.1 48	25.2 45	12.3 13	11.2 73	37.2 15	3.3 36	-0.8 91	-3.5 99	0.5 88	4.0 37
41.3 3	na --	na --	na --	na --	na --	na --	na --	na --	na --
16.9 36	23.5 51	na --	na --	na --	na --	na --	na --	na --	na --
14.7 50	23.2 52	9.7 25	13.9 63	32.7 28	4.2 31	8.1 79	na --	na --	na --
22.3 11	33.9 13	6.1 42	31.6 8	31.2 33	2.7 38	15.7 72	8.8 78	2.9 72	-0.6 61
28.8 6	38.5 6	-2.7 68	28.4 13	23.4 62	10.3 9	31.6 37	19.7 57	9.3 41	-4.8 82
21.8 13	24.0 49	9.9 23	8.5 86	35.7 19	-10.4 87	-16.4 99	-2.7 97	-6.3 98	6.6 24
na --	na --	na --	na --	na --	na --	na --	na --	na --	na --
15.1 48	26.0 41	-6.7 78	na --	na --	na --	na --	na --	na --	na --
13.8 55	24.2 48	4.2 48	13.1 66	34.9 21	3.8 34	20.9 63	16.7 65	-5.3 97	3.2 41
18.1 28	23.1 53	-1.4 65	18.5 43	24.1 60	-10.8 88	42.0 16	21.4 53	17.8 17	-2.8 71
17.7 30	23.0 53	-3.1 69	20.9 33	44.4 7	6.9 20	59.3 6	34.4 21	14.9 23	2.1 48
12.4 64	na --	na --	na --	na --	na --	na --	na --	na --	na --
9.4 80	22.7 55	-5.6 76	22.5 29	16.7 79	-0.7 53	32.8 34	47.5 9	23.1 8	17.4 8
5.9 89	na --	na --	na --	na --	na --	na --	na --	na --	na --
37.5 4	-27.0 99	-29.7 98	0.9 98	70.5 1	-27.7 99	78.7 1	184.1 1	2.5 74	48.4 1
8.9 81	22.5 56	2.7 53	11.1 73	23.4 62	na --	na --	na --	na --	na --
10.7 74	20.0 71	-26.4 97	na --	na --	na --	na --	na --	na --	na --
0.6 94	15.3 88	3.9 49	na --	na --	na --	na --	na --	na --	na --
-6.8 97	na --	na --	na --	na --	na --	na --	na --	na --	na --
41.5 3	na --	na --	na --	na --	na --	na --	na --	na --	na --
30.9 5	0.0 98	-36.8 99	na --	na --	na --	na --	na --	na --	na --
9.8 77	19.9 71	-7.5 80	15.8 53	20.7 71	-8.1 82	44.0 14	22.4 50	4.8 64	-5.5 84
12.6 62	20.6 67	13.9 9	4.5 96	36.6 16	9.1 11	4.7 83	2.5 86	-1.0 92	4.0 37
5.6 89	23.0 53	-18.1 94	23.9 25	na --	na --	na --	na --	na --	na --
17.0 35	19.7 73	10.4 21	11.4 71	na --	na --	na --	na --	na --	na --

CDA ANNUAL SUPPLEMENT - 12/31/86

FUND	IO	ASSETS (MIL$) 9/86	1st PCNT RK	2nd PCNT RK	3rd PCNT RK	4th PCNT RK
USAA TAX EX INTERMEDIATE	MB	284	6.5 80	-0.3 82	4.1 16	2.6 69
USAA TAX EX SH-TERM FD	MB	211	3.5 92	1.1 66	2.1 28	2.1 78
VALLEY FORGE FUND	GI	10	2.3 97	0.1 78	1.1 36	1.9 80
VALUE LINE FUND	AG	203	19.4 8	8.2 11	-15.9 94	7.4 5
VALUE LINE INCOME	B	154	13.6 37	5.1 28	-6.9 66	3.8 46
VALUE LINE LEVER. GROWTH	G	239	20.1 7	10.2 6	-13.2 88	7.3 5
VALUE LINE SPECIAL SIT.	AG	194	16.3 19	6.2 21	-19.7 98	6.0 11
VALUE LINE US GOV SECS	BP	117	3.6 92	0.8 71	3.1 22	2.9 65
VAN KAMPEN MERRITT-GOV	BP	3,538	5.1 86	0.4 74	3.6 19	4.1 38
VANCE, SANDERS SPECIAL	G	83	8.3 69	0.8 70	-12.9 87	-0.7 94
VANGUARD CONVERTIBLE SEC	GI	40	na --	na --	-3.7 54	3.1 63
VANGUARD FIXED INC HIYLD	BP	1,158	7.0 77	3.0 49	2.2 27	3.2 60
VANGUARD FIXED INC INVT	BP	517	5.9 83	0.8 70	2.2 27	4.8 23
VANGUARD FIXED INC GNMA	BP	1,853	3.6 91	0.2 76	3.7 18	3.8 45
VANGUARD FI SECS-SH TERM	BP	315	4.4 89	1.9 57	2.4 25	2.3 74
VANGUARD INDEX TRUST	GI	474	13.9 35	5.8 24	-7.1 67	5.7 14
VANGUARD CALIF INS TX FR	MB	46	na --	na --	4.7 12	4.8 22
VANGUARD PENNA INS TX FR	MB	84	na --	na --	4.1 16	4.2 33
VANGUARD MUNI HIGH YIELD	MB	782	9.8 59	-0.5 84	4.9 11	4.5 27
VANGUARD MUNI INSURED LT	MB	728	10.1 57	-0.8 87	4.5 14	4.0 39
VANGUARD MUNI INTERM-TRM	MB	833	7.4 74	-0.3 81	4.9 10	3.4 55
VANGUARD MUNI LONG-TERM	MB	627	9.7 60	-0.6 85	4.8 12	4.6 27
VANGUARD MUNI SHORT-TERM	MB	940	2.7 96	1.4 63	1.6 32	1.5 83
VANGUARD SPEC PORT-ENRGY	G	14	-8.2 99	7.8 13	6.1 5	7.2 6
VANGUARD SPEC PORT-GOLD	ME	54	20.0 7	-11.9 99	32.2 1	7.0 6
VANGUARD SPC PORT-HEALTH	AG	43	17.6 13	8.0 12	-6.5 64	2.3 74
VANGUARD SPEC-SVC ECON	G	49	18.9 9	7.4 15	-13.9 90	2.6 70
VANGUARD SPEC PORT-TECH	AG	13	10.5 55	1.0 68	-9.6 78	4.8 23
VANGUARD STAR FUND	B	416	9.7 60	2.2 54	-2.2 47	3.7 48
VANGUARD WORLD-INTL GR	IN	411	23.2 3	10.2 7	6.8 4	8.0 4
VANGUARD WORLD-US GR	G	167	13.5 37	2.9 49	-9.7 78	2.0 79
VENTURE INCOME PLUS	BP	62	-1.9 99	5.7 24	-5.3 59	2.9 66
VENTURE MUNI PLUS	MB	27	9.0 65	-1.1 90	0.9 37	3.3 56
WALL STREET FUND	AG	9	15.6 22	4.2 36	-12.3 86	5.2 19
WASHINGTON AREA GROWTH	G	17	18.3 10	3.9 39	-8.9 75	4.4 31
WASH. MUTUAL INVESTORS	GI	1,568	15.7 21	4.8 31	-4.4 56	5.7 13
WEALTH MONITORS FUND	G	5	na --	na --	na --	-6.9 99
WEINGARTEN EQUITY FUND	AG	160	20.3 6	13.8 3	-14.1 90	5.8 12
WELLESLEY INCOME FUND	B	399	9.1 65	2.7 51	1.2 35	4.3 32
WELLINGTON FUND	B	1,025	11.4 49	4.2 36	-2.5 48	4.3 31
WESTERGAARD FUND INC.	AG	15	14.8 28	4.6 33	-22.2 99	-0.7 94
WINDSOR FUND	GI	4,839	14.5 31	3.2 46	-0.9 43	2.6 70
WINDSOR II	GI	730	17.5 14	3.4 43	-4.9 58	5.1 20
WORLD OF TECHNOLOGY FUND	IN	8	12.8 41	5.5 25	-8.9 75	7.4 5
WORLD TRENDS	IN	58	18.1 11	5.6 25	10.2 4	2.3 75
WPG FUND	G	39	16.3 19	3.9 39	-11.8 85	4.5 28
YES FUND	BP	168	2.7 97	0.4 74	1.6 32	3.6 50

TEN YEARS OF ANNUAL RETURNS

1986		1985		1984		1983		1982		1981		1980		1979		1978		1977	
PCNT	RK	PCNT	RK	PCNT	RK	PCNT	RK	PCNT	RK	PCNT	RK	PCNT	RK	PCNT	RK	PCNT	RK	PCNT	RK
13.4	58	16.3	86	8.8	29	9.6	81	na	--	na	--	na	--	na	--	na	--	na	--
9.1	80	9.5	95	7.6	35	6.3	92	na	--	na	--	na	--	na	--	na	--	na	--
5.5	89	10.5	95	6.7	39	17.9	46	28.7	43	12.4	7	31.9	36	26.1	40	13.6	26	8.6	18
16.8	37	34.6	11	-14.7	90	-1.3	98	28.5	45	1.5	44	41.7	17	43.9	11	19.3	15	9.5	17
15.4	46	23.7	50	2.9	52	6.7	91	29.8	39	16.2	4	26.8	48	27.6	35	11.1	34	1.8	50
23.3	10	27.1	35	-9.1	83	7.9	87	28.6	44	15.9	5	30.8	38	26.2	40	27.6	4	51.3	1
5.1	90	21.1	64	-25.5	97	19.5	39	23.1	63	-2.3	60	54.3	8	43.5	12	21.2	11	12.4	14
10.7	74	21.2	63	13.7	9	6.0	93	na	--	na	--	na	--	na	--	na	--	na	--
13.8	55	22.3	57	na	--	na	--	na	--	na	--	na	--	na	--	na	--	na	--
-5.5	97	15.2	89	-14.8	91	19.3	39	16.3	79	4.7	29	36.2	27	39.7	16	23.2	8	19.8	7
na	--	na	--	na	--	na	--	na	--	na	--	na	--	na	--	na	--	na	--
16.1	41	21.9	59	7.5	35	15.7	53	28.2	46	8.2	15	3.4	85	na	--	na	--	na	--
14.3	52	22.1	58	14.6	6	6.7	91	29.1	41	9.0	12	4.5	83	0.3	91	1.9	78	5.0	32
11.8	66	20.7	67	14.0	8	9.7	80	31.5	31	na	--	na	--	na	--	na	--	na	--
11.4	69	14.9	89	14.2	8	9.1	83	na	--	na	--	na	--	na	--	na	--	na	--
18.2	27	31.2	20	6.2	41	21.3	32	21.0	70	-5.3	70	31.6	37	18.2	60	6.0	57	-7.8	94
na	--	na	--	na	--	na	--	na	--	na	--	na	--	na	--	na	--	na	--
na	--	na	--	na	--	na	--	na	--	na	--	na	--	na	--	na	--	na	--
19.7	20	21.7	61	9.7	25	10.4	76	35.9	18	-8.8	84	-11.4	95	na	--	na	--	na	--
18.6	25	19.4	75	na	--	na	--	na	--	na	--	na	--	na	--	na	--	na	--
16.2	40	17.4	82	9.5	26	6.5	92	31.1	33	-7.4	80	-10.3	95	-1.6	95	-4.5	96	na	--
19.4	21	20.8	66	8.5	31	9.5	81	38.5	14	-11.2	90	-16.0	98	-3.0	98	-6.7	99	na	--
7.4	86	7.0	96	6.8	38	5.1	95	10.1	91	8.3	14	5.3	82	4.8	83	1.9	78	na	--
12.5	63	14.4	90	na	--	na	--	na	--	na	--	na	--	na	--	na	--	na	--
49.5	2	-5.1	98	na	--	na	--	na	--	na	--	na	--	na	--	na	--	na	--
21.5	14	45.7	3	na	--	na	--	na	--	na	--	na	--	na	--	na	--	na	--
12.8	60	43.6	3	na	--	na	--	na	--	na	--	na	--	na	--	na	--	na	--
5.7	89	14.0	91	na	--	na	--	na	--	na	--	na	--	na	--	na	--	na	--
13.8	55	na	--	na	--	na	--	na	--	na	--	na	--	na	--	na	--	na	--
56.6	1	56.9	2	-1.1	64	43.1	2	5.4	95	na	--	na	--	na	--	na	--	na	--
7.6	85	36.5	8	1.2	57	24.2	24	19.8	74	-0.5	53	33.7	32	18.1	61	16.2	19	1.2	53
1.1	94	28.2	31	7.9	34	18.8	42	na	--	na	--	na	--	na	--	na	--	na	--
12.3	64	na	--	na	--	na	--	na	--	na	--	na	--	na	--	na	--	na	--
11.1	71	28.2	31	-2.3	67	13.9	63	15.8	81	-7.6	80	21.0	63	21.6	52	6.7	54	-4.3	79
16.9	36	na	--	na	--	na	--	na	--	na	--	na	--	na	--	na	--	na	--
22.5	11	32.1	17	8.3	32	26.2	19	34.7	21	6.3	23	24.0	56	14.4	70	8.0	47	-3.9	77
na	--	na	--	na	--	na	--	na	--	na	--	na	--	na	--	na	--	na	--
24.4	9	36.1	9	-6.1	77	28.9	12	30.2	37	-12.6	92	66.1	4	50.9	7	27.0	4	18.7	8
18.4	26	27.4	35	16.6	3	18.6	43	23.3	62	8.6	13	11.9	77	6.3	82	3.5	69	4.3	36
18.2	27	28.5	30	10.8	19	23.4	26	24.5	59	2.8	38	22.5	59	13.7	72	5.4	62	-4.4	80
-7.2	97	11.8	94	-13.9	90	na	--	na	--	na	--	na	--	na	--	na	--	na	--
20.2	18	28.0	32	19.5	2	30.1	10	21.8	67	16.8	4	22.5	59	22.6	49	8.9	42	1.1	53
21.4	14	na	--	na	--	na	--	na	--	na	--	na	--	na	--	na	--	na	--
16.5	39	16.5	85	-17.2	93	na	--	na	--	na	--	na	--	na	--	na	--	na	--
40.6	3	na	--	na	--	na	--	na	--	na	--	na	--	na	--	na	--	na	--
11.5	69	30.2	23	-1.6	66	18.4	43	30.6	36	-5.6	71	30.1	41	na	--	na	--	na	--
8.5	82	7.2	96	8.8	29	na	--	na	--	na	--	na	--	na	--	na	--	na	--

CDA ANNUAL SUPPLEMENT – 12/31/86

		ASSETS (MIL$) 9/86	1986 QUARTERLY RETURNS							
			1st		2nd		3rd		4th	
FUND	IO		PCNT	RK	PCNT	RK	PCNT	RK	PCNT	RK
SUMMARY BY INVESTMENT OBJECTIVE										
32 INTERNATIONAL	IN	9,271	20.1	13	8.2	19	5.2	21	5.8	25
115 AGGRESSIVE GROWTH	AG	13,500	14.2	34	6.5	29	-13.4	86	3.0	51
236 GROWTH	G	62,547	14.4	33	4.8	37	-8.5	71	3.3	48
135 GROWTH & INCOME	GI	57,333	11.9	46	4.0	42	-4.6	57	3.5	49
120 MUNICIPAL BOND	MB	57,394	8.7	66	-0.7	85	4.6	13	3.8	44
183 BOND & PREFERRED	BP	138,076	5.9	81	1.3	65	1.7	30	3.0	60
58 BALANCED	B	17,523	10.9	52	3.3	46	-2.0	47	3.4	50
18 METALS	ME	2,197	10.1	54	-8.6	96	28.5	2	2.0	58
897 TOTAL FUNDS		357,834	11.4	50	3.2	50	-3.1	50	3.4	50
STANDARD & POOR 500			14.1		5.9		-7.0		5.6	
SALOMON BROS. CORP. BOND			10.8		0.7		1.9		5.0	
U.S. TREASURY BILLS			1.6		1.5		1.3		1.3	
CONSUMER PRICES			-0.4		0.6		0.7		0.3	

TEN YEARS OF ANNUAL RETURNS

1986		1985		1984		1983		1982		1981		1980		1979		1978		1977	
PCNT	RK	PCNT	RK	PCNT	RK	PCNT	RK	PCNT	RK	PCNT	RK	PCNT	RK	PCNT	RK	PCNT	RK	PCNT	RK
45.2	7	42.1	20	-4.7	70	29.3	18	7.0	87	0.8	48	41.6	31	24.8	47	15.1	28	0.1	57
8.6	63	25.6	42	-14.4	86	19.0	46	27.1	48	-5.0	65	46.9	22	39.3	22	16.8	27	6.3	40
13.2	54	27.7	37	-1.9	63	21.3	38	23.5	57	-2.0	57	33.6	36	29.9	35	13.2	34	2.7	54
14.8	48	25.6	44	5.6	41	20.3	39	24.4	56	1.5	46	27.7	47	23.8	48	7.6	52	-0.4	60
17.1	35	18.9	73	8.5	30	10.6	77	34.9	27	-6.3	73	-12.1	96	-1.2	94	-4.2	95	7.5	21
12.4	62	20.0	68	10.8	21	10.9	74	30.6	36	5.7	27	2.9	86	2.5	88	1.4	81	4.0	38
16.0	41	24.7	47	9.9	26	18.1	50	26.4	50	4.7	34	18.8	65	16.0	64	3.7	68	1.4	51
31.6	13	-7.6	98	-27.9	97	1.7	95	48.1	17	-22.6	98	66.8	5	176.1	1	8.1	47	39.5	1
14.9	50	24.3	50	1.2	50	17.8	50	26.2	50	-0.3	50	25.8	50	24.0	50	8.9	50	3.0	50
18.6		31.7		6.2		22.5		21.6		-5.0		32.5		18.5		6.5		-7.4	
19.3		30.1		16.9		6.3		42.5		-1.2		-2.7		-4.2		-0.1		1.7	
5.8		7.3		9.8		8.9		10.9		14.2		11.4		10.0		7.1		5.2	
1.1		3.8		4.0		3.8		3.9		8.9		12.4		13.3		9.0		6.8	

Directory

CDA MUTUAL FUND DIRECTORY – 12/31/86

FUND/MGMNT	STREET	CITY/STATE	ZIP	PHONE

AIM - AIM MANAGEMENT CO

FUND/MGMNT	STREET	CITY/STATE	ZIP	PHONE
CHARTER FUND	11 GREENWAY PLAZA, #1919	HOUSTON, TX	77046	800-231-0803
CONSTELLATION GROWTH	11 GREENWAY PLAZA, #1919	HOUSTON, TX	77046	800-231-0803
CONVERTIBLE YIELD	11 GREENWAY PLAZA, #1919	HOUSTON, TX	77046	800-231-0803
GREENWAY FUND	11 GREENWAY PLAZA, #1919	HOUSTON, TX	77046	800-231-0803
HIGH YIELD SECURITIES	11 GREENWAY PLAZA, #1919	HOUSTON, TX	77046	800-231-0803
SUMMIT INVESTOR FD INC.	11 GREENWAY PLAZA, #1919	HOUSTON, TX	77046	800-231-0803
WEINGARTEN EQUITY FUND	11 GREENWAY PLAZA, #1919	HOUSTON, TX	77046	800-231-0803

ALEX - ALEX BROWN

FUND/MGMNT	STREET	CITY/STATE	ZIP	PHONE
TELEPHONE INCOME SHARES	P.O. BOX 515	BALTIMORE, MD	21203	301-727-1700

ALLIAN - ALLIANCE CAPITAL MANAGEMENT

FUND/MGMNT	STREET	CITY/STATE	ZIP	PHONE
ALLIANCE CONVERTIBLE	140 BROADWAY, 42ND FL.	NEW YORK, NY	10005	215-565-3131
ALLIANCE COUNTERPOINT	140 BROADWAY, 42ND FL.	NEW YORK, NY	10005	215-565-3131
ALLIANCE HIGH GRADE BOND	140 BROADWAY, 42ND FL.	NEW YORK, NY	10005	212-969-9000
ALLIANCE HIGH YIELD BOND	140 BROADWAY, 42ND FL.	NEW YORK, NY	10005	212-969-9000
ALLIANCE INTERNATIONAL	140 BROADWAY, 42ND FL.	NEW YORK, NY	10005	212-969-9000
ALLIANCE MORTGAGE SECS	140 BROADWAY, 42ND FL.	NEW YORK, NY	10005	212-969-9000
ALLIANCE TECHNOLOGY	140 BROADWAY, 42ND FL.	NEW YORK, NY	10005	212-969-9000
CHEMICAL FUND	140 BROADWAY, 42ND FL.	NEW YORK, NY	10005	212-902-4000
QUASAR ASSOCIATES	140 BROADWAY, 40TH FL.	NEW YORK, NY	10005	800-221-5672
SURVEYOR FUND	140 BROADWAY, 42ND FL.	NEW YORK, NY	10005	212-902-4000

AM-CAP - AMERICAN CAPITAL COMPANIES

FUND/MGMNT	STREET	CITY/STATE	ZIP	PHONE
AMERICAN CAPITAL CORP BD	P.O. BOX 3528	HOUSTON, TX	77253	713-993-0500
AMERICAN CAP COMSTOCK	P.O. BOX 3528	HOUSTON, TX	77253	713-993-0500
AMERICAN CAP ENTERPRISE	P.O. BOX 3528	HOUSTON, TX	77253	713-993-0500
AMERICAN CAP GOV SECS	P.O. BOX 3528	HOUSTON, TX	77253	713-993-0500
AMERICAN CAPITAL GROWTH	P.O. BOX 3528	HOUSTON, TX	77253	713-993-0500
AMERICAN CAPITAL HARBOR	P.O. BOX 3528	HOUSTON, TX	77253	713-993-0500
AMERICAN CAPTL HIYLD INV	P.O. BOX 3528	HOUSTON, TX	77253	713-993-0500
AMERICAN CAPITAL PACE FD	P.O. BOX 3528	HOUSTON, TX	77253	713-993-0500
AMERICAN CAPITAL OTC SEC	P.O. BOX 3528	HOUSTON, TX	77253	713-993-0500
AMERICAN CAPITAL VENTURE	P.O. BOX 3528	HOUSTON, TX	77253	713-993-0500
AMERICAN CAPITAL MUNI BD	P.O. BOX 3528	HOUSTON, TX	77253	713-993-0500
FUND OF AMERICA	P.O. BOX 3528	HOUSTON, TX	77253	713-529-0600
PROVIDENT FD. FOR INCOME	P.O. BOX 3528	HOUSTON, TX	77253	713-529-0600

AM-INV - AMERICAN INVESTORS CORP

FUND/MGMNT	STREET	CITY/STATE	ZIP	PHONE
AMERICAN INVESTORS FUND	P.O. BOX 2500	GREENWICH, CT	06836	203-531-5000
AMERICAN INVS INCOME	P.O. BOX 2500	GREENWICH, CT	06830	203-531-5000

AMA - AMA ADVISORS INC

FUND/MGMNT	STREET	CITY/STATE	ZIP	PHONE
AMA GROWTH FUND, INC.	P.O. BOX 1111	BLUE BELL, PA	19422	215-825-0400
AMA INCOME FUND, INC.	P.O. BOX 1111	BLUE BELL, PA	19422	215-825-0400
MEDICAL TECHNOLOGY FUND	P.O. BOX 1111	BLUE BELL, PA	19422	215-836-0400

AMERIN - AMERICAN INVESTMENT MGMT

FUND/MGMNT	STREET	CITY/STATE	ZIP	PHONE
DIVIDEND/GROWTH FD., INC	107 NORTH ADAMS STREET	ROCKVILLE, MD	20850	301-251-1002

FUND/MGMNT	STREET	CITY/STATE	ZIP	PHONE

AMEV - AMEV ADVISORS

AMEV CAPITAL FUND, INC.	P.O. BOX 64284	ST. PAUL, MN	55164	612-738-4276
AMEV GROWTH FUND, INC.	P.O. BOX 64284	ST. PAUL, MN	55164	612-738-4276
AMEV SPECIAL FUND, INC.	P.O. BOX 64284	ST. PAUL, MN	55164	612-738-4276
AMEV US GOV SECURITIES	P.O. BOX 64284	ST. PAUL, MN	55164	612-738-4276

AMFDA - AMERICAN FUND ADVISORS

NATL AVIATION & TECH	50 BROAD STREET	NEW YORK, NY	10004	212-482-8100
NATL TELECOMMUNICATIONS	50 BROAD STREET	NEW YORK, NY	10104	212-482-8100

AMPORT - AMERICAN PORTFOLIOS INC

VAN KAMPEN MERRITT-GOV	1001 WARRENVILLE RD.	LISLE, IL	60532	800-225-2222

AMWAY - AMWAY MANAGEMENT CO.

AMWAY MUTUAL FUND	7575 EAST FULTON ROAD	ADA, MI	49355	616-676-6000

ANALYT - ANALYTIC INVESTMENT MGMT.

ANALYTIC OPTIONED EQUITY	2222 MARTIN ST., #230	IRVINE, CA	92715	714-833-0294

BARTCO - BARTLETT COMPANY

BARTLETT BASIC VALUE FD	120 EAST 4TH STREET	CINCINNATI, OH	45202	513-621-4612

BEACON - BEACON HILL MANAGEMENT, INC.

BEACON HILL MUTUAL FUND	75 FEDERAL ST.	BOSTON, MA	02110	617-482-0795

BENHAM - BENHAM MANAGEMENT

BENHAM CALIF TF-INTERMED	755 PAGE MILL ROAD	PALO ALTO, CA	94304	800-227-8380
BENHAM CALIF TF-LONG TRM	755 PAGE MILL ROAD	PALO ALTO, CA	94304	800-227-8380
BENHAM GNMA INCOME FUND	755 PAGE MILL ROAD	PALO ALTO, CA	94304	800-227-8380
CAPITAL PRESERVATION TNT	755 PAGE MILL ROAD	PALO ALTO, CA	94304	800-227-8380

BERGER - BERGER ASSOCIATES

ONE HUNDRED FUND	899 LOGAN ST.	DENVER, CO	80203	303-837-1020
ONE HUNDRED ONE FUND	899 LOGAN ST.	DENVER, CO	80203	303-837-1020

BOSADV - BOSTON COMPANY ADV.

BOSTON CO. CAP. APPREC.	53 STATE STREET-9TH FL	BOSTON, MA	02109	800-343-6324
BOSTON CO. MANAGED INC.	53 STATE STREET-9TH FL	BOSTON, MA	02109	800-343-6324
BOSTON CO. SPEC GROWTH	53 STATE STREET-9TH FL	BOSTON, MA	02109	800-343-6324

BRNHRD - ARNOLD BERNHARD & CO.,INC.

VALUE LINE FUND	711 THIRD AVENUE	NEW YORK, NY	10017	212-687-3965
VALUE LINE INCOME	711 THIRD AVENUE	NEW YORK, NY	10017	212-687-3965
VALUE LINE LEVER. GROWTH	711 THIRD AVENUE	NEW YORK, NY	10017	212-687-3965
VALUE LINE SPECIAL SIT.	711 THIRD AVENUE	NEW YORK, NY	10017	212-687-3965
VALUE LINE US GOV SECS	711 THIRD AVENUE	NEW YORK, NY	10017	212-687-3965

CDA MUTUAL FUND DIRECTORY – 12/31/86

FUND/MGMNT	STREET	CITY/STATE	ZIP	PHONE
BRUCE - BRUCE & CO. INC.				
BRUCE FUND	20 NORTH WACKER DR.	CHICAGO, IL	60606	312-236-9160
BULLBR - BULL & BEAR GROUP, INC.				
BULL & BEAR CAP GROWTH	11 HANOVER SQUARE	NEW YORK, NY	10005	212-785-0900
BULL & BEAR EQUITY INC.	11 HANOVER SQUARE	NEW YORK, NY	10005	212-785-0900
BULL & BEAR HIGH YIELD	11 HANOVER SQUARE	NEW YORK, NY	10005	212-785-0900
BULOCK - CALVIN BULLOCK & CO				
BULLOCK AGGRES GROWTH SH	40 RECTOR ST., 16TH FLOOR	NEW YORK, NY	10006	212-513-4200
BULLOCK BALANCED SHARES	40 RECTOR ST., 16TH FLOOR	NEW YORK, NY	10006	212-513-4200
BULLOCK DIVIDEND SHARES	40 RECTOR ST., 16TH FLOOR	NEW YORK, NY	10006	212-513-4200
BULLOCK GROWTH SHARES	40 RECTOR ST., 16TH FLOOR	NEW YORK, NY	10006	212-513-4200
BULLOCK HIGH INCOME SHS	40 RECTOR ST., 16TH FLOOR	NEW YORK, NY	10006	212-513-4200
BULLOCK MONTHLY INC SHS	40 RECTOR ST., 16TH FLOOR	NEW YORK, NY	10006	212-513-4473
BULLOCK TAX-FREE SHARES	40 RECTOR ST., 16TH FLOOR	NEW YORK, NY	10006	212-513-4200
CANADIAN FUND	40 RECTOR ST., 16TH FLOOR	NEW YORK, NY	10006	212-513-4200
CALVER - CALVERT GROUP				
CALVERT EQUITY	4550 MONTGOMERY AVE-#1000	BETHESDA, MD	20814	301-951-4800
CALVERT INCOME	4550 MONTGOMERY AVE-#1000	BETHESDA, MD	20814	301-951-4800
CALVERT MANAGED GROWTH	4550 MONTGOMERY AVE-#1000	BETHESDA, MD	20814	301-951-4800
WASHINGTON AREA GROWTH	4550 MONTGOMERY AVE-#1000	BETHESDA, MD	20814	301-951-4800
CAPRES - CAPITAL RESEARCH & MANAGEMENT				
AMCAP FUND	333 S. HOPE ST.	LOS ANGELES, CA	90071	213-486-9200
AMERICAN BALANCED FUND	333 S. HOPE ST.	LOS ANGELES, CA	90071	213-486-9200
AMERICAN MUTUAL FUND	333 S. HOPE ST.	LOS ANGELES, CA	90071	213-486-9200
BOND FUND OF AMERICA	333 S. HOPE ST.	LOS ANGELES, CA	90071	213-486-9200
EUROPACIFIC GROWTH FUND	333 S. HOPE ST.	LOS ANGELES, CA	90071	213-486-9200
FUNDAMENTAL INVESTORS	333 S. HOPE ST.	LOS ANGELES, CA	90071	213-486-9200
GROWTH FUND OF AMERICA	333 S. HOPE ST.	LOS ANGELES, CA	90071	213-486-9200
INCOME FUND OF AMERICA	333 S. HOPE ST.	LOS ANGELES, CA	90071	213-486-9200
INVEST. CO. OF AMERICA	333 S. HOPE ST.	LOS ANGELES, CA	90071	213-486-9200
NEW ECONOMY FUND	333 S. HOPE ST.	LOS ANGELES, CA	90071	213-486-9200
NEW PERSPECTIVE FUND	333 S. HOPE ST.	LOS ANGELES, CA	90071	213-486-9200
TAX EXEMPT BD FD/AMERICA	333 S. HOPE ST.	LOS ANGELES, CA	90071	213-486-9200
U.S. GOV GUARANTEED SECS	333 S. HOPE ST.	LOS ANGELES, CA	90071	213-486-9200
WASH. MUTUAL INVESTORS	333 S. HOPE ST.	LOS ANGELES, CA	90071	213-486-9200
CARCAP - CARNEGIE CAPPIELLO MGMT.				
CARNEGIE CAPPIELLO GROW	1313 EUCLID AVENUE	CLEVELAND, OH	44115	216-781-4440
CARLIL - CARLISLE-ASHER MANAGEMENT CO.				
AFUTURE FUND	FRONT & LEMON ST	MEDIA, PA	19063	215-565-3131
CENSHS - CENTURY SHARES TRUST				
CENTURY SHARES TRUST	ONE LIBERTY SQUARE	BOSTON, MA	02109	617-482-3060
CIGNA - CIGNA INVESTMENT MANAGERS				
CIGNA AGGRESSIVE GROWTH	P.O. BOX 550	HARTFORD, CT	06152	203-726-6000

FUND/MGMNT	STREET	CITY/STATE	ZIP	PHONE

CONTINUATION - CIGNA INVESTMENT MANAGERS

CIGNA GROWTH FUND	P.O. BOX 550	HARTFORD, CT	06152	203-726-6000
CIGNA HIGH YIELD	P.O. BOX 550	HARTFORD, CT	06152	203-726-6000
CIGNA INCOME FUND	P.O. BOX 550	HARTFORD, CT	06152	203-726-6000
CIGNA MUNICIPAL BOND FD	P.O. BOX 550	HARTFORD, CT	06152	203-726-6000
CIGNA VALUE FUND	P.O. BOX 550	HARTFORD, CT	06152	203-726-6000
COMPANION FUND	CONNECTICUT GEN LIFE INS	HARTFORD, CT	06152	203-725-2127

CLMBIA - COLUMBIA MANAGEMENT CO.

COLUMBIA FIXED INCOME FD	P.O. BOX 1350	PORTLAND, OR	97207	503-222-3601
COLUMBIA GROWTH FUND	P.O. BOX 1350	PORTLAND, OR	97207	503-222-3601
COLUMBIA MUNICIPAL BOND	P.O. BOX 1350	PORTLAND, OR	97207	503-222-3601
COLUMBIA SPECIAL FUND	P.O. BOX 1350	PORTLAND, OR	97207	503-222-3601

COLE - COLE,AYER,MCCULLY & LIGHT INC.

NATIONAL INDUSTRIES FUND	2130 S. DAHLIA ST.	DENVER, CO	80222	303-759-2400
SIERRA GROWTH FUND	1880 CENTURY PARK EAST	LOS ANGELES, CA	90067	213-277-1450

COLONL - COLONIAL MANAGEMENT ASSOCIATES

COLONIAL ADV STRAT GOLD	ONE FINANCIAL CENTER	BOSTON, MA	02111	617-426-3750
COLONIAL EQUITY INC TR	ONE FINANCIAL CENTER	BOSTON, MA	02111	617-426-3750
COLONIAL GOV MORTGAGE	ONE FINANCIAL CENTER	BOSTON, MA	02111	617-426-3750
COLONIAL FUND	ONE FINANCIAL CENTER	BOSTON, MA	02111	617-426-3750
COLONIAL CORP CASH I	ONE FINANCIAL CENTER	BOSTON, MA	02111	617-426-3750
COLONIAL CORP CASH II	ONE FINANCIAL CENTER	BOSTON, MA	02111	617-426-3750
COLONIAL GOV SEC PLUS TR	ONE FINANCIAL CENTER	BOSTON, MA	02111	617-426-3750
COLONIAL GROWTH SHARES	ONE FINANCIAL CENTER	BOSTON, MA	02111	617-426-3750
COLONIAL INCOME	ONE FINANCIAL CENTER	BOSTON, MA	02111	617-426-3750
COLONIAL OPTION INC I	ONE FINANCIAL CENTER	BOSTON, MA	02111	617-426-3750
COLONIAL OPTION INC II	ONE FINANCIAL CENTER	BOSTON, MA	02111	617-426-3750
COLONIAL HIGH YIELD SECS	ONE FINANCIAL CENTER	BOSTON, MA	02111	617-426-3750
COLONIAL TAX EXEMPT HIYD	ONE FINANCIAL CENTER	BOSTON, MA	02111	617-426-3750
COLONIAL TAX EX INSURED	ONE FINANCIAL CENTER	BOSTON, MA	02111	617-426-3750

COMCAP - COMMONWEALTH CAPITAL MGMT

BOWSER GROWTH FUND	P.O. BOX 8687	RICHMOND, VA	23226	800-527-9500
NEWPORT FAR EAST	P.O. BOX 8687	RICHMOND, VA	23226	800-527-9500
NICHOLSON GROWTH FUND	P.O. BOX 8687	RICHMOND, VA	23226	800-527-9500

COMPOS - COMPOSITE RESEARCH & MGT

COMPOSITE BOND & STOCK	9TH FL,SEAFIRST FIN CNTR	SPOKANE, WA	99201	509-624-4101
COMPOSITE FUND	9TH FL,SEAFIRST FIN CNTR	SPOKANE, WA	99204	509-624-4101

CONCOR - CONCORD FUND INC.

CONCORD FUND	60 STATE ST.-ROOM 930	BOSTON, MA	02109	617-742-7077

CONTRY - COUNTRY CAPITAL MANAGEMENT CO.

COUNTRY CAPITAL GROWTH	1701 TOWANDA AVE.,BOX 2222	BLOOMINGTON, IL	61701	309-557-2111

COPLEY - COPLEY FINANCIAL SERVICES

COPLEY TAX-MANAGED FUND	28 STATE ST. - 38TH FL	BOSTON, NA	02107	800-336-1616

CDA MUTUAL FUND DIRECTORY - 12/31/86

FUND/MGMNT	STREET	CITY/STATE	ZIP	PHONE
CRAHAL - CRAIG-HALLUM, INC.				
GENERAL SECURITIES	133 S. 7TH ST.	MINNEAPOLIS, MN	55402	612-332-1212
CRITER - CRITERION FUNDS				
COMMERCE INCOME SHARES	333 CLAY ST., #4300	HOUSTON, TX	77002	713-751-2400
CRITERION QUAL TX FR INS	1000 LOUISIANA, #6000	HOUSTON, TX	77002	713-652-1748
INVEST. QUALITY INTEREST	333 CLAY ST., #4300	HOUSTON, TX	77002	713-751-2400
LOWRY MARKET TIMING FD	333 CLAY ST., #4300	HOUSTON, TX	77002	713-751-2400
PILOT FUND	333 CLAY ST., #4300	HOUSTON, TX	77002	713-751-2400
SUNBELT GROWTH FUND	333 CLAY ST., #4300	HOUSTON, TX	77002	713-751-2400
US GOVT HIGH YIELD TRUST	333 CLAY ST., #4300	HOUSTON, TX	77002	713-751-2400
DAYTON - DAYTON, KAHN, HEPPE, HANCOCK				
GIBRALTAR FUND, INC.	1905 ARCHITECTS BUILDING	PHILADELPHIA, PA	19103	215-988-0277
DGE&CX - DODGE & COX				
DODGE & COX BALANCED	ONE POST ST.,35TH FLOOR	SAN FRANCISCO, CA	94104	415-981-1710
DODGE & COX STOCK	ONE POST ST.,35TH FLOOR	SAN FRANCISCO, CA	94104	415-981-1710
DIMEN - DIMENSIONAL FUND ADVS.				
DFA FIXED INC PORTFOLIO	1299 OCEAN AVE, SUITE 650	SANTA MONICA, CA	90401	213-395-8005
DFA SMALL CO. PORTFOLIO	1299 OCEAN AVE, SUITE 650	SANTA MONICA, CA	90401	213-395-8005
DLAWRE - DELAWARE MANAGEMENT COMPANY				
DECATUR FUND INC-SER 1	10 PENN CENTER PLAZA	PHILADELPHIA, PA	19103	215-988-1200
DELAWARE FUND	10 PENN CENTER PLAZA	PHILADELPHIA, PA	19103	215-988-1200
DELAWARE GOV FD-USG SER	10 PENN CENTER PLAZA	PHILADELPHIA, PA	19103	215-988-1200
DELAWARE GOV FD-GNMA SER	10 PENN CENTER PLAZA	PHILADELPHIA, PA	19103	215-988-1200
DELAWARE TREAS RESERVES	10 PENN CENTER PLAZA	PHILADELPHIA, PA	19103	215-988-1200
DELCHESTER BOND FUND	10 PENN CENTER PLAZA	PHILADELPHIA, PA	19103	215-988-1200
DELTA TREND FUND	10 PENN CENTER PLAZA	PHILADELPHIA, PA	19103	215-988-1200
DMC TAX FREE-PA	10 PENN CENTER PLAZA	PHILADELPHIA, PA	19103	215-988-1200
DMC TAX FREE-USA	10 PENN CENTER PLAZA	PHILADELPHIA, PA	19103	215-988-1200
DMC TAX FREE-INSURED	10 PENN CENTER PLAZA	PHILADELPHIA, PA	19103	215-988-1200
DREXEL - DREXEL FUNDS MANAGEMENT CO.				
DREXEL BURNHAM FUND	60 BROAD ST.	NEW YORK, NY	10004	212-480-6000
DREXEL ST GOV SECURITIES	60 BROAD ST.	NEW YORK, NY	10004	212-480-6000
DREXEL ST OPTION INC FD	60 BROAD ST.	NEW YORK, NY	10004	212-480-6000
DREXEL ST EMERG GROWTH	60 BROAD ST.	NEW YORK, NY	10004	212-480-6000
DREXEL ST GROWTH	60 BROAD ST.	NEW YORK, NY	10004	212-480-6000
DRYFUS - DREYFUS CORPORATION				
DREYFUS A BONDS PLUS	ONE PENN PLAZA-37TH FL	NEW YORK, NY	10019	800-645-6561
DREYFUS CALIF TAX EXEMPT	ONE PENN PLAZA-37TH FL	NEW YORK, NY	10019	800-645-6561
DREYFUS CONVERTIBLE SECS	ONE PENN PLAZA-37TH FL	NEW YORK, NY	10019	800-645-6561
DREYFUS FUND	ONE PENN PLAZA-37TH FL	NEW YORK, NY	10019	800-645-6561
DREYFUS GNMA	ONE PENN PLAZA-37TH FL	NEW YORK, NY	10019	800-645-6561
DREYFUS GROWTH OPPORTUN.	ONE PENN PLAZA-37TH FL	NEW YORK, NY	10019	800-645-6561
DREYFUS INSURED TAX EX	ONE PENN PLAZA-37TH FL	NEW YORK, NY	10019	800-645-6561
DREYFUS INTERMDIATE MUNI	ONE PENN PLAZA-37TH FL	NEW YORK, NY	10019	800-645-6561
DREYFUS LEVERAGE	ONE PENN PLAZA-37TH FL	NEW YORK, NY	10019	800-645-6561

FUND/MGMNT	STREET	CITY/STATE	ZIP	PHONE

CONTINUATION - DREYFUS CORPORATION

DREYFUS MASS TAX EXEMPT	ONE PENN PLAZA-37TH FL	NEW YORK, NY	10019	800-645-6561
DREYFUS NY TAX EXEMPT	ONE PENN PLAZA-37TH FL	NEW YORK, NY	10019	800-645-6561
DREYFUS TAX EXEMPT BOND	ONE PENN PLAZA-37TH FL	NEW YORK, NY	10019	800-645-6561
DREYFUS THIRD CENTURY	ONE PENN PLAZA-37TH FL	NEW YORK, NY	10019	800-645-6561

DWRI - DEAN WITTER REYNOLDS INTERCAP

DEAN WITTER CALIF TX FR	1 WORLD TRADE CTR.-59TH FL	NEW YORK, NY	10048	212-902-4147
DEAN WITTER DEVELOP GROW	1 WORLD TRADE CTR.-59TH FL	NEW YORK, NY	10048	212-938-4500
DEAN WITTER DIVIDEND GRO	1 WORLD TRADE CTR.-59TH FL	NEW YORK, NY	10048	212-938-4500
DEAN WITTER HIGH YIELD	1 WORLD TRADE CTR.-59TH FL	NEW YORK, NY	10048	212-938-4500
DEAN WITTER INDUSTRY VAL	1 WORLD TRADE CTR.-59TH FL	NEW YORK, NY	10048	212-938-4500
DEAN WITTER OPTION INC	1 WORLD TRADE CTR.-59TH FL	NEW YORK, NY	10048	212-938-4500
DEAN WITTER NAT RESOURCE	1 WORLD TRADE CTR.-59TH FL	NEW YORK, NY	10048	212-938-4500
DEAN WITTER NY TX FR INC	1 WORLD TRADE CTR.-59TH FL	NEW YORK, NY	10048	212-902-4147
DEAN WITTER TX ADVANTAGE	1 WORLD TRADE CTR.-59TH FL	NEW YORK, NY	10048	212-902-4147
DEAN WITTER TAX EX SECS	1 WORLD TRADE CTR.-59TH FL	NEW YORK, NY	10048	212-902-4147
DEAN WITTER US GOV TRUST	1 WORLD TRADE CTR.-59TH FL	NEW YORK, NY	10048	212-938-4500
DEAN WITTER WORLDWIDE	1 WORLD TRADE CTR.-59TH FL	NEW YORK, NY	10048	212-938-4500

ELFUN - ELFUN TRUSTS

| ELFUN TRUSTS | P.O. BOX 7900 | STAMFORD, CT | 06904 | 203-357-4145 |

ENDOW - ENDOWMENT MANAGEMENT & RES

| OMEGA FUND | 77 FRANKLIN ST. | BOSTON, MA | 02110 | 617-357-8480 |

EQ-RE - EQUITY RESEARCH ASSOC.

| WESTERGAARD FUND INC. | 540 MADISON AVE, #805 | NEW YORK, NY | 10022 | 212-940-0218 |

ETN&HD - EATON & HOWARD,VANCE SANDERS

DEPOSITORS FUND/BOSTON	24 FEDERAL ST.-9TH FLOOR	BOSTON, MA	02110	617-482-8260
DIVERSIFICATION FUND	24 FEDERAL ST.-9TH FLOOR	BOSTON, MA	02110	617-482-8260
EATON & HOWARD STOCK	24 FEDERAL ST.-9TH FLOOR	BOSTON, MA	02110	617-482-8260
EATON VANCE GROWTH FD	24 FEDERAL ST.-9TH FLOOR	BOSTON, MA	02110	617-482-8260
EATON VANCE GOV OBLIGATN	24 FEDERAL ST.-9TH FLOOR	BOSTON, MA	02110	617-482-8260
EATON VANCE HIGH YIELD	24 FEDERAL ST.-9TH FLOOR	BOSTON, MA	02110	617-482-8260
EATON VANCE INC FD/BOST	24 FEDERAL ST.-9TH FLOOR	BOSTON, MA	02110	617-482-8260
EATON VANCE INVESTORS FD	24 FEDERAL ST.-9TH FLOOR	BOSTON, MA	02110	617-482-8260
EATON VANCE MUNICIPAL BD	24 FEDERAL ST.-9TH FLOOR	BOSTON, MA	02110	617-482-8260
EATON VANCE SPL EQUITIES	24 FEDERAL ST.-9TH FLOOR	BOSTON, MA	02110	617-482-8260
EATON VANCE TOTAL RETURN	24 FEDERAL ST.-9TH FLOOR	BOSTON, MA	02110	617-482-8260
LEVERAGE FUND OF BOSTON	24 FEDERAL ST.-9TH FLOOR	BOSTON, MA	02110	617-482-8260
NAUTILUS FUND	24 FEDERAL ST.-9TH FLOOR	BOSTON, MA	02110	617-482-8260
VANCE, SANDERS SPECIAL	24 FEDERAL ST.-9TH FLOOR	BOSTON, MA	02110	617-482-8260

EW-AXE - E.W. AXE & COMPANY,INC.

AXE-HOUGHTON INCOME	400 BENEDICT AVE.	TARRYTOWN, NY	10591	914-631-8131
AXE-HOUGHTON FUND B	400 BENEDICT AVE.	TARRYTOWN, NY	10591	914-631-8131
AXE-HOUGHTON STOCK FUND	400 BENEDICT AVE.	TARRYTOWN, NY	10591	914-631-8131

FAHNST - FAHNESTOCK MANAGEMENT CORP.

| EAGLE GROWTH SHARES | 110 WALL STREET | NEW YORK, NY | 10005 | 212-668-8000 |

CDA MUTUAL FUND DIRECTORY - 12/31/86

FUND/MGMNT	STREET	CITY/STATE	ZIP	PHONE
CONTINUATION - FAHNESTOCK MANAGEMENT CORP.				
PHILADELPHIA FUND	110 WALL STREET	NEW YORK, NY	10005	212-668-8000
FD-M&R - FUND MANAGEMENT & RESEARCH				
CONTINENTAL MUTUAL INV.	6631 E. IRONWOOD DR.	SCOTTSDALE, AZ	85253	602-991-1363
FOUNDATION GROWTH STOCK	6631 E. IRONWOOD DR.	SCOTTSDALE, AZ	85253	602-991-1363
FEDRES - FEDERATED RESEARCH CORP.				
AMERICAN LEADERS FUND	421 SEVENTH AVENUE	PITTSBURGH, PA	15219	800-245-0242
FEDERATED CORP CASH TR	421 SEVENTH AVENUE	PITTSBURGH, PA	15219	800-245-0242
FEDERATED GNMA	421 SEVENTH AVENUE	PITTSBURGH, PA	15219	800-245-0242
FEDERATED GROWTH TRUST	421 SEVENTH AVENUE	PITTSBURGH, PA	15219	800-245-0242
FEDERATED HIGH INCOME	421 SEVENTH AVENUE	PITTSBURGH, PA	15219	800-245-0242
FEDERATED HIGH YIELD TR.	421 SEVENTH AVENUE	PITTSBURGH, PA	15219	800-245-0242
FEDERATED INCOME TRUST	421 SEVENTH AVENUE	PITTSBURGH, PA	15219	800-245-0242
FEDERATED INTERM. GOV.	421 SEVENTH AVENUE	PITTSBURGH, PA	15219	800-245-0242
FEDERATED INTMED MUNI TR	421 SEVENTH AVENUE	PITTSBURGH, PA	15219	800-245-0242
FEDERATED SH-INTERM GOV	421 SEVENTH AVENUE	PITTSBURGH, PA	15219	800-245-0242
FEDERATED SH-INTERM MUNI	421 SEVENTH AVENUE	PITTSBURGH, PA	15219	800-245-0242
FEDERATED STOCK & BOND	421 SEVENTH AVENUE	PITTSBURGH, PA	15219	800-245-0242
FEDERATED STOCK TRUST	421 SEVENTH AVENUE	PITTSBURGH, PA	15219	800-245-0242
FEDERATED TAX FR INCOME	421 SEVENTH AVENUE	PITTSBURGH, PA	15219	800-245-0242
FT INTERNATIONAL	421 SEVENTH AVENUE	PITTSBURGH, PA	15219	800-245-0242
FUND FOR U.S. GOVT. SEC.	421 SEVENTH AVENUE	PITTSBURGH, PA	15219	412-288-1273
LUTHERAN BROTHER. FUND	421 SEVENTH AVENUE	PITTSBURGH, PA	15219	800-328-4552
LUTHERAN BROTHER. INCOME	625 FOURTH AVE. S.	MINNEAPOLIS, MN	55415	800-328-4552
LUTHERAN BROTHER. MUN BD	421 SEVENTH AVENUE	PITTSBURGH, PA	15219	800-328-4552
FIDEL - FIDELITY MANAGEMENT & RESEARCH				
FIDELITY AGGRESS TAX FR	82 DEVONSHIRE, 2P1	BOSTON, MA	02109	800-544-7777
FIDELITY CALIF TAX FREE	82 DEVONSHIRE, 2P1	BOSTON, MA	02109	800-544-7777
FIDELITY CONGRESS STREET	82 DEVONSHIRE, 2P1	BOSTON, MA	02109	800-544-7777
FIDELITY CONTRAFUND	82 DEVONSHIRE, 2P1	BOSTON, MA	02109	800-544-7777
FIDELITY CORP TR-ARP	82 DEVONSHIRE, 2P1	BOSTON, MA	02109	800-544-7777
FIDELITY DESTINY	82 DEVONSHIRE, 2P1	BOSTON, MA	02109	800-544-7777
FIDELITY EQUITY INCOME	82 DEVONSHIRE, 2P1	BOSTON, MA	02109	800-544-7777
FIDELITY EXCHANGE FUND	82 DEVONSHIRE, 2P1	BOSTON, MA	02109	800-544-7777
FIDELITY FLEXIBLE BOND	82 DEVONSHIRE, 2P1	BOSTON, MA	02109	800-544-7777
FIDELITY FREEDOM FUND	82 DEVONSHIRE, 2P1	BOSTON, MA	02109	800-544-7777
FIDELITY FUND	82 DEVONSHIRE, 2P1	BOSTON, MA	02109	800-544-7777
FIDELITY GOVT SECS	82 DEVONSHIRE, 2P1	BOSTON, MA	02109	800-544-7777
FIDELITY GROWTH FUND	82 DEVONSHIRE, 2P1	BOSTON, MA	02109	800-544-7777
FIDELITY GROWTH & INCOME	82 DEVONSHIRE, 2P1	BOSTON, MA	02109	800-544-7777
FIDELITY LTD TERM MUNS	82 DEVONSHIRE, 2P1	BOSTON, MA	02109	800-544-7777
FIDELITY MASS TAX FREE	82 DEVONSHIRE, 2P1	BOSTON, MA	02109	800-544-7777
FIDELITY MORTGAGE SECS	82 DEVONSHIRE, 2P1	BOSTON, MA	02109	800-544-7777
FIDELITY MUNI BOND FD	82 DEVONSHIRE, 2P1	BOSTON, MA	02109	800-544-7777
FIDELITY OVERSEAS FUND	82 DEVONSHIRE, 2P1	BOSTON, MA	02109	800-544-7777
FIDELITY SEL AMER GOLD	82 DEVONSHIRE, 2P1	BOSTON, MA	02109	800-544-7777
FIDELITY SEL BIOTECH	82 DEVONSHIRE, 2P1	BOSTON, MA	02109	800-544-7777
FIDELITY HIGH YIELD MUNI	82 DEVONSHIRE, 2P1	BOSTON, MA	02109	800-544-7777
FIDELITY HIGH INCOME FD	82 DEVONSHIRE, 2P1	BOSTON, MA	02109	800-544-7777
FIDELITY SEL CHEMICAL	82 DEVONSHIRE, 2P1	BOSTON, MA	02109	800-544-7777
FIDELITY MAGELLAN FUND	82 DEVONSHIRE, 2P1	BOSTON, MA	02109	800-544-7777
FIDELITY PURITAN FD	82 DEVONSHIRE, 2P1	BOSTON, MA	02109	800-544-7777
FIDELITY OTC PORTFOLIO	82 DEVONSHIRE, 2P1	BOSTON, MA	02109	800-544-7777

FUND/MGMNT	STREET	CITY/STATE	ZIP	PHONE

CONTINUATION - FIDELITY MANAGEMENT & RESEARCH

FUND/MGMNT	STREET	CITY/STATE	ZIP	PHONE
FIDELITY QUALIFIED DIVD	82 DEVONSHIRE, 2P1	BOSTON, MA	02109	800-544-7777
FIDELITY SEL DEF & AERO	82 DEVONSHIRE, 2P1	BOSTON, MA	02109	800-544-7777
FIDELITY SELECT ENERGY	82 DEVONSHIRE, 2P1	BOSTON, MA	02109	800-544-7777
FIDELITY SEL LEISURE ENT	82 DEVONSHIRE, 2P1	BOSTON, MA	02109	800-544-7777
FIDELITY SELECT FINL SVC	82 DEVONSHIRE, 2P1	BOSTON, MA	02109	800-544-7777
FIDELITY SELECT HEALTH	82 DEVONSHIRE, 2P1	BOSTON, MA	02109	800-544-7777
FIDELITY SEL PREC MET&MN	82 DEVONSHIRE, 2P1	BOSTON, MA	02109	800-544-7777
FIDELITY SELECT TECHNLGY	82 DEVONSHIRE, 2P1	BOSTON, MA	02109	800-544-7777
FIDELITY SEL UTILITIES	82 DEVONSHIRE, 2P1	BOSTON, MA	02109	800-544-7777
FIDELITY SPEC SITUATIONS	82 DEVONSHIRE, 2P1	BOSTON, MA	02109	800-544-7777
FIDELITY SEL BROKERAGE	82 DEVONSHIRE, 2P1	BOSTON, MA	02109	800-544-7777
FIDELITY SEL ELECTRONICS	82 DEVONSHIRE, 2P1	BOSTON, MA	02109	800-544-7777
FIDELITY SEL PROPTY/CAS	82 DEVONSHIRE, 2P1	BOSTON, MA	02109	800-544-7777
FIDELITY SEL COMPUTER	82 DEVONSHIRE, 2P1	BOSTON, MA	02109	800-544-7777
FIDELITY SEL FOOD/AGRI	82 DEVONSHIRE, 2P1	BOSTON, MA	02109	800-544-7777
FIDELITY SEL SAVINGS/LN	82 DEVONSHIRE, 2P1	BOSTON, MA	02109	800-544-7777
FIDELITY SEL SOFTWARE	82 DEVONSHIRE, 2P1	BOSTON, MA	02109	800-544-7777
FIDELITY SEL TELECOMM	82 DEVONSHIRE, 2P1	BOSTON, MA	02109	800-544-7777
FIDELITY TREND	82 DEVONSHIRE, 2P1	BOSTON, MA	02109	800-544-7777
FIDELITY THRIFT TRUST	82 DEVONSHIRE, 2P1	BOSTON, MA	02109	800-544-7777
FIDELITY VALUE FUND	82 DEVONSHIRE, 2P1	BOSTON, MA	02109	800-544-7777
FTP-EQ PORTFOLIO-GROWTH	82 DEVONSHIRE, 2P1	BOSTON, MA	02109	800-544-7777
FTP-EQ PORTFOLIO INCOME	82 DEVONSHIRE, 2P1	BOSTON, MA	02109	800-544-7777
FTP-FIXED INC. LTD PORT.	82 DEVONSHIRE, 2P1	BOSTON, MA	02109	800-544-7777

FIDMAN - FIDUCIARY MANAGEMENT

FUND/MGMNT	STREET	CITY/STATE	ZIP	PHONE
FIDUCIARY CAPITAL GROWTH	222 EAST MASON	MILWAUKEE, WI	53202	414-271-6666

FIF - FINANCIAL PROGRAMS,INC.

FUND/MGMNT	STREET	CITY/STATE	ZIP	PHONE
FINANCIAL BD-HIYLD PORT	P.O. BOX 2040	DENVER, CO	80201	303-779-1233
FINANCIAL BD-SELECT INC	P.O. BOX 2040	DENVER, CO	80201	303-779-1233
FINANCIAL DYNAMICS FUND	P.O. BOX 2040	DENVER, CO	80201	303-779-1233
FINANCIAL INDUST. FUND	P.O. BOX 2040	DENVER, CO	80201	303-779-1233
FINANCIAL INDUST. INCOME	P.O. BOX 2040	DENVER, CO	80201	303-779-1233
FINANCIAL TAX FR INC SHS	P.O. BOX 2040	DENVER, CO	80201	303-779-1233
WORLD OF TECHNOLOGY FUND	P.O. BOX 2040	DENVER, CO	80201	303-779-1233

FLAGSP - FLAGSHIP FUNDS

FUND/MGMNT	STREET	CITY/STATE	ZIP	PHONE
FLAGSHIP CORPORATE CASH	1ST NATIONAL PLAZA	DAYTON, OH	45402	513-461-0332
FLAGSHIP MICHIGAN DBL TX	1ST NATIONAL PLAZA	DAYTON, OH	45402	513-461-0332
FLAGSHIP OHIO DOUBLE TAX	1ST NATIONAL PLAZA	DAYTON, OH	45402	513-461-0332

FLDNG - FIELDING MANAGEMENT CO.

FUND/MGMNT	STREET	CITY/STATE	ZIP	PHONE
ROCHESTER TAX MANAGED FD	183 EAST MAIN ST., STE 942	ROCHESTER, NY	14604	716-442-5500

FNDRS - FOUNDERS MUTUAL DEPOSITORS

FUND/MGMNT	STREET	CITY/STATE	ZIP	PHONE
FOUNDERS EQUITY INCOME	3033 E. 1ST AVE, STE 810	DENVER, CO	80206	800-525-2440
FOUNDERS GROWTH FUND	3033 E. 1ST AVE, STE 810	DENVER, CO	80206	800-525-2440
FOUNDERS MUTUAL FUND	3033 E. 1ST AVE, STE 810	DENVER, CO	80206	303-623-1567
FOUNDERS SPECIAL FUND	3033 E. 1ST AVE, STE 810	DENVER, CO	80206	800-525-2440

CDA MUTUAL FUND DIRECTORY - 12/31/86

FUND/MGMNT	STREET	CITY/STATE	ZIP	PHONE
FRNKRE - FRANKLIN RESEARCH,INC.				
AGE HIGH INCOME FUND	777 MARINER'S ISLAND BLVD.	SAN MATEO, CA	94404	415-570-3000
FRANKLIN CALIF TAX FREE	777 MARINER'S ISLAND BLVD.	SAN MATEO, CA	94404	415-570-3000
FRANKLIN CORP CASH TR	777 MARINER'S ISLAND BLVD.	SAN MATEO, CA	94404	415-570-3000
FRANKLIN DYNATECH	777 MARINER'S ISLAND BLVD.	SAN MATEO, CA	94404	415-570-3000
FRANKLIN EQUITY FUND	777 MARINER'S ISLAND BLVD.	SAN MATEO, CA	94404	415-570-3000
FRANKLIN FEDERAL TAX FR	777 MARINER'S ISLAND BLVD.	SAN MATEO, CA	94404	415-570-3000
FRANKLIN GOLD FUND	777 MARINER'S ISLAND BLVD.	SAN MATEO, CA	94404	415-570-3000
FRANKLIN GROWTH	777 MARINER'S ISLAND BLVD.	SAN MATEO, CA	94404	415-570-3000
FRANKLIN INCOME	777 MARINER'S ISLAND BLVD.	SAN MATEO, CA	94404	415-570-3000
FRANKLIN NEW YORK TAX FR	777 MARINER'S ISLAND BLVD.	SAN MATEO, CA	94404	415-570-3000
FRANKLIN OPTION FUND	777 MARINER'S ISLAND BLVD.	SAN MATEO, CA	94404	415-570-3000
FRANKLIN U.S. GOVT. SEC.	777 MARINER'S ISLAND BLVD.	SAN MATEO, CA	94404	415-570-3000
FRANKLIN UTILITIES	777 MARINER'S ISLAND BLVD.	SAN MATEO, CA	94404	415-570-3000
FSTINV - FIRST INVESTORS MANAGEMENT CO.				
FIRST INVEST. BND APPREC	10 WOODBRIDGE CTR. DR.	WOODBRIDGE, NJ	07095	201-855-2500
FIRST INVEST. DISCOVERY	10 WOODBRIDGE CTR. DR.	WOODBRIDGE, NJ	07095	201-855-2500
FIRST INVEST. FD. GROWTH	10 WOODBRIDGE CTR. DR.	WOODBRIDGE, NJ	07095	201-855-2500
FIRST INVEST. FD. INCOME	10 WOODBRIDGE CTR. DR.	WOODBRIDGE, NJ	07095	201-855-2500
FIRST INVEST. GOV FUND	10 WOODBRIDGE CTR. DR.	WOODBRIDGE, NJ	07095	201-855-2500
FIRST INVEST. INTL SECS.	10 WOODBRIDGE CTR. DR.	WOODBRIDGE, NJ	07095	201-855-2500
FIRST INVEST. NATURL RES	10 WOODBRIDGE CTR. DR.	WOODBRIDGE, NJ	07095	201-855-2500
FIRST INVEST. NY TAX FR	10 WOODBRIDGE CTR. DR.	WOODBRIDGE, NJ	07095	201-855-2500
FIRST INVEST. NINETY-TEN	10 WOODBRIDGE CTR. DR.	WOODBRIDGE, NJ	07095	201-855-2500
FIRST INVEST. OPTION	10 WOODBRIDGE CTR. DR.	WOODBRIDGE, NJ	07095	201-855-2500
FIRST INVEST. TAX EXEMPT	10 WOODBRIDGE CTR. DR.	WOODBRIDGE, NJ	07095	201-855-2500
FSTPAC - FIRST PACIFIC ADVISORS				
FPA CAPITAL FUND	10301 WEST PICO BLVD.	LOS ANGELES, CA	90064	213-277-4900
FPA NEW INCOME	10301 WEST PICO BLVD.	LOS ANGELES, CA	90064	213-277-4900
FPA PARAMOUNT FD INC	10301 WEST PICO BLVD.	LOS ANGELES, CA	90064	213-277-4900
FPA PERENNIAL FUND	10301 WEST PICO BLVD.	LOS ANGELES, CA	90064	213-277-4900
FTY-FR - FORTY-FOUR MANAGEMENT CO.				
FORTY-FOUR WALL ST EQTY	ONE STATE STREET PLAZA	NEW YORK, NY	10004	212-344-4224
FORTY-FOUR WALL ST FUND	ONE STATE STREET PLAZA	NEW YORK, NY	10004	212-344-4224
FURMAN - ROBERT M. FURMAN				
RAINBOW FUND	19 RECTOR STREET, RM 1319	NEW YORK, NY	10006	212-509-8600
FURSEL - FURMAN SELZ MAGER DIETZ				
FUNDTRUST AGGRESSIVE	230 PARK AVENUE	NEW YORK, NY	10169	212-309-8400
FUNDTRUST GROWTH	230 PARK AVENUE	NEW YORK, NY	10169	212-309-8400
FUNDTRUST GROWTH & INC	230 PARK AVENUE	NEW YORK, NY	10169	212-309-8400
FUNDTRUST INCOME	230 PARK AVENUE	NEW YORK, NY	10169	212-309-8400
GABCO - GABELLI & COMPANY				
GABELLI ASSET FUND	655 3RD AVENUE	NEW YORK, NY	10017	212-490-3670
GATEWY - GATEWAY INVESTMENT ADVS.				
GATEWAY GROWTH PLUS FUND	P.O. BOX 458167	CINCINNATI, OH	45245	513-248-2700

FUND/MGMNT	STREET	CITY/STATE	ZIP	PHONE

CONTINUATION - GATEWAY INVESTMENT ADVS.

| GATEWAY OPTION INCOME | P.O. BOX 458167 | CINCINNATI, OH | 45245 | 513-248-2700 |

GENELC - GENERAL ELEC INVESTMENT CORP

| GENERAL ELEC S&S LT BOND | P.O. BOX 7900 | STAMFORD, CT | 06904 | 203-357-4145 |
| GENL ELEC S&S PROGRAM | P.O. BOX 7900 | STAMFORD, CT | 06904 | 203-357-4145 |

GINTEL - GINTEL EQUITY MGMT.

GINTEL CAP APPRECIATION	GREENWICH OFFICE PARK-#6	GREENWICH, CT	06830	203-622-6402
GINTEL ERISA	GREENWICH OFFICE PARK-#6	GREENWICH, CT	06830	203-622-6402
GINTEL FUND	GREENWICH OFFICE PARK-#6	GREENWICH, CT	06830	203-622-6402

GOLCON - GOLCONDA MANAGEMENT CORP

| GOLCONDA INVESTORS | 11 HANOVER SQUARE | NEW YORK, NY | 10005 | 212-785-0900 |

GRADSN - GRADISON & COMPANY INC

| GRADISON ESTABLISHED GR. | 580 BLDG.-6TH & WALNUT | CINCINNATI, OH | 45202 | 800-543-1818 |
| GRADISON OPPORTUNITY GR | 580 BLDG.-6TH & WALNUT | CINCINNATI, OH | 45202 | 513-579-5000 |

GTCAP - G T CAPITAL CORP

| G. T. PACIFIC GROWTH FD | 601 MONTGOMERY STREET | SAN FRANCISCO, CA | 94111 | 415-392-6181 |

GUARD - GUARDIAN INVT SERVICES CORP.

| GUARDIAN PARK AVE FUND | 201 PARK AVENUE SOUTH | NEW YORK, NY | 10003 | 212-598-8259 |

H&W - HOTCHKIS & WILEY

| OLYMPIC TRUST SERIES B | 800 WEST SIXTH ST., #540 | LOS ANGELES, CA | 90017 | 213-623-7833 |
| OLYMPIC TRUST TOT RETURN | 800 WEST SIXTH ST., #540 | LOS ANGELES, CA | 90017 | 213-623-7833 |

HANCOK - JOHN HANCOCK ADVISERS,INC.

HANCOCK (JOHN) BOND	101 HUNTINGTON AVE.-6TH FL	BOSTON, MA	02199	617-421-6000
HANCOCK (JOHN) GLOBAL	101 HUNTGINGTON AVE.-6TH F L	BOSTON, MA	02199	617-421-6379
HANCOCK (JOHN) GNMA	101 HUNTINGTON AVE.-6TH FL	BOSTON, MA	02199	617-421-6000
HANCOCK (JOHN) GROWTH	101 HUNTINGTON AVE.-6TH FL	BOSTON, MA	02199	617-421-6379
HANCOCK (JOHN) SPECIAL	101 HUNTINGTON AVE.-6TH FL	BOSTON, MA	02199	617-421-6379
HANCOCK (JOHN) TX EX DIV	101 HUNTINGTON AVE.-6TH FL	BOSTON, MA	02199	617-421-6379
HANCOCK (JOHN) US GOV	101 HUNTINGTON AVE.-6TH FL	BOSTON, MA	02199	617-421-6379

HARRIS - HARRIS GROUP,INC.

| ACORN FUND | 120 S. LASALLE STREET | CHICAGO, IL | 60603 | 312-621-0630 |

HARTWL - HARTWELL MANAGEMENT CO.

| HARTWELL GROWTH FUND | 515 MADISON AVENUE | NEW YORK, NY | 10022 | 212-308-3355 |
| HARTWELL LEVERAGE FUND | 515 MADISON AVENUE | NEW YORK, NY | 10022 | 212-308-3355 |

HEINE - HEINE MANAGEMENT GROUP

| LMH FUND, LTD. | 253 POST ROAD WEST, PO 830 | WESTPORT, CT | 06881 | 203-226-4768 |

CDA MUTUAL FUND DIRECTORY - 12/31/86

FUND/MGMNT	STREET	CITY/STATE	ZIP	PHONE
HERTGE - HERITAGE MANAGEMENT CO.				
AMERICAN HERITAGE FUND	115 BROADWAY #1100	NEW YORK, NY	10006	212-952-2052
INDUSTRY FUND OF AMERICA	115 BROADWAY #1100	NEW YORK, NY	10006	212-952-2052
HGM - HINGHAM MGT/GRANTHAM MAYO				
IVY INSTITUTIONAL INV FD	40 INDUSTRIAL PARK ROAD	HINGHAM, MA	02043	617-749-1416
HMI - HINGHAM MANAGEMENT INC				
IVY GROWTH FUND	40 INDUSTRIAL PARK ROAD	HINGHAM, MA	02043	617-749-1416
HOPPER - HOPPER SOLIDAY & CO				
SOVEREIGN INVESTORS	985 OLD EAGLE SCHOOL RD	WAYNE, PA	19087	215-251-0705
HSC - HEINE SECURITY CORP.				
MUTUAL BEACON GROWTH FD	26 BROADWAY	NEW YORK, NY	10004	212-908-4000
MUTUAL QUALIFIED INCOME	26 BROADWAY	NEW YORK, NY	10004	212-908-4000
MUTUAL SHARES CORP.	26 BROADWAY	NEW YORK, NY	10004	212-908-4000
HTC - HAWAIIAN TRUST COMPANY				
HAWAIIAN TAX-FREE TRUST	200 PARK AVE, SUITE 4515	NEW YORK, NY	10017	212-697-6666
HUTTON - E. F. HUTTON				
HUTTON CAL MUNICIPAL FD	71 BROADWAY-10TH FLOOR	NEW YORK, NY	10006	212-742-5000
HUTTON INV SER BASIC VAL	71 BROADWAY-10TH FLOOR	NEW YORK, NY	10006	212-742-5000
HUTTON INV SER BOND/INC	71 BROADWAY-10TH FLOOR	NEW YORK, NY	10006	212-742-5000
HUTTON INV SER SPL EQTY	71 BROADWAY-10TH FLOOR	NEW YORK, NY	10006	212-742-5000
HUTTON INV SERIES GROWTH	71 BROADWAY-10TH FLOOR	NEW YORK, NY	10006	212-742-5000
HUTTON INV SER GOV SECS	71 BROADWAY-10TH FLOOR	NEW YORK, NY	10006	212-742-5000
HUTTON INV SER PRE METAL	71 BROADWAY-10TH FLOOR	NEW YORK, NY	10006	212-742-5000
HUTTON NATL MUNICIPAL FD	71 BROADWAY-10TH FLOOR	NEW YORK, NY	10006	212-742-5000
HUTTON N.Y. MUNICIPAL FD	71 BROADWAY-10TH FLOOR	NEW YORK, NY	10006	212-742-5000
HUTTON OPTION INCOME	71 BROADWAY-10TH FL	NEW YORK, NY	10006	212-742-5000
IDS - INVESTORS DIVERSIFIED SERVICES				
IDS BOND FUND	BOX 534	MINNEAPOLIS, MN	55402	612-372-3131
IDS DISCOVERY FUND	BOX 534	MINNEAPOLIS, MN	55402	612-372-3131
IDS EQUITY PLUS FD INC.	BOX 534	MINNEAPOLIS, MN	55402	612-372-3353
IDS EXTRA INCOME	BOX 534	MINNEAPOLIS, MN	55402	612-372-3131
IDS GROWTH FUND	BOX 534	MINNEAPOLIS, MN	55402	612-372-3131
IDS MUTUAL FUND	BOX 534	MINNEAPOLIS, MN	55402	612-372-3353
IDS NEW DIMENSIONS FUND	BOX 534	MINNEAPOLIS, MN	55402	612-372-3131
IDS PROGRESSIVE FUND	BOX 534	MINNEAPOLIS, MN	55402	612-372-3353
IDS SELECTIVE	BOX 534	MINNEAPOLIS, MN	55402	612-372-3353
IDS STOCK FUND	BOX 534	MINNEAPOLIS, MN	55402	612-372-3353
INA - INA CAPITAL MANAGEMENT SVCS				
HORACE MANN GROWTH FUND	1 HORACE MANN PLAZA	SPRINGFIELD, IL	62715	217-789-2500
INTEGR - INTEGRATED RES ASSET MGMT.				
HOME INVS GOV GTD INCOME	666 3RD AVENUE	NEW YORK, NY	10017	212-551-5313

FUND/MGMNT	STREET	CITY/STATE	ZIP	PHONE

CONTINUATION - INTEGRATED RES ASSET MGMT.

INTEGRATED CAPTL APPREC	666 3RD AVENUE	NEW YORK, NY	10017	212-551-5313
INTEGRATED INSD TAX FREE	666 3RD AVENUE	NEW YORK, NY	10017	212-551-5313

INV-RE - INVESTORS RESEARCH CO.

INVESTORS RESEARCH	1900 STATE STREET	SANTA BARBARA, CA	93101	805-569-1011

INVADV - INVESTMENT ADVISERS INC.

NORTH STAR APOLLO FUND	1100 DAIN TOWER-PO BOX 357	MINNEAPOLIS, MN	55440	612-371-7780
NORTH STAR BOND	1100 DAIN TOWER-PO BOX 357	MINNEAPOLIS, MN	55440	612-371-7780
NORTH STAR REGIONAL FUND	1100 DAIN TOWER-PO BOX 357	MINNEAPOLIS, MN	55440	612-371-7780
NORTH STAR STOCK FUND	1100 DAIN TOWER-PO BOX 357	MINNEAPOLIS, MN	55440	612-371-7780

INVRES - INVESTORS RESEARCH CORP.

TWENTIETH CENTURY GIFTR	605 W. 47TH ST.	KANSAS CITY, MO	64112	816-531-5575
TWENTIETH CENTURY GROWTH	605 W. 47TH ST.	KANSAS CITY, MO	64112	816-531-5575
TWENTIETH CENTURY SELECT	605 W. 47TH ST.	KANSAS CITY, MO	64112	816-531-5575
TWENTIETH CENTURY ULTRA	605 W. 47TH ST.	KANSAS CITY, MO	64112	816-531-5575
TWENTIETH CENTURY US GOV	605 W. 47TH ST.	KANSAS CITY, MO	64112	816-531-5575
TWENTIETH CENTURY VISTA	605 W. 47TH ST.	KANSAS CITY, MO	64112	816-531-5575

INVSEC - INVESTORS SECURITY CO., INC.

OLD DOMINION INVTS TR	P.O.BOX 546	SUFFOLK, VA	23434	804-539-2396

INVSMT - INVESTMENT RESEARCH CORP.

AMERICAN GROWTH FUND	650 17TH ST.,SUITE 800	DENVER, CO	80202	303-623-6137

IRI - IRI ASSET MANAGEMENT CO.

IRI STOCK FUND	ONE APPLETREE SQUARE	MINNEAPOLIS, MN	55420	800-328-1010

JANUS - JANUS MANAGEMENT CORP.

JANUS FUND	100 FILLMORE ST, SUITE 300	DENVER, CO	80206	303-333-3863
JANUS VALUE FUND	100 FILLMORE ST, SUITE 300	DENVER, CO	80206	303-333-3863
JANUS VENTURE FUND	100 FILLMORE ST, SUITE 300	DENVER, CO	80206	303-333-3863

JL - JOHNSTON LEMON & CO

GROWTH FD OF WASHINGTON	1101 VERMONT AVENUE	WASH., DC	20005	202-842-5300

JONES - JONES & BABSON, INC.

BABSON GROWTH FUND	2440 PERSHING ROAD	KANSAS CITY, MO	64108	816-471-5200
BABSON BOND TRUST	2440 PERSHING ROAD	KANSAS CITY, MO	64108	816-471-5200
BABSON ENTERPRISE FUND	2440 PERSHING ROAD	KANSAS CITY, MO	64108	816-471-5200
BABSON VALUE FD INC.	2440 PERSHING ROAD	KANSAS CITY, MO	64108	816-471-5200
UMB BOND FUND	2440 PERSHING ROAD	KANSAS CITY, MO	64108	816-471-5200
UMB STOCK FUND	2440 PERSHING ROAD	KANSAS CITY, MO	64108	816-471-5200

JP-INV - JP INVESTMENT MANAGEMENT CO.

JP GROWTH FUND	P.O. BOX 20407	GREENSBORO, NC	27420	919-378-2451
JP INCOME	P.O. BOX 20407	GREENSBORO, NC	27420	919-378-2451

CDA MUTUAL FUND DIRECTORY - 12/31/86

FUND/MGMNT	STREET	CITY/STATE	ZIP	PHONE

KEMPER - KEMPER FINANCIAL SERVICES

FUND/MGMNT	STREET	CITY/STATE	ZIP	PHONE
INVEST. PORTFOLIOS-EQ	120 S. LASALLE ST.	CHICAGO, IL	60603	312-781-1121
INVEST. PORTFOLIOS-GOV +	120 S. LASALLE ST.	CHICAGO, IL	60603	312-781-1121
INVEST. PORTFOLIOS-HIYLD	120 S. LASALLE ST.	CHICAGO, IL	60603	312-781-1121
INVEST. PORTFOLIOS-OP IN	120 S. LASALLE ST.	CHICAGO, IL	60603	312-781-1121
KEMPER CALIF TAX FREE	120 S. LASALLE ST.	CHICAGO, IL	60603	312-781-1121
KEMPER GROWTH FUND	120 S. LASALLE ST.	CHICAGO, IL	60603	312-781-1121
KEMPER HIGH YIELD FD	120 S. LASALLE ST.	CHICAGO, IL	60603	312-781-1121
KEMPER INC & CAP PRESERV	120 S. LASALLE ST.	CHICAGO, IL	60603	312-781-1121
KEMPER INTL FD	120 S. LASALLE ST.	CHICAGO, IL	60603	312-781-1121
KEMPER MUNI BOND FD LTD	120 S. LASALLE ST.	CHICAGO, IL	60603	312-781-1121
KEMPER OPTION INCOME FD	120 S. LASALLE ST.	CHICAGO, IL	60603	312-781-1121
KEMPER SUMMIT FUND	120 S. LASALLE ST.	CHICAGO, IL	60603	312-781-1121
KEMPER TOTAL RETURN FD	120 S. LASALLE ST.	CHICAGO, IL	60603	312-781-1121
KEMPER US GOVT SECS	120 S. LASALLE ST.	CHICAGO, IL	60603	312-781-1121
TECHNOLOGY FUND	120 S. LASALLE ST.	CHICAGO, IL	60603	312-781-1121

KEYSTN - KEYSTONE MASSACHUSETTS GROUP

FUND/MGMNT	STREET	CITY/STATE	ZIP	PHONE
KEYSTONE INTL FUND	99 HIGH ST.	BOSTON, MA	02110	617-338-3200
KEYSTONE B-1	99 HIGH ST.	BOSTON, MA	02110	617-338-3200
KEYSTONE B-2	99 HIGH ST.	BOSTON, MA	02110	617-338-3200
KEYSTONE B-4	99 HIGH ST.	BOSTON, MA	02110	617-338-3200
KEYSTONE K-1	99 HIGH ST.	BOSTON, MA	02110	617-338-3200
KEYSTONE K-2	99 HIGH ST.	BOSTON, MA	02110	617-338-3200
KEYSTONE PRECIOUS METALS	99 HIGH ST.	BOSTON, MA	02110	617-742-7700
KEYSTONE S-1	99 HIGH ST.	BOSTON, MA	02110	617-338-3200
KEYSTONE S-3	99 HIGH ST.	BOSTON, MA	02110	617-338-3200
KEYSTONE S-4	99 HIGH ST.	BOSTON, MA	02110	617-338-3200
KEYSTONE TAX FREE	99 HIGH ST.	BOSTON, MA	02110	617-742-7700

KLEIN - KLEINWORT BENSON INVT MGMT

FUND/MGMNT	STREET	CITY/STATE	ZIP	PHONE
TRANSATLANTIC FUND INC.	100 WALL STREET	NEW YORK, NY	10005	800-223-4130

LD-ABT - LORD,ABBETT & COMPANY

FUND/MGMNT	STREET	CITY/STATE	ZIP	PHONE
AFFILIATED FUND	63 WALL ST.	NEW YORK, NY	10005	212-425-8720
LORD ABBETT BOND-DEBEN.	63 WALL ST.	NEW YORK, NY	10005	212-425-8720
LORD ABBETT DEV GROWTH	63 WALL ST.	NEW YORK, NY	10005	212-425-8720
LORD ABBETT TX FREE NATL	63 WALL ST.	NEW YORK, NY	10005	212-425-8720
LORD ABBETT TX FREE NY	63 WALL ST.	NEW YORK, NY	10005	212-425-8720
LORD ABBETT US GOV SECS	63 WALL ST.	NEW YORK, NY	10005	212-425-8720
LORD ABBETT VALUE APPREC	63 WALL ST.	NEW YORK, NY	10005	212-425-8720

LEGG - LEGG MASON

FUND/MGMNT	STREET	CITY/STATE	ZIP	PHONE
LEGG MASON VALUE TRUST	7 EAST REDWOOD ST/PO 1476	BALTIMORE, MD	21203	301-539-3400

LEHMAN - LEHMAN MANAGEMENT CO INC.

FUND/MGMNT	STREET	CITY/STATE	ZIP	PHONE
LEHMAN CAPITAL FUND	55 WATER STREET	NEW YORK, NY	10041	212-668-4000
LEHMAN INVESTORS FD, INC	55 WATER STREET	NEW YORK, NY	10041	212-668-4000
LEHMAN OPPORTUNITY FUND	55 WATER STREET	NEW YORK, NY	10041	212-668-4000

LEPERQ - LEPERCQ,DE NEUFLIZE & CO.,INC.

FUND/MGMNT	STREET	CITY/STATE	ZIP	PHONE
LEPERCQ-ISTEL TRUST	345 PARK AVE.	NEW YORK, NY	10154	212-702-0100

FUND/MGMNT	STREET	CITY/STATE	ZIP	PHONE
LEXGTN - LEXINGTON SECURITY MANAGERS				
LEXINGTON GOLDFUND	P.O. BOX 1515	SADDLE BROOK, NJ	07662	201-845-7300
LEXINGTON GROWTH FUND	P.O. BOX 1515	SADDLE BROOK, NJ	07662	201-845-7300
LEXINGTON GNMA NEW INC	P.O. BOX 1515	SADDLE BROOK, NJ	07662	201-845-7300
LEXINGTON RESEARCH FUND	P.O. BOX 1515	SADDLE BROOK, NJ	07662	201-845-7300
LIFINV - LIFE INVESTORS MANAGEMENT CORP				
MIDAMERICA HIGH GROWTH	P.O. BOX 1447	CEDAR RAPIDS, IA	52406	319-398-8985
MIDAMERICA MUTUAL FUND	P.O. BOX 1447	CEDAR RAPIDS, IA	52406	319-398-8511
LINDNR - LINDNER MANAGEMENT CORP.				
LINDNER DIVIDEND FUND	200 S. BEMISTON	ST. LOUIS, MO	63105	314-727-5305
LINDNER FUND	200 S. BEMISTON	ST. LOUIS, MO	63105	314-727-5305
LOOMIS - LOOMIS-SAYLES & COMPANY,INC.				
LOOMIS-SAYLES CAP. DEV.	399 BOYLSTON ST.	BOSTON, MA	02117	617-267-6601
LOOMIS-SAYLES MUTUAL	399 BOYLSTON ST.	BOSTON, MA	02117	617-267-6601
NEL EQUITY FUND	399 BOYLSTON ST.	BOSTON, MA	02117	617-267-6600
NEL GROWTH FUND	399 BOYLSTON ST.	BOSTON, MA	02117	617-267-6600
NEL RETIREMENT EQUITY	399 BOYLSTON ST.	BOSTON, MA	02117	617-267-6600
M&I - M & I INVESTMENT MGMT.				
NEWTON GROWTH FUND	330 E. KILBOURNE, #1150	MILWAUKEE, WI	53202	414-347-1141
NEWTON INCOME FUND	330 E. KILBOURNE, #1150	MILWAUKEE, WI	53202	414-347-1141
M-B-F - MUTUAL BENEFIT FINANCIAL SVC				
MUTUAL BENEFIT FUND	520 BROAD ST.	NEWARK, NJ	07101	201-481-8356
MADINV - MADISON INVT. ADVISORS				
BASCOM HILL INVESTORS	402 SOUTH GAMMON PLACE	MADISON, WI	53719	608-833-6300
MASFIN - MASSACHUSETTS FINANCIAL SVCS				
MASS. CAPITAL DEVEL.	200 BERKELEY ST.	BOSTON, MA	02116	617-423-3500
MASS. FINANCIAL BOND	200 BERKELEY ST.	BOSTON, MA	02116	617-423-3500
MASS. FINANCIAL DEVEL.	200 BERKELEY ST.	BOSTON, MA	02116	617-423-3500
MASS. FINL EMERG. GWTH.	200 BERKELEY ST.	BOSTON, MA	02116	617-423-3500
MASS. FINL GOV SEC HIYLD	200 BERKELEY ST.	BOSTON, MA	02116	617-433-3500
MASS. FINL HI INCOME	200 BERKELEY ST.	BOSTON, MA	02116	617-423-3500
MASS. FINL INTL TRUST BD	200 BERKELEY ST.	BOSTON, MA	02116	617-423-3500
MASS. FINANCIAL SPECIAL	200 BERKELEY ST.	BOSTON, MA	02116	617-423-3500
MASS. FINL TOTAL RETURN	200 BERKELEY ST.	BOSTON, MA	02116	617-423-3500
MASS. FINL SECTORS FUND	200 BERKELEY ST.	BOSTON, MA	02116	617-423-3500
MASS. INV. GROWTH STOCK	200 BERKELEY ST.	BOSTON, MA	02116	617-423-3500
MASS. INV. TRUST	200 BERKELEY ST.	BOSTON, MA	02116	617-423-3500
MFS GOVT GUARANTEED	200 BERKELEY ST.	BOSTON, MA	02116	617-423-3500
MFS GOV SECURITIES HIYLD	200 BERKELEY ST.	BOSTON, MA	02116	617-423-3500
MFS MGD MUNI-BOND HIYLD	200 BERKELEY ST.	BOSTON, MA	02116	617-423-3500
MFS MGD MUNI-BD TRUST	200 BERKELEY ST.	BOSTON, MA	02116	617-423-3500
MFS MDG MULTI-ST MASS.	200 BERKELEY ST.	BOSTON, MA	02116	617-423-3500
MFS MGD MULTI-ST N.C.	200 BERKELEY ST.	BOSTON, MA	02116	617-423-3500
MFS MGD MULTI-ST VA	200 BERKELEY ST.	BOSTON, MA	02116	617-423-3500

CDA MUTUAL FUND DIRECTORY — 12/31/86

FUND/MGMNT	STREET	CITY/STATE	ZIP	PHONE
MATHRS - MATHERS AND COMPANY,INC.				
MATHERS FUND	125 S. WACKER DR.,STE 2510	CHICAGO, IL	60606	312-236-8215
MEEDER - R MEEDER & ASSOCIATES				
FLEX FD-RETIRE GR SERIES	6000 MEMORIAL DR/PO 7177	DUBLIN, OH	43017	614-766-7000
MEESCH - MEESCHAERT CAPITAL ADV.				
MEESCHAERT CAP. ACCUM.	11 PARKER STREET	NEWTON CENTRE, MA	02159	617-785-1403
MERRIL - MERRIL LYNCH-NOMURA MGT				
MERRILL L. BASIC VALUE	P.O. BOX 9011	PRINCETON, NJ	08540	609-282-2800
MERRILL L. CALIF TAX-EX	P.O. BOX 9011	PRINCETON, NJ	08540	609-282-2800
MERRILL L. CORP DIV FUND	P.O. BOX 9011	PRINCETON, NJ	08540	609-282-2800
MERRILL L. BOND-INTERMED	P.O. BOX 9011	PRINCETON, NJ	08540	609-282-2800
MERRILL L. FEDERAL SECS	P.O. BOX 9011	PRINCETON, NJ	08540	609-282-2800
MERRILL L. INTERNATIONAL	P.O. BOX 9011	PRINCETON, NJ	08540	609-282-2800
MERRILL L. CAPITAL FUND	P.O. BOX 9011	PRINCETON, NJ	08540	609-282-2800
MERRILL L. EQUI-BOND I	P.O. BOX 9011	PRINCETON, NJ	08540	609-282-2800
MERRILL L. HIGH INC BOND	P.O. BOX 9011	PRINCETON, NJ	08540	609-282-2800
MERRILL L. PACIFIC FUND	P.O. BOX 9011	PRINCETON, NJ	08540	609-282-2800
MERRILL L. PHOENIX	P.O. BOX 9011	PRINCETON, NJ	08540	609-282-2800
MERRILL L. MUNI-BD HIYLD	P.O. BOX 9011	PRINCETON, NJ	08540	609-282-2800
MERRILL L. MUNI-BD INSD	P.O. BOX 9011	PRINCETON, NJ	08540	609-282-2800
MERRILL L. MUNI-LTD MAT	P.O. BOX 9011	PRINCETON, NJ	08540	609-282-2800
MERRILL L. SPECIAL VALUE	P.O. BOX 9011	PRINCETON, NJ	08540	609-282-2800
MERRILL L. NAT RESOURCE	P.O. BOX 9011	PRINCETON, NJ	08540	609-282-2800
MERRILL L. HIGH QUAL BD	P.O. BOX 9011	PRINCETON, NJ	08540	609-282-2800
MERRILL L. NY MUNI BOND	P.O. BOX 9011	PRINCETON, NJ	08540	609-282-2800
MERRILL L. FUND FOR TOM	P.O. BOX 9011	PRINCETON, NJ	08540	609-282-2800
MERRILL L. RETIRE BEN IN	P.O. BOX 9011	PRINCETON, NJ	08540	609-282-2800
MERRILL L. RETIRE/INCOME	P.O. BOX 9011	PRINCETON, NJ	08540	609-282-2800
SCI-TECH HOLDINGS	P.O. BOX 9001	PRINCETON, NJ	08540	212-692-2939
MIDWES - MIDWEST ADVISORY SERVICES				
ABT EMERGING GROWTH	700 DIXIE TERMINAL BLDG.	CINCINNATI, OH	45202	800-543-8721
ABT GROWTH & INCOME TR.	700 DIXIE TERMINAL BLDG.	CINCINNATI, OH	45202	800-543-8721
ABT SECURITY INCOME	700 DIXIE TERMINAL BLDG.	CINCINNATI, OH	45202	800-543-8721
ABT UTILITY INCOME FD	700 DIXIE TERMINAL BLDG.	CINCINNATI, OH	45202	800-543-8721
LG US GOV SECURITIES	700 DIXIE TERMINAL BLDG.	CINCINNATI, OH	45202	800-543-8721
MIDWEST INC-INTERMED TRM	700 DIXIE TERMINAL BLDG.	CINCINNATI, OH	45202	800-543-8721
MILWCO - MILWAUKEE COMPANY				
HEARTLAND VALUE FUND	250 E. WISCONSIN AVENUE	MILWAUKEE, WI	53202	414-347-7276
MIM - MACKENZIE INVESTMENT MGMT				
MACKENZIE INDUSTRIAL AM	1665 PALM BEACH LAKES #604	PALM BEACH, FL	33401	800-222-2274
MACKENZIE INDUSTRIAL GOV	1665 PALM BEACH LAKES #604	PALM BEACH, FL	33401	800-222-2274
MACKENZIE INDUSTRIAL OPT	1665 PALM BEACH LAKES #604	PALM BEACH, FL	33401	800-222-2274
MONTAG - MONTAG & CALDWELL				
ALPHA FUND	3565 PIEDMONT ROAD	ATLANTA, GA	30305	404-262-3480

FUND/MGMNT	STREET	CITY/STATE	ZIP	PHONE

MOSELY - MOSELEY CAPITAL MGMT.

INVEST. TRUST OF BOSTON	60 STATE STREET	BOSTON, MA	02109	617-367-5900
INV TR/BOSTON HI IN PLUS	60 STATE STREET	BOSTON, MA	02109	617-367-5900
ITB MASS TAX FREE	60 STATE STREET	BOSTON, MA	02109	617-367-5900

MTREND - MONITREND INVT MGMT INC.

MONITREND VALUE FUND	6190 POWERS FERRY RD, #600	ATLANTA, GA	30339	800-251-1970

NATFIN - NATIONWIDE FINANCIAL SVCS. INC

NATIONWIDE FUND	ONE NATIONWIDE PLAZA	COLUMBUS, OH	43216	800-848-0920
NATIONWIDE GROWTH FUND	ONE NATIONWIDE PLAZA	COLUMBUS, OH	43216	800-848-0920
NATIONWIDE BOND FUND	ONE NATIONWIDE PLAZA	COLUMBUS, OH	43216	800-848-0920

NATLIF - NATIONAL LIFE INVESTMENT MGT

SENTINEL BALANCED FUND	NATIONAL LIFE DRIVE	MONTPELIER, VT	05602	802-229-3615
SENTINEL BOND	NATIONAL LIFE DRIVE	MONTPELIER, VT	05602	802-229-3615
SENTINEL COMMON STOCK FD	NATIONAL LIFE DRIVE	MONTPELIER, VT	05602	802-229-3615
SENTINEL GROWTH FUND	NATIONAL LIFE DRIVE	MONTPELIER, VT	05602	802-229-3615

NATSEC - NATIONAL SECURITIES & RESEARCH

FAIRFIELD FUND	605 THIRD AVE.	NEW YORK, NY	10158	212-661-3000
NATL FEDERAL SECURITIES	605 THIRD AVE.	NEW YORK, NY	10158	212-661-3000
NATL SECURITIES BALANCED	605 THIRD AVE.	NEW YORK, NY	10158	212-661-3000
NATL SECURITIES BOND	605 THIRD AVE.	NEW YORK, NY	10158	212-661-3000
NATL SECURITIES CAL TX E	605 THIRD AVE.	NEW YORK, NY	10158	212-661-3000
NATL SECURITIES GROWTH	605 THIRD AVE.	NEW YORK, NY	10158	212-661-3000
NATL SECURITIES PREFERED	605 THIRD AVE.	NEW YORK, NY	10158	212-661-3000
NATL SECS REAL ESTATE	605 THIRD AVE.	NEW YORK, NY	10158	212-661-3000
NATL SECURITIES STOCK	605 THIRD AVE.	NEW YORK, NY	10158	212-661-3000
NATL SECURITIES TOT INC	605 THIRD AVE.	NEW YORK, NY	10158	212-661-3000
NATL SECURITIES TOT RET	605 THIRD AVE.	NEW YORK, NY	10158	212-661-3000
NATL SECURITIES TX EX BD	605 THIRD AVE.	NEW YORK, NY	10158	212-661-3000

NEL - NEW ENGLAND LIFE INS

NEL GOVERNMENT SEC TR	399 BOYLSTON ST.	BOSTON, MA	02117	617-267-6600
NEL INCOME	399 BOYLSTON ST.	BOSTON, MA	02117	617-267-6600
NEL TAX EXEMPT	399 BOYLSTON ST.	BOSTON, MA	02117	617-267-6600

NEUBER - NEUBERGER & BERMAN MANAGEMENT

ENERGY FUND	342 MADISON AVE	NEW YORK, NY	10173	212-850-8300
GUARDIAN MUTUAL FUND	342 MADISON AVE	NEW YORK, NY	10173	212-850-8300
LIBERTY FUND	342 MADISON AVE	NEW YORK, NY	10173	212-850-8300
MANHATTAN FUND	342 MADISON AVE	NEW YORK, NY	10173	212-850-8300
PARTNERS FUND	342 MADISON AVE	NEW YORK, NY	10173	212-850-8300

NICHOL - NICHOLAS STRONG & CO.,INC.

NICHOLAS FUND	700 N. WATER, SUITE 1010	MILWAUKEE, WI	53202	414-272-6133
NICHOLAS II	700 N. WATER, SUITE 1010	MILWAUKEE, WI	53202	414-272-6133
NICHOLAS INCOME FUND	700 N. WATER, SUITE 1010	MILWAUKEE, WI	53202	414-272-6133

CDA MUTUAL FUND DIRECTORY - 12/31/86

FUND/MGMNT	STREET	CITY/STATE	ZIP	PHONE
NIT - NORTHEAST INVESTORS TRUST				
NORTHEAST INV GROWTH	50 CONGRESS ST.	BOSTON, MA	02109	617-523-3588
NORTHEAST INV. TRUST	50 CONGRESS ST.	BOSTON, MA	02109	617-523-3588
NODCAL - NODDING CALAMOS ASSET MGMT				
NODDING CALAMOS INCOME	2001 SPRING RD., #750	OAKBROOK, IL	60521	800-251-2411
NOMURA - NOMURA CAPITAL MGMT				
NOMURA PACIFIC BASIN FD	180 MAIDEN LANE,31ST FL.	NEW YORK, NY	10038	212-208-9312
NOVA - NOVA ADVISORS				
NOVA FUND INC	TWO OLIVER STREET	BOSTON, MA	02109	617-439-6126
NUVEEN - JOHN NUVEEN & CO., INC.				
NUVEEN MUNICIPAL BOND FD	333 WEST WACKER DRIVE	CHICAGO, IL	60606	312-917-7980
OHIO - OHIO COMPANY				
CARDINAL FUND	155 EAST BROAD STREET	COLUMBUS, OH	43215	614-464-6811
CARDINAL GOVERNMENT GTD	155 EAST BROAD STREET	COLUMBUS, OH	43215	614-464-6811
OMAHA - MUTUAL OF OMAHA FUND MGT				
MUTUAL OF OMAHA AMERICA	10235 REGENCY CIRCLE	OMAHA, NB	68114	402-397-8555
MUTUAL OF OMAHA GROWTH	10235 REGENCY CIRCLE	OMAHA, NB	68114	402-397-8555
MUTUAL OF OMAHA INCOME	10235 REGENCY CIRCLE	OMAHA, NB	68114	402-397-8555
OPPCAP - OPPENHEIMER CAPITAL CORP				
QUEST FOR VALUE FUND	ONE NEW YORK PLAZA	NEW YORK, NY	10004	800-221-5833
OPPEN - OPPENHEIMER MANAGEMENT CORP.				
HAMILTON FUNDS	3410 S. GALENA	DENVER, CO	80231	303-671-3579
OPPENHEIMER A.I.M. FUND	3410 S. GALENA	DENVER, CO	80231	303-671-3408
OPPENHEIMER DIRECTORS	3410 S. GALENA	DENVER, CO	80231	303-671-3408
OPPENHEIMER EQUITY INC.	3410 S. GALENA	DENVER, CO	80231	303-671-3408
OPPENHEIMER FUND	3410 S. GALENA	DENVER, CO	80231	303-671-3408
OPPENHEIMER GOLD & SPEC.	3410 S. GALENA	DENVER, CO	80231	303-671-3408
OPPENHEIMER HIGH YIELD	3410 S. GALENA	DENVER, CO	80231	303-671-3408
OPPENHEIMER PREMIUM INC	3410 S. GALENA	DENVER, CO	80231	303-671-3408
OPPENHEIMER NY TX EXEMPT	3410 S. GALENA	DENVER, CO	80231	303-671-3408
OPPENHEIMER REGENCY	3410 S. GALENA	DENVER, CO	80231	303-671-3408
OPPENHEIMER SPECIAL FUND	3410 S. GALENA	DENVER, CO	80231	303-671-3408
OPPENHEIMER SELECT STOCK	3410 S. GALENA	DENVER, CO	80231	303-671-3408
OPPENHEIMER RETR-GOV SEC	3410 S. GALENA	DENVER, CO	80231	303-671-3408
OPPENHEIMER TARGET FUND	3410 S. GALENA	DENVER, CO	80231	303-671-3408
OPPENHEIMER TAX FREE BD	3410 S. GALENA	DENVER, CO	80231	303-671-3408
OPPENHEIMER TIME FUND	3410 S. GALENA	DENVER, CO	80231	303-671-3408
PACFIN - PACIFIC FINANCIAL RESEARCH				
CLIPPER FUND, INC.	9665 WILSHIRE BLVD., #950	BEVERLY HILLS, CA	90212	213-278-4461

FUND/MGMNT	STREET	CITY/STATE	ZIP	PHONE

PAINE - PAINE WEBBER

PAINE WEBBER AMERICA FD	1285 AVE OF THE AMERICAS	NEW YORK, NY	10019	212-437-2121
PAINE WEBBER ATLAS FD	1285 AVE OF THE AMERICAS	NEW YORK, NY	10019	212-437-2121
PAINE WEBBER CALIF TX-EX	1285 AVE OF THE AMERICAS	NEW YORK, NY	10019	212-437-2121
PAINE WEBBER FI INVT GR	1285 AVE OF THE AMERICAS	NEW YORK, NY	10019	212-437-2121
PAINE WEBBER GNMA	1285 AVE OF THE AMERICAS	NEW YORK, NY	10019	212-437-2121
PAINE WEBBER HIGH YIELD	1285 AVE OF THE AMERICAS	NEW YORK, NY	10019	212-437-2121
PAINE WEBBER OLYMPUS FD	1285 AVE OF THE AMERICAS	NEW YORK, NY	10019	212-437-2121
PAINE WEBBER TAX-EX INC	1285 AVE OF THE AMERICAS	NEW YORK, NY	10019	212-437-2121

PAM - PRESCOTT ASSET MGMT. INC.

SELECTED AMERICAN SHARES	230 WEST MONROE STREET	CHICAGO, IL	60606	312-641-7862
SELECTED SPECIAL SHARES	230 WEST MONROE STREET	CHICAGO, IL	60606	312-641-7862

PAX - PAX WORLD MANAGEMENT CORP.

PAX WORLD FUND	P.O. BOX 717	PORTSMOUTH, NH	03801	603-431-8022

PENN - PENN SQUARE MANAGEMENT CORP.

PENN SQUARE MUTUAL FUND	P.O. BOX 1419	READING, PA	19603	215-670-1419

PFS - PFS MANAGEMENT SERVICES, INC.

FARM BUREAU GROWTH FUND	5400 UNIVERSITY AVE.	DES MOINES, IA	50265	515-225-5400

PIC - PHOENIX INVESTMENT COUNSEL

PHOENIX BALANCED FD SER	1 AMERICAN ROW	HARTFORD, CT	06115	800-243-1574
PHOENIX GROWTH FUND SER	1 AMERICAN ROW	HARTFORD, CT	06115	800-243-1574
PHOENIX CONVERTIBLE FUND	1 AMERICAN ROW	HARTFORD, CT	06115	800-243-1574
PHOENIX HIGH YIELD	1 AMERICAN ROW	HARTFORD, CT	06115	800-243-1574
PHOENIX STOCK FUND SER	1 AMERICAN ROW	HARTFORD, CT	06115	800-243-1574
PHOENIX TOTAL RETURN FD	1 AMERICAN ROW	HARTFORD, CT	06115	800-243-1574

PILCAP - PILGRIM CAPITAL MANAGEMENT

PILGRIM ADJUSTABLE RATE	ONE EXECUTIVE DRIVE	FORT LEE, NJ	07024	201-461-7500
PILGRIM GNMA	ONE EXECUTIVE DRIVE	FORT LEE, NJ	07024	201-461-7500
PILGRIM HIGH YIELD FD	ONE EXECUTIVE DRIVE	FORT LEE, NJ	07024	201-461-7500
PILGRIM MAGNACAP FUND	ONE EXECUTIVE DRIVE	FORT LEE, NJ	07024	201-461-7500
PILGRIM PREFERRED	ONE EXECUTIVE DRIVE	FORT LEE, NJ	07024	201-461-7500

PIMC - PRINCOR INVT. MGMT. CO.

PRINCOR CAP ACCUMULATION	711 HIGH ST.	DES MOINES, IA	50307	515-247-5711
PRINCOR GOV SECS INCOME	711 HIGH ST.	DES MOINES, IA	50307	515-247-5711
PRINCOR GROWTH FD, INC.	711 HIGH ST.	DES MOINES, IA	50307	515-247-5711

PIONER - PIONEERING MANAGEMENT CORP.

PIONEER BOND FUND	60 STATE ST.	BOSTON, MA	02109	617-742-7825
PIONEER FUND	60 STATE ST.	BOSTON, MA	02109	617-742-7825
PIONEER II	60 STATE ST.	BOSTON, MA	02109	617-742-7825
PIONEER THREE	60 STATE ST.	BOSTON, MA	02109	617-742-7825

CDA MUTUAL FUND DIRECTORY – 12/31/86

FUND/MGMNT	STREET	CITY/STATE	ZIP	PHONE
PORTFO - PORTFOLIOS, INC.				
ARMSTRONG ASSOCIATES	311 N. MARKET ST., STE 205	DALLAS, TX	75202	214-744-5558
PRICE - T. ROWE PRICE & ASSOCIATES,INC				
PRICE (ROWE) EQUITY INC	100 E. PRATT ST.	BALTIMORE, MD	21202	301-547-2000
PRICE (ROWE) GROWTH&INC.	100 E. PRATT ST.	BALTIMORE, MD	21202	301-547-2000
PRICE (ROWE) GROWTH STK.	100 E. PRATT ST.	BALTIMORE, MD	21202	301-547-2000
PRICE (ROWE) HI YLD BOND	100 E. PRATT ST.	BALTIMORE, MD	21202	301-547-2000
PRICE (ROWE) INTERNATL.	100 E. PRATT ST.	BALTIMORE, MD	21202	301-547-2000
PRICE (ROWE) NEW AMERICA	100 E. PRATT ST.	BALTIMORE, MD	21202	301-547-2000
PRICE (ROWE) NEW ERA	100 E. PRATT ST	BALTIMORE, MD	21202	301-547-2000
PRICE (ROWE) NEW HORIZ.	100 E. PRATT ST.	BALTIMORE, MD	21202	301-547-2000
PRICE (ROWE) NEW INCOME	100 E. PRATT ST.	BALTIMORE, MD	21202	301-547-2000
PRICE (ROWE) TAX FR HIYD	100 E. PRATT ST.	BALTIMORE, MD	21202	301-547-2000
PRICE (ROWE) TX FREE INC	100 E. PRATT ST.	BALTIMORE, MD	21202	301-547-2000
PRICE (ROWE) TXFR SH-INT	100 E. PRATT ST.	BALTIMORE, MD	21202	301-547-2000
PRUBAC - PRUDENTIAL BACHE				
PRU-BACHE ADJ RATE PFD	100 GOLD ST.-ROOM 5040	NEW YORK, NY	10942	212-214-1230
PRU-BACHE EQUITY FUND	100 GOLD ST.-ROOM 5040	NEW YORK, NY	10942	212-214-1230
PRU-BACHE GLOBAL FUND	100 GOLD ST.-ROOM 5040	NEW YORK, NY	10942	212-214-1230
PRU-BACHE GOV SECURITIES	100 GOLD ST.-ROOM 5040	NEW YORK, NY	10942	212-214-1230
PRU-BACHE HIGH YIELD	100 GOLD ST.-ROOM 5040	NEW YORK, NY	10942	212-214-1230
PRU-BACHE HIYLD MUNI	100 GOLD ST.-ROOM 5040	NEW YORK, NY	10942	212-214-1230
PRU-BACHE GR OPPORTUNITY	100 GOLD ST.-ROOM 5040	NEW YORK, NY	10942	212-214-1230
PRU-BACHE INCOMEVERTIBLE	100 GOLD ST.-ROOM 5040	NEW YORK, NY	10942	212-214-1230
PRU-BACHE OPTION GROWTH	100 GOLD ST.-ROOM 5040	NEW YORK, NY	10942	212-214-1230
PRU-BACHE GNMA FUND	100 GOLD ST.-ROOM 5040	NEW YORK, NY	10942	212-214-1230
PRU-BACHE RESEARCH FUND	100 GOLD ST.-ROOM 5040	NEW YORK, NY	10942	212-214-1230
PRU-BACHE UTILITY FUND	100 GOLD ST.-ROOM 5040	NEW YORK, NY	10942	212-214-1230
PUTNAM - PUTNAM MANAGEMENT COMPANY,INC.				
PUTNAM CALIF TAX EX	ONE POST OFFICE SQUARE	BOSTON, MA	02109	617-423-4960
PUTNAM CCT ARP	ONE POST OFFICE SQUARE	BOSTON, MA	02109	617-423-4960
PUTNAM CCT DSP	ONE POST OFFICE SQUARE	BOSTON, MA	02109	617-423-4960
PUTNAM CONVERT INC-GR TR	ONE POST OFFICE SQUARE	BOSTON, MA	02109	617-423-4960
PUTNAM ENERGY RESOURCES	ONE POST OFFICE SQUARE	BOSTON, MA	02109	617-423-4960
PUTNAM INFOR SCIENCES	ONE POST OFFICE SQUARE	BOSTON, MA	02109	617-423-4960
PUTNAM INTL EQUITIES	ONE POST OFFICE SQUARE	BOSTON, MA	02109	617-423-4960
PUTNAM (GEORGE) FD. BOS.	ONE POST OFFICE SQUARE	BOSTON, MA	02109	617-423-4960
PUTNAM FD FOR GROWTH/INC	ONE POST OFFICE SQUARE	BOSTON, MA	02109	617-423-4960
PUTNAM GNMA PLUS	ONE POST OFFICE SQUARE	BOSTON, MA	02109	617-423-4960
PUTNAM HEALTH SCIENCES	ONE POST OFFICE SQUARE	BOSTON, MA	02109	617-423-4960
PUTNAM HIGH INCOME GOV	ONE POST OFFICE SQUARE	BOSTON, MA	02109	617-423-4960
PUTNAM HIGH YIELD	ONE POST OFFICE SQUARE	BOSTON, MA	02109	617-423-4960
PUTNAM INCOME FUND	ONE POST OFFICE SQUARE	BOSTON, MA	02109	617-423-4960
PUTNAM INVESTORS FUND	ONE POST OFFICE SQUARE	BOSTON, MA	02109	617-423-4960
PUTNAM NY TAX EXEMPT	ONE POST OFFICE SQUARE	BOSTON, MA	02109	617-423-4960
PUTNAM VISTA FUND	ONE POST OFFICE SQUARE	BOSTON, MA	02109	617-423-4960
PUTNAM OPTION INCOME I	ONE POST OFFICE SQUARE	BOSTON, MA	02109	617-423-4960
PUTNAM OPTION INCOME II	ONE POST OFFICE SQUARE	BOSTON, MA	02109	617-423-4960
PUTNAM TAX EXEMPT INC	ONE POST OFFICE SQUARE	BOSTON, MA	02109	617-423-4960
PUTNAM US GOV SECURITIES	ONE POST OFFICE SQUARE	BOSTON, MA	02109	617-423-4960
PUTNAM VOYAGER FUND	ONE POST OFFICE SQUARE	BOSTON, MA	02109	617-423-4960

FUND/MGMNT	STREET	CITY/STATE	ZIP	PHONE
QUEST - QUEST ADVISORY CORP.				
PENNSYLVANIA MUTUAL FUND	1414 AVE OF THE AMERICAS	NEW YORK, NY	10019	212-355-7311
ROYCE VALUE FUND, INC.	1414 AVE OF THE AMERICAS	NEW YORK, NY	10019	212-355-7311
RC - RUANE CUNNIFF & CO				
SEQUOIA FUND	1370 AVENUE OF AMERICAS	NEW YORK, NY	10019	212-245-4500
REA - JAMES B REA, INC.				
REA GRAHAM FUND	1100 GLENDON AVE., #1625	LOS ANGELES, CA	90024	213-471-1917
REVIEW - REVIEW MANAGEMENT CORPORATION				
OVER-THE-COUNTER SEC.	P.O. BOX 1537	FT WASHINGTON, PA	19075	215-643-2510
RIGHT - RIGHTIME ECONOMETRICS INC				
RIGHTIME FUND	BENSON EAST OFFICE PLAZA	JENKINTOWN, PA	19046	215-572-7288
SACHS - MORTON H SACKS & CO				
FAIRMONT FUND	1346 SOUTH THIRD ST.	LOUSIVILLE, KY	40208	502-636-5633
SAFECO - SAFECO SECURITIES,INC.				
SAFECO EQUITY FUND	SAFECO PLAZA	SEATTLE, WA	98185	800-426-6730
SAFECO GROWTH FUND	SAFECO PLAZA	SEATTLE, WA	98185	800-426-6730
SAFECO INCOME FUND	SAFECO PLAZA	SEATTLE, WA	98185	206-545-5526
SAFECO MUNICIPAL BOND FD	SAFECO PLAZA	SEATTLE, WA	98185	206-545-5526
SAXON - SAXON WOODS ASSET MANAGEMENT				
EVERGREEN FUND	550 MAMARONECK AVE.	HARRISON, NY	10528	212-828-7700
EVERGREEN TOTAL RETURN	550 MAMARONECK AVE.	HARRISON, NY	10528	212-828-7700
SBSF - SPEARS BENZAK SALOMON&FARRELL				
SBSF FUND	10 ROCKEFELLER PLAZA	NEW YORK, NY	10020	212-903-1200
SCHROD - SCHRODER INCORPORATED				
CHEAPSIDE DOLLAR FD LTD	ONE STATE STREET	NEW YORK, NY	10004	212-269-6500
SCUDER - SCUDDER,STEVENS & CLARK				
SCUDDER CALIF TAX FREE	175 FEDERAL ST.	BOSTON, MA	02110	617-482-3990
SCUDDER CAPITAL GROWTH	175 FEDERAL ST.	BOSTON, MA	02110	617-482-3990
SCUDDER DEVELOPMENT FUND	175 FEDERAL ST.	BOSTON, MA	02110	617-482-3990
SCUDDER GLOBAL	175 FEDERAL ST.	BOSTON, MA	02110	617-692-2939
SCUDDER GOV MORTGAGE SEC	175 FEDERAL ST.	BOSTON, MA	02110	617-692-2939
SCUDDER GROWTH & INCOME	175 FEDERAL ST.	BOSTON, MA	02110	617-482-3990
SCUDDER INCOME FUND	175 FEDERAL ST.	BOSTON, MA	02110	617-482-3990
SCUDDER INTERNATIONAL FD	175 FEDERAL ST.	BOSTON, MA	02110	617-482-3990
SCUDDER NEW YORK TAX FR	175 FEDERAL ST.	BOSTON, MA	02110	617-482-3990
SCUDDER MANAGED MUNI BD	175 FEDERAL ST.	BOSTON, MA	02110	617-482-3990
SCUDDER TX FR TARGT 1990	175 FEDERAL ST.	BOSTON, MA	02110	617-482-3990
SCUDDER TX FR TARGT 1993	175 FEDERAL ST.	BOSTON, MA	02110	617-482-3990

CDA MUTUAL FUND DIRECTORY – 12/31/86

FUND/MGMNT	STREET	CITY/STATE	ZIP	PHONE
SD - STRATEGIC DISTRIBUTORS				
STRATEGIC CAPITAL GAINS	P.O. BOX 20066	DALLAS, TX	75220	800-527-5027
STRATEGIC INVESTMENTS	P.O. BOX 20066	DALLAS, TX	75220	800-527-5027
STRATEGIC SILVER	P.O. BOX 20066	DALLAS, TX	75220	800-527-5027
SECPAC - SECURITY PACIFIC				
PACIFIC HORIZON AGGRE GR	767 FIFTH AVENUE	NEW YORK, NY	10153	800-645-3515
PACIFIC HORIZON CAL TAX	767 FIFTH AVENUE	NEW YORK, NY	10153	800-645-3515
PACIFIC HORIZON HIYLD BD	767 FIFTH AVENUE	NEW YORK, NY	10153	800-645-3515
SECRES - SECURITIES MANAGEMENT & RES				
AMERICAN NATIONAL GROWTH	TWO MOODY PLAZA	GALVESTON, TX	77550	409-763-2767
AMERICAN NATL INC FUND	TWO MOODY PLAZA	GALVESTON, TX	77550	409-763-2767
SECRTY - SECURITY MANAGEMENT COMPANY				
SECURITY ACTION FD	700 HARRISON ST.	TOPEKA, KS	66636	913-295-3127
SECURITY INC FD-CORP BD	700 HARRISON ST.	TOPEKA, KS	66636	913-295-3127
SECURITY EQUITY FUND	700 HARRISON ST.	TOPEKA, KS	66636	913-295-3127
SECURITY INVESTMENT FUND	700 HARRISON ST.	TOPEKA, KS	66636	913-295-3127
SECURITY OMNI FUND	700 HARRISON ST.	TOPEKA, KS	66636	913-295-3127
SECURITY ULTRA FUND	700 HARRISON ST.	TOPEKA, KS	66636	913-295-3127
SELIG - SELIGMAN J W & CO				
SELIGMAN CAPITAL FUND	ONE BANKERS TRUST PLAZA	NEW YORK, NY	10006	212-912-8200
SELIGMAN CALIF TAX EX HI	ONE BANKERS TRUST PLAZA	NEW YORK, NY	10006	212-912-8200
SELIGMAN CAL TAX EX QUAL	ONE BANKERS TRUST PLAZA	NEW YORK, NY	10006	212-912-8200
SELIGMAN COMMUNICATIONS	ONE BANKERS TRUST PLAZA	NEW YORK, NY	10006	212-912-8200
SELIGMAN COMMON STOCK FD	ONE BANKERS TRUST PLAZA	NEW YORK, NY	10006	212-912-8200
SELIGMAN GROWTH FD	ONE BANKERS TRUST PLAZA	NEW YORK, NY	10006	212-912-8200
SELIGMAN GOV GUARANTEED	ONE BANKERS TRUST PLAZA	NEW YORK, NY	10006	212-912-8200
SELIGMAN HIGH YIELD BOND	ONE BANKERS TRUST PLAZA	NEW YORK, NY	10006	212-912-8200
SELIGMAN INCOME FD	ONE BANKERS TRUST PLAZA	NEW YORK, NY	10006	212-912-8200
SELIGMAN SECURED MTG	ONE BANKERS TRUST PLAZA	NEW YORK, NY	10006	212-912-8200
SELIGMAN TX EX LOUISIANA	ONE BANKERS TRUST PLAZA	NEW YORK, NY	10006	212-912-8200
SELIGMAN TAX EX MARYLAND	ONE BANKERS TRUST PLAZA	NEW YORK, NY	10006	212-912-8200
SELIGMAN TAX EX MASS	ONE BANKERS TRUST PLAZA	NEW YORK, NY	10006	212-912-8200
SELIGMAN TAX EX MICH	ONE BANKERS TRUST PLAZA	NEW YORK, NY	10006	212-912-8200
SELIGMAN TAX EX MINN	ONE BANKERS TRUST PLAZA	NEW YORK, NY	10006	212-912-8200
SELIGMAN TAX EX NATL	ONE BANKERS TRUST PLAZA	NEW YORK, NY	10006	212-912-8200
SELIGMAN TAX EX NEW YORK	ONE BANKERS TRUST PLAZA	NEW YORK, NY	10006	212-912-8200
SELIGMAN TAX EX OHIO	ONE BANKERS TRUST PLAZA	NEW YORK, NY	10006	212-912-8200
SENTRY - SENTRY INVESTMENT MANAGEMENT				
SENTRY FUND	1800 NORTH POINT DR.	STEVENS POINT, WI	54481	715-346-7129
SHEAR - SHEARSON MANAGEMENT				
AMERICAN TELECOMM TR GR	53 STATE STREET-9TH FL	BOSTON, MA	02109	800-451-2010
AMERICAN TELECOMM TR INC	53 STATE STREET-9TH FL	BOSTON, MA	02109	800-451-2010
SHEARSON AGGRESSIVE GRTH	53 STATE STREET-9TH FL	BOSTON, MA	02109	617-956-9700
SHEARSON APPRECIATION	53 STATE STREET-9TH FL	BOSTON, MA	02109	617-956-9700
SHEARSON CALIF MUNICIPAL	53 STATE STREET-9TH FL	BOSTON, MA	02109	617-956-9700
SHEARSON FUNDAMENTAL VAL	53 STATE STREET-9TH FL	BOSTON, MA	02109	617-956-9700
SHEARSON GLOBAL OPPORT	53 STATE STREET-9TH FL	BOSTON, MA	02109	617-956-9700

FUND/MGMNT	STREET	CITY/STATE	ZIP	PHONE

CONTINUATION - SHEARSON MANAGEMENT

SHEARSON HIGH YIELD	53 STATE STREET-9TH FL	BOSTON, MA	02109	617-956-9700
SHEARSON LG-TRM GOV SECS	53 STATE STREET-9TH FL	BOSTON, MA	02109	617-956-9700
SHEARSON MANAGED GOVTS	53 STATE STREET-9TH FL	BOSTON, MA	02109	617-956-9700
SHEARSON MANAGED MUNI BD	53 STATE STREET-9TH FL	BOSTON, MA	02109	617-956-9700
SHEARSON SPEC EQTY GR	53 STATE STREET-9TH FL	BOSTON, MA	02109	617-956-9700
SHEARSON NEW YORK MUNI	53 STATE STREET-9TH FL	BOSTON, MA	02109	617-956-9700
SHEARSON SPEC INTL EQ	53 STATE STREET-9TH FL	BOSTON, MA	02109	617-956-9700
SHEARSON SPEC EQTY PLUS	53 STATE STREET-9TH FL	BOSTON, MA	02109	617-956-9700
SHEARSON SPEC INTERM GOV	53 STATE STREET-9TH FL	BOSTON, MA	02109	617-956-9700
SHEARSON SPEC TAX EX INC	53 STATE STREET-9TH FL	BOSTON, MA	02109	617-956-9700
SHEARSON SPL OPTION INC	53 STATE STREET-9TH FL	BOSTON, MA	02109	617-956-9700

SHERMN - SHERMAN,DEAN RESEARCH & MGT

SHERMAN, DEAN FUND	6061 N.W. EXPRESSWAY	SAN ANTONIO, TX	78201	512-734-1488

SIEBEL - SIEBEL CAPITAL MANAGEMENT

EQUITEC SIEBEL TOTAL RET	80 EAST SIR FRANCES DRAKE	LARKSPUR, CA	94939	800-445-9020

SIGMA - SIGMA MGMT INC

ISI GROWTH FUND	P.O. BOX 23330	OAKLAND, CA	94623	415-832-1400
ISI INCOME FUND	P.O. BOX 23330	OAKLAND, CA	94623	415-832-1400
ISI TRUST FUND	P.O. BOX 23330	OAKLAND, CA	94623	415-832-1400
SIGMA CAPITAL SHARES	3801 KENNETT PIKE	WILMINGTON, DE	19807	302-652-3091
SIGMA INCOME SHARES	3801 KENNETT PIKE	WILMINGTON, DE	19807	302-652-3091
SIGMA INVESTMENT SHARES	3801 KENNETT PIKE	WILMINGTON, DE	19807	302-652-3091
SIGMA SPECIAL FUND	3801 KENNETT PIKE	WILMINGTON, DE	19807	800-441-9490
SIGMA TRUST SHARES	3801 KENNETT PIKE	WILMINGTON, DE	19807	302-652-3091
SIGMA VENTURE SHARES	3801 KENNETT PIKE	WILMINGTON, DE	19807	302-652-3091
SIGMA WORLD	3801 KENNETT PIKE	WILMINGTON, DE	19807	302-652-3091

SIS - STRATEGIC INVT. SERVICES

YES FUND	2151 EAST D ST. #201C	ONTARIO, CA	91764	714-988-0695

SM-BAR - SMITH,BARNEY ADVISORS,INC.

SMITH, BARNEY EQUITY	1345 AVE. OF THE AMERICAS	NEW YORK, NY	10105	212-356-2631
SMITH, BARNEY INC. & GR.	1345 AVE. OF THE AMERICAS	NEW YORK, NY	10105	212-356-2631

SMC - SCHIELD MANAGEMENT CO.

SCHIELD AGGRESS GROWTH	P.O. BOX 17007	DENVER, CO	80217	800-826-8154
SCHIELD VALUE PORTFOLIO	P.O. BOX 17007	DENVER, CO	80217	800-826-8154

SOGEN - SOGEN SECURITIES CORP

SOGEN INTERNATIONAL FUND	520 MADISON AVE	NEW YORK, NY	10022	212-832-0022

SR&F - STEIN,ROE & FARNHAM

STEIN R&F CAPITAL OPPOR.	300 WEST ADAMS	CHICAGO, IL	60606	800-621-0320
STEINROE DISCOVERY FUND	300 WEST ADAMS	CHICAGO, IL	60606	800-621-0320
STEINROE HIGH-YIELD BOND	300 WEST ADAMS	CHICAGO, IL	60606	800-621-0320
STEINROE HIGH-YIELD MUNI	300 WEST ADAMS	CHICAGO, IL	60606	800-621-0320
STEINROE INTERMED MUNI	300 WEST ADAMS	CHICAGO, IL	60606	800-621-0320

CDA MUTUAL FUND DIRECTORY - 12/31/86

FUND/MGMNT	STREET	CITY/STATE	ZIP	PHONE

CONTINUATION - STEIN,ROE & FARNHAM

STEINROE MANAGED BOND FD	300 WEST ADAMS	CHICAGO, IL	60606	800-621-0320
STEIN R&F STOCK	300 WEST ADAMS	CHICAGO, IL	60606	800-621-0320
STEINROE SPECIAL FUND	300 WEST ADAMS	CHICAGO, IL	60606	800-621-0320
STEINROE MANAGED MUNI FD	300 WEST ADAMS	CHICAGO, IL	60606	800-621-0320
STEIN R&F TOTAL RETURN	300 WEST ADAMS	CHICAGO, IL	60606	800-621-0320
STEINROE UNIVERSE FUND	300 WEST ADAMS	CHICAGO, IL	60606	800-621-0320

ST-B&M - STATE BOND & MORTGAGE

STATE BOND COMMON STOCK	100-106 N. MINNESOTA ST.	NEW ULM, MN	56073	507-354-2144
STATE BOND DIVERSIFIED	100-106 N. MINNESOTA ST.	NEW ULM, MN	56073	507-354-2144
STATE BOND PROGRESS FUND	100-106 N. MINNESOTA ST.	NEW ULM, MN	56073	507-354-2144

ST-ST - STATE STREET RESEARCH & MGT

| STATE STREET GROWTH | ONE FINANCIAL CTR. 38TH FL | BOSTON, MA | 02110 | 617-482-3920 |
| STATE STREET INV. CORP. | ONE FINANCIAL CTR. 38TH FL | BOSTON, MA | 02110 | 617-482-3920 |

STDLEY - STUDLEY,SHUPERT & CO. INC.

| COMMONWEALTH - PLANS A&B | ONE WINTHROP SQUARE | BOSTON, MA | 02110 | 617-482-6500 |
| COMMONWEALTH - PLAN C | ONE WINTHROP SQUARE | BOSTON, MA | 02110 | 617-482-6500 |

STDMAN - STEADMAN SECURITY CORPORATION

STEADMAN AMERICAN INDUS.	1730 K STREET N.W.	WASHINGTON, DC	20036	202-223-1000
STEADMAN ASSOCIATED	1730 K STREET N.W.	WASHINGTON, DC	20036	202-223-1000
STEADMAN INVESTMENT	1730 K STREET N.W.	WASHINGTON, DC	20036	202-223-1000
STEADMAN OCEANOGRAPHIC	1730 K STREET N.W.	WASHINGTON, DC	20036	202-223-1000

STFARM - STATE FARM INVESTMENT MGT

| STATE FARM BALANCED | ONE STATE FARM PLAZA | BLOOMINGTON, IL | 61701 | 309-766-2029 |
| STATE FARM GROWTH FUND | ONE STATE FARM PLAZA | BLOOMINGTON, IL | 61701 | 309-766-2029 |

STRMGT - STRATTON MANAGEMENT CO.

| STRATTON GROWTH FUND | P.O. BOX 550 | BLUE BELL, PA | 19422 | 215-542-8025 |
| STRATTON MONTHLY DIV SHS | P.O. BOX 550 | BLUE BELL, PA | 19422 | 215-542-8025 |

STRONG - STRONG/CORNELIUSON CAP. MGMT.

STRONG INCOME FUND	815 EAST MASON STREET	MILWAUKEE, WI	53202	800-558-1030
STRONG INVESTMENT FUND	815 EAST MASON STREET	MILWAUKEE, WI	53202	800-558-1030
STRONG OPPORTUNITY FUND	815 EAST MASON STREET	MILWAUKEE, WI	53202	800-558-1030
STRONG TOTAL RETURN FUND	815 EAST MASON STREET	MILWAUKEE, WI	53202	800-558-1030

TAMCO - TENNECO ASSET MANAGEMENT CO.

CASHMAN FARRELL VALUE FD	P.O. BOX 2511	HOUSTON, TX	43215	713-757-5806
FUND OF THE SOUTHWEST	P.O. BOX 2511	HOUSTON, TX	77201	713-757-5674
INVESTORS INCOME	P.O. BOX 2511	HOUSTON, TX	77001	713-757-5674
PBHG GROWTH FUND	P.O. BOX 2511	HOUSTON, TX	77001	713-757-5806
U.S. TREND FUND, INC.	P.O. BOX 2511	HOUSTON, TX	77201	713-757-5674

TEMPLE - TEMPLETON INVESTMENT COUNSEL

| TEMPLETON FOREIGN FUND | 700 CENTRAL AVE-PO 33030 | ST PETERSBURG, FL | 33733 | 813-823-8712 |

FUND/MGMNT	STREET	CITY/STATE	ZIP	PHONE

CONTINUATION - TEMPLETON INVESTMENT COUNSEL

FUND/MGMNT	STREET	CITY/STATE	ZIP	PHONE
TEMPLETON GROWTH FUND	700 CENTRAL AVE-PO 33030	ST PETERSBURG, FL	33733	800-237-0738
TEMPLETON GLOBAL I	700 CENTRAL AVE-PO 33030	ST PETERSBURG, FL	33733	813-823-8712
TEMPLETON GLOBAL II	700 CENTRAL AVE-PO 33030	ST PETERSBURG, FL	33733	813-823-8712
TEMPLETON WORLD FUND	700 CENTRAL AVE-PO 33030	ST PETERSBURG, FL	33733	813-823-8712

THOMSN - THOMSON MCKINNON

FUND/MGMNT	STREET	CITY/STATE	ZIP	PHONE
THOMSON MCKINNON GROWTH	1 NEW YORK PLAZA	NEW YORK, NY	10004	212-482-7070
THOMSON MCKINNON INCOME	1 NEW YORK PLAZA	NEW YORK, NY	10004	212-482-7070
THOMSON MCKINNON OPPORT.	1 NEW YORK PLAZA	NEW YORK, NY	10004	212-482-7070

TUCKER - TUCKER ANTHONY MGMT CORP

FUND/MGMNT	STREET	CITY/STATE	ZIP	PHONE
FREEDOM GOLD & GOV TRUST	THREE CENTER PLAZA	BOSTON, MA	02108	617-725-2000
FREEDOM REGIONAL BANK FD	THREE CENTER PLAZA	BOSTON, MA	02108	617-725-2000

UNIFID - UNIFIED MANAGEMENT CORP.

FUND/MGMNT	STREET	CITY/STATE	ZIP	PHONE
UNIFIED GROWTH FUND	600 GUARANTY BLDG.	INDIANAPOLIS, IN	46204	317-634-3301
UNIFIED INCOME FUND	600 GUARANTY BLDG.	INDIANAPOLIS, IN	46204	317-634-3301
UNIFIED MUNI FD-GENERAL	600 GUARANTY BLDG.	INDIANAPOLIS, IN	46204	317-634-3301
UNIFIED MUNI FD-INDIANA	600 GUARANTY BLDG.	INDIANAPOLIS, IN	46204	317-634-3301
UNIFIED MUTUAL SHARES	600 GUARANTY BLDG.	INDIANAPOLIS, IN	46204	317-634-3301

UNITED - UNITED SERVICES ADVISORS

FUND/MGMNT	STREET	CITY/STATE	ZIP	PHONE
US GOLD SHARES FUND	P.O. BOX 29467	SAN ANTONIO, TX	78229	800-824-4653
US GOOD AND BAD TIMES FD	P.O. BOX 29467	SAN ANTONIO, TX	78229	800-824-4653
US GROWTH FUND	P.O. BOX 29467	SAN ANTONIO, TX	78229	800-824-4653
US INCOME FUND	P.O. BOX 29467	SAN ANTONIO, TX	78229	800-824-4653
US LOCAP FUND	P.O. BOX 29467	SAN ANTONIO, TX	78229	800-824-4653
US NEW PROSPECTOR FUND	P.O. BOX 29467	SAN ANTONIO, TX	78229	800-824-4653
US PROSPECTOR FUND	P.O. BOX 29467	SAN ANTONIO, TX	78229	800-824-4653

USAA - USAA FUND MANAGEMENT CO.

FUND/MGMNT	STREET	CITY/STATE	ZIP	PHONE
USAA MUTUAL FD GROWTH	P.O. BOX 33338	SAN ANTONIO, TX	78265	800-531-8483
USAA MUTUAL FD INCOME	P.O. BOX 33338	SAN ANTONIO, TX	78265	800-531-8483
USAA SUNBELT ERA FUND	P.O. BOX 33338	SAN ANTONIO, TX	78265	800-531-8483
USAA TAX EX HIGH YIELD	P.O. BOX 33338	SAN ANTONIO, TX	78265	800-531-8483
USAA TAX EX INTERMEDIATE	P.O. BOX 33338	SAN ANTONIO, TX	78265	800-531-8483
USAA TAX EX SH-TERM FD	P.O. BOX 33338	SAN ANTONIO, TX	78265	800-531-8483

VALMGT - VALLEY FORGE MANAGEMENT CO.

FUND/MGMNT	STREET	CITY/STATE	ZIP	PHONE
VALLEY FORGE FUND	1375 ANTHONY WAYNE DR.	WAYNE, PA	19087	215-688-6839

VANECK - VAN ECK MANAGEMENT CORP.

FUND/MGMNT	STREET	CITY/STATE	ZIP	PHONE
INTERNATIONAL INVESTORS	122 E. 42ND ST.	NEW YORK, NY	10017	212-687-5200
WORLD TRENDS	122 EAST 42ND STREET	NEW YORK, NY	10168	212-687-5200

VENADV - VENTURE ADVISORS INC.

FUND/MGMNT	STREET	CITY/STATE	ZIP	PHONE
NEW YORK VENTURE FUND	P O BOX 1688	SANTA FE, NM	87501	800-545-2098
RETIREMENT PLANNING-BOND	309 JOHNSON STREET	SANTA FE, NM	87501	505-983-4335
RETIREMENT PLANNING-EQ	309 JOHNSON STREET	SANTA FE, NM	87501	505-983-4335
VENTURE INCOME PLUS	309 JOHNSON STREET	SANTA FE, NM	87501	505-983-4335

CDA MUTUAL FUND DIRECTORY - 12/31/86

FUND/MGMNT	STREET	CITY/STATE	ZIP	PHONE
CONTINUATION - VENTURE ADVISORS INC.				
VENTURE MUNI PLUS	P.O. BOX 1688	SANTA FE, NM	87501	505-983-4335
VGUARD - VANGUARD GROUP				
EXPLORER FUND	P.O. BOX 2600	VALLEY FORGE, PA	19482	215-648-6000
EXPLORER II	P.O. BOX 2600	VALLEY FORGE, PA	19482	215-648-6000
MORGAN (W.L.) GROWTH	P.O. BOX 2600	VALLEY FORGE, PA	19482	215-648-6000
NAESS & THOMAS SPECIAL	P.O. BOX 2600	VALLEY FORGE, PA	19482	212-269-6500
PRIMECAP FUND	P.O. BOX 2600	VALLEY FORGE, PA	19482	215-648-6000
QUALIFIED DIVD PORTF I	P.O. BOX 2600	VALLEY FORGE, PA	19482	215-648-6000
QUALIFIED DIVD PORTF II	P.O. BOX 2600	VALLEY FORGE, PA	19482	215-648-6000
QUALIFIED DIVD PORT III	P.O. BOX 2600	VALLEY FORGE, PA	19482	215-648-6000
TRUSTEES COMM EQ-INTL	P.O. BOX 2600	VALLEY FORGE, PA	19482	215-648-6000
TRUSTEES COMM EQ-US PORT	P.O. BOX 2600	VALLEY FORGE, PA	19482	215-648-6000
VANGUARD CONVERTIBLE SEC	P.O. BOX 2600	VALLEY FORGE, PA	19482	215-648-6000
VANGUARD FIXED INC HIYLD	P.O. BOX 2600	VALLEY FORGE, PA	19482	215-648-6000
VANGUARD FIXED INC INVT	P.O. BOX 2600	VALLEY FORGE, PA	19482	215-648-6000
VANGUARD FIXED INC GNMA	P.O. BOX 2600	VALLEY FORGE, PA	19482	215-648-6000
VANGUARD FI SECS-SH TERM	P.O. BOX 2600	VALLEY FORGE, PA	19482	215-648-6000
VANGUARD INDEX TRUST	P.O. BOX 2600	VALLEY FORGE, PA	19482	215-648-6000
VANGUARD CALIF INS TX FR	P.O. BOX 2600	VALLEY FORGE, PA	19482	215-648-6000
VANGUARD PENNA INS TX FR	P.O. BOX 2600	VALLEY FORGE, PA	19482	215-648-6000
VANGUARD MUNI HIGH YIELD	P.O. BOX 2600	VALLEY FORGE, PA	19482	215-648-6000
VANGUARD MUNI INSURED LT	P.O. BOX 2600	VALLEY FORGE, PA	19482	215-648-6000
VANGUARD MUNI INTERM-TRM	P.O. BOX 2600	VALLEY FORGE, PA	19482	215-648-6000
VANGUARD MUNI LONG-TERM	P.O. BOX 2600	VALLEY FORGE, PA	19482	215-648-6000
VANGUARD MUNI SHORT-TERM	P.O. BOX 2600	VALLEY FORGE, PA	19482	215-648-6000
VANGUARD SPEC PORT-ENRGY	P.O. BOX 2600	VALLEY FORGE, PA	19482	215-648-6000
VANGUARD SPEC PORT-GOLD	P.O. BOX 2600	VALLEY FORGE, PA	19482	215-648-6000
VANGUARD SPC PORT-HEALTH	P.O. BOX 2600	VALLEY FORGE, PA	19482	215-648-6000
VANGUARD SPEC-SVC ECON	P.O. BOX 2600	VALLEY FORGE, PA	19482	215-648-6000
VANGUARD SPEC PORT-TECH	P.O. BOX 2600	VALLEY FORGE, PA	19482	215-648-6000
VANGUARD STAR FUND	P.O. BOX 2600	VALLEY FORGE, PA	19482	215-648-6000
VANGUARD WORLD-INTL GR	P.O. BOX 2600	VALLEY FORGE, PA	19482	215-648-6000
VANGUARD WORLD-US GR	P.O. BOX 2600	VALLEY FORGE, PA	19482	215-648-6000
WELLESLEY INCOME FUND	P.O. BOX 2600	VALLEY FORGE, PA	19482	215-648-6000
WELLINGTON FUND	P.O. BOX 2600	VALLEY FORGE, PA	19482	215-648-6000
WINDSOR FUND	P.O. BOX 2600	VALLEY FORGE, PA	19482	215-648-6000
WINDSOR II	P.O. BOX 2600	VALLEY FORGE, PA	19482	215-648-6000
VOYAGR - VOYAGER ASSET MGMT INC.				
DOUBLE EXEMPT FLEX FUND	100 SOUTH FIFTH ST., #2300	MINNEAPOLIS, MN	55402	612-341-6748
WADDEL - WADDELL & REED,INC.				
UNITED ACCUMULATIVE FUND	P.O. BOX 1343	KANSAS CITY, MO	64141	816-283-4000
UNITED CONTL. INCOME FD.	P.O. BOX 1343	KANSAS CITY, MO	64141	816-283-4000
UNITED BOND FUND	P.O. BOX 1343	KANSAS CITY, MO	64141	816-283-4000
UNITED GOLD & GOVERNMENT	P.O. BOX 1343	KANSAS CITY, MO	64141	816-283-4000
UNITED GOV SECURITIES FD	P.O. BOX 1343	KANSAS CITY, MO	64141	816-283-4000
UNITED HIGH INCOME FUND	P.O. BOX 1343	KANSAS CITY, MO	64141	816-283-4000
UNITED INCOME FUND	P.O. BOX 1343	KANSAS CITY, MO	6^^41	816-283-4000
UNITED INTL. GROWTH FUND	P.O. BOX 1343	KANSAS CITY, MO	64141	816-283-4000
UNITED MUNICIPAL BOND FD	P.O. BOX 1343	KANSAS CITY, MO	64141	816-283-4000
UNITED MUNI HIGH INCOME	P.O. BOX 1343	KANSAS CITY, MO	64141	816-283-4000
UNITED NEW CONCEPTS FUND	P.O. BOX 1343	KANSAS CITY, MO	64141	816-283-4000
UNITED RETIREMENT SHARES	P.O. BOX 1343	KANSAS CITY, MO	64141	816-283-4000

FUND/MGMNT	STREET	CITY/STATE	ZIP	PHONE

CONTINUATION - WADDELL & REED,INC.

| UNITED SCIENCE & ENERGY | P.O. BOX 1343 | KANSAS CITY, MO | 64141 | 816-283-4000 |
| UNITED VANGUARD FUND | P.O. BOX 1343 | KANSAS CITY, MO | 64141 | 816-283-4000 |

WALL - WALL STREET MANAGEMENT CORP.

| WALL STREET FUND | 641 LEXINGTON AVE-21ST FL. | NEW YORK, NY | 10022 | 212-319-9400 |

WEALTH - WEALTH MONITORS MGMT. CO.

| WEALTH MONITORS FUND | 1001 E. 101ST TERRACE-#220 | KANSAS CITY, MO | 64131 | 816-941-7990 |

WEBSTR - WEBSTER MANAGEMENT CO.

KIDDER P. EQUITY INCOME	20 EXCHANGE PLACE	NEW YORK, NY	10005	212-510-5028
KIDDER P. GOVT INCOME	20 EXCHANGE PLACE	NEW YORK, NY	10005	212-510-5028
KIDDER P. SPECIAL GROWTH	20 EXCHANGE PLACE	NEW YORK, NY	10005	212-510-5028
KIDDER P. NATL TX-FR INC	20 EXCHANGE PLACE	NEW YORK, NY	10005	212-510-5028
KIDDER P. N.Y. TX-FR INC	20 EXCHANGE PLACE	NEW YORK, NY	10005	212-510-5028

WEISS - WEISS,PECK & GREER

| TUDOR FUND | ONE NEW YORK PLACE | NEW YORK, NY | 10004 | 800-223-3332 |
| WPG FUND | ONE NEW YORK PLACE | NEW YORK, NY | 10004 | 212-908-9500 |

WHEAT - WHEAT SECURITIES

| SOUTHEASTERN GROWTH FUND | P.O. BOX 30 | RICHMOND, VA | 23206 | 804-649-2311 |

WMBLR - WILLIAM BLAIR & COMPANY

| GROWTH INDUSTRY SHARES | 135 S. LASALLE ST | CHICAGO, IL | 60603 | 312-346-4830 |

WORLD - WORLD ADVISORS

| PERMANENT PORTFOLIO | P.O. BOX 478 | PACIFIC GROVE, CA | 93950 | 707-778-7325 |

WS&W - WOOD,STRUTHERS & WINTHROP,INC.

DE VEGH MUTUAL FUND	140 BROADWAY, 11TH FLOOR	NEW YORK, NY	10271	212-504-4006
NEUWIRTH FUND	140 BROADWAY, 42ND FLOOR	NEW YORK, NY	10271	212-504-4006
PINE STREET FUND	140 BROADWAY 11TH FLOOR	NEW YORK, NY	10271	212-504-4006

Index

ET'D

N

A113 0829418 7

HG 4530 .H386 1988

Haslem, John A.

The investor's guide to
mutual funds